Education
and Social Crisis

PERSPECTIVES ON TEACHING DISADVANTAGED YOUTH

Edited by

Everett T. Keach, Jr.
Associate Professor, Department of Elementary Education, University of Minnesota

Robert Fulton
Professor, Department of Sociology, University of Minnesota

William E. Gardner
Associate Professor, Department of Secondary Education, University of Minnesota

John Wiley & Sons, Inc.   *New York*   *London*   *Sydney*

Preface

America is undergoing a vast social revolution in which the educator can play a helpful part. Being fought along many different fronts and in many different areas, this struggle grows out of the determination of the Negro and other disadvantaged persons to attain the full rights of citizenship and dignity of the self. The educator's role, though less headline-making than that of Martin Luther King, Megdar Evars, or James Reeb, is no less important in that it consolidates the rights won at the high costs paid by these men and many like them.

Educators and teachers face a challenge to open the shutters that darken the mind. Only when man is able to see the light and respect his fellow man can the public rights and private lives of all be wholly secure. As members of the educational profession we must be clear on the values and ideological premises that supply the foundations for the objectives and goals to which the nation aspires. Our position is aptly crystallized in Gunnar Myrdal's now famous phrase, "The American Creed." A belief in the rights and privileges regarded as ethically, morally, and socially legitimate for all Americans underlies everything we seek to accomplish.

Our objectives derive directly from this "Creed." Through the educative process we attempt to reduce, if not eliminate, the social and emotional barriers which prevent all disadvantaged groups from attaining fully these rights and priviliges.

However, these objectives are more readily expressed than realized. The painfully slow admission of the Negro to full participation in American public life underlines this fact. The voice of hatred still sounds aloud and shrill in this country. Men, women, and children are assaulted and murdered for daring to press for equal rights for Negroes. As teachers we must not turn our backs on such ugly conduct but rather confront it directly and recognize the depth and tenacity of the hostility that exists in many parts of the country toward members of minority groups.

Yet, although the ramifications of prejudice are complex and the roots of hostility are deep and often beyond our control, we teachers have a part to play in mitigating their effects on students who belong to minority groups. Success depends not only on our awareness of the diverse problems which trouble these students but also on our courage and creativity in making the appropriate efforts to overcome them.

The readings presented in this book are intended to help open many of the gates to learning which are still closed to members of the minorities. It is hoped that these selections will lead to a better basis for solving the educational problems faced by disadvantaged children. The readings are organized into three parts. Part I, "Cultural Values and Family Life of Disadvantaged Youth," provides the reader with background material on the culture and life styles of these groups—Negro, Puerto Rican, Mexican-American, urban and rural poor. Among them the majority of America's socially and educationally disadvantaged children are found. Part II, "Problems Facing Disadvantaged Youth in the Schools," illustrates the effects of these subcultures upon a child's ability to succeed in the educational environment of the nation's schools. Part III, "Programs and Progress in Meeting Educational Needs of Disadvantaged Youth," explores the role of the school in its relationship to disadvantaged children and surveys the different programs developed to meet the special needs of these youth.

Introductions written by the editors serve to put each part into perspective as well as to explicate its several expositions. We, the editors, wish to thank the contributors to this volume and their publishers for permission to reprint their essays. Thanks also are due to Mrs. Judith Hillesland and Miss Susan Romlin for their secretarial assistance. Finally, we wish to thank our wives, Dorothy Keach, Julie Ann Fulton, and Marcia Gardner for their friendly advice and criticism as well as their forebearance throughout the preparation of this book.

May, 1967

Everett T. Keach, Jr.
Robert Fulton
William E. Gardner

Contents

vii

PART III: PROGRAMS AND PROGRESS IN MEETING THE
EDUCATIONAL NEEDS OF DISADVANTAGED YOUTH

Contributors

Ernest H. Austin, Jr., Professor of Education, Department of Curriculum and Instruction, College of Education, University of Tennessee, Knoxville, Tennessee

David P. Ausubel, Professor of Psychology, Department of Educational Psychology, University of Illinois, Urbana, Illinois

James Baldwin, author, New York, New York

Dorsey Baynham, author, Falls Church, Virginia

Basil Bernstein, Reader in Sociology of Education, University of London, Institute of Education, London, England

John H. Burma, Chairman and Professor of Sociology, Department of Sociology, Grinnell College, Grinnell, Iowa

Charles J. Calitri, Professor of Education, School of Education, Hofstra University, Hempstead, New York

Ruth Shonle Cavan, Professor of Sociology, Department of Sociology and Social Work, Rockford College, Rockford, Illinois

Kenneth B. Clark, Director, Social Dynamics Research Institute, The City University of New York, New York, New York

Virgil A. Clift, Professor of Education, New York University, New York, New York

Werner Cohn, Associate Professor of Sociology, University of British Columbia, Vancouver, B.C., Canada

Robert L. Curry, Associate Professor and Director of Reading Laboratory, College of Education, University of Oklahoma, Norman, Oklahoma

Delmo Della-Dora, Professor of Education, National Teacher Education Center, Eastern Michigan University, Ypsilanti, Michigan

Dan W. Dodson, Director, Center for School Studies, New York University, New York, New York

Louise G. Daugherty, Assistant Superintendent, Department of Special Education, Chicago Public School System, Chicago, Illinois

James H. Duggins, Compensatory Teacher, Mission High School, San Francisco, California

Robert W. Edgar, Professor of Education, Queens College of the City University of New York, Flushing, New York

Sophie L. Elam, Assistant Professor of Education, Department of Education, The City College of the City University of New York, New York, New York

Paul Friggens, Roving Editor, *Reader's Digest,* Pleasantville, New York

Morsley Giddings, Research Associate, Center for Urban Education, New York, New York

*Roscoe Giffin,** formerly Professor of Sociology, Berea College, Berea, Kentucky

Regina Goff, Assistant Commissioner, Office of the Disadvantaged and Handicapped, Department of Health, Education and Welfare, Office of Education, Washington, D.C.

James W. Guthrie, Special Assistant to the Assistant Secretary for Legislation, Department of Health, Education and Welfare, Washington, D.C.

Robert J. Havighurst, Professor of Education, University of Chicago, Chicago, Illinois

Suzanne Keller, Associate Professor of Sociology, Vassar College, Poughkeepsie, New York

James A. Kelly, Assistant Professor, Teachers College, Columbia University, New York, New York

Otto Klineberg, Centre International De Relations Entre Groupes Ethniques, Paris, France

George F. Kneller, Professor of Education, University of California, Los Angeles, California

Solomon Kobrin, Research Sociologist, Illinois Institute for Juvenile Research, Chicago, Illinois

Lorenzo Lisonbee, Associate Principal, Camelback High School, Phoenix, Arizona

Donald Lloyd, Vice President, Programed Learning: Resources Development Corporation, East Lansing, Michigan

Bernard Mackler, Research Associate, Center for Urban Education, New York, New York

David O. Montague, Assistant Principal, Elk Grove Senior High School, Elk Grove, California

John Niemeyer, President, Bank Street College of Education, New York, New York

* Deceased.

Eleanor Pavenstedt, formerly affiliated with the Department of Child Psychiatry, School of Medicine, Boston University, Boston, Massachusetts

Lee Rainwater, Professor of Sociology and Anthropology, Washington University, St. Louis, Missouri

Frank Riessman, Professor of Psychology, Bard College, Annandale-on-Hudson, New York

Donald W. Robinson, Associate Editor, *Phi Delta Kappan,* Bloomington, Indiana

Frank E. Ross, Associate Professor of English, Eastern Michigan University, Ypsilanti, Michigan

Marjorie B. Smiley, Director, Gateway English, Hunter College, New York, New York

Robert K. Thomas, Carnegie Cross-Cultural Educational Project of the University of Chicago, Tahlequah, Oklahoma

Horacio Ulibarri, Assistant Professor of Education, The University of New Mexico, Albuquerque, New Mexico

Bennetta B. Washington, Director, Women's Centers Division, Job Corps, Washington, D.C.

Rosalie Wax, Associate Professor of Anthropology, Department of Anthropology, The University of Kansas, Lawrence, Kansas

Marianne Wolman, Instructor, Pacific Oaks Friends School, Pasadena, California

Miles V. Zintz, Professor of Education, The University of New Mexico, Albuquerque, New Mexico

Part I: CULTURAL VALUES AND FAMILY LIFE OF DISADVANTAGED YOUTH

To say a child is disadvantaged is to speak in relative terms. Havighurst defines the socially disadvantaged child as one who is handicapped in the task of growing up and living a competent and satisfying life in urban, industrial society. It is his opinion that as many as 30 per cent of the children in such major metropolitan centers as New York, Chicago, and Detroit would fall into the category of "socially disadvantaged."

Pavenstedt describes the child-rearing practices of certain urban lower-class families and thereby further illustrates the meaning of the expression "socially disadvantaged." The "socially disadvantaged" child is seen by him as the product of a disorganized, multiproblem home with a family environment that militates against the child's capacity and willingness to learn.

The perceptive essay, "Spanish-speaking Children," by Burma, introduces us to the different worlds of the Mexican, Mexican-American, Spanish-American, and Puerto Rican children. Burma's brief but trenchant review of the life situation of Spanish-speaking children summons educators to broaden the concept "socially disadvantaged" to include not only the economically deprived but also those children who, by reason of cultural background, are unable to participate fully and adequately in American society. The problems of Spanish-speaking children are not unlike those of children everywhere, but the difficulties they face in assimilating into the dominant American society, with its cultural and linguistic expectations, frequently assume such proportions as to make their full participation in American life a virtual impossibility.

What may be said for Spanish-speaking children can also be said for children in the Negro slums. Rainwater's article, "The Crucible of Identity: The Negro Lower Class Family," provides an insight for description and analysis of slum Negro family patterns—a description which allows us to perceive more clearly the meaning and implications of the concept "socially disadvantaged."

1

In addition to the articles specifically dealing with the various life styles of socially disadvantaged children, we have included an article by Kneller entitled, "Education and Cultural Values." His essay, which introduces this part, is intended to provide a structure upon which the other articles build. It is hoped, moreover, that the inclusion of his article will substantially assist the reader in developing an increased awareness of the many difficulties of contact and cooperation with children of different social, ethnic, and racial backgrounds.

Briefly, Kneller outlines three aspects of the relation of cultural values to education, which he sees as immediately relevant to our concern with the socially disadvantaged child. The first of these is the discrepancy between a culture's values and its actual practices—such as the discrepancy, for example, between our society's definition of success (wealth and its symbols) and the actual means for attaining them. The second issue is the conflict in values generated by cultural change. Kneller cites the values of the Puritan ethic juxtaposed with those of our modern industrial society, geared as it is to a philosophy of consumption and abundance. The third issue, which is of particular interest to us, is the disparity between the dominant values of the culture and the values of various minority groups within it.

It is Kneller's observation that many Americans live outside the dominant white, Anglo, middle-class, American culture. Separated from this culture by poverty, language, education, and race, these alienated minorities have little faith in the culture, and ultimately, do not aspire to it. This alienation from the majority culture, especially among citizens of non-European ancestry (Mexican-Americans, American Indians, and Negroes) strikes at the very root of national existence, as well as at such cultural values as quality, personal freedom, and dignity of the self. This theoretical perspective of dominant versus minority values allows us to visualize the part played by the containing culture in defining and delineating the opportunities and life chances of certain racial, social, and ethnic groups. For instance, the Negro's struggle for equal status in the major spheres of American life, one might argue, may be thwarted and frustrated in part by the identity sometimes given him by interpretations of Christian doctrine. As the putative descendant of Ham, the Negro is believed by some churches to be accursed and to derive his inferior position in society by divine ordinance. Yet, at the same time, it must also be said that Christianity has been the fount of much of the emotional fervor and rationale for the civil rights movement. The striking divergence within the Judaeo-Christian ethic, which recognizes the worth and dignity of every man and yet gives rise to self-righteous certitude and intolerance, cannot be ignored by the educator.

The emergence of the Black Muslim movement is an example of

the way many Negroes have reacted to the dual image of "inferior but equal" imposed on them by the white majority. The Muslim's repudiation of the white Christian civilization as incurably corrupt is, in part, a reaction to this ambivalence. Moreover, the glorification of the black man and the rejection of all things white are the reverse image of a bias deeply ingrained in our culture—that is, the pre-eminence of white over black. God, truth, beauty, virtue, chastity, and honesty are associated in our culture with whiteness, whereas the Devil, falsehood, ugliness, evil, promiscuity, and dishonesty are expressed by various shades of black.

Examples are familiar to all of us. Polite people tell "white" lies, hold "white-collar jobs," visit the "White House" in Washington, and proudly announce on occasion that they are "free, white, and 21." On the other hand, disliked individuals are "blacklisted" or "blackballed" from clubs and associations. Every family has its "black sheep" who may, on occasion, be hauled off in a "Black Maria" to the accompaniment of "black looks" from relatives and friends.

These examples of color bias emphasize the force of language in our lives and the very significant part it plays in shaping our relations with others. In Negro-white relations in this country language has often served to keep the races apart as effectively as any physical barricade. However, langauage also has a potentiality for growth and change. The examples cited are "live" words which evoke an emotion or stimulate an attitude. But in our language there are words and phrases now "dead" which lack the power to evoke a feeling or an attitude where they once had the force to do so. Who among us has been to a "Dutch auction"? We are unfamiliar with that expression; it has no emotional significance for us. How many of us, however, have ever been "Jewed-down"? Here the meaning is known and the phrase is "alive" with emotion. And yet both expressions refer to the same thing—to be taken advantage of unfairly. The difference is, of course, that the Dutch-English wars are over, whereas Jewish-Gentile feelings still simmer.

When we appreciate that a Dutch treat is not a treat at all, a Dutch door is only half a door, a Dutch oven is a pot, and a Dutch widow is not an attractive warm individual but a bamboo and cotton contraption to keep one cool while sleeping, we become aware of words as weapons which sometimes can be beaten into useful and colorful tools of the language. Inasmuch as teachers are keepers of the language, we can make a significant contribution to improving relationships between people by remaining alert to language's power and force and by resisting its influence when used to the detriment of our fellow citizens. In this regard, we can point with some satisfaction and optimism to the disappearance of the Uncle Tom shows, to the waning of derogatory cartoons and prints, such as those by

Currier and Ives, to the virtual end of the minstrel show, and to the end of the "Amos and Andy" image of the Negro which, until quite recently, was standard fare in all communications media.

At a more immediate and personal level, there are aspects of a child's experience with language which also deserve mention. In discussing the socialization of the lower-class Negro child, Bernstein identifies two forms of communication or styles of verbal behavior: one which may encourage and the other which may thwart a child's capacity and desire to learn.[1] The "restrictive" style is stereotyped, limited, and condensed—a language of implicit meaning and non-specific clichés. "Elaborate" styles, however, are those in which communication is individualized and specific, allowing for a wider and more complex range of thought and discrimination. In Bernstein's opinion the "restrictive" style largely typifies lower-class Negro family life. The result is that the imagination, curiosity, and intellectual assertiveness of the Negro child are blunted and discouraged. The lower-class Negro child is therefore doubly "trapped" by language—that of other people as well as his own.

What may be said of the language barriers facing the lower-class Negro child and their effects upon his motivation and capacity to learn can be extended to the other aspects of Negro life. The caste line in America has denied the Negro access to the mainstream of the economy. Although this situation has improved recently, it is nevertheless true that the average Negro child has little contact with people who have meaningful, satisfying, or secure employment. His family life does not include the typical work pattern of the white, middle-class family. Instead, his parents and other adult models are restricted to the edges of the occupational structure and share little in the tenets and rationalizations of the work ethos. The Negro child does not experience the relationship between effort and advancement. Although he works hard and makes an extra effort to keep a job, neither virtue necessarily promises promotion or advancement. Moreover, the work reserved for the Negro child is frequently without value or importance and, more often than not, uninspiring, fatiguing, and poorly rewarded. The Negro child soon learns that effort, aspiration, or deferred gratification is not necessarily either good or rewarding.[2] The middle-class white child, in contrast, has had demonstrated to him, both in his home and school environments, the direct relationship between effort and achievement.

Furthermore, the number of Negro families without fathers is also of great importance. The Negro child often comes from a mother- or female-dominated household. As a result, many Negro children have few, if any, close male models of behavior. Superimposed upon the twin burdens of racial prejudice and discrimination, Negro children may suffer further handicaps because of anxieties over broken homes and poverty which inhibit learning and satisfactory living. That Negro children are often low achievers and early school dropouts comes as no surprise. What should surprise us is that their learning efficiency, aspiration levels, and attainments are as high as they are! As Lazarsfeld has written:

"The underprivileged youth has seen less, read less, heard about less, his or her whole environment experiences fewer changes than the socially privileged and he simply knows of fewer possibilities." [3]

But as Adams and Friedrich caution about Negro children:

"Unless the gap between the culture level of the white middle-class and these children lessens, they will continue to be cheated out of the full richness of whatever educational opportunities are presented them. They will bring to their learning less motivation, less background to give it meaning, and far less expectation of success than does the average school pupil—with the result that they will learn far less as they go along and will "drop out" of school *mentally* years before they, as teenagers, drop out *physically*." [4]

We cannot leave this discussion without reference to the larger social context within which the private struggle of the disadvantaged student goes on. This struggle does not occur *in vacuo*, but rather, is part of a social network which ultimately both enfolds and affects us all.

Americans are becoming an urban people. Sixty-one per cent of the population lived in metropolitan areas in 1960. By 1980, it is estimated that 70 to 75 per cent of our total population will be living in cities of 50,000 or more or in areas which feed into these cities.[5] Many observers have noted that this metropolitan growth has served to give rise to, as well as to intensify, many social problems in education. The schools must cope with growing socioeconomic and social segregation of the urban communities. Such segregation, if allowed to continue unchecked, constitutes not only a threat to our ideal of equal educational opportunity for all, but also, conceivably, to the basic democratic structure of American society.

The process whereby social segregation of our urban communities occurs may be described as follows: the growth of a city sees an increased concentration of lower-class people in areas of poorest housing, typically in the central or oldest part of the city. Persons whose incomes permit them to move out of these slum neighborhoods locate farther from the city's center. Similarly, people in middle-class neighborhoods of the central city move to the suburbs and to what they believe to be a more congenial environment. Thus the city's growing population proceeds to divide itself along social-class lines with the lower classes at the center of the city and successively higher socioeconomic groups at progressively greater distances from the core.[6] Discrimination, restrictive housing practices, private convenants, and designated ghettos merely add to and complicate this process, the end result of which is even greater stratification of residential areas along ethnic, racial, and class lines. The schools tend to become homogeneous enclaves assuming the quality and character of the area in which they are located. Some schools become entirely middle-class in character, while others become lower-class.[7] It is the urban lower-class school, a product of the growth of low economic areas in the great urban centers, that presents the problems to which these readings are addressed.

Conant reports that half the children from deprived neighborhoods drop out of school in grades 9, 10, and 11. Moreover, he points out that per pupil expenditure in deprived schools is less than half the per pupil expenditure in privileged schools, and that compared to the 70 professionals per 1000 pupils in privileged schools there are only 40 or fewer professionals per 1000 pupils in deprived schools.[8] Such economic segregation in American public schools has been growing since 1950, and is reflected particularly in the increasing percentage of middle- and lower-class schools and a decreasing percentage of mixed-class schools.[9] The question arises as to whether equality of opportunity can exist in economically and racially segregated schools. Opportunity for upward social mobility, a characteristic regarded as essential for a democracy, is undermined by lower-class schools. Recent findings indicate that mingling youth of different backgrounds in the same school contributes to a sense of democracy.[10]

Wilson reports on research conducted in eight high schools of the San Francisco-Oakland area which supports the proposition that pupils of a lower-class school have lower educational aspirations than they would have in a mixed- or middle-class school.[11] A boy of a given I.Q. is more likely to go to college if he is in a mixed-class school or a middle-class school rather than in a lower-class school.[12]

Complementing Wilson's findings are Sexton's data.[13] The latter demonstrate that curricula, educational standards, equality of teaching, educational facilities and materials, and academic achievement of the children are directly related to the socioeconomic status of the majority of children attending a particular school. These findings support the proposition that academic achievement varies directly with socioeconomic status.

Goodwin Watson has said that the American public school is a curious hybrid:

"It is managed by a school board drawn largely from upper-class circles; it is taught by teachers who come largely from middle-class backgrounds; and it is attended mainly by children from working-class homes. These three groups do not talk the same language. They differ in their manners, power and values." [14]

These studies suggest the extent and complexity of the problems confronting our society in its search for equal education for all. The solutions to these multidimensional problems will not come to hand readily, however. Although recent events in the fields of civil rights, employment, law, and legislation invite optimism regarding the future, the task of assuring equality of opportunity in education, as elsewhere, is far from accomplished.

As teachers, we see the school as the crucible in which the citizens and workers of tomorrow are tested. It is therefore incumbent upon us to understand and to view realistically the opportunities, or their absence, available to our different citizens. If we are to use the school successfully as a setting in which new formulas for citizenship and participation in American life are developed, we must be prepared to work to bring about a closer union between what is espoused in the open classroom and what is practiced in the closed society.

References

1. Basil Bernstein, "A Public Language: Some Sociological Implications of a Linguistic Form," *British Journal of Sociology,* **10** (1959), 311–327.
2. Allison Davis, *Social Class Influence on Learning* (Cambridge: Harvard University Press, 1962), *passim.*
3. Quoted in Genevieve Knupfer, "Portrait of the Underdog," in *Class, Status and Power,* ed. by Reinhard Bendix and Seymour M. Lipset (Glencoe, Ill.: Free Press, 1963), p. 263.
4. Fern Adams and Jeanette Friedrich, "Summary of Literature and Development of Guidelines for Diagnosis of Culturally Disadvantaged Pupils," Office of the Los Angeles County Superintendent of Schools, Division of Research and Guidance, Summer 1963, p. 1.
5. Robert Havighurst, "Metropolitan Development and the Educational System," *School Review,* **60** (1961), 251.
6. *Ibid.,* p. 252. See also Oscar Handlin, *The Newcomers* (New York: Doubleday and Co., 1962).
7. Robert Havighurst, "Metropolitan Development and Educational Problems," in Robert Havighurst and Bernice Neugarten, eds., *Society and Education* (Boston: Allyn and Bacon, 1962), chapter 13.
8. James B. Conant, *Slums and Suburbs* (New York: McGraw-Hill, 1961), p. 3.
9. Robert Havighurst and Bernice Neugarten, eds., *op. cit., passim.*
10. Alan B. Wilson, "Class Segregation and Aspirations of Youth," *American Sociological Review,* **24** (1959), *passim.*
11. *Ibid.,* p. 838.
12. *Ibid.,* p. 839.
13. Patricia C. Sexton, *Education and Income: Inequalities of Opportunity in our Public Schools* (New York: Viking Press, 1961), *passim.*
14. Goodwin Watson.

1. Education and Cultural Values

GEORGE KNELLER

A culture's values are its ideals of what is worth striving for. Some of them are precise, such as the value of honesty, whereas others are hard to delineate, like our belief in the supreme worth of the individual. Some, like patriotism, are constantly on men's lips, whereas others, such as the belief that reality can be measured, are rarely acknowledged.

Of the diversity of cultural values there is no doubt.[1] Consider the value of competitiveness, which seems so necessary to the American way of life. Americans are constantly urged to get ahead; our aim is always to win, always to get there first, always to climb one more rung on an endless ladder of prosperity and success. (This is not, of course, to deny that the American is not also pulled by contrary values, such as that of group harmony and cooperation.) Yet, to many primitive peoples competition is abhorrent. Hopi life, for instance, is based on cooperation among men and with nature. A Hopi child is taught never to win a game or to excel his classmates.[2] Among the Mixtecans of Juxtlahuaca, Mexico, envy and competitiveness are minor

Reprinted from George Kneller, *Educational Anthropology: An Introduction,* Chapter 7, (New York: John Wiley & Sons, 1964), by permission of the author and publisher.

crimes. A Mixtecan in a position of authority does not give orders to his fellows. If he suggests a course of action, he does so as one dispensing knowledge, not as one dominating others through personality or position. Group decisions are the result of consensus rather than majority rule.[3]

Although the values of our culture pervade our lives, they do not mold us alike. For one thing, cultural change is far from symmetrical; hence, conflicting values coexist within the same culture, and different values are affirmed by different individuals. Social groups differ in certain of their values, and in a pluralist society especially, a person is exposed to a wide range of such values. Furthermore, each person's private experiences leave their unique imprint on the values of his culture as he sees them.

The average man finds it difficult to regard his values with detachment. In his childhood he learns to regard them as universal and absolute, and, therefore, not to be compromised, for the child cannot understand that something is good unless he is also led to believe that it is good for all men everywhere. The idea, for example, that certain acts, such as lying, may be wrong in general but justified on occasion is too sophisticated for a ten-year-old to grasp. Moreover, having been absorbed for the most part unconsciously in the process of enculturation, these values have entered into the personality of the mature man and have done much to mold it.

Those values acceptable to all members of a culture tend to be very general and, for this reason, difficult to realize fully. Consider some values on which nearly all Americans would agree: that all men should have an equal opportunity to realize their talents; that all men should possess certain rights and freedoms (such as freedom of religion and equality before the law); that problems should be solved rationally and, where appropriate, democratically; and that, if such values are observed, life can be made better for all. But do all Americans really get an equal chance to make something of their lives? Are they all treated alike by the law? And can they be?

THREE ISSUES FOR EDUCATION

Three aspects of the relation of values to culture are particularly relevant. One is the discrepancy between a culture's values and its actual practices—the discrepancy, that is, between ideal and manifest or "actualized" culture. The second is the conflict in values generated by cultural change. The third is the disparity between the dominant values of the culture and the values of minorities within the culture. Let us consider each in turn.

Ideal versus Manifest Culture

THE CONFLICT IN CULTURE. Since no culture is fully integrated, its ideals are bound to vary from its practices. Every culture legitimizes for its members certain goals as well as certain norms (modes of behavior) for attaining them. These norms are not necessarily the most efficient, either for the individual or for the group—most cultures, for instance, prohibit the use of force or fraud to achieve their goals—but they are compatible, as a rule, with the existing values and institutions of the culture. These norms vary, too, in the weight that they carry, for they may be prescribed, preferred, or merely permitted.

Yet, because a culture legitimizes certain norms, it does not follow that they always are observed. The less efficient the norms become as means of reaching the culture's goals, the less the norms tend to be observed. In addition, the more a culture impels its members to concentrate on its goals and the less it emphasizes the norms for attaining them, again the less these norms are observed. The culture thus is threatened by disorganization, until eventually it may reach a state that Durkheim called *anomie*, or normlessness, when the official norms no longer answer to the realities of life in the culture.[4]

In America certain success goals, especially those connected with wealth and its symbols (the summer home, the winter cruise, the private airplane), are acclaimed far more emphatically than the institutionalized means for attaining them. Our culture insists that if a man works hard and overtime, he will succeed in life—that is, he will make a lot of money. Yet, only a few men can get rich by working long and hard, for "rich" is a relative term and the rich, by definition, must necessarily be few. (In a country of millionaires only billionaires are wealthy.) This is not to mention such other barriers to success as social class and racial or ethnic origin, which may not make hard work futile but considerably limit the benefits to be gained by it. Thus, despite the fact that the culturally sanctioned norm of hard work rarely leads to the wealth it is supposed to, all men are urged, nevertheless, to strive for success as the culture defines it. The result may be not only anxiety or frustration but also antisocial behavior, as men seek more effective ways than the official norms to gratify the success drives implanted in them.

Of itself, lack of opportunity does not cause deviant behavior; it is the combination of inadequate opportunity and the acclamation of success goals not for a few but for the whole population. The culture holds out certain goals for all its members, yet the conditions of culture render the approved means of reaching these goals ineffective for most people. The culture, in short, arouses expectations that can rarely be fulfilled in the ways it provides.

Let me mention a few more discrepancies between the theory and practice of American culture. On the one hand, we extol free enterprise. On the other, a few large firms dominate the economy; broad sectors of this economy, such as defense and aviation, are financed by the Federal government; and the small, independent businessman, praised in the chambers of commerce, is crushed by the economics of mass production. Again, individualism is prized but togetherness is practiced. In addition, youngsters are encouraged to date early and marry late, yet premarital intercourse is frowned upon. Then, as I stated earlier, there is the popular disdain of the teacher, who is "too theoretical" and insufficiently "practical," but who, nevertheless, becomes suspect if he enters the arena of politics or the marketplace of industry and commerce.

THE CONFLICT IN EDUCATION. In a thousand and one ways American schools transmit and reinforce the values of their culture. Since most teachers and administrators come from the middle class, much educational practice reflects, however covertly, middle-class attitudes.[5] Although schoolmen differ in many respects, all nevertheless embody certain values, such as the importance of adult authority, the need for order and discipline, the value of knowledge and of educational achievement, and such middle-class traits as neatness, politeness, correct speech, and respect for property. The culture's values are also subtly manifested in the school curriculum. Courses in civics convey the values of an open democracy, collective action, and the possibility of improving the human lot. Courses in history tend to depict the culture in a favorable light.[6]

A school's activities and organization also convey accepted values.[7] In the classroom the child learns to be punctual, write legibly, use paper sparingly, and be quiet when the teacher is speaking. Raising his hand to make suggestions and answer questions reinforces the drive to compete and excel. In games he learns to play fair and to take his turn with others. In clubs he learns the prestige of being an officer. From school festivities he acquires loyalty to his school and solidarity with fellow students. Nevertheless, being exposed to these values does not guarantee that he absorbs them as his own; other factors interfere, such as the special norms of the peer group, the unpopularity of certain teachers, and perhaps parental apathy toward his education.

Inevitably, the school finds itself caught in the conflict between ideal and manifest culture. Should it educate the child in the direction of certain theoretically desirable objectives or should it condition him to the existing realities of the culture? According to the democratic ethos, people should cooperate to get things done, but in most of our society they compete. Hence, the school oscillates between encouraging children to cooperate and encouraging them to compete, and does not take a firm stand for either value. We extol the idea that everyone should have an equal opportunity to pursue the career most suited to his talents, yet, in most careers, it is disproportionately difficult for a woman to succeed. As a result, the school wavers between encouraging girls to become the career women that officially they are entitled to be and training them to be the housewives most of them become. There is also the discrepancy between the belief that education should liberate the mind of every student, no matter what his background, and the fact that colleges are selective in their admission policies. Hence, the school swings between educating for intellectual development and educating for adjustment to further schooling.

Perhaps the greatest gulf is between the ideal of equality and the fact of segregation. Not only are many schools and social institutions segregated still, but even in the greater part of the country where segregation officially does not exist, it is difficult for a Negro student to get as good an education as a white student, partly because schools in Negro neighborhoods tend to be poorly staffed and poorly administered, partly because the predominantly white schools are pervaded by white attitudes to which the Negro student is unaccustomed. Other ethnic minorities, such as Mexicans and Puerto Ricans, are in a similar plight.[8]

Traditional versus Emergent Values

THE CONFLICT IN CULTURE. As a culture changes—from, say, agrarianism to industrialism—either some or all of its values will change or become reinterpreted, although not necessarily together or immediately. The transformation of the United States into an affluent society has juxtaposed the values of the Puritan ethic with those of an industrial society geared to abundance. In order to provide for its own growth, business must constantly persuade people to consume ever larger quantities of nonessentials. As a result, abstinence is retreating before consumption, thrift before installment buying.[9] Sexuality, once the prime example of abstinence, is being stimulated more and more by dress, advertising, and mass entertainment. Belief in the importance of the future is yielding to the view that the present should be enjoyed since the future is uncertain. Self-reliance is giving way to group-mindedness.

Some critics, it is true, deny that the nucleus of the American value system has changed at all. This nucleus, say Talcott Parsons and Winston White, is the concept of "instrumental individualism," or the belief that a person should aim at the kinds of success that benefit his society.[10] Today, they maintain, a person is still expected to work hard and not relax until he has achieved success. What has changed are the specific ends to be achieved and the means for achieving them. At one time, the goal was monetary profit by means of investment, and the type was the entrepreneur. Now the goal is high competence in a specialized role within a large organization, a goal attained by performing the role responsibly in order to meet approval. The type is the flexible, other-directed executive. Nevertheless, whether the values emerging from the social and economic changes of the twentieth century are replacing fundamental American values or merely reinterpreting them, the fact remains that these values exist and are at odds with the values—or interpretations—emphasized formerly.

THE CONFLICT IN EDUCATION. The conflict between traditional and emergent values frequently manifests itself in a discrepancy between the intent and the actual effect of teaching, between the effect the teacher wishes to have, and probably thinks he has, and the effect he actually does have.[11] In Spindler's view, educators tend on the whole to be less traditional in their values than the general public.[12] Young teachers especially lean most strongly toward emergent values, followed by older teachers and then by administrators. School boards tend to be the most conservative, since they generally consist of older members of the community who have succeeded in life and, therefore, tend to support the values of the established order. Students may be more or less conservative than their teachers, depending to some extent on whether the value orientation of their families is traditional or emergent. If it is traditional, children will tend to hold traditional values less firmly than their parents; if emergent, they will tend to embrace emergent values more wholeheartedly. On the other hand, children may also take up extreme traditional or emergent positions as part of a rebellion against their parents or adults in general.

Having experienced and, to some extent, internalized these cultural conflicts, teachers, as cultural transmitters, tend to pass them on to their students, thereby frustrating or obscuring many intended goals of education. As a rule they do not transmit these conflicts deliberately but rather reflect unconsciously the state of contemporary culture. Indeed, these conflicts permeate the whole subculture of education, most obviously in the design of curricula, in methods of teaching, in textbooks and teaching aids, in student-teacher relations, and in the professional training of teachers.

Consider some examples. Social studies are designed to acquaint the student, among other things, with the theory and practice of American democracy; yet frequently, in the name of doing things democratically in the classroom, they fail to train the capacity for independent, abstract thought, which democracy also needs. They tend, moreover, to reinforce those habits of group behavior already firmly embedded in the emergent value pattern.

Textbooks, too, often communicate unintended meanings. Dorothy Lee has examined one home economics textbook and fifteen state and city manuals in use in elementary and secondary schools. She mentions a number of discrepancies.[13] One book declares that it seeks to help the student "share meaningful experiences in the home." Although it provides a host of details on various household activities, such as choosing recipes, finishing seams, and doing laundry, it says nothing about the people who share these activities or who are being helped. Another book states that its goal is to help the student to enjoy the home "creatively" and to "appreciate" family living, yet it treats housework as something to be done as efficiently as possible, so that one can have more leisure time away from it. Another states that it seeks to develop a mature personality (which one would suppose called for some attention to the life of the intellect and the imagination), yet it emphasizes the external traits, congenial to the other-directed personality, of grooming, manners, popularity, making friends, and using one's time efficiently. All these textbooks, then, contain matter that is at odds with their declared goals.

Turning to classroom procedures, we find that many teachers seek to transmit the cultural heritage by permissive methods that produce a degree of freedom at variance with the attentiveness the teachers need if they are to communicate the heritage effectively. Jules Henry, for instance, describes elementary-school teachers who unconsciously transmit the cultural phenomenon of "intragroup aggression." [14] Here the group turns on its own members, who do not resist this aggression in the manner of the inner-directed individualist but rather learn to live with it. He cites a fifth-grade teacher who devoted one period to hearing short reports, which members of the class were asked to criticize. The teacher intended the experience to develop skill in writing and reporting and, one presumes, to help students to learn from criticism. In fact, however, no constructive criticism was forthcoming; nor did the teacher seek it out. As a result, and quite contrary to the teacher's intention, the children indulged in destructive criticism of one another's work, and the habit of intragroup aggression, already partly internalized from the culture, was reinforced. Furthermore, in their relations with students many teachers seek to be leaders and counselors; but in order to do this, they often curry student favor and affection to such an extent that they can no longer maintain discipline.

Inheriting, as a rule, the traditional values of the middle or lower-middle class, the prospective teacher enters the subculture of a training institution whose values are generally emergent. This institution tends to regard the prime end of education as enabling the child to work and play harmoniously with the other members of his group— often to the detriment of individual growth. The future teacher is thus in a position similar to that of an acculturating population, which somehow must handle the conflict between its own culture and the new culture that it is increasingly accepting.

The teacher may react in a number of ways. If he feels threatened by the new values, he may reaffirm his old values the more emphatically and project them uncompromisingly in the classroom. He may also overcompensate in the opposite direction by accepting the new values uncritically and seeking group harmony at all costs. If he is not given to introspection, he may internalize both sides of the conflict unconsciously without synthesizing them into a consistent value pattern of his own. In the latter case he will oscillate between different methods of handling groups and individuals and, through his inconsistencies, will make trouble for himself and his pupils. Finally, if he is thoughtful and stable, he may acknowledge the conflict but not feel threatened by it, in which case he will synthesize elements of both patterns into a coherent system of his own. In the classroom he will follow a *via media* between extreme individualism and extreme groupism. Spindler believes that this type of teacher is becoming more numerous although unfortunately he is still in a minority. [15]

In Spindler's view the first two types of teacher transmit too narrowly; the former because, contrary to his declared knowledge and intentions, he communicates effectively only with middle-class children who share his values; the latter because he aims at a group harmony that pays little attention to individuals. Both teachers may stimulate a few children, but they will fail to influence the majority. The third type communicates to many children in many ways, but is too weak and too inconsistent to transmit the culture effectively. The fourth teacher, on the other hand, having consciously synthesized the best elements of both value patterns, is able to reach more children in more ways; hence, he "transmits along many channels."

To tackle the problem of unconsciously transmitted cultural conflicts, Spindler recommends what he calls "cultural therapy." [16] In a few cases the cultural therapist can study the teacher privately and in his classroom and, by showing him how internalized values are narrowing his attitudes, can help him to deepen and broaden his approach. However, since this operation consumes much time and energy, Spindler suggests that the information gained in these cases should be put at the disposal of student teachers in foundations courses in order to help them examine their internalized values before the classroom calls these values into action.

But here a dilemma arises, for the cultural conflicts transmitted to children in the school are also beneficial in that they contribute to variations in personalities and, hence, to cultural innovation. One solution is for the teacher to acknowledge these conflicts more explicitly, even in the act of transmitting them, or, better, to transmit only selected conflicts. But there is a danger here too, for if we can control the conflicts that we transmit, we will be prone to transmit the culture too narrowly and, hence, to induce conformity. Suppose, on the other hand, that the teacher seeks to be eclectic and thereby to stimulate as many children as possible. Can he at the same time transmit the cultural heritage effectively to each of these children? We are left, then, with a theoretical problem which educators have still to solve: In order to encourage individual differences and, at the same time, avoid unconscious conflict in the student, teachers must know and control the conflicts they

transmit; yet, if they can do this, they are in a position to induce an undesirable conformity.

Dominant versus Minority Values

THE CONFLICT IN CULTURE. Many Americans live outside the dominant American culture, which is roughly that of the middle class.[17] They have not been brought up in it, and they do not aspire to it. Many of them are separated from it by poverty and many by race, and a high proportion are undereducated.[18] Since education has done little for them, many have little faith in what it can do for their children; and those who are eager to have their children well educated can give them little help, since they lack formal schooling themselves. This alienation from the majority culture is especially severe among those of non-European ancestry, of whom I shall consider the Mexican American and the American Negro in particular.[19]

Except that both belong to subcultures, Negroes and Mexicans have little in common. Traditionally, the Negro has been closer than the Mexican to the life around him, and his culture more clearly reflects the dominant American values. The Mexican tends to hold himself aloof. Under discrimination, against which the Negro may protest, the Mexican withdraws, often covering his retreat with politeness. The Mexican tends not to attend school conferences and PTA meetings. When the school asks him to cooperate in seeing that his son arrives on time or that his daughter does her homework, he often replies that he *intends* to do so. Politeness and procrastination are his way of avoiding conflict.[20]

Mexican culture, writes Ruth Landes, is more authoritarian than Negro culture. Unlike most other American children, white and Negro, Mexican children are expected to wait for adult direction, usually that of parents or elder siblings, rather than to exercise their own initiative. Hence, writes Landes, if they are to behave with initiative in the schools, they must be taught how to set aside their traditional habits of deference. Their teachers, too, must handle them more firmly than they would other American children. School counselors must expect to make more decisions for them. School officers must follow up their decisions by seeing parents personally and getting in touch with them by letter and phone—ways that other Americans would find interfering and even overbearing.[21]

The Negro woman, continues Landes, enjoys a freedom similar to that of the white woman. Negro parents are not surprised when their children are taught by women teachers and follow certain dating habits actually encouraged by the school. Mexican women, on the other hand, especially if young and unmarried, are not expected to hold positions of authority. Hence, Mexican parents are often disconcerted when their older children are instructed by young, unmarried female teachers and affronted when their daughters acquire some of the sexual independence of the normal American girl.[22]

A child of the white middle class tends to bring to his school a very different outlook from that of the lower-class child, white or colored. From infancy on he has been more carefully fed, clothed, and guarded by parents who have the time and money to spend on him. Tenderness and understanding, pride and affection, have been shown him from the beginning. He is confident and at ease in a world in which he assumes that he will succeed as a matter of course.

Having absorbed the drive and directedness of his parents, he is purposeful and self-confident.

The children of the poor have rarely known such solicitude. Their parents have not had time to give it to them—the father physically tired and perhaps chronically unemployed, the mother at work or overburdened with household chores. The world of the white middle class is indifferent to them, perhaps even hostile. Having little to aim for, they lack ambition; they feel alienated from the wider society; and they have little sense of purpose. Mexicans excepted, they are less disciplined, especially sexually, than middle-class children and express themselves more forcibly and brusquely. Instead of restraining their inclinations in order to strive for future goals, they tend to live for the moment.

THE CONFLICT IN EDUCATION. The typical American school is imbued with middle-class values. It expects children to be polite, to follow the conventions, and to respect other people's property. It encourages hard work, sportsmanship, and, above all, ambition. To all these values the middle-class child is already accustomed. His teachers, members of the middle class themselves, respond to him with understanding and appreciation. But to the lower-class child many of these values are alien. He does not feel himself a part of the school, because the values of the school are not his. Hence, talented lower-class children rarely do so well in school as middle-class children of equal and even lesser ability, and some of them drop out even when they are intellectually capable of continuing.[23]

The school's middle-class culture sets the lower-class child at a disadvantage in innumerable ways. The language of the school is unfamiliar to him. His textbooks, too, appeal to middle-class attitudes, especially that of ambition, and their illustrations often depict middle-class people in middle-class situations. He is not at ease with his teachers, who dress, talk, and think differently and appreciate different things. The subjects that he studies—grammar, history, and science —seem to him to have little or no bearing on the sordid and sometimes desperate circumstances with which he must cope when out of school. The very procedures of the school may violate the canons to which he is accustomed.[24]

How are educators to surmount the cultural differences that hinder effective communication? First, in order to understand the expectations that children bring to school, educators must study the cultures in which the children are reared. They must use this knowledge to develop appropriate techniques for all aspects of the educational process. They will find that many problems spring not from the fractiousness of the pupil or his parents, but rather from the latters' misinterpretation of ways of speech and action to which they are unaccustomed. Ruth Landes tells the case of an intelligent but unruly Korean-American boy who was nearly excluded from his school because the school authorities did not comprehend the cultural traditions of his Korean father. Unaware of the veneration accorded by Koreans to the head of the household, school representatives tried persistently to reach the mother. Finally, when the father was approached in the manner to which he was accustomed, he cooperated with the school in controlling the child.[25]

The teacher must also examine the influence of culture on his own behavior. Unless he knows the cultural signals that he himself is sending out, he gains little from perceiving the signals of his pupils. Ideally, this self-examination should be carried out during his training, although to the thoughtful, actual teaching experience will be the great enlightener.[26]

Since he feels alienated from the wider society, the lower-class child, and especially the minority child, often lacks the drive to aim at vocational goals that he is otherwise capable of attaining. It should, therefore, be the responsibility of the school counselor to foster vocational ambitions receiving little or no encouragement from parents, community, or peers.[27] He should provide an example of successful male adulthood, which the lower-class boy can imitate and, in so doing, develop long-term ambitions of his own as well as the personality traits needed to attain them. Other means of encouraging ambition, both academic and vocational, are to increase the scholarship aid offered by institutions of higher education, to acquaint the student with examples of successful professional persons from his own racial, ethnic, or class background, and to encourage parents to sympathize with the newly awakened ambitions of their children.

If the school can interest parents in their children's education, it has gone a long way toward overcoming cultural differences.[28] Teachers and administrators must gain the confidence of parents who regard the school as merely another alien power determining their lives. To this end, the school should offer parents courses in such practical subjects as speech, shorthand, typing, sewing, and millinery, as well as refresher courses in reading, arithmetic, and such other academic subjects as will enable them to help their children in school work. It should also encourage them to take courses in budgeting, food preparation, furniture repair, household tasks, and family relations generally.

CULTURAL VALUES AND EDUCATIONAL THOUGHT

Progressivism

Let us turn finally to the views of educational theorists on the question whether or not the school should promote certain of the culture's values. The progressive educator maintains that since all circumstances and societies change and since there is no permanent human nature, all values are necessarily provisional. Right action consists less in adherence to fixed standards than in action based on reflection. The student, then, should learn not values as such, but rather how to discover them through reflective thinking. He should not be conditioned to apply a fixed code of conduct to the varied and elastic circumstances of life; rather he should learn to appraise in advance the probable consequences to himself and to others of the alternative courses of action available to him in particular situations. The teacher should propose the traditional values of Western culture as hypotheses—good ones, to be sure, since they have long served to adjust men to circumstances and to one another, but as hypotheses nevertheless—which the student should test to see whether they help him to solve his present problems.[29]

The progressive educator believes that in a pluralist democracy the school cannot rightly dictate what the student's hierarchy of values should be. Nevertheless, it can influence the student's choice of values by inviting him to consider certain values rather than others as part of his general education. To insure that all students share the common experience of getting to grips with these values in a contemporary setting, the teacher must use a wide variety of methods and materials. Otherwise, given, say, a single book to read, each student will simply seize on the ideas that meet his particular interest instead of sharing the same general experience with his fellows.[30]

In any other-directed culture, social and cultural change is liable to get out of hand, since people lack firm values for assessing which changes are desirable and which are not. Few progressives any longer maintain that stability can be found in the process of change itself. In order, then, to find his own hierarchy of values, the student must be taught how to examine the values motivating much contemporary behavior, so that he will not accept the behavior of those around him without assessing its assumptions and consequences. He must study various aspects and problems of the contemporary culture, such as advertising, the automobile, and divorce, in order to understand the values that they imply and to judge them for himself. By studying current behavior and artifacts rather than abstract or historical issues, he is better able to work out for himself a realistic hierarchy of values relevant to the world he must live in.[31]

Conservatism

The conservative view of values in education takes two forms, the *perennialist* and the *essentialist*. Perennialists, believing in an absolute hierarchy of values, maintain that, contrary to present practice, it is the school's duty to inculcate these values. In Hutchins' words:

The prime object of education is to know what is good for man. It is to know the goods in their order. There is a hierarchy of values. The task of education is to help us understand it, establish it, and live by it.[32]

The essentialist view is that although the school should not give overt moral training, nevertheless, in developing the intellect it is cultivating the important moral values of intellectual honesty and reflective thinking. The school should also influence the moral character of its students by insuring that its own activities are conducted according to moral standards that the students clearly understand. Thus, it should encourage students to be honest in their work; it should reward them according to actual performance; and it should give high prestige to serious intellectual activities. Harry Broudy states that the school gives moral education when it encourages devotion to truth and reason, assists the pupil to use his talents to the full, and initiates self-knowledge by making the student think about himself and personally test his own abilities.[33]

The conservative point of view is also defended by I. B. Berkson, who rejects the progressive contention that the child should be allowed to form his own hierarchy of values. The school, he says, should teach the values of Western culture, which are more reliable than the judgments of a student.[34] He also criticizes the progressive attempt to train the character by imitating situations in real life. He points out that the main moral issues of adult life, such as those concerned with marriage or one's career, are too complex for the school to duplicate at all adequately. Instead, the school should train the character in two ways: by teaching the child contemporary mores, thereby producing social stability, and by teaching him the enduring ideals of the culture, thereby enabling him to criticize and improve these mores when he is an adult.[35]

Both types of conservatism maintain that it is the parents' responsibility to teach the child certain values that he later may assess for himself. To bring him up without fixed standards is not to emancipate but to confuse him. Meanwhile, the school should give him the intellectual training he needs if he is to weigh these values objectively in later life. Although parents should not pretend for the child's sake to hold values in which they do not believe, it is still their responsibility to instill those in which they do believe.

References and Notes

1. For an account of how different cultures interpret the notion of equality, see Dorothy Lee, "Equality of Opportunity as a Cultural Value," in *Freedom and Culture,* Prentice-Hall, Englewood Cliffs, New Jersey, 1959, pp. 39–52.
2. Wayne Dennis, *The Hopi Child,* Appleton-Century, New York, 1940.
3. Kimball Romney and Romaine Romney, "The Mixtecans of Juxtlahuaca, Mexico," in Beatrice B. Whiting, ed., *Six Cultures: Studies of Child Rearing,* Wiley, New York, 1963, p. 565.
4. Robert K. Merton, "Social Structure and Anomie," *Social Theory and Social Structure,* The Free Press of Glencoe, New York, 1957, p. 135:
   With such differential emphases upon goals and institutional procedures, the latter may be so vitiated by the stress on goals as to have the behavior of many individuals limited only by considerations of technical experience. In this context, the sole significant question becomes: Which of the available procedures is most efficient in netting the culturally approved value?

5. Robert J. Havighurst, "Social Class and the American School System," in George Z. F. Bereday and Luigi Volpicelli, eds., *Public Education in America: A New Interpretation of Purpose and Practice,* Harper, New York, 1958, p. 86:
   > They (teachers) attempt to serve as trustees of the educational system in the interests of the entire society *as they understand these interests.* This means that they tend to favor the teaching of middle class skills and attitudes in the schools, and that they favor types of education which promote social mobility.
6. Cf. Penelope Leach, "Teaching Tolerance," *International Review of Education,* **X,** No. 2 (1964), 196–197.
7. Cf. Frederick Elkins, *The Child and Society: The Process of Socialization,* Random House, New York, 1958, pp. 59–60.
8. Cf. Ruth Landes, "Culture and Education," in George F. Kneller, ed., *Foundations of Education,* Wiley, New York, 1963, pp. 320–352.
9. Cf. George Dearborn Spindler, *The Transmission of American Culture,* The Burton Lectures, 1957, Harvard University Press, 1959, p. 6, and "Education in a Transforming American Culture," in George D. Spindler, ed., *Education and Culture: Anthropological Approaches,* Holt, Rinehart and Winston, New York, 1963, pp. 136–137.
10. Talcott Parsons and Winston White, "The Link Between Character and Society," in Seymour Martin Lipset and Leo Lowenthal, eds., *Culture and Social Character: The Work of David Riesman Reviewed,* The Free Press of Glencoe, New York, 1961, pp. 89–133.
11. Of course, not all such discrepancies are the result of a conflict in cultural values. The pupil may simply not respond in the way the teacher anticipates. Compare Jules Henry's discussion of three kinds of attitudes, "indeterminate," "antithetical," and pseudo-complementary," which the teacher may arouse unconsciously: "A Cross-Cultural Survey of Education," *Current Anthropology,* I, No. 4 (July 1960), 301–302.
12. George D. Spindler, "Education in a Transforming American Culture," in George D. Spindler, ed., *Education and Culture: Anthropological Approaches,* Holt, Rinehart and Winston, New York, pp. 139–141. See also George D. Spindler, *The Transmission of American Culture,* The Burton Lecture, 1957, Harvard University Press, 1959.
13. Dorothy Lee, "Discrepancies in the Teaching of American Culture," in George D. Spindler, ed., *Education and Culture: Anthropological Approaches,* Holt, Rinehart and Winston, New York, 1963, pp. 173–191.
14. Jules Henry, "Attitude Organization in Elementary School Classrooms," *American Journal of Orthopsychiatry,* **XXVII** (January 1957), 117–133.
15. George D. Spindler, *The Transmission of American Culture,* The Burton Lecture, 1957, Harvard University Press, 1959, pp. 27–28.
16. *Ibid.,* p. 49.
17. A considerable proportion belong to the "forgotten fifth" of the nation who live below the poverty line. In 1962 thirty million Americans lived in families with annual incomes of under $3,000—less than $60 a week. Five million more unattached Americans had annual incomes of less than $1,500 a year. Of the poor families 47 per cent lived in the South, 25 per cent in the North Central region, 17 per cent in the Northeast, and 11 per cent in the West. Nearly half of all nonwhite Americans live in poverty. *New York Times,* January 21, 1964.
18. About six out of ten heads of families in the poverty group have had eight years of school or less. Expressed differently, nearly 40 per cent of heads of families with no more than eighth grade education belong to the poverty group, whereas fewer than 10 per cent of those with more than a high-school education belong to this group. *New York Times,* January 9, 1964.

19. Since my concern in this article is with cultural, rather than physical, anthropology, I consider race here as a social and cultural, not as a genetic, phenomenon. Whether the Negro's present cultural deficiencies are genetically as well as environmentally conditioned is an area of controversy that I cannot enter. See correspondence to *Science*, **CXLII** (December 13, 1963), 1419–1420, and **CXLIII** (January 24, 1964), 306–308.
20. Ruth Landes, "Culture and Education," in George F. Kneller, ed., *Foundations of Education*, Wiley, New York, 1963, p. 328.
21. *Ibid.*, pp. 341–342.
22. *Ibid.*, pp. 332–333, 345. However, in urban communities in Mexico this is ceasing to be true (author).
23. In one study Robert J. Havighurst found that for every high-school dropout from the upper and upper-middle classes there were about 32 from the upper-lower and lower-lower classes. Moreover, fifteen students entered college from the two top social classes for every one from the two lower classes. Havighurst also found that, when the proportion of middle-class children in a school approached or fell below 40 per cent, their parents began either to leave the neighborhood or to enroll their children in private schools. Robert J. Havighurst et al., *Growing Up in River City*, Wiley, New York, 1962, pp. 50–53.
24. For instance, in the 1930's Otto Klineberg discovered that some children of the Plains Indians had failed in the Indian schools because they would not act competitively in the way their white teachers wanted them to. Although each child was expected to recite publicly and be praised for his display of knowledge, none did so because this was felt to be boastful and a public shaming of one's kinsmen. See Otto Klineberg, *Race Differences,* Harper, New York, 1935 and later editions, quoted by Ruth Landes, "Culture and Education," in George F. Kneller, ed., *Foundations of Education,* Wiley, New York, 1963, p. 324.
25. *Ibid.*, p. 330.
26. *Ibid.*, pp. 336–340. According to Landes, teachers of Mexican and Puerto Rican children should, if possible, learn Spanish. Although, clearly, these students must master English, they should not be penalized for reverting to their own language, particularly in conversation among themselves. If they are to retain the pride in self to which they are entitled and which is necessary for effective learning, their language must be treated with the respect it deserves and not as an inferior argot used to deceive or shut out their teachers. A command of Spanish can win for a teacher the affection and trust of pupils on whom other teachers have little influence.
27. Cf. David P. Ausubel, "A Teaching Strategy for Culturally Deprived Pupils: Cognitive and Motivational Considerations," *The School Review,* Winter 1963, 462–463.
28. Cf. Clemmont E. Vontress, "Our Demoralizing Slum Schools," *Phi Delta Kappan,* **XLV,** No. 2 (November 1963), 81. Vontress says that if parents do not respond to the school's invitations, the school must move its activities into the neighborhood, setting up "Education Appreciation" workshops in whatever halls they can find. See also Frederick Shaw, "Educating Culturally Deprived Youth in Urban Centers," *ibid.*, 93. In addition to winning the support of parents, Shaw maintains that the school should seek the backing of the whole community. To do so, it may set up programs of activities for youth in the afternoons and for adults in the evenings. It may also enlist the help of other public and private agencies, such as libraries, neighborhood service organizations, YMCA's and YWCA's. In serving the needs of the whole community the school contributes visibly and positively to the lives of the adults and youngsters whose attitude to education materially influences the behavior of the school's students.

29. George R. Geiger, "An Experimentalist Approach to Education," in Nelson B. Henry, ed., *Modern Philosophies and Education,* The Fifty-fourth Yearbook of the National Society for the Study of Education, University of Chicago Press, 1955, p. 161.
30. Cf. Harold L. Hodgkinson, *Education in Social and Cultural Perspectives,* Prentice-Hall, Englewood Cliffs, New Jersey, 1962, pp. 133–134.
31. *Ibid.,* p. 138. Hodgkinson mentions the case of some school children in Hagerstown, Maryland, who were given constant practice during school hours in watching television critically, with the result that they became much more selective in the programs they watched out of school. He writes:

    "Here the school has unintentionally built into many students a hierarchy of values which allows them to be selective instead of being inundated by a steady flow of one program after another. If it can be done unintentionally, why could not the school intentionally develop a program to promote sophistication in analysis of a wide range of social behaviors?"
32. Robert M. Hutchins, *The Conflict in Education in a Democratic Society,* Harper New York, 1953, p. 71.
33. Harry S. Broudy, *Building a Philosophy of Education,* Prentice-Hall, Englewood Cliffs, New Jersey, 1961, p. 241.
34. I. B. Berkson, *The Ideal and the Community: A Philosophy of Education,* Harper, New York, 1958, p. 244.
35. *Ibid.*

2. Who Are the Socially Disadvantaged?

ROBERT J. HAVIGHURST

In all of our big cities, and in many smaller cities and rural counties, educators are trying to find better ways of teaching a group of children and youth who are variously called ["culturally deprived," "intellectually deprived," or "socially disadvantaged." This is a major movement, which enlists a large amount of money and time of skilled teachers and also a considerable amount of research effort.]

There is consensus that this group of children and their families present a great social problem, perhaps the greatest of our domestic social problems. It is important that the problem be seen clearly.

Different writers and different workers in this area have defined the target group somewhat differently. The group is sometimes described (and frequently enough to cause confusion in the minds of readers) as being all children of manual workers. But few if any educators care to call this large working-class group, some two-thirds of the child population, "socially disadvantaged."

A more useful definition of the "socially disadvantaged" can be arrived at in the way that is demonstrated in this article. [Children with social disadvantages have always been present in any society.] However, probably the numbers are unusually large in the present American society, because of its urbanism and the changes in the labor force which make it difficult for youths aged 16 to 20 to find employment.]

The question which is the title of this chapter may be answered in various ways. One way is to illustrate by describing some cases of social disadvantages.

Suppose we observe two mothers riding with their 4-year-old children on a bus. The mothers want to teach their children to sit properly on a bus seat while the bus starts and stops suddenly.

Case A

Mother: Hold on tight to your seat.
Child: Why?
Mother: Hold on tight.
Child: Why?
Mother: You'll fall.
Child: Why?
Mother: I told you to hold on tight, didn't I?

Case B

Mother: Hold on tightly, darling.
Child: Why?

Reprinted from the *Journal of Negro Education,* Vol. 33 (Summer 1964), pp. 210–217, by permission of the publisher and author.

Mother: If you don't you will be thrown forward and then you'll fall.

Child: Why?

Mother: Because if the bus stops suddenly you'll jerk forward and bump against the seat in front.

Child: Why?

Mother: Now hold on tightly, darling, and don't make such a fuss.

The first thing that strikes the observer of these two cases is that the mother in Case A does not try to explain to the child. Thus the child does not have an opportunity to learn the "why" of things, and if this kind of situation occurs again and again, the child may lose the habit of asking, "Why?" The next thing is that the vocabulary in Case A is more restricted than that in Case B. Thus the child does not get practice in extending his vocabulary. Perhaps the next thing that will be noticed is that there is a difference in the *relation* between child and mother in the two situations. In Case A the mother asserts her authority through categorical statements. She does not really try to explain why the child should hold on tight, but *orders* the child to do so. The mother's authority is invoked almost at once, with the result that the natural curiosity of the child is pushed back, and the child is learning *not* to think for himself. In Case B the mother attempts to satisfy the child's curiosity with explanations. Although she finally resorts to her authority, she has first given the child a chance to learn about the world in a relationship which permits him to challenge authority with his questions.

The child who experiences language and social relations of Case A during his early years is likely to develop a different kind of mind than the child who experiences language and social relations of Case B. The child in Case A is socially disadvantaged when compared with the child in Case B.

DISADVANTAGED FOR WHAT?

Disadvantage is a relative term. When we speak of a child as being *socially disadvantaged* we mean that he has a disadvantage relative to some other child for some kind of social life. As the term is used it means disadvantaged for living competently in an urban, industrial, and democratic society. [The socially disadvantaged child is one who is handicapped in the task of growing up to lead a competent and satisfying life in the American society.]

Consider, for example, Michael, who is a ten-year-old boy living in an ordinary town. His father is a truck driver, and makes a good income, though he must be away from home, frequently for days at a time. Michael's mother stays at home and does her best to give her three children a good start in life. She looks after the children faithfully, and wishes they had enough money to rent a house in a "better" part of town where the neighbors had nicer children and there were not so many Saturday night fights and Monday morning hangovers.

When Michael was seven years old he was put into an experimental second grade class consisting of 18 children who had failed the first grade by not learning to read at the proper grade level. Instead of making them repeat the first grade, the principal put them all in one class with a teacher who volunteered to work with them, and with a social worker who spent a day a week visiting the homes of the children. Michael had an IQ of 97. He began to read by Thanksgiving of the second year, and soon was reading at a second grade level. He liked especially the trips his group took to the public library, where the children's librarian read to them and encouraged them to borrow books and take them home. Michael read about 20 children's books by the spring of the year. But he forgot to return his books on time, and one day his mother received a post card telling her that there was a 16-cent fine for overdue books. She sent Michael to the library with the money, but told him, "Don't you ever go near that library again. They didn't have a right to fine you."

To Michael's mother, a fine was a bad thing. She associated it with the punishment some of her neighbors suffered when they got drunk and had a fight at a nearby tavern and were arrested and fined "for being drunk and disorderly." She was raising her children to avoid this kind of life, and she did not think Michael was guilty of a crime by keeping the library books too long.

Michael got along fairly well in school; his grades were average, and he was a good boy. One day, when he was in the fifth grade, he was playing after school and he spied the social worker who used to visit his home when he was in the experimental second grade. He greeted her, and said, "Miss Jansen, please come to my house and see my books." He took her into his home and showed her a set of Britannica Junior books. "These are all mine," he said. "My dad pays five dollars a month for them." The social worker said, "That's wonderful, Michael, and do your folks read to you from these books?" "Oh, no," said Michael, "they don't like to read much, and, besides, they said that these are my books, for me to read. Of course, I can't understand everything, but I've been reading about the animals of the world."

Just then, Michael's mother came in and greeted the social worker warmly. "We'll never forget how much you helped us when Michael was in the second grade," she said, "and don't you think these books are wonderful?"

This was a case of social disadvantage, and illustrates the fact that parents may take very good care of their children in an emotional sense, but still deprive them of a good intellectual start in life. This mother and father simply did not *know* how to help their children do well in school. In spite of their good intentions, they deprived Michael of the use of the library, which might have been a major intellectual resource for him, and then they splurged by getting him a children's encyclopedia but they did not set an example of reading, and they did not read to him to help him learn to read.

WHO ARE THE SOCIALLY DISADVANTAGED?

The socially disadvantaged children may be defined and described in three ways: in terms of certain family characteristics relating directly to the child, in terms of their personal characteristics, or in terms of the social group characteristics of their families.

Family Characteristics

Compared with other children whose families give them average or better advantages for getting started in modern urban life, the socially disadvantaged child lacks several of the following:

A *family conversation which:* answers his questions and encourages him to ask questions; extends his vocabulary with words and with adjectives and adverbs; gives him a right and a need to stand up for and to explain his point of view on the world.

A *family environment which:* sets an example of reading; provides a variety of toys and play materials with colors, sizes, and objects that challenge his ingenuity with his hands and his mind.

Two parents who: read a good deal; read to him; show him that they believe in the value of education; reward him for good school achievement.

Bernstein [1] has studied the language behavior of families that relate to the intellectual development of their children. He distinguishes between two forms or *types* of language. (These language types are statistically related to social class, as will be pointed out later.) One form of language is called *restricted* and the other form is called *elaborated.* A family which employs restricted language gives a child a language environment characterized by the following:

1. Short, grammatically simple, often unfinished sentences with a poor syntactical form stressing the active voice.

2. Simple and repetitive use of conjunctions (so, then, because).

3. Little use of subordinate clauses to break down the initial categories of the dominant subject.

4. Inability to hold a formal subject through a speech sequence; thus a dislocated informational content is facilitated.

5. Rigid and limited use of adjectives and adverbs.

6. Constraint on the self-reference pronoun; frequent use of personal pronoun.

7. Frequent use of statements where the reason and conclusion are confounded to produce a categoric statement.

8. A large number of statements/phrases which signal a requirement for the previous speech sequence to be reinforced: "Wouldn't it? You see? You know?" etc. This process is termed "sympathetic circularity."

9. Individual selection from a group of idiomatic phrases or sequences will frequently occur.

10. The individual qualification is implicit in the sentence organization; it is a language of implicit meaning.

On the other hand, a family which employs an *elaborated* language gives the child a language environment characterized by the following:

1. Accurate grammatical order and syntax regulate what is said.

2. Logical modifications and stress are mediated through a grammatically complex sentence construction, especially through the use of a range of conjunctions and subordinate clauses.

3. Frequent use of prepositions which indicate logical relationships as well as prepositions which indicate temporal and spatial contiguity.

4. Frequent use of the personal pronoun "I."

5. A discriminative selection from a range of adjectives and adverbs.

6. Individual qualification is verbally mediated through the structure and relationships within and between sentences.

7. Expressive symbolism discriminates between meanings within speech sequences rather than reinforcing dominant words or phrases, or accompanying the sequence in a diffuse, generalized manner.

8. A language use which points to the possibilities inherent in a complex conceptual hierarchy for the organizing of experience.

A child who has learned a *restricted* language at home is likely to have difficulty in school, where an *elaborate* language is used and taught by the teacher; and the difficulty of the child is likely to increase as he goes further in school, unless he learns the elaborate language that is expected in the school. On the other hand, the child who has had experience with an elaborate language from his earliest years has a relatively easy time in school because he must simply go on developing the kind of language and related thinking which he has already started.

Personal Characteristics

The family environment with the characteristics just cited tends to produce children with certain personal deficits. Martin Deutsch [2] has studied such children with techniques of the experimental psychologists, and he finds them to have inferior auditory discrimination, inferior visual discrimination, inferior judgment concerning time, number, and other basic concepts. He finds that this inferiority is not due to physical defects of eyes and ears and brain, but is due to inferior *habits* of hearing and seeing and thinking. Presumably, the family environment of these children did not teach them to "pay attention" to what was being said around them, or to the visual scene. Then, when they came to school, their school performance suffered because they had not learned to "listen" to the teacher and other important people or to "see" the things they are shown in the school.

Social Group Characteristics

We introduce the social group characteristics of socially disadvantaged children last so as to avoid giving the impression that there is a hard-and-fast relation between socioeconomic status, or some other group characteristic, and social disadvantages for the child. Although there are statistical relations and very important ones between socioeconomic status and social disadvantages of children, there are so many individual exceptions to the statistical generalizations that any educational policy aimed at identifying socially disadvantaged children should avoid reliance upon general socioeconomic characteristics as the decisive criteria.

Above all, it is important to avoid the error of saying that all children of working class families are socially disadvantaged. Approximately 65 per cent of the children of this country are living in working-class homes. That is, their fathers or mothers do manual work for a living. The great majority of these families give their children a fairly good start for life in an urban industrial democratic society. Their children are adequately fed and clothed. They are loved and protected by their parents. They learn to respect teachers and to like school. They do fairly well or better than that in school.

Although working-class children as a group are somewhat different from the children of white-collar workers, it would not be reasonable to say that the [working-class children are socially disadvantaged or culturally deprived. Working-class children as a group score slightly below children of white-collar families in intelligence tests; they fall slightly below on tests of school achievement; they attain somewhat less formal education.] But the differences are relatively small, and become even smaller when the socially disadvantaged children are removed and the majority of working-class youth who remain are compared with white-collar children.

Most working-class families participate fully in the American mass or core culture. This is certainly not a culture of deprivation. While the differences between the upper working-class and the middle-class are real and they are interesting, these differences should not be described in terms of social advantage or social disadvantage. The great amount of movement of people across the boundary between these two classes as they grow up is evidence that the differences between these two classes are not fundamental ones.

Who, then, are the socially disadvantaged when we attempt to describe them in terms of observable social groups? They are groups with the following characteristics:

1. They are at the bottom of the American society in terms of income.
2. They have a rural background.
3. They suffer from social and economic discrimination at the hands of the majority of the society.
4. They are widely distributed in the United States. While they are most visible in the big cities, they are present in all except the very high income communities. There are many of them in rural areas.

In racial and ethnic terms, these groups are about evenly divided between whites and nonwhites. They consist mainly of the following:

1. Negroes from the rural South who have migrated recently to the Northern industrial cities.
2. Whites from the rural South and the Southern mountains who have migrated recently to the Northern industrial cities.
3. Puerto Ricans who have migrated to a few Northern industrial cities.
4. Mexicans with a rural background who have migrated into the West and Middle West.
5. European immigrants with a rural background, from East and Southern Europe.

Altogether these groups make up about 15 per cent of the United States population. Since they tend to have large families, their children make up as much as 20 per cent of the child population. Not all socially disadvantaged children come from these groups, but the great majority do. Not all children in these groups are socially disadvantaged, but the great majority are.

HOW MANY ARE SOCIALLY DISADVANTAGED?

There is an infinite graduation of social advantage-disadvantage, and therefore any quantitative estimate of the number of socially disadvantaged children and youth must be a personal rather than a scientific statement.

The writer would place the number of socially disadvantaged children at about 15 per cent of the child population. One basis for this estimate is the proportion of unemployed, out-of-school youth between the ages of 16 and 20. These young people have been relatively unsuccessful in school and in the labor market. The great majority of them come from the social groups listed above. There are about 11 per cent of boys and 17 per cent of girls in this group. The boys are clearly maladjusted to society. Some of the girls are not; they are simply doing what girls have done for a long time, helping out at home while waiting to get married. But these figures place a minimum on the numbers of socially disadvantaged youth. There are a few others who have jobs which are below their capacity or are disadvantaged in other ways—enough to bring the total up to about 15 per cent.

Since these children and their families tend to concentrate in the large cities, while upper-income people tend to move out from the cities to the suburbs, the socially disadvantaged children are in big cities in larger proportions than 15 per cent. Probably *30 per cent of the children* in such cities as New York, Chicago, Philadelphia, Washington, Detroit, Cleveland, and Baltimore fall into the socially disadvantaged category.

DO THE SOCIALLY DISADVANTAGED HAVE SPECIAL ADVANTAGES?

In discussions of education for the socially disadvantaged there is a good deal of sentimental talk about the "valuable" or the "positive" characteristics of the cultures from which these children come, and about the desirability of developing school programs that allow the child to profit from these positive qualities.

It is said that this kind of child is "physically oriented"—that he likes action rather than words. It is said that he has nonlanguage skills that can serve him for learning. It is said that he can perceive (see, hear, and smell) in superior fashion. It is said that he has more of certain kinds of creativity. It is said that he has a different "mental style" from that of children who do well in the ordinary school.

This set of propositions is conceivably correct. The child growing up in a rural culture certainly gains some skills that are likely to be more highly developed than they would be if he grew up in a city. Every culture has characteristics that are positive in its own situation. For example, in a study of Hopi Indian children of the American Southwest, it was found that their drawings were superior in many ways to the drawings of American white children. A university art teacher made systematic comparisons of the drawings and found that, according to his own criteria of good children's art, the Hopi drawings were superior to those of Midwest white children of the middle-class. Yet the same Hopi children were inferior to Midwest children on a verbal test of intelligence. Thus one might make use of this positive quality of the Hopi children in developing schools to fit them for participation in the surrounding American culture.

However, there is substantial doubt that the socially disadvantaged children in our big cities have *any* positive qualities of potential value in urban society in which they are systematically better than the children of families who participate fully in the mass culture. The writer does not know any comparative study which shows American lower-lower class children to be superior in any positive respect to American upper working-class or middle-class children. As a group they are inferior in tests of spatial perception, for example, as well as in tests of vocabulary and arithmetic. It is true that the difference between the socially disadvantaged and the mass culture majority is less on tests of certain non-verbal skills than on tests of more verbal and abstract abilities. This fact might suggest that the socially disadvantaged could learn more rapidly and efficiently if they had more concrete experience on which to base their vocabulary and their reasoning skills. This is probably true, but it does not argue for a difference in "mental style" and therefore a difference in school curriculum. It argues for more building of "readiness" for reading and arithmetic in the pre-school and primary grades.

CONCLUSION

The *socially disadvantaged* children can be defined and discovered at an early age. Although social disadvantage and social advantage are concepts which shade into each other, it is possible to make working distinctions which are a basis for identification of some 30 per cent of the children of the big cities as socially disadvantaged. These are not necessarily working-class, or lower-class children. The majority of children of working-class families are not socially disadvantaged as the term is used in this discussion.

[The socially disadvantaged children tend to come from families that are poor, and that are recent immigrants to the big cities. They are a group that need special attention in the schools and special help to assist them to overcome the disadvantages conferred on them by their families.]

References

1. Bernstein, Basil. "Language and Social Class," *British Journal of Sociology* (1960), 11, 271–276.
    Bernstein, Basil. "Social Class and Linguistic Development: A Theory of Social Learning," pp. 288 ff. in *Economy, Education and Society*, A. H. Halsey, J. Floud, and C. A. Anderson (Eds.) (New York: The Free Press of Glencoe, 1961).
    Bernstein, Basil. "Social Class, Linguistic Codes and Grammatical Elements," *Language and Speech*, 5, 221–240 (October–December, 1962). "Elaborated and Restricted Codes: Their Origins and Some Consequences," *American Anthropologist* (1964).
2. Deutsch, Martin P. "The Disadvantaged Child and the Learning Process," in *Education in Depressed Areas*, A. Harry Passow (Ed.) (New York: Bureau of Publications, Teachers College, Columbia University, 1963).

3. The Nature and Values of Culturally Different Youth

CHARLES J. CALITRI

It is imbedded in the very heart of our American democracy that we must work at the task of improving the lives of our people who find themselves on a lower economic, social, and educational level than the great middle-class majority. There will always be classes; there will always be groups of people composing strata, even though the conditions and the characteristics of those strata may constantly change. As one group finds its way out of the prize fighting ring into professional baseball and then places some of its sons and daughters among the teachers, lawyers, doctors, engineers, and business leaders, another group forms at the lower economic level, either imported from a hungry or despotic land, or home-grown among the displaced persons of industrial towns that lose their factories and farm lands that turn into empires whose fields and orchards are harvested by itinerant laborers and pickers.

If we set aside the derelicts for

Reprinted from *Improving English Skills of Culturally Different Youth in Large Cities,* edited by Arno Jewett, et al. (Washington, D.C.: United States Department of Health, Education and Welfare, Office of Education, 1964), pp. 1–9, by permission of the publisher and author.

whom there can be only succor and welfare, then the lowest level remains the lowest; but it is constantly rising even as our entire society rises, so that the migrant workers of 1962 are no longer Steinbeck's "Joads" of the thirties. In the large cities the tenements and walkups are being leveled and replaced by large housing projects where there is grass and where ceilings do not crack and fall. Yet the bottom is still there, consisting of those people who have not had time, opportunity, or perhaps the desire to become like those of us who set the goals, form the tastes, select the art forms, and establish the values which are written into our laws and customs.

It is true that the prescription for how an American citizen shall behave, by what standards he shall live, and by what morality he shall abide are determined largely by those who have come out of schools and colleges and been brought up in middle- and upper-class families. Behind those institutions are centuries of man's learning and living, where knowledge and tradition have been brought together to make up the ways of our adjusting to one another and the world.

It is because of that history, evolved

from a Judaeo-Greco-Roman-Christian-Democratic complex, that we are not content to let things happen as they will. We are compelled to influence our people to adopt our basic cultural and political values, especially those embodied in our Constitution and national documents. This is as it should be. It remains only that we learn how to bring about these changes without harming others and ourselves.

One of the dangerous by-products of the attempt to raise the "cultural" and educational levels of those who are different is that, in the attempt to make them over, our teachers strip them of diginity, of individuality, and of self.

Not too many months ago a group of Puerto Rican boys were sitting at a table in a corner of a New York City high school cafeteria discussing Cuba's Castro. At other tables, nearby but somehow distantly separated, other boys of other origins looked across, some annoyed, some sneering, some hostile.

"What's the monkey talk for? Why don't they use English?"

And why not? Since they had first come to school, those Puerto Ricans had been admonished daily by their teachers to "talk" English otherwise they "would never learn the language."

Somewhere else in another school a group of Negro youths were speaking in a strange kind of bop, that mysterious new language built upon some of the roots and forms used by Negroes more than a hundred years ago, but updated now with musical terms and common words carrying hidden meanings.

In each instance, their language was a deliberate attempt to exclude outsiders from invading their privacy. Wherever there is a congregation of people, isolated for one reason or another from the main culture, language seems to become a weapon and a wall, a bulwark for the preservation of dignity and self. It does not begin that way. Language starts with the need of men to go beyond the communion of existence, where eyes and nose and skin are sufficient to carry identifying messages to the brain so that a man knows where he is and what he feels. Language begins out of a necessity to express what is inside the self and to communicate it to someone outside the self. When there are many men living in the same time and place, who by their living together are forced to share burdens, to witness experiences in concert, to react to outer dangers as a group, language becomes the means of survival. Further developed, it becomes an art form of a people by which they reveal to one another whatever secret and irrepressible emotions and ideas have emerged out of the activity of the glands and brain.

It is here that language becomes the personal property of the individual and of groups of men and women, setting them apart as persons and as people. Because language does belong to a man, we dare not take it away. We may not demand that it be supplanted with another language, nor be suppressed, nor ridiculed. Those are destructive ways.

We may only respect the language as a part of the human being, and perhaps ask that another language be added; but such an addition can occur only if the reasons for it are understood and accepted.

The language of a minority group has the same relationship to the establishment of a sense of self as the identifying club jacket has for the teen-age club or gang. When Spanish-speaking youths from Puerto Rico or Mexico defy the strictures of their teachers and the scornful glances of their non-Spanish schoolmates saying, "Why should I learn English? My language is Spanish"; and when the Puerto Rican goes further saying, "Besides I am an American citizen as much as you are," what are they saying to us? What feelings have been ruffled, what deep emotions irritated, what beliefs challenged, and what inner sense of dignity insulted?

Too often these situations have occurred. We, the teaching group, and we, the native-to-these-streets group, have somehow held ourselves higher than the newcomers. We have made them understand not that we welcome them as they are, whatever they are, but that we wish to make them over in order that they may become like us.

The Puerto Rican islands in Manhattan, the Mexican sections of California and the Southwest, the Negro Harlems of all our big cities in the North and Midwest, the three main rivers of migration running up and down the two shores and the center line of our Nation following ripen crops—these are not very different from the Delancey Street ghettos and the Little Italys of the early 1900's. All exist because people who understand each other's ways hold themselves together against other people who would either cast them out, wall them in, absorb them, or eat them up with words like *assimilation* and *Americanization*. People do not want to be Americanized in the same way that they can be atomized, and they do not want to feel that they must develop cultural tastes and abilities to replace what they already have.

How rigid we are, we of the educated American middle class! We make Carol Kennicotts of all those who come to our main streets, or else we impose the costume and the makeup of our little stages upon all the young actors who come to play with us, pushing them into a faceless chorus line.

We tell them they must speak as

we do, read as we do, follow our customs, and adopt our moral values. We attempt to impose our music and art upon them and insist that they admire our technology as if the very differences that make them what they are, individuals in their own right, make them less than we instead of only different.

The problem, then, is one not only of language and reading, but also of socialization—and beyond that, it is a problem of values and philosophy.

How far shall we go with the announced educational ideal of creating a citizenry of well-rounded men and women? How round shall we make them, turning them into marbles that can be rolled on the earth? How far shall we push to achieve the images of excellence we have before our eyes? What kind of happiness shall we insist upon their pursuing? And how profitable must their leisure time activity be? (Or do we forget that, if it is profitable and active, it is no longer leisure but work?)

On the other hand, to what extent shall we encourage difference and provide the atmosphere in which the eccentricities and the individualities of each human being may be developed for whatever purposes that impel him from the inside out? How strongly shall we adhere to the concept that a man's life belongs to him alone and he alone can determine how it shall be lived, setting up only the proviso that he not interfere with or harm any other person in the living?

I do not believe that these questions are incompatible with one another. I do not believe that we must decide for the "good citizen" over the "rugged individual," but much of our practice has been just that kind of choosing.

Perhaps it is one of the elements in the nature of man that he must feel the superiority of his way over all others, or else consider himself inferior. Perhaps it is programed into the ambivalent ego of man, which sees itself both superior and inferior at the same time, that he must hold tightly to what he is and try to change those over whom he has control, whether it be through the domination of a teacher, the weight of majority numbers, or the length of time lived in the neighborhood. In any case, these thoughts lead us to the question of what to do with those who are not all like us.

If that sense of self is in us, it is also in those who are culturally different; and this is the cause of difficulty because that very knowledge of being numerically inferior, new to a place, less affluent, or lower on a social scale, inspires a battery of defenses designed to protect the ego itself. Man finds it very difficult to admit that there are those who stand above him. The poor man says the rich cannot be happy with his wealth. The illiterate says the egghead does not know which end is up when it comes to practical things. The man who has been forced by his physician and his heart attack to give up smoking says all those who smoke are idiots.

So those who are culturally different from the majority among whom they are forced to live must resent and reject efforts which they suspect are directed toward making them change, if accompanying those efforts there are indications of disapproval and denigration. Unfortunately, with intentions that are sincere and humanitarian and altruistic, we who teach or are involved in education in any of a hundred ways manage to demonstrate that we do not accept those who are different for what they are.

How do we do this? Perhaps one of the classical criticisms of Americans abroad will demonstrate it. "You think everyone must learn to speak English, so that when you come to our hotels you will be understood," an Italian said. "Why do you not bother to learn our language if you are going to travel in our country?"

"Americans think the whole world belongs to them," a French storekeeper said. "No, I cannot accept American dollars. You will have to change them into new francs."

To bring it closer to home, into the very heart of a family, let us consider the teenage child who rejects classical music as being square. It is not because he was born with a dislike for the tones and rhythms of the concerto or the symphony, but because he had been made to feel that his jazz, swing, rock 'n' roll, bop, or twist are looked down upon by his parents when they ask him, "Why don't you play something decent?" We do not really intend to say that his music is indecent. We mean only to say that we have outgrown it, that its sound is different from the sounds we have come to enjoy, that it is too loud, and that it is somehow associated in our minds with behavior systems which we cannot approve. We mean also to tell him that we find richer meanings, finer skills, and more intellectual stimulation in the more classical forms. Because we love him, we want our child to enjoy this too; but we tried to take something away from him in the process, because a teenager's music belongs to him, is part of whatever he is, and he considers an attack upon it to be an attack upon himself.

Cultural differences mean differences in value systems, and it should be evident that I do not separate the culturally different only in terms of national, migrational, or social scale groups. Teenage children are culturally different from the adults who are their parents and teachers. The problems which attend the concept of differences are universal. Difference leads to conflict; conflict leads to offense and defense where the larger force is almost compelled by the nature of things to absorb the smaller force, and the lesser force is compelled to resist. It cannot permit itself to be assimilated out of existence.

Thus what we mean by education, the leading away from whatever is, becomes a battle joined until we are capable of seeing the process of learning and teaching as an interaction rather than the submission of one group to another.

The child has a reality which is the life he is living. He has himself and the world outside of himself which he takes in through his senses and re-fashions in his brain according to whatever has happened during past experiences. If we would be effective in our school communication with him, then we must admit the reality of that self in our classrooms.

But where is there a reflection of this child and of the world in which he exists? What textbook confronts him with reality? Where can he see himself? And where are those pleasant sensations which have pleased him in his own world, with which he can be motivated to enjoy this other world of school?

Our fears of exposing young people to the kinds of truths their parents might find objectionable, or for which pressure groups might attack us, force us to feed a bland diet of tasteless foods, where bitter and strong flavors have already titillated young adult taste buds. We are in competition with television and motion pictures; with newspapers, magazines, and paperbacks; with crowds of friends on street corners, at beach parties, and in cellar basements. We

have our pupils from homes where unhappiness is a reality, where there are unpleasant emotions which make it impossible for them to recognize a stewed prune kind of world where no child hates his father or peers. In most of our classes, then, we dare not cater to the interests of our students even though we know that those interests will sharpen their perceptions, irritate their nerve endings, and activate their brains.

How much worse it is when the child comes to us from another language, or another segment of our society, or a traveling home with another set of values and with a much stranger concept of the world. How much more difficult when his language patterns, even in English, are built upon conceptual differences, so that a cup sits on the table because in his experience there is no need for a saucer! How much more difficult if his schooling must follow the trailer camps and the crops, of if his color pushes him into a corner apart from the clear white faces which belong to the clean white world of textbook illustrations!

So, having tried to impose our language upon young people, rejecting their mother tongue, or their peer group's meta-language, and being prevented in most places from at least dealing with truths that they will understand, we are forced out of our desire to give them something, to place before them pictures of ideals that cannot be matched. We defeat them with our assault of honesty, goodness, integrity, bravery, and courage as the qualifications of humanity, setting up for them images of excellence which are impossible of imitation. This we have managed to do for all youths, not only those who are considered culturally different.

We hold forth such values in almost uncompromising fashion, pretending that these lie behind the precepts which any fine American must follow. In doing so, we are telling them that, whatever dishonest act they may commit, whatever anger or spite they may feel against sibling or parent or neighbor, whatever fear they exhibit or act of cowardice they may perform simply because they are not superhuman, they face condemnation. We are telling them further that they are not worthy to be in the world as we see it.

This is no exaggeration. Where in the textbooks will a youth have revealed to him the weaknesses of a Washington or the inadequacies of a Lincoln? Where will he find it said that men are not always strong, that there are times which encourage cowardice because the desire to live is stronger than the desire to be heroic at a particular moment in a particular battle? Until what semester must he wait before some teacher will make an acknowledgment that our heroes were also people like Lord Jim or Fleming, and that during World War II our soldiers were capable of inhuman acts? I do not know whether we are to be forgiven or not for wanting to hide these aspects of our character which are not praiseworthy.

I have no intention of demeaning either our country's heroes or the values of our society and culture. There are characteristics of human behavior which we do admire, as a nation and a people, and there is value to our trying to emulate them. But admonition and preachment are not effective teaching methods, and the half truths of history and the fiction of shoddy fiction are both forms of exhortation. I do intend to point out that, if we are to have any success in our educational exchange with youth, then our share must be the honesty of things as they are.

Therefore, we must know how things are. Most of us who have become teachers have spent from two to five years learning about children. Where we have been fortunate, we have been taught by professors who themselves had some knowledge gained from classrooms and from facing the problems of the active teacher. In that way, if we remember what we have been taught and what we were when we were youths, then we come with some measure of competence for the teaching of youth. But how many of us have studied enough anthropology to be able to recognize the differences and accept the behavior patterns of people from another world? How many of us have been prepared by field experiences in sociology to realize what constitute the elements of a migratory population? Are we prepared to accept, without blanching, a set of values different from our own and then do no more than point out the differences, laying down no moral platitudes?

It is the failure to recognize the possibilities and the implications of cultural differences that makes for a failure with young people. We need to know, before they come to our classes, what Puerto Rican children are like and what we may expect from them. We need to know them as a cultural entity and as individuals within that culture so that their inordinate sense of dignity not be affronted and their nationalistic yearnings not be stepped on; for their sense of already having been rejected by the new people of their new environment has made them wary of us.

We need to know that there are Negro youths who have been buffeted by their white neighbors so that they have grown a hatred for the white world, and we must learn to listen to them, trying desperately to discover what they are saying when they behave in a way that seems peculiar to us. What is the source of their defiance or their sullenness? How much do they resent the lip service some of us give to civil rights?

We need to know how to admit that there is color, not try to wipe it away as if it did not exist with a pretense that all men are the same. All men are not the same and children know it better than adults. More than that, we have to understand our own unconscious prejudices, those glances and withdrawals which communicate what we feel regarding people of different origins, even as our minds are telling us we feel nothing and our mouths are telling others that we love them.

We have to understand the fact that culturally different does not mean devoid of culture, and that children of Negro, Mexican, uneducated, bookless, and houseless families do not come to us with nothing. Let me repeat—they come with selves and with a sense of belonging to whatever group is theirs. They, too, have parents and they, too, have brothers and sisters; and in some cases they, too, have individual beds which they do not have to share with four other persons. They, too, have television and have seen motion pictures, and in these respects they are the same as any other youths.

Finally, we have to understand that many of them come to us, too often, with shattered dignity and frightened selves and that their hostility is too deep to be seen by our eyes. They have learned long ago that one can hide things from strangers who have not yet discovered how to look at other people and know what they are seeing.

These are the ones we must cultivate, must help to grow a trust in us which they justly do not have. Because until we have recognized that the values by which they have lived are often directly in contrast with the values of our society, and until we can accept their behavior, however strange and antisocial it may be from our point of view, we can never hope to help them. Perhaps we must even question ourselves and our motives once again, looking carefully at some of the concepts we have held closely in our hearts and minds.

There are other questions which we must ask ourselves. If we are convinced that one must know how to read in our society and to speak so that he can simply get along with those who do not know his language, we must remember that the language of the United States is English, not Spanish, or the Negro meta-language, or the dialects of the migratory workers. The question, then, is how much must we accomplish; where do we set the limits of our goals? Shall we try to make every child, regardless of his origin or his subgroup, an appreciator of fine literature, feeding him *Silas Marner*, or even Salinger because the books are there and he "must read for pleasure"? Must every American learn to derive his pleasure from this type of reading? Must every American learn syntax? Must they all speak with round tones and in perfect sentences? Or is there room in our world for those who will manage to communicate in less than formal ways?

The final question is for all teachers and educational administrators, for all members of the adult society who are concerned about younger people. Just what do we want to do with, or to, or for our children? What do we expect of them? What kind of world can we anticipate and what do we imagine will be their role in it? It is at this point, if we are wrong, that we can erect impassable walls for ourselves. When we are dealing not only with young people who are already different from us because of their age, but also with those who have differences which are a result of color, national origin, occupation, educational level, or economic status our answers need to be clear, realistic, and as right as our intelligence can make them.

When we have found our answers and our new perspectives, or even reinforced those ideas which we already have through a new examination of this problem, then we can go about helping those youths who need our inspiration and our confidence. Then we can create images for them, not solely out of the legendary excellences of our history, but out of ourselves—sympathetic, honest, capable, and understanding selves—with whom these young people can first of all communicate and finally, we hope, wish to emulate.

4. Factors Relating to the Education of Culturally Deprived Negro Youth

VIRGIL A. CLIFT

Educators in our major cities have devised programs of various types to help school children overcome cultural deprivation. Some of these programs are noble attempts to meet a new challenge; however, it is now obvious that some people who are trying to solve this problem are limited in their knowledge of the social realities that have contributed to cultural deprivation. Without this information, it is impossible to develop a rationale or a proper theoretical basis for action.

Much of the current thinking about the problems of the culturally deprived in urban areas is focused on the Negro. Cultural deprivation should not be viewed as a racial problem, but rather as a social problem. It is a problem that relates to the total society because it can be attributed to multidimensional factors in the broader society.

It is this writer's view that the ego development of individuals in each subculture (including subcultures in the Negro minority) is directly influenced by the special nature and quality of multidimensional cutural factors which are uniquely character-

Reprinted from *Educational Theory,* Vol. 14 (April 1964), pp. 76–82, by permission of the publisher and author.

istic of the group. Therefore, cultural deprivation is not specific to racial groups, but to cultural factors. Ausubel states the position thus: [1]

"Many of the ecological features of the segregated Negro subculture that impinge on personality development in early childhood are not specific to Negroes as such, but are characteristic of most lower-class populations. This fact is not widely appreciated by white Americans and hence contributes to much anti-Negro sentiment: many characteristic facets of the Negro's value system and behavior pattern are falsely attributed to his racial membership, whereas they really reflect his predominant membership in the lower social class."

In this article special emphasis is focused on the cultural deprivation of Negro children in urban areas. The reasons for citing references and statistical examples for this group are: (1) There is much more data available on this minority than any other. Social scientists, many of whom have been Negroes, have developed an extensive body of information about the special or unique social forces affecting this group. Consequently, we can-

39

not speak as authoritatively about some of the other populations such as the white mountaineer, the recent European immigrant, the Eskimo, the American Indian, the Mexican, or the oriental minorities. (2) The Negro population represents a very large minority. (3) The value orientation and traditions of the group are American. Their religion as well as their vices are American, and they are not influenced by a culture foreign to America as would be immigrants, American Indians, and others. (4) Certain formal and informal channels of social mobility are closed to the Negro. It has always been easier for the European immigrant to lose his brogue, Americanize his name, select a new neighborhood for his residence, join the right church, and benefit immediately because these things have brought a change in status and enabled him to move up the ladder in social stratification and become fully accepted. These channels of mobility are closed for the Negro because he cannot change skin pigmentation. Color places restrictions on employment, income, housing, and even aspiration and self-esteem.

In each subculture there are special cultural factors which are unique and which play a profound role in ego development. Therefore, there exists no such thing as a general concept of education which will meet adequately the needs of various subcultures. The social scientists have furnished us with useful information on particular populations which must be taken into consideration as we plan to make education adequate and effective for a particular group. We know from social research, for example, that social stratification (and the way in which it occurs) differs from one group of culturally deprived youth to another. We now understand better some of the factors operating in various groups which contribute to status. We know that social class relates to differential behavior.

Before dealing more specifically with factors operating in a subculture, we should consider several forces operating in the total society which contribute to and accentuate cultural deprivation. We shall deal briefly with five of the most important of these.

1. *Mass migration to cities has increased the urban population and helped to change many characteristics of the city.* According to the 1960 census,[2] 69.9% of the population was urban as compared with 56.6% in 1940.

Associated with urban living, the lower socioeconomic groups face problems of housing, employment, income, education, and injury to self-esteem. For a very large segment of the urban population, the only choice at present is to live in deteriorating slum neighborhoods which are characterized by crime, tensions, frustrations, poverty, and infectious ignorance. Migration of any group to the city has always contributed to these problems, and this was especially true of the European immigrant of the last century. The present migration to the city consists primarily of Negroes.

According to Silberman,[3] in 20 years the Negro population of New York City has increased nearly two and one-half times, to 1,100,000 or 14% of the city's population. In Philadelphia, Negroes have doubled to over one-half million, or 26%; in Detroit it has tripled to over one-half million, or over one-third the total population. The Negro population outside the Deep South has tripled since 1940, and most of this population has migrated to city slums because the people involved had no other choice.

Mayer and Holt,[4] sociologists at

Wayne State University, challenge the widespread assumption that racial segregation in housing is steadily diminishing north of the Mason-Dixon Line. They claim that most major industrialized Northern cities are actually now more segregated than they were 30 years ago. Their study showed, for example, in Detroit in 1930, 51% of all Negro residents lived in predominantly white areas. In 1930, 15.8% of the Negroes lived in Negro ghettos. In 1960, Negro ghettos held 23% of the Negro population. The reason for this pattern is partly economic and this brings us to a second factor in the total society which relates to cultural deprivation.

2. *Employment and income reflect the effects of automation and the demand for more education.* Automation is causing the displacement of men by machines. The unskilled and semiskilled worker, those traditionally in the lowest income brackets, are today faced with an economic crisis without precedent.

Some very significant changes have taken place in the last ten years in the distribution of persons among the major occupation groups. In 1962, 47.7% of the white workers had risen into professional, technical, managerial, and white-collar clerical and sales jobs, whereas only 18.2% of the Negro workers were in these occupations.[5] This means that 82% of the Negro work force was in semiskilled, unskilled, service occupations, rural nonfarm, and farm jobs. A. Phillip Randolph, Vice-President, AFL-CIO, reports, "At present there is no single skilled craft in which Negroes constitute even 2% of the workers."[6]

In comparing incomes, the ratio is reversed. As has been true for decades, whites earn twice as much in wages as do Negroes. Whitney Young (National Urban League)[7] pointed out in 1962 that the average annual Negro income was $3,233, or 54% of the average white family's income of $5,835, whereas ten years ago the proportion was 57%. Young used median income figures for urban areas which do not highlight differentials that exist because of the changed percentage distribution of people over the major occupation groups.

When dealing with this problem as it contributes to cultural deprivation, we should look also at the incomes of the rural population for nonwhites, because this represents the source of many migrants to the urban area. According to the 1962 Department of Commerce statistics, the money income of rural nonwhite families and unrelated individuals was as follows: A total of 60.5% had an income of less than $4,000 and 31.7% had an income of less than $2,000. On the other hand, 36.6% of the white families had an income of over $7,000 and 15.3% had incomes of $10,000 and over.[8] The educational implication here is clear. When and if the children from the lowest income groups get into the school cafeteria, a more compelling concern may be to get something to eat, rather than to bother with good table manners, which seem to them to be insignificant trifles.

3. *The rapid development of and increase in man's knowledge is without parallel.* It is estimated that man's knowledge doubles every decade, that more new knowledge has been developed during the past two decades than during the entire period from the dawn of civilization to the turn of the twentieth century, and that 90% of all the scientists who have ever lived throughout civilization are alive today. This means that the role of the school is changing. The amount of knowledge to be acquired by students in the academic curriculum is

much greater and is increasing progressively. Students must read much faster, and much more, than formerly was expected. The school is confronted with the problem of helping students to acquire this vast increase in knowledge. But teachers know little more about learning and achievement motivation than they knew decades ago. The result is that the school differentiates and provides an academic program for those who, for some reason, acquire knowledge readily. Other students are placed in classes and in schools where academic achievement is expected to be low, and is indeed low. Therefore, the gap between those students who perform at a very high academic level and those who achieve at a low level is wider.

4. *There is considerable evidence that the school reflects quite accurately the place of parents in social stratification.* If we know the income and occupation of a student's father, we can predict whether or not he will go to college almost as well as by using intelligence scores.[9] Conant has pointed out: "The contrast in the money available to the schools in a wealthy suburb and to the schools in a large city jolts one's notion of the meaning of equality of opportunity."[10] He also found that preparation for college had become the purpose of the suburban school.

In addition to the inequities in financial support, Havighurst[11] reports a close relationship between progress through school and social class. He found that for every high school dropout from the upper and upper-middle classes, there were about 32 from the upper-lower and the lower-lower classes. The ratio of those entering college from the two top social classes as compared with the two lower classes was 15 to 1. Havighurst indicated also that when the proportion

of middle-class children in a school approaches or drops below 40%, their parents begin to move out of the neighborhood or to enroll their children in private schools. Chandler[12] also discussed area of residence, social class background of students, and inequities in financial support to schools as factors causing the school to contribute to social rigidity. He adds: "Most of the schools, except those in economically favored suburbs, are understaffed, both qualitatively and quantitatively."

The above indicates that the school is failing in its responsibility to the able child of certain occupational and income groups. The culturally deprived child cannot escape the slums easily; schools in slum districts do not prepare white-collar workers; low family incomes will not provide equality of opportunity for children. All too often culturally deprived children have little to give them a sense of aspiration or direction. They have few models to follow which give them reason to assume that education offers a way out of the slums. Yet we have in most cases no reason to assume that these children have less academic ability than any others.

5. *The nature and character of the city have changed and are changing.* Our cities are responsible for three-fourths of our manufacturing capacity; they produce 90% of our national income; they contain the greatest universities, our finest schools, and outstanding libraries. In our cities we find our greatest and most creative minds in the arts, sciences, economics, and politics; our cities are indeed the decision-making centers of the nation. The super metropolitan complex called the "megalopolis" has developed. For example, the megalopolis along the Northeastern Seaboard extends 500 miles from Massachusetts

to Virginia, crossing ten state boundaries, and includes 32 adjoining population centers.[13] It contains 20% of the nation's population, its residents pay 27% of the Federal income taxes, and it accounts for 30% of the country's manufacturing. Gottmann [14] found the cities he studied as being "on the average the richest, best educated, best housed, and best serviced in the world."

On the other hand, the city seems to represent a hodgepodge of ambiguities, inconsistencies, and contradictions. Lewis Mumford [15] characterized the modern American metropolis as "dehumanized," representing "purposeless materialism," seamy political life, and uncontrolled technology. For others it means deteriorating slums, ignorance, tensions, frustrations, and a "mad rush." The city also represents a series of one-class neighborhoods ranging from slums and suburbs.

Another paradox in urban life can be seen in the suburbs with their economic, cultural, and educational advantages. However, they are not free from social disease. In them, we can find rampant materialism, false values, immorality, disinterest in self-government, juvenile delinquency, high rates of emotional instability among youth and adults, and extensive and expensive educational programs in isolation from social and political problems.

EDUCATIONAL PROBLEMS

Out of this background emerge problems which the educator must face with educational practice based on sound theory. Too much of what has gone on in the past was initiated because it was thought to be expedient or because of pressure from one group or another.

The school has become the dominant institution in the control and socialization of youth because it is a major force in determining status transitions of youth. The school is reinforcing the social class pattern of the neighborhood in which it is located; and, in our large cities, where *de facto* restrictions continue to create segregated housing, the school is reinforcing a caste system along race lines. The urban school is faced with the problem of preparing youth for a type of society that is different from that of two decades ago. According to Riessman,[16]

"In 1950, approximately one child out of every ten in the fourteen largest cities of the United States was 'culturally deprived.' By 1960, this figure had risen to one in three. This ever increasing trend is due to their rapid migration to urban centers. By 1970, it is estimated that there may be one deprived child for every two enrolled in schools in the large cities."

In conclusion, two major classifications of problems are raised for consideration:

1. *How are we to desegregate the urban school?* An answer to this question must be formulated within a theoretical framework that makes sense. The harsh facts in the situation are these: *De facto* segregation does in fact perpetuate the group stigma and it is a means of enforcing a negative self-evaluation on Negroes as individuals and as a group.

Dan Dodson says,[17]

"It is basically through the mechanism of the public school that members of a group occupying an inferior position in our society can achieve equal opportunities. Help in breaking down economic, social and cultural barriers should begin with the public schools."

Kenneth Clark [18] stresses a different emphasis:

"It was found that as minority group children learn the inferior status to which they are assigned—as they observe that fact that they are almost always segregated and kept apart from others who are treated with more respect by the society as a whole—they react with feelings of inferiority and a sense of personal humiliation. The minority group child is thrown into a conflict with regard to his feelings about himself and his group. He wonders whether his group, and he himself, are worthy of no more respect than they receive. This conflict and confusion leads to self-hatred and to rejection of his own group."

In another connection, Dodson [19] raises another issue for consideration.

"A third thing about which there is confusion is the import of the *de facto* segregated school. Conant, in *Slums and Suburbs,* draws a clear distinction between *de facto* and *de jure* segregation, and indicates his belief that there is nothing wrong with segregated schools, provided they reflect the neighborhood; are not the result of assignment because of race; and provided they offer as high a quality of education as do the other schools which are not segregated. On the other hand, there is little, if any, evidence to indicate that a *de facto* segregated school can be made equal in its educational progress. If the entire culture conceives a "Jim Crow" school as inferior, does not this in fact make it so? If it does, does not the requirement that a youth attend it violate his civil rights? I believe it does."

This being the case, our responsibility in ending *de facto* segregation goes far beyond mixing schools with children of different national origins, racial identity, or social class. This leads us to the second major problem.

2. *What specifically in the organization and program of the school will help children to overcome cultural deprivation?* When children have been transferred out of their districts to eliminate segregation, usually they have been placed in sections of classes or in curricula which indeed did segregate them again within the desegregated school to which they had been transferred.

In view of the emerging social realities in employment, housing, and other multidimensional forces it seems clear that education for the culturally deprived should consist of more than improved guidance, greater emphasis on reading and communication skills, and contacts with teachers who have a missionary spirit and sympathetic attitude. These things are very important without a doubt, but they do not reach the more fundamental factors relating to cultural deprivation.

An adequate program for the culturally deprived cannot be provided until teachers and administrators can answer the following questions and relate educational programs to the answers: What is the differential quality of cultural deprivation from social class to social class? What are the changes in the status systems that will effectuate a more positive attitude in regard to academic achievement and desirable behavior? How do status systems and other culture-related factors affect ego development? What are the culturally institutionalized differences in interpersonal relations for the culturally deprived child? What are the types of achievement motivation that are socially sanctioned for individuals of a given social class of certain ethnic identity? What specifically can be done to overcome psychological degradation and injury to self-esteem which results from the negative valuation society places on individuals because of their race? In what ways have cultural forces made the cognitive orientation and functioning different for children of minority status?

These are difficult questions, but we must find answers to them if the public school in America is to continue to be a force in helping all people to achieve equal opportunities.

References

1. David P. Ausubel and Pearl Ausubel, "Research on Ego Development Among Segregated Negro Children: Implications for Education." (Mimeographed) Bureau of Educational Research (University of Illinois, 1962), p. 4.
2. *Statistical Abstract of the United States, 1962.* U.S. Department of Commerce, Bureau of the Census (Washington: Supt. of Documents, Government Printing Office, 83rd Edition, 1962), p. 21.
3. Charles E. Silberman, "The Negro in Our Cities," *Fortune* (March 1962).
4. Albert J. Mayer and Thomas F. Holt, *Time* (Nov. 9, 1962), p. 62.
5. *Statistical Abstract of the U.S., ibid.* (1962), p. 227.
6. A. Philip Randolph, "The Unfinished Revolution," *Progressive* (Dec. 1962), Vol. 26, p. 24.
7. *Ibid.,* p. 24.
8. *Statistical Abstract, op. cit.,* p. 227.
9. Harold L. Hodgkinson, *Education in Social and Cultural Perspectives* (Englewood Cliffs: Prentice-Hall, Inc., 1962), p. 86.
10. James B. Conant, *Slums and Suburbs: A Commentary on Schools in Metropolitan Areas* (New York: McGraw-Hill Book Co., 1961), pp. 145–146.
11. Robert J. Havighurst, et al., *Growing Up in River City* (New York: John Wiley and Sons, 1962), pp. 50–53.
12. B. J. Chandler, L. J. Stiles, and J. I. Kitsuse, eds., *Education in Urban Society* (New York: Dodd, Mead & Co., 1962), pp. 10–12.
13. Jean Gottmann, *Megalopolis: Urbanized Northeastern Seaboard of the United States* (New York: Twenty Century Fund, 1961).
14. *Ibid.,* p. 7.
15. Lewis Mumford, *The City in History: Its Origins, Its Transformations and Its Prospects* (New York: Harcourt, Brace & World, 1961).
16. Frank Riessmann, *The Culturally Deprived Child* (New York: Harper & Bros., 1962), p. 1.
17. Dan W. Dodson, "The New Rochelle Decision," *Journal of Educational Sociology,* Vol. 36, No. 6 (Feb. 1963), p. 265.
18. Kenneth B. Clark, "Segregated Schools in New York City," *Journal of Educational Sociology,* Vol. 36, No. 6 (Feb. 1963), p. 245.
19. Dan Dodson, "Preparing for Desegration," *Journal of Educational Sociology,* Vol. 36, No. 6 (Feb. 1963), p. 274.

5. Lower-Class Families

RUTH SHONIE CAVAN

THE FAMILY'S PAST

Even more brief than the history of the middle-class family is that of the lower-class family. The European origin a generation or two ago gives a finite beginning to the American phase of the family, often within the memory of the older members. Dispersion of family members as they migrate from job to job breaks the connecting ties between related nuclear families. Correspondence is irregular, and visits are made only at long intervals. There are virtually no written family records. For a minority at the lowest range, however, stability rather than mobility is common, for an impoverished and dependent class marks the lowest status in the social hierarchy. This class is too dependent upon social institutions and too completely enmeshed in poverty even to migrate with the hope of finding work. It has a history, not in its own family possessions, but in the records of social agencies and in the legends of the community that identify certain families as permanently worthless. Some of these families have been in the active case

Reprinted from *The American Family* by Ruth Shonle Cavan (New York: Thomas Y. Crowell, 1963), pp. 141–153 (Copyright © 1963 by Thomas Y. Crowell Co.), by permission of the publisher and author.

46

load of social agencies off and on for two or three generations.

THE FAMILY UNIT

The family unit consists of the husband, wife, and their unmarried adult children and minor children. In some respects, the stable and continuing family unit is the mother and minor children. The death rate, especially of the men, is higher in the lower classes than in the middle or upper classes; therefore there are more widows. In addition, the marriage bond is weak; desertions, separations, and divorces destroy the family unit. Almost without exception, the mother keeps the children, and the father is the one to withdraw. Now marriages—legal or common-law—bring a new man into the family as husband but rarely as a genuine replacement of the original father. Occasionally, there may be a succession of husbands. Thus, even in the event of a stepfather, the core of the family remains the mother and her children.

Especially in the Negro lower-lower class, temporary liaisons and common-law marriages are practiced without feelings of guilt. Attention is called to the middle-class attitude toward these marriages and the high rate of illegitimate births that result. The lower-lower class, however, does not regard the children as unwanted or handicapped, since the mother assumes responsibility for their rearing and relief agencies assist financially. Sociologists and anthropologists recognize the female-based family as a subtype of the American family.[2] Another term, "matrifocal family," has been applied to Negro families in the Caribbean, emphasizing the transient character of the adult male and the stability of the mother's household, not only for children, but also for adult sons who may be between liaisons.[3] Freilich's analysis links the matrifocal family of the Caribbean with the background of slavery; a similar relationship can be seen in the lower-lower-class Negro family in the United States.

In the lower-class matrifocal family, the grandmother may be included in the household group. Otherwise, ties with grandparents and collaterals are weak, although at a time of family crisis, usually with economic implications, they strengthen, and one branch of the family gives sanctuary to a stranded branch. When the conditions change, the families separate. In as much as crises fraught with economic strain are more frequent in the lower-class family than in the family of any other class, these temporary mergings and withdrawals are fairly common.

CULTURAL DIVERSITY

The lower class as a whole is a variegated group: families with a lengthy American background who somehow or other have failed to make the grade; newly arrived immigrant groups in the cities who, because of lack of vocational training and language difficulties, come into American society at the lower-class level; remnants of earlier ethnic groups who have failed to adjust to American culture at a higher level; groups that

come into cities from other sections of the United States where they have been economically and culturally deprived (southern Negroes and "poor whites" from the hills of the southern border states). When the ethnic groups are included, the variations of language, culture, and religion are great. An illustration is found in the religious affiliations of the lower class. In Jonesville, the upper-lower class had affiliations with nine different churches with slightly over half the class having no church membership.[4] In the lower-class, membership in the same nine churches is represented, but only 28 per cent had church affiliations. Diversity is also shown by birthplace of the class members. In Yankee City, both upper-lower and lower-lower class contained 30 per cent who were foreign-born.[5] The upper-lower class had 28 per cent, and the lower-lower class 38 per cent, who were born outside of Yankee City (although for the most part nearby or in other parts of New England). No other social class in Yankee City included as few Yankee City-born members. The ethnic and racial groups, largely concentrated in the two lower classes, consisted of nine stocks, representing many different languages, cultural values, and religions: Irish, French Canadians, Jewish, Italian, Armenian, Greek, Polish, Russian, and Negro.

Confusion and conflicts are reduced by the tendency for families with the same cultural background to cluster together, living perhaps in distinct and separate communities. Sometimes the majority of persons residing in one community work in the same industry, thus further reducing contacts. The lower classes, then, somewhat resemble a mosaic of cultural groups, each with a distinctive and group-centered life of its own. When groups meet, conflicts may arise; among adolescents and youths, especially male, physical conflicts may be sought, either in free-for-all or planned battles, or on another level through competitive groups sports. When marriages occur between members of different or opposed cultural groups, the conflict may be carried over into either an inter- or an intrafamily conflict.

Regardless of these differences, the general pattern of economic status and insecurity, the necessity for each member of the lower class to become self-sufficient, and the lack of community prestige and influence produce certain family similarities that characterize the lower classes.

ECONOMIC BASIS

Inherited wealth is unheard of in the lower classes. Income is primarily from wages earned through semiskilled and unskilled labor. These are the jobs that may be entered easily and that are easily refilled if the worker leaves. The workers are at the mercy of even slight changes in the market and may be laid off without ceremony because they are easily replaced. Much seasonal work is also done by lower-class workers. Income is not only low but uncertain; consequently, savings are small, and an accumulation of family wealth impossible.

The lower-class family is the one that experiences the economic life cycle observed by Rountree in his study of the English laborer.[6] In the life cycle of the family, early manhood and womanhood when courtship and marriage occur is a period of relatively adequate income; the youth is young and vigorous, the wife is able to work, and there are no children or only one child. The second stage comes when the number of children increases and the wife drops out of employment, while expenses mount; this is a period of insecurity and per-

haps downright poverty. As the children come into adolescence and begin to work, comes the third stage; the family income is larger and many home improvements are made, as the accumulated moderate incomes from several workers may make a respectable total. In the fourth stage, as children marry and leave home, income decreases but so also do expenses. With old age the cycle comes to a close with the old couple again facing the poverty and insecurity they knew in their childhood. Savings are small or do not exist, and payments under Old Age Assistance or Old Age and Survivors' Insurance are often inadequate even for minimum essentials.

When savings are possible, as among the more thrifty upper-lower-class families they may go into the purchase of a small home. In some cities this home is a small frame house with a basement flat and a second floor flat, in one of which the family lives, the other being rented for additional income. In other cities, the upper-lower-class family buys a small plot in an unincorporated area beyond the city and there, unhampered by municipal building ordinances, constructs a small house often of second-hand materials and without plumbing, electricity, or gas, although these may be added later. But the proportion of lower-class families who own homes is small. In Elmtown, 35 per cent of the upper-lower-class families and 19 per cent of the lower-lower-class families, as compared with 66 per cent of lower-middle-class families, owned their homes.[7] In Yankee City, only 6 per cent of lower-lower-class families owned homes.[8]

Only rarely are savings sufficient to tide the family over an emergency, such as a major operation of the chief wage earner or a long-continued period of unemployment. A limited degree of security may be gained when the wage earner is eligible for unemployment insurance. Even the upper-lower-class family may have to apply for relief during an emergency, and the lower-lower-class family may be on and off relief as a permanent feature of life. Relief, therefore, is accepted as a possibility or even a probability and is sought without the deep shame and loss of self-respect with which the occasional middle-class person reluctantly approaches a welfare office. Moreover, it is sought before the family has lowered its standard of living or threatened its future security through the exhaustion of resources that typifies the middle-class family in economic distress. The lower-class family has few resources to be exhausted, and life on relief often represents only a slight diminution of the customary standard of living. The attitude of realistic acceptance of economic insecurity is expressed in these words by one lower-class father: "There's never been a time when I could be sure that I could care for my family. And my father was that way before me, too." [9]

Regular or intermittent employment for all members of the family who can work is not only the common practice but is believed to be normal and necessary. It is also accepted by both husbands and wives that wives should be employed a large part of the time, even when the children are small. The necessity for women to work is increased also by the number of families in which the father is dead or has deserted either temporarily or permanently. The mother, with whatever aid she can secure from social agencies or relatives, must pick up the economic responsibility for herself and her children.

The extent of employment of lower-class mothers can be seen from a comparison of the percentage of wives who are employed, according to the income of their husbands. The figures are for wives aged 20–44 who are living with their husbands. When the husband's income was less than $1,000 per year, 43 per cent of wives worked. With increase in level of income, the percentage of working wives dropped. For example, when the husband's income was between $3,000 and $5,000 per year, 35 per cent of wives worked. The drop continued; when the husband's income was $10,000 or more, only 16 per cent of wives worked. Mothers with children under six years of age were much less likely to work than those with no children or older children. But among families in which the husband's income was less than $3,000, approximately a fourth of the mothers with children under six years old were employed.[10]

Children also work without question. Their work is not in support of an ideal of thrift and industry, as in the middle class, but from necessity. Since the educational ideals of the family usually are low, parents expect children to leave school and begin to work as soon as the law permits. Younger children are expected to secure after-school, Saturday, and vacation jobs. Moreover, the children find it difficult to relate the training they receive in the average public school to the realities of their lives and are only too ready to find a legitimate excuse for ending their formal education. Since they have neither a sound liberal education nor vocational training, they enter unskilled or semiskilled work and thus repeat in their lives the cycle followed by their parents. In securing work, the children answer newspaper ads or approach the employment office as the only contact between adolescent and employer. Since the father's employment is on an impersonal and often impermanent basis, he is unable to provide an occupational opening for his children.

RESIDENTIAL STABILITY

Lower-class families have less residential stability than those in higher classes. Many are newcomers seeking a better living than they had in some other community—for example, rural migrants. Those who are able to build achieve a certain stability for a period of perhaps 10 to 20 years. But the house may be lost through mortgage foreclosure, or sold if a job is lost and another found in some other community, or sold as old age approaches. Those who rent move frequently, and those who do not own furniture but live in small furnished rooms or flats move most often of all. Nevertheless, in each community some lower-class families have held that status over a period of generations without rising in the social scale. In Elmtown, many lower-class families have been residents of the community as long as the upper-class families, and, like the upper-class families, are linked in the public mind with the past behavior of their ancestors.[11] The legends that cling to these permanent lower-lower families are notorious, however, rather than laudatory: a murder, chronic drunkenness, or family abuse on the part of the grandfather hangs over the present generation, giving a pattern for the children and lowering community expectation of achievement from them.

Although we think of home-ownership and residential stability as adding to a family's prestige, for great numbers of the lower class such stability is a handicap. For one thing, it fixes them in a class level that has little to offer them or their children. For another, it reduces their economic opportunities. The semiskilled or un-skilled laborer must be a ready migrant if he is to have work all the time. Tied to one locality, he may be unemployed a much higher percentage of the time than if he is mobile.

MARRIAGE

Young people in the lower classes marry at an earlier age than in other classes. In Yankee City the average age in the upper-lower class was 24 years and in the lower-lower 23, or four or five years younger than in the upper-upper class.[12] In Elmtown, where all the marital ages were lower than in Yankee City, men married in their early twenties and girls in their late teens in the upper-lower class and in the very early twenties and middle teens in the lower-lower class.[13]

Marriages tend to occur between members of the same class, but if there is out-class marriage it is upward, since there is no lower class into which marriage may be made. Thus the attractive girl or the enterprising youth may marry into a family somewhat above his own in social status. Since each marriage starts a new and independent nuclear family, however, the decision is more or less in the hands of the couple as to whether the future family pattern follows that of the lower or the higher class.

Marriage occurs with less preliminary social contact and with less ritual as to ceremony than in the middle or upper classes. Eligible girls and men do not meet in a debut as in the upper class nor through supervised mixed-group activities as in the middle class; they do not even meet at school, for many have left school before mid- or late adolescence. The street corner, the tavern, or the factory provides the locale, and individual initiative brings youths and girls together. Courtship is short, often sexually exciting, and ends with a marriage that is announced to family and friends after it has occurred. The economic status of the husband may be low, for the criterion of selection is personal and sexual attraction rather than economic and social suitability.[14]

FAMILY ORGANIZATION

In the normal family unit of husband, wife, and children, the father is the head of the family. Lower-class families are more nearly patriarchal than families in any other class. The husband asserts his authority more thoroughly and more harshly than in higher classes, keeping wife and children in submission by physical force if necessary. He is the final authority and disciplinarian to whom the mother refers in her daily training of children; except in times of stress, he is the chief wage earner and controls the purse; he makes the final decisions for the family.

Nevertheless, it is the mother who rears the children, and it is with her that the children remain if the family disintegrates. The father, however, may make rules for the rearing of the children, which the mother enforces in his absence. The mother's role also is that of housekeeper, and the husband does not expect to participate in housekeeping tasks after he comes from work. The roles of husband and wife are more sharply drawn than in the middle class where there is more sharing in planning and often in execution of the plans.

The husband and wife have a life of their own which takes precedence over the demands of their children. The bond between them is personal and sexual in nature. Having fewer interests, husband and wife have less of a companionship and friendship re-lationship than the middle-class husband and wife achieve. Children, though important and welcome in the lower-class family, nevertheless have less family importance than in the middle-class family. They are definitely subordinate to the parents, who neither cater to them nor sacrifice for their education and cultural development as middle-class parents do. Moreover, the expectation is strong that children will leave school after fulfilling the minimum legal requirements in order to work and contribute to the family until the day of their marriage.

Although the obligations are more simple than in higher social classes, the roles of husband and wife are specific. The husband earns the living if he is able to do so, supports his family, is not cruel but may be strict, and is faithful to his wife (although discreet deviations are tolerated, especially in the lower-lower group). The wife bears and rears the children, keeps house, earns money if her husband is unable to earn all that is needed, and is faithful to her husband. If these obligations are broken, the offended party may and often does leave, opening the way for a possible divorce. As has already been stated, the children almost without exception remain with the mother. Since the husband may find work almost as readily in another city as the one where his estranged or divorced wife lives, he often leaves, thus obstructing any attempts of the wife to secure support for herself or their children. The wife therefore finds herself facing the roles of both father and mother to her children. Sometimes she and the children are absorbed back into her parental family where she may serve a useful function if her parents are old; or collateral relatives may give her room and board for a time, although rarely are they able to give cash help if she lives elsewhere. The mother faces three possible solutions: to work for the support of herself and her children; to remain at home with them and apply for Aid to Dependent Children, a form of public relief; or to remarry.

The role of the second husband is a peculiar and unstable one. He is husband to his wife but not father to her children. He does not assume authority over them, nor do they recognize him as their father; however, he may be friendly with them and help support them. If he attempts to discipline his stepchildren, conflict may result, with the mother siding with her children in their rejection of his authority. Sometimes the solution is found by placing the children with relatives who are willing to accept them, or by permitting very young children to be adopted. At other times, the second marriage breaks on the rocks of family conflict.

Family life in the lower class is less stable than in the middle or upper classes. Separations, often without divorce, are frequent. The very fact that after a separation the marriage may be resumed without formality adds to the instability. One separation may follow another, often being in the nature of desertion by the father who moves out leaving the mother and children without support. With longer periods of separation, but no legal termination of the marriage through divorce, temporary alliances or more permanent common-law marriages may replace legal marriage. The death rate is higher in the lower classes than in classes where there are both more economic security and better health practices; and it is higher for men than for women. Widows, often with young children, are frequent. Another disturbing fac-

tor is the presence in the lower classes of detached men who have come into this country from abroad or have moved into certain industrial areas seeking work in proportions that disturb the natural sex ratio by providing an excess of men. Some of these men have wives and children elsewhere; others are unmarried; some are non-Caucasian. Seeking not only sexual satisfaction but the practical homemaking advantages that a woman can provide in the way of food, mending, laundry, and a homelike place to spend evenings and holidays, many of these men are willing to become partners to temporary or illicit household arrangements. As job opportunities change or the desire comes to return home, they leave with as little ceremony as they came. In many families, although illegal unions are unknown, divorce or death breaks the family leaving a parent and perhaps children. Remarriage may follow, with the usual difficulties of adjustment. The instability of the lower-class family is reflected in the rate of broken homes. In the upper-lower class in Elmtown, 33 per cent of the homes were broken, and in the lower-lower class 56 per cent.[15]

One may question why separations and divorces are disproportionately frequent in the lower classes. One possible answer is that stresses and strains are more frequent. The family lives closer to the thin line that lies between sufficiency and poverty. Ill health and disease are of more common occurrence. Homes are small and allow little freedom of movement or privacy.

Another plausible reason lies in personality development. As will be discussed later in this chapter, lower-class children are encouraged and openly taught by their parents to be aggressive. They are expected by their families to fight for status in their play groups, to elbow others aside in securing work, and to employ small trickery in shopping and entering movies. Life in the lower classes demands aggression for survival. These aggressive attitudes are vented not only toward the outside world but also within the family circle. Brother competes with brother for clothing, food, and the most comfortable chair or bed; parents compete with children, and children with parents. Aggressive individualism, tempered by a certain practical kind of familism in time of crisis, becomes habitual. Cooperation, conciliation, and compromise, common in the middle- and upper-class family, are neither taught to the child nor demonstrated in his family. Any encroachment upon the individual or his rights as he conceives them brings an aggressive reaction inside the family as well as outside.

Another personality trait of the lower class is withdrawal when faced with overwhelming odds. The boy or girl who finds school work difficult or unpleasant does not wait until the legal age to leave school, but truants and perhaps becomes adept at evading the attendance officer. Many adolescent lower-class boys and girls leave home to evade parental control; they sleep in hallways, or, in the summer, in vacant lots, or secure work and rent a cheap room. Boys may tramp across the country, working and begging alternately as they go. When marriage becomes a trial, the husband tends to follow the same pattern and withdraws. The wife less often leaves as she feels emotional ties to and responsibility for her children.

LOWER-CLASS CHILDREN

Lower-class families have a higher average of children than any other social class. Using education of married women as a crude criterion of social-class status, in 1957 the average number of children for women with less than eight years of education was 3.8, and with eight years, 2.8, which was also the average for the nation. However, women with one to three years of college averaged 1.9 and those with four or more years of college, 1.6. Thus the average number of children among the best educated women was less than half the average among the most poorly educated. In the small city of Elmtown in the 1940's, the average number of children was 5.6 in the lower-lower class family and 4.3 in the upper-lower-class family.[16]

Studies show that lower-class families state that they want three or four children, spaced about two years apart. Those with larger families have more children less because they want them than because of ineffective methods of contraception.[17] One study showed that 75 per cent of the upper-lower-class families but only a third of lower-lower-class families used contraceptive techniques effectively. Their interview responses showed that they were ignorant of how contraceptives work; some women were afraid that a diaphragm inserted in the vagina might "get lost" in their bodies; some men objected to reduced pleasure when a condom was used. Even when effective types of contraceptives were used, they were often used sporadically, indicating a failure to realize that only one omission of the contraceptive might result in pregnancy.

Factors other than ignorance and carelessness are also present. By the accident of national origin, many lower-class families are descendants of recent immigrants from Catholic countries; they adhere to the Catholic prohibition against artificial control of conception. In addition, the use of contraceptives presupposes a certain degree of sophistication, self-discipline, and sometimes expenditure that is contrary to the lower-class culture. Another factor contributing to the high birth rate is that children are regarded as assets to the family in that they begin to earn early in life. Also, lower-class values do not demand the heavy expenditures of middle-class families for prenatal care, hospital delivery, pediatric supervision, dental work, special educational classes in childhood, and college education. These have become routine necessities of child rearing in the middle class; they are regarded as superfluities by the lower-class family.

Another factor is the early age of marriage, especially for girls, at a time when sex drives are strong and fertility high. The early marriage also lengthens the total span for childbearing.

Finally, the general attitude in many lower-class families is that children are a natural outcome of marriage. The mother especially finds satisfaction in producing children and lavishes affection on them, particularly if her relationship with her husband is not completely satisfying to her emotionally.

The training of lower-class children differs from that of middle- and upper-class children, both in objectives and methods. The objective is to develop a tough-minded, hard-fisted individual, able to compete to the point of personal conflict in support of individual rights and privileges. When these rights are not challenged, the lower-class person is orderly and law-abiding. The little boy is not taught, as is the middle-class boy, to wait until he is struck before he fights, nor to seek the protection of parent, teacher, or policeman. He is expected to be able to take care of himself at an early age. The little girl, likewise, is taught to be self-sufficient, to protect her virtue by a sharp tongue and her fists if necessary.[18]

At an early age both boys and girls are allowed to extend their activities into the community without the supervision of parents or other adults. They play in the neighborhood at night and attend movies alone at an age when middle-class children are carefully sequestered in house or yard by their parents. They learn to ride the bus across the city, shop for their mothers, care for younger brothers and sisters, make change, avoid automobiles, earn money, and otherwise look after themselves and contribute to the utilitarian functions of the family while still well below teen age. Conversely, they are not taught certain duties and aspirations that have high value in the middle-class family and that middle-class children are urged and coerced into learning—regularity of school attendance, ambition for at least high school graduation, excessive neatness and cleanliness both of person and the child's room, and avoidance of fighting unless attacked.

As stated in the discussion of the middle-class family, the methods of training differ between the two classes. The lower-class mother rears her children with a combination of leniency and impulsive aggressiveness. One might say that she treats her children more naturally and more in accord with her own emotional needs than does the middle-class mother who trains her children with the child psychologist always peeping over her shoulder. The mother responds to the personal relationship between herself and each child, whereas the middle-class mother tries to do what is "best for the child," often denying her own feelings in the process. The lower-class child is less likely to view himself as a person of special value for whom parental sacrifices are justified. He plays a subordinate role in the family, gaining in status when he reaches an age to contribute financially.

Ritual is less used in the lower-class family than in the family of any other class. Nevertheless, only in the very lowest levels is ritual nonexistent. The celebration of Christmas is a form of ritual if repeated year after year in characteristic fashion. Catholic families tend to follow religious rituals that reinforce in the family the teachings of the Church. However, many of the rituals that reflect leisure (as the after-dinner coffee of the middle-class-family) or that regulate relations between family members (as the standing of the child when an older person enters the room) are unknown. Houses are crowded; duties crowd fast one upon another; tensions are often unresolved. The members of the family may seek avoidance of each other through outside activities rather than find satisfaction in a closely integrated family pattern of rituals.

UPWARDLY MOBILE UPPER-LOWER CLASS—THE NOUVEAU BOURGEOISIE

A portion of the upper-lower class is upwardly mobile into the lower-middle class. The process, observed especially since the end of World War II, rests on the high percentage of employment among upper-lower or blue-collar workers, higher incomes not only in number of dollars but also in buying power, and the widespread practice of buying goods on the installment plan. The ambitious blue-collar worker therefore is able to acquire some of the material goods of the lower-middle class and to move into a lower-middle class residential area.[19] He does not as readily acquire the values and ways of behaving of the middle class. When an individual family makes the physical move into a middle-class area, the members may be rejected by neighbors, schools, and other institutions, which often results in feelings of insecurity, frustration, and perhaps aggression.

Another result of upward mobility involving a large amount of installment buying is the potential economic insecurity. A long period of unemployment for the chief wage-earner may send the family rapidly downward in status.

Limited upward mobility also may be carried out by a larger group than the family; for example, when families of lower status move into a newly built lower-middle-class suburb or other community, or when an industry moves and houses its blue-collar workers in a community of much better quality than the one from which they came.[20] Families then give each other support but do not quickly or automatically become middle class. The slow process of changes in values and behavior must still be accomplished.

CRISES

That lower-class families are subject to many types of crises has been implied in the preceding discussion. Frequent unemployment, the higher illness rate than in other social classes, the higher birth rate that results in the more frequent introduction of a new member into the family circle, delinquency of younger members of the family, occasional or chronic alcoholism, and aggressiveness between neighbors or relatives as well as personal clashes within the family are some of the conditions that cause a breakdown of the folkways of the lower-class family and require the family to readjust itself in some way. The lower-class family is rarely equipped by education or training to resolve a personal crisis on the verbal level. Verbal emotional explosions may relieve inner tensions but add to the disruption; and sometimes the verbal expression moves into physical aggressiveness against or between offending persons. Thus, the husband may beat his wife, or the wife may throw china at her husband; children may be beaten; neighborhood fights may occur; and occasionally, in one of these personal clashes, someone is killed. Such aggressions not only widen the breach but often serve to bring the crisis to the attention of the neighbors or the police. Crises that emanate from lack of money are also frequent and difficult to resolve because the family lacks accumulated savings and finds it impossible, or nearly so, to establish credit.

Lower-class crises tend to be prolonged and often result in serious damage to family unity. The family tends to disintegrate under the pressure of the crisis, although later it may re-form. The husband may desert when a new baby threatens to upset the household routine or to impose extra expense, but he may return six months or a year later. The adolescent boy or girl may run away but be sent home by some social agency or the police of another community. At other times the disintegration is permanent, and the family may appeal to official agencies for help. The wife may bring suit against her husband for nonsupport or obtain a divorce; she may ask for financial relief or aid in controlling rebellious children.

The official agency usually enters into the situation, however, after other efforts have been made to solve the problems. The lower-class family does not keep its problems to itself. Less reticent about its problems, less proud of its status than the middle-class family, the lower-class family tends to seek outside aid, but not of a professional nature in the first instance. The druggist, the bartender, and relatives are approached for advice or financial assistance. Only when they fail are the legal and social agencies approached.[21]

SPECIAL CHARACTERISTICS

The lower class as a whole abides by the common mores of our society and meets such expectations as family self-support (except, perhaps, in times of great crisis), legal monogamous marriages, conformity to laws, participation in community institutions (such as sending their children to school) and affiliations with some type of church connection.

There is a small substratum, however, that deviates from the class and family mores. These families might be illustrated by families of beggars, pauperized families that violate the sex mores through unofficial polygyny or the practice of incest, or in which prostitute mothers teach their daughters to become prostitutes, and criminal families. These families may belong to small groups that have developed mores of their own and a philosophy that cushions them against a feeling of guilt or rationalizes their conduct. Other families are composed of demoralized individuals in the sense that they do not have a system of mores, have not developed a conscience or superego, but live close to their natural needs and impulses.

THE LOWER CLASS AS A POPULATION POOL

The lower class forms a population pool from which higher strata—chiefly middle-class—draw replacements necessitated by their lower reproductive rate. The excess members in lower-class families originate partly from the high birth rate and partly from immigrant groups, which usually enter the American social-class system as unskilled workers at the lower-class level.

References

1. W. Lloyd Warner and Associates, *Democracy in Jonesville* (New York: Harper, 1949), p. 24.
2. Walter B. Miller, "Implications of Urban Lower-Class Culture for Social Work," *Social Service Review,* 33 (September, 1959), 219–236.
3. Morris Freilich, "Serial Polygyny, Negro Peasants, and Model Analysis," *American Anthropologist,* 63, No. 5, pt. I (October, 1961), 955–975.
4. Warner and Associates, *op. cit.,* pp. 154–155.
5. W. Lloyd Warner and Paul S. Lunt, *The Social Life of a Modern Community* (New Haven: Yale University Press, 1941), pp. 209, 211.
6. B. S. Rountree, *Poverty: A Study of Town Life* (London: Longmans, 1922).
7. August Hollingshead, *Elmtown's Youth* (New York: Wiley, 1949), pp. 97, 104, 116.
8. Warner and Lunt, *op. cit.,* p. 448.
9. Earl L. Koos, "Class Differences in Family Reactions to Crisis," *Marriage and Family Living,* 12 (1950), 77. In contrast to the above is the atttitude of the middle-class man, quoted by Koos: "I'd shoot myself before I'd go to the county welfare office and apply for help."
10. *1960 Handbook on Women Workers,* Women's Bureau Bulletin No. 275 (Washington, D.C.: Government Printing Office, 1960), p. 41. The figures are for 1958–1959.
11. Hollingshead, *op. cit.,* pp. 113–114.
12. Warner and Lunt, *op. cit.,* p. 255.
13. Hollingshead, *op. cit.,* pp. 106, 116.
14. For a detailed discussion of preparation for marriage, see Chapter 12.
15. Hollingshead, *op. cit.,* pp. 106, 117.
16. Hollingshead, *op. cit.,* pp. 106, 116.
17. Lee Rainwater and Karol Kane Weinstein, "A Qualitative Exploration of Family Planning and Contraception in the Working Class," *Marriage and Family Living,* 22 (1960), 238–242.
18. An excellent comparative statement of middle-class and lower-class child training is given in W. Allison Davis and Robert J. Havighurst, *Father of the Man* (Boston: Houghton Mifflin, 1947).
19. Robert H. Bohlke, "Social Mobility, Stratification Inconsistency, and Middle Class Delinquency," *Social Problems,* 8 (Spring, 1961), 351–363. The study reviews earlier studies and is generally applicable to upward mobility.
20. For an interesting study of such a move, see Bennett M. Berger, *Working Class Suburb: A Study of Auto Workers in Suburbia* (Berkeley: University of Calif., 1960).
21. Earl L. Koos, "Middle-class Family Crisis," *Marriage and Family Living,* 10 (1948), 25, 40.

6.　The Social World of the Urban Slum Child: Some Early Findings

SUZANNE KELLER

Throughout its history, this country has been settled largely, though not exclusively, by men and women seeking to escape the stings of poverty, unemployment, overcrowding in rapidly expanding cities, poor hygiene, and social discrimination and turmoil. Many came to make their fortunes and many succeeded. But after a century or two it turned out that even the "land of opportunity" had room for poverty and for slums and knew unemployment, ignorance, and failure. Periodically, the awareness that there are millions of city poor in the richest industrial society in the world comes as a shock only to be displaced by more immediate concerns. The prosperity since World War II, the rising standard of living, and extensive social and geographical mobility among large segments of the population are chiefly responsible for this relative neglect.

But the poor survive. In a metropolis like New York about 25 per cent of the families would be considered poor by any standards—underfed, un-

Reprinted from *The American Journal of Orthopsychiatry*, Vol. 33 (1962), pp. 823–831 (Copyright, The American Orthopsychiatric Association, Inc.), by permission of Dr. Keller and the copyright holder.

deremployed, ill-educated, and socially and economically marginal.[1] Children continue to be born in Negro ghettos; mothers are deserted; families are on relief in a society that has put self-reliance and self-support among its cardinal virtues. Social and economic deprivation go hand in hand with other frightening problems—with crime and delinquency, with illiteracy, and ill health. It is the poorest children who do least well in school, who care least about learning, and who swell the ranks of youthful delinquents, drug addicts, and the mentally and emotionally disabled. Poverty has always had its cost and its price. Its victims are many. Its most innocent victims are the children raised under its influence.

This article describes some aspects of the lives of underprivileged New York City public school children. Though the numbers involved are small, a general pattern may be discerned which, rather than any statistical uniformity, is of interest here. I will describe the social and family backgrounds of these children, their ambitions, achievements and activities, and their perceptions of themselves and their future. And since I had access to both Negro and white children I will also describe their discernible similarities and differences.

The data are drawn from a larger study of the verbal and intellectual development of some 250 school children from various social and cultural backgrounds. The purpose of this study, carried out by the Institute for Developmental Studies, was to ascertain the influence of social and familial factors on the development of basic cognitive and verbal skills in young children. It arose out of a concern for the hundreds of thousands of children who annually fail to benefit from instruction in the city's public schools by failing to learn their three R's, which are considered a part of their birthright. Failure in the first grade is usually only a prelude to failure in the fifth, and failure in school is all too often a forerunner of failure in life.

As is well known, most of the standard achievement and intelligence tests, the school curricula, and the children's books are based on the capacities and problems of middle-class children who are used as a yardstick for all children. It is also known, however, that these children are by no means typical of all children in their life experiences, family relationships, and socioeconomic opportunities. Numerically, at any rate, the lower-class children outnumber them. And if the middle-class child were an "ideal type" of child for our society, then, by definition, the majority of children fall far short of this ideal.

Educators, psychologists, psychiatrists and, of course, parents have long been aware of this fact and attempts are being made to take the differential experiences, motivations, and life chances into account when preparing and evaluating programs for teaching children from underprivileged backgrounds. But in order to do so systematically, it is necessary to know what

the typical life experiences of underprivileged children are. This article is an attempt to provide some relevant information.

The children studied are 46 first- and fifth-grade children currently living and attending public school in the poorer sections of New York City. Both colored and white children are included, though in view of the incompleteness of the larger study from which they are drawn, they are not equally represented. By means of an Index of Social Class developed at the Institute, based on occupational and educational level of the main support of the family, and on a Crowding Index, these children were all classified as Level IV on a ten-level stratification continuum, which might be considered as somewhere at the top of the lower-lower class stratum or at the bottom of the upper-lower class stratum.

The children were seen in the schools for several hours, during which they took a number of tests tapping their verbal, intellectual, and conceptual abilities. Their parents received questionnaires by mail and the children themselves gave accounts of their typical weekend activities and their life at home. It must be pointed out that the major purpose of the larger study was to compare test performances on various measures, and not to obtain full and comprehensive information on socioeconomic backgrounds. The background measures, in fact, permit at best only a rough classification of the socioeconomic levels of the children. But, although these measures are gross, they do depict some aspects of life in the slums of Harlem and in some of the poorer white sections in the changing neighborhoods of Brooklyn and Manhattan. One-fifth of the families were interviewed in their own homes.

The following summary is divided into two parts: an overall comparison, and a comparison of Negroes and whites separately. Four areas are discussed: (1) social and economic characteristics of the families, such as size, available space, regional origins of the parents, and educational and occupational attainments; (2) the children's after-school and weekend activities; (3) the children's self-perceptions; and (4) parental aspirations for the children.

SOCIAL AND ECONOMIC BACKGROUNDS

The children were selected on a roughly comparable basis. Three factors: the educational and occupational attainments of their parents and a Crowding Index were used. On all three of these they fell on the lower end of a socioeconomic continuum, although gross measures such as these hardly tap more than a fraction of the characteristics associated with lower-class life. The breadwinners in these families were employed as porters, short-order cooks, unskilled and semi-skilled factory workers, and maintenance and service workers. A few were bus or taxi drivers, clerks, or self-employed. The somewhat higher occupational positions of the self-employed were offset by overcrowded living conditions and conspicuously low educational attainments. One out of six of the breadwinners was unemployed at the time of the study and these families were receiving welfare assistance. On the average, the parents of the children had not gone beyond the first year of high school, and the mothers had somewhat more schooling than the fathers.

Family size, nativity, and family composition showed some important variations within the group. Less than three-fifths of these families conformed to the model American type of two parents with between two and three children;

more than two-fifths were large families with six to ten members. The average number of persons per room in the household was 1.2; this went as high as 1.5 persons per room for the larger families.

These families are not by and large the poor immigrant of half a century ago. These poor are Americanized, the majority born and raised on native ground. They also have been poor for a long time—two-thirds have held their current low-level jobs for six years or more, one-third for as long as ten years or more. Nor have they experienced extensive job mobility—one-half have had no other job during the past ten years, and none more than three jobs during that time. If either rapid horizontal or vertical mobility is characteristic of workers at higher levels and at the lowest levels, it does not, apparently, characterize these.

These are among the poorest elements of the population, they hold low-level jobs, they have had such jobs for a number of years, and they typically have not finished high school. Their actual chances for upward mobility are therefore objectively low. Thus their own subjective appraisals for such mobility are interesting. When asked to classify themselves in one of three groups, those going up, those going down in the world, and those doing neither, fully two-thirds felt they were going up in the world, three-tenths felt they were at a standstill, and only 2 per cent stated that they were going downhill. The ethic of success is very much in evidence.

LIFE OUTSIDE OF SCHOOL

All 46 children live in homes that contain both radio and television sets and all utilize both media regularly and frequently. Three-fourths had spent at least two hours (and a sizable proportion, as many as five) before their television sets the previous day watching a variety of entertainment programs—cartoons, the fights, Westerns, a few adult shows such as "I Love Lucy" and "Hitchcock Presents," and some of the better known comedians. The larger society seems to come to these children via entertainment and escapist stories on television. The children are familiar, even in the first grade, with the names of programs and of leading characters—a fact which might be used in school instruction.

This emphasis on peer-group entertainment also runs through their accounts of typical weekend activities. These children are between the ages of five and 13, years crucial for the acquisition of skills and information and the development of any talents they may possess. Life is not yet as serious as it will one day be, responsibilities are at a minimum, and the mind is receptive to new experiences and to the exploration of the natural and the social world. Yet hardly any of these children mention using their time to prepare themselves for something— they play, they watch television, they see films, and they listen to music on the radio. Sometimes they visit relatives and go to church on Sundays. They do not read, they do not study, they do not take lessons, they do not get instruction in any of the things that interest many children at these ages.

There is clearly a lack of sustained interaction with adult members of their families—a fact corroborating the findings of studies by Esther Milner, Walter B. Miller, and others. Only about one-half, for example, regularly eat one meal with one or both parents, the rest either eat alone or with brothers and sisters only. This robs them of one of the important socializing and intellectually stimulating experiences of childhood. According to Bossard and Boll,[2] the family meal is a focus for a number of important emotional, cultural, and educational experiences. Participation and interaction with significant others in an organized way helps shape the personality and sensitizes the participants to each other's needs and inclinations. Organized conversation helps shape vocabulary, influences the development of verbal facility and subtlety, and determines a whole set of complex attitudes and feelings about the use of language. The family meal also serves as an acculturating agency, for, in their interaction, the members teach each other and develop a way of seeing themselves and the world in which they live. The family meal has been described as a forum, as a clearing house for information, as a school for life, and as an opportunity to act out deeper personality needs. Such experiences were absent in the lives of at least one-half of the lower-class children here discussed.

SELF-PERCEPTIONS

Compared to middle-class children these children are evidently handicapped, both in their objective living conditions and in their opportunities for learning outside of school, either from their parents and other family members through sustained relationships and contacts, or through organized activities other than play, or from passive response to the mass media. Presumably, this will affect their self-perceptions and their school performance.

The Self-Concept and Motivation Test of the Institute contains ten incompleted sentences, each relating to some wish, judgment or evaluation of the child. One in particular seems to tap the self-image of the child by comparison with other children: "When I look at other boys and girls, and then look at myself, I feel. . . ." In all, 28 of 46 responses (or 60 per cent) were unfavorable to the child, and only 14 of the 46 (30 per cent) were favorable. The favorable responses read: "I feel good, happy, the same." The unfavorable ones read: "I feel ashamed, sad, heart-broken." The proportion of unfavorable self-references, moreover, increases from 55 per cent in the first grade to 65 per cent in the fifth. These children typically express a low self-esteem, drawing unfavorable comparisons between themselves and their schoolmates. If such self-deprecation is representative of the feelings of most young children from lower socioeconomic backgrounds, it suggests one potential source for early school failure.

PARENTAL ASPIRATIONS FOR THEIR CHILDREN

A number of studies have shown that parents may abandon their hopes for conspicuous achievements only to project them the more intensely onto their children.[3] These parents, too, conform to this pattern. When they were asked to indicate a first and a second choice of possible future occupations, although they could have nothing but vague hopes and expectations about the occupational future of their young children, their replies provide some insight into their ambitions and hopes. In their choices for the boys, fully two-thirds of the parents currently engaged in unskilled and semiskilled labor or unemployed hoped that their sons would become professional men such as doctors, lawyers, engineers, or business executives. Parents of girls most frequently mentioned such traditional feminine callings as nursing and teaching.

As to the amount of schooling they would like their children to obtain, here again aspirations were high. Eight-tenths of the parents wish their children to acquire a college degree. Only one-tenth would be satisfied with a high school diploma.

These responses compare interestingly with those given in private interviews in the homes of the ten families who had not answered the mail questionnaire. When asked what they considered the best sort of job to have, security and steady work, rather than prestige, power, or riches, received greatest emphasis. Ideally, then, on the fantasy level perhaps, these parents would like to see their sons get to the top. More realistically, they will be satisfied if their children manage to do what they themselves have failed to do—get a steady and secure job.

In sum, the children described in this paper come from large families living in relatively crowded quarters in the midst or on the edge of poverty. Only two out of three are being supported solely by their fathers' earning in low-level jobs, and one out of six are currently exposed to the stings of their parents' unemployment and the mixed blessings of public assistance. The majority of the parents, most of whom are native born, have been in this relatively deprived status for a long time—two-thirds for more than six years, one-third for more than ten. Nor has there been the sort of rapid job mobility one has come to expect from the official statistics on national trends, for, most of these people had held at most two other jobs at similar levels during the previous ten years.

All of this might lead to a pervasive sense of discouragement among them— and well it may, for we have no data to tap these feelings directly. Such discouragement is not, however, translated into resignation or indifference toward upward mobility; for, fully two-thirds of the group believe that they are on the way up in the world and a bare 2 per cent feel that things are going downhill. These great expectations are further reflected in the high hopes they have for their children, whom they would like to see graduating from college and entering one of the professions. Whether these desires reflect concrete plans or unrealistic fantasies about the future cannot be assessed.

What else do we know about these children, most of whom do poorly in school about which they care very little? Television seems to be a rather persistent influence. They like to play and they have friends. But they have little sustained contact with adults, they have few organized conversations with other adults the way middle-class children do, and few participate in shared family activities. Even at meal times, one-half of these children are alone or in the company of their brothers and sisters. It is interesting that, although these children are poor, they are not starving—the foods typically eaten at breakfast and dinner include a considerable variety of nutritionally adequate foods although amounts were not indicated.

Poverty, today, probably extends more to housing, to lack of spending money, to lack of comforts and to a constricted milieu for learning and exploring the world. A city, especially a metropolis, would seem to be a fascinating place in which to grow up, but one would not believe this from these accounts of restricted movement and the monotonous repetitiveness of activities—TV and more TV, play with other children, movies, and, as the single organized activity beside school, church on Sunday for one-half of the group. Their world seems to be small and monotonous, though not necessarily unhappy.

This constriction of experience and the poverty of spirit it engenders may account for the below normal I.Q. scores of this group of poor children by the time of the fifth grade (mean I.Q. is 88.57 on Lorge Thorndike nonverbal I.Q. test; in first grade, Lorge

Thorndike I.Q. mean scores were 96.56) confirming countless other studies that have shown a similar scholastic and verbal inferiority for children from underprivileged environments. It may also account for the high degree of negative self-evaluations already discussed.

In recent years there has been talk of the existence of a lower-class culture that performs much the same function for its members as any culture does: It defines the world, structures perceptions and habitual reactions, sets goals and standards, and permits people to evaluate and approve each other's conduct. This means that lower-class culture patterns, while substantially different from middle-class patterns, nevertheless provide a web of shared meanings for those subject to its rewards and penalties. Still, cultural relativism ignores the fact that schools and industry are middle-class in organization and outlook. If lower-class children conform to the "focal concerns" [4] of their milieu they will typically be misfits in the schools they attend. Short of adapting the public school to the cultural milieu of different groups, the children of this background will be at a disadvantage.

Clearly these children have a profound initial handicap in the scholastic competition with middle-class children. This initial disadvantage rarely turns to later advantage—instead, they become negativistic or bored and fail to learn the rudiments of the verbal and intellectual skills expected of adults in an industrial society.

The discrepancy in preschool orientation of social class is duplicated within the lower class by race. Using the same index of socioeconomic status, we find that even when gross socioeconomic factors are controlled, Negroes and whites do not live in comparable social environments.

For one thing, lower-class Negro (Level IV on the Index) children come from larger families than white children (nearly one-half, as compared to one-third among the white children, have at least three brothers or sisters). Thus an already low income must stretch farther for one group than for the other. More significantly, only one-half the Negro children were supported solely by the earnings of their fathers, whereas fully nine-tenths of the white children had fathers who could assume the traditional male role of chief breadwinner. In addition, three times as many Negro as white children at the same socioeconomic level live in families where the adults are currently unemployed and receiving welfare and other types of aid for the indigent. In educational attainment, too, the white families were somewhat at an advantage, the fathers of the white children having on the average one more year of schooling than the Negro fathers, and the white mothers having one-half a year more. In each group, however, the mothers were somewhat better educated than the fathers.

One of the striking differences occurs with regard to place of birth. Three-fourths of the Negro parents were geographically mobile, two-thirds having been born in the South and one-tenth outside the United States. None of the white children came from mobile families—all had parents both of whom had been born in the North.

As regards occupational mobility, however, Negro families were more likely to have held their present low-level jobs for a long time. In fact, whereas more than half the white families were at this low level for less than six years more than half the Negro families had been there for six years or more. Thus, although Negro families at this level were more mobile geographically, they were less mobile occupationally. This does not, apparently, diminish their belief in their own success. Fully three-fourths of the Negro families, as against only one-third of the white families, felt that they were going up in the world. Only one-fifth of the Negro families felt that they were at a standstill, but three-fifths of the white families felt this way. Negro lower-class children are thus raised in objectively inferior homes in which subjective appraisals of life's chances are much higher than among a comparable group of white families. Without more extensive data it is impossible to account for this discrepancy, although two possibilities suggest themselves. One relates to the differential geographical mobility of Negro families, which may lead them to expect other types of mobility as well. That is, they may have migrated to New York in the hope of improving their standing. The other relates to the relative standing of two equally low-level socioeconomic groups in the larger world.

Level IV has been described as somewhere at the top of the lowest and most underprivileged stratum, or at the bottom of the upper-lower stratum. But while the two groups were objectively at the same socioeconomic level, their status relative to most others of their rate is quite different. The majority of white persons in this country are above the lower-lower-class level but the same does not hold true for Negroes. This means, then, that the top of the lower-lower class is an exceedingly low status for most of the white families but perhaps a relatively high one for the Negro families. In other words, the white families may feel relatively deprived by comparison with others, whereas the Negro families may feel relatively favored. Further exploration on a larger sample should clarify this. It would be interesting, for example, to see whether this expressed optimism is also characteristic of the very low socioeconomic group among Negroes.

The most striking finding regarding the children themselves concerns the self-perceptions of the fifth graders. Negro children definitely exhibit more negative self-evaluations than do white children; 30 per cent of the white children but fully 80 per cent of the Negro children draw unfavorable self-other comparisons, paralleling findings from a number of other studies.[5]

These fifth-grade Negro children had also been evaluated by their teachers and some of their observations are relevant. More than half were judged to have little motivation for school work, to be typically sad or preoccupied, and to be working below capacity in school. The interplay between self-perception and school achievement must be explored further, particularly in view of the fact that the parents

of the Negro children were very much concerned about their children's work, for although nearly all the white families were satisfied with their children's school work, only one-half of the Negro families were. This may be yet another indication of the greater ambitiousness of the Negro families already noted.

These preliminary results reveal rather striking differences between Negro and white school children at the same socioeconomic level in their objective living conditions, parental aspirations, and their self-evaluations. Similarly, by inference, lower-class children, irrespective of race, differ sharply in their preparation for school from the ideal middle-class children with whom they must compete. Presumably, in both instances, this will exert a negative effect on intellectual interests and ambitions and may thus help account for the long-demonstrated correlation between socioeconomic deprivation and school failure.

References

1. In 1957, for example, 4.5 per cent of the Caucasians and 7.8 per cent of the Negroes in New York City were unemployed; 27 per cent of all families earned less than $4000 annually; 55 per cent of all Negro families earned less than $4000 annually; 12 per cent of all households had female heads. These figures are taken from *Characteristics of Population and Labor Force, New York State 1956 and 1957*, Vol. II, New York City. 1960. New York State Department of Labor, New York.
2. J. H. S. Bossard and E. S. Boll, *The Sociology of Child Development*, Ch. 13 (New York: Harper and Brothers, 1960).
3. E. Chinoy, *Automobile Workers and the American Dream* (New York: Random House, 1955).

   S. M. Lipset and R. Bendix, *Social Mobility in Industrial Society*, Chapter IX (University of California Press, Berkeley and Los Angeles, Calif., 1962).

   F. Zweig, *The Worker in an Affluent Society* (New York: The Free Press of Glencoe, 1961), p. 21.
4. W. B. Miller, "Lower class culture as a generating milieu of gang delinquency," *Journal of Social Issues* (1958), 14:5–19.
5. For a summary of such studies, see R. M. Drager and K. S. Miller, "Comparative psychological studies of Negroes and whites in the United States," *Psychological Bulletin* (1960), 57(5): 382–383.

7. The Impact of Cultural Factors on Selected Problems of Adolescent Development in the Middle and Lower Class

SOLOMON KOBRIN

Three common problems of adolescent development are here examined in relation to the differential cultural patterning of their resolution in the middle class and the lower class. In its ideal typical form each class exhibits a distinctive set of norms, values, and concerns generating different modes of response to the problems of adolescent development which occur uniformly in all social class groups. For the training of the young the social and cultural system of the middle class is organized to foster impulse control, planfulness, and achievement in the interest of maximizing status. Essential in the attainment of these goals is acceptance by the young of adult authority. In contrast, the social and cultural system of the lower class is uncommitted to a positive program of child training and by virtue of this fact fosters impulse expression, aggressivity, and independence from adult authority. These features define the elements of the two subcultural systems relevant for the present discussion.[1]

Reprinted from *The American Journal of Orthopsychiatry*, Vol. 33 (April 1962), pp. 387–390 (Copyright, The American Orthopsychiatric Association, Inc.), by permission of Mr. Kobrin and the copyright holder.

ADULT AUTHORITY AND THE EARLY ADOLESCENT PERIOD

The Developmental Problem [2]

The period of early adolescence is relatively free of serious problems, and ordinarily exhibits an easy and stable accommodation across the generational line. This period is commonly regarded as characterized by a minimum of parent-child conflict. There prevails, instead, a situation of mutual respect for each other's spheres of responsibility and values resulting from the rather sharp divergence of interests. This contrasts with the situation in later adolescence when the interests of the young person tend to parallel and ultimately to merge with those of the adult as the requirements of sexual and occupational adjustment come increasingly into focus. As this takes place, the accommodation of the earlier period is dissolved, and what had existed formerly as latent cross-generational hostility then becomes explicit and calls for an effort at a new accommodation.

Cultural Factors in Its Resolution

The cultural experiences of middle- and lower-class children during the period of early adolescence exhibit crucial differences affecting the readiness with which the accommodation required in the later phase of the adolescent period is accomplished. The middle-class mode of child rearing surrounds the child, during both the prepubertal and early adolescent period, with a wide network of adult supervised training and socializing institutions. The young person pursues the separate and independent interests of his juvenile world within these structures which function, on the whole, under the relentless surveillance of adults. The freedom of the child is thus a qualified one in which he is subtly conditioned to accept the primacy of adult authority. In contrast, the freedom of the lower-class child, commonly expressed in the spontaneity of his street life, is unqualified by a similar omnipresent spirit of adult surveillance. Inescapably this results in his failure to acquire a similar conditioning to an implicit acceptance of adult authority. When, therefore, he moves into the struggle of later adolescence to come to terms with the more stringent demands of adult authority he tends to be distinctively handicapped in his task of assimilating the requisite elements of an adult identity, although he is not necessarily more rebellious than his middle-class counterpart. This feature of the differential impact of cultural conditioning is not unrelated to the relatively high rates of delinquents in the urban lower class.

THE ROLE OF ADULT MODELS IN THE RESOLUTION OF AMBIVALENCE RESPECTING DEPENDENCE AND INDEPENDENCE

The Developmental Problem

As is known, the adolescent comes in time to want independence with respect to the whole range of adult objects and interests, and will not readily accept dictation as to what he should value. However, in the very newness of his interests he needs, and senses his need for, guidance and advice. However, he can accept the dependency implicit in such guidance only by segregating the dependency of the new type from infantile dependency. For this reason parents are generally unacceptable (or only ambivalently acceptable) for this purpose. Consequently, he needs and will readily idealize a non-parental adult who meets this requirement.

Cultural Factors in Its Resolution

Nonparental adults capable of filling the role described are everywhere in short supply, although they are relatively more available to middle-class youth. In the lower class such figures are notably in short supply. The cultural factors operating systematically to reduce the availability of such adult figures in the lower-class milieu are, first, the cultural strangeness of professional personnel provided in part for this purpose (teachers, group workers, recreation workers, etc.) based primarily on the divergence between middle-class and lower-class concerns, values and goals; and, second, the absence of a culturally based interest in the lower class with the problem of child rearing. Although age-graded segregation to some degree is a cultural universal, the definition of the problem of child training as a legitimate object of concern in a cultural system operates to reduce isolation on the basis of age grades. In the lower class there appears to be relatively little tendency on the part of adults to take a serious interest in child rearing as a distinctive problem area, due, probably, to the prevailing truncated view of the future. This results in a tendency in boys in lower-class communities to select their role models from the next oldest age group, with a consequent tendency for the traditions of street life, including its delinquent patterns, to be transmitted relatively intact.

PHASE RELATIONS OF DEPENDENCY AND AUTONOMY

The Developmental Problem

In meeting the problems of adolescent development all viable cultural systems must possess workable practices for meeting three types of contingencies: (1) the regression of the adolescent to dependent modes of response and behavior; (2) the thrust toward autonomy through independent modes of response and behavior, and (3) the alternate phasing of the two. The security of the person, at the deepest levels, is bound up with the availability of dependency relationships; his achievement of autonomy with opportunity for independent decision and action; and the progressive attainment of maturity with an appropriate phasing of the alternation of the two modes. Clinical observation suggests the hypothesis that each phase is intrinsically disorganizing for its alternate, and that systematic differential receptivity in parents and other adult figures to either dependency modes or autonomy modes tends to limit and in extreme cases to undermine an appropriate resolution of the phase relation problem.

Cultural Factors in Its Resolution

Middle-class and lower-class subcultural systems may be differentiated in the distribution of their receptivity to dependency and autonomy in adolescents. Parents in both class subcultures are equally subject to the requirement of the general culture that they produce a new generation of competent and responsible adults. However, by virtue of the heavy investment in their children as a means of status maintenance and potential mobility, middle-class parents in contrast to lower-class parents

are expectedly more protective and controlling in their relations with their children, and hence accept relatively more readily the dependency phases of adolescent development. Lower-class parents, being less invested in their children as instruments of status maintenance and mobility, are less protective and controlling in their relations with their children, and accept relatively more readily the autonomy phases of adolescent development. As a result, the dependency phases of adolescent experience are more protracted and prominent in the middle class, the autonomy phases in the lower class. This inference, based on observation of the two subcultural systems, is supported by the essentially psychological observation that the single most problematic aspect of adolescent development among middle-class adolescent youth centers on the establishment of their independence. The complementary observation with respect to lower-class adolescent youth, infrequently made, is that their developmental problem centers on the management of their dependency needs. As a consequence, their autonomy, so fully supported by their social and cultural system, has a qualitatively different character from that found in the psychologically mature middle-class adult.

Hypothetically, the autonomy of the lower-class adult may be expected to be compromised and tainted by an attraction to random forms of group support, expressive of what may be termed an unsatisfied psychological hunger for dependency relationships. This view would be supported by studies, for example, which have shown a correlation between educational level, an index of class affiliation, and susceptibility to nonrational types of crowd action. Another example is furnished by the observations of Walter Miller, a cultural anthropologist, who has noted a structured defensive expression of dependency hunger in the street boy's aversion to all forms of adult authority and control.[3] The primacy of the peer group in the street life of lower-class youth offers further evidence on this point.

References

1. Davis, Allison and Robert J. Havighurst, "Social Class and Color Differences in Child Rearing." *American Sociology Review* (1946), 11:698–710.
2. The statement of the developmental problem concerned in the first two topics has been freely adapted from Irene Josselyn, "The Adolescent and His World" (New York: Family Service Association of America, 1952).
3. Miller, Walter, "Lower Class Culture as a Generating Milieu of Gang Delinquency." *Journal Social Issues* (1958), 14, 3:5–19.

8. A Comparison of the Child-Rearing Environment of Upper-Lower and Very Low-Lower Class Families

ELEANOR PAVENSTEDT

The observations reported are descriptive of two socioeconomic groups at the two extremes of the lower class of an urban population on the East coast. You will see that there is a vast difference in the functioning of the families in the organized, stable, often upwardly mobile upper-lower class group and the deprived, disorganized "multiproblem" families of the very low, lower-class group. We are bringing this contrast to your attention in the hope that it will lead to a differentiated range of educational enrichment programs now being set up for deprived children.

These observations were made during home visits to families in the course of two different projects. The stable upper-lower class group constituted the bulk of the research population of a longitudinal study in child development. The disorganized families in the low, lower-class group have received our assistance since 1955; they became

Reprinted from *The American Journal of Orthopsychiatry*, Vol. 35 (January 1965), pp. 89–98 (Copyright, The American Orthopsychiatric Association, Inc.), by permission of Dr. Pavenstedt and the copyright holder.

the subjects of a demonstration project in 1960. For the sake of clarity we will refer to these two as "the stable group" and the "disorganized group."

Both studies were planned by child psychiatrists and were staffed by the usual child guidance disciplines, including a pediatrician, nurses with special training in mental health, educators, and an anthropologist. The overall theoretical framework was psychoanalytic. Both studies initially were concerned with preschool children, since then followed into the first grades of grammar school. The mothers of the stable group were contacted in the prenatal clinic of a private hospital to which they had elected to come for care around their first pregnancy and delivery. In contrast, the families of the disorganized group already had one to three children under six when they first came to our attention on the obstetrical service of a city hospital or after having been referred by a community agency.

The 30 stable families lived mostly in flats or in three- and four-family houses. About 25 per cent of them lived in the same skid row environment as the multiproblem families but never identified themselves with the neighborhood. Their goal was to move into the suburbs, and many of them by now (eight to ten years later) have achieved it. All were American-born from various ethnic backgrounds: Italian, Greek, Syrian, Negro, Irish and Anglo-Saxon. They were 85 per cent Catholic—Roman and Orthodox.

Since we accepted into the study only young families living separately where the mothers planned to stay at home, most Negro subjects we screened had to be eliminated.

In the history obtained of the courtship, the young couple's conscious goals seldom went beyond simple security. All of them wanted children and usually had some idea of the size family they would like, but they seldom had formulated ambitions for their children nor did they discuss matters of child-rearing together. The immediate future (the trousseau, preparations for the wedding and the apartment) were matters of great concern. Often both sides of the family helped. The apartments—usually in poor housing—were clean, bright, and colorful but showed little taste. There were no books; only a few copies of such magazines as *True Love,* etc. Rarely was there any expressed interest in national or world affairs, despite the fact that the radio often was turned on high in the kitchen and the TV in the parlor. Bowling and roller-skating had been the chief interests of the mothers prior to marriage. The movies and visiting with family members and occasional friends now took their place. Intellectual interests on the part of a young man were viewed with suspicion.

When we first saw them, the women were still in factory, clerical, or sales jobs engaged in upon leaving school. About half of them had graduated from high school. They were reluctant to cease working in the seventh month of pregnancy, fearing the loss of companionship, routine activity and their relative financial independence. Many of the men were taking courses under the G.I. bill to improve their employment. Most abandoned these as they were confronted by the cost of the delivery and the responsibility of becoming fathers. Instead, they took on extra jobs to supplement their small salaries from factory work, house painting, truck driving, mechanical repair work, etc. Only one man expressed his dissatisfaction later with the monotony and hopelessness of his occupational lot and one other continued to improve his situation with considerable support from a capable wife.

Psychological testing of the mothers revealed restriction of the personality as a general characteristic. We uncovered many circumscribed phobias of which the subjects themselves were hardly aware. We found it difficult to involve the young fathers in the study and would not have dared to propose psychological testing to them. They were, as a group, self-conscious and often timid with little confidence or push.

Born into this environment, the children lacked intellectual stimulation. Our presence in their lives aroused their mothers' interest in many aspects of the children's development that otherwise would have passed unheeded. They bought toys at first resembling the developmental testing material and later the play material to which we had exposed them, including picture books and story books. Many of the mothers soon had families of two and three children. With a baby to carry and a toddler or two to propel down steep, ricketty stairs, most mothers preferred to remain at home, especially when they were pregnant. The streets where they lived offered little safety and no attraction. The husbands, by and large, did the weekly marketing; with their help Saturdays often were devoted to thorough housecleaning. Grandparents' and other relatives' homes were the most frequent destinations of Sunday trips. When the children were old enough to enjoy them, they were taken to children's amusement parks. The Greek women talked of their large group picnics but rarely attended them when the children were young. There were no trips to airports, to railroad stations, to the harbor or to zoos to give the children some experience with the world around them. Only a small number of the families vacationed in the country in the summer.

In this particular section of the population, mothers bottle-feed their children. Although they prop occasional bottles very early, they hold the children at many feedings. Before birth many mothers said they would let their babies scream so as not to spoil them. When the time came, however, they responded immediately to the infant's cry. The appropriateness of the response depended on the clarity of the child's cues and the mother's mothering gifts. After the first two months, however, many mothers returned to housekeeping routines and no longer tolerated as much interference with these tasks. The degree to which this was carried on depended again more on the individual mother's personality than on cultural usages. The same was true of permissiveness in self-feeding and messing with food.

Details of health care, i.e. bowel management, feeding, dressing, etc., were outlined by the pediatrician on our staff, but we observed that the mothers were just as likely to heed the advice of family members and neighbors. The majority were fairly adaptable as regards toilet training; they

abandoned their efforts when the child showed no readiness to respond or objected strenuously.

The children of this group were overtly neglected only by a few mothers who had serious character problems and then only briefly and under stress. As infants they seldom were separated. Later the mothers usually had one evening away from home while father or another relative baby-sat. The families were greatly concerned for the welfare of their children. The father who rebelled against his work told us he lived for his children. In most of these families they were the first concern.

Language development covered the normal range on the Gesell, Merrill-Palmer, Binet, and Wechsler intelligence tests. These mothers talked to their children from an early age. In fact, they projected adult comprehension and responses onto the infants, sometimes even the newborn. Smiling gave rise to considerable social interaction and pleasure. Response to and encouragement of vocalizations were frequent but not always present. Some mothers encouraged and welcomed motor development whereas others often unwittingly discouraged it, depending on their need to hurry the children along or to infantilize them. The same was true of education toward independence. However, all the children were feeding themselves by the time they were two and dressing themselves before they were three.

Fathers often became more involved in actually playing with the children, whereas the mothers participated only verbally while carrying on their housework. The extent to which the mothers entered into their children's fantasies was again a factor of the mothers' personality makeup. Considerable permissiveness was granted the children around coming into the parental bed at night.

The concept that children needed to be trained, to be taught to obey and conform was universal. Fear of delinquent behavior was widespread. There were many different methods used to instill parental standards. There was not a single home where the mother and father failed to ask themselves how they best could reach and manage their child, even though impulsivity, impatience, and anger might break through at times and interfere with their plans. They never lost sight of their parental role. Except for short periods of special stress or depression, the children were carefully and affectionately supervised.

The mothers' voices often were raised. They accused themselves of yelling at the children. This was perhaps the most frequent deterrent used. Physical punishment was rejected by only a few of the parents, and spankings sometimes were administered at a surprisingly early age. There was more teasing than we had had any awareness of. Some mothers in this group were determined to control their child, particularly a son,[1] from very early in life. Although the children sometimes bore the brunt of a parent's feelings toward another adult, a sincere effort was made to deal equitably with the child. Some mothers ruefully shared wih us their awareness of such displacement of anger to the child.

As their children came of school age, parents showed more concern that they conform to the teacher's expectations than about learning per se. While teachers described mothers as cooperative and wanting to help and to do well for their children, it was often the fathers who took poor achievement more seriously and even helped their children with homework. Mothers frequently were protective, particularly of boys. In their adaptation to

school, none of the children appeared to have discipline or behavior problems. In first grade some of them encountered difficulty in learning, but they managed to make sufficient improvement when pressure was brought to bear so that none of them had to repeat.

Let us turn now to the disorganized, grossly deprived, multiproblem families of our demonstration project. The women of this group, when first encountered by the writer in a reformatory, were inadequately diagnosed as schizoid personality or narcissistic character disorder. The ineffectiveness of our welfare, custodial, and protective agencies in altering their lives and those of their children lay clearly exposed.

When they were re-encountered on the obstetrical service of a city hospital and found to be unreferrable because of their failure to maintain constructive contacts with social agencies, we decided to go into their homes. We found them very suspicious and guarded but nevertheless accessible.

The anthropologist on our project called their culture fringe-skid row, or preferred to speak of it as a protoculture since there are no values, rituals, or directions.

As long as the staff consisted of only family workers, we were unable to obtain a clear picture of the children. The adults in the families were in constant crises. They completely absorbed the workers. We knew only that (contrary to what one might expect) the small children were seldom overtly aggressive, or destructive, or engaged in sexual exploits. We had seen them as shadowy, underfed little waifs with meaningless smiles, seldom toilet-trained, climbing into the laps of our visitors at every opportunity and attempting to ingratiate themselves.

It took months or often a year of

skillful, especially adapted casework in the homes before the parents would allow their three- and four-year-olds to come to our nursery school.

When they finally allowed the teachers to pick up the children, no recognition was given either by the children or by the parents to the fact that they were leaving for the first time with people they hardly knew for a place they had seen only a few times. No goodbyes were said, no mother came to the window and no child spoke about his mother or home during the better part of two months. It gradually became clear that their *separation anxiety*, shared no doubt by the mothers, was so overwhelming that the thought of separation had to be completely avoided. After several months of attendance when they had begun to relate to their teacher the theme of desertion dominated their play. By now many of the mothers, too, were bidding their children goodbye.

This shared fear of separation gives us a clue to the intensity of distrust and suspicion these families feel toward organized, i.e. middle-class, society. The proposal that their children come to our nursery school aroused a fear that they would be exposing themselves to dangers from outside against which experience had shown they were powerless. Their self-image was so degraded that they expected to be criticized and punished, deprived of their privacy and even of their children.

The marriages in this group do not follow racial, ethnic or religious lines. Separations, desertion, divorce, abandonment, and neglect of children are commonplace. At other times parents defend themselves fiercely against having their children removed from the home. Petty crimes, alcoholism, prostitution, and cohabitation often bring agents of the law down upon them. They feel rejected by the church whose laws they have offended. Most of them are chronic public relief clients and feel under critical scrutiny by social service agencies. Only the medical and para-medical professions minister to their needs without asking embarrassing questions or assuming a critical position, but these professional people also are feared.

Many of these families lived in housing projects. A few families lived in rooming houses where they shared bathroom facilities with other, often undesirable, boarders. When they lived in run-down "apartment" houses, the housing was only *sometimes* worse than in the other group, but the inside of the apartments was strikingly different. Disorder and evidence of household tasks begun but left unfinished often gave an impression of chaos. There was an occasional desultory attempt to brighten up the room with colorful paper curtains or ornaments, soon faded and dirty. In a number of the homes, the shades remained drawn the better part of the day. Bits of food and dirty dishes were found anywhere, and the smell of urine often pervaded the place. In many homes the beds had shabby stained mattresses and odd bits of blankets. The blaring of TV sets was deliberately used as a protection against the visitor and was toned down as he or she came to be accepted.

The youngest child usually was found in his crib in a back room. Diapers were changed infrequently. As often as not, a partially full bottle was somewhere in the crib beyond the baby's reach. During our visits, crying often remained unheeded while the mother discussed her own worries and needs, or she would hold the baby with little attention to his comfort. The outstanding characteristic in these homes was that activities were impulse-determined; [2] consistency was totally absent. The mother might stay in bed until noon while the children also were kept in bed or ran around unsupervised. Although families sometimes ate breakfast or dinner together, there was no pattern for anything. Until children had learned not to mess with food, the mothers fed them and prevented them from holding the spoon. Curiously enough, they always dressed their children, who were completely passive and expected to be dressed. Most children ran around in an undershirt and diapers until they were about two and a half years old. Then they were dressed, and only then let out to play. Once out-of-doors they received no supervision. We saw them standing around, holding onto some outdoor toy and watching other children play. Sometimes the mother called them to have something to eat or when it was getting dark. The children often came running in to ask for money to buy candy or ice cream. We saw children crying from some injury dash into the apartment, run past mother to their bed and continue to scream there. The mothers seldom inquired about their injuries or attempted to comfort them. Ridicule was as likely to be the response. There were no toys in children's rooms; the beds left little space to play. What toys there were usually were kept on shelves beyond the children's reach.

Poor planning on the mother's part made it necessary to wash large piles of clothes daily. The children apparently often wore each other's clothes to judge from the fit. None of the children owned anything; a recent gift might be taken away by a sibling without anyone's intervening. The parents often failed to discriminate between the children. A parent, incensed by the behavior of one child, was seen dealing a blow to another child who was closer. Communication by means of words hardly existed. Directions were indefinite or hung unfinished in mid-air. Reprimands were often high-pitched and angry. The children usu-

ally were put to bed immediately after supper, regardless of their age. Although boys and girls slept in the same bed, a great issue was made of not looking at each other while undressing or bathing. As the children outgrew babyhood, the parents differentiated very little between the parent and child roles. The parents' needs were as pressing and as often indulged as were those of the children. There was strong competition for the attention of helpful adults. All this grimness was interspersed with attempts at mothering which were not maintained because of the mother's tension and lack of self-control. Many of these mothers seemed to think nothing of leaving the home for hours on end with a four- or five-year-old in charge of the babies.

Children in such an environment have to learn to cope for themselves, and these children were extraordinarily adept in certain areas. Extremely skillful at reading their cues, they focused on adults and manipulated them so as to obtain the attention, praise, food, money or whatever else they wanted. Some people thought of this as "object hunger," i.e. the longing for a person who would provide an affectionate, giving relationship. No doubt the absence of anyone sufficiently attentive to the child to allow him to relate had led to this extreme alertness. However, the element of avoiding the adult's anger and sudden impulsive reactions contributed to it as well. They recognized a drunk on the street and were careful to keep their distance. They also manipulated other children and were able to gain possession of another child's toy without raising an outcry. As soon as they were allowed out, they ran errands, usually with a slip of paper. They learned early that you obtained things for money. They soon learned to keep secrets, to cover up for their parents and to say, "Mother isn't here," or, "Mother has a headache," when she was intoxicated.

In our nursery school we had ample opportunity to observe these children. We already have mentioned the total absence of separation anxiety at first. Actually all emotions were veiled. The children masked pleasure by clowning and grimacing and showed no distress when hurt. They wore wide smiles quite inappropriately. When disappointed or angry, they would fade away. When upset or anxious, they might become paralyzed or engage in some frantic repetitive activity. Nevertheless, many of them, surprisingly well-dressed for nursery school, had a certain charm.

Many of them formed their words so poorly that it was at first almost impossible to understand them at three and four years of age. Words were used imitatively and often quite out of context. Instructions, when attended to, were at times repeated but not translated into action. Concrete demonstrations were necessary.

The children were overly obedient in many instances. They never expected their requests to be fulfilled and might wander off while the adult was engaged in helping them. They failed to discriminate between adults and would just as soon run to a stranger. They didn't know the teachers' names and there was no carryover from day to day. There was considerable pseudo-independence and self-sufficiency but no negativism or self-assertion. They were hyper-alert to sounds outside and to the gestures of adults around them.

Rivalry seemed the only determinant for the choice of a toy. It was immaturely handled and the children failed to become involved in play except briefly when an adult was right there. For a long time, however, they did not allow the teacher to be close to them. No questions were asked, no problem-solving activity engaged in.

Often they would repeat the same movements indefinitely.

They usually were well-coordinated in gross motor activity but lack of concern about harm to their bodies disguised this proficiency. They suddenly fell and bruised themselves and seemed never to learn from past experience. Even in fine motor coordination they were better equipped than appeared at first. This was demonstrated as soon as they felt free enough to choose their own activity, but was much less in evidence when they had a task imposed on them. An outstanding trait was their great sense of rhythm. As with autistic children, they could be reached by music and could much more readily memorize a verse when it was set to music. They listened attentively and responded with rhythmic body movements.

The siblings seldom comforted or helped each other in trouble unless a younger sibling appealed directly to an older one. Then encouragement, praise or assistance was promptly forthcoming. A girl three and a half years old reported quite casually that when the baby cried during the night the parents wouldn't hear the infant; the girl then would get milk from the refrigerator, warm it and feed the baby. From what she had observed of the child's activities at home the nursery school teacher felt this was a credible report.

The children were unbelievably greedy when food was presented to them. There was little evidence of fantasy. Animation of inanimate objects went far beyond the age norm. Suggestions about a picture of a dog (such as "take him down, put him on the floor") occurred daily.

The saddest, and to us the outstanding characteristic of this group with adults and children alike, was the self-devaluation. One little boy, when encouraged by the teacher to have her put his name on his drawing, wanted her to write "shitty Billy." Their lack of confidence in their ability to master was painfully reenacted with each new encounter.

CONCLUSION

We see a vast difference in child-rearing practices among these two sub-groups of the lower socioeconomic class. In the stable group we found parents assuming the parental role, children were cherished, cared for and trained in an organized home with daily routines.

Maturation of the child's total development proceeded as an epigenetic process. The children were the focus of the mothers' feelings; they were mutually involved with each other, and the father participated as well in this relationship, as did the siblings. Most of them learned to trust others and to look after themselves. Deviations of development, where they occurred, were tied to pathology of the parental personalities or of the individual child's equipment. Although initiative and self-assertion sometimes were lacking, especially in the boys, they were by age six ready to profit from first-grade public or parochial school instruction and able to participate in a learning experience.

Many of them, as toddlers, had appeared to us alert and capable. Since, according to most psychologists, developmental tests do not correlate with later intelligence tests, we cannot claim that good native intelligence was paralyzed as a result of absence of stimulation. We can only say that their cognitive development did not proceed as their early functioning had led us to anticipate. We had the impression that they learned in school because it was expected of them, seldom because they were excited about what their new skills might open up to them. Motivation to acquire knowledge was not often present, but a willingness to work for good marks and to please the teacher and parents was there.

This stable upper lower-class group is definitely educable. The parents rapidly shared in our interested observations and bought our toys for their children. If one could involve these families in enrichment programs and persuade them of the advantages of intellectual development for their children, one might be tapping a reliable resource for our man-power requirements since their overall personality development is at a reasonable level of maturity. The developmental point of view can enrich the study of socio-cultural groups and add another dimension to our preventive measures.

In the disorganized families, impulse-ridden adults led a chaotic existence in which the mothers barely managed to maintain a home (we had not accepted families unless the mother expressed a desire to do something for her children). The children seemed to have no individual personality for the parents. They never learned to trust and were constantly on the alert for the adults' reaction. Without anyone to relate to, they failed to learn communication and came to grips only with certain very circumscribed areas of their reality. They were immature little drifters.

We were unable to deter the parents in their determination to send the children to school just as soon as they were eligible to go—at five or five and a half. In large classes with their extreme concreteness of thinking they failed to grasp directions. Suspicion and anxiety concerning the adult's intentions made them unable to attend to the teacher's instructions. As failure followed failure, they grew very anxious and shunned any learning task. It was impossible after six months in school for our psychologist to obtain the cooperation of several of the children in order to test them, for instance. Their mothers screamed at them, or shamed them when they came home with poor papers. Teachers (who said many of their children came to school hardly knowing their family names or where they lived) became understandably discouraged about teaching these abashed and disoriented children.

Upon superficial appraisal, it is not easy to distinguish between these two groups of children. They come from the same neighborhood and are equally well dressed. Yet they must be separated, for they require a totally different approach. Between these two groups there are, no doubt, many strata, each with a little more organization and internal stability than the one below.

Fortunately educators have become aroused to the plight of these deprived children. It is difficult to estimate how many of them now being offered special preparatory training are children from as grim an environment as the one we have been dealing with. In order to teach these children anything that will really take root, the teachers will have to overcome the children's distrust and demonstrate very con-

cretely to them that they are consistently helpful adults who can be relied upon. In some new programs teachers are spending considerable time with the parents. Before they call upon the parents to encourage their children and exhort them to fulfill their supportive parental role, they will have to fill some of the parents' own needs. When one has never been given to, one cannot be expected to give. These parents, while superficially conforming, will be suspicious of teachers, for they, too, are representatives of the feared, middle-class, governing group.

The education of these children represents a complex task, since developmental issues other than the cognitive ones have to be dealt with. Progress cannot be expected to be maintained unless the parents receive help through especially adapted casework and group work.[3]

Perhaps a massive approach from the schools can convince the parents that society attributes some value to them and to their children. Only after we have altered their self-image can we expect them to find some value in their children. And only then will the children be able to sustain feelings of self-confidence and self-respect.

References

1. Bayley, Nancy and E. S. Schaefer. Relationships between socioeconomic variables and the behavior of mothers toward young children. **1960.** *Jour. Genet. Psychol.* **96:** 61–77.
2. See Kaufman, I. and B. S. Reiner. **1959.** Character Disorders in Parents of Delinquents. Family Service Association of America. New York, N.Y.
3. Although publications from Wiltwyck School for Boys, Inc. deal with the families of delinquents, their findings are relevant:
   Minuchin, S. The acting-out child and his family. Presented at the William Alanson White Institute, 1962.
   Minuchin, S., E. Auerswald, C. H. King and C. Rabinowitz. **1963.** The study and treatment of families who produce multiple acting-out boys. *Amer. Jour. Orthopsychiat.*
   Auerswald, E. Developmental effects of poverty on children of hard-core urban families: implications for nosology and treatment. Presented at the Annual Meeting of the American Orthopsychiatric Association, Chicago, Ill. March, 1964.

9. Newcomers from the Southern Mountains

ROSCOE GIFFIN

Some people stoutly maintain that there is nothing which distinguishes Southern Mountain people from any one else in the United States. I think, however, that going to church on Saturday night in the summertime and families with eight and ten children are indicators of significant cultural differences.

Despite this evidence and much more which is available, people of and from this area are often very resistant to being given any specific identification. For purposes of this presentation they will be identified as Southern Mountain Newcomers. . . .

There are important variations among the approximately 7,000,000 people in the Appalachian South which complicates the task of making valid generalizations. A third difficulty is the lack of adequate research data to document some of the hypotheses.

MAGNITUDE AND CAUSES OF THE MIGRATION FROM THE SOUTHERN MOUNTAINS

The Southern Mountain States have long been an important source of popu-

Reprinted from the report of the Institute of Cultural Patterns of Newcomers (Chicago: Welfare Council of Metropolitan Chicago, 1959), pp. 15–40, by permission of the publisher and the author's estate.

lation for such industrial states of the Midwest as Illinois, Michigan, Indiana, and Ohio. I have estimated that nearly 800,000 people have moved out of the counties in the Appalachian South between 1950–1956. Not all of these have come north by any means, for Southern cities are also growing. But there is much evidence that the road north has attracted a great many of them.

Many factors are involved in this population movement. Perhaps if we classify them by area or origin and area of destination, the factors can be summarized readily. Within the mountain states in which these people originate the following factors are operative. First, dissatisfaction with the possibilities of life there is increasing as a result of receiving and accepting the knowledge and values of urban living. Second, the population carrying capacity of the resources of the area are already strained to such a point that further population increases will reduce the already low levels of living. The area as a whole is characterized by high birth rates, declining agricultural resources, and only a few opportunities for industrial employment. A third cause of the outmigration is the rapid mechanization of coal-mining and the declining demand for coal. . . .

Most of the (migrants) are young

and in reasonably good health. They thus offer many years of productive labor. Despite all the handicaps for urban living which their situational background imposes upon them, we can take encouragement from the evidence that, like most other people, they have a capacity to learn the ways and demands of a new environment.

They have no responsibility for the fact that they are "Old American" stock, but in the scales of group membership by which people are judged in America, the balance is tipped in favor of such groups. I have received numerous favorable reports of the work of Southern Mountain men in factories and with machinery. This particular strength comes almost as a "natural" to men who have been reared on the near-subsistence farm of the mountains or who have worked in mines and logging woods. Their ability to keep their elderly cars and trucks operating is evidence of a mechanical ability and ingenuity which few people I know possess.

PLACES OF RESIDENCE ARE DOMINANTLY RURAL AND RELATIVELY ISOLATED IN A MOUNTAINOUS REGION

The social, economic, and political manifestations of a rural background have been noted frequently in recent research studies, such as those of the Detroit Area Study.

A recent Indianapolis study which showed that the limited capacity of southern migrants to make new friends constituted one of their major sources of adjustment difficulty.

For many . . . concerned with the adjustment problems of such migrants as these, the difficulties are those of involving them in programs of churches, neighborhood centers, or helping their children develop a feeling of belonging in large urban schools. The areas of our great cities in which the South-

ern Mountain people concentrate are generally lacking in active churches. The buildings may be there, but their congregations have moved away. In many cases the staffs of such churches have done all they knew to get the newcomers to participate.

I know of a Cincinnati case where only one family from the hills attended church after seven years of concentrated effort by the church staff. Finally, the staff gave up and turned to the task of ministering to its own membership. But I'm sure it will not be long before this church moves out to the suburbs where its membership is.

There are no easy remedies for this problem. One difficulty seems to be the tendency of rural people to define large impersonal organizations as unfriendly. Also, there is the fact that they simply are not accustomed to regular church attendance as are many urban people. For many in the mountain areas, going to church has been something you do only in the summer while the revivals are being held. . . .

MOST OF THE AREA MUST BE CHARACTERIZED AS ONE OF LOW ECONOMIC PRODUCTIVITY

The meaning of a thin economic base for urban adjustment can perhaps only be understood as we gain some comprehension of the effects of poverty upon attitudes and behavior. Although most of our knowledge of these effects are derived from studies of urban poverty, there are many insights which can be appropriated and applied to the case of rural poverty.

Not all mountain families have adequate food, nor are their houses always warm in winter despite the general abundance of fuels. Allison Davis has shown how from such circumstances come anxiety patterns which may show up as excesses of eating and getting warm when resources are abundant instead of rational budgeting for future needs. I wish I had a nickel for every time I've heard a middle-class mountain person of secure income condemn the improvidence of coal mining families. Poverty seems to develop a certain defensive hardening and insensitivity which James Plant interprets as a product of insecurity and deprivation. There is no reason why we should not expect to find all of these manifestations among the Southern Mountain Newcomers. . . .

THE RELATIVELY LARGE FAMILIES PERFORM NUMEROUS FUNCTIONS THROUGH A SYSTEM OF ROLES ALLOCATED BY AGE AND SEX IN WHICH THE FATHER IS GENERALLY THE AUTHORITY CENTER AND MOTHER THE AFFECTION CENTER

Both in terms of structure and function the extended families to which this proposition refers are in conflict with the need to prepare children for migration. In place of rigid systems of role allocation, there is a need for flexibility, and instead of activities mainly in concert with other members of the family, there is a need for variety of personal contacts. Rather than seeking to bind its members to it by continual involvement in activities centering in the family, a major function should be to prepare children emotionally for leaving home by a gradual process of separation and new experiences.

But the ties that pull these people towards their childhood home are not only those of family. There are also the bonds to place, to the beauty and serenity of the hills. As one who left behind the mountain grandeur of Colorado in exchange for those broad, green plains of Urbana, Illinois, I think I can empathize with the writer of "The Hills of Home." And also with the mountain man who left a good Indiana farm to return to Kentucky because he just couldn't get along without some hills to "lean his eyes agin" when he got up in the morning. . . .

CHILD-REARING PRACTICES ARE GENERALLY PERMISSIVE IN THE EARLY YEARS OF LIFE AND CONTINUE FOR BOYS IN REGARD TO THEIR OUTSIDE ACTIVITIES AND CHOICES OF AGE-RELATED ACTIVITIES

Research studies on this point are few and far between, but the writings of various novelists and able observers all seem in line with my own numerous observations on the permissive character of parent-child relations. One of the most interesting documents in this field was written by a former New York City nursery school teacher, Claudia Lewis, in her book, *Children of the Cumberlands.* Perhaps such permissiveness is but a general characteristic of families with numerous children, crowded living quarters, and limited and uncertain incomes. Numerous studies of lower class urban families point to this conclusion. . . .

In the hills the children seem to be rather free to roam about the roads, woods, and streams doing much as they please. This is not necessarily a healthy pattern, but it does not exist amidst the variety of dangers of the city. Transplanted to the city such permissiveness becomes neglect. In view of the small living quarters available to most of these newcomers and their own behavioral patterns, there is an obvious need for play areas, made safe both by absence of traffic and by the presence of adult supervision.

HOUSES ARE GENERALLY SMALL AND CHEAPLY CONSTRUCTED

Both in absolute size and more importantly in terms of the number of persons per dwelling unit, the houses of the area must be classed as "small." I have run some data through my slide rule and come up with a few figures which might be thought of as an Index of Crowding. For the mountain counties of Kentucky the index ranges from 100 up to nearly 125, but for the urban counties it ranges around 70. In the midwestern states the index stands at about 60. It is no exaggeration to say that living space per occupant in Leslie County, Kentucky, is less than half that available, on the average, in Illinois.

In such crowded houses there is an obvious problem of order. How families of four, six, eight children even keep out of each other's way in such small quarters remains a mystery to me. In my own interviewing experience in the mountains, I've yet to enter a home in which the beds were not made, regardless of the time of day. And remember living room and bedroom may all be the same.

There is some evidence that such order is purchased at the price of harsh authoritarianism which demands conformity from the children, and the repression of hostility among the family members. The scope of this authority among farm families extends also to the work-sets. One careful student of mountain culture who lived in many homes while gathering his data has offered the hypothesis that the displacement of repressed feelings may explain the widespread bickering, lawin', and various forms of conflict which are so obviously present in Southern Mountain neighborhoods.

RELIGIOUS BELIEFS AND PRACTICES ARE DOMINATED BY THE FUNDAMENTALIST AND LITERALIST INTERPRETATIONS OF THE BIBLE, AND ALTHOUGH NOT PROMOTED BY ACTIVE CHURCH ORGANIZATIONS, THESE BELIEFS PERMEATE THE SOCIETY

It is considerably easier to provide evidence for the low level of church participation than for the idea of religious beliefs permeating the society. Membership rates in the eastern mountain area of Kentucky are probably not much above 20 per cent of the population, and when we note further the infrequency of services for rural churches and the general shortage of pastors, it is evident that participation rates will be well below those of our urban areas.

The degree to which religion permeates the society is difficult to measure. It's something you learn about as you listen to and talk with people, as you listen to school children, note the signs along the highways and in the country stores. The following summarizes the matter well: "To an outsider coming in, it is a source of wonder how universally religion is recognized in the mountains. Practically everyone acknowledges its claims, whether he does anything about them or not. Almost no one opposes or deprecates religion."

Emphasis on a hereafter, lovely in its promise of tangible goods and a reversal of the ranks of the present society, has been noted frequently by observers of religious behavior among the poor. Rural church services in the mountains among the various "holiness" groups are noted for their extremes of emotional display. To interpret this as a culturally acceptable outlet for normally restrained emotions would seem to be a logical extension of the preceding analysis.

EDUCATION THROUGH THE SCHOOLS HAS BEEN SERVING THE RATHER MINIMAL NEEDS FOR THE 3 R'S IN A FAMILY-CENTERED, LOW PRODUCTIVITY ECONOMY INFUSED WITH OTHER WORLDLY VALUES

Throughout the rural farm areas of the Southern States the proportion of adults aged 25 and over whose formal schooling stopped before the completion of the eighth grade averages close to 75 per cent. In rural nonfarm regions two-thirds is a fair approximation.

In recent years much interest has been focused on the dropout problem. In one study of the percentage of children enrolled in the fifth grade in 1943–1944 who graduated eight years later from high school, Wisconsin topped the list with 80 per cent; Illinois was 65, well above the national average of 52. The Southern States with mountain counties ranged from a low in Georgia of 22 per cent to 41 in West Virginia. The Kentucky figure of 35 per cent means that only 35 out of every 100 in the fifth grade as of 1943–1944 finished high school within eight years. We are on the upward road in this regard but the vista that I see ahead is long and steep.

Such data can only mean that the vast majority of the Southern Mountain Newcomers will have received inadequate formal education, judged by urban standards. For both the teachers of children and those who would find some way to involve the older newcomers in adult education, getting acceptance of the value of schooling is a difficult undertaking. Most of our schools are probably oriented to the values of the middle class and taught by representatives of this class. Such values are not part of the experience world of most people from the mountains, and their values are, conversely, not part of the experience world of their teachers and those who would help them.

The present concern with dropouts, and the discovery of the extent to which this is concentrated among lower status persons has intensified the concern of educators to find some way to bridge these cultural worlds. We have plenty of evidence that these people have adequate learning capacity. The problem is one of getting them to accept the values and experiences which the educational system has to offer.

THE LEISURE TIME OF ADULTS AND CHILDREN IS NOT USUALLY ORGANIZED AROUND COMPETITIVE ACTIVITIES

Rural life in the mountains has a relaxed quality about it which may lead one to the erroneous conclusion that they never work hard. This is far from the truth as anyone knows who has shared in the tasks of a household of numerous children but devoid of running water, automatic heating, and the like. The largely unmechanized agriculture requires a large output of energy, and those who cut the timber from precipitous mountain slopes or mine the coal are hardly engaged in sedentary occupations. Such activities surely do not call for a game of golf or tennis, when the day's work is over. "Jus' settin' " on the porch is much more appropriate. . . .

IT IS EXPECTED THAT FEAR, PAIN, AND HARDSHIP WILL NOT BE EXPRESSED, AND DEMONSTRATIONS OF AFFECTION AND JOY ARE SUBJECT TO CULTURAL CONTROLS

I have no statistical measurement of the extent to which mountain people are conditioned to repress open expression of the feelings associated with hardship, pain, and fear. Pride is of course involved in these phenomena, but one psychiatric social worker has written of the way in which coal miners drive themselves back to the mines, never admitting their fears, until for some the repressions come forth as a characteristic neurosis.

And then I recall a conversation with a Red Cross worker in Hazard, Kentucky, during the great flood there one January and February. She spoke of having worked in disaster situations in many parts of the nation, but she had never encountered people so unwilling to reveal the extent to which they had been damaged by the flood. Perhaps some of the high rejection rates noted by Selective Service in this area is a result of the patterned emphasis on not admitting the need for medical care and taking steps to get it. . . .

The need the children show for openly expressed affection is an observation which has been impressed on me repeatedly and which others who visit mountain schools notice. To get close to a warmly affectionate adult, to touch the person—these seem experiences of great value to mountain children. From what I know of their family life, this search for affection is understandable.

THE RIGHTS OF INDIVIDUALS TO INDEPENDENCE OF BELIEF AND ACTION ARE TO BE VIGOROUSLY DEFENDED AGAINST CRITICISM AND INTERFERENCE BY OTHERS

The two aspects of this proposition probably find their best documentation in novels and stories of mountain life, plus the daily newspapers of the region. Both the independence and vigorous defense of this independence probably have their cultural roots in isolated rural living, historic rebellion against the landed classes of the seaboard states and the cotton economy of the South, and the permissiveness of child-rearing practices.

I find such independence manifesting itself in the "right-to-differ." One expects this right for himself, and extends it to others. But those who differ must adopt a laissez-faire attitude toward each other's differences. Among many examples of this spirit let me cite a few. On learning about a unique way of house construction proposed by a visitor whose idea had been subject to much scoffing by urban acquaintances, one mountain man remarked,

"It's a free country, ain't it? A man's got a right to do what he wants. . . ."

Racial integration in schools has taken place in numerous mountain counties of eastern Kentucky and West Virginia without serious difficulties. For about 30 years following the Civil War the student body of Berea College was about equally divided between white and Negro, and our integration today, though on much smaller scale, has been without difficulty. I submit that such events as I have mentioned could not have occurred unless the culture of these people had given them the expectation of accepting the different.

To have someone out of the South make such a statement today must indeed give rise to honest doubts. I am aware that there are thousands of low-status whites coming into northern cities bearing a heavy load of prejudice towards all sorts of differences. But I do not believe my mountain neighbors have been the victims of this spiritual disease quite so intensively. Those responsible for programs calling for integration where Southern Mountain Newcomers are involved can, I believe, act with the confidence that clearly stated and well-administered programs will be accepted with tolerance.

CONCLUSION

As with other migrant groups who have come to Chicago, a considerable amount of acculturation of the newcomers is to be expected; many of their children will lose most evidences of their mountain background. But many of them will simply exchange the status of "newcomer from the Southern Mountains" for the status of lower class.

We have every reason to expect the continuation of this migration-stream if the following assumptions hold true: first, the continued growth of employment opportunities in the Chicago Metropolitan Area; second, the continuation of the high effective fertility rate now present in the mountains.

Our economic analyst has concluded that eastern Kentucky has presently twice as many people as can be adequately employed. There is good reason to believe this applies to much of the rest of the mountain South. Presently most of these people are deeply attached to the values of land ownership and farming. Industrial employment will not attract them except on terms far beyond what employers would be willing to offer. If the expectations of these people ever rise above the level which can be met by staying on their small farms, the potential stream of out-migrants will have expanded greatly.

The satisfactoriness both for the newcomers and for the oldtimers of future movements of population groups such as this one would seem to depend upon the following conditions. First, if helping agents can obtain and make use of insights into not only the cultural background of the newcomers but also the meaning of the urban situation for them, then a more beneficial adjustment for all can result. Second, I believe there is no doubt that a better solution must be found for the problems of housing and residential areas than has yet been achieved. Third, the youngsters in the mountains need to be prepared for urban adjustment through improving and extending their formal education, through diversifying their social and cultural experiences with other people, and through orienting and training them for the possible kinds of employment the city has to offer.

The accomplishment of this tremendous task requires resources far beyond those which can be supplied by any of the states from which these folks come. Is it possible that those states which get the best years of the newcomers' lives might transfer resources to the states which are responsible for preparing them for adult living?

10. Spanish-Speaking Children

JOHN H. BURMA

Children from Spanish-speaking backgrounds are very much like any other children, and basically their problems are the same as those of ordinary Anglo-American children, with the significant addition of acculturation, culture conflict, and assimilation. These latter may be significantly out of proportion, for they may lead to difficulties which otherwise would not have arisen or would not have been as acute.

In this discussion no inviolately rigorous use of the terms Mexican, Mexican American, or Spanish-speaking people feasible, because of the confused use of these terms by the general public. Therefore, the noun "Mexican" will be used to mean a native of Mexico, usually an adult; the term "Mexican American" will mean a native-born citizen of Mexican ancestry, a naturalized citizen, or a child who emigrated from Mexico early in his life. "Spanish-speaking people" is used to refer inclusively to Mexicans, Mexican Americans, Puerto Ricans, and Spanish Americans. Where the group is mixed, the attempt is to designate it according to the majority of the members.

Reprinted from *The Nation's Children*, edited by Eli Ginzberg (New York: Columbia University Press, 1960), Vol. III, pp. 78–102 (Copyright © 1960 Golden Anniversary White House Conference on Children and Youth, Inc.), by permission of the publisher and author.

THE MEXICAN AMERICAN CHILD

There are in the United States today approximately 3.5 million people of Mexican origin or ancestry (the census makes no exact count) of whom possibly 1.5 million are children and youth. This large number of Mexican American youth exists because Mexicans have been likely to emigrate as families, and because of the relatively high birth rate of Mexican families. Mexican immigration was only a trickle until about 1915, but large numbers came between then and 1930. From 1930 to 1940 this flow reversed itself to emigration, but turned again after 1940 and has continued strongly for twenty years. The majority of adults in this group were born in Mexico, but the majority of youth were born in the United States.

Approximately 40 per cent of Mexican American youth live in Texas, another 40 per cent in California, and the remainder in Colorado, Arizona, New Mexico, Illinois, Kansas, Michigan, New York—in fact, in almost every state. In numerous school districts of Texas, California, and New Mexico, Spanish-speaking children make up one-fourth or more of the total students. As a rule there exist social and residential segregation wherever there are large numbers of Mexican Americans, although where their number is small, there usually is little or no segregation. Throughout Texas, California, and the other states with large Mexican American population, the Mexican American child suffers a special and serious handicap in becoming a successful American citizen as the result of being segregated by Anglos and of segregating himself from Anglos. It is the child growing up under these conditions with whom we are here most concerned, whether he lives in rural Texas or the slums of New York City. A relatively small proportion of Spanish-speaking children are from Puerto Rico; these will be discussed at the end of this chapter.

Family and Home

As with all children, the family of the Mexican American child is of great importance in his development. Historically the Mexican family has been of the extended type, including grandparents, uncles and aunts, and cousins. This has the effect of giving the child a wide circle from whom he may receive emotional support, warmth of acceptance, stability, and a real feeling of belonging. These contributions are much to be desired (and have been suggested as probable factors in the lower rate of psychoses found among Mexican Americans). In this sense it is unfortunate that the extended family system runs counter to the American middle-class nuclear family pattern, hampers acculturation and assimilation, and tends to limit the individual largely to contacts with family members. These are serious handicaps for a child who is marginal (i.e., living on edges of two cultures but wholly in neither) and has contributed to the retention of the "colony" (colonia) housing pattern among Mexican Americans. The extended family and the colonia help explain why most Mexican American children have few

if any Anglo friends. In the past, most recreation was found in the home and most free time was spent in the home; this is still true, but is observably decreasing. The extended family pattern is itself in a state of decline; the third generation does not want it as a day-to-day relationship, but only as a matter of frequent family get-togethers.

Other changes are occurring in behavior and attitudes toward matters relating to the family. Families plan for, and have, fewer children. The role of godparents in the life of the child is becoming negligible. There is an increasing desire by the Mexican American to function as an individual rather than as a subordinate unit in an extended family structure. This leads to "unfilial" behavior, and some consequent misunderstanding and estrangement between generations. This may become particularly acute before the marriage of the children, for under the extended family system marriage is a matter of group concern and activity; under the nucleated family system marriage is a private concern.

As acculturation increases there are changes in family roles. The father becomes less dominant, and shows more affection for the wife and children; the wife is less subordinate as the result of mutual sharing of authority and discipline; the education of the wife equals or surpasses that of the husband; the possibility of the wife working outside the home is looked upon with more favor. The gap between the freedom permitted boys and girls, although still great, is decreasing; girls are less strictly supervised, but still are more closely watched than are boys; supervision of both is least among the lower class. "Nice" girls are now permitted more dating than previously—which was almost nil—but still much less than Anglo girls. In most of these matters class differences are quite observable, with the lower and upper classes, for different reasons, most closely approaching the Anglo norm; the middle class is slowest to change, seeming to feel that their prized "family respectability" requires the perpetuation of the older attitudes and behavior patterns.

Sometimes an additional cleavage between generations results when parents who cling tenaciously to the old culture have children who seek rapid, complete assimilation. This not only causes heartache, but may leave the second generation without adequate adult models or adult guidance, and foster the formation of gangs, whose influence on the child and control of his behavior then are greater than they normally would be.

Important to any family is the home and the neighborhood in which it lives. Almost always in the Southwest, and commonly elsewhere, the Mexican immigrant lives in a segregated subcommunity. By whatever name is it known, this area is substandard and its reputation, among Anglos, is not a savory one. Nearly all these *colonias* are below the average of their parent city in such things as size and quality of housing, electricity, inside toilets, and piped hot water. The families of migratory agricultural workers have a poorer situation, for in the spring they leave their shacks for the even worse housing available to migratory laborers. Here and there public housing projects have been provided to improve this situation, but probably two-thirds to three-fourths of all Mexican American children live in substandard houses located in substandard communities. The lighter, the more well-to-do, and the more assimilated he and his parents are, the less the discrimination and the less likely he is to live in such an area.

Education

The educational opportunities and activities of any child are of great significance; this is especially true if he is the child of immigrant parents coming from a country of low average education and entering a country of high average education. Adult Mexican immigrants brought with them an average of about five years of formal education, the attitude that neither sex, particularly girls, needed a high-school education, and little belief in the general value of education for anyone except well-to-do and professional people.

Thus the chief problem relating to the education of Mexican American children before 1930 was that of getting them into school. This problem was solved with reasonable success, but there next arose the problem of segregated schools. In many areas in Texas, California, and some other parts of the Southwest, Mexican American children were required to attend segregated schools or were placed in segregated classrooms. As usual, "segregated" meant second class or worse, and from the 1930s to the middle '40s the removal of these barriers was a major concern. During the 1946–1948 period, various federal courts ruled against this segregation, and in the succeeding dozen years desegregation has become almost complete. Segregation sometimes still exists through gerrymandering and the fact that schools near Mexican subcommunities are likely to be labeled "Mexican" schools and hence shunned by Anglos.

Today the chief problem is early dropout of Mexican American students. Enrollments are good in the primary grades but then decline so that by high school they probably average no more than half the potential. Low income is a serious barrier, and since many of these parents have had little formal education they are not successful in explaining to their children why they should graduate from high school— if indeed the parents see this as desirable.

Part of the explanation for this problem also is to be found in the fact that Mexican American pupils typically are overage for their grade placement. Either they have missed school to follow the crops, or their language handicaps have been too severe, or they started late and always have been overage. In some cases, as the child reaches adolescence the disparity between his age and that of his schoolmates is magnified for him and is a significant factor in his lack of desire to remain in school. In others, behavior which would be normal two grades ahead is viewed as alarmingly precocious by Anglo mothers who do not take into account the normal significant differences between the behavior of a twelve-year-old girl and that of a fourteen-year-old girl, even if they happen to share the same school room.

From the standpoint of the children themselves, probably their chief educational problem is their linguistic handicap. The normal educational procedure is to admit children to school at six or seven, carry on all teaching in English, and trust that they will learn the language and the content material simultaneously. This does occur under optimum conditions; i.e., when the child is bright, strongly motivated and encouraged, sympathetically taught, and wholeheartedly included by his classmates in all activities. Unfortunately such a situation is rather rare, and most commonly the child learns both language and content imperfectly. Often this language handicap, difficult at any time, becomes progressively worse until it becomes insurmountable and the child

fails repeatedly and finally leaves school.

This linguistic difficulty of Mexican American pupils was used as a rationalization by those who wished educational segregation for social reasons. It was stated that segregation gave the Spanish-speaking student a "language benefit." Today professional opinion is virtually unanimous that the best way to teach English is to place the child in a class where most of the children speak English.

Another educational problem, much less dramatic than language, but equally significant, is the average Mexican American child's relatively low economic, social, and cultural level. These factors are serious handicaps for any child, and the superimposition on them of bilingualism, cultural conflicts, and assimilation problems often has unfortunate results. Teachers report occupational orientation and health education as problems frequently encountered. Some of the more alert school systems report considerable difficulty in presenting the Mexican cultural heritage adequately either to the majority or minority groups. Certainly an indispensable element in a complete school program for mixed schools must be the education of Anglo children to some appreciation of the Mexican culture. Most states with large numbers of Mexican American students now publish guides to aid teachers with Spanish-speaking students.

In addition to these difficulties, a significant number of Mexican American children must move about with their parents who are engaged in migratory agricultural labor. This means at best shifting schools several times, and at worst attending school only a few months of the year. Under a situation of permanent or temporary mobility the child and his parents must value education very highly to make the necessary effort and sacrifices so that the child can attend school regularly. Various educational experiments have been tried in coping with the migrant child, but none has been outstandingly successful, so the great bulk of such children attend regular community schools. Here they create problems. Sometimes they cause serious, if temporary, overcrowding. They present a difficult challenge to teachers to provide a program which has meaning and value for them, permits them to learn at their own level and pace, and which takes into account their special needs without jeopardizing the program of the permanent pupil. The best solution, a highly flexible, individualistic learning program, is good for the permanent children as well as the migrants, but unfortunately, such a program is difficult to organize and staff, and expensive to maintain.

To be successful in such a program, a school must plan an adequate method. This may be done by a "big brother" system, by a classroom host and hostess, by special use of Spanish-speaking permanent students, and by practical study units on cotton, vegetables, beets, purchasing, health, family living—and Mexico. The school must have available class materials on a wide range of levels, so the migrant child may begin where he is fitted to begin and may receive individual assistance as he needs it. Account must be taken of bilingualism by emphasizing the use of oral English, yet protecting the child with a limited knowledge of the language; respect should be shown for Spanish, and at least a smattering of it should be taught to Anglo children.

In general, the educational picture for Mexican American children is a constantly brightening one. Segregation is disappearing, and schools and teachers are better equipped and more deeply motivated to handle special problems. Mexican American standards of living are improving and migratory labor is decreasing. A rapidly increasing number of pupils are children of native-born parents and bring to school a considerable knowledge of American customs and language. In short, at the chief points of tension the strain is gradually lessening, and at the same time better techniques for dealing with these problems are being developed and more widely used.

Delinquency

Wherever there are sizable numbers of Mexican American youth, they have the reputation of being more delinquency-prone than Anglo youth. Although this is likely to be exaggerated, it does exist. Delinquency is related in some way to a number of factors: living in slum or substandard areas, employment of both parents away from home, educational difficulties, association with persons who break the law, low family income, poor recreation, the power of the gang, lack of occupational opportunity, lack of strict supervision, culture conflict, movement from rural to urban areas, family disorganization. All these impinge upon the average Mexican American youth more than the average Anglo youth, and hence we predict and find a higher delinquency rate among Mexican Americans. For example, most youth are rather strongly motivated to make money, to be liked, and to "be somebody." There are many avenues to achieve these goals and most of them are socially acceptable. A high proportion of the socially approved avenues are virtually closed, however, to Mexican American youth, while none of the socially disapproved avenues are closed. Thus the chances of the Mexican American youth choosing one of the disapproved methods of goal-seeking are greater than they are for the average Anglo boy—through no fault of his own but because of societal factors over which he has no control.

For all immigrants and their children, cultural differences or culture conflict are potential sources of disorganization, and this is true for Mexican Americans. For example, in Mexico it is normal for men and boys to idle on the street corner in the evening, amusing themselves and getting the day's news. In this country if boys spend much time loafing on the streets in the evenings they are likely to get into trouble with the law. Moreover, in Mexico the pattern was to release the boy from most parental controls when he was around sixteen, so that he might "become a man"; this usually meant sex, gambling, alcohol, and potentially some fighting. It was assumed that the boy would have his fling for a year or two, get it out of his system, and marry and settle down to become a respectable adult. In the United States if this kind of release occurs at the same age, the boy is only half through high school, and may be four to six years away from settling down as an adult. Here he is considered a delinquent and may be sent to a training school.

In the past fifteen years the spotlight has been on Mexican American gangs as products and producers of delinquency. From San Antonio to Los Angeles these youngsters are called *pachucos*, or simply *'chucs*, and are looked down upon by Anglos and by some Mexican Americans. Usually they are marginal persons, lost between the old Mexican world which they do not accept and the new American world which does not accept them. The core of the *pachuco* world is the neighborhood gang, not the home or school, and the members of the gang feel for it a great attachment. Their rejection of parts of the Mexican culture is closely related to the cleavage be-

tween this age group and the parent group. It is particularly unfortunate that the isolation from the parent group usually occurs before the youngsters have achieved access to Anglo society. Whenever this type of situation occurs, teen-aged gangs are strong and prevalent. Their members go out of their way to make themselves visible and to demonstrate "belonging," by ducktail and fender haircuts, special clothes, whiskers, sunglasses ("shades"), self-tattoos, and a special language, *pachucana*—part Spanish, part English, part jive, part manufactured or invented. Not all Mexican American youth who sport some of these external characteristics are actual *pachucos;* for many of them the true *pachucos* are just a reference group, one to which they feel some psychic kinship, or to which they aspire eventually, but with which they presently have no direction connection.

Group workers and probation officers say most *pachucos* are not antisocial, but are so painfully social that they are willing to make great sacrifices to achieve acceptance, status, and "belonging." The strength, uniqueness, and social cohesion of these groups undoubtedly are increased by language and cultural factors.

It must not be assumed from the foregoing paragraphs that there is a wholesale revolt among Mexican American youth against their parents. This is far from true, and the situation is a great deal more complex than such an oversimplification might indicate. Both parents and children agree on the desirability of rapid assimilation and uphold many of the attitudes and goals of Anglo culture. In such families the parents may speak only English to their children, and both may be motivated strongly toward education and upward mobility. They may seek Anglo friends, residence outside the *colonia*, and

Anglo jobs. In school these children tend to achieve better than the average, to be liked by their teachers, and to find some small acceptance by the Anglo students.

The attitudes of other Mexican American youth toward this group of "squares" range from acceptance, jealousy, and grudging emulation on one extreme to almost hate on the other. Many *pachucos,* however, retain much *Mexicanissmo* and indicate great pride in their parents' cultural heritage. Anyone who turns his back on this heritage (speaking English only, for example) may be termed a *falso,* is thought to consider himself "too good for the rest of us," and may expect to be roughed up occasionally if he lives in a *pachuco* neighborhood. In actuality the great majority of Mexican American youth fall between the "squares" and the *pachucos* on the continuum. They seek assimilation, but not avidly, and retain, partly by inertia, a considerable amount of the old culture. They attend school dutifully, if without much enthusiasm, and have hopes (realistic or not) of finishing high school and getting a "good" job. Only for the "square" group is there any hope of attending college. Members of the great middle group may engage in delinquent acts, but their frequency and seriousness are likely to be considerably less than are those of the true delinquent. Obviously it is this middle group who offer the greatest hope and challenge to concerned agencies and individuals. This group has all kinds of problems, but most of them are not insurmountable in size or of such depth that they cannot be alleviated by known, normal means.

Culture

Of the various problems faced by Mexican American youth, none are more clearly different from those of Anglo youth than the ones related to acculturation, assimilation, culture conflict, and marginality. In the United States we tend to pay lip service to the concept of cultural pluralism—numerous separate cultures coexisting in cooperative harmony—but in actual practice most Americans tacitly expect cultural conformity and look down upon anyone whose language, color, or ways of life differ from the majority norm. This leads to pressure on any culturally different group to acculturate and to become assimilated.

Some immigrants to America fled from their homeland or in other ways forever severed their ties with the old country. For them and their children, acquisition of the new culture was the only possibility they saw for a secure future. Such motivation has not been strong for all groups; some (Chinese, Italians, Mexicans, etc.) have contained many individuals who looked upon themselves as temporary residents and who anticipated a return to the homeland within a few years. For such persons a transfer of loyalty would be both undesirable and impractical. Elements of the new culture were accepted or rejected in terms of utility only, and any which were in serious conflict with the old culture would not be accepted; the less change and adjustment necessary, the better.

Many Mexican immigrants entered the United States with the full intention of returning to Mexico. Men brought their families with them not because they intended to "settle" but to keep the family unit intact during their sojourn. They and their children were Mexicans and intended to remain so. Under these circumstances acculturation has little utility and would have negative effects if carried too far.

Immigrants from across the seas had to accumulate a great deal of money before renewing their family and cultural ties by a visit to the "old country"; not so with the Mexican immigrant who may return to Mexico easily. Thus the accessibility of Mexico has hindered among Mexican Americans the acculturation to be found in other groups. Yet some Mexican immigrants intended from the first to become American citizens, to live here the rest of their lives, and have expected their children to do the same. These persons consciously have sought acculturation and have achieved it as rapidly as any other group. Thus second generation Mexican American children come from homes which represent both a wide range of attitudes toward acculturation and a wide range of actual acculturation. When the parents, through intent, inertia, or ignorance, cling to the old culture, and the children are sent to a public school which endeavors to inculcate in them middle-class Anglo attitudes, values, and culture patterns, misunderstanding and conflict at home and at school are almost inevitable.

It has been observed that there are three cultures with which the Mexican American child is concerned: the Anglo, the Mexican, and the Mexican-American. The Mexican-American culture often acts as a bridge for the immigrant child; he can acquire it much more easily than the Anglo culture. In general, the Mexican-American culture contains large portions of Anglo material culture and Anglo mass culture, and large portions of Mexican nonmaterial culture. The second generation boy usually has accepted much Anglo material culture, i.e., he understands and wants a bicycle, air rifle, and comic books. As a participant in our mass culture he may play Tarzan, be able to give you the batting average of Mickey Mantle, or be a rock-'n-roll addict. The material culture and mass culture are wide but shallow; the

child's real problems come with the more fundamental ethical and value aspects of nonmaterial culture, for it is here that serious confusion or conflict occurs.

The public school, which is by far the chief acculturative agency for Mexican American children, usually teaches Anglo middle-class attitudes, values, and norms as if they were Absolute Truth; to the extent that the school is successful, the child accepts these and either drops or refuses to adopt many of the attitudes, values, and norms presented by his family. Granted complete good will within the family, which is as unrealistic an assumption as it would be among Anglo families, conflict in these matters is inevitable. Hence the typical Mexican American youth of the second or third generation is marginal; this marginality is an anomalous condition, likely to lead to misunderstanding, frustration, and disorganization. Fortunately marginality is dynamic rather than static, and tends to reach a peak and then decline to a less disorganizing level. It is the child who is half-and-half, rather than 10 per cent and 90 per cent, who suffers most from marginality.

Some of the social disorganization found among marginal Mexican Americans results because such youth have freed themselves from creeds, beliefs, and other social controls which operate within the framework of the old culture, and yet have not acquired wholly the folkways, mores, and social controls of the new Anglo culture. Thus they may suffer from *anomie,* be relatively free from self-discipline or value internalization, and be more easily influenced by matters of the moment. Aimless or delinquent behavior is the frequent result, although strong, disciplined men, dreamers and reformers, as well as hoodlums, alcoholics, and criminals have come from such environments.

Marginality of children may be prolonged by parents who wish to have "the best of both cultures." At first glance this is a laudable goal; in practice it frequently works out unsatisfactorily. Basic to the failure of any such goal is the fact that cultures do not consist of many unrelated bits and pieces, but rather are a weblike, organic whole. Bits may not be abstracted from the whole with impunity, even if other bits arbitrarily are put into place. Thus it appears necessary for the Mexican American to make up his mind which culture he wishes for his own, rather than to drag on, willy-nilly, with unrelated parts of each.

A good illustration is bilingualism; for no one would argue that it is undesirable to know more than one language. Mexican American youngsters are not really taught Spanish, and commonly they read it very imperfectly, write it phonetically and incorrectly, and speak with poor grammar, construction, and vocabulary; and if they take academic Spanish in high school they meet with little more success than they do in English courses. Since such children as a rule also know English imperfectly, they have a mastery of no language. An increasing number of ambitious second generation persons who now are parents do not teach their children Spanish in the home; they fear the child will learn neither language well, and if a choice must be made, they prefer English.

Certainly conflicting values of the two or three cultures with which the Mexican American child has contact is a disorienting factor for him. Neither the Mexican nor the American culture has truly systematic values; each has some contradictory elements. Confusion of values is serious enough to warrant considerable attention by philosophers, social psychologists, educators, and psychiatrists, when only one culture is involved, how much more serious it is when the child is expected to grope toward a workable, acceptable pattern within the maze of two such cultures! That he confronts frustration, confusion, misconception, and disorganization is to be accepted as a matter of course at the same time it is greatly deplored.

THE PUERTO RICAN CHILD

The second largest group of Spanish-speaking children in America today are the Puerto Ricans. Twenty years ago there were only a few scattered thousands on the mainland, and few of them were children. In 1955 there were between one-half to two-thirds of a million here (despite wild estimates of "millions"), with an estimated 80 per cent of the total in New York City alone, including 40,000 to 50,000 children enrolled in the New York City schools. There, in Chicago, and in most major cities between, are found sizable numbers of Puerto Rican youth. Like other immigrant groups of the past, Puerto Ricans are poor, uneducated, lack occupational skills, have little facility with the English language, suffer disproportionately from social problems, and live in the least desirable sections of the city with their high delinquency rates, in part because of discrimination, segregation, and exploitation. Puerto Rican children and youth have serious enough problems to warrant our attention. Except that a high proportion of Puerto Rican youth are themselves immigrants, and that they are concentrated much more heavily in large urban areas, the situations and problems of Puerto Rican and Mexican American youth are in many respects similar.

Like the Mexican family the Puerto

Rican family undergoes changes with immigration. The father's authority over the wife and children declines, freedom of wife and children increases, and for the children freedom sometimes becomes license and incorrigibility. With this group, too, there is likely to be a hiatus between generations which increases misunderstanding and conflict; in part this is the result of the greater acculturation of the child and his consequent marginality, confusion, and disorientation of values and norms. As is so common and so tragic in such cases, usually parents and children each sincerely believe that they are right and the other wrong. Many Puerto Rican women work outside the home, because there is need for additional income or because there is no male breadwinner. This means children too frequently are without the mothers' care during the day, and left with neighbors or in day nurseries, or wait on the streets after school until the parent returns.

The environment of large numbers of Puerto Rican children in the New York City and Chicago school systems has caused more problems than one would expect, because of the attempt to put into practice new educational philosophies. Instead of the older rapid assimilation philosophy, the new philosophy maintains that the cultural and social contributions which Puerto Ricans and other groups can make should be utilized; that education for all children need not mean the same education for all children, but rather individualized instruction, assistance, and remedial work geared to the needs and interests of each child; and that teaching should encompass the total development of the individual for his best total adjustment. These philosophies and goals, although highly desirable, do create extra problems whenever large numbers of young-

sters as different as the Puerto Rican children enter a school system. Inevitably the school to which the Puerto Rican child is assigned is much different from the one with which he or his parents were familiar in Puerto Rico, and many of the values and norms peripheral to education are different (such as participation of girls in after-school programs), so that tri-cornered misunderstandings between parent, school, and child easily arise, but are not so easily resolved.

Some of the techniques which have been evolved to meet these problems in New York City include the use of Spanish-speaking interpreters at registration time and other methods of making the parents and child feel accepted, booklets in Spanish to explain the school's aims and rules, the use of a buddy or big brother system, assignment to orientation or vestibule classes where emphasis is placed on remedial and language arts work and from which the student is moved when he is ready, a conscious attempt to involve parents as much as possible in school activities and interests, and the use of special Spanish-speaking guidance counsellors.

Unlike the Mexican Americans, Puerto Ricans never have been subjected to educational segregation, but the quality of the school systems from which the immigrant children come is such that they usually are retarded a year or more. The fact that these young people have special needs for vocational training, health, and hygiene, and community awareness makes their satisfactory education even more difficult. Almost without exception Puerto Rican students have serious linguistic handicaps, despite the fact that immigrant children have been taught some English in the Puerto Rican schools.

One of the most frustrating aspects of mainland living for many immigrant

Puerto Rican children is our color bar. On the island three groups are recognized: the white, the Negro, and the *grifo*, who is mixed; there is not much discrimination against the Negro, and almost none against the *grifo* except socially; the *grifo* thinks of himself as somewhat above the Negro. When a *grifo* comes to the mainland, he finds himself not only classed as a Negro, which threatens his status, but also subjected to far more discrimination than was directed against the Negro on his home island. The results may be confusion, bitterness, frustration, aggression, or a "don't care" or "what's the use" attitude. By mainland standards from a third to a half of Puerto Ricans are colored—considerably more than by island standards. The Puerto Rican mulatto child is not only subjected to discrimination on the mainland, he faces difficulty in thinking of himself as originally Puerto Rican and Spanish, since he is looked upon by most people as a Negro. His problem of self-evaluation and self-concept may lead to psychic disturbance. Certainly this is one reason for Puerto Rican gang membership; in the gang he is accepted for what he is, stands on his own merit, and has security.

In general the problems of the Puerto Rican child are basically those which most of our immigrants have faced and overcome in the past: language handicaps, overcrowded housing in slum and delinquency areas, poverty and all its secondary aspects, discrimination and low status, educational difficulties, recreational inadequacy, and the problems of acculturation, assimilation, and culture conflict. The historic pattern on the East Coast has been for the immigrant group to settle in an ethnic slum area and there to reproduce for a generation the culture patterns of the old country. The younger people gradually move away to undifferentiated housing areas until the ethnic area, as an area, no longer exists. The "white" Puerto Ricans are following this traditional pattern, and the social world of the Negro Puerto Ricans, at first bounded by the apartment house and the street, expands more slowly. This change comes more easily for those who live outside the New York City area. The assimilation of Puerto Rican youth is hindered in New York by the absence of concrete, homogeneous norms to which to adjust. The kaleidoscope pattern of New York City produces neither a clear norm to which to conform nor the social controls conducive to conformity which may be found elsewhere. Lack of homogeneity of behavior, however, is not always a serious handicap in a heterogeneous social world.

Coming late, as they do, in our stream of immigrants, Puerto Rican children benefit from the wisdom gained by trial-and-error techniques used on other groups. Metropolitan schools and social agencies know better how to handle such problems than before. The Puerto Rican immigrant child brings with him knowledge of some elements of American mass culture acquired in Puerto Rico, and at least some knowledge of the language on which to build. He already is a citizen, and suffers little more from divided loyalty than does a transplanted Texan. For a significant number, their color will be a serious handicap from their school days forward. In short, Puerto Rican children suffer all the handicaps of any children living under comparable socioeconomic conditions, plus special problems which are cultural and racial in nature; yet they have better and more sympathetic assistance in meeting all these problems than any previous group on the East Coast. There is every reason to believe that their problems will decline in the future.

THE SPANISH AMERICAN CHILD

Although relatively fewer in number, the problems and prospects of Spanish American children also are of importance. There are in New Mexico several tens of thousands of Spanish American children. Although they are tenth generation native American, this group until a generation ago had clung tenaciously to its own variation of Spanish culture, and hence its children have most of the problems of Mexican American or Puerto Rican children, at least in terms of cultural differences. They suffer a mixture of ethnic and class discrimination, but not in overwhelming degree. They, too, must choose which culture to follow, and consequently are typically marginal, with all that this implies. On the other hand, many of them live in stable families in their own small agricultural communities, or in cities like Albuquerque and Santa Fe where their numbers are so great that they do not feel isolated.

Like other Spanish-speaking children their greatest handicap, other than poverty and its secondary results, is their language difficulty in school, which results in an average achievement less than that of Anglo children. Spanish Americans are a proud group, but this has not prevented many adolescent boys from needing the psychic security received from gang membership, and so-called *pachucos* are as common in cities in New Mexico as in California or Texas.

Although these children are now and for some time in the future will be handicapped by poverty, lack of economic opportunity, linguistic inadequacy, marginality, and culture conflict, their opportunities and outlook seem at least as good as those of Mexican American or Puerto Rican youth.

11. Crucible of Identity: The Negro Lower-Class Family

LEE RAINWATER

As long as Negroes have been in America, their marital and family patterns have been subjects of curiosity and amusement, moral indignation and self-congratulation, puzzlement and frustration, concern and guilt, on the part of white Americans.[1] As some Negroes have moved into middle-class status, or acquired standards of American common-man respectability, they too have shared these attitudes toward the private behavior of their fellows, sometimes with a moral punitiveness to rival that of whites, but at other times with a hard-headed interest in causes and remedies rather than moral evaluation. Moralism permeated the subject of Negro sexual, marital, and family behavior in the polemics of slavery apologists and abolitionists as much as in the Northern and Southern civil rights controversies of today. Yet, as long as the dialectic of good or bad, guilty or innocent, overshadows a concern with who, why, and what can be, it is unlikely that realistic and effective social planning to correct the clearly desperate situation of poor Negro families can begin.

This article is concerned with a description and analysis of slum Negro family patterns as these reflect and sustain Negroes' adaptations to the economic, social, and personal situation into which they are born and in which they must live. As such it deals with facts of lower-class life that are usually forgotten or ignored in polite discussion. We have chosen not to ignore these facts in the belief that to do so can lead only to assumptions which would frustrate efforts at social reconstruction, to strategies that are unrealistic in the light of the actual day-to-day reality of slum Negro life. Further, this analysis will deal with family patterns which interfere with the efforts slum Negroes make to attain a stable way of life as working- or middle-class individuals and with the effects such failure in turn has on family life. To be sure, many Negro families live *in* the slum ghetto, but are not *of* its culture (though even they, and particularly their children, can be deeply affected by what happens there). However, it is the individuals who succumb to the distinctive family life style of the slum who experience the greatest weight of deprivation and who have the greatest difficulty responding to the few self-improvement resources that

Reprinted by permission from *Daedalus*, published by the American Academy of Arts and Sciences, Brookline, Massachusetts. Vol. 94, No. 4, *The Negro American*.

make their way into the ghetto. In short, we propose to explore in depth the family's role in the "tangle of pathology" which characterizes the ghetto.

The social reality in which Negroes have had to make their lives during the 450 years of their existence in the western hemisphere has been one of victimization "in the sense that a system of social relations operates in such a way as to deprive them of a chance to share in the more desirable material and non-material products of a society which is dependent, in part, upon their labor and loyalty." In making this observation, St. Clair Drake goes on to note that Negroes are victimized also because "they do not have the same degree of access which others have to the attributes needed for rising in the general class system—money, education, 'contacts,' and 'know-how.'" [2] The victimization process started with slavery; for 350 years thereafter Negroes worked out as best they could adaptations to the slave status. After emancipation, the cultural mechanisms which Negroes had developed for living the life of victim continued to be serviceable as the victimization process was maintained first under the myths of white supremacy and black inferiority, later by the doctrines of gradualism which covered the fact of no improvement in position, and finally by the modern Northern system of ghettoization and indifference.

When lower-class Negroes use the expression, "Tell it like it is," they signal their intention to strip away pretense, to describe a situation or its participants as they really are, rather than in a polite or euphemistic way. "Telling it like it is" can be used as a harsh, aggressive device, or it can be a healthy attempt to face reality rather than retreat into fantasy. In any case, as he goes about his field work, the participant observer studying a ghetto community learns to listen carefully to any exchange preceded by such an announcement because he knows the speaker is about to express his understanding of how his world operates, of what motivates its members, of how they actually behave.

The first responsibility of the social scientist can be phrased in much the same way: "Tell it like it is." His second responsibility is to try to understand why "it" is that way, and to explore the implications of what and why for more constructive solutions to human problems. Social research on the situation of the Negro American has been informed by four main goals: (1) to describe the disadvantaged position of Negroes, (2) to disprove the racist ideology which sustains the caste system, (3) to demonstrate that responsibility for the disadvantages Negroes suffer lies squarely upon the white caste which derives economic, prestige, and psychic benefits from the operation of the system, and (4) to suggest that in reality whites would be better rather than worse off if the whole jerry-built caste structure were to be dismantled. The successful accomplishment of these *intellectual* goals has been a towering achievement, in which the social scientists of the 1920's, '30's, and '40's can take great pride; that white society has proved so recalcitrant to utilizing this intellectual accomplishment is one of the great tragedies of our time, and provides the stimulus for further social research on "the white problem."

Yet the implicit paradigm of much of the research on Negro Americans has been an overly simplistic one concentrating on two terms of an argument:

White cupidity———→Negro suffering.

As an intellectual shorthand, and even more as a civil rights slogan, this simple model is both justified and essential. But, as a guide to greater understanding of the Negro situation as human adaptation to human situations, the paradigm is totally inadequate because it fails to specify fully enough the *process* by which Negroes adapt to their situations as they do, and the limitations one kind of adaptation places on possibilities for subsequent adaptations. A reassessment of previous social research, combined with examination of current social research on Negro ghetto communities, suggests a more complex, but hopefully more vertical model:

White cupidity
creates
Structural Conditions Highly Inimical to Basic Social Adaptation (low-income availability, poor education, poor services, stigmatization)
to which Negroes adapt
by
Social and Personal Responses which serve to sustain the individual in his punishing world but also generate aggressiveness toward the self and others which results in
Suffering directly inflicted by Negroes on themselves and on others.

In short, whites, by their greater power, create situations in which Negroes do the dirty work of caste victimization for them.

The white caste maintains a cadre of whites whose special responsibility is to enforce the system in brutal or refined ways (the Klan, the rural sheriff, the metropolitan police, the businessman who specializes in a Negro clientele, the Board of Education). Increasingly, whites recruit to this cadre middle-class Negroes who can soften awareness of victimization by their protective coloration. These special cadres, white and/or Negro, serve the very important function of enforc-

ing caste standards by whatever means seems required, while at the same time concealing from an increasingly "unprejudiced" public the unpleasant facts they would prefer to ignore. The system is quite homologous to the Gestapo and concentration camps of Nazi Germany, though less fatal to its victims.

For their part, Negroes creatively adapt to the system in ways that keep them alive and extract what gratification they can find, but in the process of adaptation they are constrained to behave in ways that inflict a great deal of suffering on those with whom they make their lives, and on themselves. The ghetto Negro is constantly confronted by the immediate necessity to suffer in order to get what he wants of those few things he can have, or to make others suffer, or both—for example, he suffers as exploited student and employee, as drug user, as loser in the competitive game of his peer-group society; he inflicts suffering as disloyal spouse, petty thief, knife- or gun-wielder, petty con man.

It is the central thesis of this article that the caste-facilitated infliction of suffering by Negroes on other Negroes and on themselves appears most poignantly within the confines of the family, and that the victimization process as it operates in families prepares and toughens its members to function in the ghetto world, at the same time that it seriously interferes with their ability to operate in any other world. This, however, is very different from arguing that "the family is to blame" for the deprived situation ghetto Negroes suffer; rather we are looking at the logical outcome of the operation of the widely ramified and interconnecting caste system. In the end we will argue that only palliative results can be expected from attempts to treat directly the disordered family patterns to be described. Only a change in the original "inputs" of the caste system, the structural conditions inimical to basic social adaptation, can change family forms.

Almost thirty years ago, E. Franklin Frazier foresaw that the fate of the Negro family in the city would be a highly destructive one. His readers would have little reason to be surprised at observations of slum ghetto life today:

". . . As long as the bankrupt system of southern agriculture exists, Negro families will continue to seek a living in the towns and cities. . . . They will crowd the slum areas of southern cities or make their way to northern cities where their families will become disrupted and their poverty will force them to depend upon charity." [3]

THE AUTONOMY OF THE SLUM GHETTO

Just as the deprivations and depredations practiced by white society have had their effect on the personalities and social life of Negroes, so also has the separation from the ongoing social life of the white community had its effect. In a curious way, Negroes have had considerable freedom to fashion their own adaptations within their separate world. The larger society provides them with few resources but also with minimal interference in the Negro community on matters which did not seem to affect white interests. Because Negroes learned early that there were a great many things they could not depend upon whites to provide they developed their own solutions to recurrent human issues. These solutions can often be seen to combine, along with the predominance of elements from white culture, elements that are distinctive to the Negro group. Even more distinctive is the *configuration* which emerges from those elements Negroes share with whites and those which are different.

It is in this sense that we may speak of a Negro subculture, a distinctive *patterning* of existential perspectives, techniques for coping with the problems of social life, views about what is desirable and undesirable in particular situations. This subculture, and particularly that of the lower-class, the slum, Negro, can be seen as his own creation out of the elements available to him in response to (1) the conditions of life set by white society and (2) the selective freedom which that society allows (or must put up with given the pattern of separateness on which it insists).

Out of this kind of "freedom" slum Negroes have built a culture which has some elements of intrinsic value and many more elements that are highly destructive to the people who must live in it. The elements that whites can value they constantly borrow. Negro arts and language have proved so popular that such commentators on American culture as Norman Mailer and Leslie Fiedler have noted processes of Negro-ization of white Americans as a minor theme of the past thirty years.[4] A fairly large proportion of Negroes with national reputations are engaged in the occupation of diffusing to the larger culture these elements of intrinsic value.

On the negative side, this freedom has meant, as social scientists who have studied Negro communities have long commented, that many of the protections offered by white institutions stop at the edge of the Negro ghetto: there are poor police protection and enforcement of civil equities, inadequate schooling and medical service, and more informal indulgences which whites allow Negroes as a small price for feeling superior.

For our purposes, however, the most

important thing about the freedom which whites have allowed Negroes within their own world is that it has required them to work out their own ways of making it from day to day, from birth to death. The subculture that Negroes have created may be imperfect but it has been viable for centuries; it behooves both white and Negro leaders and intellectuals to seek to understand it even as they hope to change it.[5]

Negroes have created, again particularly within the lower-class slum group, a range of institutions to structure the tasks of living a victimized life and to minimize the pain it inevitably produces. In the slum ghetto these institutions include prominently those of the social network—the extended kinship system and the "street system" of buddies and broads which tie (although tenuously and unpredictably) the "members" to each other—and the institutions of entertainment (music, dance, folk tales) by which they instruct, explain, and accept themselves. Other institutions function to provide escape from the society of the victimized: the church (Hereafter!) and the civil rights movement (Now!).

THE FUNCTIONAL AUTONOMY OF THE NEGRO FAMILY

At the center of the matrix of Negro institutional life lies the family. It is in the family that individuals are trained for participation in the culture and find personal and group identity and continuity. The "freedom" allowed by white society is greatest here, and this freedom has been used to create an institutional variant more distinctive perhaps to the Negro subculture than any other. (Much of the content of Negro art and entertainment derives exactly from the distinctive characteristics of Negro family life.) At each stage in the Negro's experience of American life—slavery, segregation, *de facto* ghettoization—whites have found it less necessary to interfere in the relations between the sexes and between parents and children than in other areas of the Negro's existence. His adaptations in this area, therefore, have been less constrained by whites than in many other areas.

Now that the larger society is becoming increasingly committed to integrating Negroes into the main stream of American life, however, we can expect increasing constraint (benevolent as it may be) to be placed on the autonomy of the Negro family system.[6] These constraints will be designed to pull Negroes into meaningful integration with the larger society, to give up ways which are inimical to successful performance in the larger society, and to adopt new ways that are functional in that society. The strategic questions of the civil rights movement and of the war on poverty are ones that have to do with how one provides functional equivalents for the existing subculture before the capacity to make a life within its confines is destroyed.

The history of the Negro family has been ably documented by historians and sociologists.[7] In slavery, conjugal and family ties were reluctantly and ambivalently recognized by the slave holders, were often violated by them, but proved necessary to the slave system. This necessity stemmed both from the profitable offspring of slave sexual unions and the necessity for their nurture, and from the fact that the slaves' efforts to sustain patterns of sexual and parental relations mollified the men and women whose labor could not simply be commanded. From nature's promptings, the thinning memories of African heritage, and the example and guilt-ridden permission of the slave holders, slaves constructed a partial family system and sets of relations that generated conjugal and familial sentiments. The slave holder's recognition in advertisements for run-away slaves of marital and family sentiments as motivations for absconding provides one indication that strong family ties were possible, though perhaps not common, in the slave quarter. The mother-centered family with its emphasis on the primacy of the mother-child relation and only tenuous ties to a man, then, is the legacy of adaptations worked out by Negroes during slavery.

After emancipation this family design often also served well to cope with the social disorganization of Negro life in the late nineteenth century. Matrifocal families, ambivalence about the desirability of marriage, ready acceptance of illegitimacy, all sustained some kind of family life in situations which often made it difficult to maintain a full nuclear family. Yet in the hundred years since emancipation, Negroes in rural areas have been able to maintain full nuclear families almost as well as similarly situated whites. As we will see, it is the move to the city that results in the very high proportion of mother-headed households. In the rural system the man continues to have important functions; it is difficult for a woman to make a crop by herself, or even with the help of other women. In the city, however, the woman can earn wages just as a man can, and she can receive welfare payments more easily than he can. In rural areas, although there may be high illegitimacy rates and high rates of marital disruption, men and women have an interest in getting together; families are headed by a husband-wife pair much more often than in the city. That pair may be much less stable than in the more prosperous segments of Negro and white communities but it is more likely to exist among rural Negroes than among urban ones.

The matrifocal character of the Negro lower-class family in the United States has much in common with Caribbean Negro family patterns; research in both areas has done a great deal to increase our understanding of the Negro situation. However, there are important differences in the family forms of the two areas.[8] The impact of white European family models has been much greater in the United States than in the Caribbean both because of the relative population proportions of white and colored peoples and because equalitarian values in the United States have had a great impact on Negroes even when they have not on whites. The typical Caribbean mating pattern is that women go through several visiting and common-law unions but eventually marry; that is, they marry legally only relatively late in their sexual lives. The Caribbean marriage is the crowning of a sexual and procreative career; it is considered a serious and difficult step.

In the United States, in contrast, Negroes marry at only a slightly lower rate and slightly higher age than whites.[9] Most Negro women marry relatively early in their careers; marriage is not regarded as the same kind of crowning choice and achievement that it is in the Caribbean. For lower-class Negroes in the United States marriage ceremonies are rather informal affairs. In the Caribbean, marriage is regarded as quite costly because of the feasting which goes along with it; ideally it is performed in church.

In the United States, unlike the Caribbean, early marriage confers a kind of permanent respectable status upon a woman which she can use to deny any subsequent accusations of immorality or promiscuity once the marriage is broken and she becomes sexually involved in visiting or common-law relations. The relevant effective status for many Negro women is that of "having been married" rather than "being married"; having the right to be called "Mrs." rather than currently being Mrs. Someone-in-Particular.

For Negro lower-class women, then, first marriage has the same kind of importance as having a first child. Both indicate that the girl has become a woman but neither one that this is the last such activity in which she will engage. It seems very likely that only a minority of Negro women in the urban slum go through their child-rearing years with only one man around the house.

Among the Negro urban poor, then, a great many women have the experience of heading a family for part of their mature lives, and a great many children spend some part of their formative years in a household without a father-mother pair. From Table 1 we see that in 1960, forty-seven per cent of the Negro poor urban families with children had a female head. Unfortunately cumulative statistics are hard to come by; but, given this very high level for a cross-sectional sample (and taking into account the fact that the

Table 1

PROPORTION OF FEMALE HEADS FOR
FAMILIES WITH CHILDREN BY RACE,
INCOME, AND URBAN-RURAL
CATEGORIES

	Rural	Urban	Total
Negroes			
Under $3000	18%	47%	36%
$3000 and over	5%	8%	7%
Total	14%	23%	21%
Whites			
Under $3000	12%	38%	22%
$3000 and over	2%	4%	3%
Total	4%	7%	6%

Source: U.S. Census: 1960, PC (1) D. U. S. Volume, Table 225; State Volume, Table 140.

median age of the children in these families is about six years), it seems very likely that as many as two-thirds of Negro urban poor children will not live in families headed by a man and a woman throughout the first eighteen years of their lives.

One of the other distinctive characteristics of Negro families, both poor and not so poor, is the fact that Negro households have a much higher proportion of relatives outside the mother-father-children triangle than is the case with whites. For example, in St. Louis Negro families average 0.8 other relatives per household compared to only 0.4 for white families. In the case of the more prosperous Negro families this is likely to mean that an older relative lives in the home providing baby-sitting services while both the husband and wife work and thus further their climb toward stable working- or middle-class status. In the poor Negro families it is much more likely that the household is headed by an older relative who brings under her wings a daughter and that daughter's children. It is important to note that the three-generation household with the grandmother at the head exists only when there is no husband present. Thus, despite the high proportion of female-headed households in this group and despite the high proportion of households that contain other relatives, we find that almost all married couples in the St. Louis Negro slum community have their own household. In other words, when a couple marries it establishes its own household; when that couple breaks up the mother either maintains that household or moves back to her parents or grandparents.

Finally we should note that Negro slum families have more children than do either white slum families or stable working- and middle-class Negro families. Mobile Negro families limit their fertility sharply in the interest of bringing the advantages of mobility more fully to the few children that they do have. Since the Negro slum family is both more likely to have the father absent and more likely to have more children in the family, the mother has a more demanding task with fewer resources at her disposal. When we examine the patterns of life of the stem family we shall see that even the presence of several mothers does not necessarily lighten the work load for the principal mother in charge.

THE FORMATION AND MAINTENANCE OF FAMILIES

We will outline below the several stages and forms of Negro lower-class family life. At many points these family forms and the interpersonal relations that exist within them will be seen to have characteristics in common with the life styles of white lower-class families.[10] At other points there are differences, or the Negro pattern will be seen to be more sharply divergent from the family life of stable working- and middle-class couples.

It is important to recognize that lower-class Negroes know that their particular family forms are different from those of the rest of the society and that, though they often see these forms as representing the only ways of behaving given their circumstances, they also think of the more stable family forms of the working class as more desirable. That is, lower-class Negroes know what the "normal American family" is supposed to be like, and they consider a stable family-centered way of life superior to the conjugal and familial situations in which they often find themselves. Their conceptions of the good American life include the notion of a father-husband who functions as an adequate provider and interested member of the family, a hard working home-bound mother who is concerned about her children's welfare and her

husband's needs, and children who look up to their parents and perform well in school and other outside places to reflect credit on their families. This image of what family life can be like is very real from time to time as lower-class men and women grow up and move through adulthood. Many of them make efforts to establish such families but find it impossible to do so either because of the direct impact of economic disabilities or because they are not able to sustain in their day-to-day lives the ideals which they hold.[11] While these ideals do serve as a meaningful guide to lower-class couples who are mobile out of the group, for a great many others the existence of such ideas about normal family life represents a recurrent source of stress within families as individuals become aware that they are failing to measure up to the ideals, or as others within the family and outside it use the ideals as an aggressive weapon for criticizing each other's performance. It is not at all uncommon for husbands or wives or children to try to hold others in the family to the norms of stable family life while they themselves engage in behaviors which violate these norms. The effect of such criticism in the end is to deepen commitment to the deviant sexual and parental norms of a slum subculture. Unless they are careful, social workers and other professionals exacerbate the tendency to use the norms of "American family life" as weapons by supporting these norms in situations where they are in reality unsupportable, thus aggravating the sense of failing and being failed by others which is chronic for lower-class people.

Going Together

The initial steps toward mating and family formation in the Negro slum take place in a context of highly developed boys' and girls' peer groups. Adolescents tend to become deeply involved in their peer-group societies beginning as early as the age of twelve or thirteen and continue to be involved after first pregnancies and first marriages. Boys and girls are heavily committed both to their same sex peer groups and to the activities that those groups carry out. While classical gang activity does not necessarily characterize Negro slum communities everywhere, loosely-knit peer groups do.

The world of the Negro slum is wide open to exploration by adolescent boys and girls: "Negro communities provide a flow of common experience in which young people and their elders share, and out of which delinquent behavior emerges almost imperceptibly." [12] More than is possible in white slum communities, Negro adolescents have an opportunity to interact with adults in various "high life" activities; their behavior more often represents an identification with the behavior of adults than an attempt to set up group standards and activities that differ from those of adults.

Boys and young men participating in the street system of peer-group activity are much caught up in games of furthering and enhancing their status as significant persons. These games are played out in small and large gatherings through various kinds of verbal contests that go under the names of "sounding," "signifying," and "working game." Very much a part of a boy's or man's status in this group is his ability to win women. The man who has several women "up tight," who is successful in "pimping off" women for sexual favors and material benefits, is much admired. In sharp contrast to white lower-class groups, there is little tendency for males to separate girls into "good" and "bad" categories.[13] Observations of groups of Negro youths suggest that girls and women are much more readily referred to as "that bitch"

or "that whore" than they are by their names, and this seems to be a universal tendency carrying no connotation that "that bitch" is morally inferior to or different from other women. Thus, all women are essentially the same, all women are legitimate targets, and no girl or woman is expected to be virginal except for reason of lack of opportunity or immaturity. From their participation in the peer group and according to standards legitimated by the total Negro slum culture, Negro boys and young men are propelled in the direction of girls to test their "strength" as seducers. They are mercilessly rated by both their peers and the opposite sex in their ability to "talk" to girls; a young man will go to great lengths to avoid the reputation of having a "weak" line.[14]

The girls share these definitions of the nature of heterosexual relations; they take for granted that almost any male they deal with will try to seduce them and that given sufficient inducement (social not monetary) they may wish to go along with his line. Although girls have a great deal of ambivalence about participating in sexual relations, this ambivalence is minimally moral and has much more to do with a desire not to be taken advantage of or get in trouble. Girls develop defenses against the exploitative orientations of men by devaluing the significance of sexual relations ("he really didn't do anything bad to me"), and as time goes on by developing their own appreciation of the intrinsic rewards of sexual intercourse.

The informal social relations of slum Negroes begin in adolescence to be highly sexualized. Although parents have many qualms about boys and, particularly, girls entering into this system, they seldom feel there is much they can do to prevent their children's sexual involvement. They usually confine themselves to counseling somewhat hopelessly against girls becoming pregnant or boys being forced into situations where they might have to marry a girl they do not want to marry.

Girls are propelled toward boys and men in order to demonstrate their maturity and attractiveness; in the process they are constantly exposed to pressures for seduction, to boys "rapping" to them. An active girl will "go with" quite a number of boys, but she will generally try to restrict the number with whom she has intercourse to the few to whom she is attracted or (as happens not infrequently) to those whose threats of physical violence she cannot avoid. For their part, the boys move rapidly from girl to girl seeking to have intercourse with as many as they can and thus build up their "reps." The activity of seduction is itself highly cathected; there is gratification in simply "talking to" a girl as long as the boy can feel that he has acquitted himself well.

At sixteen Joan Bemias enjoys spending time with three or four very close girl friends. She tells us they follow this routine when the girls want to go out and none of the boys they have been seeing lately is available: "Every time we get ready to go someplace we look through all the telephone numbers of boys we'd have and we call them and talk so sweet to them that they'd come on around. All of them had cars you see. (I: What do you do to keep all these fellows interested?) Well nothing. We don't have to make love with all of them. Let's see, Joe, J. B., Albert, and Paul, out of all of them I've been going out with I've only had sex with four boys, that's all." She goes on to say that she and her girl friends resist boys by being unresponsive to their lines and by breaking off relations with them on the ground that they're going out with other girls. It is also clear from her comments that the girl friends support each other in resisting the boys when they are out together in groups.

Joan has had a relationship with a boy which has lasted six months, but she has managed to hold the frequency of intercourse down to four times. Initially she managed to hold this particular boy off for a month but eventually gave in.

Becoming Pregnant

It is clear that the contest elements in relationships between men and women continue even in relationships that become quite steady. Despite the girls' ambivalence about sexual relations and their manifold efforts to reduce its frequency, the operation of chance often eventuates in their becoming pregnant.[15] This was the case with Joan. With this we reach the second stage in the formation of families, that of premarital pregnancy. (We are outlining an ideal-typical sequence and not, of course, implying that all girls in the Negro slum culture become pregnant before they marry but only that a great many of them do.)

Joan was caught despite the fact that she was considerably more sophisticated about contraception than most girls or young women in the group (her mother had both instructed her in contraceptive techniques and constantly warned her to take precautions). No one was particularly surprised at her pregnancy although she, her boy friend, her mother, and others regarded it as unfortunate. For girls in the Negro slum, pregnancy before marriage is expected in much the same way that parents expect their children to catch mumps or chicken pox; if they are lucky it will not happen but if it happens people are not too surprised and everyone knows what to do about it. It was quickly decided that Joan and the baby would stay at home. It seems clear from the preparations that Joan's mother is making that she expects to have the main responsibility for caring for the infant. Joan seems quite indifferent to the baby; she shows little interest in mothering the child although she is not particularly adverse to the idea so long as the baby does not interfere too much with her continued participation in her peer group.

Establishing who the father is under these circumstances seems to be important and confers a kind of legitimacy on the birth; not to know who one's father is, on the other hand, seems the ultimate in illegitimacy. Actually Joan had a choice in the imputation of fatherhood; she chose J. B. because he is older than she, and because she may marry him if he can get a divorce from his wife. She could have chosen Paul (with whom she had also had intercourse at about the time she became pregnant), but she would have done this reluctantly since Paul is a year younger than she and somehow this does not seem fitting.

In general, when a girl becomes pregnant while still living at home it seems taken for granted that she will continue to live there and that her parents will take a major responsibility for rearing the children. Since there are usually siblings who can help out and even siblings who will be playmates for the child, the addition of a third generation to the household does not seem to place a great stress on relationships within the family. It seems common for the first pregnancy to have a liberating influence on the mother once the child is born in that she becomes socially and sexually more active that she was before. She no longer has to be concerned with preserving her status as a single girl. Since her mother

is usually willing to take care of the child for a few years, the unwed mother has an opportunity to go out with girl friends and with men and thus become more deeply involved in the peer-group society of her culture. As she has more children and perhaps marries she will find it necessary to settle down and spend more time around the house fulfilling the functions of a mother herself.

It would seem that for girls pregnancy is the real measure of maturity, the dividing line between adolescence and womanhood. Perhaps because of this, as well as because of the ready resources for child care, girls in the Negro slum community show much less concern about pregnancy than do girls in the white lower-class community and are less motivated to marry the fathers of their children. When a girl becomes pregnant the question of marriage certainly arises and is considered, but the girl often decides that she would rather not marry the man either because she does not want to settle down yet or because she does not think he would make a good husband.

It is in the easy attitudes toward premarital pregnancy that the matrifocal character of the Negro lower-class family appears most clearly. In order to have and raise a family it is simply not necessary, though it may be desirable, to have a man around the house. Although the AFDC program may make it easier to maintain such attitudes in the urban situation, this pattern existed long before the program was initiated and continues in families where support comes from other sources.

Finally, it should be noted that fathering a child similarly confers maturity on boys and young men, although perhaps it is less important for them. If the boy has any interest in the girl, he will tend to feel that the fact that he has impregnated her gives him an additional claim on her. He will be stricter in seeking to enforce his exclusive rights over her (though not exclusive loyalty to her). This exclusive right does not mean that he expects to marry her, but only that there is a new and special bond between them. If the girl is not willing to accept such claims, she may find it necessary to break off the relationship rather than tolerate the man's jealousy. Since others in the peer group have a vested interest in not allowing a couple to be too loyal to each other, they go out of their way to question and challenge each partner about the loyalty of the other, thus contributing to the deterioration of the relationship. This same kind of questioning and challenging continues if the couple marries and represents one source of the instability of the marital relationship.

Getting Married

As noted earlier, despite the high degree of premarital sexual activity and the rather high proportion of premarital pregnancies, most lower-class Negro men and women eventually do marry and stay together for a shorter or longer period of time. Marriage is an intimidating prospect and is approached ambivalently by both parties. For the girl it means giving up a familiar and comfortable home that, unlike some other lower-class subcultures, places few real restrictions on her behavior. (While marriage can appear to be an escape from interpersonal difficulties at home, these difficulties seldom seem to revolve around effective restrictions placed on her behavior by her parents.) The girl also has good reason to be suspicious of the likelihood that men will be able to perform stably in the role of husband and provider; she is reluctant to be tied down

by a man who will not prove to be worth it.

From the man's point of view the fickleness of women makes marriage problematic. It is one thing to have a girl friend step out on you, but it is quite another to have a wife do so. Whereas premarital sexual relations and fatherhood carry almost no connotation of responsibility for the welfare of the partner, marriage is supposed to mean that a man behaves more responsibly, becoming a provider for his wife and children even though he may not be expected to give up all the gratifications of participation in the street system.

For all of these reasons both boys and girls tend to have rather negative views of marriage as well as a low expectation that marriage will prove a stable and gratifying existence. When marriage does take place it tends to represent a tentative commitment on the part of both parties with a strong tendency to seek greater commitment on the part of the partner than on one's own part. Marriage is regarded as a fragile arrangement held together primarily by affectional ties rather than instrumental concerns.

In general, as in white lower-class groups, the decision to marry seems to be taken rather impulsively.[16] Since everyone knows that sooner or later he will get married, in spite of the fact that he may not be sanguine about the prospect, Negro lower-class men and women are alert for clues that the time has arrived. The time may arrive because of a pregnancy in a steady relationship that seems gratifying to both partners, or as a way of getting out of what seems to be an awkward situation, or as a self-indulgence during periods when a boy and a girl are feeling very sorry for themselves. Thus, one girl tells us that when she marries her husband will cook all of her meals for her and she will not have any housework; another girl says that when she marries it will be to a man who has plenty of money and will have to take her out often and really show her a good time.

Boys see in marriage the possibility of regular sexual intercourse without having to fight for it, or a girl safe from venereal disease, or a relationship to a nurturant figure who will fulfill the functions of a mother. For boys, marriage can also be a way of asserting their independence from the peer group if its demands become burdensome. In this case the young man seeks to have the best of both worlds.[17]

Marriage as a way out of an unpleasant situation can be seen in the case of one of our informants, Janet Cowan:

Janet has been going with two men, one of them married and the other single. The married man's wife took exception to their relationship and killed her husband. Within a week Janet and her single boy friend, Howard, were married. One way out of the turmoil the murder of her married boy friend stimulated (they lived in the same building) was to choose marriage as a way of "settling down." However, after marrying the new couple seemed to have little idea how to set themselves up as a family. Janet was reluctant to leave her parents' home because her parents cared for her two illegitimate children. Howard was unemployed and therefore unacceptable in his parent-in-law's home, nor were his own parents willing to have his wife move in with them. Howard was also reluctant to give up another girl friend in another part of town. Although both he and his wife maintained that it was all right for a couple to step out on each other so long as the other partner did not know about it, they were both jealous if they suspected anything of this kind. In the end they gave up on the idea of marriage and went their separate ways.

In general, then, the movement toward marriage is an uncertain and tentative one. Once the couple does settle down together in a household of their own, they have the problem of working out a mutually acceptable organization of rights and duties, expectations and performances, that will meet their needs.

Husband-Wife Relations

Characteristic of both the Negro and white lower class is a high degree of conjugal role segregation.[18] That is, husbands and wives tend to think of themselves as having very separate kinds of functioning in the instrumental organization of family life, and also as pursuing recreational and outside interests separately. The husband is expected to be a provider; he resists assuming functions around the home so long as he feels he is doing his proper job of bringing home a pay check. He feels he has the right to indulge himself in little ways if he is successful at this task. The wife is expected to care for the home and children and make her husband feel welcome and comfortable. Much that is distinctive to Negro family life stems from the fact that husbands often are not stable providers. Even when a particular man is, his wife's conception of men in general is such that she is pessimistic about the likelihood that he will continue to do well in this area. A great many Negro wives work to supplement the family income. When this is so the separate incomes earned by husband and wife tend to be treated not as "family" income but as the individual property of the two persons involved. If their wives work, husbands are likely to feel that they are entitled to retain a larger share of the income they provide; the wives, in turn, feel that the husbands have no right to benefit from the purchases they make out of their own money. There is, then, "my money" and "your money." In this situation the husband may come to feel that the wife should support the children out of her income and that he can retain all of his income for himself.

While white lower-class wives often are very much intimidated by their husbands, Negro lower-class wives come to feel that they have a right to give as good as they get. If the husband indulges himself, they have the right to indulge themselves. If the husband steps out on his wife, she has the right to step out on him. The commitment of husbands and wives to each other seems often a highly instrumental one after the "honeymoon" period. Many wives feel they owe the husband nothing once he fails to perform his provider role. If the husband is unemployed the wife increasingly refuses to perform her usual duties for him. For example one woman, after mentioning that her husband had cooked four eggs for himself, commented, "I cook for him when he's working but right now he's unemployed; he can cook for himself." It is important, however, to understand that the man's status in the home depends not so much on whether he is working as on whether he brings money into the home. Thus, in several of the families we have studied in which the husband receives disability payments his status is as well-recognized as in families in which the husband is working.[19]

Because of the high degree of conjugal role segregation, both white and Negro lower-class families tend to be matrifocal in comparison to middle-class families. They are matrifocal in the sense that the wife makes most of the decisions that keep the family going and has the greatest sense of responsibility to the family. In white as well as in Negro lower-class families women tend to look to their female relatives for support and counsel, and to treat their husbands as essentially uninterested in the day-to-day problems of family living.[20] In the Negro lower-class family these tendencies are all considerably exaggerated so that the matrifocality is much clearer than in white lower-class families.

The fact that both sexes in the Negro slum culture have equal right to the various satisfactions of life (earning an income, sex, drinking, and peer-group activity which conflicts with family responsibilities) means that there is less pretense to patriarchal authority in the Negro than in the white lower class. Since men find the overt debasement of their status very threatening, the Negro family is much more vulnerable to disruption when men are temporarily unable to perform their provider roles. Also, when men are unemployed the temptations for them to engage in street adventures which might have repercussions within the marital relationship are much greater. This fact is well-recognized by Negro lower-class wives; they often seem as concerned about what their unemployed husbands will do instead of working as they are about the fact that the husband is no longer bringing money into the home.

It is tempting to cope with the likelihood of disloyalty by denying the usual norms of fidelity, by maintaining instead that extra-marital affairs are acceptable as long as they do not interfere with family functioning. Quite a few informants tell us this, but we have yet to observe a situation in which a couple maintains a stable relationship under these circumstances without a great deal of conflict. Thus one woman in her forties who has been married for many years and has four children first outlined this deviant norm and then illustrated how it did not work out:

My husband and I, we go out alone and sometimes stay all night. But when I get back my husband doesn't ask me a thing and I don't ask him anything. . . . A couple of years ago I suspected he was going out on me. One day I came home and my daughter was here. I told her to tell me when he left the house. I went into the bedroom and got into bed and then I heard him come in. He left in about ten minutes and my daughter came in and told me he was gone. I got out of bed and put on my clothes and started following him. Soon I saw him walking with a young girl and I began walking after them. They were just laughing and joking right out loud right on the sidewalk. He was carrying a large package of hers. I walked up behind them until I was about a yard from them. I had a large dirk which I opened and had decided to take one long slash across the both of them. Just when I decided to swing at them I lost my balance—I have a bad hip. Anyway, I didn't cut them because I lost my balance. Then I called his name and he turned around and stared at me. He didn't move at all. He was shaking all over. That girl just ran away from us. He still had her package so the next day she called on the telephone and said she wanted to come pick it up. My husband washed his face, brushed his teeth, took out his false tooth and started scrubbing it and put on a clean shirt and everything just for her. We went downstairs together and gave her the package and she left.

So you see my husband does run around on me and it seems like he does it a lot. The thing about it is he's just getting too old to be pulling that kind of stuff. If a young man does it then that's not so bad—but an old man, he just looks foolish. One of these days he'll catch me but I'll just tell him, "Buddy you owe me one," and that'll be all there is to it. He hasn't caught me yet though.

In this case, as in others, the wife is not able to leave well enough alone; her jealousy forces her to a confrontation. Actually seeing her husband with another woman stimulates her to violence.

With couples who have managed to stay married for a good many years, these peccadillos are tolerable although they generate a great deal of conflict in the marital relationship. At earlier ages the partners are likely to be both prouder and less inured to the hopelessness of maintaining stable relationships; outside involvements are therefore much more likely to be disruptive of the marriage.

Marital Breakup

The precipitating causes of marital disruption seem to fall mainly into economic or sexual categories. As noted, the husband has little credit with his wife to tide him over periods of unemployment. Wives seem very willing to withdraw commitment from husbands who are not bringing money into the house. They take the point of view that he has no right to take up space around the house, to use its facilities, or to demand loyalty from her. Even where the wife is not inclined to press these claims, the husband tends to be touchy because he knows that such definitions are usual in his group, and he may, therefore, prove difficult for even a well-meaning wife to deal with. As noted above, if husbands do not work they tend to play around. Since they continue to maintain some contact with their peer groups, whenever they have time on their hands they move back into the world of the street system and are likely to get involved in activities which pose a threat to their family relationships.

Drink is a great enemy of the lower-class housewife, both white and Negro. Lower-class wives fear their husband's drinking because it costs money, because the husband may become violent and take out his frustrations on his wife, and because drinking may lead to sexual involvements with other women.[21]

The combination of economic problems and sexual difficulties can be seen in the case of the following couple in their early twenties:

When the field worker first came to know them, the Wilsons seemed to be working hard to establish a stable family life. The couple had been married about three years and had a two-year-old son. Their apartment was very sparsely furnished but also very clean. Within six weeks the couple had acquired several rooms of inexpensive furniture and obviously had gone to a great deal of effort to make a liveable home. Husband and wife worked on different shifts so that the husband could take care of the child while the wife worked. They looked forward to saving enough money to move out of the housing project into a more desirable neighborhood. Six weeks later, however, the husband had lost his job. He and his wife were in great conflict. She made him feel unwelcome at home and he strongly suspected her of going out with other men. A short time later they had separated. It is impossible to disentangle the various factors involved in this separation into a sequence of cause and effect, but

we can see something of the impact of the total complex.

First Mr. Wilson loses his job: "I went to work one day and the man told me that I would have to work until 1:00. I asked him if there would be any extra pay for working overtime and he said no. I asked him why and he said, 'If you don't like it you can kiss my ass.' He said that to me. I said, 'Why do I have to do all that?' He said, 'Because I said so.' I wanted to jam (fight) him but I said to myself I don't want to be that ignorant, I don't want to be as ignorant as he is, so I just cut out and left. Later his father called me (it was a family firm) and asked why I left and I told him. He said, 'If you don't want to go along with my son then you're fired.' I said O.K. They had another Negro man come in to help me part time before they fired me. I think they were trying to have him work full time because he worked for them before. He has seven kids and he takes their shit."

The field worker observed that things were not as hard as they could be because his wife had a job, to which he replied, "Yeah, I know, that's just where the trouble is. My wife has become independent since she began working. If I don't get a job pretty soon I'll go crazy. We have a lot of little arguments about nothing since she got so independent." He went on to say that his wife had become a completely different person recently; she was hard to talk to because she felt that now that she was working and he was not there was nothing that he could tell her. On her last pay day his wife did not return home for three days; when she did she had only seven cents left from her pay check. He said that he loved his wife very much and had begged her to quit fooling around. He is pretty sure that she is having an affair with the man with whom she rides to work. To make matters worse his wife's sister counsels her that she does not have to stay home with him as long as he is out of work. Finally the wife moved most of their furniture out of the apartment so that he came home to find an empty apartment. He moved back to his parents' home (also in the housing project).

One interesting effect of this experience was the radical change in the husband's attitudes toward race relations. When he and his wife were doing well together and he had hopes of moving up in the world he was quite critical of Negroes; "Our people are not ready for integration in many cases because they really don't know how to act. You figure if our people don't want to be bothered with whites then why in hell should the white man want to be bothered with them. There are some of us who are ready; there are others who aren't quite ready yet so I don't see why they're doing all of this hollering." A scarce eight months later he addressed white people as if he spoke for two hours into a tape recorder, "If we're willing to be with you, why aren't you willing to be with us? Do our color make us look dirty and low down and cheap? Or do you know the real meaning of 'nigger'? Anyone can be a nigger, white, colored, orange or any other color. It's something that you labeled us with. You put us away like you put a can away on the shelf with a label on it. The can is marked 'Poison: stay away from it.' You want us to help build your country but you don't want us to live in it. . . . You give me respect; I'll give you respect. If you threaten to take my life, I'll take yours and believe me I know how to take a life. We do believe that man was put here to live together as human beings; not one that's superior and the one that's a dog, but as human beings. And if you don't want to

live this way then you become the dog and we'll become the human beings. There's too much corruption, too much hate, too much one individual trying to step on another. If we don't get together in a hurry we will destroy each other." It was clear from what the respondent said that he had been much influenced by Black Muslim philosophy, yet again and again in his comments one can see the displacement into a public, race relations dialogue of the sense of rage, frustration and victimization that he had experienced in his ill-fated marriage.[22]

Finally, it should be noted that migration plays a part in marital disruption. Sometimes marriages do not break up in the dramatic way described above but rather simply become increasingly unsatisfactory to one or both partners. In such a situation the temptation to move to another city, from South to North, or North to West, is great. Several wives told us that their first marriages were broken when they moved with their children to the North and their husbands stayed behind.

"After we couldn't get along I left the farm and came here and stayed away three or four days. I didn't come here to stay. I came to visit but I liked it and so I said, 'I'm gonna leave!' He said, 'I'll be glad if you do.' Well, maybe he didn't mean it but I thought he did. . . . I miss him sometimes, you know. I think about him I guess. But just in a small way. That's what I can't understand about life sometimes; you know—how people can go on like that and still break up and meet somebody else. Why couldn't—oh, I don't know!"

The gains and losses in marriage and in the post-marital state often seem quite comparable. Once they have had the experience of marriage, many women in the Negro slum culture see little to recommend it in the future, important as the first marriage may have been in establishing their maturity and respectability.

The House of Mothers

As we have seen, perhaps a majority of mothers in the Negro slum community spend at least part of their mature life as mothers heading a family. The Negro mother may be a working mother or she may be an AFDC mother, but in either case she has the problems of maintaining a household, socializing her children, and achieving for herself some sense of membership in relations with other women and with men. As is apparent from the earlier discussion, she often receives her training in how to run such a household by observing her own mother manage without a husband. Similarly she often learns how to run a three-generation household because she herself brought a third generation into her home with her first, premarital, pregnancy.

Because men are not expected to be much help around the house, having to be head of the household is not particularly intimidating to the Negro mother if she can feel some security about income. She knows it is a hard, hopeless, and often thankless task, but she also knows that it is possible. The maternal household in the slum is generally run with a minimum of organization. The children quickly learn to fend for themselves, to go to the store, to make small purchases, to bring change home, to watch after themselves when the mother has to be out of the home, to amuse themselves, to set their own schedules of sleeping, eating, and going to school. Housekeeping practices may be poor, furniture takes a terrific beating from

the children, and emergencies constantly arise. The Negro mother in this situation copes by not setting too high standards for herself, by letting things take their course. Life is most difficult when there are babies and preschool children around because then the mother is confined to the home. If she is a grandmother and the children are her daughter's, she is often confined since it is taken as a matter of course that the mother has the right to continue her outside activities and that the grandmother has the duty to be responsible for the child.

In this culture there is little of the sense of the awesome responsibility of caring for children that is characteristic of the working and middle class. There is not the deep psychological involvement with babies which has been observed with the working-class mother.[23] The baby's needs are cared for on a catch-as-catch-can basis. If there are other children around and they happen to like babies, the baby can be over-stimulated; if this is not the case, the baby is left alone a good deal of the time. As quickly as he can move around he learns to fend for himself.

The three-generation maternal household is a busy place. In contrast to working- and middle-class homes it tends to be open to the world, with many nonfamily members coming in and out at all times as the children are visited by friends, the teenagers by their boy friends and girl friends, the mother by her friends and perhaps an occasional boy friend, and the grandmother by fewer friends but still by an occasional boy friend.

The openness of the household is, among other things, a reflection of the mother's sense of impotence in the face of the street system. Negro lower-class mothers often indicate that they try very hard to keep their young children at home and away from the streets; they often seem to make the children virtual prisoners in the home. As the children grow and go to school they inevitably do become involved in peer-group activities. The mother gradually gives up, feeling that once the child is lost to this pernicious outside world there is little she can do to continue to control him and direct his development. She will try to limit the types of activities that go on in the home and to restrict the kinds of friends that her children can bring into the home, but even this she must give up as time goes on, as the children become older and less attentive to her direction.

The grandmothers in their late forties, fifties, and sixties tend increasingly to stay at home. The home becomes a kind of court at which other family members gather and to which they bring their friends for sociability, and, as a by-product, provide amusement and entertainment for the mother. A grandmother may provide a home for her daughters, their children, and sometimes their children's children, and yet receive very little in a material way from them; but one of the things she does receive is a sense of human involvement, a sense that although life may have passed her by she is not completely isolated from it.

The lack of control that mothers have over much that goes on in their households is most dramatically apparent in the fact that their older children seem to have the right to come home at any time once they had moved and to stay in the home without contributing to its maintenance. Though the mother may be resentful about being taken advantage of, she does not feel she can turn her children away. For example, sixty-five-year-old Mrs. Washington plays hostess for weeks or months at a time to her forty-year-old daughter and her small children, and to her twenty-three-year-old granddaughter and her children. When these daughters come home with their families the grandmother is expected to take care of the young children and must argue with her daughter and granddaughter to receive contributions to the daily household ration of food and liquor. Or, a twenty-year-old son comes home from the Air Force and feels he has the right to live at home without working and to run up an eighty-dollar long-distance telephone bill.

Even aged parents living alone in small apartments sometimes acknowledge such obligations to their children or grandchildren. Again, the only clear return they receive for their hospitality is the reduction of isolation that comes from having people around and interesting activity going on. When in the Washington home the daughter and granddaughter and their children move in with the grandmother, or when they come to visit for shorter periods of time, the occasion has a party atmosphere. The women sit around talking and reminiscing. Though boy friends may be present, they take little part; instead they sit passively, enjoying the stories and drinking along with the women. It would seem that in this kind of party activity the women are defined as the stars. Grandmother, daughter, and granddaughter in turn take the center of the stage telling a story from the family's past, talking about a particularly interesting night out on the town or just making some general observation about life. In the course of these events a good deal of liquor is consumed. In such a household as this little attention is paid to the children since the competition by adults for attention is stiff.

Boy Friends, Not Husbands

It is with an understanding of the problems of isolation which older mothers have that we can obtain the best insight into the role and function of boy friends in the maternal household. The older mothers, surrounded by their own children and grandchildren, are not able to move freely in the outside world, to participate in the high life which they enjoyed when younger and more foot-loose. They are disillusioned with marriage as providing any more secure economic base than they can achieve on their own. They see marriage as involving just another responsibility without a concomitant reward—"It's the greatest thing in the world to come home in the afternoon and not have some curly headed twot in the house yellin' at me and askin' me where supper is, where I've been, what I've been doin', and who I've been seein'." In this situation the woman is tempted to form relationships with men that are not so demanding as marriage but still provide companionship and an opportunity for occasional sexual gratification.

There seem to be two kinds of boy friends. Some boy friends "pimp" off mothers; they extract payment in food or money for their companionship. This leads to the custom sometimes called "Mother's Day," the tenth of the month when the AFDC checks come.[24] On this day one can observe an influx of men into the neighborhood, and much partying. But there is another kind of boy friend, perhaps more numerous than the first, who instead of being paid for his services pays for the right to be a pseudo family member. He may be the father of one of the women's children and for this reason makes a steady contribution to the family's support, or he may simply be a man whose company the mother enjoys and who makes reasonable gifts to the family for the time he spends with them (and perhaps implicitly for the sexual favors he receives). While the boy friend does not assume fatherly authority within the family, he often is known and liked by the children. The older children appreciate the meaningfulness of their mother's relationship with him—one girl said of her mother's boy friend:

"We don't none of us (the children) want her to marry again. It's all right if she wants to live by herself and have a boy friend. It's not because we're afraid we're going to have some more sisters and brothers, which it wouldn't make us much difference, but I think she be too old."

Even when the boy friend contributes ten or twenty dollars a month to the family he is in a certain sense getting a bargain. If he is a well-accepted boy friend he spends considerable time around the house, has a chance to relax in an atmosphere less competitive than that of his peer group, is fed and cared for by the woman, yet has no responsibilities which he cannot renounce when he wishes. When women have stable relationships of this kind with boy friends they often consider marrying them but are reluctant to take such a step. Even the well-liked boy friend has some shortcomings—one woman said of her boy friend:

"Well he works; I know that. He seems to be a nice person, kind hearted. He believes in survival for me and my family. He don't much mind sharing with my youngsters. If I ask him for a helping hand he don't seem to mind that. The only part I dislike is his drinking."

The woman in this situation has worked out a reasonably stable adaptation to the problems of her life; she is fearful of upsetting this adaptation by marrying again. It seems easier to take the "sweet" part of the relationship with a man without the complexities that marriage might involve.

It is in the light of this pattern of women living in families and men living by themselves in rooming houses, odd rooms, here and there, that we can understand Daniel Patrick Moynihan's observation that during their mature years men simply disappear; that is, that census data show a very high sex ratio of women to men.[25] In St. Louis, starting at the age range twenty to twenty-four there are only seventy-two men for every one hundred women. This ratio does not climb to ninety until the age range fifty to fifty-four. Men often do not have real homes; they move about from one household where they have kinship or sexual ties to another; they live in flop houses and rooming houses; they spend time in institutions. They are not household members in the only "homes" that they have—the homes of their mothers and of their girl friends.

It is in this kind of world that boys and girls in the Negro slum community learn their sex roles. It is not just, or even mainly, that fathers are often absent but that the male role models around boys are ones which emphasize expressive, affectional techniques for making one's way in the world. The female role models available to girls emphasize an exaggerated self-sufficiency (from the point of view of the middle class) and the danger of allowing oneself to be dependent on men for anything that is crucial. By the time she is mature, the woman learns that she is most secure when she herself manages the family affairs and when she dominates her men. The

man learns that he exposes himself to the least risk of failure when he does not assume a husband's and father's responsibilities but instead counts on his ability to court women and to ingratiate himself with them.

IDENTITY PROCESSES IN THE FAMILY

Up to this point we have been examining the sequential development of family stages in the Negro slum community, paying only incidental attention to the psychological responses family members make to these social forms and not concerning ourselves with the effect the family forms have on the psychosocial development of the children who grow up in them. Now we want to examine the effect that growing up in this kind of a system has in terms of socialization and personality development.

Household groups function for cultures in carrying out the initial phases of socialization and personality formation. It is in the family that the child learns the most primitive categories of existence and experience, and that he develops his most deeply held beliefs about the world and about himself.[26] From the child's point of view, the household *is* the world; his experiences as he moves out of it into the larger world are always interpreted in terms of his particular experience within the home. The painful experiences which a child in the Negro slum culture has are, therefore, interpreted as in some sense a reflection of this family world. The impact of the system of victimization is transmitted through the family; the child cannot be expected to have the sophistication an outside observer has for seeing exactly where the villains are. From the child's point of view, if he is hungry it is his parents' fault; if he experiences frustrations in the streets or in the school it is his parents' fault; if that world seems incomprehensible to him it is his parents' fault; if people are aggressive or destructive toward each other it is his parents' fault, not that of a system of race relations. In another culture this might not be the case; if a subculture could exist which provided comfort and security within its limited world and the individual experienced frustration only when he moved out into the larger society, the family might not be thought so much to blame. The effect of the caste system, however, is to bring home through a chain of cause and effect all of the victimization processes, and to bring them home in such a way that it is often very difficult even for adults in the system to see the connection between the pain they feel at the moment and the structured patterns of the caste system.

Let us take as a central question that of identity formation within the Negro slum family. We are concerned with the question of who the individual believes himself to be and to be becoming. For Erikson, identity means a sense of continuity and social sameness which bridges what the individual "*was* as a child and and what he is *about to become* and also reconciles his *conception of himself* and his community's recognition of him." Thus identity is a "self-realization coupled with a mutual recognition." [27] In the early childhood years identity is family-bound since the child's identity is his identity *vis-à-vis* other members of the family. Later he incorporates into his sense of who he is and is becoming his experiences outside the family, but always influenced by the interpretations and evaluations of those experiences that the family gives. As the child tries on identities, *announces* them, the family sits as judge of his pretensions. Family members are both the most important judges and the most critical ones, since who he is allowed to become affects them in their own identity striving more crucially than it affects anyone else. The child seeks a sense of valid identity, a sense of being a particular person with a satisfactory degree of congruence between who he feels he is, who he announces himself to be, and where he feels his society places him. [28] He is uncomfortable when he experiences disjunction between his own needs and the kinds of needs legitimated by those around him, or when he feels a disjunction between his sense of himself and the image of himself that others play back to him. [29]

"Tell It Like It Is"

When families become involved in important quarrels the psychosocial underpinnings of family life are laid bare. One such quarrel in a family we have been studying brings together in one place many of the themes that seem to dominate identity problems in Negro slum culture. The incident illustrates in a particularly forceful and dramatic way family processes which our field work, and some other contemporary studies of slum family life, suggests unfold more subtly in a great many families at the lower-class level. The family involved, the Johnsons, is certainly not the most disorganized one we have studied; in some respects their way of life represents a realistic adaptation to the hard living of a family nineteen years on AFDC with a monthly income of $202 for nine people. The two oldest daughters, Mary Jane (eighteen years old) and Esther (sixteen) are pregnant; Mary Jane has one illegitimate child. The adolescent sons, Bob and Richard, are much involved in the social and sexual activities of their peer group. The three other children, ranging in age from twelve to fourteen, are apparently also moving into this kind of peer-group society.

When the argument started Bob and Esther were alone in the apartment with Mary Jane's baby. Esther took exception to Bob's playing with the baby because she had been left in charge; the argument quickly progressed to a fight in which Bob cuffed Esther around, and she tried to cut him with a knife. The police were called and subdued Bob with their nightsticks. At this point the rest of the family and the field worker arrived. As the argument continued, these themes relevant to the analysis which follows appeared:

1. The sisters said that Bob was not their brother (he is a half-brother to Esther, and Mary Jane's full brother). Indeed, they said their mother "didn't have no husband. These kids don't even know who their daddies are." The mother defended herself by saying that she had one legal husband, and one common-law husband, no more.

2. The sisters said that their fathers had never done anything for them, nor had their mother. She retorted that she had raised them "to the age of womanhood" and now would care for their babies.

3. Esther continued to threaten to cut Bob if she got a chance (a month later they fought again, and she did cut Bob, who required twenty-one stitches).

4. The sisters accused their mother of favoring their lazy brothers and asked her to put them out of the house. She retorted that the girls were as lazy, that they made no contribution to maintaining the household, could not get their boy friends to marry them or support their children, that all the support came from her AFDC

check. Mary Jane retorted that "the baby has a check of her own."

5. The girls threatened to leave the house if their mother refused to put their brothers out. They said they could force their boy friends to support them by taking them to court, and Esther threatened to cut her boy friend's throat if he did not cooperate.

6. Mrs. Johnson said the girls could leave if they wished but that she would keep their babies; "I'll not have it, not knowing who's taking care of them."

7. When her thirteen-year-old sister laughed at all of this, Esther told her not to laugh because she, too, would be pregnant within a year.

8. When Bob laughed, Esther attacked him and his brother by saying that both were not man enough to make babies, as she and her sister had been able to do.

9. As the field worker left, Mrs. Johnson sought his sympathy. "You see, Joe, how hard it is for me to bring up a family. . . . They sit around and talk to me like I'm some kind of a dog and not their mother."

10. Finally, it is important to note for the analysis which follows that the following labels—"black-assed," "black bastard," "bitch," and other profane terms—were liberally used by Esther and Mary Jane, and rather less liberally by their mother, to refer to each other, to the girls' boy friends, to Bob, and to the thirteen-year-old daughter.

Several of the themes outlined previously appear forcefully in the course of this argument. In the last year and a half the mother has become a grandmother and expects shortly to add two more grandchildren to her household. She takes it for granted that it is her responsibility to care for the grandchildren and that she has the right to decide what will be done with the children since her own daughters are not fully responsible. She makes this very clear to them when they threaten to move out, a threat which they do not really wish to make good nor could they if they wished to.

However, only as an act of will is Mrs. Johnson able to make this a family. She must constantly cope with the tendency of her adolescent children to disrupt the family group and to deny that they are in fact a family—"He ain't no brother of mine"; "The baby has a check of her own." Though we do not know exactly what processes communicate these facts to the children it is clear that in growing up they have learned to regard themselves as not fully part of a solidary collectivity. During the quarrel this message was reinforced for the twelve-, thirteen-, and fourteen-year-old daughters by the four-way argument among their older sisters, older brother, and their mother.

The argument represents vicious unmasking of the individual members' pretenses to being competent individuals.[30] The efforts of the two girls to present themselves as masters of their own fate are unmasked by the mother. The girls in turn unmask the pretensions of the mother and of their two brothers. When the thirteen-year-old daughter expresses some amusement they turn on her, telling her that it won't be long before she too becomes pregnant. Each member of the family in turn is told that he can expect to be no more than a victim of his world, but that this is somehow inevitably his own fault.

In this argument masculinity is consistently demeaned. Bob has no right to play with his niece, the boys are not really masculine because at fifteen and sixteen years they have yet to father children. Their own fathers were no goods who failed to do any-

thing for their family. These notions probably come originally from the mother, who enjoys recounting the story of having her common-law husband imprisoned for nonsupport, but this comes back to haunt her as her daughters accuse her of being no better than they in ability to force support and nurturance from a man. In contrast, the girls came off somewhat better than the boys, although they must accept the label of stupid girls because they have similarly failed and inconveniently become pregnant in the first place. At least they can and have had children and therefore have some meaningful connection with the ongoing substance of life. There is something important and dramatic in which they participate, while the boys, despite their sexual activity, "can't get no babies."

In most societies, as children grow and are formed by their elders into suitable members of the society they gain increasingly a sense of competence and ability to master the behavioral environment their particular world presents. But in Negro slum culture growing up involves an ever-increasing appreciation of one's shortcomings, of the impossibility of finding a self-sufficient and gratifying way of living.[31] It is in the family first and most devastatingly that one learns these lessons. As the child's sense of frustration builds he too can strike out and unmask the pretensions of others. The result is a peculiar strength and a pervasive weakness. The strength involves the ability to tolerate and defend against degrading verbal and physical aggressions from others and not to give up completely. The weakness involves the inability to embark hopefully on any course of action that might make things better, particularly action which involves cooperating and trusting attitudes toward others. Family members become potential enemies to each other, as the frequency of observing the police being called in to settle family quarrels brings home all too dramatically.

The conceptions parents have of their children are such that they are constantly alert, as the child matures, to evidence that he is as bad as everyone else. That is, in lower-class culture human nature is conceived of as essentially bad, destructive, immoral.[32] This is the nature of things. Therefore any one child must be inherently bad unless his parents are very lucky indeed. If the mother can keep the child insulated from the outside world, she feels she may be able to prevent his inherent badness from coming out. She feels that once he is let out into the larger world the badness will come to the fore since that is his nature. This means that in the identity development of the child he is constantly exposed to identity labeling by his parents as a bad person. Since as he grows up he does not experience his world as particularly gratifying, it is very easy for him to conclude that this lack of gratification is due to the fact that something is wrong with him. This, in turn, can readily be assimilated to the definitions of being a bad person offered him by those with whom he lives.[33] In this way the Negro slum child learns his culture's conception of being-in-the-world, a conception that emphasizes inherent evil in a chaotic, hostile, destructive world.

Blackness

To a certain extent these same processes operate in white lower-class groups, but added for the Negro is the reality of blackness. "Black-assed" is not an empty pejorative adjective. In the Negro slum culture several distinctive appellations are used to refer to oneself and others. One involves the terms, "black" or "nigger." Black is generally a negative way of naming, but nigger can be either negative or positive, depending upon the context. It is important to note that, at least in the urban North, the initial development of racial identity in these terms has very little directly to do with relations with whites. A child experiences these identity placements in the context of the family and in the neighborhood peer group; he probably very seldom hears the same terms used by whites (unlike the situation in the South). In this way, one of the effects of ghettoization is to mask the ultimate enemy so that the understanding of the fact of victimization by a caste system comes as a late acquisition laid over conceptions of self and of other Negroes derived from intimate, and to the child often traumatic, experience within the ghetto community. If, in addition, the child attends a ghetto school where his Negro teachers either overtly or by implication reinforce his community's negative conceptions of what it means to be black, then the child has little opportunity to develop a more realistic image of himself and other Negroes as being damaged by whites and not by themselves. In such a situation, an intelligent man like Mr. Wilson (quoted on pages 113–114) can say with all sincerity that he does not feel most Negroes are ready for integration—only under the experience of certain kinds of intense personal threat coupled with exposure to an ideology that places the responsibility on whites did he begin to see through the direct evidence of his daily experience.

To those living in the heart of a ghetto, black comes to mean not just "stay back," but also membership in a community of persons who think poorly of each other, who attack and manipulate each other, who give each other small comfort in a desperate world. Black comes to stand for a sense of identity as no better than these destructive others. The individual feels that he must embrace an unattractive self in order to function at all.

We can hypothesize that in those families that manage to avoid the destructive identity imputations of "black" and that manage to maintain solidarity against such assaults from the world around, it is possible for children to grow up with a sense of both Negro and personal identity that allows them to socialize themselves in an anticipatory way for participation in the larger society.[34] This broader sense of identity, however, will remain a brittle one as long as the individual is vulnerable to attack from within the Negro community as "nothing but a nigger like everybody else," or from the white community as "just a nigger." We can hypothesize further that the vicious unmasking of essential identity as black described above is least likely to occur within families where the parents have some stable sense of security, and where they therefore have less need to protect themselves by disavowing responsibility for their children's behavior and denying the children their patrimony as products of a particular family rather than of an immoral nature and an evil community.

In sum, we are suggesting that Negro slum children as they grow up in their families and in their neighborhoods are exposed to a set of experiences—and a rhetoric which conceptualizes them—that brings home to the child an understanding of his essence as a weak and debased person who can expect only partial gratification of his needs, and who must seek even this level of gratification by less than straight-forward means.

Strategies for Living

In every society complex processes of socialization inculcate in their members strategies for gratifying the needs with which they are born and those which the society itself generates. Inextricably linked to these strategies, both as cause and effect of them, are the existential propositions which members of a culture entertain about the nature of their world and of effective action within the world as it is defined for them. In most of American society two grand strategies seem to attract the allegiance of its members and guide their day-to-day actions. I have called these strategies those of *the good life* and of *career success*.[35] A good life strategy involves efforts to get along with others and not to rock the boat, a comfortable familism grounded on a stable work career for husbands in which they perform adequately at the modest jobs that enable them to be good providers. The strategy of career success is the choice of ambitious men and women who see life as providing opportunities to move from a lower to a higher status, to "accomplish something," to achieve greater than ordinary material well-being, prestige, and social recognition. Both of these strategies are predicated on the assumption that the world is inherently rewarding if one behaves properly and does his part. The rewards of the world may come easily or only at the cost of great effort, but at least they are there.

In the white and particularly in the Negro slum worlds little in the experience that individuals have as they grow up sustains a belief in a rewarding world. The strategies that seem appropriate are not those of a good, family-based life or of a career, but rather *strategies for survival.*

Much of what has been said above can be summarized as encouraging three kinds of survival strategies. One is the strategy of the *expressive life style* which I have described elsewhere as an effort to make yourself interesting and attractive to others so that you are better able to manipulate their behavior along lines that will provide some immediate gratification.[36] Negro slum culture provides many examples of techniques for seduction, of persuading others to give you what you want in situations where you have very little that is tangible to offer in return. In order to get what you want you learn to "work game," a strategy which requires a high development of a certain kind of verbal facility, a sophisticated manipulation of promise and interim reward. When the expressive strategy fails or when it is unavailable there is, of course, the great temptation to adopt a *violent strategy* in which you force others to give you what you need once you fail to win it by verbal and other symbolic means.[37] Finally, and increasingly as members of the Negro slum culture grow older, there is the *depressive strategy* in which goals are increasingly

constricted to the bare necessities for survival (not as a social being but simply as an organism).[38] This is the strategy of "I don't bother anybody and I hope nobody's gonna bother me; I'm simply going through the motions to keep body (but not soul) together." Most lower-class people follow mixed strategies, as Walter Miller has observed, alternating among the excitement of the expressive style, the desperation of the violent style, and the deadness of the depressed style.[39] Some members of the Negro slum world experiment from time to time with mixed strategies that also incorporate the stable working-class model of the good American life, but this latter strategy is exceedingly vulnerable to the threats of unemployment or a less than adequate pay check, on the one hand, and the seduction and violence of the slum world around them, on the other.

References

1. This article is based in part on research supported by a grant from the National Institutes of Mental Health, Grant No. MH-09189, "Social and Community Problems in Public Housing Areas." Many of the ideas presented stem from discussion with the senior members of the Pruitt-Igoe research staff—Alvin W. Gouldner, David J. Pittman, and Jules Henry—and with the research associates and assistants on the project. I have made particular use of ideas developed in discussions with Boone Hammond, Joyce Ladner, Robert Simpson, David Schulz, and William Yancey. I also wish to acknowledge helpful suggestions and criticisms by Catherine Chilman, Gerald Handel, and Marc J. Swartz. Although this paper is not a formal report of the Pruitt-Igoe research, all of the illustrations of family behavior given in the text are drawn from interviews and observations that are part of that study. The study deals with the residents of the Pruitt-Igoe housing projects in St. Louis. Some 10,000 people live in these projects which comprise forty-three eleven-story buildings near the downtown area of St. Louis. Over half of the households have female heads, and for over half of the households the principal income comes from public assistance of one kind or another. The research has been in the field for a little over two years. It is a broad community study which thus far has relied principally on methods of participant observation and open-ended interviewing. Data on families come from repeated interviews and observations with a small group of families. The field workers are identified as graduate students at Washington University who have no connection with the housing authority or other officials, but are simply interested in learning about how families in the project live. This very intensive study of families yields a wealth of information (over 10,000 pages of interview and observation reports) which obviously cannot be analyzed within

the limits of one article. In this article I have limited myself to outlining a typical family stage sequence and discussing some of the psychosocial implications of growing up in families characterized by this sequence. In addition, I have tried to limit myself to findings which other literature on Negro family life suggests are not limited to the residents of the housing projects we are studying.

2. St. Clair Drake, "The Social and Economic Status of the Negro in the United States," *Daedalus* (Fall, 1965), p. 772.

3. E. Franklin Frazier, *The Negro Family in the United States* (Chicago, 1939), p. 487.

4. Norman Mailer, "The White Negro" (City Light Books, San Francisco, Calif., 1957); and Leslie Fiedler, *Waiting For The End* (New York, 1964), pp. 118–137.

5. See Alvin W. Gouldner, "Reciprocity and Autonomy in Functional Theory," in Llewellyn Gross (ed.), *Symposium of Sociological Theory* (Evanston, Ill., 1958), for a discussion of functional autonomy and dependence of structural elements in social systems. We are suggesting here that lower-class groups have a relatively high degree of functional autonomy *vis à vis* the total social system because that system does little to meet their needs. In general the fewer the rewards a society offers members of a particular group in the society, the more autonomous will that group prove to be with reference to the norms of the society. Only by constructing an elaborate repressive machinery, as in concentration camps, can the effect be otherwise.

6. For example, the lead sentence in a *St. Louis Post Dispatch* article of July 20, 1965, begins "A White House study group is laying the ground work for an attempt to better the structure of the Negro family."

7. See Kenneth Stampp, *The Peculiar Institution* (New York, 1956); John Hope Franklin, *From Slavery to Freedom* (New York, 1956); Frank Tannenbaum, *Slave and Citizen* (New York, 1946); E. Franklin Frazier, *op. cit.;* and Melville J. Herskovits, *The Myth of the Negro Past* (New York, 1941).

8. See Raymond T. Smith, *The Negro Family in British Guiana* (New York, 1956); J. Mayone Stycos and Kurt W. Back, *The Control of Human Fertility in Jamaica* (Ithaca, N. Y., 1964); F. M. Henriques, *Family and Colour in Jamaica* (London, 1953); Judith Blake, *Family Structure in Jamaica* (Glencoe, Ill., 1961); and Raymond T. Smith, "Culture and Social Structure in The Caribbean," *Comparative Studies in Society and History,* Vol. VI (The Hague, The Netherlands, October 1963), pp. 24–46. For a broader comparative discussion of the matrifocal family see Peter Kunstadter, "A Survey of the Consanguine or Matrifocal Family," *American Anthropologist,* Vol. 65, No. 1 (February 1963), pp. 55–56; and Ruth M. Boyer, "The Matrifocal Family Among the Mescalero: Additional Data," *American Anthropologist,* Vol. 66, No. 3 (June 1964), pp. 593–602.

9. Paul C. Glick, *American Families* (New York, 1957), pp. 133 ff.

10. For discussions of white lower-class families, see Lee Rainwater, Richard P. Coleman, and Gerald Handel, *Workingman's Wife* (New York, 1959); Lee Rainwater, *Family Design* (Chicago, 1964); Herbert Gans, *The Urban Villagers* (New York, 1962); Albert K. Cohen and Harold M. Hodges, "Characteristics of the Lower-Blue-Collar Class," *Social Problems,* Vol. 10, No. 4 (Spring 1963), pp. 303–334; S. M. Miller, "The American Lower Classes: A Typological Approach," in Arthur B. Shostak and William Gomberg, *Blue Collar World* (Englewood Cliffs, N. J., 1964); and Mirra Komarovsky, *Blue Collar Marriage* (New York, 1964). Discussions of Negro slum life can be found in St. Clair Drake and Horace R. Cayton, *Black Metropolis* (New York, 1962), and Kenneth B. Clark, *Dark Ghetto* (New York, 1965); and of Negro community life in small-town and rural settings in Allison Davis, Burleigh B. Gardner, and Mary Gardner, *Deep South* (Chicago, 1944), and Hylan Lewis, *Blackways of Kent* (Chapel Hill, N. C., 1955).

11. For general discussions of the extent to which lower-class people hold the values of the larger society, see Albert K. Cohen, *Delinquent Boys* (New York, 1955); Hyman Rodman, "The Lower Class Value Stretch," *Social Forces,* Vol. 42, No. 2

(December 1963), pp. 205 ff; and William L. Yancey, "The Culture of Poverty: Not So Much Parsimony," unpublished manuscript, Social Science Institute, Washington University.

12. James F. Short, Jr., and Fred L. Strodtbeck, *Group Process and Gang Delinquency* (Chicago, 1965), p. 114. Chapter V (pages 102–115) of this book contains a very useful discussion of differences between white and Negro lower-class communities.

13. Discussions of white lower-class attitudes toward sex may be found in Arnold W. Green, "The Cult of Personality and Sexual Relations," *Psychiatry*, Vol. 4 (1941), pp. 343–348; William F. Whyte, "A Slum Sex Code," *American Journal of Sociology*, Vol. 49, No. 1 (July 1943), pp. 24–31; and Lee Rainwater, "Marital Sexuality in Four Cultures of Poverty," *Journal of Marriage and the Family*, Vol. 26, No. 4 (November 1964), pp. 457–466.

14. See Boone Hammond, "The Contest System: A Survival Technique," Master's Honors paper, Washington University, 1965. See also Ira L. Reiss, "Premarital Sexual Permissiveness Among Negroes and Whites," *American Sociological Review*, Vol. 29, No. 5 (October 1964), pp. 688–698.

15. See the discussion of aleatory processes leading to premarital fatherhood in Short and Strodtbeck, *op. cit.*, pp. 44–45.

16. Rainwater, *And the Poor Get Children, op. cit.*, pp. 61–63. See also, Carlfred B. Broderick, "Social Heterosexual Development Among Urban Negroes and Whites," *Journal of Marriage and the Family*, Vol. 27 (May 1965), pp. 200–212. Broderick finds that although white boys and girls, and Negro girls become more interested in marriage as they get older, Negro boys become *less* interested in late adolescence than they were as preadolescents.

17. Walter Miller, "The Corner Gang Boys Get Married," *Trans-action*, Vol. 1, No. 1 (November 1963), pp. 10–12.

18. Rainwater, *Family Design, op. cit.*, pp. 28–60.

19. Yancey, *op. cit.* The effects of unemployment on the family have been discussed by E. Wright Bakke, *Citizens Without Work* (New Haven, Conn., 1940); Mirra Komarovsky, *The Unemployed Man and His Family* (New York, 1960); and Earl L. Koos, *Families in Trouble* (New York, 1946). What seems distinctive to the Negro slum culture is the short time lapse between the husband's loss of a job and his wife's considering him superfluous.

20. See particularly Komarovsky's discussion of "barriers to marital communications" (Chapter 7) and "confidants outside of marriage" (Chapter 9), in *Blue Collar Marriage, op. cit.*

21. Rainwater, *Family Design, op. cit.*, pp. 305–308.

22. For a discussion of the relationship between Black Nationalist ideology and the Negro struggle to achieve a sense of valid personal identity, see Howard Brotz, *The Black Jews of Harlem* (New York, 1963), and E. U. Essien-Udom, *Black Nationalism: A Search for Identity in America* (Chicago, 1962).

23. Rainwater, Coleman, and Handel, *op. cit.*, pp. 88–102.

24. Cf. Michael Schwartz and George Henderson, "The Culture of Unemployment: Some Notes on Negro Children," in Schostak and Gomberg, *op. cit.*

25. Daniel Patrick Moynihan, "Employment, Income, and the Ordeal of the Negro Family," *Daedalus* (Fall 1965), pp. 760–61.

26. Talcott Parsons concludes his discussion of child socialization, the development of an "internalized family system" and internalized role differentiation by observing, "The internalization of the family collectivity as an object and its value should not be lost sight of. This is crucial with respect to . . . the assumption of representative roles outside the family on behalf of it. Here it is the child's family membership which is decisive, and thus his acting in a role in terms of its values for 'such as he.'" Talcott Parsons and Robert F. Bales, *Family, Socialization and Interaction Process* (Glencoe, Ill., 1955), p. 113.

27. Erik H. Erikson, "Identity and the Life Cycle," *Psychological Issues,* Vol. 1, No. 1 (1959).

28. For discussion of the dynamics of the individual's *announcements* and the society's *placements* in the formation of identity, see Gregory Stone, "Appearance and the Self," in Arnold Rose, *Human Behavior in Social Process* (Boston, 1962), pp. 86–118.

29. The importance of identity for social behavior is discussed in detail in Ward Goodenough, *Cooperation and Change* (New York, 1963), pp. 176–251, and in Lee Rainwater, "Work and Identity in the Lower Class," in Sam H. Warner, Jr., *Planning for the Quality of Urban Life* (Cambridge, Mass., forthcoming). The images of self and of other family members is a crucial variable in Hess and Handel's psychosocial analysis of family life; see Robert D. Hess and Gerald Handel, *Family Worlds* (Chicago, 1959), especially pp. 6–11.

30. See the discussion of "masking" and "unmasking" in relation to disorganization and re-equilibration in families by John P. Spiegel, "The Resolution of Role Conflict within the Family," in Norman W. Bell and Ezra F. Vogel, *A Modern Introduction to the Family* (Glencoe, Ill., 1960), pp. 375–377.

31. See the discussion of self-identity and self-esteem in Thomas F. Pettigrew, *A Profile of the Negro American* (Princeton, N. J., 1964), pp. 6–11.

32. Rainwater, Coleman, and Handel, *op. cit.,* pp. 44–51. See also the discussion of the greater level of "anomie" and mistrust among lower-class people in Ephraim Mizruchi, *Success and Opportunity* (New York, 1954). Unpublished research by the author indicates that for one urban lower-class sample (Chicago) Negroes scored about 50 per cent higher on Srole's anomie scale than did comparable whites.

33. For a discussion of the child's propensity from a very early age for speculation and developing explanations, see William V. Silverberg, *Childhood Experience and Personal Destiny* (New York, 1953), pp. 81 ff.

34. See Ralph Ellison's autobiographical descriptions of growing up in Oklahoma City in his *Shadow and Act* (New York, 1964). The quotations at the beginning of this article are taken from pages 315 and 112 of this book.

35. Rainwater, "Work and Identity in the Lower Class," *op. cit.*

36. *Ibid.*

37. Short and Strodtbeck see violent behavior in juvenile gangs as a kind of last resort strategy in situations where the actor feels he has no other choice. See Short and Strodtbeck, *op. cit.,* pp. 248–264.

38. Wiltse speaks of a "pseudo depression syndrome" as characteristic of many AFDC mothers. Kermit T. Wiltse, "Orthopsychiatric Programs for Socially Deprived Groups," *American Journal of Orthopsychiatry,* Vol. 33, No. 5 (October 1963), pp. 806–813.

39. Walter B. Miller, "Lower Class Culture as a Generating Milieu of Gang Delinquency," *Journal of Social Issues,* Vol. 14, No. 3 (1958), pp. 5–19.

40. This line of argument concerning the employment problems of Negroes, and poverty war strategy more generally, is developed with great cogency by James Tobin, "On Improving the Economic Status of the Negro," *Daedalus* (Fall 1965), and previously by Gunnar Myrdal, in his *Challenge to Affluence* (New York, 1963), and Orville R. Gursslin and Jack L. Roach, in their "Some Issues in Training the Employed," *Social Problems,* Vol. 12, No. 1 (Summer 1964), pp. 68–77.

41. See Chapter 6 (pages 111–153) of Kenneth Clark, *op cit.,* for a discussion of the destructive effects of ghetto schools on their students.

42. See the discussion of "moral danger" in Lee Rainwater, "Fear and the House-as-Haven in the Lower Class," *Journal of the American Institute of Planners,* February 1966.

12.   The Overlooked Positives of Disadvantaged Groups

FRANK RIESSMAN

I have been interested in the problems of lower socioeconomic groups for about fifteen years, during most of which time there has been a lack of concern for the educational problems of children from low-income families. In the last five years, however, this attitude has changed markedly. There is now an enormous interest in this problem by practitioners and academic people. I think we are on the point of a major breakthrough in terms of dealing with this question.

After appraising a good deal of the recent work that has been done on the education of disadvantaged children, I feel that there is a considerable agreement regarding many of the recommendations for dealing with the problem, although there are some very different emphases. What is missing, however, is a theoretic rationale to give meaning and direction to the action suggestions. I should like to attempt to provide the beginnings of such a rationale.

I think that a basic theoretic approach here has to be based on the culture of lower socioeconomic groups

Reprinted from the *Journal of Negro Education*, Vol. 33 (Summer 1964), pp. 225–231, by permission of the publisher and author.

and more particularly the elements of strength, the positives in this culture. The terms "deprived," "handicapped," "underprivileged," "disadvantaged," unfortunately emphasize environmental limitations and ignore the positive efforts of low-income individuals to cope with their environment. Most approaches concerned with educating the disadvantaged child either overlook the positives entirely or merely mention in passing that there are positive features in the culture of low socioeconomic groups, that middle-class groups might learn from, but they do not spell out what these strengths are, and they build educational programs almost exclusively around the weaknesses or deficits.

I want to call attention to the positive features in the culture and the psychology of low income individuals. In particular, I should like to look at the cognitive style, the mental style or way of thinking characteristics of these people. One major dimension of this style is slowness.

SLOW VS. DULL

Most disadvantaged children are relatively slow in performing intellectual tasks. This slowness is an important feature of their mental style and it needs to be carefully evaluated. In considering the question of the slowness of the deprived child, we would do well to recognize that in our culture there has probably been far too much emphasis on speed. We reward speed. We think of the fast child as the smart child and the slow child as the dull child. I think this is a basically false idea. I think there are many weaknesses in speed and many strengths in slowness.

The teacher can be motivated to develop techniques for rewarding slow pupils if she has an appreciation of some of the positive attributes of a slow style of learning. The teacher should know that pupils may be slow for reasons other than because they are stupid.

A pupil may be slow because he is extremely careful, meticulous, or cautious. He may be slow because he refuses to generalize easily. He may be slow because he cannot understand a concept unless he does something physically, for example, with his hands, in connection with the idea he is trying to grasp.

The disadvantaged child is typically a physical learner and the physical learner is generally a slower learner. Incidentally, the physical style of learning is another important characteristic of the deprived individual and it, too, has many positive features hitherto overlooked.

A child may be slow because he learns in what I have called a one-track way. That is, he persists in one line of thought and is not flexible or broad. He does not easily adopt other frames of reference, such as the teachers, and consequently he may appear slow and dull.

Very often this single-minded individual has considerable creative potential, much of which goes unrealized

because of lack of reinforcement in the educational system.

Analysis of the many reasons for slowness leads to the conclusion that slowness should not be equated with stupidity. In fact, there is no reason to assume that there are not a great many slow, gifted children.

The school in general does not pay too much attention to the slow gifted child but rather is alert to discover fast gifted children. Excellence comes in many packages and we must begin to search for it among the slow learners as well as among the faster individuals.

My own understanding of some of the merits of the slow style came through teaching at Bard College, where there is an enrollment of about 350 students. There I had the opportunity of getting to know quite well about 40 students over a period of four years. I could really see what happened to them during this time. Very often the students I thought were slow and dull in their freshman year achieved a great deal by the time they became seniors. These are not the over-all bright people who are typically selected by colleges, but in some area, in a one-track way, these students did some marvelous creative work. It was too outstanding to be ignored. I discovered in talking with students that most of them had spent five or six years in order to complete college. They had failed courses and made them up in summer school. Some had dropped out of college for a period of time and taken courses in night school. These students are slow learners, often one-track learners, but very persistent about something when they develop an interest in it. They have a fear of being overpowered by teachers in situations where they do not accept the teacher's point of view, but they stick to their own particular way of seeing the problem. They do not have a fast pace, they do not catch on quickly, and they very often fail subjects.

At the present time, when there is a measure of public excitement for reducing the four-year college to three years, I would submit that many potentially excellent students need a five or six year span to complete a college education.

The assumption that the slow pupil is not bright functions, I think, as a self-fulfilling prophecy. If the teachers act toward these pupils as if they were dull, the pupils will frequently come to function in this way. Of course, there are pupils who are very well developed at an early age and no teacher can stop them. But in the average development of the young person, even at the college level, there is need for reinforcement. The teacher must pick up what he says, appeal to him, and pitch examples to him. Typically this does not occur with the slow child. I find in examining my own classroom teaching that I easily fall into the habit of rewarding pupils whose faces light up when I talk, who are quick to respond to me, and I respond back to them. The things they say in class become absorbed in the repertoire of what I say. I remember what they say and I use it in providing examples, etc. I do not pick up and select the slower pupil and I do not respond to him. He has to make it on his own.

In the teacher training program, future teachers should be taught to guard against the almost unconscious and automatic tendency of the teacher to respond to the pupil who responds to him.

HIDDEN VERBAL ABILITY

A great deal has been said about the language or verbal deficit supposedly characteristic of disadvantaged children. Everybody in the school system, at one time or another, has heard that these children are inarticulate, nonverbal, etc. But is not this too simple a generalization? Are not these children quite verbal in out-of-school situations? For example, that the educationally deprived child can be quite articulate in conversation with his peers is well illustrated by the whole language developed by urban Negro groups, some of which is absorbed into the main culture via the Beatnick and the musician, if you dig what I mean.

Many questions about the verbal potential of disadvantaged children must be answered by research. Under what conditions are they verbal? What kind of stimuli do they respond to verbally? With whom are they verbal? What do they talk about? What parts of speech do they use? Martin Deutsch of New York Medical School is doing some very significant research trying to specify these factors and I surveyed some of his findings in my book, *The Culturally Deprived Child*. I think Deutsch is getting at some very interesting things. One technique he uses is a clown that lights up when the children say something. "Inarticulate" children can be very verbal and expressive in this situation.

Disadvantaged children are often surprisingly articulate in role-playing situations. One day when I was with a group of these youngsters, sometimes mistaken for a "gang," I asked them, "Why are you sore at the teachers?" Even though I was on good terms with them, I could not get much of a response. Most of them answered in highly abbreviated sentences. However, after I held a role-playing session in which some of the youngsters acted out the part of the teachers while others acted out the parts of the pupils, these "inarticulate" youngsters changed sharply. Within a half-hour they were bubbling over with very verbal and very sensitive answers to the questions I had asked earlier. They were telling me about the expressions on the teachers' faces that they did not like. They reported that they knew the minute they entered the room that the teacher did not like them and that she did not think they were going to do well in school. Their analyses were specific and remarkably verbal.

However, the quality of language employed has its limitations and I think herein lies the deficit. As Basil Bernstein indicates, the difference is between formal language and public language, between a language in a written book and the informal, everyday language. There is no question in my mind that there is a deficit in formal language. Since this deficit is fairly clear, the question might be asked, why make such an issue of the positive verbal ability to these children.

The reason is that it is easy to believe, that too many people have come to believe, that this formal deficit in language means that deprived people are characteristically nonverbal.

On the other hand, if the schools have the idea that these pupils are basically very good verbally, teachers might approach them in a different manner. Teachers might look for additional techniques to bring out the verbal facility. They might abandon the prediction that deprived children will not go very far in the education system and predict instead that they can go very far indeed because they have very good ability at the verbal level. In other words, an awareness of the positive verbal ability—not merely potential—will lead to demanding more of the disadvantaged child and expecting more of him.

EDUCATION VS. THE SCHOOL

There is a good deal of evidence that deprived children and their parents have a much more positive attitude toward education than is generally believed. One factor that obscures the recognition of this attitude is that although deprived individuals value education, they dislike the school. They are alienated from the school and they resent the teachers. For the sake of clarity, their attitude toward education and toward the school must be considered separately.

In a survey conducted a few years ago, people were asked, "What did you miss most in life that you would like your children to have?" Over 70 per cent of the lower, socioeconomic groups answered, "Education." The answer was supplied by the respondents, not checked on a list. They could have answered "money," "happiness," "health," or a number of things. And I think this is quite significant. Middle-class people answer "education" less frequently because they had an education and do not miss it as much.

A nationwide poll conducted by Roper after World War II asked, "If you had a son or daughter graduating from high school, would you prefer to have him or her go on to college, do something else, wouldn't care?" The affirmative response to the college choice was given by 68 per cent of the "poor," and 91 per cent for the more prosperous. The difference is significant; but 68 per cent of the poorer people is a large, absolute figure and indicates that a large number of these people are interested in a college education for their children.

Why then do these people who have a positive attitude toward education hold a negative attitude toward the school? These youngsters and their parents recognize that they are second-class citizens in the school and they are angry about it. From the classroom to the PTA they discover that the school does not like them, does not respond to them, does not appreciate their culture, and does not think they can learn.

Furthermore, these children and their parents want education for different reasons than those presented by the school. They do not easily accept the ideas of expressing yourself, developing yourself, or knowledge for its own sake. They want education much more for vocational ends. But underneath there is a very positive attitude toward education and I think this is predominant in the lower socioeconomic Negro groups. In the Higher Horizons program in New York City the parents have participated eagerly once they have seen that the school system is concerned about their children. One of the tremendously positive features about this program and the Great Cities programs is the concern for disadvantaged children and the interest in them. This the deprived have not experienced before, and even if the programs did nothing else, I believe that the parents and the children would be responsive and would become involved in the school because of the demonstrated concern for them.

SOME WEAKNESSES

A basic weakness of deprived youngsters that the school can deal with is the problem of "know-how." Included here is the academic "know-how" of the school culture as well as the "know-how" of the middle class generally: Knowing how to get a job, how to appear for an interview, how to fill out a form, how to take tests, how to answer questions, and how to listen.

The last is of particular importance. The whole style of learning of the deprived is not geared to respond to oral or written stimuli. These children respond much more readily to visual kinesthetic signals. We should remodel the schools to suit the styles and meet the needs of these children. But no matter how much we change the school to suit their needs, we nevertheless have to change these children in certain ways; namely, reading, formal language, test taking, and general "know-how."

These weaknesses represent deficiencies in skills and techniques. However, there is one basic limitation at the value level, namely the anti-intellectual attitudes of deprived groups. It is the only value of lower socio economic groups which I would fight in the school. I want to make it very clear that I am very much opposed to the school spending a lot of time teaching values to these kids. I am much more concerned—and in this I am traditional—that the schools impart skills, techniques, and knowledge rather than training the disadvantaged to become good middle-class children.

However, I think there is one area indigenous to the school which has to be fought out at some point with these youngsters; that is, their attitude toward intellectuals, toward knowledge for its own sake, and similar issues.

These children and their parents are pretty much anti-intellectual at all levels. They do not like "eggheads." They think talk is a lot of bull. I would consciously oppose this attitude in the school. I would make the issue explicit. There would be nothing subtle or covert about it. I would at some point state clearly that on this question the school does not agree with them and is prepared to argue about the views they hold.

OTHER POSITIVE DIMENSIONS

In my book, *The Culturally Deprived Child,* and in various speeches, I have elaborated more fully on these and other positive dimensions of the culture and style of educationally deprived people. A brief list would include the following: cooperativeness and mutual aid that mark the extended family; the avoidance of the strain accompanying competitiveness and individualism; the equalitarianism, in informality and humor; the freedom from self-blame and parental overprotection; the children's enjoyment of each other's company and lessened sibling rivalry, the security found in the extended family and a traditional outlook; the enjoyment of music, games, sports, and cards; the ability to express anger; the freedom from being word-bound; an externally oriented rather than an introspective outlook; a spatial rather than temporal perspective; an expressive orientation in contrast to an instrumental one; content-centered not a form-centered mental style; a problem-centered rather than an abstract-centered approach; and finally, the use of physical and visual style in learning.

SUMMARY AND IMPLICATIONS

I have attempted to reinterpret some of the supposedly negative aspects (e.g., slowness) that characterize the cognitive style of disadvantaged individuals. I have given particular attention to the untapped verbal ability of these individuals and have indicated the basic weaknesses of the disadvantaged child that the school must overcome, such as the lack of school know-how, anti-intellectualism, and limited experience with formal language. Others which should be noted here are poor auditory attention, poor time perspective, inefficient test-taking skills, and limited reading ability.

The school must recognize these deficiencies and work assiduously to combat them. They are by no means irreversible, but even more important, because neglected, the positive elements in the culture and style of lower socioeconomic groups should become the guide lines for new school programs and new educational techniques for teaching these children.

There are a number of reasons why it is important to emphasize the positive:

1. It will encourage the school to develop approaches and techniques, including possibly special teaching machines, appropriate for the cognitive style of deprived children.

2. It will enable children of low income backgrounds to be educated without middle-classifying them.

3. It will stimulate teachers to aim high, to expect more, and work for more from these youngsters. Thus, it will constrain against patronization and condescension, and determinate, double-track systems where the deprived child never arrives on the main track.

4. It will function against the current tendency of overemphasizing both vocational, nonacademic education for children of low-income background.

5. It will provide an exciting challenge for teachers if they realize that they need not simply aim to "bring these children up to grade level," but rather can actually develop new kinds of creativity.

6. It will make the school far more pluralistic and democratic because different cultures and styles will exist and interact side by side. Thus, each can learn from the other and the empty phrase that the teacher has much to learn from deprived children will take on real meaning. General cultural interaction between equal cultures can become the hallmark of the school.

7. It will enable the teacher to see that when techniques, such as role-playing and visual aids, are used with deprived children, it is because these techniques are useful for eliciting the special cognitive style and creative po-

tential of these children. All too often these techniques have been employed with the implicit assumption that they are useful with children who have inadequate learning ability.

8. It will lead to real appreciation of slowness, one-track learning, and physical learning as potential strengths which require careful nurturing. The teacher will have to receive special training in how to respond to these styles, how to listen carefully to the one-track person, how to reward the slow learner, etc. Special classes for slow learners will not culminate in the removal of these youngsters from the mainstream of the educational process on a permanent second track, and longer periods of time in school and college can be planned for these students without invidious connotations.

Dr. Irving Taylor, who has been concerned with various types of creativity in our American society, has observed that the mental style of the socially and economically disadvantaged learners resembles the mental style of one type of highly creative persons. Our schools should provide for the development of these unique, untapped national sources of creativity.

Part II: PROBLEMS FACING DISADVANTAGED YOUTH IN THE SCHOOLS

Traditionally, schools in American society have been concerned with the development and perpetuation of middle-class values and attitudes. If the reader takes a moment to review his educational experiences in the public schools he will surely recall the behaviors of his teachers in their efforts to implement the curriculum, the negative and positive sanctions they used to motivate him to succeed, and the nature of the content considered requisite for his survival in his future world. He will then understand the middle-class approach to a way of life.

Students of middle-class origins or from families ascribing to middle-class status travel in our society through the public school system with few, if any, major problems of adjustment. However, the child who is a stranger to the behaviors and values of the middle class finds himself in the position of an "alien" in the schools. The chief reason for this is because the behavior patterns manifested by disadvantaged children do not parallel those acceptable to our public schools. In far too many cases, children who suffer the disadvantages of belonging to a subculture experience a phenomenon known as "culture clash."

The disastrous effects of the "culture clash" begin for the disadvantaged children immediately upon entering into the cultural milieu of the middle-class-oriented public school. Many teachers, unaware of the differences between the life styles of the disadvantaged and those promoted by the schools, embark upon a process of unconscious discrimination. They plan a curriculum that rests on the assumption that all of the children have had a similar range of experiences in the family, neighborhood, and community. From the readings in Part I of this book, one cannot fail to be impressed with some of the differences in life styles which exist among children representing several subcultures. Ulibari explores the extent of teacher awareness of these differences in the initial article in Part II.

A more intimate look at the interaction between members of two cultures living on our soil is presented by Wax and Thomas. Their discussion of the cultural barriers to effective communication illustrates the problem encountered in the classroom by the teacher and the child when each of them adheres to a different set of cultural pressures.

Perhaps the greatest problem experienced in our schools by the educationally disadvantaged child is that of intellectual retardation. Reared in an environment that lacks many of the books, magazines, toys, and other objects found in the more advantaged homes, he has not had the opportunity to acquire a foundation of the basic concepts and skills which teachers take for granted in their classroom instruction.[1] The lack of cognitive readiness among the average educationally disadvantaged students quickly forces them into the "slow" category of students. Ausubel and Klineberg comment on the effects of environment on the disadvantaged individuals' intellectual achievement.

The disadvantaged child's out-of-school environment, in addition to limiting his cognitive development, penalizes him in his opportunities to develop language skills. Coming frequently from a family that is nonverbal, he has slight opportunity to engage in conversations involving the lengthy sentences heard in middle-class homes. The monosyllabic nature of conversations occurring in his exchanges with parents, siblings, and others in his environment seriously restricts his ability to communicate with teachers in the public schools. Lengthy sentences spoken by the teacher confuse and frustrate him. Consequently, we find him inattentive and daydreaming—or engaging in antisocial behavior—during those portions of the day when his teacher is involved in the various verbal acts of explaining, questioning, and advising.

When he speaks to the teacher, he is urged to "use better English," for his teacher finds it difficult to listen to—and understand—the monosyllabic nature of his speech mixed with those metaphors, syntactical irregularities, and "jargon" common among his subculture.

The interesting research by Bernstein describing the relationship between social class and linguistic codes lends support to the notion that the disadvantaged student will suffer from unconscious or conscious discrimination by the school. Use by the educationally deprived individual of a linguistic code different from the one promoted by the school has more than once prompted teachers to say, with an air of resignation, "They just don't understand."

The lower-class child, on the other hand, using a language pattern that is functional for his communcation needs in his out-of-school environment, may react to the school's pressures to adopt a new pattern in a number of ways. Two of the most common behaviors are withdrawal from classroom activities or striking out to "get back at the teacher." Cohn suggests the type of interaction that may develop if the teacher is not aware of the functional aspects of lower-class children's language patterns.

The educational deprivation of the disadvantaged child also becomes apparent in other areas of the curriculum. In a study of the arithmetic concepts of kindergarten children drawn from different socioeconomic areas, Montagne dramatizes the effect of one's environment upon one's ability to form mathematical concepts. Curry's study of scholastic achievement of sixth-grade students focuses attention on the relationships existing between social and economic deprivation and school achievement.

Confronted by the constancy of failure brought about by the traditional school's philosophy of instruction and its curriculum content, many children from minority subcultures begin to develop feelings of alienation. Goff's study illustrates the feeling of inadequacy experienced by the lower-class child in relation to the curriculum. The decrease in self-confidence accompanying increasing age suggests that the school probably provides few opportunities for nurturing the ego of the child from the educationally deprived home. As we have noted in the previous descriptions of the disadvantaged child's home life, few opportunities are provided for him to rebuild his feeling of confidence in relation to the school's curriculum. In fact, he probably enters the school with a negative self-concept.

"Possession of a stunted, warped self-concept is perhaps the most stubborn and persistent obstacle to self-fulfillment for the minority group youngster. It is a consequence of being socialized into a stigmatized second class citizen status, of being unquestioningly ascribed a variety of inadequacies and inferiorities so persistently that one comes to conceive of himself as being an inadequate and second-class order of humanity. . . . Belief in their own inferiority is frequently shared by parents and by other adult fellow minority group members, since they have themselves been socialized to this conception in this country, and since, furthermore, they have not encountered anything which would lead them seriously to question this stigmatization.[2]

Parents of disadvantaged children, many of whom are school failures themselves, look upon the school with suspicion and distrust. For many of them, the school represents a major symbol of failure.[3] Although some of the adults in the families may have graduated from secondary schools, the examples that this training has "paid off" are too few. Even with public school training, they are prevented by economic and social barriers from experiencing the "good life." Trying unsuccessfully to overcome these roadblocks, the disadvantaged often become disillusioned with many of our social institutions—including the schools. This disillusionment pervades the environment of the disadvantaged child. As a consequence, he is susceptible to the apathy that arises from this condition, just as a child in any cultural group is susceptible to the forces that are part of his cultural group.

The apathy engendered by constant failure is interpreted as a lack of motivation by the teacher. The deprived child's unwillingness to participate in activities that do no offer immediate or foreseeable gratifications—his orientation to the present—is viewed by the teacher as further evidence that "he does not want to amount to anything in life." Conditioned by the socialization process that takes place in his home and neighborhood, the child is suspicious of talk, books, and other phenomena associated with the classroom. His inability to speak, read, and deal with the abstractions woven into the standard curriculum of the school reinforces his feelings, and those of the teacher, that he is intellectually inferior.

The problem of acculturation as experienced by the Indian and the Puerto Rican introduces still another barrier to the successful development of a self-concept. The articles by Elam and Zintz should help the prospective or in-service teacher to acquire an increased sensitivity to additional factors that may influence the development of a positive self-concept among a segment of the disadvantaged.

In the instance of both the Puerto Rican, newly transplanted from a rural to an urban area, and the Indian, recently moved from a conservative Indian community to one of our cities, there are major cultural divergencies to be resolved. The Indian's time-honored tradition of living in harmony with nature, for example, clashes sharply with the school's concern for training individuals to gain mastery over nature. Puerto Rican girls may be faced with serious problems of adjustment when, after being taught at home to be compliant, are encouraged by teachers to be outgoing and competitive.

In the final article, Wax describes some of the factors operating in withdrawal from school. In her study, the reader will note that more frequently than school personnel would like to believe, the dropout considers himself to be a "pushout." Her discussion of the process that alienates the Oglala Sioux boy from the schools warns of the inadequacies the schools must overcome if they are to be an effective social institution for representatives of minority subcultures.

References

1. An illuminating description of the variables existing in the homes of the educationally disadvantaged is found in Charles E. Silterman, "Give Slum Children A Chance, A Radical Proposal, *Harper's*, **228**, 37–42 (May 1964).
2. Hobart, Charles E., "Underachievement Among Minority Group Students: An Analysis and a Proposal," *Phylon*, **24**, No. 2, 184–185 (Summer, 1963).
3. This topic is developed further in Gordon P. Liddle and Robert E. Rockwell, "The Role of Parents and Family Life," *Journal of Negro Education*, **33**, 311–317 (1964 Yearbook).

13. Teacher Awareness of Sociocultural Differences in Multicultural Classrooms

HORACIO ULIBARRI

ABSTRACT. Three levels of sensitivity are found among the teachers of Anglo-American, Spanish-American, and Indian children in New Mexico toward the sociocultural differences of these ethnic groups: a tremendous amount of awareness, awareness but not real sensitivity to the differences, and no awareness. The greatest awareness was shown toward differences in oral proficiency; and the least, toward differences in psychological needs, civic responsibility, and economic efficiency.

The public schools in the United States were created to serve all the children of all the people in order that the youth might more ably participate in American society. With the acceptance of the principle of educating the whole child, the functions of the schools have been greatly expanded. Ideally, all these services are primarily aimed to help the individual child develop to his full potential. The practical application, however, is different. Upon closer analysis, one may find

Reprinted from *Sociology and Social Research*, Vol. 45 (October 1960), pp. 49–55, by permission of the publisher and author. This article is a condensation of a doctoral dissertation accepted in August 1959, at New Mexico Highlands University.

great discrepancies in the educational opportunities available to the children of different social and cultural backgrounds.

Among the variables jeopardizing equalized educational opportunity are the social-cultural backgrounds of the students. The schools have been complacent to a large degree in presenting only a small aspect of the American culture, namely, the middle-class values and orientations, as the sum total of the curricula in the schools.[1] The teachers themselves, generally, have a middle-class orientation.[2] These two factors, the middle-class orientation of the curriculum and the middle-class life-style of the teachers, place students of lower-class and/or different ethnic backgrounds at a disadvantage when competing with middle-class students.[3]

The problem of equalizing educational opportunity may be resolved to the extent that teachers have empathy for, and insight into, classroom behavior and to the extent that they provide a curriculum that satisfies the needs of students from all sociocultural backgrounds.

In New Mexico, the problem is greatly accentuated because of the large number of children coming from

Indian and Spanish cultural backgrounds. These minority groups, namely, the Navajo, Apache, and Pueblo Indians, and the Spanish-Americans, are in a state of transition and moving rapidly toward acculturation and assimilation. The extent of acculturation, however, seems to vary from almost no acculturation to complete acculturation. As with most other minority groups, these minority groups in New Mexico are being assimilated into the lower classes of Anglo Society. Thus, they present some of the same problems that the lower classes present as well as some unique problems of their own. There are a number of children coming from traditional homes who enter school with all cultural orientations of the parents and with no knowledge of the English language. Nor is the problem resolved as the child progresses through school. It seems that the child is able to absorb some of the values promulgated by the school while still retaining, in large measure, the orientations of the traditional culture.

On first observation, this dual participation in both cultures would not seem to constitute a problem. But as the child develops into maturity, he finds himself confronted with orientations and expectations from the home and the school that are often opposing and contradictory. This factor engenders a personality conflict and disorganization in the individual which has expression in more basic behavioral patterns.

Thus, in New Mexico, the teachers need, for maximum effectiveness in their teaching, not only an understanding of child growth and development but also a deep insight into the cultural orientations and value configurations of these groups as they are expressed in traditional and transitional behavioral patterns. This study has attempted to measure the extent to which teachers are aware of sociocultural factors that impinge on the education of children of these minority groups. A major premise of this study was that the ineffectiveness of the public schools in the education of minority groups, such as the Indians and the Spanish-Americans in New Mexico,[4] has been the result in large measure from the failure to consider sufficiently the cultural orientations, the value configurations, and the behavior arising therefrom in the development of the curricula.

A stratified sample of 100 teachers, who were currently teaching Anglo, Spanish-American, and Indian children, was selected for interviewing. The interview schedule was made with the use of a questionnaire that covered the following areas: (1) psychological needs of children in relation to sociocultural differences, (2) cultural orientations as they affected children's classroom behavior, (3) social conditions prevailing among the groups, and (4) educational problems pertinent to the three ethnic groups. Each item had three five-point scales—one for each group—which enabled the subjects to draw comparisons among the three groups. The following is an item from the questionnaire used in the interview.

11. The concept of life-space entails the following three aspects: (1) the physical environment that the child lives in; (2) the artifacts, i.e., the material things that he manipulates; and (3) the persons with whom he interacts.

In your way of thinking, how enriching is the life-space of the following children?

Indian	1 2 3 4 5
Spanish-American	1 2 3 4 5
Anglo	1 2 3 4 5

To encircle "1" on the continuum would indicate that the teacher feels that the life-space is extremely meager and limiting; to encircle "5" would indicate that the teacher believes that the child has a very rich background to experience for understanding concepts taught in school.

Each item was analyzed statistically. The mean for each scale gave a rank to each ethnic group. The standard deviation showed the extent to which teachers agreed in assigning such a rank to each group. The coefficient of concordance [5] indicated the amount of agreement or disagreement among teachers in assigning similar ranks to the three ethnic groups. A high coefficient of concordance indicated a high degree of agreement in assigning similar ranks to the groups. A low coefficient of concordance indicated a low agreement in assigning similar ranks.

When this analysis was completed, the results were compiled in terms of implications for education. This was done because several items had a bearing to several educational areas. Educational areas covered in the analysis were (1) curriculum, (2) language, (3) life-space, (4) motivation and achievement, (5) intergroup relations, and (6) personality disorganization.

CURRICULUM

All the items in the questionnaire had some relationship to the problems in curriculum. The teachers' responses on all items indicated consistent lack of awareness of the effect of sociocultural factors on pupil behavior. Their responses also indicated that some teachers were not in agreement with practices and recommendations advanced by educational theorists.

The general lack of sensitivity on the part of the teachers in the sample indicated that they were not sure of the nature of sociocultural problems presented by these ethnic groups. This lack of awareness points to a strong probability of having a general curriculum for everybody regardless of sociocultural backgrounds. If these teachers follow the general trends in the country, the possibilities are that the curriculum implemented will be geared strongly toward middle-class values.

LANGUAGE DIFFERENCES

One item in the questionnaire considered oral proficiency in the use of the English language among the three groups. The teachers showed marked awareness in indicating that real and wide differences existed among the groups. However, in response to another item, the teachers failed to show that there existed any differences among the three ethnic groups in ability to use the regular textbooks for instruction.

Lack of proficiency in the use of oral English is rather self-evident; and, hence, the sensitivity may be really superficial. This suggests an awareness of an obvious phenomenon without an understanding of the underlying causes or the adapting of methodology because of it. The teachers' responses to the item concerning differences in ability to use regular textbooks seem to confirm this supposition. The results of this item point to the possibility that the same textbook is being used within a grade level regardless of differences in reading abilities of the children.

LIFE-SPACE

Several items attempted to measure teachers' awareness to differences in life-space of the pupil groups considered. One item compared the out-of-school environment of the various groups with the school environment. The teachers appeared to be strongly aware of the effect of the differences of out-of-school environment upon pupils. The teachers indicated that the Anglo pupils have a superior out-of-school environment, that is, one which is closer and more compatible to the school environment than that of the Spanish-Americans or Indians. The teachers, in another item, failed to show sensitivity toward richness or meagerness in the life-space of the three groups. A third item relating to the concept of life-space attempted to interrelate the vicarious experiences in the classroom with the direct firsthand experiences of the children. In this item, the teachers again failed to differentiate, with any assurance, how meaningful the classroom experiences became to the children because of their firsthand experiences out of school. The teachers, in other words, believe that all children get equally meaningful experiences in the classroom despite the differences in direct life experiences of the three groups.

Thus, the last two items tended to negate the responses of the first item in which the teachers showed marked sensitivity to differences in out-of-school environment of the three groups. The contradictions in responses to the three interrelated items indicate that, although teachers may be aware of out-of-school factors as they affect pupils, they apparently do not see any connection of these factors with in-school performance, nor do they know what to do about them.

Lack of sensitivity toward the child's life-space indicates that the curriculum may not be meaningful to a large number of children. When children have only a meager range of direct experiences to which they can relate the vicarious experiences of the classroom, the formulation of meaningful constructs is very difficult. There is a great possibility that teachers will start with what they consider common experiences for all, but which may actually exclude the majority. Thus, teachers

may think their teaching is quite effective. Apparently, teachers are prone to believe that there is a commensurate amount of learning with a given amount of pedagogy.

MOTIVATION AND ACHIEVEMENT

Several items attempted to measure whether teachers are sensitive to factors affecting pupil motivation and achievement. Two items showed that teachers did not differentiate the types of curricula needed to meet the psychological differences of the three ethnic groups. They stated that the same type of curriculum could essentially satisfy the psychological needs of Indian and Spanish-speaking children just as it did for the Anglo children. They further stated that the present curriculum was meeting these needs.

The teachers were somewhat undecided with respect to the true value placed on education by the parents from the three ethnic groups. The teachers failed to recognize any substantial differences in the amount of motivation the children from each ethnic group received from the parents. A large number of teachers thought that there was some difference in the financial means at the disposal of each ethnic group for further education, but many did not. Furthermore, the teachers believed that most of the children, regardless of ethnic origin, were achieving at grade level.

The lack of sensitivity regarding values placed on education by minority groups points to the possibility that teachers may not know obstacles or aids that may thwart or enhance the motivation of children from different ethnic groups for maximum school achievement. Generally, teachers reflect middle-class values. These middle-class values are comprised, in part, of achievement and success, competition, and aggressiveness. The teachers, therefore, use praise, competitiveness, and pressure as some of their motivating practices. Children from different cultural backgrounds may not have internalized any of these values and may not respond to these types of motivation. Hence, if teachers are unaware of cultural differences in the motivation of children, motivational structures such as drive, reward and punishment, and level of aspiration may become very unreal to children with cultural orientations different from those of middle-class society.

INTERGROUP RELATIONS

Two items considered intergroup relations among the different ethnic groups. In one item, the teachers agreed very strongly that the children were practicing school-taught concepts of citizenship in their out-of-school life. In another item, the teachers agreed that the three groups, that is, the Indian, the Spanish-American, and the Anglo, were interacting with a minimum of tension and intergroup conflict.

The possible outcome of unawareness regarding problems of intergroup relationships is that the intergroup cleavages will remain indefinitely and will, perhaps, become more rigid. In effect, instead of helping the situation, the schools will be perpetuating the minority status of the Indian and Spanish-American. The need exists for orientation of teachers concerning majority-minority human relationship problems as well as to find ways and means of establishing better relations among the groups. This is imperative if the groups acculturating through the educational process are not going to be denied the rights and privileges that the school teaches them to appreciate and desire.

PERSONALITY DISORGANIZATION

An attempt was made to measure teachers' sensitivity toward differences in satisfying the psychological needs of the children from the three ethnic groups. These items have a relationship to personality disorganization of minority group members.

The teachers very strongly agreed that the psychological needs of all the children in school could be met within a singular curricular design. Moreover, the teachers strongly indicated that the school was essentially meeting the psychological needs of the three ethnic groups equally well.

The outcome of these items may indicate that teachers are not exactly sure of the nature of psychological needs or of the process of personality development. How the total sociocultural background defines the psychological needs of each child, and to a great extent prescribes the manner in which these needs should be met, incorporates an area of knowledge drawn from anthropology, sociology, and psychology that teachers need to know in much more detail than they appear to know at present.

Similarly, as evidenced from the responses, teachers need an understanding of the concept of marginality, the process of disassociation, and of personal disorganization. Without these concepts, the behavior of children from minority groups may not be fully understood. At the same time, no preventive steps can be taken without an appreciation of the dual roles that the children are playing—at home and at school. There is real danger that the school will unconsciously bring about personality disorganization among its students because of its insistence on inculcating middle-class values and its belittling or ignoring of the subculture.

CONCLUSIONS

At least three levels of sensitivity were detected among the teachers in the sample toward sociocultural differences of the three ethnic groups considered. At one level, the teachers revealed a tremendous amount of awareness; at another, the teachers were somewhat aware but not really sensitive to sociocultural factors; and at still a deeper level, the teachers were not sensitive at all to sociocultural factors as they impinge on classroom behavior of the different ethnic groups.

The level at which the teachers showed great sensitivity was the area concerned with overt behavioral practices and artifacts of the three cultures. Thus, they were very sensitive to differences in oral proficiency in the use of the English language, and were quite ready to differentiate between the home and school environment in relation to the three ethnic groups.

At the second level, which perhaps is more abstract and of deeper signifi-cance, the teachers tended to show very little awareness of sociocultural factors affecting classroom behavior. The teachers showed very little sensitivity to differences among the three groups in issues concerning health, meaningfulness of classroom experi-ences, values placed on education, and reading abilities of the three ethnic groups.

The third level at which teachers indicated little or no sensitivity to socio-cultural differences was concerned with psychological needs and their satisfac-tion in relation to sociocultural orienta-tions, scientific interpretation of natural phenomena, civic responsibility, inter-group relationships, economic efficiency, and achievement at grade level.

References

1. Allison Davis, *Social Class Influences upon Learning* (Cambridge: Harvard University Press, 1949).
2. W. Lloyd Warner, *American Life: Dream and Reality* (Chicago: University of Chicago Press, 1953), pp. 176–180.
3. William O. Stanley, *et al.*, *Social Foundations of Education* (New York: The Dryden Press, 1956), pp. 129–179.
4. Research Study entitled "The Adjustment of Indian and Non-Indian Children in the Public Schools of New Mexico," College of Education, University of New Mexico, Albuquerque.
5. Sidney Siegel, *Non-parametric Statistics for the Behavioral Sciences* (New York: McGraw Hill Book Co., 1956), pp. 235–37.

14.   American Indians and White People

ROSALIE H. WAX and ROBERT K. THOMAS

As the Hughes have pointed out, when people come into troublesome contact with each other, popular and scholary attention is usually focused on only one of them. Thus the realtionship between Indians and the persons of European extraction, known as whites, is commonly termed the "Indian problem." Although these authors agree that such emphasis is natural, they call attention to the fact that the unit of racial or ethnic relations is no single people, but the situation—the frontier of contact of the two or more peoples inhabiting a community or region.[1]

This article is an attempt to describe one of the more intimate aspects of just such a frontier situation, namely what happens when American Indians and white people meet in the course of their day-to-day activities and try to communicate with each other. It does not attempt to define the major areas of difference between Indian and white American culture or personality, nor does it discuss the major reasons for conflict and hostility between the two, but rather tries to explain how and why they find talking to each other difficult. It is, therefore, directed as much to the Indian as to the white reader.

We are aware that there are signifi-

Reprinted from *Phylon,* Vol. XXII, No. 4 (Winter 1961) pp. 305–317, by permission of the publisher and authors.

cant differences in behavior and personality among the various kinds of Indians and, likewise, among the various kinds of white men, and that interesting exceptions may possibly be found to all of our generalizations. Nevertheless, our observations have convinced us that most white men who live in the United States share ideas and practices about proper behavior that are very different from those shared by most Indians.

Social discourse is one of the areas where Indians and whites most easily misunderstand each other. Placed in an informal social gathering, such as a small party where he knows only the host, the Indian will usually sit or stand quietly, saying nothing and seeming to do nothing. He may do this so naturally that he disappears into the background, merging with the wall fixtures. If addressed directly, he will not look at the speaker; there may be considerable delay before a reply, and this may be pitched so softly as to be below the hearing threshold of the white interlocutor; he may even look deliberately away and give no response at all.

In this same situation, the white man will often become undiscourageably loquacious. A silent neighbor will be peppered with small shop talk in the hope that one of his rounds will trigger an exchange and a conversa-

145

tional engagement. If the neighbor happens to be an Indian, his protracted silence will spur the white to even more extreme exertions; and the more frantic the one becomes the less the response he is likely to elicit from the other.

Ironically, both parties are trying hard to establish communication and good feeling. But, like Aesop's would-be friends, the crane and the fox, each employs devices that puzzle, alienate, and sometimes anger the other.

From childhood, white people and Indians are brought up to react to strange and dangerous situations in quite different ways. The white man who finds himself in an unstructured, anxiety-provoking situation is trained to react with a great deal of activity. He will begin action after action until he either structures the situation, or escapes from it, or simply collapses. But the Indian, put in the same place, is brought up to remain motionless and watch. Outwardly he appears to freeze. Inwardly, he is using all of his senses to discover what is expected of him— what activities are proper, seemly, and safe. One might put it this way: In an unfamiliar situation a white man is taught to react by agressive experimentation—he keeps moving until he finds a satisfactory pattern. His motto is "Try and try again." But the Indian puts his faith in observation. He waits and watches until the other actors show him the correct pattern.

Once he has picked up the cues and feels relatively certain that he can accomplish what is expected, the Indian may respond with a sudden energy and enthusiasm that can bewilder his white parents. For example, at a party given for a group of Indian college students by the white members of a faculty, the Indian students sat and said virtually nothing. The faculty members did their best to draw out their expressionless and noncommittal guests. Even the stock questions of school and educational plans brought little response. At length in desperation, the faculty members talked to each other.

After refreshments were served, the party broke into small clusters of guests, and in each cluster an Indian student did most of the talking. He delivered a modest but well-organized address describing his educational plans. From questions put to him, each had concluded that his role at the party was to paint his academic future. When opportunity offered, he gave the faculty members exactly what he thought they wanted.

The active experimenting disposition of many white men and the motionless alertness of Indians may be related to different cultural attitudes toward what white people call success or failure. Indian friends tell us that they do not praise or reward their children for doing what is proper or right, they are expected to behave well, for this is "natural" or "normal." Thus a "good" Indian child reflects no special credit on himself or on his parents. He is simply behaving as a child of his people should behave.[2] On the other hand, the "bad" or ill-intentioned child is censured and the child who makes mistakes is shamed, which, in an Indian community, is a grave punishment. As one sophisticated Indian remarked: "As a result of the way they are raised, very few Indians will try to do something at which they're not good (adept). It takes a lot of courage.

As an example, he cited a phenomenon, common in his tribe, of men gathering to help a relative build a house.

"You watch a housebuilding among my people. You see some men struggling with the work of erecting the structure, and, over there, sitting on the grass, may be a man, just watching, never lending a hand, even with the heaviest work. They get the structure up, and all of a sudden there's that man on the roof, working away, laying shingle—because what he knows how to do is lay shingle. All these men that were there are kin come to help with the housebuilding, but each person only offers his assistance in what he knows he can do." [4]

He also reminded us of how an Indian girl who had been making tortillas at a picnic immediately stopped when two highly skilled girls began to help her. She excused herself and disappeared. But a white girl who knew nothing of Indian cookery pitched in and was quite embarrassed by her lack of skill.

Many other examples of the Indians' reluctance to exhibit clumsiness or ineptitude before others appear in the literature. For example, Nash relates how a Maya girl learns to operate weaving or spinning machines in a factory by silently observing the operator. Only when she feels competent will the observer take over and run the machine.

"She will not try her hand until she feels competent, for to fumble and make mistakes is a cause for "verguenza"—public shame. She does not ask questions because that would annoy the person teaching her, and they might also think she is stupid." [3]

Again, Macgregor mentions that an Indian school track team was reluctant to run because they knew they could not win, and a basketball team did not want their parents and neighbors to come to an interschool game for fear they would laugh at their mistakes and failure to win. [5]

Perhaps it will be reassuring to the Indian to realize that the reckless torrents of words poured out by white people are usually intended as friendly or, at least, social gestures. The more ill at ease a white man becomes, the more he is likely to talk. He is not nearly so afraid of making mistakes as is the Indian and it is almost impossible (by Indian standards) to embarrass or "shame" him. By the same token, he will rarely hold an Indian's mistakes against him. Conversely, the white person who has had little experience in talking with Indians should find it heartening to know that the silence and downcast eyes with which his first conversational gambits may be received spring from shyness and, often, from courtesy. He is not being snubbed or ignored; on the contrary, his words and actions are being observed with minute care. Once the Indian has discovered what his response ought to be, he will make it. This may take a little time, but the person who is not willing to spend a little time ought not to try to talk to Indians.

The oversensitive white man may take comfort in the fact that the Indian who wishes to insult him will generally make his intentions quite clear. The Indian who looks away when you address him is being considerate—to stare into your face might embarrass you. But the Indian who treats you as if you were invisible is putting you beneath the notice of a highly observant man.

In every human relationship there is some element of influence, interference, or downright compulsion. The white man has been and is torn between two ideals: on the one hand, he believes in freedom, in minding his own business, and in the right of people to make up their minds for themselves; but, on the other hand, he believes that he should be his brother's keeper and not abstain from advice, or even action, when his brother is speeding down the road toward perdition, death, or social isolation due to halitosis. The Indian society is unequivocal: interference of any form is forbidden, regardless of the folly, irresponsibility, or ignorance of your brother.

Consequently, when the white man is motivated as his brother's keeper, which is most of the time when he is dealing with Indians, he rarely says or does anything that does not sound rude or even hostile to the latter. The white, imbued with a sense of righteousness in "helping the down trodden and backward," does not realize the nature of his conduct, and the Indian cannot tell him, for that, in itself, would be "interference" with the white's freedom to act as he sees fit.

In general sense, coercion has been and is a fundamental element in the social orders of the Western world. Social theorists have characterized the state as that national institution that effectively claims the legitimate monopoly of violence. Lesser institutions utilize a variety of corporeal and spiritual sanctions to effect cooperative action, and the economy prides itself on utilizing the lash of need and the lure of wealth. These characteristics of Western social structure have stimulated the more idealistic to the proposal of new communities in which the elimination of brute compulsion would ensure the release of the creative energies of man; but so deeply entrenched is this system of hierarchial and enforced organization that these are ridiculed as "utopian." In contrast, many of the Indian societies were organized on principles that relied to a great extent on voluntary cooperation and lacked the military or other coercive instrumentalities of the European.

Recent years have seen a marked shift in the general American social patterns. The use of physical violence has been curtailed and the emphasis has shifted toward verbal manipulation; this has been evident in such diverse areas as the armed services, business corporations, educational institutions, and the family. Educational movies shown to children at school impress them with the fact that the admirable leader is the boy or girl who can "get other children to do what he (the leader) wants them to do by convincing them that they really want to do what he (the leader) wants them to do." Children are taught by parents and playmates that their success in most areas of life will depend on their skill as an influence on or manipulator of others. Thus white children begin to practice influencing other people very early in life and they conscientiously try to improve their skills, if we may judge by the letters sent to columnists asking for advice on how to get parents, dates, spouses, or children to do things that (one assumes) these parents, dates, spouses, or children are not particularly eager to do.

This ability is justly valued by the white people since a great deal of modern industrial and organizational work could not be carried on without it. For example, an office manager or foreman finds himself in charge of a group of people, of different religious and ethnic backgrounds, different ages and temperaments, and widely varying moral and ethical views. If he is going to get the job done he must find some way of getting all of these folks to work together, and he does this by being an extraordinarily flexible, agreeable, and persuasive influencer.

Perhaps because these "human relation skills" are a social replacement for physical force, white people tend to be insensitive to the simple fact that they are still interpersonally coercive. The "nondirective" teacher still wants the children to work as a group and on the project for which she has the materials and skills. Similarly, the would-be hostess who will not listen to an excuse and interprets a refusal as a personal affront may not realize that she is forcing her guests to do what they do not wish to do. Even when white people do not wish to accomplish some end, their conversational patterns are structured along coercive lines. Thus, as a casual party, the man who remarks that he plans to buy a pear tree may anticipate that someone will immediately suggest that he buy a peach tree instead. If he remarks that he is shopping for a new car, someone will be happy to tell him exactly what kind of a car he ought to buy. The same thing happens if he ventures an opinion about music or politics. Someone is bound to inform him (in a friendly way, of course) that he ought to be listening to, reading, or attending something for which he has no particular inclination. Perhaps these patterns of conversation entertain white people because they play with the forms that are so serious in their society. The man who can out-advise the other is "one-up," and the loser is expected to take his defeat with good grace.

The Indian defines all of the above behavior, from the gentlest manipulation to the most egregious meddling, as outside the area of proper action. From earliest childhood he is trained to regard absolute noninterference in interpersonal relations as decent or normal and to react to even the mildest coercion in these areas with bewilderment, disgust, and fear.

Although most sensitive white persons who have lived with Indians are aware of this phenomemon, we have found none that have successfully described it in gereral terms.[6] Under these circumstances it might be wise to follow the Indian pattern of communication and describe the Indian "ethnic of noninterference" by examples.

One of the more spectacular examples is the behavior of Indian passengers in an automobile. If the car is the property of the driver, no passenger ever considers giving him suggestions or directions. Even though a rock slide or a wandering steer may have blocked the right of way, no one says a word. To do so would be "interference." Consequently, accidents can occur which might have been prevented had any one of several passengers chosen to direct the attention of the driver to the hazard or obstacle. As the car rolls merrily into the ditch all that may be heard is a quiet exhalation of breath.

An example of this "ethic" was noted over thirty years ago among the Pit River Indians of California and recorded by Jaime de Angulo:

"I have heard Indians say: "That's not right what he's doing, that fellow . . ." "What d'you mean it's not right?" "Well . . . you ain't suppose to do things that way . . . it never was done that way . . . there'll be trouble." "Then why don't you stop him?" "Stop him? How can I stop him? It's his way."[7]

A more personal example was given by an Indian friend. The friend was living with his wife's family and customarily drove to work every morning. One morning at breakfast he noticed that his sister-in-law, Mary, had dressed up as if she were going to town. Curious, he asked his wife: "Is Mary going any place?" "Oh yes," said his wife, "She's going to Phoenix."

"Does she have a lift to the bus station?" asked our friend. "No," said his wife.

Our friend then asked his sister-in-law if she would like him to give her a lift on his way to work and she accepted. After driving for some time, our friend suddenly became aware of the fact that he had automatically driven directly to work, passing right by the bus station without stopping. His sister-in-law was calmly looking out of the window. She had made no comment when he overshot the bus station and she made none now. Without a word, he turned the car around and took her to the bus station.

Characteristic Indian "noninterference" was shown by Mary, not only when she did not comment on the fact that her brother-in-law was passing the bus station but also in her behavior before they set out. To have asked her brother-in-law to take her to the bus station would have constituted an indelicate attempt to influence him. Perhaps he would not wish to take her with him. By asking him she might "force" him to refuse and thus cause him embarrassment and discomfort. Again, if he took her unwillingly he would feel resentment toward her. By dressing up she could communicate her desires in a way that he could accept or reject without arousing any "bad feelings." That is, he could invite her to go along or he could "be occupied" and go without her.

Great delicacy and sensitivity of feeling are essential to even a moderate standard of Indian good manners. If one is extending invitations to a get-together one does not urge people to come; such urging would be "interfering," for, if they wish to come, they will come. Again, under ordinary circumstances, one does not address another human being unless he has given some indication that he is willing to give you his attention. Thus, if one wishes to begin a conversation, even with a spouse or relative, one first puts oneself in his line of vision. If he does not acknowledge your presence this is a sign that he is occupied and you wait or go away. To address him while he is talking to someone else or meditat-

ing would be gross interference. If one is talking with a friend and he unwittingly brings up a delicate or painful subject, one lets him know this by pretending not to hear, by looking away, or by changing the subject. Most Indians follow these rules of etiquette unconsciously. Even so-called assimilated Indians follow them in part and are not aware that they do so.[8]

A profound respect for the interests, occupations, and responsibilities of other human beings begins to show itself even in the very young Indian child. We have, for example, conversed with Indian parents for hours, while half a dozen children played around us, and, not once, did any of the children address a word to us. A little girl of three or four might leave the play group for a while and lean against an adult relative or sit in a lap. But only in a grave emergency did she try to attract the attention of an adult, and even then she tried not to interrupt what they were doing. Thus, if a bold child wanted to know if it might have a piece of the watermelon that an adult was cutting, he might creep up and whisper into his mother's ear.

We have asked a number of Indians how it is that even very young children do not bother older people. We are usually told something like this: "When I think about it, I see you're right. We never did bother grown-up people when I was a kid. It's funny because I can't remember that anybody said anything to us about it. We just didn't do it."

Such statements suggest that the Indian child is taught very early not to interfere with or bother older people who are otherwise occupied and that both instruction and learning may proceed on a subconscious level. Indeed, we have noticed that even little toddlers do not make the loud and vigorous attempts to monopolize their parent's attention which are characteristic of so many white infants.

Since the human infant must be taught to demand the attention of its parents and since Indian parents simply do not respond to "interfering" demand, it is possible that many Indian infants never learn some of the coercive and aggressive oral and verbal techniques available to children in other cultures. We do not suggest that Indain children lack aggression, but rather that their culture gives them virtually no opportunity to express it by interfering with the activities of others. On the other hand, they are taught consideration through the example of their elders, for Indian adults consistently treat children with the same respect they expect for themselves. To interrupt a child at play, or force it to do something against its will but "for its own good," are contrary to all precepts of Indian child-rearing.[9] Indeed, Erikson tells of an Indian man reared by whites who felt that his wife ought to forbid his children to use profanity. His wife, reared as an Indian, regarded her husband's interfering attitude as evidence that he was sick in mind.[10]

Indians rarely discipline their children in a fashion noticeable to white persons. In the few cases where Rosalie Wax has seen an Indian child punished, parental disapproval was directed against "interference." In one case an Indian boy of about six who played a great deal with white children repeatedly interrupted a conversation between Indian elders. At first he was ignored or gently set aside. When, after five or six rejections he was still persisting, his father addressed him directly: "Son," he said, "You're making it hard for all of us." This boy's father says regretfully that he thinks his son will grow up to be a white man. "When my wife or I show disapproval, it no longer makes any impression on him.

He behaves just like the white boys he plays with."

In another case R. Wax was engaged in a conversation with an Indian man. His wife, a woman of notorious impatience, wished to go home. Not venturing to intrude herself, she sent her five-year-old daughter to tell Papa to come home. Papa, though very fond of his little girl, behaved as if he neither saw nor heard her. I noticed that the child was very distressed and frightened, but I did not realize at this time how severely her father was rebuking her.

By this time some non-Indian readers may have concluded that the upbringings of Indian children must be harsh indeed and that the little tykes creep through their days behind a wall of silence created by adults. Nothing, of course, could be farther from the truth. Indian parents are by no means "busy" all the time, and when they are unoccupied they like nothing better than to coddle, play with, and talk to little children.[11] Moreover, when an Indian gives anyone, child or adult, his attention, he gives all of it. Thus, when he is interacting with an adult, the child is not only treated with the warmth and indulgence noted by so many observers but he is given an attention that is absolute. As we have already noted, this intense concentration on the emotional and intellectual overtones of a personal relationship also characterizes adult interaction. Thus, there really is no such thing as a casual or dilatory conversation between Indians. If they are not "en rapport" they are worlds apart; if they are giving their attention, they use every sense to the utmost.

As we have noted, the first impluse of an Indian who encounters an interferer (with whom he is on terms of friendship) is to withdraw his attention. If the ill-mannered person does not take the hint, the Indian will quietly go away. If it is impossible for him to leave, he does his best to make himself inconspicuous. By disappearing he avoids provoking the disturbed individual to further outbursts and also avoids embarrassing him by being a witness to his improper behavior. Simultaneously, he rebukes him in a socially sanctioned manner. In the past an entire community might withdraw from an incorrigible meddler and leave him quite alone.

Perhaps because these social sanctions are usually effective in an Indian community, Indians have not yet developed devices for dealing with an interferer who claims to be peaceable but aggressively refuses to permit them to withdraw. They can only marvel at his bizarre behavior and wish that he would go away. Sometimes, when prodded past endurance, Indian women will lose their self-control and try to drive out intruders with harsh words and even physical force.

Since the white man from infancy has been encouraged to defend himself and "face up" to unpleasant things, he almost invariably interprets the Indian's withdrawal from his verbal "attacks," not as an unostentatious rebuke, but as evidence of timidity, irresponsibility, or even, as a tendency to "flee from reality." [12] This Indian trait more than any other seems to baffle the white man, for though he has been exposed to Christian doctrine for many, many centuries, he still cannot begin to understand the man who will not fight back.

We regret that some social scientists are among the least perceptive persons in this particular matter. (Perhaps their training makes them over prone to equate a disappearing informant with personal failure.) For example, we have seen a social scientist of some repute attempt to initiate a discussion with Indians by suggesting that they no longer possessed any culture of their own but were unrealistically clinging to an impoverished "reservation" culture. What they ought to do, he went on to say, was to leave the reservations and become assimilated. When this remark was received in expressionless silence, the scientist suggested that this "lack of response" supported his point, for no one present had been able to defend the existence of their culture. The faces of the Indians became even more impassive, but the scientist did not notice that the feet and legs of some of the young men from the Plains tribes had begun to tremble as with the ague. A white person in the audience could no longer control his impulse to interfere, and, in the ensuing debate, much of the Indians' tension was dissipated.

On another occasion a psychiatrist whose initial overtures had been observed in silence by his Indian audience began to prod them with remarks intended to arouse their anger. The Indian men, as usual, made themselves inconspicuous. A few stole out of the meeting. But some of the women lost their tempers and the session ended in a loud and rather vulgar brawl.

After these incidents we talked with both the white and Indian participants. Both of the social scientists assured us that they had merely been trying to elicit a response from the Indians and the second one seemed naively pleased with the "discovery" that "they'll only react if you get them mad." The Indians seemed to feel that it was best to ignore the whole thing. As one older man remarked: "You do not take the words of an insane person seriously or get angry at him."

The reader, by now, may be able to appreciate the blunt truth of a statement made by a middle-aged Apache who was attending a college class on the behavior of ethnic groups. Hoping to stimulate a discussion of accommodation and assimilation, the instructor asked: "What develops when two different peoples meet?" Laconically, the Apache replied: "Bad feelings."

One cannot examine a situation as distressing as the Indian and white frontier of sociable contact without wondering what might be done to make it less painful for both parties. To tell most white people that they can get along with Indians fairly well if they do not interfere is almost like telling them to give up breathing. It is, perhaps, equally difficult for an Indian to appreciate that "mean" and "crazy" deeds of the white men do not necessarily have the same significance as the mean or crazy deeds of an Indian.

We have noted that there is less tension and distress in those situations in which the atmosphere of power and authority in which the Indian and the white man usually meet is mitigated or absent. Thus, the white man often finds it easier to get along with the Indian when he is gambling, trading, partying, or simply "chewing the rag." This is not because there is anything particularly friendly or brotherly in these activities but because they represent some of the few remaining social situations in which the white man cannot always immediately assume an authoritative or interfering role. In such situations the Indian learns to make allowances for or take advantage of the white man's restlessness, his incomprehensible "pride," and his reckless "courage." The white man, for his part, learns to accommodate himself to the slow pace, sudden temperamental outbursts, and unexpected disappearances of the Indian.

We have noted that most white people who have a tolerably good relationship with Indians consciously or unconsciously subscribe to the notion that white men ought to keep their noses out of Indian matters. However else they may behave seems to make little difference. Thus one of the finest field workers known to us is an anthropologist of so gentle and unaggressive a nature that one sometimes wonders how he can maintain himself in the modern world. When he is in the field, the Indians spend a good deal of their time seeing that he comes to no harm. Another white man has no tact at all and breaks some rule of Indian decorum in almost every sentence he utters. Both men, however, subscribe to noninterference in Indian matters and both are admired and liked by Indians.

On the matter of interaction between groups composed of Indians and whites, we have noted that "good feelings" are more likely to arise when the situation is clearly defined as one of contact. By this we mean that the participants from both groups come to realize that they are interacting in an entirely new situation, alien to both, and that their comfort, enjoyment, and accomplishment will depend on their ingenuity in inventing new forms and rules applicable to this new situation.

It is remarkable how rapidly and spontaneously new social forms comfortable to both parties may be defined, provided that both parties strongly desire to act or play together. We were, for example, unable to accomplish much in the Workshop on American Indian Affairs until we redefined the teaching-learning situation, and we were obliged to do that before we could participate in picnics and dances at which both white people and Indians could have a good time. It is possible that such "accommodating" contact situations are established more frequently than social scientists realize. Their recognition and study might help to throw light on problems of great importance.

We are aware that we have presented a picture and analysis of Indian child-rearing practices not entirely compatible with those of certain other observers. However, we think that the significant differences are quantitative rather than qualitative and rest on the fact that we emphasize what other scholars have overlooked.

We agree with Dorothy Lee that it is misleading to call Indian child-rearing practices "permissive" or "indulgent." [13] It might be more accurate to say that it usually does not occur to Indian parents to permit or forbid their children to do anything, much less permit or forbid them to move their bowels. White parents, on the other hand, see themselves as "permitters" and "forbidders." Nevertheless, from the Indian point of view, they leave vast and very important areas of their children's behavior completely unstructured. Thus one might suggest that in both cultures parents and elders subject infants and children to an intensive and careful training, but that they use very different methods and emphasize very different skills.

Again, we believe that Erikson has overlooked something very important when he depicts Sioux upbringing as one in which the child is introduced to social discipline "in the form of a tradition of unrelenting public opinion" only after an infancy in which he "is allowed to be an individualist" and is subject to no frustration of impulse.[14]

According to our observations, Sioux and other Indians begin to train their children to be highly sensitive social beings long before they can talk and, perhaps, even before the age when white infants are subjected or oral and anal frustrations. Here we again agree with Lee in the view that Indian training in social sensitivity and in respect for others begins at birth, and, apparently, is reinforced with every interpersonal experience.

Perhaps, on occasion, too intense a focus on a formidable theoretical framework may serve to blur important aspects of the phenomena one intends to observe. This may be especially so with an alien culture. Thus a people who do not practice the classic Freudian instinctual disciplines may be characterized as lacking in discipline, whereas the fact that they may practice a kind of subliminal "sleep-training" on their children (as do the Papago) may be overlooked. On the other hand, we may anticipate that, in time, cross-cultural studies will help to refine and develop our existing body of theory.

References

1. Everett Cherrington Hughes and Helen MacGill, Hughes. *Where Peoples Meet* (Glencoe, Ill.: Free Press, 1952) pp. 18–19.
2. We have not heard an Indian use the old-fashioned term, "decent," in this context though we note that Kluckhohn used it to describe the Indian point of view (cited in Dorothy B. Lee, *Freedom and Culture*, Englewood Cliffs, New Jersey, 1959, p. 130). We find it apt since in the white society of a generation ago, decent behavior was expected of children and brought no reward whereas indecent behavior was severely punished.

   The Indian conception that decent or proper behavior deserves no particular notice or praise is nevertheless rarely appreciated by white people. We, for example, have heard teachers and other professionals complain that their Indian students and clients never thanked them for their work and devotion. And Margaret Mead remarks that to Indians "All government employees, no matter how honest, how tireless, how enthusiastic, would be voted as merely 'doing their duty' and given neither laurels nor thanks." This Indian behavior does not reflect hostility or ingratitude. It merely reflects the Indian view that medals or laurel wreaths are not given to people for doing what they ought to do (Margaret Mead, *The Changing Culture of an Indian Tribe,* New York, 1932; cited by Erik H. Erikson in "Observations on Sioux Education," *Journal of Psychology,* **VII,** 1939), 123.

3. Manning Nash, *Machine Age Maya,* Memoirs of the American Anthropological Association, No. 87 (1958), pp. 26–27, 46.

4. Debo, Angie. *The Five Civilized Tribes of Oklahoma:* report on social and economic conditions. Philadelphia: Indian Rights Association, 1951; p. 10.

5. Gordon Macgregor, *Warriors Without Weapons* (Chicago, 1946), p. 137.

6. Lowie's examples of the attitude of Indian parents toward their children's property is, we think, an example of non-interference (*Primitive Society,* New York, 1925, pp. 233–34). See also Paul Radin, *The Trickster,* (New York, 1956), pp. 9 and 55, n, 9. On p. 153 Radin suggests that part of the Trickster Cycle criticizes the chief, since "one of his functions was to interfere in all kinds of situations." MacGregor's statement that the Indian respects the individual's accountability to himself for his own actions is helpful and Lee's remark on individual autonomy and social structure are extremely acute. Indeed, only Lee seems to see that Indian "respect for the individual" is an integral part of Indian "respect for social structure" (MacGregor, *op. cit.,* p. 65, No. 7; Dorothy Lee, *op. cit.,* Chap. I). Erikson (*op. cit.*) has made an uncommon attempt to describe how white people and Indians see each other and often notices the Indians' reaction to "interference" without quite understanding what is going on.

7. "Indians in Overalls," *Hudson Review,* **III** (1956), 369.

8. Some fine descriptions of the extremely delicate interaction demanded in Eskimo communities may be found in the works of Peter Freuchen.

9. White people frequently interpret this consideration as indifference or gross indulgence. As Macgregor remarks: (Indian) Parents do not force their children to conform because 'mother knows best' or to avoid damaging the parents' reputation or self-esteem. A child who runs away from school is usually not asked why he came home. Likewise, a grown son who leaves the reservation aid and is not heard from in years is rarely questioned on his return about what he has been doing (*op. cit.,* p. 67, n. 7).

10. Erikson, *op. cit.,* p. 130.

11. The men of some tribes do not play with little children, but they usually seem to enjoy talking to them.

12. Even Erikson, who is far more aware of the withdrawing disposition of the Indian than are most other white men, does not see that it is, to the Indian, a matter of self-evident good manners. See for example, his complex discussion in *op. cit.,* pp. 124–125.

13. *Op. cit.,* p. 6.

14. *Op. cit.,* pp. 152–153.

15. The Effects of Cultural Deprivation on Learning Patterns

DAVID P. AUSUBEL

The distinctive learning patterns of the culturally deprived child are a reflection of selective retardation in his intellectual development. In considering, therefore, how the learning of the disadvantaged differs from that of other children, and what implications this has for the use of instructional materials, we must examine the selective effects of environmental deprivation on the development of intelligence and the extent to which such effects are both reversible and irreversible.

CULTURAL DEPRIVATION AND INTELLECTUAL DEVELOPMENT

Neither the contribution of the cultural environment to intellectual development nor the modifiability of children's relative intellectual ability as measured by intelligence tests is seriously disputed any longer. Whatever the individual's genic potentialities are, cognitive development occurs largely in response to a variable range of stimulation requiring incorporation, accommodation, adjustment, and reconciliation. The more variable the environment to which individuals are exposed, the higher is the resulting level

Reprinted from *Audiovisual Instruction,* Vol. 10 (January 1965), pp. 10–12, by permission of the publisher and author.

of effective stimulation. Characteristic of the culturally deprived environment, however, is a restricted range and a less adequate and systematic ordering of stimulation sequences. The effects of this restricted environment include poor perceptual discrimination skills; inability to use adults as sources of information, correction, and reality testing, and as instruments for satisfying curiosity; an impoverished language-symbolic system; and a paucity of information, concepts, and relational propositions.

Hence, once we grant that the IQ represents a multiply determined functional capacity in the development of which experiential and motivational factors play an important regulatory role, it is superfluous to inquire whether it can be modified—both qualitatively and quantitatively—by significant variation in such factors. The more relevant questions at this point are the extent of the modification that is possible and the conditions under which it occurs, that is, how late in the course of cultural deprivation appropriate experience can reverse intellectual retardation and what the most suitable kind of experience is for this purpose.

It is in the area of language development, and particularly with respect to the abstract dimension of verbal functioning, that the culturally deprived child manifests the greatest degree of intellectual retardation. Many factors contribute to this unfortunate developmental outcome. The culturally deprived home, to begin with, lacks the large variety of objects, utensils, toys, pictures, etc., that require labeling and serve as referents for language acquisition in the middle-class home. The culturally deprived child is also not spoken to or read to very much by adults. Hence, his auditory discrimination tends to be poor, and he receives little corrective feedback regarding his enunciation, pronunciation, and grammar. Furthermore, the syntactical model provided him by his parents is typically faulty. Later on, when new concepts and transactional terms are largely acquired verbally, that is, by definition and context from speech and reading rather than by abstraction from direct concrete experience, he suffers from the paucity of abstractions in the everyday vocabulary of his elders; from the rarity of stimulating conversations in the home; from the relative absence of books, magazines, and newspapers; and from the lack of example of a reading adult in the family setting.

It is small wonder, therefore, that the abstract vocabulary of the culturally deprived child is deficient in range and precision, that his grammar and language usage are shoddy, that his attentivity and memory are pooly developed, and that he is impoverished in such language-related knowledge as the number concepts, self-identity information, and understanding of the physical, geometric, and geographical environments. Social class differences in language and conceptual measures also tend to increase with increasing age, thus demonstrating the cumulative effects of both continued environmental deprivation and of initial deficit in language development.

The culturally deprived child's entire orientation to language is also different from that of the middle-class child. He responds more to the concrete, tangible, immediate, and particularized properties of objects and situations than to their abstract, categorical, and relational properties. His speech is instigated more by the objects and actions he sees than by abstract ideas emanating from within, and he makes more ancillary use of nonverbal forms of communication. In short, the language of the culturally deprived child is more concrete, expressive, and informal than that of the middle-class child, showing signs of impoverishment mainly in its formal, abstract, and syntactical aspects.

However, the most important consequence of the culturally disadvantaged child's retardation is his slower and less complete transition from concrete to abstract modes of thought and understanding. This transition normally begins to occur in our culture during the junior high school period. As a result, preadolescent and adolescent children are able to understand and manipulate relationships between abstractions directly, i.e., without the benefit of reference to current or immediately prior concrete-empirical experience. Thus they are no longer limited to semiabstract, intuitive, and particularized thought, and can formulate more precise, abstract, and general propositions that embody all possible hypothetical relationships between categorical variables.

This transition takes place more slowly and less completely in culturally deprived children for two reasons. First, the culturally deprived child lacks the necessary repertoire of clear and stable abstractions and transactional terms that is obviously prerequisite for the direct manipulation and understanding of relationships between abstractions. Second, for lack of adequate practice, he has not acquired sufficient facility in relating abstractions to each other *with* the benefit of concrete-empirical props, so that he can later dispense with their assistance at the same age as his environmentally more favored contemporaries. Because concrete thought operations are necessarily more time consuming than their abstract-verbal counterparts, and also because of his distractibility, unfamiliarity with formal language, impaired self-confidence, and unresponsiveness to time pressure, the culturally deprived child typically works more slowly than the middle-class child in an academic setting.

THE EFFECTS OF CULTURAL DEPRIVATION ARE PARTLY IRREVERSIBLE

To avoid unrealistic expectations regarding the possibilities of educational amelioration, it is important for persons working with disadvantaged children both to appreciate that the effects of cultural deprivation on intellectual development are *partly* irreversible and to understand why this must necessarily be so. In the first place, since current and future rates of intellectual development are always conditioned or limited by the attainment of development, existing developmental deficits tend to become cumulative in nature. The child who has an existing deficit in growth incurred from past deprivation is less able to profit developmentally from new and more advanced levels of environmental stimulation. Thus, irrespective of the adequacy of all other factors—both internal and external—his deficit tends to increase cumulatively and to lead to permanent retardation.

New growth, in other words, always proceeds from the existing phenotype, that is, from already actualized capacity, rather than from potentialities

inherent in the genotype. It makes no difference in terms of this limiting influence whether the attained efficiency is attributable to inferior genic endowment or to inadequate environment. If, as a result of a consistently deprived environment during the early formative years, superior intellectual endowment is not actualized, the attained deficit in functional capacity significantly limits the extent to which later environmental stimulation, even if normal in quantity and quality, can increase the rate of cognitive growth. Hence, an individual's prior success or failure in developing his intellectual capacities tends to keep his future rate of growth relatively constant.

In addition to the limiting condition of attained level of development or of existing degree of deficiency, we must consider the further limiting factor of the organism's degree of plasticity or freedom to respond developmentally in a given direction in response to appropriate environmental stimulation. Generally speaking, the plasticity of intelligence tends to decrease with increasing age. At first, intelligence is a relatively undifferentiated capacity that can develop in several different directions. But as children grow older, particularly during preadolescence and adolescence, it becomes increasingly more differentiated as shown by the decreasing intercorrelations among the subtests of a given intelligence scale. Another indication of the trend toward the progressive differentiation of abilities is the fact that ten-year-old boys of high socioeconomic status make higher scores than ten-year-old boys of low socioeconomic status on tests of both verbal *and* mechanical ability, but at age 16 are only superior on the verbal tests. Furthermore, the verbal ability scores of boys who drop out of school at the age of 17 tend to decline, whereas their scores on tests of mechanical aptitude continue to improve. Thus by the time an individual reaches adolescence, differential factors of interest, relative ability, specialization of training, motivation, success and failure experience, and cultural expectation operate selectively to develop certain potential abilities and to leave others relatively undeveloped.

Once intelligence undergoes definite relative commitment in the various aforementioned channels, the individual is less responsive to stimulation in areas of minimal development than he was in the original undifferentiated state. Thus, for example, if because of inadequate stimulation during early and middle childhood, genic potentialities for verbal intelligence fail to be adequately actualized, other facets of intelligence (e.g., mechanical, social) which are more satisfactorily stimulated become differentially more highly developed. At this point, therefore, the development of the individual's verbal intelligence is not only limited by his existing deficiency in the verbal area, but also by the fact that his once undifferentiated intelligence has been definitely committed in other directions, and is hence less free than previously to respond to an enriched verbal environment. Hence it is evident that the possibility for complete reversibility of environmentally induced retardation in verbal intelligence decreases as children advance in age. This is not to say, of course, that later enrichment is entirely to no avail; but, in my opinion, some of this failure in developmental actualization is irreversible and cannot be compensated for later, irrespective of the amount of hyperstimulation that is applied.

AMELIORATIVE USE OF INSTRUCTIONAL MATERIALS

The hypothesis of cumulative development deficit implicitly assumes the continued operation of a learning environment, the stimulating value of which remains average or below average during the crucial formative years. Hence, despite the twin limiting effects in disadvantaged pupils of attained deficit in intellectual development and of increasing differentiation of intelligence on subsequent responsiveness to cognitive stimulation, it is completely consistent with the above theoretical analysis to hypothesize that an *optimal* learning environment could arrest and even reverse in part the existing degree of retardation. Such an environment must obviously be adequately stimulating, must be specially geared to the deprived individual's particular level of readiness in each subject-matter area and intellectual skill, as well as to his over-all level of cognitive maturity, and presupposes much individualized attention and guided remedial effort. This, of course, is a far cry from the kind of learning environment that culturally deprived children typically enjoy. In actual practice their existing intellectual deficit is usually compounded by the fact that not only are they less able than their peers to profit from appropriate new experience, but they also are usually overwhelmed by exposure to learning tasks that exceed by far their prevailing level of cognitive readiness. Hence, since they do not function at the required level of cognitive maturity and do not possess the necessary background of knowledge required for efficient learning, they typically fail, lose self-confidence in their ability to learn, become thoroughly demoralized in the school situation, and disinvolve themselves from it.

An optimal learning environment for culturally deprived pupils focuses therefore on two complementary aspects of cognitive readiness for learning—readiness in terms of general level of intellectual functioning and readiness in terms of specific subject-matter background. Appropriate use of instructional materials can enhance each aspect of readiness.

General unreadiness for school learning among culturally disadvantaged children largely reflects their slower and less complete transition from concrete to abstract modes of thought during the junior and senior high school years. Thus, in the presentation of abstract ideas and relational propositions, it is important for instructional materials and audiovisual aids to provide more concrete-empirical props and opportunities for direct physical manipulation of objects and situations than would be considered desirable in a more typical classroom. Such props, for example, might include generous use of such techniques as Cuisenaire rods, the abacus, schematic models and diagrams, and role-playing activities; and in the teaching of mathematics and science, much reliance would be placed on applicability to common problems in the immediate environment and on supportive illustrations and analogies drawn from everyday experience. It should be appreciated however, that these techniques are merely ways of facilitating the transition to a more abstract level of cognitive functioning. We do not want to induce permanent dependence on concrete-empirical props or to be satisfied with this state of affairs as our ultimate objective.

Specific subject-matter unreadiness among culturally deprived children is a consequence of their failure to master the basic intellectual skills and to acquire an adequate foundation of integrative concepts and principles in the hierarchically organized disciplines. It is essential, therefore, that the initial selection of learning materials take account of pupils' *existing* state of knowledge and sophistication in the various subject-matter areas, no matter how primitive this happens to be. Once the appropriate starting point is ascertained, continued subject-matter readiness can then be assured by using structured, sequentially organized materials and by insisting on mastery of all ongoing lessons before new learning tasks are introduced. These latter teaching strategies can, in turn, be implemented most effectively through programed instruction.

The careful sequential arrangement and gradation of difficulty characteristic of programmed instruction maintains readiness by insuring that each attained increment in learning serves as an appropriate foundation or anchoring post for the learning and retention of subsequent items in the ordered sequence. In addition, competent programming of materials presupposes maximum attention to such matters as lucidity, organization, and the explanatory and integrative power of substantive content. The programmed instruction format also promotes readiness by making it possible to insure that the presentation of new material is always deferred until that degree of consolidation or overlearning required for efficient sequential learning is attained. This is accomplished by self-pacing, by frequent testing and the provision of feedback, and by furnishing adequately spaced reviews and opportunity for differential practice of the more difficult components of a task.

Advocacy of programmed instruction as best suited to the needs of the culturally deprived pupil does not necessarily imply endorsement of the small-frame format typical of most teaching machine programs and programmed textbooks. As a matter of fact, in terms of both the logical requirements and meaningful learning and the actual size of the learning task that can be conveniently   accommodated   by   the learner, the frame length typically used by teaching machines is artificially and unnecessarily abbreviated. It tends to fragment the ideas presented in the program so that their interrelationships are obscured and their logical structure is destroyed.

Neither does endorsement of programmed instruction imply that the effectiveness of the method is attributable to the mechanical reinforcement of rote verbal responses. Quite the contrary! Programmed instruction is effective in school learning precisely because its emphasis on lucidity of presentation, sequential arrangement, clarification, consolidation, and integration of related materials enhances meaningful learning processes. For example, in the learning of grammar through repetitive practice with feedback of the principal syntactical forms in written and spoken discourse, the learning be-

comes transferable only if the program requires the learner to appreciate the precise relationships between the verbal manipulations he practices and the changes in meaning that he induces by such manipulations. Mere ability rotely to emit the correct forms as ends in themselves, apart from their relationship to meaning, results in learning that is restricted to the specific practice frames under consideration.

Adequate attention to the two factors of readiness specified above—through the appropriate use of instructional materials—can go a long way toward assuring effective learning for the first time, toward arresting or partly reversing the course of culturally induced retardation in intellectual development, and toward restoring the disadvantaged child's educational morale and confidence in his ability to learn.

16. Negro-White Differences in Intelligence Test Performance: A New Look at an Old Problem

OTTO KLINEBERG

I have written this article at the suggestion of the Society for the Psychological Study of Social Issues (SPSSI), Division 9 of the American Psychological Association. It is based in part on some of my own earlier publications and in part on a chapter which I have prepared for a forthcoming book; it represents an attempt to bring up to date a psychological analysis of an old problem. The substantial number of recent publications in this field, some of which have attracted considerable popular attention; the many "letters to the editor," the unfortunate tendency, all too frequently, to stray from an interpretation of the data to an attack on the ethnic origins or the alleged political positions of the persons involved; the accusation of a "conspiracy"; and finally, the practical implications which have been drawn for public policy—all of these developments have made a factual reappraisal desirable. I had hoped that this might be done by another psychologist, one less closely identified with a definite stand on one side of this issue. As the next best thing, I have tried to look, as honestly as my own biases would

Reprinted from *American Psychologist,* 18 (April 1963) pp. 198–203, by permission of the publisher and author.
162

permit, at the evidence which has accumulated on both sides. It goes without saying that I am writing as an individual, and that neither the Council nor the memberhip of SPSSI should be held responsible for what follows.

THE ISSUE

I shall restrict my discussion of Negro-white differences to that aspect of the issue on which we, as psychologists, may claim to speak with professional competence, namely, the interpretation of the results obtained from the application of mental tests. There are other aspects of at least equal importance: whether, for example, there is any acceptable indication of biological superiority or inferiority; whether one can argue from the nature of a culture to the genetic factors responsible, etc. On these and related questions the anthropologists are better qualified than we are to express a judgment. I leave these matters, therefore, with the single reminder that the American Anthropological Association has taken the position that there is no scientifically acceptable basis for a genetic hierarchy among ethnic groups.

As far as mental tests are concerned, the issue is *not* one of whether *on the average* Negro children obtain lower test scores than whites. Of that there can be no doubt. My own earlier survey (Klineberg, 1944), in which I was greatly aided by Kenneth B. Clark, was based on 27 studies, and led me to the conclusion that an IQ of 86 represented the approximate Negro median. Shuey (1958), after a much more thorough and complete survey, obtained substantially similar results; on verbal group tests alone, she located no fewer than 72 studies, based upon tests of 36,000 colored children, and her estimate of the average IQ is 85. (I might add parenthetically that in my own earlier survey I found median IQs for children of Italian, Portuguese, and Mexican parentage at or below those of American Negroes, and those of American Indians definitely below.) Shuey's estimate is therefore very close to mine.

The addition of so many further studies has, however, supplied very little new insight. One is reminded of the *Literary Digest* poll in connection with the Roosevelt-Landon electoral contest in 1936; on the basis of more than 2,000,000 ballots, it was predicted that Landon would win an overwhelming victory. As is well known, there was a systematic bias in the sample. The addition of another 100 studies of Negro children would not strengthen Shuey's (1958) conclusion that there are "some native differences between Negroes and whites as determined by intelligence tests" (p. 318), if some systematic error entered into the test results.

As far back as 1933, Garrett and Schneck in their book on *Psychological Tests* reminded us that "the examiner must always remember that comparisons are permissible only when environmental differences are absent, or at least negligible" (p. 24). This appears to be the crucial issue. What comparisons of Negroes and whites have been made under such conditions?

THE ARGUMENT FOR "SOME NATIVE DIFFERENCES"

There are three major studies cited by Shuey and others as demonstrating that differences persist even when environmental factors have been "equated." (I have put this word in quotation marks for reasons which will appear later.) One of these is by Myrtle Bruce (1940), who matched Negroes and whites in a rural community in southern Virginia on the Sims Socioeconomic scale, and still found a difference, with a resulting mean IQ on the Binet of 86 for the whites and 77 for the Negroes. Those who have used Bruce's results have not always gone on to note her careful qualifications.

"Although the white and Negro samples for social status still show statistical differences in IQ on each of the three intelligence tests, this fact cannot be considered proof of the superiority of the white group, since the equation of the two groups *is not entirely valid*" (p. 20, italics supplied).

Even a quick look at her graph on page 20 shows more whites at the upper levels and more Negroes at the lower. Bruce herself "is inclined to believe that there is an innate difference between the particular white and Negro groups studied" (p. 97). She does not, however, extend this conclusion to the ethnic groups in general; she speaks, for example, of the skewness of the Negro IQ distribution as something which "prevents this study from being used as evidence for the superiority of the white race to the Negro race" (p. 97).

Suppose, however, that the two groups had really been "equated" for their scores on a satisfactory socioeconomic scale. Can this possibly be regarded as taking care of all the relevant environmental variables? This appears to be the assumption underlying the study by McGurk (1951) in New Jersey and Pennsylvania. Negro and white high school seniors were matched for socioeconomic level, and still there was a difference, the Negroes overlapping the white means by 29%. This would be an important finding (as would also the demonstration that there was about as much difference between the two groups on test items identified as "cultural" and "noncultural," respectively) if socioeconomic level were all that mattered. Can anyone really believe that? Do motivation, self-confidence, opportunity for wider experience, and other related factors count for nothing?

In a recent critical review, Dreger and Miller (1960) insist that it is not enough to equate ethnic groups in terms of social class and economic variables; that there is a caste as well as a class difference; that even those Negroes whose economic status is higher than that of most white persons will still in most cases be prevented from living the same kind of life in all respects; these writers insist that many other factors may also be important. Incidentally, they emphasize that they "are not taking sides at this point in the hereditary-environment controversy. . . ." (p. 367). They show their impartiality in a striking and (to me) slighty painful manner by stating that "Shuey does the same rationalizing from an hereditarian standpoint that Klineberg did in his earlier 'review' from an environmental standpoint" (p. 364). To return to McGurk, it is impossible to accept the contention that all relevant environmental factors have been considered, just because socioeconomic status has been controlled.

The third study which has figured prominently on this side of the argument is by Tanser (1939). This was conducted in Kent County, Ontario,

Canada, where the Negroes have lived since before the Civil War; Tanser writes that they are on a level with the whites in regard to "every political and social advantage." On the Pintner-Paterson tests, the mean white IQ was 109.6, the Negro, 91; on the Pintner nonlanguage test, the means were 111 and 95; on the National Intelligence Test the respective figures were 104 and 89. On this last test, 20% of the Negroes and 56% of the whites reached or surpassed the *National* test norms. (Tanser's study is unfortunately not available to me in Paris; I have quoted these figures from Shuey.)

If Tanser is right with regard to "every political and social advantage," these results must be taken seriously. A comment by Anastasi (1958) is, however, pertinent.

"Nevertheless significant differences were found in the socio-economic level of the two groups. Moreover, it is reported that the white children attended school more regularly than the Negro, a difference often associated with social class differences. Thus within the entire sample of white children tested, school attendance averaged 93.38%; within the Negro sample, it averaged 84.77%" (pp. 556–557).

I have only one comment to add. I was born in Canada, and lived there the first 25 years of my life. I would have said that Negroes were reasonably well off there, but emphatically not that they lived under conditions of complete equality or that the social environment was free of prejudice. I would have thought that Canada was in this respect similar to the northeastern United States, with Negroes occupying about the same relative position. As a matter of fact Chant and Freedman (1934) report a correlation of .98 between scale values assigned to the same list of ethnic groups, including Negroes, by Canadian as by American students. I do not know Kent County, Ontario, and I cannot take it for granted that the same attitudes would be found there. I cannot help wondering, however, whether this particular Canadian community can be so exceptional. I would like to see a replication of this study, with full attention to social and sociological variables, and to patterns of personal development and interpersonal relations. In the meantime, Tanser's results cannot be dismissed, but they appear to me to be outweighed by the evidence on the other side.

THE ARGUMENT AGAINST NATIVE DIFFERENCES

The evidence against the assumption of native differences in intelligence test performance between Negroes and whites still seems to me to be very convincing. The relevant studies, most of which are already well known and will therefore be presented in brief outline, include the following.

Among infants during the first year of life the earlier finding by McGraw (1931) was that southern Negro babies showed inferiority on the Hetzer-Wolf tests. McGraw concludes:

"It is significant that with even the very young subjects, *when environmental factors are minimized* (italics supplied), the same type and approximately the same degree of superiority are evidenced on the part of the white subject as that found among older groups."

In New Haven, however, where Negro mothers obtained more adequate nourishment and where the general economic level of the families had improved, Pasamanick (1946) found no Negro inferiority or retardation. A follow-up of 40 cases at a mean age of about two years still showed no retardation (Knobloch and Pasamanick, 1953; Pasamanick and Knobloch, 1955). Using different tests, Gilliland (1951) also reports no significant differences between Negro and white infants in Chicago.

For preschool children, Anastasi and d'Angelo (1952), found no significant differences on Goodenough Draw-a-Man IQ between samples of Negroes and whites attending Day Care Centers in New York City. Dreger and Miller (1960) comment:

"With due recognition of the limitations of the Goodenough as a test of intelligence, we may yet regard Anastasi and d'Angelo's results as a challenge to nativist theories of intellectual differences between the races (p. 366).

It is as the children get older that differences in test performance appear. Surely this is to be expected on the basis of the cumulative effect of an inferior environment. Such an effect has been demonstrated in the case of white children as well. To mention only one example out of many, Sherman and Key (1932) found a striking decrement with age among white children living in the "hollows" of the Blue Ridge Mountains; there was a Pintner-Cunningham IQ of 84 at ages 6–8; 70 at 8–10; and 53 at 10–12. This is a much more dramatic drop than any with which I am familiar in the case of Negro children; it shows what *can* happen when a poor environment persists over a long period.

Conversely, when the environment improves, test scores go up. In the case of Negro children they do not usually go up all the way to meet the white norms, but this is to be expected if the discriminatory treatment persists, and even *for a time* if discrimination were to be completely eliminated. The atmosphere in the home, the conversation around the dinner table, the use of leisure time, the books read and discussed—these and other factors contributing to "intelligence" cannot be expected to change over night or even possibly in one generation. With this in mind, the changes that have been reported in Negro IQs become all the more impressive.

When my students and I indicated (Klineberg, 1935) that test scores of southern Negro children improved in proportion to their length of residence in New York City, we were perfectly aware that they still did not reach the white norms, and we pointed that out. Could anyone have expected them to do so under Harlem living conditions, and in Harlem schools as they were at that time? Could anyone possibly suggest that in New York or in Philadelphia, where Lee (1951) obtained similar results, there is *no* discrimination against Negroes? There was improvement, however, because there was *less* discrimination than where they came from.

In some cases, the improvement has even been dramatic. Shuey (1958, p. 87) points out that in my review of Negro intelligence testing (Klineberg, 1944) I gave special prominence to a study by W. W. Clark in Los Angeles (1923). This I did because of the striking finding that the Negro children attending five elementary schools obtained an average National Intelligence Test IQ of 104.7 as compared with an IQ of 106 for all the children in fifteen schools. Shuey indicates that she wrote to Clark asking for further details, and was informed by him that "the *National* norms available in 1922 were probably *about 5 per cent too high*" (p. 87, italics supplied). Surely

5% does not change the results greatly. Besides, in that case the results for the comparison group of 15 schools would also have to be reduced by a similar proportion.

I also wrote to Clark for further information, and he indicated that the obtained IQs were too high, but that he could not determine by how much. The fact remains that if they were too high for the Negroes, they were also too high for the rest of the Los Angeles school population. Clark's original article indicates that there was *no significant difference* shown in the intelligence level of the Negro children and the fifteen schools in general, nor were there significant differences in reading comprehension, arithmetic ability, spelling, as well as educational accomplishment in general. He writes: "The average accomplishment and range of accomplishment for Negro children are practically the same as for the total population of the fifteen schools."

Shuey reports further that research conducted in Los Angeles Public Schools in 1928 (unpublished) revealed a median IQ for Negro children of 95. If that is the case, it is difficult to understand Clark's finding of "no significant difference." Even if we accept this estimate, however, the fact remains that in the relatively friendly climate of Los Angeles, Negro IQs have shown a tremendous leap upwards. Compare even this lower estimate of 95 with the 76 reported by Bruce for rural Virginia. Could "selective migration" account for this large difference? Shuey writes:

"If we were correct in assuming an IQ difference of about 9 points between northern and southern Negro children, then about half of two-thirds of the difference may reasonably be attributed to environmental factors and the remainder to selective migration" (p. 314).

Here the difference is 19 points, and "half of two-thirds" would suggest that Shuey would accept an improvement of 10 to 12 points in IQ as attributable to the superior environment. I am putting this figure at its most conservative, since I have found no acceptable evidence for this kind of selective migration, but even then the environmental rise is clear, and it is considerable.

The desegregation of elementary schools, particularly in the border states and cities where the process has more than a "token" character, gives us another opportunity to see what an improved educational environment may accomplish. This situation has been studied in Washington, D. C., although the measures used were tests of achievement rather than of intelligence. Stallings (1960) writes:

"The Washington study showed that during the five years following integration, marked progress has been made in academic achievement . . . a gain was made in the median score for every (school) subject tested at every grade level where the tests were given.

With regard to Louisville, Kentucky, Omer Carmichael, Superintendent of Public Schools, reported (1959) as follows:

"When we tested, we looked at the results the year before desegregation and then looked at them after the second year of desegregation and found that the Negro in all grades had improved—and by an amount that was statistically significant."

This does not mean that average differences between Negroes and whites have disappeared; it does mean that they have been reduced. Nor has this occurred as the result of "pulling down" the white level. Carmichael reports that there "was a slight improvement for the whites; a substantial improvement for the Negroes." For the difference to disappear completely, much more has to happen. (Even among whites, the difference in the IQ of occupational classes is substantial.) Until that "more" has happened, we have no right to assume that Negroes are, on the average, innately inferior.

AVERAGES AND INDIVIDUALS

In many of the recent analyses of ethnic differences, including the extensive one by Shuey, a great deal of emphasis has been placed on the extent of overlapping. Her own estimate is that the median overlap among school children was between 10 and 20%. (In McGurk's study it was 29%, and presumably in Clark's it was close to 50%.) As every psychology student (but unfortunately not every layman) knows, this refers to the percentage of the "inferior" group who reach or exceed the mean of the "superior." As Anastasi (1958) points out:

"If 30 per cent of the Negroes reach or exceed the white median, the percentage who reach or exceed the lowest score of the white group will be approximately 99. Under these conditions, therefore, the ranges will overlap almost completely" (p. 549).

Clearly, then, statements to the effect that there was "only 20% overlap" obscure the degree of similarity in the total distributions.

This fact comes out strikingly when one looks more closely at Bruce's findings on the Juhlmann-Anderson scale. For the total population examined (521 whites and 432 Negroes), the range in IQ was 52 to 129 for the former and 39 to 130 for the latter. When equated on the Sims scale, the range was 51 to 115 for the whites, and 41 to 130 for the Negroes. On the Binet, the two ranges were 51 to 125, and 51 to 130; on the Grace Arthur scale, 46 to 140, and 51 to 120, respectively. On three out of these four comparisons, one or more Negroes obtained higher scores than *any* of the whites; on two out of the four, one or more whites obtained scores as low as, or lower than, those of *any* Negro.

Let us suppose for the purpose of this argument (a supposition for which I perceive no acceptable evidence) that there is a difference in averages due to genetic factors. What about the individuals who "overlap"? I learned my statistics from a good teacher, a former psychologist at Columbia University, who kept reminding us not to forget the range when we compared two distributions. We were both students of that wise man, R. S. Woodworth, for whom the essence of psychology, as I understood him, was the behavior and characteristics of the individual. In one of his texts (1929) he defined psychology as the scientific study of the activities of the individual.

It is perhaps beyond the scope of this chapter to consider the practical implications of psychological research on Negro-white differences and similarities, but I hope I may be permitted one observation. Lines of demarcation between groups of people, in employment, in education, in opportunities for development, based on alleged differences in averages which are essentially abstractions, do violence to the facts of individual capacities and potentialities. At the most, group differences are obscure and uncertain; we are faced with the living reality of individual human beings who have a

right to the opportunity to show what they can do when they are given an equal chance. Perhaps I am allowing my own value system to influence me to look at the whole range of individual variations and not just at averages. I should have thought, however, that concern with the individual represented one value on which all psychologists might find themselves in agreement.

CONCLUSION

I can only conclude that there is no scientifically acceptable evidence for the view that ethnic groups differ in innate abilities. This is not the same as saying that there are no ethnic differences in such abilities. In the first place, I do not feel that mental tests can by themselves alone be used to prove this negative proposition. Perhaps in the future new techniques will be developed, better than our present tests, less subject to possible variations in interpretation, more conclusive in their results. I doubt that this would really change the picture, but the possibility must be kept open. Second, it is exceedingly difficult ever to prove the absence of something, because one can never be certain that all relevant factors have been taken into account. We can, however, say to those who have claimed to find evidence for ethnic differences in innate mentality: You have not proved your case. You have not been able to demonstrate that such differences exist.

We can go a little farther than that. We can point to the improvement in achievement when conditions of life improve. We can emphasize the tremendous variations within each ethnic group, much greater than the differences between groups even under discrepant environmental stimulation. We can insist that since innate psychological differences between ethnic groups have never been satisfactorily demonstrated, we have no right to act as if they had been. The science of psychology can offer no support to those who see in the accident of inherited skin color or other physical characteristics any excuse for denying to individuals the right to full participation in American democracy.

References

Anastasi, Anne. *Differential psychology* (3rd ed.). New York: Macmillan, 1958.

Anastasi, Anne and R. Y. D'Angelo, A comparison of Negro and white preschool children in language development and Goodenough Draw-a-Man IQ. *J. genet. Psychol.*, 1952, **81**, 147–165.

Bruce, M. Factors affecting intelligence test performance of whites and Negroes in the rural South. *Arch. Psychol.*, New York, 1940, No. 252.

Carmichael, O. Television Program of Sept. 13, 1959. Report, Dec. 15, 1959, Southern Regional Council, Atlanta.

Chant, S. N. F., and Freedman, S. S. A quantitative comparison of the nationality preferences of two groups. *J. soc. Psychol.*, 1934, **5**, 116–120.

Clark, W. W. Los Angeles Negro children. *Educ. Res. Bull., Los Angeles*, 1923, **3** (2), 1–2.

Dreger, R. M. and Miller, K. S. Comparative psychological studies of Negroes and whites in the United States. *Psychol. Bull.*, 1960, **57**, 361–402.

Garrett, H. E., and Schneck, M. R. *Psychological tests, methods and results.* New York: Harper, 1933.

Gilliland, A. R. Socioeconomic status and race as factors in infant intelligence test scores. *Child Developm.*, 1951, **22**, 271–273.

Klineberg, O. *Negro intelligence and selective migration.* New York: Columbia Univer. Press, 1935.

Klineberg, O. (Ed.) *Characteristics of the American Negro.* New York: Harper, 1944.

Knobloch, H. and Pasamanick, B. Further observations on the behavioral development of Negro children. *J. genet. Psychol.*, 1953, **83**, 137–157.

Lee, E. S. Negro intelligence and selective migration: A Philadelphia test of Klineberg's hypothesis. *Amer. sociol. Rev.*, 1951, **61**, 227–233.

McGraw, M. B. A comparative study of a group of southern white and Negro infants. *Genet. Psychol. Monogr.*, 1931, **10**, 1–105.

McGurk, F. C. J. *Comparison of the performance of Negro and white high school seniors on cultural and non-cultural psychological test questions.* Washington, D. C.: Catholic Univ. America Press, 1951.

Pasamanick, B. and Knobloch, H. Early language behavior in Negro children and the testing of intelligence. *J. abnorm. soc. Psychol.*, 1955, **50**, 401–402.

Pasamanick, B. A comparative study of the educational development of Negro infants. *J. genet. Psychol.*, 1946, **69**, 3–44.

Sherman, M., and Key, C. B. The intelligence of isolated mountain children. *Child Developm.*, 1932, **3**, 279–290.

Shuey, A. M. *The testing of Negro intelligence.* Lynchburg, Va.: J. P. Bell, 1958.

Stallings, F. H. Atlanta and Washington: Racial differences in academic achievement. Report No. L-16, Feb. 26, 1960, Southern Regional Council, Atlanta.

Tanser, H. A. *The settlement of Negroes in Kent County, Ontario, and a study of the mental capacity of their descendants.* Chatham, Ont.: Shepherd, 1939.

Woodworth, R. S. *Psychology* (Rev. ed.). New York: Holt, 1929.

17. Subcultural Patterns Which Affect Language and Reading Development

DONALD LLOYD

My approach to the effect of cultural differences on reading and language will not be that of the researcher, either in social science or in linguistics. It will be the approach of a literary scholar thrust into teaching masses of freshmen, who concluded that the creation of literacy in the young is a problem involving whole persons in their cultural setting, and who set out to discover what scholarship had to say about that. Since no one field of study touches the human being and his language at all points, what I have to say will be interdisciplinary. It will also be theoretical and high minded, but with some leavening of experience.

We speak of culturally divergent youth and also of culturally disadvantaged youth. These are not quite the same things, and I wish to distinguish between them. A person may be culturally divergent without being disadvantaged thereby, or he may be culturally disadvantaged without being divergent—or he may be both

Reprinted from Arno Jewett et al. (Eds.) *Improving English Skills of Culturally Different Youth In Large Cities* (Washington, D.C.: U.S. Dept. of Health, Education and Welfare, Office of Education, 1964), pp. 110–119, by permission of the author.
170

at once. We can make some grievous errors if we assume that cultural divergency necessarily means cultural disadvantage. There is a long history of Chinese and Japanese migrants to the United States who have successfully assimilated our values without abandoning their own, and who have made almost no contribution to the history of juvenile delinquency. Cultural strength meets cultural strength, we might say, and accommodates it, in the main happily. A similar situation exists with many of the present migrants coming to Miami from Cuba. They have a language problem, but it is temporary; they assimilate rapidly without excess damage to their pride.

The migrant Puerto Rican, on the other hand, is both culturally divergent and culturally disadvantaged. Coming to a different world using a different language, he has a difficult time maintaining his self-respect, as he faces the way of life he finds and the place he is expected to accept in the continental United States. The migrant southern white and Negro in our northern cities are culturally disadvantaged without being in any important way culturally divergent or divergent in language. We head into trouble if we think of these three situations as "similar" rather than "different." They *are* different.

For the Cuban, assimilation is on a level. He may even find that accented or broken English has commercial value for him. The Puerto Rican, however, meets a cultural monolith set mainly against him. A stranger and afraid, he penetrates the lowest level of the "have nots" in American society. The better he assimilates to that level the more difficult his further penetration may be. The migrant American is in a sociological sense culturally divergent, but only as any American assimilated to any American subgroup is. He is limited as much by his own expectations as by anything external to himself and his group. In terms of language, finally, the differences he shows are in themselves so trivial as to lay no special burden on him. His language problems are created in the schools and forced on him there.

Economic and social change has brought many new faces into the penniless, prolific, migrant populations of our great cities: unemployment brought about by automation alone seems to be creating a new mass of hard-core unemployables of low education and unneeded manual skills. In the United States, as everywhere in the world, the cities also seem to promise a life, bad as it is, preferable to hanging on in the countryside where life is even harsher. And there are always the refugees.

Forgive me for reviewing all this, which is surely known to you as well as to me, but I find it necessary to set my own thought into perspective. Other social forces affect these people also. Year by year the level of educational attainment creeps higher in the United States; nowadays more than half of each high school graduating class goes on to some kind of higher education. Thus each year more older people become a little more obsolescent in their education and a little more resistant to retraining. As the high school diploma drops a little in value, the value of each lower grade drops also. Yet even the present flood of college graduates fails to meet the need for cultivated brainpower. Handpower less, brainpower more—handpower less, machines more. Whatever happens in the suburbs, bad things happen in the cities. In Detroit, for example, half the 1958 graduating class of Miller High School had, up to 1961, never had a job. What of the ones who dropped out that year without finishing high school?

Our subject, then, turns out to be the literacy of children born to the have-not population in the older and more run-down sections of our great cities, what we should aim at, and how we should approach it. But even after saying so much, I cannot extract the thread of language and deal with it alone. A have-not population is not monolithic and homogeneous; it is a congeries of subcultures, defensively oriented in a hostile society. These cultures have their values, and these values are not all bad. Belongingness is a value; one must belong somewhere. Sharing is a value; at the table of the poor, there is always room for one more. Endurance is a value; it is good to get through one day more. Faith, loyalty, and silence are values; society is an enemy; say nothing to the cops. Companionship is a value, even in misery; you have to mean something to somebody. And love, in its myriad forms and expressions, is a value.

When children come to school from coherent groups which intercommunicate by means of a foreign language, the educational problem ought to be relatively simple, unless the school, as representative of the larger community, expresses contempt for the group and its language. If the group is large—as the Spanish-speaking population of the South and Southwest is large—then it is only common sense to teach the language of the groups to nonspeakers at the same age-levels as the foreign-speaking youngsters in English classes. It does a great deal for these children to be allowed to act as informants. Older children may be given special work in English as a foreign language. Modern techniques for this instruction have been quite well worked out. Very young children need have no special attention; left to themselves, they will work their way into the give- and-take of school life, and shortly their English will not be distinguishable from that of their schoolmates.

It is, then, the spoken English of the central city which concerns us as it is used by the children who live there. It is different from the English of college-educated teachers, different in its sounds, in its "grammar," and in its usage. The children have different terms for the same things, and terms for many things and processes not mentioned by adults, at least not in public and not in mixed company. Yet these differences, subcultural in origin if you will, are not and need not be factors interfering with the literacy of these children. They will not stand in the way of reading and writing if they are accepted and let alone without remark. They are trivial surface differences compared to the great mass of underlying similarities between the language of these children and the language of educated adults. Many of them, in fact, are features of child language and will pass out of use as the child matures. All are, of course, provided by the community in which the child is immersed. When you fight them, you take on the community—not the larger community only, but the

community of the school itself, of the turbulent, boisterous school corridors and playgrounds, and of the street; the community to which it is the child's normal and proper desire to belong, to fit into, to disappear in.

There are two main reasons for accepting the speech of the child, simply and noncommittally, during his early language education and, indeed, throughout all of it. The first is that it is his means of assimilating to all those persons to whom such security as he has is tied. He is, as I have said elsewhere, a kind of delegate from a speech community—an ambassador, as it were. When you touch him, you touch all those members of his family and his friends through him. Though his parents may say, "Git on down to that school and let them learn you some good English," they may not tolerate much of it when he brings it into the house. His playmates will tolerate it even less. I am not against introducing such discord into a child's life if it leads to some desirable educational objective, but in this case it does not. Not much good will come to a colored youngster by "learning to talk like all us white folks"; our vocabulary may not lead *him* to success. Change of speech will accompany or follow, not precede, his decision to make his way out of the world into which he was born. In any event, each person must *at all times* read his own speech on the page when he writes. To change his speech in the process of leading him to literacy is to multiply the problems of literacy beyond his ability to cope with them.

The second reason for accepting the child's speech is that changing it is not necessary to reading instruction. He shares with his teacher all the features of language important to reading, no matter what dialect he speaks or what dialect his teacher uses. Obviously children who speak midland, southern, southwestern, mountain, and rural dialects can learn to read without giving up their local speechways; otherwise, the schools in the areas from which they have migrated to the cities might as well close down. Persons speaking all the dialects represented by in-migrants to the cities proceed to the highest degrees in universities in their home areas and to great national prominence. Standard written and printed English is the same for all of us, and I doubt that any English speech in the United States, cultivated or uncultivated, is closer to it than any other. A pretty good representation of London English of the fifteenth century, standard written English fits any modern spoken English quite loosely. Humanity adjusts so well to incongruities that northerner, southerner, New Englander, and people along the eastern seaboard—not to speak of the English, Irish, Scotch, Welsh, East Indians, and South Africans—all think that they speak what is written and that others do not.

There is considerable literature on the language learning of children. Scholars generally agree that the child who goes to school is in full command of the system of his language—as presented to him by his family and community—and has it so thoroughly internalized that he uses it without thought. He thus has it *in him* to apply to the process of becoming literate. As he learned his speech from experience with people who speak within and about a milieu, we may expect that he will learn written language from reading books composed within and about human society. His speaking vocabulary when he comes to school is already old and already beyond measure; he needs only to learn how the words that he knows (their pronunciation varying as their place varies

within intonation patterns) relate to writing and print. It is reasonable to assume that as he learned the syntax and vocabulary of speech through engaging in the processes of hearing and speaking, he will learn the grammar and vocabulary of writing through engaging in reading and writing, and not through dictionary study, word lists, and grammar. Our problem is to set him as free in reading and writing as he is in hearing and speaking.

I come at last, then to words and their meanings. A theory of language and reading must, of course, embody a theory of words and meanings compatible with the whole. That is, if one thinks, as I do, that children learn words from reading and do not learn reading from word-study, he ought to be able to state his reasons. Here I must go back to a chapter in *American English in Its Cultural Setting*,[7] "Meaning, Structural and Otherwise," for my rationale. To me, the word is simply one element in a hierarchy of elements which make up the sentence, in itself of no particular importance.

For many years I puzzled over the question of how the stream of noises which make up the sentence can communicate meaning. I decided, finally, that the sentence is a handy-dandy meaning generator, the words within it conveying meaning not so much by what they assert as by what they deny and exclude. This is a kind of reversal.

In effect, the sentence is a kind of game of 20 questions. You recall that it is possible in that game, within 20 questions (if they are well chosen), to zero in on a particular person or object in the mind of someone else: when animal or mineral is stated, half your problem is eliminated. Then by taking one-half the terrestrial globe, you exclude the other half, and by eliminating large masses of possibilities, you finally get down to the point where an educated guess has a high probability of success.

The sentence operates similarly. Words are highly abstract items; each has a wide range of recorded significances—which is to say that outside a sentence, a word has no valid specific significance. If I give you the word *man* in isolation, you cannot possibly guess what meaning I have in mind for it. In the sentence, "Man has lived on this earth for fifty thousand years," *man* obviously means the human race; the term embraces *woman* as well. In the sentence, "Man never manages to get along with woman," *man* indicates the male half of the human race. I can run you through a dozen sentences, in each of which *man* has a different significance.

Indeed, all common words are multireferential; to express specific meaning, their range of possible significance must be curbed. The instrument for doing this curbing is the sentence, and the device is like the game 20 questions. Each meaning-element (intonation, pattern of order, function, word-class, and word) cuts away from each other meaning element anything which is incompatible with itself. In the end, the shrewd hearer or reader may know everything about a word except exactly what it does mean—its place in the sentence, in the subunit, in the word-class, and in the general area in which it is significant. In fact, he may be so close that he mistakes it for its exact opposite.

One illustration should suffice. A colleague came to me troubled about a student. He had assigned the general subject, "The special virtue of one character in the Odyssey." This student, a girl, had chosen Penelope, and had written about her *promiscuity*. That was Penelope's virtue. The writer had spoken of her fidelity to her husband, her rejection of the suitors, her

devices for stalling—weaving the web by day and unweaving it by night—and all her singleminded defense of her chastity. These, to the student, were summed up in the term *promiscuity*. The teacher said, "What shall I do? Send her to the dictionary?" I said, "No. Tell her what it means. She will say, "Oh migod.' " He did and she did. Note that she knew everything about the word, down to the area in which it had meaning, but she chose the exact opposite of its significance. When she seemed furthest off, she was actually as close as she could get—without being right.

The means by which we learn words from reading has been defined by Martin Joos of the University of Wisconsin as "bridging the gap with the minimal semantic burden necessary." Thus if we meet the word *stroll* in "He strolled in the garden," we can use *was* to carry the minimal semantic burden, reading "He was in the garden." Later we may meet, "He strolled through the town," and we have added a sense of motion: "He moved in some as yet unspecified way through the town." Little by little, as we meet the word in different contexts, we will narrow its meaning-range down until we have it cold. The linguistic principle here is that the meaning of a form lies as much in its distribution—in kinds and classes of other words and structural signals among which it appears—as in the history of experiences with its distribution. Many words can give significance to a sentence on a minimal basis without reflecting other significances relevant in other contexts.

From all this, you will have little trouble in defining my general stance on reading instruction. Reading instruction must be closely tied to speech in order to be successful. It should begin with familiar materials, the more familiar the better. It should not involve an attempt to change the children's speech, because that speech is the teacher's strongest ally. The child must learn to see the way that he normally talks in the print on the page. Instruction should relate to the total speech system, dealing honorably with the fluctuating relations between letters and the sounds of actual speech. It should rest heavily on intonation, and the students should be provided with intonation contours rather than permitted to puzzle out their own. The teacher should talk out in normal speech patterns what is on the page, and encourage the children to do so also. No "reading singsong" should be permitted to develop. Reading instruction should consist almost entirely of reading, and not of related but ineffectual busywork. Words should never be treated in isolation. Words should be handled in signal groups that are also meaning groups. At any stage, the teacher should settle on general meanings of sentences, passages, and whole stories, rather than on specific meanings of specific words —meanings which may not be the same for the same words in the next passage.

In order to operate this way, teachers must know the *sound system* of English, especially and specifically that of the children's speech—and they should let it alone. Reading instruction should not be combined with speech correction, or with an effort to change the dialectal peculiarities of the children's speech toward any other, regardless of the difference in prestige. Reading teachers should know the syntax of English speech well enough to manipulate the language somewhat at various syntactical levels and to create patterns for practice.

And finally, reading teachers should have enough uninhibited "ham" in them, enough of the dramatic impulse, to exaggerate, to push loud stresses up to extra loud and high pitches up to extra high: "The *sky* is falling," said Henny-Penny. "Let's go tell the *King!*" "Let's," said Foxy-Loxy, "but *first,* let's stop at *my* house for *dinner.*" And teachers should nourish the dramatic impulse in every child, the impulse to push his own loud stresses up and his own high pitches higher, and to emphasize the strong, unsteady, slightly loping, thoroughly internalized rhythm of his native speech. And they should make sure that every reading lesson is a lesson *in* reading, not a lesson *about* reading.

If reading actually is, as I believe it is, a native language process, then the youngster, who must carry to the page the signals that he finds on the page (if he is ever to find them there), can be helped to discover in his own free speech all he needs to make him a good reader. For the nature of each language is compulsive on the native speaker; he must work in terms of it. The teacher, too, must work in terms compatible with the native language, the familiar speech of the child. He must do so knowledgeably; otherwise, he will blunder along with it unawares. He will criss-cross it irrelevantly without knowing that he is doing so, or he will blunder head-on into it.

We cannot afford such blunders. Our society places increasing demands upon literacy as we become more and more the makers, the custodians, and the managers of machines. In our world of vast and ever vaster organizations, literacy becomes day by day more essential to meaningful citizenship. Each reading cripple is a badly wounded person, a social reject in his own mind and in the minds of others. We cannot afford such cripples. If blundering with language tends to favor the development of reading cripples, reading instruction is obligated to discover the harmonies of language and move in harmony with them.

With all these regularities of language working for them, it is clear that it is not the dialectal or subcultural patterns of the culturally different children which affect their reading development. These youngsters have the main bases for learning which are brought to school by all children except very special ones (who require special treatment beyond the capabilities of the classroom reacher). They can be led into literacy; if they are not, they may well be led into delinquency. I have seen a rather closely held study of children in trouble which provided all information about each child: age, crime, previous crimes, kind of family, sibling relationship, church affiliation, and so on. In all these factors no consistency is to be found; the child may be from a good or poor home, may have one or both parents, may be first, middle, or last child, may or may not be a churchgoer, and so on. One thing only is consistent: each child was from two to seven grades below his proper level in reading. In our society, the value placed on literacy is so high that failure to read well produces a badly wounded person who may hit back in one way or another.

There is one subcultural factor which does affect the language development of these children, and it is one which I wish to touch on now. This factor is the set of attitudes toward language held by the teachers whom Allison Davis would call "aspiring middle class"—as many teachers are. These attitudes are partly learned in the school and college training of English teachers with its monolithic fixation on "correct English" as the main proper outcome of education in English and the language arts. It is

fixation so deep that it is not felt as a subject for question; it overrides whatever work in child development, educational psychology, or methods the teacher may have had, even if these have been more enlightened about language than usual. It is a fixation often nourished in the teacher's own sense that only by parting with his origins, learning correct English, and moving out of the neighborhood has he been able to cut himself off from the foreign, rural, or working-class ways of his parents. And it frequently expresses itself as a demonstration of real love and concern for the children that they, too, should come up and out and away from a manner of life that is poverty-stricken, universally condemned, and deadened. Negro teachers especially, insisting that they cannot even understand the children whom they understand only too well, bear down brutally on the divergent phonology, "grammar," and usage of Negro children, communicating their own tension to the construction of the child's ultimate trauma about language. In most instances all the mores of the school sustain them in this unfortunate practice where they should resist it. The alternative to this overemphasis on conformity to "middle-class" speech, too, is unfortunate—the idea that the children are so low on the intelligence scale that their case is hopeless, and that the most the school can do is prepare them for the same manual occupations their parents engage in, keeping them off the streets and out of trouble as long as possible.

Certainly not every "linguistic approach" to the reading and language development of culturally different children will make them happy readers and writers. Linguists themselves tend to teach as they were taught rather than use the knowledge which descriptive linguistics provides. Much in current linguistics, misapplied in the classroom, tends to reinforce precisely those practices which will impede rather than advance the learning of the children. But if linguistic findings as a whole are drawn on and employed in a manner consistent with findings in other social sciences and psychology to create an environment favorable to language learning in the schools, then a whole new posture on the part of the teacher becomes possible. It is a posture much decried among the right-wing educational theorists: it is fundamentally nondisciplinary and permissive in regard to speech, marked by a courteous and studious respect for the children's speechways, to the extent of defining and recording exactly what they do say. It involves a great deal of reading with and to the children, to provide them with the delights and cultural nourishment other children get at home—the fairy tales, rhymes, and legends of literature. It begins where they are in language, wherever they are. It rests on the really rich and viable culture that almost any child car-ries within him to school, and it respects that culture. It relates the children's actual language to the printed page, and it lets the reading child talk the way his parents talk instead of "sounding out words" painfully, one by one, tonelessly, with strange and difficult sounds.

At present, if a child is in trouble with the community, the police, or the school, the school shows its harshest face to him in the language arts and English class. It is here that he finds that least praise and the most blame. The subcultural patterns which bring this about are not those of the children and they are not unchangeable. It is the patterns of the teachers which must change. Rather than let the athletic field or the shop represent the one place these children can excel, we can let them in on literacy. To do so, teachers need new knowledge, new attitudes, and new materials; but if the tieup between reading difficulties and delinquency is as close as it seems to be, we have no choice but to find out what we need to know and do what we need to do about reading.

References

Lefevre, Carl. "Language Patterns and Their Graphic Counterparts: A Linguistic View." A paper read at the Sixth Annual Convention of the International Reading Association, St. Louis, Missouri, May 6, 1961. Published in *Changing Concepts of Reading Instruction: International Reading Association Conference Proceedings,* Vol. 6, 1961.

Lefevre, Carl. "Reading Instruction Related to Primary Language Learnings: A Linguistic View." A paper read at the Golden Anniversary Convention of the National Council of Teachers of English, Chicago, Illinois, Nov. 25, 1960. Published in the *Journal of Developmental Reading,* Spring, 1961.

Lloyd, Donald J. Pure and applied linguistics—an overview. *Hexagon.* Chicago: Chicago Teachers College North, 1962.

Lloyd, Donald J. "Reading American English Sound Patterns," *Proceedings of the Chicago Area Reading Association,* 1962. Monograph No. 104. Evanston, Ill.: Row, Peterson, and Company, 1962.

Lloyd, Donald J. and Warfel, Harry R. *American English in Its Cultural Setting.* New York: Knopf, 1956.

Smith, Henry Lee, Jr. *Superfixes and Syntactic Markers.* Monograph Series on Language and Linguistics, No. 9. Washington, D.C.: Georgetown University, Dec. 1957, pp. 7–24.

Smith, Henry Lee, Jr. and George L. Trager, *Outline of English Structures, Studies in Linguistics,* Occasional Papers, No. 3.

Trager, Edith Crowell. "Superfix and Sememe: English Verbal Compounds." *General Linguistics,* Vol. 2, No. 1, Fall, 1956, pp. 1–14.

Warfel, Harry R. *Language, A Science of Human Behavior.* Cleveland, Ohio: Howard Allen, Inc., 1962.

18. Linguistic Codes, Hesitation Phenomena and Intelligence

BASIL BERNSTEIN

INTRODUCTION

In previous papers (Bernstein, 1959, 1961a, 1961b) attempts have been made to find a way of analysing some of the interrelationships between social structure, language use, and subsequent behaviour. In some way the form of the social relationship acts selectively on the speech possibilities of the individual and again in some way these possibilities constrain behaviour. Luria (1959, 1961) has explored both theoretically and experimentally the regulative function of speech. I take it that a proposition central to his view is that when a child speaks he voluntarily produces changes in his field of stimuli and his subsequent behaviour is modified by the nature of these changes. I shall here propose that forms of spoken language in the process of their learning initiate, generalise, and reinforce special types of relationship with the environment and thus create for the individual particular dimensions of significance. One of the tasks of the sociologist would be to seek the social origins of particular linguistic forms and to examine their regulative function.

Reprinted from *Language and Speech*, Vol. 5, Part 1 (October–December 1962), pp. 31–46, by permission of the publisher and author.

This task would become an attempt to reduce the interrelationships between social structure, language use, and individual behaviour to a theory of social learning. Such a theory should indicate *what* in the environment is available to be learned, the *conditions* of learning, and the *constraints* on subsequent learning. From this point of view the social structure transforms language possibilities into a specific code which elicits, generalises, and reinforces those relationships necessary for its continuance.

DEFINITION OF THE CODES

Two general types of code can be distinguished: *elaborated* and *restricted*. They can be defined, on a linguistic level, in terms of the probability of predicting for any one speaker which structural elements will be used to organise meaning. In the case of an elaborated code, the speaker will select from a relatively extensive range of alternatives, and therefore the probability of predicting the pattern of organising elements is considerably reduced. In the case of a restricted code the number of these alternatives is often severely limited, and the probability of predicting the pattern is greatly increased.

On a psychological level the codes may be distinguished by the extent to which each facilitates (elaborated code) or inhibits (restricted code) the orientation to symbolise intent in a verbally explicit form. Behaviour processed by these codes will, it is suggested, develop different modes of self-regulation and so different forms of orientation. The codes themselves are functions of a particular form of social relationship or, more generally, qualities of social structures.

SOCIOLOGICAL CONDITIONS FOR THE TWO CODES

The pure form of a restricted code would be one where the lexicon and hence the organising structure, irrespective of its degree of complexity, are wholly predictable. Examples of this pure form would be *ritualistic modes of communication*—relationships regulated by protocol, religious services, the opening gambits at a cocktail party, conversations about the weather, a mother telling her children stories, etc. It is clear that in the pure form of the restricted code individual intent can only be signaled through the nonverbal components of the situation, i.e., intonation, stress, expressive features, etc. Specific verbal planning will be minimal.

What is more often found is a restricted code [1] where prediction is only possible at the structural level. The lexicon will vary from one case to another, but in all cases it is drawn from a narrow range. The social forms which produce this code will also vary, but the most general condition for its development will be based upon some common set of closely shared identifications, self-consciously held by the members, where immediacy of the relationship is stressed. It follows that

these social relationships will be of an exclusive character. The speech is played out against a background of communal, self-consciously held interests which removes the need to verbalise subjective intent and make it explicit. The meanings will be condensed. Examples of the use of this code are to be found in the peer group of children and adolescents, criminal subcultures, combat units in the armed services, senior common rooms, between married couples of long standing, etc. In these social relationships the sequences will tend to be well organised at both the structural and lexicon levels. Verbal planning will tend to be reduced and the utterances fluent. The nonverbal component (expressive features) will be a major source for indicating changes in meaning. These expressive features will tend to reinforce a word or phrase rather than finely discriminate between meanings. The utterances will be well ventilated. They will tend to be *impersonal* in that the speech is not specially prepared to fit a particular referent. How things are said rather than what is said becomes important. The intent of the listener may be taken for granted. Finally, the content of the speech is likely to be concrete, descriptive, and narrative rather than analytical and abstract. The major function of this code is to reinforce the *form* of the social relationship (a warm and exclusive relationship) by restricting the verbal signaling of individuated responses. [2]

An elaborated code has its origins in a form of social relationship which increases the tension on the individual to select from his linguistic resources a verbal arrangement which closely

---

[1] In different ways Vigotsky (1939), Malinowski (1923) and Sapir (1931) have drawn attention to this form of speech.

[2] One important channel for individuated responses is humor, wit, or the joking relationship. These channels allow an individuated response, but an important effect is to reinforce the solidarity of the social relationship.

fits specific referents. The code becomes a vehicle for individuated responses. If a restricted code facilitates the construction and exchange of *social* symbols, then an elaborated code facilitates the construction and exchange of *individuated* symbols. The verbal planning function associated with this code promotes a higher level of structural organisation and lexicon selection. The preparation and delivery of relatively *explicit* meaning is the major purpose of the code. This does not necessarily mean that the content will be abstract, although this is inherent among the possibilities regulated by this code, but that the code will facilitate the verbal transmission and elaboration of the individual's experience. The condition of the listener will *not* be taken for granted, for the individual through verbal planning will modify his speech in relation to the specific requirements of the listener. This is not to say that such modification will always occur, but that the possibility exists. The code induces, through its regulation, a sensitivity to the implications of separateness for the organisation of experience. Finally, the expressive features which accompany the speech will tend to discriminate finely between meaning within sequences.

FORMAL SOCIOLOGICAL CONDITIONS FOR THE EMERGENCE OF THE TWO CODES

A *restricted* code is particularistic with reference to meaning and to the social structure which controls its inception. The speech model for this code is universalistic, for its use depends on the characteristics of a form of social relationship which can arise at any point in the social structure. An *elaborated* code is universalistic with reference to its meaning and *potentially* universalistic with reference to the social structure which controls its

inception. The speech model for this code in contemporary societies is particularistic. This does not mean that its origin is to be sought in the psychological qualities of the model, but that the model is an incumbent of a specialised position which is a function of the general system of social stratification. The models for the two codes lie in different sociological dimensions. In principle this is not necessary; it happens to be the case at the moment.

In terms of learning the codes are different. The abbreviated structures of a restricted code may be learned informally and readily. They become well-habituated. The greater range of and selection from structural alternatives associated with an elaborated code normally require a much longer period of informal and formal learning. An elaborated code is universalistic with reference to its meaning inasmuch as it summarises *general* social means and ends. A restricted code is particularistic with reference to its meaning inasmuch as it summarises *local* means and ends. The degree of elaboration is thus a function of the generality of the means and ends, whereas the degree of restriction is a function of the parochialness of the social means and ends. Thus because a restricted code is universalistic with respect to its model, all people have access to the code and to its local condensed meanings, but because an elaborate code is particularistic with respect to its model only some people have access to the code and to the potential universalistic character of its meanings. Access to an elaborated code will depend not on psychological factors but on specialised social positions within the social structure, by virtue of which a particular type of speech model is made available. Normally, but not inevitably, these positions will coincide with a stratum seeking, or already possessing, access to the major decision-making areas of the social structure.

The distinctions which have been drawn in terms of the availability of the speech model and the subsequent differences in coding are useful in isolating the general conditions for a special case of a restricted code. This is where the speech model is particularistic and the meaning is also particularistic. *In this situation the individual is wholly constrained by the code.* He has access to no other. It is with this situation that this article is concerned.

The sociological conditions may be summarised as follows:

1. Restricted code (lexicon prediction: ritualism.
   (a) restricted code (high structural prediction).
       Model: universalistic; meaning particularistic.
   (b) restricted code (high structural prediction).
       Model: particularistic; meaning particularistic.
2. Elaborated code (low structural prediction).
       Model: particularistic; meaning universalistic.

DEFINITION OF THE TERM "CODE"

At this point it is necessary to define the sense in which the word "code" is used. The following is both an attempt at definition and an attempt to show the relationship with verbal planning.

In the model represented in Figure 1, the section below the line represents the signal store in which interrelated verbal and nonverbal signals are contained. Above the line, E and D represent the usual encoding and decoding processes controlled and integrated by the verbal planning function (VP).

When A signals to B it is suggested that at least the following takes place:

ORIENTATION: *B* scans the incoming message for a pattern of dominant signals. (This is the beginning of the verbal planning sequence.)

Associations to the pattern of dominant signals control.

Selection from the signal store (V + NV).

ORGANISATION and integration of signals (V + NV) to produce a sequential reply.

The term "code" as I use it implies the principles which regulate these three processes. It follows that restricted and elaborated codes will es-

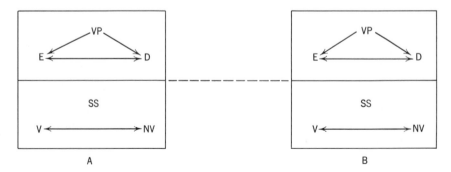

A   B

FIGURE 1.

tablish different kinds of control which crystallise in the nature of verbal planning. The latter is a resultant of the conditions which establish the patterns of orientation, association, and organisation. The originating determinants of this trio would be the form of the social relationship or more generally the quality of the social structure. This would allow the following postulate: the form of the social relationship acts selectively on the type of code, which then becomes a symbolic expression of the relationship and proceeds to regulate the nature of the interaction. Simply, the consequences of the form of the social relationship are transmitted and sustained by the code on a psychological level. Strategic learning would be elicited, sustained, and generalised by the code which would mark out what has to be learned and would constrain the conditions of successful learning.

It is clear that what is made available to be learned, the conditions of learning, and the subsequent constraints are different in the two codes. Individuals will, of course, shift from one to the other according to the form of the social relationship and so their usage is independent of the personality and intelligence of the speakers. These factors may influence the *level* within each code, but the latter is not inevitably a function of these psychological factors. This is a point of some importance if the situation of an individual who is wholly constrained by a restricted code (structural prediction) is considered. The general condition for this code, it will be remembered, is where both the model and the meaning are particularistic. In this country, it is suggested, this is the situation of the lower working-class, including rural groups. Together these groups represent 29% of the population. An elaborated code is associated with the middle-class and adjacent social strata. These codes, however, are not neces-

sarily clear functions of social class, but in advanced industrialised societies the association will have a high degree of probability. Class is only one of many principles of social stratification and differentiation.

Thus in this country children from these respective social strata will be exposed to different orders of learning and so their resultant modes of self-regulation and orientation will be different, irrespective of their levels of innate intelligence. The net effect of the constraint of a restricted code will be to depress potential linguistic ability, raise the relevance of the concrete and descriptive level of response, and inhibit generalising ability at the higher ranges. At the same time it will reinforce the solidarity of the developing child with his peers, which in turn will reinforce the solidarity of the code. Children from the middle-class and adjacent social strata will be exposed to both a restricted and an elaborated code and so to the possibilities symbolised by both these codes.

An experiment was designed to see whether these two codes were associated with social class and more particularly to see whether the orientation to use one or the other was independent of measured intelligence. At this point a problem arose of the measures which would discriminate the two codes in other than linguistic terms. Measures were required which would throw light upon the major controls of the codes, that is, would illuminate the verbal planning functions. The research, originated and systematically developed by Goldman-Eisler (1954, 1958a,b,c, 1961a,b) into the nature of hesitation phenomena, seemed the most promising technique. Her work has demonstrated a relationship between levels of coding activities and hesitation behaviour. She has found that the habit strength of speech sequences can be inferred from the hesitation phenomena. Levels of verbal planning thus become susceptible to objective measurement and discrimination. In terms of this work the following predictions were made about the hesitation phenomena associated with *elaborated* and *restricted* codes when speakers were subject to a group discussion situation.

1. Holding Verbal and Nonverbal I.Q. constant, working-class groups would pause less frequently and spend less time pausing than middle-class groups.

2. Holding Nonverbal I.Q. constant, working-class groups would pause less frequently and spend less time pausing than middle-class groups.

3. Irrespective of Nonverbal I.Q. the hesitation phenomenon of working-class subjects would be similar.

4. A general relationship would be found between the two I.Q. tests for the working-class group: the verbal scores would be severely depressed in relation to the scores at the higher ranges of the nonverbal test. It was expected that this general relationship would not hold for the middle-class group.

DESCRIPTION OF THE EXPERIMENT

Two extreme social groups were chosen for linguistic comparison. One group consisted of 61 male subjects between 15 and 18 years of age, matched for education and occupation but whose homes were distributed between inner and outer London. These subjects were compulsory students at a day release college where they attended one day a week to receive a general nonvocational education. They were employed as messengers and none had received a grammar school education. This group will be referred to as working-class. The second group consisted of 45 male subjects matched for age with the first group, all pupils at one of the six major public schools. These boys represented a reasonable cross section of the upper school with respect to educational attainment and particular subject interest. This group will be referred to as middle-class.

The two groups were given the Raven Progressive Matrices 1938 (a nonverbal measure of intelligence) and the Mill Hill Vocabulary Scale Form I Senior. These tests were selected so as to afford a comparison with 309 working-class subjects who had previously been tested (Bernstein, 1958). From the two major groups five subgroups were selected which would permit the following comparisons (see Table 1).

1. General interclass comparison.
2. Class comparisons with nonverbal intelligence held constant.
3. Class comparisons with verbal and nonverbal intelligence held constant.
4. Comparisons between different I.Q. profiles holding class constant.

Table 1

Group		Subjects	Verbal I.Q.	S.D.	Nonverbal I.Q.	S.D.	Age
Middle Class	1	5	125.0	1.81	123.8	2.75	16.2
	2	5	108.0	2.72	123.0	2.24	16.0
Working Class	3	5	105.0	2.14	126.0	0.0	15.6
	4	4	97.5	2.60	123.0	3.08	16.5
	5	5	100.00	4.60	100.6	3.20	16.2

A tape-recorded, relatively undirected discussion was taken with all groups on the topic of the abolition of capital punishment. It was possible to make a comparative analysis of the speech forms associated with the two major groups and the variations associated with the subgroups. It was thought that the working-class group would find the test situation threatening and that this would interfere with the speech, and consequently all working-class groups had two practice discussions (one a week) before the test discussion. This was not the case for the middle-class groups as such trials were impracticable. The working-class groups were drawn from four different forms and the subgroups contained members with varying degrees of personal contact. The social and educational contact of the middle-class group was not known. The probability of this highly selected group with varying characteristics containing members all of whom were in the same form or house was low, for the Upper School is very large and there are six houses. As far as possible the boys set the level of discussion, and the research worker intervened when a particular sequence was exhausted, when a boy was monopolising the discussion, or when voluntary contributions came to an end. The number of such interventions was considerably greater for the working-class groups for the last-mentioned reason. In order to permit maximum freedom little attempt was made to standardize the questions put to the groups. The major aim was to get the boys talking and to permit the groups themselves to establish the level of coding difficulty.

RESULTS OF THE INTELLIGENCE TESTING FOR THE MAJOR GROUPS

These results have been published in detail elsewhere (Bernstein, 1960) and only a summary will be given here.

For the working-class group all the verbal I.Q. scores are within the average range of the test, but 36 subjects (59%) scored above average on the nonverbal test and 11 subjects (18%) scored between 120–126 + I.Q. points. In other words, 18% of the group made scores which placed them in the top 5% of the population. A general relationship held. The higher the score on the nonverbal test, the greater the discrepancy between the scores on the two tests. In relation to the higher ranges of the Matrices test the language scores were severely depressed. This general relationship between the two tests for the working-class group was *not* found for the middle-class group. The mean scores for the two tests at different ranges matched each other very closely.

SPEECH SAMPLE

The speech sample consisted, for each group, of the next 1800 words approximately which followed the first five minutes of the discussion. An utterance was considered to be from the time a subject commenced to talk until he finished. The utterances were divided into long and short. The latter were sequences containing forty syllables or more and the former were sequences of between ten and forty syllabels. This division follows from the work of Goldman-Eisler (1954), who found that the hesitation phenomena associated with short utterances is unstable. The two categories of utterance have been analysed separately and only the results of the long utterances will be given here.

METHOD

Visual recordings of the speech were made on teledeltos paper and the speech on the magnetic tape was then synchronised with these visual records. Measurements were made from them of the following quantities for each utterance:

1. The number of words.
2. The number of syllables.
3. The articulation rate: this time is based on the rate of vocal speech utterance exclusive of pauses.
4. The mean number of words per pause (W/P). This gives a measure of the phrase length or frequency of pauses.
5. The mean pause duration per word per utterance (P/W).
6. The mean word length in number of syllables. Pauses with a duration of under 0.25 second were ignored.

ORGANISATION OF THE SUBGROUPS

Information about the subgroups is contained in Table 2. The difference in numbers in groups 4 and 5 arose because one member from each group failed to contribute a long utterance and one member from group 4 was absent from the college on the day of the study. It is perhaps of interest that the two members who failed to make a long utterance were both members of the working-class group.

The arrangement of the groups for the purpose of the analysis was different from the original grouping. One subject each from group 1 and from group 2 was exchanged, two subjects were shifted from group 4 to group 3, and one from group 3 was placed in group 4. This was necessary in order to make a better match between group 2 and group 3 to see whether the lower verbal I.Q. of group 4 would affect the hesitation phenomena. Although the original sample was approximately 1800 words for each group, this rearrangement altered considerably the balance of speech analysed for each group. The number of words also differs because the number of short utterances contributing to the total varied with each group. The very large standard deviation for the mean number of words in group 1 and group 3 is the result of one subject from each of these groups contributing a mean of 217.3 words and 194.3 words respectively. If these subjects' utterances are subtracted from the totals of their respective groups, then the only major significant difference in the mean number of words for each group is between group 3 and group 5. The low total of words for group 2 was because one of the subjects, who in this analysis now appears in group 1, uttered a total of 652 words. He took up much of the discussion time. The total for group 4 is low because one of the original members contributed a total of 777 words, but for the purposes of the analysis this subject is included in group 3. As all the measures used in the analysis are ratios, the real differences between the groups in absolute number of words is not so important as differences in the mean number of utterances contributed by each subject. For the critical com-

Table 2

Group	Subjects	Number of Utterances	Mean No. of Utterances	Number of Words	Mean No. of Words	S.D.
1	5	21	4.2	1885	99.4	59.33
2	5	19	3.8	1242	64.4	8.06
3	5	22	4.4	2205	101.2	46.89
4	3	12	4.0	793	61.9	27.80
5	4	24	6.0	1329	54.8	5.86

parisons there is little difference. In group 5 the mean number of utterances is somewhat higher.

Finally, the rearranging of the subjects could not in any way alter the results of the major class comparisons. The exchange of one subject between group 1 and group 2 made no difference, for the scores on all relevant measures corresponded with the scores of the groups to which they were attached. This was also the case for the exchanges between group 3 and group 4.

RESULTS

The results are summarised in Table 3. One tail t tests were used as the direction of the differences was predicted in all comparisons.

Mean Differences

There is no significant difference between the articulation rates for any of the comparisons, except for the intra middle-class comparison where the difference is at borderline significance at the 0.05 level of confidence. This is in line with the findings of Goldman-Eisler (1961) for this measure. She has found that this rate is a constant of great rigidity inasmuch as it does not respond to changes in the level of verbal planning, as do pauses, but only to the effect of practice.

Differences in mean phrase length, mean pause duration per word, and mean word length were found for the class groups matched for nonverbal intelligence. The working-class group uses a longer phrase length, a shorter mean pause duration, and a considerably shorter word length.

The same pattern of differences was found (at a higher level of confidence for the hesitation phenomena and at a somewhat reduced level of confidence for mean word length) for the over-all comparison between the class groups. The only difference between the working-class groups $(3 + 4$ v. $5)$, two of whom had an advantage of over 20 nonverbal I.Q. points, was in mean pause duration. The working-class group with the average I.Q. profile spends less time pausing.

The mean difference of 7.5 verbal I.Q. points is associated with no difference in the hesitation phenomena and mean word length for the working class groups matched for nonverbal intelligence.

Differences were found between the two middle-class groups matched for high nonverbal intelligence, for mean phrase length, and mean word length. The group with high verbal intelligence used a longer phrase length and word length than the group with low verbal intelligence.

When the I.Q. profile was held constant and middle- and working-class groups were compared, differences at a high level of confidence were found for mean phrase length and mean pause duration. No differences were found for mean word length. The working-class group used a considerably longer phrase length (3.8 more words to the phrase) and spent much less time pausing (0.06 second) than the middle-class group.

Scatter

The scatter about the mean for pause duration per word is considerably smaller for all the working-class groups. It is greatest for group 1, that is, the middle-class group with the superior I.Q. scores on both tests.

The scatter about the mean for phrase length is considerably and significantly less $(p > 0.05)$ for group 2 when this group is compared with group 1 or group 3.

DISCUSSION

The first point of interest is that this technique of analysis discriminates between the groups and that the hesita-

Table 3

Group	Articulation Rate					Phrase Length				
	Mean	S.D.	Mean	S.D.	t	Mean	S.D.	Mean	S.D.	t
1+2 v 3+4	6.2	0.80	6.3	0.60	0.27 n.s.	6.3	2.00	8.9	1.92	2.69 $p > 0.01$
1+2 v 3+4+5	6.2	0.80	6.2	0.58	0.00 n.s.	6.3	2.00	9.3	2.07	3.29 $p > 0.005$
3+4 v 5	6.3	0.60	5.8	0.23	1.47 n.s.	8.9	1.92	10.0	2.28	0.87 n.s.
3 v 4	6.2	0.32	6.7	0.78	1.11 n.s.	8.9	1.91	8.9	1.69	0.00 n.s.
1 v 2	6.6	0.61	5.8	0.63	1.82 n.s.	7.6	2.14	5.1	0.49	2.33 $p > 0.025$
2 v 3	5.8	0.63	6.2	0.32	1.14 n.s.	5.1	0.49	8.9	1.91	3.87 $p > 0.005$

Group	Pause Duration per Word					Word Length				
	Mean	S.D.	Mean	S.D.	t	Mean	S.D.	Mean	S.D.	t
1+2 v 3+4	0.12	0.05	0.08	0.02	1.90 $p > 0.05$	1.30	0.06	1.21	0.06	2.90 $p > 0.01$
1+2 v 3+4+5	0.12	0.05	0.07	0.03	2.94 $p > 0.005$	1.30	0.06	1.23	0.07	2.33 $p > 0.025$
3+4 v 5	0.08	0.02	0.05	0.01	2.50 $p > 0.025$	1.21	0.06	1.25	0.05	0.85 n.s.
3 v 4	0.08	0.02	0.07	0.02	0.02 n.s.	1.20	0.06	1.23	0.05	0.61 n.s.
1 v 2	0.11	0.06	0.14	0.04	0.83 n.s.	1.34	0.05	1.26	0.05	2.28 $p > 0.05$
2 v 3	0.14	0.04	0.08	0.02	2.74 $p > 0.025$	1.26	0.05	1.20	0.06	1.50 n.s.

tion behaviour is independent of measured intelligence for this small sample and with reference to a discussion situation.

All predictions were confirmed except that relating to the hesitation pattern associated with the working-class groups independent of the level of nonverbal intelligence of the members. For this group, nonverbal IQ is related to the ability to tolerate delay associated with coding.

Since frequency of pauses (phrase length) refers to the amount of monitoring of the sequences [3] and thus to the number of intervals during which alternative possibilities are available, and duration refers to the relative difficulty of selecting the next sequence, the two measures yield an index of coding difficulty. Duration also refers to the ability to tolerate delay and the resulting tension associated with coding difficulty. Word length yields a crude indication of the informational value of the output (Goldman-Eisler, 1958).

It would follow that the longer the phrase, the more well-organised the sequence and the more likely that the units will readily condition each other, their pairing being the result of common verbal conditioning within a community (Goldman-Eisler, 1958). In a fascinating paper Goldman-Eisler (1961b) has demonstrated that summarising (abstracting and generalising from perceived events) requires more time in pausing than does description. Fluency and hesitation would seem to discriminate between two kinds of speech and differentiate levels of verbal planning. These propositions were derived from data obtained in rigorous experimental conditions and checked against the content of the speech. In evaluating the results of the present experiment conducted in relatively free conditions some caution is required. Furthermore the content of the speech has yet to be analysed. The interpretations are therefore expectations about the organisation of the content.

In all interclass comparisons matched or not for nonverbal intelligence, there are clear-cut differences in the hesitation phenomena which presumably indicate differences in verbal planning. In the critical comparison between the classes in which the I.Q. profile is held constant, the differences are even sharper. This would seem to mean at least that for the middle-class group, in this comparison, the conditions exist for greater lexicon and structural selection and thus greater appropriateness between the speech sequences and their referents. Further, the middle-class group can tolerate the delay normally associated with increasing information even though at this stage the informational value of the speech is not known. This delay was not associated with a marked drop in output.[4] The hesitation behaviour of the working-class group would seem to rule out the possibilities available to the middle-class group. The verbal planning orientations are different. Inasmuch as the word lengths for these groups are not significantly different, nor are their vocabulary scores, the differences in verbal planning orientation can be considered independent of passive and active vocabulary.

The intraclass comparisons indicate that for the working-class group matched for nonverbal intelligence but who differ by a mean of 7.5 verbal I.Q. points, no differences for the hesitation measures and word length occur. It is considered that these groups share a similar verbal planning orientation

---

[3] It is assumed that frequency of pauses is an index of the degree of monitoring.

[4] One member of the working-class group in this comparison failed to contribute any long utterances.

despite the difference in verbal I.Q. There is considerable restriction of the scatter for the measure of mean pause duration. There are very few relatively long pauses, and this is even more pronounced in the working-class group with an average I.Q. profile. The latter group makes significantly shorter pauses and this is the only measure which discriminates this group from the working-class groups who have an advantage of over 20 nonverbal I.Q. points. This raises an interesting point. Differences in verbal I.Q. between the middle-class groups are associated with differences in phrase and word length and possibly articulation rate, whereas differences in nonverbal I.Q. are associated with differences in pause duration. The monitoring processes are affected in one case and only the interval between *similar* monitoring in the other. It would seem that for the average working-class group the delay between impulse and verbal signal is very short and the control (selection) of the subsequent sequences is reduced. Presumably the middle-class group with low verbal intelligence, relative to the middle-class group with high verbal intelligence, was in a situation of coding difficulty and responded by shortening the phrase length in order to avail themselves of a greater number of intervals during which alternative selections could be made. The difference between the articulation rates for the middle-class groups may be related to how well-practiced the arguments selected were. The low verbal group would appear to have much difficulty at all coding levels, but the members perserved in their orientation.

The behaviour of the middle-class group with the superior IQ profile is of interest. In comparison with the working-class groups matched for nonverbal I.Q. there is no difference in

the hesitation pattern but only in word length $(p > 0.005)$.[5] However, the scatter for the measure of mean pause duration is significantly different $(p > 0.05)$. In fact, 52.4% of the utterances made by this middle-class group have a mean pause duration of 0.09 second or over. The figure for the working-class is 34.3%. Over half the utterances contain relatively longer pauses. In other words, this middle-class group can avail itself of longer pauses. Although there is no significant difference, the mean phrase length of this middle-class group is shorter by 1.3 words per phrase. These results are taken to mean that the middle-class group produced a higher level of speech organisation, lexicon selection, and information for similar monitoring (pause frequency) and that where necessary the delay associated with coding could be tolerated.

If now this discussion is related to the theory briefly outlined in the introduction, it is clear that the derivations have been confirmed. Middle-class and working-class subjects in this small sample are orientated to different levels of verbal planning which control the speech process. These planning orientations are independent of intelligence as measured by two reliable group tests and by word length. They are thus independent of psychological factors and inherent in the linguistic codes which are available to normal individuals. In psychological terms, the codes are stabilised by the planning functions and reinforced in the speaking. They are highly resistant to change as they encapsulate the major effects of socialisation.

From this point of view the general relationship between the verbal and

[5] It is thought that this difference in length of word would be associated with a greater complexity of organisation, lexicon selection, and informational output.

nonverbal intelligence scores attained by members of the lower working-class stratum becomes somewhat more understandable. This does not rule out the role of innate factors; rather it becomes more difficult to evaluate their relationship to behaviour when the individual is limited to a restricted code and the educational process requires, at least, an orientation to an elaborated code. Children who already have this orientation are in a situation of symbolic development; those without it are in a situation of symbolic change.

For various reasons, in particular the occupation of the mother before marriage and the role differentiation within the family, there will not be a one-to-one correlation between the use of a restricted code and the working-class stratum, but the probability is certainly very high.[6]

The analysis of hesitation phenomena developed by Goldman-Eisler has discriminated between the proposed codes, has illuminated the nature of verbal planning processes, and has provided an objective means for their assessment.

CONCLUSIONS

Two linguistic codes have been proposed, *elaborated* and *restricted*. These codes are regarded as functions of different social structures. They are considered to entail qualitatively different

[6] A more general description of the use of this code would be that the speech model is particularistic and the meaning channeled through the model also particularistic.

verbal planning orientations which control different modes of self-regulation and levels of cognitive behavior. Social class differences in the use of these codes were postulated and the hesitation phenomena associated with them predicted.

Speech samples were obtained and the hesitation phenomena analyzed from a discussion situation involving small groups of middle-class and working-class subjects with varying I.Q. profiles.

Major Results

1. Over-all social class differences were found. The working-class subjects used a longer mean phrase length, spent less time pausing, and used a shorter word length.

2. Holding nonverbal intelligence constant, social class differences were found in the same direction.

3. Holding verbal and nonverbal intelligence constant, social class differences were again found in the same direction, but not for word length.

4. Within the middle-class group, the subgroup with superior verbal intelligence used a longer mean phrase length, a faster rate of articulation, and a longer word length.

5. Within the working-class group, the subgroup with the average IQ profile spent less time pausing.

The major predictions were confirmed. The results were considered as supporting evidence for the two codes and the different verbal planning orientations which are entailed.

References

Bernstein, B. (1958). Some sociological determinants of perception. *Brit. J. Sociol.*, **9**, 159.

Bernstein, B. (1959). A *public* language: some sociological implications of a linguistic form. *Brit. J. Sociol.* **10**, 311.

Bernstein, B. (1960). Language and social class. *Brit. J. Sociol.*, **11**, 217.

Bernstein, B. (1961a). Aspects of language and learning in the genesis of the social process. *J. Child Psychol. & Psychiat.*, **1**, 313.

Bernstein, B. (1961b). Social class and linguistic development: a theory of social learning. In *Economy, Education and Society*, eds. A. H. Halsey, Floud, J. and Anderson, A. (New York), 288.

Goldman-Eisler, F. (1954). On the variability of the speed of talking and on its relation to the length of utterances in conversations. *Brit. J. Psychol.*, **45**, 94.

Goldman-Eisler, F. (1958a). Speech analysis and mental processes. *Language and Speech*, **1**, 59.

Goldman-Eisler, F. (1958b). Speech production and the predictability of words in context. *Quart. J. exp. Psychol.*, **10**, 96.

Goldman-Eisler, F. (1958c). The predictability of words in context and the length of pauses in speech. *Language and Speech*, **1**, 226.

Goldman-Eisler, F. (1961a). The significance of changes in the rate of articulation. *Language and Speech*, **4**, 171.

Goldman-Eisler, F. (1961b). Hesitation and information in speech. In *Information Theory, 4th London Symposium* (London), 162.

Luria, A. R. and Yudovich, F. (1959). Speech and the Development of Mental Processes in the Child (London).

Malinowski, B. (1923). The problem of meaning in primitive languages. In C. K. Ogden and I. A. Richards, *The Meaning of Meaning* (London).

Sapir, E. (1931). Communication. In *Encyclopedia of the Social Sciences*, **4** (New York), 78.

Vigotsky, L. S. (1939). Thought and speech. *Psychiatry*, **2**, 29.

19. Social Class, Linguistic Codes, and Grammatical Elements

BASIL BERNSTEIN

Table 1

Group		Subjects	Verbal I.Q.	S.D.	Nonverbal I.Q.	S.D.	Average Age
Middle-class	1	5	125.0	1.81	123.8	2.75	16.2
	2	5	108.0	2.72	123.0	2.24	16.0
Working-class	3	5	105.0	2.14	126.0	0.00	15.6
	4	4	97.5	2.60	123.0	3.08	16.5
	5	5	100.0	4.60	100.6	3.20	16.2

DESCRIPTION OF THE EXPERIMENT

Only a summary will be given here, as the study has been described in detail in the previous article. Five subgroups were selected from two parent samples with the characteristics shown in Table 1. The members of the main sample were drawn from a public school and a day release college. The pupils of the latter were all educated in secondary modern schools, none had achieved any formal examination certificate, and all were employed as messenger boys. This group will be referred to as working-class and the first as middle-class. The mean age of the subjects was sixteen. A tape-recorded relatively undirected discussion on the topic of abolition of capital punishment was taken with the five subgroups.

SPEECH SAMPLE

The speech sample consisted for each group of the 1800 words, approximately, which followed the first five minutes of the discussion. Long and short utterances were distinguished according to whether the utterance was between ten and forty syllables or over forty syllables. The distribution is shown in Table 2. In order that close I.Q. comparisons could be made there was an interchange of one member between groups 1 and 2 and between groups 3 and 4. Groups 2 and 3 are matched for verbal and nonverbal I.Q.

Reprinted from *Language and Speech*, Vol. 5, Part 4 (October–December 1962), pp. 221–240, by permission of the publisher and author.

193

Table 2

UTTERANCES (NUMBER AND TYPE)

Group	1	2	3	4	5	1 + 2	3 + 4	3 + 4 + 5
Long	21	19	22	12	24	40	34	58
Short	24	8	14	9	19	32	23	42
Total	45	27	36	21	43	72	57	100
Mean No. of words	48.8	52.9	68.8	49.6	39.8	50.3	61.8	52.3

The membership of the original groups differed slightly from the membership shown in Table 1. This shift partly accounts for the differences in the total number of words analysed for each group. The lower number of words in group 2 is the result of shifting one original member who contributed 590 words and who took up much of the time of the discussion to group 1. A similar reason accounts for the low number of words in group 4.

Two members of the working-class sample, one from group 4 and one from group 5, were omitted from the analysis as neither contributed a long utterance and the total number of words for each was under 90 words. This results in the difference in the total number of words between groups 1 + 2 and groups 3 + 4 and reduces the aggregate number of words for groups 3, 4, and 5.

Not all the words spoken were used for the analysis. All group comparisons, except those for personal pronouns, are based upon a speech sample which excludes all words repeated, fragments (false starts and sequences which could be deleted without altering the meaning), sequences such as "I mean" and "I think" and terminal sequences such as "isn't it," "you know," "ain't it," "wouldn't he," etc. One personal pronoun count included the "I think" and the terminal sequences. The terminal sequences, for reasons which will be given later, are called *sympathetic circularity* sequences and are indicated by the abbreviation S.C. Table 3 contains a summary of the information relating to omission. It can be seen that the percentage of words removed from each group does not vary greatly. The general effect of the words and sequences excluded was to bring the social class speech samples closer together.

Table 3

Group	Total No. of Words	No. of Words Omitted	No. of Words Analysed	Percentage Omitted
1(5)	2194	196	1998	8.9
2(5)	1429	139	1290	9.7
3(5)	2478	283	2195	11.4
4(3)	1042	84	958	8.1
5(4)	1709	123	1586	7.2
1 + 2(10)	3623	335	3288	9.3
3 + 4(8)	3520	367	3153	10.5
3 + 4 + 5(12)	5229	490	4739	9.4

STATISTICAL ANALYSIS

The nature of the distributions indicated that nonparametric tests of significance were more appropriate as these tests do not require that the data be normally distributed and the variance be homogeneous. The Mann-Whitney u test of significance was used, for it is considered the most powerful of the nonparametric tests and a most useful alternative to the parametric t test when the researcher wishes to avoid the t test's assumptions (Seigal, 1956). The grammatical elements were expressed as proportions of the appropriate populations. The distribution of the proportions for the various measures indicates that for the over-all sample the scores attained on the various measures are independent of the number of words.

Only when the comparison indicated a significant difference between the major class groupings ($1 + 2$ v. $3 + 4 + 5$) were the subgroups examined. Intraclass comparisons were made to test the consistency of the interclass differences. In the previous article a number of interclass comparisons were redundant in that given an over-all significance between the class groups only a limited inspection may be made of the subgroups. Thus in this analysis groups 2 and 3 (the subgroups matched for verbal and nonverbal I.Q.

but differing in terms of social class) were compared; group 1 v. 2 and 4 v. 5 were compared, respectively, to test intraclass consistency. Tables of significance are not given (for reasons of space) where no difference exists between the major class comparisons and where the difference is so clear that statistical examination is unnecessary. One-tail tests were used as the direction of the differences was predicted on all tests.

RESULTS

No differences between the major class comparisons ($1 + 2$ v. $3 + 4 + 5$) were found for the proportion of finite verbs, nouns, different nouns, prepositions, conjunctions, and adverbs. No count was made for different finite verbs as the writer found it difficult to decide the principle by which these verbs with their attendent stems could be classified.

I mean, I think, and S.C. sequences. I mean.

This sequence was excluded from the analysis as it was considered a simple reinforcing unit of the previous or subsequent sequence and likely to be an idiosyncratic speech habit. Table 4 indicates the findings, but of the 26 sequences for group 3, 22 were contributed by one subject; of the 11 se-

Table 4

Group	I mean	I think	SC	I think and S.C.	I think and S.C. as Percentage of Words
1	10	21	4	25	1.25
2	5	22	4	26	1.82
3	26	11	35	48	2.10
4	2	3	15	18	1.88
5	11	3	17	20	1.26
1 + 2	15	43	8	51	1.55
3 + 4	28	14	50	64	2.03
3 + 4 + 5	39	17	67	84	1.77

quences for group 5, 8 were contributed by one subject; of the 10 for group 1, 7 were contributed by one subject. The "I think" and S.C. sequences are not idiosyncratically distributed and their function is different.

I think.

There is clear evidence that this sequence is used more frequently by the middle-class groups and especially by group 2.

S.C. Sequences.

These sequences are used much more frequently by the working-class groups and within this group less frequently by group 5.

"I think" plus S.C. sequences.

If these sequences are added and the result expressed as a percentage of the number of words for each group, then the differences between the major class groups is very small. Inspection of the table indicates that this results from the low frequency of these combined sequences in group 1 and group 5.

Subordination (Table 5)

The method used to assess the use of subordination was pointed out to the writer in discussion with Dr. Frieda Goldman-Eisler. The first step was to isolate a unit which could readily be observed with a minimum of ambiguity in the two major speech samples. This

was done by terming a proposition any sequence which contained a finite verb whether or not the subject was implicit or explicit. The implicit verb at the beginning of an utterance was not counted, for example, "Not really. . . ." When two finite verbs were associated with the same subject this counted as two propositions. If the number of such finite verbs is then divided into the total number of analysed words for each group, a mean proposition length is obtained. There was no difference between the major class groups on this measure. The number of subordinations linking two finite verbs was counted and the proportion of subordinations to finite verbs was assessed for each subject. In this analysis the role of the "I think" and S.C. sequences becomes important. The latter would tend to decrease the proportion of the former to increase it. Inasmuch as these sequences are class patterned the results would be prejudiced. They were omitted in both the finite verb and subordination counts. The effect of this omission brought the two speech samples closer together.

Table 5 indicates that the difference in use of subordination when groups 1 + 2 is compared with groups 3 + 4 + 5 is significant at above the 0.001 level of confidence. The difference between groups 2 and 3 is significant at the 0.008 level of confidence. The intraclass differences are not significant.

No comparison was made of differ-

Table 5

SUBORDINATION

Group	n	n	u	P
1 + 2 v. 3 + 4 + 5	10	12	6	0.001
1 v. 2	5	5	8	n.s.
2 v. 3	5	5	1	0.008
4 v. 5	3	4	3	n.s.

Table 6

COMPLEXITY OF VERBAL STEM

Group	n	n	u	P
1 + 2 v. 3 + 4 + 5	10	12	23	0.02
1 v. 2	5	5	12	n.s.
2 v. 3	5	5	3	0.028
4 v. 5	3	4	5	n.s.

ences in sentence length, for no reliable method for distinguishing the samples on this measure was available. A method appropriate for groups 1 and 2 would have been inappropriate for groups 3, 4, and 5. The method of double juncture was too sophisticated in terms of the skills of the research worker.

Complexity of the Verbal Stem (*Table 6*)

This count was based upon the number of units in the verbal stem excluding the adverbial negation. Verbal stems containing more than three units were counted for each subject and expressed as a proportion of the total number of finite verbs uttered (excluding the verbs in the "I think" and S.C. sequences). A verb plus an infinitive was counted as a complex verbal stem. The results indicate that groups 1 and 2 select more complex verbal stems than do groups 3, 4, and 5. The difference is significant beyond the 0.02 level of confidence. Group 2 selects more complex stems than does group 3 and the difference is significant at the 0.028 level of confidence. The intraclass differences are not significant.

Passive Voice (*Table 7*)

Major class differences in the proportion of passive verbs to total finite verbs was found and the difference is significant beyond the 0.02 level of confidence. The middle-class use a greater proportion of passive verbs and this holds when group 2 is compared with group 3 at the 0.048 level of confidence. The intraclass differences are not significant.

Uncommon Adverbs (*Table 8*)

An arbitrary classification was used to distinguish uncommon adverbs. Adverbs of degree and place, "just," "not," "yes," "no," "then," "how," "really," "when," "where," "why," were excluded from the total number of adverbs and the remainder, excluding repetitions, was expressed as a proportion of the total number of analyzed

Table 7

PASSIVE VOICE

Group	n	n	u	P
1 + 2 v. 3 + 4 + 5	10	12	21	0.02
1 v. 2	5	5	5	n.s.
2 v. 3	5	5	4	0.048
4 v. 5	3	4	4	n.s.

Table 8

UNCOMMON ADVERBS

Group	n	n	u	P
1 + 2 v 3 + 4 + 5	10	12	2	0.001
1 v 2	5	5	12	n.s.
2 v 3	5	5	0	0.004
4 v 5	3	4	3	n.s.

words used by each subject. This remainder was termed "uncommon adverbs." A greater proportion of the adverbs of the middle-class are uncommon and the difference is significant beyond the 0.001 level of confidence. This difference, at the 0.004 level of confidence, holds when group 2 is compared with group 3. The intraclass differences are not significant.

Total Adjectives (Table 9)

The proportion of all adjectives to total analyzed words is greater for the middle-class group and the difference is significant beyond the 0.01 level of confidence. This difference holds at the 0.004 level of confidence when group 2 is compared with group 3. The intraclass differences are not significant.

Uncommon Adjectives (Table 10)

An arbitrary classification was again used to distinguish uncommon adjectives. Numerical and demonstrative adjectives and "other" and "another"

were excluded from the total number of adjectives and the remainder excluding repetitions was expressed as a proportion of the total number of analysed words used by each subject. The middle-class use a higher proportion of uncommon adjectives to total analysed words than do the working-class groups and the difference is significant beyond the 0.001 level of confidence. This difference holds at the 0.008 level of confidence when group 2 is compared with group 3. The intraclass differences are not significant.

Prepositions, Of (Table 11)

No difference was found, it will be remembered, in the proportion of prepositions to total analysed words. For reasons to be given in the discussion the use of "of" was of interest. The prepositions "of" and "in" combined account for over 34% of the total prepositions used. The relative use of "of" in relation to "in" and "into" was assessed by expressing the proportion of

Table 9

TOTAL ADJECTIVES

Group	n	n	u	P
1 + 2 v 3 + 4 + 5	10	12	16	0.01
1 v 2	5	5	11	n.s.
2 v 3	5	5	0	0.004
4 v 5	3	4	3	n.s.

Table 10

UNCOMMON ADJECTIVES

Group	n	n	u	P
1 + 2 v 3 + 4 + 5	10	12	4	0.001
1 v 2	5	5	11	n.s.
2 v 3	5	5	1	0.008
4 v 5	3	4	5	n.s.

"of" (excluding "of" in "sort of") to the total of "of" and "in" and "into." The middle-class groups use a higher proportion of "of" than do the working-class groups and the difference is significant beyond the 0.01 level of confidence. The difference holds at the 0.008 level of confidence when group 2 is compared with group 3. No difference is found when the two middle-class groups are compared, but group 5 uses a higher proportion of this preposition than does group 4. The difference between these two groups is at the 0.028 level of confidence.

Uncommon Conjunctions (*Table 12*)

An arbitrary division was made. All conjunctions other than "and," "so," "or," "because," "also," "then," "like" were classified uncommon and the result was expressed as a proportion of total conjunctions. The middle-class groups use a higher proportion of uncommon conjunctions than do the working-class group and the difference is significant

beyond the 0.01 level of confidence. The difference holds at the 0.008 level of confidence when group 2 is compared with group 3. The intraclass differences are not significant. Much less faith is placed in this finding than in any of the others as the numbers are small and whether certain conjunctions are classified as types of adverbs will affect the result.

Personal Pronouns

Two different assessments of the proportion of personal pronouns were made. The first included all personal pronouns and therefore those to be found in the "I think" and S.C. sequences. The second excluded those personal pronouns contained in the "I think," S.C., and direct speech sequences. Two different assessments were also made of the relative proportions of "I" and "you" combined with "they." The first expressed these pronouns as proportions of total pronouns and the second as proportions of the

Table 11

OF

Group	n	n	u	P
1 + 2 v. 3 + 4 + 5	10	12	19	0.01
1 v. 2	5	5	11	n.s.
2 v. 3	5	5	1	0.008
4 v. 5	3	4	0	0.028

Table 12

UNCOMMON CONJUNCTIONS

Group	n	n	u	P
$1 + 2$ v $3 + 4 + 5$	10	12	18	0.01
1 v 2	5	5	12	n.s.
2 v 3	5	5	1	0.008
4 v 5	3	4	3	n.s.

total number of analysed words. The latter assessment was necessary to see whether those particular pronouns were used more frequently; the former merely establishes which of these pronouns *within* the personal pronoun group is selected more frequently.

All Personal Pronouns (Table 13)

The middle-class groups use a smaller proportion of all personal pronouns than do the working-class groups (Table 13a). The difference is significant beyond the 0.05 level of confidence. The intraclass differences are

Table 13

Group	n	n	u	P
(a) All Personal Pronouns				
$1 + 2$ v. $3 + 4 + 5$	10	12	29	0.05
1 v. 2	5	5	5	n.s.
2 v. 3	5	5	6	n.s.
4 v. 5	3	4	4	n.s.
(b) I: Personal Pronouns				
$1 + 2$ v. $3 + 4 + 5$	10	12	13	0.001
1 v. 2	5	5	5	n.s.
2 v. 3	5	5	3	0.028
4 v. 5	3	4	5	n.s.
(c) I: Words				
$1 + 2$ v. $3 + 4 + 5$	10	12	30	0.05
1 v. 2	5	5	7	n.s.
2 v. 3	5	5	3	0.028
4 v. 5	3	4	5	n.s.
(d) You and They: Personal Pronouns				
$1 + 2$ v. $3 + 4 + 5$	10	12	23	0.01
1 v. 2	5	5	11	n.s.
2 v. 3	5	5	6	n.s.
4 v. 5	3	4	2	n.s.
(e) You and They: Words				
$1 + 2$ v. $3 + 4 + 5$	10	12	14	0.001
1 v. 2	5	5	12	n.s.
2 v. 3	5	5	3	0.028
4 v. 5	3	4	4	n.s.

not significant, neither is the difference in the proportions when group 2 is compared with group 3. The middle-class groups use a higher proportion of the pronoun "I" to total personal pronouns (Table 12*b*) and the difference is significant beyond the 0.001 level of confidence. This difference holds when group 2 is compared with group 3 at the 0.028 level of confidence. The intraclass differences are not significant. These differences hold when "I" is expressed as a proportion of the total number of words but at a lower level of significance (0.05) for the major class comparison (Table 13*c*).

When "you" and "they" are combined and expressed as a proportion of the total number of personal pronouns (Table 13*d*) it is found that the working-class group use a higher proportion of the combined pronouns. The difference is significant beyond

the 0.01 level of confidence. No significant differences are found for the intraclass comparisons nor between groups 2 and 3. However, when "you" and "they" are expressed as a proportion of the total number of *words* it is found that the working-class groups use a higher proportion and this differences is now significant beyond the 0.001 level of confidence. The difference holds when group 2 is compared with group 3 and is significant beyond the 0.028 level of confidence. The intraclass differences are not significant (Table 13*e*).

Selected Personal Pronouns (Minus Pronouns in I think, S.C. Sequences, and Direct Speech Sequences)
(Table 14)

The middle-class groups use a smaller proportion of total selected pronouns than do the working-class groups

Table 14

Group	n	n	u	P
(*a*) Selected Personal Pronouns				
1 + 2 v. 3 + 4 + 5	10	12	33	0.05
1 v. 2	5	5	5	n.s.
2 v. 3	5	5	11	n.s.
4 v. 5	3	4	4	n.s.
(*b*) I: Personal Pronouns				
1 + 2 v. 3 + 4 + 5	10	12	31	0.05
1 v. 2	5	5	12	n.s.
2 v. 3	5	5	3	0.028
4 v. 5	3	4	4	n.s.
(*c*) I: Words				
Not Significant				
(*d*) You and They: Personal Pronouns				
1 + 2 v. 3 + 4 + 5	10	12	23	0.01
1 v. 2	5	5	11	n.s.
2 v. 3	5	5	6	n.s.
4 v. 5	3	4	2	n.s.
(*e*) You and They: Words				
1 + 2 v. 3 + 4 + 5	10	12	19	0.01
1 v. 2	5	5	12	n.s.
2 v. 3	5	5	5	n.s.
4 v. 5	3	4	3	n.s.

(Table 14) and the difference is significant beyond the 0.05 level of confidence. No significant difference is found for the intraclass comparisons nor when group 2 is compared with group 3. The middle-class groups use a higher proportion of the pronoun "I" to total selected personal pronouns (Table 14b) and the difference is significant beyond the 0.05 level of confidence. The difference holds when group 2 is compared with group 3 at the 0.28 level of confidence. No significant difference is found for the intraclass comparisons.

No significant difference is found when "I" is expressed as a proportion of words.

When "you" and "they" are combined and expressed either as a proportion of selected personal pronouns or of words (Table 14d and e) the proportion of these combined pronouns is higher for the working-class group and the difference for both assessments is significant beyond the 0.01 level of confidence. In neither case are the intraclass differences significant nor when group 2 is compared with group 3.

The exclusion of personal pronouns in the above sequences brings the speech samples closer together. Direct speech sequences were excluded from the count because their content tends to be concrete, e.g., "The judge says, 'I shall send you away for six months.' " It is thought that the proportion of selected personal pronouns to words gives a better indication of how concrete the speech samples were.

Personal Pronouns—Summary

In both counts of total personal pronouns the combined middle-class groups use a smaller proportion. In both counts the middle-class groups more frequently select "I" among the personal pronouns, but only in the case of all personal pronouns does this group

use "I" more frequently. In both counts and for both words and personal pronouns the working-class groups use "you" and "they" more frequently. These groups both select and use these personal pronouns more often. The lack of significance in the case of "I" when expressed as a proportion of selected pronouns to words is the result of the exclusion of the "I think" sequences. The critical result is that the differences in the over-all use of personal pronouns and the selections made within them holds when the two speech samples are brought close together by excluding the "I think" and S.C. sequences. No over-all class differences were found for the remaining personal pronouns. The relatively low level of significance both for total personal pronoun counts and for the use of "I" must be taken to mean that these findings are only suggestive.

DISCUSSION

The results will be discussed in relation to the two general linguistic codes mentioned at the beginning of this article. For a more detailed account of the social origins and behavioural implications of these codes the reader is referred to previous papers (Bernstein, 1961a; 1961b; 1962).

The codes are defined in terms of the probability of predicting which structural elements will be selected for the organization of meaning. The structural elements are highly predictable in the case of a restricted code and much less so in the case of an elaborated code. It is considered that an elaborated code facilitates the verbal elaboration of intent, whereas a restricted code limits the verbal explication of intent. The codes themselves are thought to be functions of different forms of social relations or more generally qualities of different social structures. A restricted code is generated by a form of social relationship based upon a range of closely shared identifications self-consciously held by the members. An elaborated code is generated by a form of social relationship which does not necessarily presuppose such shared, self-consciously held identifications with the consequence that much less is taken for granted. The codes regulate the area of discretion available to a speaker and so differently constrain the verbal signalling of difference.

The community of like interests underlying a restricted code removes the need for intent to be verbally elaborated and made explicit. The effect of this on the speech is to simplify the structural alternatives used to organise meaning and restrict the range of lexicon choice. A restricted code can arise *at any point* in society where its conditions may be fulfilled, but a special case of this code will be that in which the speaker is *limited* to this code. This is the situation of members of the lower working-class, including rural groups. An elaborated code is part of the life chance of members of the middle-class; a middle-class individual simply has access to the two codes, a lower working-class individual access to one.

It follows from this formulation that orientation toward the use of these codes is independent of measured intelligence and is a function of the form social relationships take.

The results of this study clearly indicate that the class groups are differently oriented in their structural selections and lexicon choices. Furthermore, this difference is relatively consistent within the social class subgroups. Within the working-class subgroups (3, 4, and 5) the difference of over 20 nonverbal I.Q. points does not produce any major disturbances in the consistency of the results. Similarly the difference

of 17 verbal I.Q. points between the two middle-class groups (1 and 2) does not affect the orientation of the speech as reflected in the measures used. This does not mean that within the middle-class groups there are no differences in content but that the low verbal middle-class group is at least oriented to making types of selection at both the lexicon and organisational level which are in the same direction as those made by the high verbal middle-class group.[1] It is very clear that group 2 and group 3 (the class groups matched for verbal and nonverbal intelligence) are oriented to different selection and organisation procedures.

It is thought that the constraints on selection procedures found in the working-class speech samples may well be found in speech samples of a restricted code independent of the class membership of the speakers. The data will now be discussed in more detail.

The restriction on the use of adjectives, uncommon adjectives, uncommon adverbs, the relative simplicity of the verbal form and the low proportion of subordinations supports the thesis that the working-class subjects relative to the middle-class do not explicate intent verbally and inasmuch as this is so the speech is relatively nonindividuated. The difference in the proportion of selected personal pronouns to words suggests that the content of the speech is likely to be descriptive and narrative and this possibility is increased by the low proportion of subordinations.

The class differences in the relative preference for "I" or "you" and "they" are of interest. Even when the speech samples are brought close together (that is, when the "I think" and S.C. sequences are omitted) the middle-class select "I" more frequently among the

[1] This subgroup used longer words as measured by syllable length (Bernstein, 1962).

personal pronouns than do the working-class; whereas the working-class select "you" and "they" more frequently among personal pronouns and these pronouns are *used* more frequently in the speech. These relative preferences reach a higher level of significance when they are expressed as proportions of *all* personal pronouns and words.

The use of "they" is not simply the result of the tension between in-group and out-group. It is not the case that "they" is used solely to distinguish non-members of the group. Inasmuch as referents are not finely differentiated then the global term "they" will be adopted as a general label. The non-specificity implied by "they" is a function of the lack of differentiation and the subsequent concretising of experience which characterises a restricted code as a whole. On the one hand, too high a level of abstraction is used ("they"), yet on the other, speakers are often involved in the consideration of a series of individual concrete cases. What appears to be lacking is the intervening series of successive levels of abstraction. The lack of specification also implies that there is possibly some implicit agreement about the referent such that the elaboration is redundant. In this sense "they" is based upon "we." How much is redundant will depend upon the community of interests generated by "we."

The use of "you" (second person plural) may also arise out of the concretising of experience. It offers a formal subject which facilitates a ready identification on the part of the listener. The content of the statement is presented in such a way that the listener can translate this in terms of his experience. Contrary to expectation, "one" was not used by the middle-class groups. Even if "one" is used, it is often not the psychological equivalent of

"you"; for "one" may involve a differentiation of own experience from that which is the subject of the discourse. This is not to say that "one" may not be reduced to "me," but "one" at least extends the invitation to an objective consideration.

The constraint on the use of "I" is not easy to understand nor is it easy to demonstrate what is thought to be understood. It may be that if an individual takes as his reference point rigid adherence to a wide range of closely shared identifications and expectations, the area of discretion available is reduced and the differentiation of self from act may be constrained. Looked at from another point of view the controls on behaviour would be mediated through a restricted self-editing process. If, on the other hand, the controls are mediated through a less constrained self-editing process, the area of discretion available to the individual in particular areas is greater. It may well be that such different forms of mediation, in themselves functions of the form social relationships take, are responsible for the differential use of the self-reference pronoun. If this were to be the case, then the relative infrequency of "I" would occur whenever the form of social relationship generated a restricted code. The degree of restriction of the code would affect the probability of the use of "I." If individuals are limited to a restricted code, one of its general effects may be to reduce the differentiation of self.

The data indicated that although no difference was found in the proportion of prepositions to words, the middle-class group selected a higher proportion of the preposition "of" to "of" plus "in" and "into." These prepositions account for a much greater proportion of the total prepositions than do any other three. In earlier work it had been suggested that an elaborated code would be associated with greater selection of prepositions symbolising logical relationships than with those indicating spatial or temporal contiguity. "Of" has also an adjectival quality and it may be that the restraint on this form of qualification is also responsible for the relatively infrequent use of the preposition "of" in the working-class groups. There is a hint that this may be the case. With the working-class groups the average group (5) selected a higher proportion of this preposition and it is this group which uses a higher proportion of adjectives although the difference is not significant.

Of particular interest is the class distribution of the S.C. sequences. It is thought that these sequences will occur more frequently whenever a restricted code is used. The meanings signaled in this code tend to be implicit and so condensed, with the result that there is less redundancy. A greater strain is placed upon the listener which is relieved by the range of identification that the speakers share. The S.C. sequences may be transmitted as a response of the speaker to the condensation of his own meanings. The speaker requires assurance that the message has been received and the listener requires an opportunity to indicate the contrary. It is as if the speaker is saying "Check—are we together on this?". On the whole the speaker expects affirmation. At the same time, by inviting agreement, the S.C. sequences test the range of identifications which the speakers have in common. The agreement reinforces the form of the social relationship which lends its objective authority to the significance of what is said. This also acts to reduce any uncertainty which the speaker may have had when the message was first planned. This uncertainty may not only arise out of the change in the level

of coding. Inasmuch as a restricted code is generated by the sense of "we-ness" then at the point where a speaker is giving reasons or making suggestions, the form of the social relationship undergoes a subtle change.

A shift from narative or description to reflection—from the simple ordering of experiences to abstracting from experience—also may signal a shift from we-centered to individuated experience. If this is so, then this shift introduces a measure of social isolation for the speaker which differentiates the speaker from his group in a way similar to a figure-ground relation. Inasmuch as the group is based upon a closely shared self-consciously held identification the change in the role relationships of the members is clearly indicated. The unspoken affirmation which the S.C. signal may receive reduces the sociological strain upon the speaker. In a discussion situation which invites the verbal signaling of individuated experience, the "we-ness" of the group is modified in direct relation to such individuated signaling. The S.C. sequences may then function as feelers toward a new equilibrium for the group; that is, toward a new balance in the role relationship of the members. This analysis is wholly consistent with the use of these sequences as an idiosyncratic speech habit of an individual. The point here is that they are released relatively frequently by all individuals if they are constrained by a particular form of social relationship which generates a restricted linguistic code.

Thus groups 3, 4, and 5, the working-class groups, who it is considered are limited to a restricted code, will use such sequences frequently. The uncertainty of the appropriateness of the message, for these groups, in a discussion situation will probably be relatively great. This will add to the sociological strain inherent in producing a verbally individuated message. As a consequence, the frequency of S.C. sequences may be expected to be great.

The middle-class groups are oriented to an elaborated code which is appropriated to a formal discussion situation. This code facilitates the verbal explication of meaning and so there is more redundancy. In a sense, any speaker is less dependent upon the listener because he has taken into account the requirements of the listener in the preparation of his speech. The form of the social relationship which generates this code is such that a range of discretion must be available to the members if it is to be produced at all. Further, the members' social history must have included practice and training for the role which such social relationships require. Role does not refer to the specific role within a discussion group but more generally to the particular role relationships consequent upon the use of an elaborated code. These role relationships receive less support from implicit identifications shared by the participators. The orientation of the individual is based upon the expectation of psychological difference, his own and others. Individuated speech presupposes a history of a particular role relationship if it is to be prepared and delivered appropriately. Inasmuch as difference is part of the expectation, there is less reliance or dependence on the listener; or rather this dependency is reduced by the explication of meaning. The dependency underpinning the use of a restricted code is upon the closely shared identifications which serve as a backcloth to the speech. The dependency underpinning the use of an elaborated code is upon the verbal explication of meaning. The sources of strain which are inherent in these codes, and thus in the social relationships which generate them, are different. Thus the use of S.C. sequences in an elaborated code

will tend to be relatively infrequent.

In the light of this argument, of what significance is the frequency of "I think" sequences which are associated, it is thought, with the use of an elaborated code and so differentiates groups 1 and 2 from groups 3, 4, and 5?

The preface "I think" is probably as much an indication of semantic uncertainty as the S.C. sequences are in a restricted code. The former sequence does not usually require affirmation; in fact such return signaling is often inappropriate. It invites a further "I think" on the part of the listener. The sequence signals difference and relates the sequence to the person. It symbolises the area of discretion which the form of the social relationship permits. It translates in palpable form the sociological relationship constraining the participators. The egocentric basis of the interaction is raised like a flag. At the same time this sequence, just like the S.C. sequences, may indicate the strain in the social interaction, but in this case the strain is taken wholly by the individual.

Table 4 indicates that group 2 used more "I think" sequences than group 1, the high verbal middle-class group.[2] In the previous report the analysis of hesitation phenomena indicated that group 2 relative to group 1 used a shorter phrase length and a slower rate of articulation. This was taken to mean that group 2 were in a situation of coding difficulty. If the S.C. and "I think" sequences are functional equivalents in different codes, then the total number of such sequences might give an index of coding difficulty. Table 4 indicates the percentage occurrence of this combination. Group 1, the high verbal middle-class group, and group 5, the average working-class group, have very much lower percentages. There

[2] The number of S.C. sequences produced are too small for comparison.

is little objective data which can be used to support the hypothesis that these groups were under less coding difficulty. However, group 5 in relation to all the other subgroups used a much shorter pause duration per word, which suggests that the speech was well organised and of a high habit strength.

Finally, these sequences may set up different constraints on the flow of communication, particularly on its logical development and elaboration. Inasmuch as the S.C. sequences, which are generated basically by uncertainty, invite implicit affirmation of the previous sequence, they tend to close communication in a particular area rather than facilitate its development and elaboration. The sequences tend to act to maintain the reduction in redundancy and so the condensation of meaning. The "I think" sequence, on the other hand, allows the listener far more degrees of freedom and may be regarded as an invitation to the listener to develop the communication on his own terms. The sequence facilitates the development and elaboration of the the communication and so the logical development and exploration of a particular area. The content analysis of the speech samples may throw some light upon this function of the "I think" and S.C. sequences. These sequences, then, in the light of the above argument, play an important role in maintaining the equilibrium which characterises the different codes.

If this analysis is appropriate, then the role of "I think" and the S.C. sequences (where they are not idiosyncratic habits) can only be understood in terms of the two codes of which they are a part. As the codes are functions of different forms of social relationships, or more generally, qualities of different social structures, then the function of these sequences must receive sociological analysis. Different

orienting media, different forms of dependency, different areas of discretion inhere in these codes and thus the sources of strain in the relationships are also different. Psychological factors will affect the frequency with which different individuals take up the options represented by the sequences. At this point it would be better to conceptualise these sequences as egocentric and sociocentric signals.

As language is a patterned activity, the consistency of the findings for the two codes is partly to be expected. To attempt to assess the relative contribution of the various measures to the stability of the code is beyond the scope of this article. It is thought that the best single indicator of the two codes is the proportion of subordinations to finite verbs and this measure is, of course, implied in the original definition of the codes.

It may seem that this discussion of the results is somewhat unbalanced in the sense that it has been almost limited to the personal pronouns and the egocentric and sociocentric sequences. This is because in previous papers attention has been given to the findings on the other measures. An attempt has been made to relate the results to conditions more general than social class. Class is a particular but not a necessary exemplar of the codes. The latter are more strictly functions of social hierarchy.

CONCLUSION

The findings clearly indicate that for this small sample of subjects, speech orientation to the two codes and verbal planning processes which they entail are independent of measured intelligence indicated by the tests used. The mean difference of over 20 nonverbal I.Q. points between the working-class groups 3, 4, and 5 does not disturb the orientation of the speech. The mean difference of 17 verbal I.Q.

points between the middle-class groups 1 and 2 again does not distrub the orientation of the speech of these groups. This does not mean that the quality of the speech is necessarily the same but that the class groups differ in terms of the level of structure and lexicon from which selections are made.

The results fall into main groups in terms of the directions of the differences found for the various measures. *m* after the finding on a particular measure indicates that the result holds only for the major class comparison (1 + 2 v. 3 + 4 + 5).

"You" and "they" combined as a proportion of total personal pronouns(m).

"You" and "they" combined (total personal pronouns) as a proportion of total number of words.

"You" and "they" combined as a proportion of total selected personal pronouns(m).

"You" and "they" combined (selected personal pronouns) as a proportion of total number of words(m).

Sociocentric Sequences

The significance of the difference for the above results is at the 0.05 level

GROUP A
Middle-class groups used a high proportion of the following:

Subordinations
Complex verbal stems
Passive voice
Total adjectives

Uncommon adjectives
Uncommon adverbs
Uncommon conjunctions
Egocentric sequences

"of" as a proportion of the sum of the prepositions 'of', 'in' and 'into'. (This finding is *not* consistent within the working-class group.)

"I" as a proportion of all personal pronouns.

"I" as a proportion of total number of words.

"I" as a proportion of total selected pronouns.

Where the level of significance of the difference for the major class comparisons is 0.05, the finding should be regarded only as suggestive. In the above group results this applies to 'I' as a proportion of total selected personal pronouns and 'I' as a proportion of words.

GROUP B
The working-class groups use a higher proportion of the following:

Total personal pronouns(m).
Total selected personal pronouns(m).

of confidence in the case of total personal and selected pronouns.

No significant differences were found for the proportion of finite verbs, nouns, adverbs, prepositions, conjunctions, and the proportion of the selected personal pronoun "I" to number of words.

It should be remembered, when assessing the results, that the working-class sample was reduced by two subjects as these subjects contributed too few words to justify analysis.

Although the findings for the class comparisons are not related to the number of words, the results must be placed in the perspective of a very small speech sample. The consistency of the findings for the two class groups suggests that if the speech samples were increased it would be a little unlikely for the working-class groups to change their level of verbal planning and maintain it. The topic of the discussion may also have affected some of the elements measured, and the relationship with the researcher could probably have affected the quality and amount of speech. The topic may have had a different significance for the two class groups. The working-class may have tended to identify with the criminal and the middle-class with law and principles of justice. The point is not that such identifications may occur but rather their effect on speech. One can identify with the criminal but not necessarily be limited to speech with the characteristics associated with the present findings.

It will be remembered that the arrangement of the original groups was different from the arrangement for this analysis. In the case of groups 1 and 2 and groups 3 and 4 internal changes within the class groups were made in order to control more adequately for verbal I.Q. Whilst the scores the exchanged members received were appropriate to the groups to which they were attached, the possibility that the middle-class group of average verbal ability (group 2) may have been af-fected by the presence of the high verbal subject cannot be ruled out. On the other hand, the original groups 3 and 4 contained the possibility of a similar disturbance, but perhaps more limited in its effect for the verbal I.Q. range was narrower. The important question is whether the groups were sufficiently stretched by the discussion to allow for the possibility of changes in the level of the speech. The researcher is confident that the conditions for changes in the level existed in all groups. The measures used in this report are too insensitive to allow the measurement of variations within a given level. It is clear, however, that a longer speech sample, obtained from many more subjects under different conditions, including written work, is required.

With these reservations in mind, it is considered that the results of the analysis of the hesitation phenomena and of the simple grammatical analysis presented in this article are supportive evidence for the two codes and their social class relationship.

References

Bernstein, B. (1962). Linguistic codes, hesitation phenomena and intelligence. *Language and Speech,* **5,** 31.

Bernstein, B. (1961a). Social class and linguistic development: a theory of social learning. In *Education, Economy and Society,* ed. A. H. Halsey, J. Floud and A. Anderson (New York), 228.

Bernstein, B. (1961b). Social structure, language and learning, *Educational Research,* **3,** 163.

Siegel, S. (1956). Non-parametric Statistics (New York).

20. On the Language of Lower-Class Children

WERNER COHN

It is a commonplace observation that the language of lower-class children differs remarkably from the standard English in which most school business is transacted. Difficulties caused by the differences in language probably countribute to the fairly widespread disaffection of lower-class children from our public school culture. All too often these children do not succeed in our schools, do not know the satisfaction enjoyed by children of the higher classes, and in general, are unable to use much that the school teaches.

Lower-class English may be viewed as an inferior version of standard English; or the two may be considered as points on a continuum that ranges from the most formal to the most free; or standard and lower-class English may be regarded as entirely separate modes of expression. Each approach has it uses; here we shall regard the language of the lower class as a separate dialect, related to, but distinct from, standard English. This way of looking at these speech differences, we believe, can contribute to a more adequate common education for all our children.

The British sociologist B. Bernstein recently argued rather forcefully that lower-class language is inferior to standard English.[1] He showed that the language as well as the general perceptual apparatus of the lower classes ordinarily permits only gross intellectual distinctions. In contrast, standard English and the generally more refined perceptual apparatus of the middle and upper classes facilitate fine distinctions. Bernstein prefers to regard lower-class speech as an inferior form of the standard language; he does not like to think in terms of a separate lower-class dialect.

But students of Hawaiian-English speech have shown that it is quite possible to acknowledge perceptual deficiencies in lower-class language and yet think of it as a separate dialect. Reinecke and Tokimasa described the general confusion of grammatical forms in Hawaiian English and in such lower-class speech forms as those used by many Negroes in the South.[2] Such radical simplifications in language structure, these authors point out, make it almost impossible to formulate intellectual generalizations in lower-class speech. These scholars, together with Hormann,[3] another Hawaiian sociologist, insist on treating Hawaiian English as a separate dialect. We would also hold that to speak of a certain inferiority of the lower-class language need not deny it the respect due a dialect. The assertions of Bernstein and the Hawaiian investigators concerning the intellectual deficiencies in lower-class speech are convincing. But there is always a danger in our culture of equating intellectual shortcomings with moral shortcomings.[4]

A first step toward a morally neutral consideration of the two types of language may be taken by inquiring into their function. Students of the problem seem to agree that standard English, which has a more elaborate syntax, is far superior to lower-class English for purely intellectual purposes. The finer distinctions to which Bernstein has pointed, the greater exactness shown by Reinecke and Tokimasa and others, as well as the common experience of most of us, demonstrate that standard English is much better adapted for those analytic and scientific functions that Susanne Langer has described as discursive thought.[5] Moreover, practically the whole permanent depository of formal knowledge is laid down in standard language. Access to this depository requires familiarity with forms of standard language. Discursive thought, couched in standard language, seems to be required for the study of science and for all those "rational" activities to which our higher classes are dedicated. The reason for the quotation marks around *rational* becomes apparent when we consider that competitive business, advertising, and warmaking, are among the higher-class pursuits made possible by our discursive standard English.

What are the uses of lower-class English? Is there communication of anything—of anything worthwhile—that is not "discursive"? Intimate and satisfying personal communication among lower-class parents, children, and friends is carried on almost exclusively by means of lower-class speech. It may be argued that, since the higher classes seem to use standard English for the same purposes, lower-class speech is not absolutely necessary. This objection, even if it were true, would not dispute the usefulness of lower-class speech, though it would question its indispensability.

Actually, lower-class speech is at times used by the higher classes for a variety of purposes. Bernstein noted that the difference between the speech of higher- and lower-class youngsters does not lie in an absolute language distinction, but in the acquisition by the higher classes of standard English in addition to the common lower-class forms. The emotive capacities of lower-class speech, so well adapted to lower-class communication needs, are frequently enlisted also by higher-class people for non-discursive purposes.[6]

Members of the higher classes often borrow from lower-class vocabulary—obscene expressions, for example—while retaining essentially standard English syntax. More extensive borrowing, which involves not only vocabulary but syntax as well, appears in creative writing. Some writers use lower-class language forms to reproduce common speech realistically. But others, like Faulkner, seem to choose lower-class language for its greater emotive expressiveness.

Further light is thrown on the division of labor between lower-class and standard English when we consider certain differences in values of lower and higher classes. A study by Leanna K. Baker[7] showed that middle-class boys generally held to a Puritan ethnic of business obligation, while lower-class children were more prone to emphasize personal attachments and to display considerably more generosity in peer-group relationships. One might say that the lower-class boys tended toward an ethnic of *Gemeinschaft,* or community, while middle-class boys tended toward an ethic of the prevailing *Gesellschaft* of our business society, that is, an ethic of legalistic obligations.[8] This difference would suggest that lower-class English, in its more casual grammatical habits, may carry less demanding, less competitive, and possibly more generous modes than the standard language.

All these considerations lead us to certain practical suggestions concerning lower-class English in the public schools. Most of our proposals have been borrowed from writers on the Hawaiian-English dialect, writers we have already mentioned.

First, it would seem that a moralistic depreciation of lower-class English mirrors an undesirably ethnocentric depreciation of lower-class values. Class antagonism on the part of middle-class teacher toward lower-class children is one of the most important contributing factors in the alienation of the lower classes from our public schools. Actually, one suggestion can be stated rather simply: it is necessary and important for the teacher to understand and respect lower-class speech if he wishes to gain the confidence and respect of lower-class children.[9] Individuals in authority who disparage this language endanger the emotional security of lower-class children in their charge. Lower-class language is the only language with which lower-class children are thoroughly familiar and with which they communicate with their parents. It is the carrier of the most important emotional attachments.

This is not to say that standard English should not be taught in our public schools to children of all classes. As we have seen, standard English is important for all intellectual disciplines. But one cannot teach a new language to people whose native tongue one

scorns. Hormann's advice for Hawaii seems applicable to our problem:

"Pedagogically, a systematic knowledge of the local dialect would make possible the development of better techniques for teaching standard English. In grammar, for instance, the structure of the local dialect can be worked out inductively by the pupils. These pupil-discovered rules can then be used to bridge the gap to the structure of standard English. This is the way many of us learn a foreign language when it is efficiently taught." [10]

To teach lower-class children the alien tongue that we call standard English involves more than technical problems of educational method. The purposes of standard English and formal learning are ordinarily not related to the self-image of the lower-class child; he does not usually think of himself as the kind of person who would speak this stilted-sounding standard language. The problem is probably too large for the school system alone to handle; the whole social structure is involved, particularly our patterns of social mobility and the values of lower-class culture. These considerations, which lie beyond the scope of this article, are mentioned only to indicate the complexity of the problem and the need for scepticism concerning easy solutions.

It should not be difficult for higher-class children to learn to respect and use lower-class speech. For these children know and often use lower-class language. The teacher who has a rational approach to the differences between the two languages, the teacher who is unhampered by moralistic and snobbish attitudes, can help children overcome their ambivalence toward language expression. If he succeeds, the great power of lower-class language to express emotions, a power ordinarily exploited with a clear conscience only by novelists, would become available to all and could extend the range of expressed feelings and perceptions.

The writer does not expect his suggestions to find wide acceptance at this time. We fear lower-class speech and are inclined to give it no quarter. The more precarious our social status in the higher classes—that is, the closer we are to the line that divides the middle from the lower classes or the more recent our ascent from the lower strata —the more insistent we are on the purity of our linguistic credentials. Such insecurity is perhaps especially troublesome to public school teachers, whose separation from the lower classes is often recent and precarious.

Linguistic snobbishness is part of the price we pay educationally for being chained to the demands of our social-class system. But our culture also has a tradition of resisting considerations of social class in dealing with people.[11] Our tradition of emphasizing personal needs of individuals rather than outward social esteem contains the promise of a more rational handling of language problems and a more adequate public school education for all our children.

References

1. B. Bernstein, "Some Sociological Determinants of Perception, An Enquiry into Sub-Cultural Differences," *British Journal of Sociology,* IX (1958), 159–74.

2. John E. Reinecke and Aiko Tokimasa, "The English Dialect of Hawaii," *American Speech,* IX (1934), 48–58; 122–30. *See also* John E. Reinecke, " 'Pidgin English' in Hawaii: A Local Study in the Sociology of Language," *American Journal of Sociology,* XLIII (1938), 778–89.

3. Bernhard Hormann, "Speech, Prejudice, and the School in Hawaii" in *Community Forces in Hawaii,* ed. Bernhard L. Hormann (Honolulu: University of Hawaii, 1956), pp. 232–37. This article appeared originally in 1947 in *Social Process in Hawaii.*

4. The "intellectual inferiority of the lower classes," of course, is an oversimplification. The great complexity of this problem was classically discussed by Allison Davis in *Social Class Influence upon Learning,* (Cambridge, Massachusetts: Harvard University Press, 1948). For a more recent discussion and review of the literature, see Seymour B. Sarason and Thomas Gladwin, "Psychological and Cultural Problems in Mental Subnormality: A Review of Research," *Genetic Psychology Monographs,* LVII (1958), 3–290.

5. Susanne K. Langer, *Philosophy in a New Key,* (Cambridge, Massachusetts: Harvard University Press, 1942), Chaps. IV and V.

6. Compare the quotation from a university department chairman in Theodore Caplow and Reece J. McGee, *The Academic Marketplace* (New York: Basic Books, 1958), p. 160.

7. Reported by Albert K. Cohen, *Delinquent Boys* (Glencoe, Illinois: Free Press, 1955), pp. 105 ff.

8. Compare Ferdinand Toennies, *Community & Society, Gemeinschaft und Gesellschaft* (East Lansing, Michigan: Michigan State University Press, 1957). A new edition of a work that originally appeared in 1887.

9. Compare Norman A. McQuown, "Language-Learning from an Anthropological Point of View," *Elementary School Journal,* LIV (1954), 402–8.

10. Bernhard Hormann, *op. cit.,* p. 234.

11. Werner Cohn "Social Stratification and the Charismatic," *Midwest Sociologist,* XXI (1958), 12–18.

21. Arithmetic Concepts of Kindergarten Children in Contrasting Socioeconomic Areas

DAVID O. MONTAGUE

"We are living in a world of change." This has become one of the trite sayings of our day. But no other statement seems to tell the story of this era so straight forwardly. In a mere twenty years the world has passed through the atomic age and into the space age.

While technology has progressed rapidly, the ability of our society to develop the potential of each individual has failed to keep pace. We spend a great deal of time talking about the so-called disadvantaged children. These boys and girls, who come from lower-class, socially impoverished circumstances, account for a high proportion of our school failures and school dropouts. These children struggle with reading and learning disabilities, as well as life adjustment problems (Ref. 1, p. 1). The culture of their environment is different from the culture that has molded the school and its educational theory. The child who enters school under such circumstances is so poorly prepared to produce what the school demands that initial failures are almost inevitable.

What effect do differences in socioeconomic background have on kindergarteners' arithmetic concepts? Four kindergarten classes took part in a study to explore this question. The classes had a total of 82 pupils. At the time of the study the children were in their seventh month of school.

All the children lived in a California city in the San Francisco Bay Area. Fifty-one of them came from a low socioeconomic section of the city. Thirty-one came from a high socioeconomic area of the city. The group of pupils from the low socioeconomic classes was composed of 32 Negroes, 14 Caucasians, and five Orientals. The group of pupils from the high socioeconomic classes was composed of 29 Caucasians and two Orientals.

In doing research in educationn, especially in the classroom, the teacher is a variable that is most difficult to control. In this study the two teachers involved were very comparable. Each had more than fifteen years of experience, more than eight of those years in teaching kindergarten. Both women were over thirty-five years old and had comparable educational backgrounds.

Reprinted from *The Elementary School Journal* (April 1964), pp. 393–397, by permission of The University of Chicago Press. Copyright 1964 by the University of Chicago.

Both were considered "top quality teachers" by their principals, and both had been teaching in their respective schools for eight years. Each teacher expressed a preference for the socio-economic area in which she was teaching.

At each school the kindergarten classes were divided into morning and afternoon classes. In the low socio-economic area, 26 pupils from the morning class and 25 pupils from the afternoon class were given the test on arithmetic concepts. An attempt had been made to group the morning and afternoon classes by ability. In the high socioeconomic area 11 pupils from the morning class and 20 pupils from the afternoon class were given the test on arithmetic concepts.

The district had not formally adopted a curriculum for the kindergarten. However, for several years the kindergarten teachers had been meeting to coordinate their programs, and they were in the process of formulating an overall curriculum guide for the kindergarten.

Neither teacher had a formal outline for arithmetic instruction. But as opportunities arose, each teacher spent time on arithmetic concepts. Neither teacher tried to devote a specified amount of time each day to developing arithmetic concepts.

The principal of each school granted the researcher permission to discuss the study with all the kindergarten teachers. Two teachers who were comparable were chosen after all expressed a desire to participate.

The researcher visited each of the four kindergarten classes to become acquainted with the pupils. Since classes met for half a day, each teacher had two classes. The arithmetic test was administered to each class by the researcher during the week of March 25, 1963.

The Arithmetic Concepts Inventory for Kindergarten and Entering First Grade by Arden K. Ruddell, of the School of Education, University of California, Berkeley, was used. This test consists of five sections. The following items are typical of what the child was asked to do in each section:

Enumeration

Look at the row of clown faces.
Make a mark on two of the clowns.

Quantitative Relationships

Look at the row of boxes with apples in them.
Make a mark on the box that has the most apples in it.

Symbol Recognition

Look at the row of balls.
How many balls are there?
(Be sure that every child is told that there are three balls.)
Make a mark on the number that tells there are three balls.

Social Usage

In the row by the umbrella, make a mark on the square.

Problem Solving

Look at the row of tables.
One table has two apples on it, the next table has one apple on it.
Make marks on the empty table to show how many apples there are all together.

The inventory has a reliability coefficient of .89. In analyzing the data, a *t* test of the difference between mean scores was used. Only the .01 level of confidence was considered significant.

The inventory was administered to each class in two sittings. The first 27 questions were administered during

Table 1

MEAN AGE OF KINDERGARTEN CHILDREN IN CONTRASTING SOCIOECONOMIC AREAS

Group	Number of Pupils	Mean Age (in Months)	Standard Deviation	Standard Error of the Mean	t
Low socioeconomic	51	69.55	3.81	.54	1.04
High socioeconomic	31	68.68	3.46	.63	

the first part of the half-day session; the last 17 questions were given during the last part of the session. About 90 minutes elapsed between the end of the first set of questions and the beginning of the last set of questions.

In comparing the ages of the children in each school, a *t* test of the difference between the means indicated no significant difference. (See Table 1)

There was no readily available information on the pupils that would ac-curately rate their intelligence. According to Davis no intelligence test has yet been devised that is culture free (Ref. 2, p. 65). He wrote: "Recent research indicates that many slum children, who do poorly in school and in present intelligence tests, have greater real or native intelligence than many children from higher income families" (Ref. 3, p. 294).

Several phenomena enter into the system of acts that constitute a pupil's response to an intelligence test. One

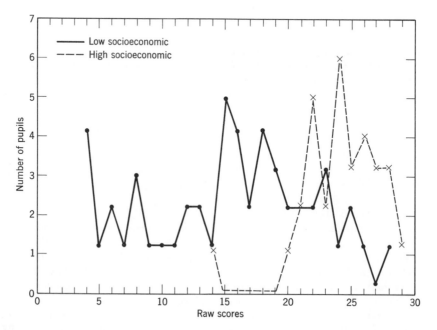

FIGURE 1. Scores on an inventory of arithmetic concepts administered to kindergarteners from contrasting socioeconomic areas.

Table 2

MEAN SCORES ON AN INVENTORY OF ARITHMETIC CONCEPTS ADMINISTERED TO
KINDERGARTENERS FROM CONTRASTING SOCIOECONOMIC AREAS

Group	Number of Pupils	Mean Score	Standard Deviation	Standard Error of the Mean	t
Low socioeconomic	51	15.35	6.51	.92	8.23 *
High socioeconomic	31	24.16	2.98	.54	

* Significant at the .01 level of confidence.

of these, according to Davis, is the hereditary phenomenon. Davis wrote: "There is no evidence that such hereditary factors are segregated by socioeconomic levels" (Ref. 2, pp. 63–64). It is therefore assumed that there was no significant difference in the "native or real" intelligence of the two groups of children.

Figure 1 shows the mean scores the kindergarteners made on the inventory of arithmetic concepts. The great range is evident from the chart. The pupils from the low socioeconomic school had scores ranging from 4 to 28, a range of 24 points. The mean score for this group of fifty-one pupils was 15.35. The pupils from the high socio-economic area had scores ranging from 14 to 29, a range of 15 points. The mean scores for this group of thirty-one pupils was 24.16.

The mean scores the kindergarteners made on the inventory of arithmetic concepts were compared by using a *t* test. Table 2 summarizes the results.

There was a significant difference at the .01 level of confidence in the mean scores made by kindergarteners of differing socioeconomic areas in the inventory of arithmetic concepts.

The scores were analyzed further by comparing the mean scores of children of the same sex in the contrasting socioeconomic areas. Table 3 shows

Table 3

MEAN SCORES ON AN INVENTORY OF ARITHMETIC CONCEPTS ADMINISTERED TO
KINDERGARTEN GIRLS AND BOYS FROM CONTRASTING SOCIOECONOMIC AREAS

Group	Number of Pupils	Mean Score	Standard Deviation	Standard Error of the Mean	t
Girls					
Low socioeconomic	28	15.86	6.03	1.21	6.35 *
High socioeconomic	14	24.5	2.26	.63	
Boys					
Low socioeconomic	23	14.74	6.9	1.47	5.37 *
High socioeconomic	17	23.88	3.45	.86	

* Significant at the .01 level of confidence.

the mean scores of the kindergarten girls and boys. The difference is significant at the .01 level of confidence for each sex.

The mean scores made on an inventory of arithmetic concepts by kindergarteners from a high socioeconomic area and a low socioeconomic area showed a significant difference at the .01 level of confidence. This difference was also significant when the scores of boys and girls were compared. Kindergarteners in the high socioeconomic area scored significantly higher on the inventory. The findings indicate a relationship between arithmetic concepts held by kindergarteners and the socioeconomic areas from which the children came.

The implications of this study are indicated in a statement by Deutsch, who wrote: "A child from any circumstance who has been deprived of a substantial portion of the variety of stimuli which he is maturationally capable in both the formal and contentual equipment required for learning" (Ref. 1, p. 8).

Being deprived of the background and the educational experience that help build arithmetic concepts, the disadvantaged child enters school in need of individualized help. The study revealed the great range in scores of the children in the kindergarten attended by children from a low socioeconomic area. This finding implies a need for a much lower pupil-teacher ratio in this type of class to permit individualized instruction. Children in the low socioeconomic areas also need opportunities to have experiences that are basic to forming arithmetic concepts.

As researchers identify the many factors that promote learning, the school that has disadvantaged children must expose them to these factors.

References

1. Martin Deutsch, *The Disadvantaged Child and the Learning Process: Some Social, Psychological and Developmental Considerations.* A paper prepared for Ford Foundation "Work Conference in Curriculum and Teaching in Depressed Urban Areas." New York: Columbia University, 1962.
2. Allison Davis, *Social-Class Influence upon Learning.* Cambridge, Massachusetts: Harvard University Press, 1948.
3. Allison Davis, "Poor People Have Brains, Too," *Phi Delta Kappan,* XXX (April, 1949), 294–295.

22. The Effect of Socioeconomic Status on the Scholastic Achievement of Sixth-Grade Children

ROBERT L. CURRY

INTRODUCTION

For several decades investigations have been conducted which were designed to determine the relationship between socioeconomic status and scholastic achievement. These investigations (Bryan, 1941; Coleman, 1940; Collins and Douglass, 1937; Gough, 1946; Shaw, 1943) have indicated the existence of a definite relationship between intellectual ability and scholastic achievement. In addition, Garrison (1932) completed a study which indicated that socioeconomic status has a greater effect on scholastic achievement than intellectual ability. The common assumption has been that socioeconomic status was associated with scholastic achievement regardless of the intellectual ability level.

The purpose of this study was to determine whether the differences in scholastic achievement were significant between groups of sixth-grade children when the groups were of comparable intellectual ability but differed in socioeconomic status.

The subjects used in this investigation were 360 sixth-grade students who

Reprinted from *British Journal of Educational Psychology*, Vol. **32** (February 1962), 46–49, by permission of the publisher and author.

were randomly selected from 2,623 subjects from 33 elementary schools in a large city in the South-West United States. The subjects were Caucasians with American-born parents. In addition, they had no school record of serious emotional maladjustment and had attended the same elementary school the previous academic year.

The California Test of Mental Maturity was used to determine the intellectual ability level of the subjects, and they were assigned to one of three intellectual ability groups designated as follows: high (I.Qs. of 116 and above), medium (I.Qs. in the 94–107 range), or low (I.Qs. of 85 and below). Each of the intellectual ability groups was further divided on the basis of socioeconomic status which was determined by use of the *Questionnaire by which Socioeconomic Information was Secured from Parents*, described by Eells and others (1951). Subjects were then assigned to the upper, middle, or lower socioeconomic group. Each group consisted of an equal number of boys and girls to prevent any bias because of sex. Table 1 provides a distribution of subjects on the bases of socioeconomic status and intellectual ability.

The California Achievement Test, Elementary Battery, was used as a

219

Table 1

DISTRIBUTION OF SUBJECTS ON THE BASES OF SOCIOECONOMIC
STATUS AND INTELLECTUAL ABILITY

Intellectual Ability Groups	Socioeconomic Status			Totals
	Upper	Middle	Lower	
High	50	50	22	122
Medium	50	50	50	150
Low	14	40	34	88
Totals	114	140	106	360

measure of the scholastic achievement of the subjects. This test gives level of achievement in the areas of reading, arithmetic, language, and total achievement. Raw scores for each of the achievement areas were used for statistical analyses purposes.

Within the high, medium, and low intellectual ability groups t tests were computed between the upper and middle, upper and lower, and the middle and lower socioeconomic status groups in reading, arithmetic, language, and total achievement. A total of thirty-six t tests was computed with twelve being related to each of the intellectual ability groups. The .05 level was used to determine statistical significance.

RESULTS

Table 2 provides an analysis of the data for all intellectual ability groups.

Table 2

ANALYSIS OF DATA FOR THE THREE INTELLECTUAL ABILITY GROUPS

Intellectual Ability Group	Achievment Area	Socioeconomic Status Groups			t-ratios		
		Upper	Middle Means	Lower	Upper–Middle	Upper–Lower	Middle–Lower
High	Reading	118.1	116.2	114.9	1.04	1.34	0.58
	Arithmetic	82.6	77.7	79.8	0.92	0.95	0.70
	Language	61.3	59.3	59.7	1.45	1.02	0.21
	Total	262.0	253.1	254.4	1.98	1.44	0.22
Medium	Reading	100.1	98.9	96.8	0.38	1.17	0.63
	Arithmetic	66.4	66.3	63.1	0.02	1.72	0.57
	Language	51.9	51.8	47.1	0.06	2.84 *	2.49 *
	Total	218.3	217.2	206.9	0.19	2.17 *	1.66
Low	Reading	82.1	70.2	58.1	2.50 *	4.11 *	2.99 *
	Arithmetic	48.1	46.6	41.7	0.37	2.06	1.66
	Language	42.4	36.2	32.9	2.20 *	3.03 *	1.52
	Total	172.7	153.1	132.8	1.99	3.55 *	2.62 *

* Denotes significance at the .05 level.

In the high intellectual ability group there were no statistically significant differences in scholastic achievement between the three socioeconomic groups.

In the medium-intellectual ability group, differences in language achievement were found to be statistically significant between the upper and lower and the middle and lower socioeconomic status groups. Also, the difference in the area of total achievement between the upper and lower socioeconomic status groups was found to be statistically significant. Other differences in achievement were not found to be statistically significant. When differences were statistically significant the results always indicated greater achievement for the higher of the two socioeconomic status groups being compared.

In the low intellectual ability group, differences in reading achievement were statistically significant between the upper and middle, upper and lower, and middle and lower socioeconomic status groups. In language achievement the differences were statistically significant between the upper and middle and the upper and lower socioeconomic status groups. Also, in total achievement the differences were statistically significant between the upper and lower and the middle and lower socioeconomic groups. Other differences were not statistically significant. Significant differences also indicated greater achievement for the higher of the two socioeconomic groups being compared.

CONCLUSIONS

From the results of this investigation the following conclusions were made:

1. Socioeconomic status seems to have no effect upon the scholastic achievement of sixth-grade students when the students have high intellectual ability. High-intellectual ability offsets any deficiency which may be created by lower social and economic conditions.

2. Social and economic factors have an effect upon language achievement in the medium intellectual ability group. Both the upper and middle socioeconomic status groups achieve a greater amount than the lower socioeconomic status group. Similarly, in total achievement, the upper socioeconomic status group achieves a greater amount than the lower socioeconomic status group.

3. In the low intellectual ability group, social and economic factors have an effect on achievement in reading, language, and total achievement. In reading the upper socioeconomic status group shows a greater amount of achievement than the middle and lower socioeconomic status groups, and the middle socioeconomic status group shows greater achievement than the lower socioeconomic group. In language the upper socioeconomic status group achieves more than the middle and lower socioeconomic groups. In the area of total achievement, the upper socioeconomic group achieves greater than the lower socioeconomic group.

4. As the intellectual ability decreases from high to low, the effect of social and economic conditions on scholastic achievement increases greatly.

5. Achievement in arithmetic seems to be relatively free from the influence of social and economic conditions since no significant differences were found within any of the intellectual ability groups.

References

1. Allen, Mildred M. (1944). Relationship between Kuhlmann-Anderson intelligence test and academic achievement in Grade IV. *Journal of Educational Psychology,* **35,** 229–39.
2. Bryan, Ruth (1941). *A Study of the Relationship Between Socio-Economic Status and Scholastic Achievement.* Unpublished Master's Thesis, University of Iowa.
3. Coleman, Hubert A. (1940). The relationship of socio-economic status to the performance of junior high school students. *Journal of Experimental Education,* **9,** 61–63.
4. Collins, Joseph H., and Douglass, Harl, R. (1937). The socio-economic status of home as a factor in success in the junior high schools. *Elementary School Journal,* **38,** 107–13.
5. Eells, Kenneth, et al. (1951). *Intelligence and Cultural Differences,* Chicago: University of Chicago Press.
6. Garrison, K. C. (1932). The relative influence of intelligence and socio-cultural status upon the information possessed by first-grade children. *Journal of Social Psychology,* **3,** 362–67.
7. Gough, Harrison, G. (1946). The relationship of socio-economic status to personality inventory and achievement test scores. *Journal of Educational Psychology,* **37,** 527–40.
8. Line, W., and Glen, J. S. (1935). Some relationships between intelligence and achievement in the public schools. *Journal of Educational Research,* **33,** 582–87.
9. Shaw, Duane C. (1943). The relation of socio-economic status to educational achievement in grades four to eight. *Journal of Educational Research,* **37,** 197–201.

23. Some Educational Implications of the Influence of Rejection on Aspiration Levels of Minority Group Children

REGINA M. GOFF

This article is concerned with the social pressure of rejection as it acts as a barrier to effective intellectual and social functioning of minority group children. The purpose is to consider approaches in guidance which may offset attitudes and action patterns which follow rejection, and which subsequently interfere with goals or aspiration levels of the individual who is rejected.

The term "rejection" is used in the sense of a feeling state which represents a response to specific overt action patterns such as being barred from activities and institutions freely attended by others. The act of rejecting is essentially one of dispatching annoyers to which the designated individual responds with discomfort. An assumption made is that attitudes have a pervasive effect on behavior; that goals personally anticipated have an "inner structure" [1] which reflects attitudes of confidence; that experiences subsequent to the original goal-setting may depress attitudes and thus deflect

Reprinted from *Journal of Experimental Education*, Vol. 23 (December 1954), pp. 179–183, by permission of the publisher and author.

the individual from anticipated paths leading to the attainment of the goal. Furthermore, ways of thinking concerning the self become habituated through time in terms of social reinforcements. The individual thus learns to place values on himself in terms of positive or negative experiences. It is the desire here to indicate how educational experience may contribute to positive conditioning with reference to the self.

In analysis of the problem, there is presented, first, an exploration of the probable strength of intervening annoyers and interferences through an appraisal of the picture which a designated group of children have of themselves. This includes, among other things, their own evaluations of their abilities and the concomitant goals which they have set. This is followed by a consideration of actual achievement as it is found in adult members of the same group. The probable strength of annoyances in forestalling the realization of goals may be indicated by the consistency or discrepancy existing between goals of young group members and actual achievement as it is found in mature

223

members of the same group. The approach thus followed includes a presentation of original, empirical data on the children studied and a summary of the findings, followed by a comparative statement of the status of adult members of the same group, and finally, interpretations and implications with reference to offsetting the effects of rejection.

DESCRIPTION OF THE STUDY

One hundred twenty children, including 60 boys and 60 girls, were interviewed in Durham, North Carolina, in the summer of 1951. Represented in the group were 6- to 8-year-old children and those aged 12 to 14. Equal numbers were in each group. Two age groups were used in order to note any changes in attitudes or outlook during the years of growing awareness, deepening perception, the acquisition of new knowledge, and new realizations concerning individual abilities. Upper and lower income groups are also represented in recognition of the fact that individuals in different social and economic groups "act in response to their cultural training, to their particular system of socioeconomic rewards." [2] Contrasts in social experiencing and training result in subjective intellectual and emotional reactions which, in turn, result in contrast in thought, feeling, and action.

Questions asked centered around successes or failures in competitive out-of-school activities (games and sports) in which they freely engaged, ranking of the self in relation to in-school academic performance, ambitions, goals, or aspiration levels, and major wishes held. Where one places himself reflects personal feelings of potentialities, confidence, and worth of self. Ambitions or goals are natural consequents of self-evaluation. That there may be wishful

thinking rather than objective, realistic evaluations, is a possibility. Nevertheless, such thinking furnishes a basis for action. In-school and out-of-school performances were considered to note any possible differences in ranking of the self in freely chosen activities and those which are adult imposed tasks. Wishes, revealing unfulfilled desires or "formulated aspirations" indicate sensitivity to lacks. This ego involved sensitivity provides vulnerable areas in personality structure on which negative pressures may make immediate and noticeable inroads.

The qualitative data from the interviews are categorized and later quantified in terms of percentage in various categories. In order to obtain significant differences in responses according to age level and economic bracket, where appropriate, the chi-square technique was employed.

In giving results obtained, it is recognized that 6- to 8-year-old children, because of limited experience, may present fanciful conjectures. Nevertheless, if such should be the case, it is not amiss to place credence in responses inasmuch as fantasy has its origin in experience, real or vicarious, and thought patterns emerge from such content. It may be added that 12- to 14-year-old children may voice social expectations or approved of goals rather than true individual expectancies. However, in 46 per cent of the cases, the ambitions of children differed from parental expectations of them, which might indicate some genuine personal concern on the part of the subjects.

STATEMENT OF FINDINGS

I. Competency in in-school and out-of-school activities

    A. In freely chosen out-of-school activities, lower income children indicated a decrease in confidence with increase in age (significant at the .01 level of probability).

B. Feelings of inadequacy in relation to school subjects were notable in the low income group. But 33 percent of the girls as each age level felt competent, while 63 per cent of the younger boys and 37 per of the older had feelings of academic success.

C. Upper income girls indicated rising assurance with age increase in relation to both in-school and out-of-school activities. (Significant at the .02 level of probability.)

D. There was no significant difference in levels of confidence expressed by 6- 8-year-old, lower and upper income boys. Older upper income boys expressed more assurance in relation to school subjects than the comparable lower income group. (Significant at the .02 level of probability.) However, there was greater reluctance on the part of upper income boys to make decisive statements concerning out-of-school activities. Statements such as "Maybe I do as well," "Sometimes," were typical.

E. Results obtained indicate that feelings of worth exist to some extent in all groups and are found most often in younger children. In the upper income group, children rank themselves as equally competent or better than their peers more often than they rank themselves as decisively less capable.

F. Lower income girls hold least feelings of assurance and self-esteem.

II. Ambitions held, presented according to age, sex, and income level, and in order of first three preferences

A. Lower income group:

Boys: 6–8—Firemen and policemen (26%); brickmasons, builders, mechanics (24%); lawyers (20%)

12–14—Big league ball players (40%); doctors (27%); contractors, builders (14%)

Girls: 6–8—Teachers (34%); movie stars, dancers, models (15%); cooks (14%)

12–14—Teachers (30%); movie stars, dancers, models (15%); secretarial activities (10%)

B. Upper income group:

Boys: 6–8—Policemen and firemen (34%); builders and mechanics (32%); agents in real-estate offices (14%)

12–14—Doctors and lawyers (46%); scientists, "biologists," "chemists" (20%); architects (10%)

Girls: 6–8—Teachers (34%); nurses (26%); home makers, mothers (24%)

12–14—Teachers (37%); movie stars (27%); secretaries (14%)

C. Seventy-nine per cent of the lower income boys and 33 per cent of the girls felt that they would reach their goals, while 53 per cent of the upper income boys and 67 per cent of the girls made decisive statements of assurance.

D. Lower income children held money and lack of opportunity as major interferences, while the upper income children named ill-health, physical disabilities, bad luck, and death as possible interventions.

E. Lower income girls expressed least security with reference to probable success.

III. Expression of wishes presented in order of first three choices

A. Lower income group:

Boys: 6–8—Toys (Only wish expressed)

12–14—Money, clothes

Girls: 6–8—Clothing, food, homes

12–14—Improved physical appearance, homes, families, and money

B. Upper income group:

Boys: 6–8—Toys, pets

12–14—A wide spread of desires was reported from the acquisition of Eagle Scout badges, success in occupation, money for philanthropic purposes, to more sober wishes for good health to eternal life

Girls: 6–8—Toys, pets

12–14—As above, wishes were divergent with no heavy localization in any particular category. These included distribution from personal luxuries and travel to fulfillment of social needs; "places for colored children to swim," skating rinks, admittance to the "big library."

C. Particularly in the lower income group were findings similar to those of Gray [3] in which wishes were more in terms of the material and concrete than in terms of the abstract: happiness, health.

SUMMARY OF FINDINGS

A glance at trends throughout the findings reveals, with reference to lower income girls, a straight-line relationship between low confidence levels, little anticipation of success, and feelings of deprivation as revealed by wishes in areas which contribute to inner securities. Similarly, a thread of continuity appears to run through the findings with reference to the remainder of the group reporting. In general, feelings of confidence are expressed more often than not, positive attitudes of competence exist more frequently than negative ones, ambitions are directed toward occupations which yield substantial economic returns, success in areas of performance are most often expected, and wishes generally are in terms of further self-enhancement.

While these children have no doubt experienced ego-deflation in their movements in the larger world, they evidently see them as isolated from the context of life of the future. There probably exist at these ages no generalized notions of the impact which a totality of rejecting episodes of the larger world may have on the fruition of ambitions. When asked to state conditions which might interfere with the realizations of goals, all but two mentioned rejecting experiences and conflict in intergroup relations although a much larger number had no doubt experienced unfavorable situations.

THE ADULT POPULATION

If we now turn to the adult population of Negroes in American life, we find only 2.6 per cent of the total group in the professions with more than half of this number in the teaching occupations and the remainder spread thinly as doctors, trained ministers, and lawyers. Discriminatory and rejecting practices in industry have leveled the ranks of Negro workers to unskilled and semiskilled employment. Hardly 5 percent of the total Negro population can be considered in the upper income bracket. How much of the discrepancy which we note between children's confidence levels, their ambitions and wishes toward improvement and adult reflection of lack of fruition of these can be attributed to outright techniques of economic and social discrimination and rejection, or to misjudgment of ability, and how much to apathy or a giving up in the process of development is hardly discernible. Yet the question appears worthy of consideration. It is highly probable that aspiration levels are lowered, confidences shaken, and wishes abandoned because of psychological omissions in training and guidance. It is also likely that much by way of prevention of wastage of ability and warping of personality could be achieved if, before their inception, efforts were made to offset negative attitudinal patterns which are barriers to achievement. While the Negro group was used for the illustrative purposes, it would appear appropriate to assume that the same principles apply to any individuals in comparable unfavorable situations, for common causes are present despite other variables.

INTERPRETATIONS AND EDUCATIONAL IMPLICATIONS

As indicated, lower income children showed a marked feeling of inadequacy in relation to school subjects. It is possible that attitudinal patterns stem most directly from early home and cultural influences. In other words, these children have learned a particular response pattern. They have no social heritage akin to scholarly production, nor perhaps do they even have family exposures which reflect a tradition of schooling. Such omissions generate an unfamiliarity with abstract symbols and attendant feelings of shyness concerning them. The discernible trend to feel more at ease in physical games and sports may be worthy of attention. The school might recognize the role of feelings of competence in physical activities from the point of view using these initial security reactions for the development of generalized feelings of adequacy. Praise and commendation following successful endeavor in deliberately chosen games which require thought as well as skill, with this requirement pointed out to the child, releases latent streams of inspiration which invoke motivation to tackle problems with similar requirements in other areas. A greater measure of successful anticipation will accompany effort, and early tendencies to feel incompetent in relation to diverse tasks will be eased.

Incidentally, a factor influencing attitudes toward success in out-of-school activity is absence of adult domination and censure. The child, relieved of the tension of straining for goals set by adults, unreservedly directs attention and enthusiasm to the experience at hand. Also, he probably chooses those activities in which he has demonstrated his competence. Teachers might well assume a "background" or "hands off" attitude, thus avoiding unnecessary intrusions which set up emotional restraints.

The discernible trend of decrease in confidence level with increase in age in lower income children has implications for the basic problem—the probable force of the impact of rejection. Greater receptivity, less resistance to social depressors characterize the individual who already has initial feelings of inadequacy and whose confidence level is continuously lowering. In such instances, there are hardly notions of success freely entertained nor high goals set with reference to the larger competitive world. Lower income girls merit special attention, for their reactions indicate a greater sensitivity with reference to the self. A cue is given here for the building of thought patterns, outgrowths of experience, which negate feelings of self-limitations. Otherwise, circumstances of rejection will be accepted as a natural consequence of imagined inadequacy. A capable person may thus never discover latent abilities and, as a consequent waste inherent talents.

The contrast furnished by the upper income girls, in which there is increase in self-confidence with age increase, may reflect among other things more considerate classroom treatment. Not infrequently, children from "better families" are academically favored or given a place of importance which serves to nourish the ego and to influence effort and output. If the difference in feelings of competence can be attributed in part, to interpersonal parent-child, teacher-pupil relations, it is incumbent upon parents and teachers to begin in the early stages of the child's life, particularly with low-income children, to contrive planned

activities that provide opportunity for independent performances which give status in the respective groups. This in turn provides satisfactions which bolster the ego.

Older upper-income boys revealing less confidence than girls in the same group, no doubt have a greater attunement with reality. There is more movement and mingling outside the home and classroom with greater opportunity for sharp person to person comparisons and increased awareness of group standards. Outlooks, as a result, are less hopeful.

As indicated, feelings of worth exist to some extent in all groups. Where found, these positive attitudes may be thought of as "security anchors" which, if strengthened, may, figuratively speaking, provide a basis for the building of a reserve of "ego energy" which in turn holds the individual fast when he is faced with annoyers designed to deflate.

It is interesting to note in relation to occupational choices that irrespective of socioeconomic level and the roles of parents, ambitions of children were directed away from more menial types of employment. The increasingly large number of picture magazines and comic strips high-lighting activities of the world outside the home may have some bearing on choices made. An influence, too, may be the recent advent of a few Negroes in occupational avenues previously closed to them. An indication of social direction of a given time is revealed by the beliefs and values held by the children of the culture.

A question sometimes arises with reference to the advisability of giving the growing child a full view of the social world of which he is a part, and of his possible position and treatment within it. As stated earlier, the Negro child voiced little evidence of seeing a relationship between future success in chosen fields and his particular group membership. Is it wise to tell a child of underprivileged parents and deprived homes, or a child of a minority group that he might not be invited to play with some children whose parents consider them better; that he will not be allowed to enter some theaters and restaurants; that adult members of his group are not welcome to live in some neighborhoods and may be bombed out; that there are industries and firms which will not hire them? Is there a risk of unduly planting seeds of inferiority and antagonism? Is it better to let the individual smack up against the culture without forewarning? Perhaps either approach as stated is inadequate. However, if revealing the culture carries with it a "readiness for"; a full view of the larger world appears feasible. An approach tinged with self-pity or hatred, rather than understanding, is detrimental. However, if the growing individual were made aware of annoyances and interferences, there would more likely be whole-hearted cooperation in training designed to weaken the impact. Furthermore, there would follow increased determination to succeed in desired ends.

Though recurring patterns of rejection, mobilized by the culture, have persisted through time, few behavioral responses conceived of as psychological defenses have been suggested for withstanding them. However, such insightful training seems a possibility. Teacher training institutions might consider even further than at present the social and psychological role of future teachers, and emphasize the meaning of social morality, the study of social-psychological problems, principles of mental hygiene and guidance, and dynamics in human relations. The examination of causal sequences in behavior attempts to offset the effects of known but uncontrollable causes, the utilization of experimental data in the area of human relations, and use of findings from sociopsychological studies in child guidance would all appear to be aids in filling the notable gaps in the training of minority group children.

References

1. Kurt Lewin, et al. "Levels of Aspiration" in *Personality and Behavior Disorders,* Vol. II (New York: Ronald Press, 1944), p. 335.
2. Allison Davis. "Light from Anthropology," in *Cultural Groups and Human Relations,* Conference on Educational Problems of Special Cultural Groups (New York: Bureau of Publications, Teachers College, Columbia University, 1951), p. 84.
3. S. Gray, "Wishes of Negro Children," *Journal of Genetic Psychology,* LXIV (1944), pp. 225–237.

24. Acculturation and Learning Problems of Puerto Rican Children

SOPHIE L. ELAM

Many studies have been made and much has been said about the Puerto Rican child in cities. Although there are characteristics common to Puerto Rican children, these are by no means very different from those of other minority and emigrant children in the lower economic range. Problems of acculturation of emigrant groups are not new in our society, but invariably there is an urgency about them which is reflected in the many problems in the school and the community.

Perhaps as we look back at other migrations and note how these have been assimilated, it is possible to reflect that people who, like the Puerto Ricans, have recently come out of a rural peasant cultural pattern of living find acculturation more difficult than those who come from an urban center. It may well be that rural peoples tend to be tradition-oriented, while those from metropolitan communities are more other-directed so that they more readily respond to the cues available to them in our culture.

Acculturation is basically a problem of accommodation to a whole new set of patterns and being. It is actually the changeover from one culture to another. Culture is primarily a learning which is begun at birth and which provides the base for living. It permeates all behavior, from the simple fundamentals of eating and dressing and talking to the more complex and involved patterns of communication, use of symbols, and the development of a value system. Culture is also considered to be a determinant of the way one perceives oneself and others. It involves the totality of living from the biological to the social and intellectual. And the greatest complexity of the adjustment lies largely in the social sphere. ". . . under situations of stress or strain, of rapid change and consequent disorientation there is likely to be an increase in manifest ill health." [1]

Despite the vast network of our communications in mass media each emigrant group maintains almost intact its social constructs. For the adult who is already completely oriented to a way of life and whose whole gamut of responses is organized around the expected cues in his culture, the transition is difficult enough. He must select from the new what has resemblance to the familiar and add to this repertoire, by trial and error the new learnings as they are needed. He tends

Reprinted from *Teachers College Record*, Vol. 61 (February 1960), pp. 258–264, by permission of the publisher and the author.

to remain in his own ethnic and cultural clusters, both in industry and in neighborhood living, as witness the conclaves of Puerto Ricans in our cities.

But for the child who is still in the process of learning his social role and the inherent responses, the transition —often in only a few hours from the known to the unknown; from the simple to the complex environment; from rural areas to the cosmopolitan city— creates an even greater problem. It is the children who manifest the greatest degree of maladjustment.[2]

When the culture process is interrupted or suddenly changed, learning seems to cease. The new setting often destroys the foundations of security. It is therefore little wonder that the child who is an emigrant has not completely learned the culture of the land of origin before he is thrust into the new world, with a brand-new set of learning conditions to deal with. He is also usually the child of a family that is socially and economically disadvantaged and is therefore heir to all the insecurity, fears, and instabilities of our society to a larger degree than others. Both he and the adults in his family pursue a day-to-day existence with the attendant problems of inadequate housing, clothing, and nourishment. His parents too are caught in the crosscurrents of adjustment: to find jobs though they may be unskilled; to find housing at a cost they can afford when there is little available; to hold onto their own culture in a setting which neither understands nor is able to accept this culture.

The Puerto Rican child is thus caught between the two cultures, that of his people and the one which he must meet every day in the school. Sometimes he must respond to one that contradicts his own. The little girl who has been compliant is now expected to be active and responsive,

to take the initiative, to face new people and situations on her own. In the school room she is expected to talk and play with boys and to socialize more freely with her peers. There are rewards in our culture for this, but when she goes home she is forbidden to go out on the street to play. At home there is no reward for enterprising deeds, but rather the awaited and expected punishment. The emigrant child's age and sex roles and his developmental tasks are not the same as ours. If he adjusts to one, he negates the other, and as a result may lose his sense of identity with his family. The rewards we offer for these "disloyalties" are perhaps not as satisfying, nor can they be easily integrated into the patterns of the home and the other culture. We do, in fact, tend to create "culture conflict"—the battle of the supremacy of cultures in the family and the clash of roles between parents and children.[3]

Parents play the primary role in transmitting culture to the child. This is part of the socialization process. The child identifies with the parent and internalizes the learnings. In the new environment the parent is no longer in tune with the prevalent culture. He cannot command his child's involvement since the new society does not value his contribution to the socialization of his own child. The dichotomies and dualisms we create tend to whip the dog we taught to eat.

I

Such a situation is evident in the story of Ana, the sixth of eight children in a family.* She was eight years

* The cases described below are derived from the operation of a training program for undergraduates in Education at the City College of New York. Students serve as leaders for groups of children in a community group work program. The names of all cases described here are fictitious.

old when she came to the mainland. Ana's mother is the strong and managing figure in the family—a traditional Puerto Rican mother who holds her daughters in rigid control. They are not allowed out on the street; they must not talk to other people, particularly boys. Even the older girls are kept in this strict regimen. Ana could perhaps have developed some ease in interchange, but the mother's restrictions were so forceful that the girl's only recourse was to deny all contact. As a result, no one was able to reach out to Ana. She went on to junior high school, where she is barely passing. In addition, she has developed even more reticence and isolates herself. She has frequent headaches and stomach upsets, and is absent from school very often.

This is a rather extreme example of the frequently found conflict in social roles particularly in reference to the upbringing of girls. Since the neighborhoods in which these families settle are often socially disorganized, there is a kind of justification for the fears of the parents which further constricts the life of the girls and the younger children. It is important in working with Puerto Rican parents to help them find ways to protect their children without completely depriving them of social interchange. However, the traditions are so firmly imbedded in the structure of their living that this is difficult to achieve. It is equally difficult to help growing children find the channel between outright rebellion and complete submission, hence they live in an atmosphere of conflict and indecision. It is at this point that they either compliantly submit and lose the ability to relate to their own peer group, or completely leave their families and join the peer group, thereby losing the support which they still need so much.

The language disability which pervades all these problems is very real. It is also a measure of the emotional stability of the person at this time of pressure. The differential rates of language learning are not only the result of age differentials and intelligence levels (the younger child learning more rapidly than the older and the brighter child learning faster than the duller) but also cues to the general level of the individual's emotional adjustment and the resolution of cultural identification and conflicts. Language is one of the tools for learning which the emigrant child lacks. He is left with only the cues he can obtain from nonverbal communication; the expressive gestures which may convey some meaning for him. Here too, however, a facial expression or a gesture may mean something else to him, since gestures are also a language and are richly colored by each culture with specific meanings. Meanwhile he must manage without the necessary cues for directing his behavior.

As a result of these handicaps the child begins to feel inadequate. He cannot solve all the problems of adjustment to a new land, new language, new living, and new culture. He cannot seek support from his parents since they too are faced with the identical problems and with the added responsibility of founding their families in this new land. Therefore, if the child fails he suffers further indignity. He may reason that it is better not to try. Then one has not failed. Or better still, it is possible to remain so indifferent, uninvolved, and apathetic that one evades all responsibility for functioning in a setting fraught with failure and with many demands that one cannot meet.[4] This kind of "culture shock" is frequently found in great or small degree in many of our children and families.

The school is brought face to face

with all these problems. There may be some variation in the nature of these difficulties in different families or individuals, but the total problem is present in every child the school works with who has recently arrived from Puerto Rico. Neither the school nor the teacher has been trained to see behavior in the light of these causes. Rather, they tend to meet each situation separately either as a discipline question or as an education problem. Our training practices in education have dealt chiefly with the child who is native to our land and has no outstanding language problem. The child of the lower economic and social strata is also rarely dealt with in our academic courses. Most of our textbooks are written by middle-class professors for middle-class teachers of middle-class children. We tend to think of education as primarily establishing literacy and the ability to deal with the daily techniques of middle-class living in urban centers.

Education, although drawn from many other disciplines, for a long time tended to ignore the findings in anthropology, social psychology, and clinical psychology. Or at least it has not found a way to integrate these findings into the educational and developmental sequence usually taught in the teacher-preparation courses. We tend to divide sharply our disciplines at the college level, thus making it more difficult to provide an interdisciplinary approach to problems that the school faces. It seems hardly necessary to point out that if we are to work with a large number of children from a given culture we must, at the very least, learn something of the specifics of that culture, and of how it pervades the entire personality and its perceptions in new situations. Learning how Puerto Rican children dance, or play ball, or count in Spanish will not make the teacher aware of how Puerto Rican children view their inadequacy in learning the fundamentals of arithmetic, or how and why it is so difficult for them to retain the fact that three and four are seven, or remember that our *j* does not sound like *h*. There needs to be rather the concept of "fundamental education to cover the whole of living; to teach not only new ways but the need and the incentive for new ways." [5]

How does it feel to be unable to comprehend the cues in this new setting? How do anxiety and insecurity affect a child's readiness to learn? How do people acquire a new culture without stress and destruction to their sense of well-being? The findings and skills of anthropology, sociology, and social and clinical psychology will help us interpret this kind of defeat, and better still, to learn to look for these problems. They will perhaps also sharpen our focus and help us find the educational methods which are best employed for reaching these children who really so desperately want to achieve. The individual caught in the maelstrom of conflicting cultures and feelings can be helped to move from inadequacy and near panic (as in "culture shock") to independence and courage.

II

In our work we encounter many children who reflect these problems. Rafael, a boy of two, saw his father migrate to the States. His mother left when he was three. When he was four his younger sister was sent to the mainland to join the family. He and his grandmother lived in Puerto Rico until he was seven. All these years of separation seemed to have given him the feeling of being unwanted. When he arrived here his mother was again unavailable to him, since she worked long hours away from home. During his first two years in this country he made few friends, and seemed to his teacher unable to learn. Carmen, his younger sister, was much more competent than he, and carried on much of the interchange for him and other members of the family with the new and strange world. Rafael was frequently sick and remained at home with his old grandmother to care for him. In the third year of his stay he seemed able to come to terms with his new country—to emerge from his chrysalis. Now he is lively and takes an interest in what goes on around him. He greets adults and children alike with warmth and friendliness, and his work at school has begun to show the real potential that he possesses.

Elsa is another child who experienced the privation of her mother's departure. When Elsa was two, her mother left for the United States, leaving her children to the care of their maternal grandmother. At three Elsa was brought to the mainland but since her mother was working the children were left in the care of a woman living in the same apartment house. Elsa's initial adjustment to school was so poor that when she was in the second grade the school notified the mother that something had to be done. The child was hyperactive, inattentive, and created too much distraction in the classroom. The mother sent Elsa back to Puerto Rico to live with an aunt for a year. When Elsa returned, her adjustment to school, and her learning achievement were no better. At this time Elsa is being referred to a child guidance clinic.

These are only two cases among the many which we encounter in the schools. The pattern of emigration here depicted is usual in the Puerto Rican family. Early deprivation of the mother creates social and emotional problems which are very difficult to overcome, even with care and concern by the school and other agencies.

Many Puerto Rican children arrive after a period of separation from their mothers or both parents. Thus the emotional concomitants are disabling before the schools in this country even begin to work with the children. Exploration of conditions in each of the new families might alert the schools to the problems and perhaps gear the school situation to help these children. They syndrome of this difficulty has already been fully described by such writers in this field as John Bowlby and Lauretta Bender. It includes a range of behavior: apathy, lack of social responsiveness, depressed intellectual functioning (discussed by William Goldfarb), inability to form meaningful relationships, hyperactivity, aggression, and lowered intellectual potential.

III

The Alvarez family presents a different picture, yet it also has within it all the problems of adjustment to a new environment. There were four children in this family, who lived originally in a rural community on the Island. The father worked in the sugar cane fields; they had a small house, a cow, and chickens. Miguel, the father, migrated to the United States eight years ago. Two years later, Rosa, the mother, leaving the children on the island, came to set the new home. After a few months of separation all the children were brought to the mainland.

The father had no skills, but he found employment as a dishwasher and has remained in that work. He is always employed but does not earn enough to care fully for his growing family. Two children were born here and the entire family lives in a partly furnished apartment (they have never been able to save enough to buy the requisite furniture). The Department of Public Welfare helps to subsidize the family, but even with this help the budget is too small to provide adequate bed linen, blankets, and warm winter clothing. All the children are slender and the school records indicate poor nutrition for all the school-age children.

Frequently the members of the family are prey to the upper respiratory illness so common to Puerto Rican families. Maria, the thirteen-year-old daughter, must then remain at home to help care for the mother and children. She had so many absences from school that the teachers complained they could not really help her.

Maria is a tall, stoop-shouldered girl with large dark eyes, pale olive skin, and a slow, hesitant manner. She attended an after-school club program for three years but always remained on the outskirts of the group, although nearly all the club members are of Puerto Rican background. She uttered hardly a word. When she was ten Maria had the first of a series of minor epileptic attacks and is now attending the Seizure Clinic regularly. (This is another common ailment among newly emigrant families, who refer to this illness as "attaques." It may be another manifestation of the somatic effects of the stress of adjustment.)

Maria has repeated the sixth grade and even now has achieved a reading level of only third grade. Her ability in mathematics is even lower than her reading level. This girl saw herself as completely inadequate in every aspect of her living. She never undertook anything for fear of failure. It was only after a year of intensive work with Maria and her family, using nearly every resource in the community, that Maria gained any sense of competence.

There were many health problems in the family for which nursing, nutritional guidance, and hospital care had to be obtained. Fortunately, though the mother speaks no English and is completely illiterate, she is deeply concerned for her children, has much warmth and affection to give, and is eager to help her family adjust to the new environment. She is able to overcome the traditional patterns and encourages Irma to participate in clubs and activities.

The problem of family finances was partially solved by additional funds allotted for special diets for several of the children. The family was encouraged to make application for public housing. The social service resources were made available for Maria by the Catholic Big Sisters, and Maria is now assured of a permanent relationship to meet her emotional needs.

A special program was set up to give Maria opportunities for relationships with children in the group club program, and a special worker was assigned to act in a supportive role for the child as she began to make the transition to active participation. A remedial program in reading was also arranged. From the start it was felt that Maria had much more potential than her low IQ indicated. She seemed quite creative with art materials. As all this enrichment was made available she began to awake from her long passive role and to look out and see people. She clamored for help in her school work; she wanted to achieve. She began to take a more active role with her peers. Even her slow, hesitant manner and walk changed. She ran now and jumped; she had a close friend; and she had abandoned her role on the periphery of the group.

Although there are still many problems in the Alvarez family and Maria has a long way to go, we have already some sense of the potential of the child and the possibility that she can move more rapidly now toward the achievement of a large part of that potential. She will probably never achieve all that is possible for her. But having studied Maria we can continue with the other children and help each one of them. They are younger and there may be a better chance to bring to fruition more of their potential. Perhaps the second generation of this family will achieve greater self-actualization. The school has to meet the needs of many children. Now it is the Puerto Rican child, as it was once the Irish, the Italian, the Jewish groups in other tides of emigration. In each child there will be problems which stand in the way of learning. It is only as the school and the community come to know the family and its needs that these newcomers can be helped. It will be through the school, together with many other agencies and with a view to the totality of the child and his family, that the acculturation will come about.

References

1. Margaret Mead, *Cultural Patterns and Technological Change* (New York: Mentor Books, 1955).
2. *Ibid.*, p. 281.
3. *Ibid.*, p. 254.
4. A. Anastasi and Cordova, F. A., "Some Effects of Bilingualism upon the Intelligence Test Performance of Puerto Rican Children in New York City," *Journal of Educational Psychology*, **44**, pp. 1–19.
5. Margaret Mead, *op. cit.*, p. 253.

25. Problems of Classroom Adjustment of Indian Children in Public Elementary Schools in the Southwest

MILES V. ZINTZ

New Mexico is the home of several ethnic groups whose life ways through past centuries have been very different. The Pueblo Indian groups have lived in the middle Rio Grande Valley for centuries—perhaps a thousand years. The Navajos and Apaches migrated southward down the western side of North America not later than the fifteen hundreds. The Spanish Americans established homes in the Rio Grande Valley and the capitol of New Mexico at Santa Fe in the later years of the seventeenth century. Finally, the "Anglos" established trade routes and homesteads, and through the years, definitely made theirs the dominant culture of the state. This dominance is of recent date, however, and many of the problems of acculturation, or amalgamation of cultures, have not been resolved.

As recently as ten years ago, Congress made provision for educating Indian children in public school facilities in place of former arrangements provided by the Bureau of Indian Affairs

Reprinted from *Science Education*, Vol. 46 (April 1962), pp. 261–269, by permission of the publisher and the author.

through civil service appointment of teachers. This provision necessitated providing classroom space, materials of instruction, and reimbursement for average per pupil costs at the local level. The Federal government underwrites this cost in the same way in which it formerly paid the cost of educating Indian children in Indian schools.

This change in the educational plan for Indian children came about as a result of testing and evaluation programs conducted in the Bureau which had shown clearly that Indian children educated in public schools were able to achieve better than those educated in Bureau schools. The works of Peterson,[1] Anderson,[2] and Coombs[3] showed clearly the lack of educational achievement and also pointed up the very different cultural values of these children as they related to the motivations and expectations of American school teachers.

The Bureau of Indian Affairs had shown its concern about both of these problems—lack of educational achievement and the differences in cultures—and has completed significant studies in analyzing them. During Collier's ad-

237

ministration in the Bureau, funds were obtained for a comprehensive Indian Education Research Project.

The Indian Education Research Project, a joint activity of the United States Office of Indian Affairs and the Committee on Human Development of the University of Chicago, was begun in 1941 to study personality development of Indians in their native environments. The hope was that an interdisciplinary approach, utilizing anthropology, psychology, linguistics, and education, might prognosticate directions toward more effective Bureau of Indian Affairs Administration. Several very valuable publications resulted from this research:

1. *Warriors Without Weapons, A Study of the Society and Personality Development of the Pine Ridge Sioux,* by MacGregor, 1946;

2. *The Hopi Way, The Education of the Hopi Indian Child,* by Thompson and Joseph, 1944;

3. *The Children of the People, The Navajo Individual and His Development,* by Leighton and Kluckhohn, 1948;

4. *The Desert People, A Study of the Papago Indians,* by Jospeh, Spicer, and Chesky, 1949.

Hundreds of Indian children were given individually administered intelligence tests. The Grace Arthur Point Performance Scale and the Goodenough Draw-a-Man were two of the tests used. In all this testing, Indian children did demonstrate normal intelligence. Based on such evidence, Havighurst wrote in 1957:

"The conclusion which is drawn by most social scientists from the data on Indian cultures and Indian intelligence is that the American Indians of today have about the same innate equipment for learning as have the white children of America. But in those Indian tribes which have preserved their traditional cultures to some extent, there is a limited motivation of children for a high level performance in schools and colleges." [4]

The day-to-day work of classroom teachers of Indian children should certainly have been affected if these publications had been studied carefully and if teachers had apprized themselves of the pertinent information.

In the present study, then, lack of basic intelligence was not recognized as a factor in the poor achievement of minority groups in the elementary schools. This study, conducted under a three-year research grant from the United States Office of Education, Cooperative Research Branch, had five major purposes:

1. To identify, define, and describe factors of cultural and environmental differences between Indians and non-Indians.

2. To find ways to alleviate conflicts which arise because of differences in culture. Child behavior must be interpreted in terms of causal factors—or must be understood in light of the child's life values.

3. To plan for the adjustment of the school curriculum in light of cultural differences and conflicts. Understanding the English language is, of course, a primary problem.

4. To increase understanding and cooperation of parents in all problems listed above in cultural differences, value conflicts, language barriers, and the school curriculum.

5. To improve teacher preparation (pre-service and in-service) in view of the intercultural problems to be faced.

The first objective necessitated a careful scrutiny of the body of anthropological literature that would help to reveal the life values, or cultural beliefs, of the various minority ethnic groups to be taught in the schools. This necessitated an attempt on the part of educators to synthesize findings of anthropologists translated into a sociological frame of reference in order to provide the information needed by classroom teachers. These sociocultural differences included not only overt behaviors in dress, customs, attitudes, and language, but also, more difficult to assess, covert behaviors in beliefs, knowledges, and ideals. These cultural differences needed to be described in terms of basic institutions in each different social group—family living, church affiliation, economy, politics, health, education, and recreation. This body of knowledge would be helpful to both pre-service and in-service classroom teachers who were about to become the teachers of these children from minority groups in New Mexico.

This study presupposed that Indian children were different. It presupposed that teachers were inadequately prepared to understand or accept the dissimilar cultural values. The values of most teachers are middle-class values. This means that teachers come from homes where the drive for achievement and success causes parents to "push" their children to climb the ladder of success; where "work for work's sake" is important; and where everyone is oriented to future-time values. To teach the child successfully, the teacher must recognize that the child may come to school with a radically divergent set of values, and the teacher must try to understand, not disparage, these values.

Some contrasting values of the school teacher and the traditional values of the Pueblo Indian child are cited here. The child's values and the teacher's may be generalized to considerable degree as following the pattern of:

1. *Harmony with* nature as juxtaposed with *mastery over* nature.

2. *Present time* orientation rather than *future time* orientation.

3. Inclusion of mythology, fear of the supernatural, and sorcery rather than a total commitment to a scientific explanation of all natural phenomena.

4. A level of aspiration to follow in the ways of the old people; to cooperate and maintain the status quo rather than to develop a keen sense of competition and climb the ladder of success.

5. To value anonymity and submissiveness rather than individuality and aggression.

6. To work to satisfy present needs and to be willing to share rather than always working to "get ahead" and save for the future.

The Navajo, too, has traditionally learned to try to live in harmony with nature. An unhurried inexactness with time schedules has resulted from using the sun as a measure of time rather than having clocks (while Navajo people accept Indian time for Indians, they expect the *Bilagaana* to be *on time!*). About saving, one should not have too much. Then people (witches) won't take it away from you or make you sick. You might also be thought of as selfish or stingy. The Navajo society is based on a matrilineal, consanguinal, extended family organization. Success rests more in being a good person than in acquiring things.

Understanding cultural differences extends beyond any stereotyping of all Indians into one general category. There are observable differences between Pueblos and Navajos, for example. The tight, complex social fabric of the Pueblo villages may be *contrasted* with a kind of comparative individualism of the Navajo. The age-old sufficiency and resistance to change of the Pueblo may be *contrasted* with the adaptability and the cultural borrowing of the Navajo. The Pueblo might appear to have adopted many non-Indian ways without even sensing any inroads into his religious beliefs and practices, while in *contrast*, the Navajo may, more like the Anglo neighbor, hinge his total interaction of social institutions on the economy which he is rapidly copying from the Anglo.[5]

It is necessary at this point to recognize that New Mexico Indians as individuals do not all conform to generalized patterns. Acculturation takes place on a long continuum of behaviors —all the way from those who still very completely fit the traditional patterns to those whose life style is completely middle-class, or they have become bicultural. The serious problems lie in the twilight zone of social disorganization.

There are those non-Indians who challenge this research with observations that "These people should be allowed to preserve their own culture" and "If they want to go back to the reservation, they have a perfect right to do so." These observations, with some nostalgic overtones, must be countered with reality in present-day society. Consider the Navajo, for example:

1. Navajo adults over 25 years of age have, on the average, only a second-grade level of formal education.

2. Little exposure to English as a language of communication except in the school environment is apt to leave the individual poorly equipped to compete in the labor market off the reservation.

3. The reservation can support no more than a third of the Navajo population if they are to, in any measure, approximate the usually expected standard of living.

4. Their cultural institutions are changing: the matrilineal family is breaking up; their traditional economy is rapidly being destroyed; their health practices are rapidly incorporating white man's medicine; certain curing ceremonies encompassed in religious practice are becoming obsolescent; and a tribal council is bringing conformity to previously autonomous segregated groups.

The research study hoped to define for teachers those differences with the hope that understanding might ease the conflict.

It was also necessary to encompass the educational problems of the Spanish-American people of the Rio Grande Valley in this research. Today in New Mexico there are a great number of unacculturated Spanish Americans. There are a great number of old people who do not speak the English language. Among the young there are many who stopped their formal education early and, as a result, do not speak the English language fluently and do not begin to understand the Anglo folkways and mores. As some of these people are exposed to, and accept, the value system of the Anglo society, they lose more of the Spanish-American values, generally speaking. Some exist in a half-Spanish, half-Anglo world; others have accepted Anglo values and are, practically speaking, acculturated. About the only things they have retained of the traditional Spanish-American culture are the language and the foods they like.

In the traditional Spanish-American culture pattern were people who placed great value on:

1. "Getting through" this temporal life so that they could enjoy the rewards of the life hereafter.

2. A "work a little; rest a little" attitude.

3. Following in one's father's footsteps.

4. Being satisfied with the present.

5. Being particularistic in nature, recognizing the emotional response in dealing with others and their needs—not competing at the expense of the feelings of others, perhaps.

A middle class is now beginning to arise among the Spanish-American people. Many of these people, whose families have previously felt that they could not, now really believe that they, too, can climb the ladder of success. Pressures within the Spanish-American group itself are now greater, and many more of the young people are responding to challenges of formal education. The cultural status of the Spanish-American group is rapidly changing.

Too, as Spanish-American families acquire the artifacts of the middle-class family—new cars for which monthly payments must be made, television sets, the convenience of bathrooms—the desire to have and to keep these artifacts places the individual in a position where he must extend himself more and more into the dominant culture.

That Spanish-Americans are successfully acquiring these new orientations has been demonstrated by those who have emerged from the typical traditional culture as doctors, scientists, lawyers, and college professors. These, however, are still the rare exceptions. Too many today terminate their educations before they finish high school. Only a very small percentage finish college.

Such schools as the Presbyterian Menaul Boarding School in Albuquerque, in which the children leave the home and stay at the school, have probably been helpful in speeding the acculturation process. Many Spanish-American children go home to parents who love them, but who do not value the formal education and say, in sym-

pathy, to the child, "They make you work *so* hard." If a trusted parent puts the emphasis on how hard the work is, rather than on the value of having done the work, the child is likely to be less motivated to complete it.

Saunders summarizes one of his addresses concerning the cultural history of the Spanish-American in this way:

"The Spanish-speaking people of the Southwest, like all the rest of us, have come a long way in the past hundred years. The changes they have undergone can be dramatically symbolized in terms of contrasts; the thatch roofed hut and the skyscraper; the horse-drawn wagon and the stratocruiser; the wooden hoe and the mechanical cotton picker; the corrido singer and the juke box; the open fireplace and the atomic pile. The social distance they have traversed is greater than that between the most isolated village in New Mexico and the heart of downtown San Antonio. They have not all moved at the same rate, nor are they at the same point now. But they all are upon the same road and moving in the same direction. *And there will be no turning back.*" [6]

This discussion of cultural differences may well be concluded with a word of caution based on Henry's discussion of his Cross-Cultural Outline of Education. American teachers have experienced the desire for upward mobility in the social structure, the adherence to a rigid set of values by which they *judge* the behaviors of all children, and vague allegiance to what may be termed the Protestant ethic. This has caused teaching as a method of cultural transmission to be a *continuous narrowing* of the learners' perceptual field with respect to what values, beliefs, and attitudes are right, proper, and acceptable is directly opposed to the world view and the concept of broadening a child's appreciations of the interactions of man in a world community.[7]

EDUCATIONAL RETARDATION

Beyond this description of the cultural differences and their effect on the behaviors of children in classrooms, the research study investigated two problems related to curriculum. The first was to establish current evidence in the public schools of the patterns of educational retardation, and the second was to devise tests to measure the abilities of the children from the minority ethnic groups to understand facets of English as the language of the school.

The work of Tireman,[8] Sininger,[9] Sanchez,[10] Coombs,[11] and Boyce[12] had shown, through the years, a general tendency for pupils to become more and more educationally retarded as they progress through the schools, with many of these students either dropping out or becoming hopelessly lost in the high school. Educational retardation may be defined as the extent to which students fail to achieve academically according to their capacity for such achievement. Children of normal intelligence are expected to move through the public school grades on an extremely homogeneous age-in-grade scale. Academic performance at grade-placement for children in the normal range of intelligence indicates achievement that is neither retarded nor accelerated.

The results of the current testing program reinforce the previous findings that as minority ethnic group children progress through the school grades, their achievement falls farther and farther behind. Not only are these students from one to two years overage for their grades, on the average, but they are also educationally retarded an additional one to two years in achievement on standardized tests. In two of four selected high schools, half of the eleventh and twelfth grade students were in the bottom decile when compared to national norms on a survey reading test.

The testing program showed that groups of Anglo children scored from approximate grade placement to one-half year of retardation in achievement. Spanish-American students were, on the average, one year educationally retarded in fifth and sixth grade, but they were an additional year overage in grade. Indian children tended to be two to three years retarded in reading ability in sixth grade and were one to two years overage in grade.

In the *Navajo Yearbook*, Young has also emphasized that one of the major problems in the field of Navajo education is that of educational retardation. This educational retardation made itself strongly felt with the transfer of Indian children to public schools. Pub-school personnel were concerned that Navajo children accepted for enrollment be "up to grade." Of 9,751 children whose records were analyzed in December, 1957, only 6 per cent were "up to grade," 40 per cent were retarded at least one year, and 54 per cent were retarded two or more years.[13]

It is apparent from data obtained in 1960 that there continues to be one full year of over-ageness for all minority ethnic groups. This is not as significant, however, as the indication that even though the sample children were over-age in grade, they were an additional one and one-half to two years retarded in achievement as measured by a survey reading test. Overageness and retardation must be combined to determine the full extent of educational retardation. This severity of educational retardation follows the same pattern recognized by Sanchez, Tireman, and Sininger three decades previously.

UNDERSTANDING OF ENGLISH AS THE LANGUAGE OF THE SCHOOL

The teaching of English as a second language encompasses at least three facets: (1) the memorization of, and drill on, the common speech utterances of the second language; (2) the extension of vocabulary in the second language beyond the initial levels required in such common utterances; and (3) the reading and writing of the second language.

In the present study only a small amount of work was done in this area. This work centered on testing knowledge of facets of English vocabulary—investigating semantic difficulties as found in common idiomatic expressions, multiple meanings of common words, simple analogies, and opposites. Four masters' theses measuring these abilities indicated that Indian and Spanish-American children are significantly handicapped in comparison with Anglo children with whom their performances were compared. Fourth grade Anglo children with unilingual backgrounds performed statistically significantly better on all these tests than did Indian and Spanish-American sixth grade children enrolled in public school classes.[14] Selected items are included here for illustrative purposes.

1. *Understanding the idiom in the English language.* Idioms taken from *expressions in the English language.*

Mother will *piece out* the supper.
Tom knew he was *saved by a hair.*
His plan *fell through.*
"O.K.," he retorted, *"Don't bite my head off."*
He won't be *worth his salt* for a long time to come.
Mr. Bird chuckled, "Now I've *let the cat out of the bag."*

The idioms were interpreted in a completely literal sense by those for whom English was the second language.

2. *Understanding commonly used slang expressions in English language.*

Mr. Jones really *cramps my style.*
When everyone else quit, I was *stuck with the job.*
He is great for *talking through his hat.*
It's about time to quit fooling around and *talk turkey.*
Tom likes to *pull your leg* every chance he gets.

These slang expressions will surely be baffling if translated in a completely literal way.

3. *Understanding all the uses of the same little English word.*

The boy will *run* a race.
The disease has *run* its course.
The fence *runs* east and west.
The man *runs* a garage.
The boy has *run* a splinter in a finger.
He will *run* out of money.
He will *run* up a bill.
He may *run* across an old friend.
He can knock a home *run.*
There was a *run* on the bank.
He is not the common *run* of persons.

Run has some seventy-five uses in the elementary school dictionary.

4. *Testing multiple meanings of the same word.* Most children for whom English is a foreign language have difficulty with multiple meanings of the same word. A multiple choice test was devised asking children to identify the *incorrect* use of a word.

1. a. It came in a *plain* package.
   b. The answer is *plain* to everyone.
   c. The *plain* wore off his new coat.
   d. The house was built on a high *plain.*

2. a. Don't *hold* me.
   b. Look in the *hold* of the ship.
   c. The cup can *hold* water.
   d. Your clothes are full of *hold*.

3. a. He hurt my *left* hand.
   b. There is nothing *left*.

   c. We put *left* in the pan.
   d. We *left* the city.

5. *Lack of adequate word meanings for words heard orally.* Children often misunderstand the word given completely when they attempt to use words orally in sentences.[15]

blot	Where blood come.	(clot)
spool	A place where there is water.	(pool)
habit	We habit be quiet.	
rack	When we go fast we rack the car.	(wreck)
won	The Indians have a wigwon.	(wigwam)
tasks	They cut the tasks of the elephant.	(tusks)
bushel	The name of a big bush.	
climate	The natives climate the trees to get coconuts.	(climbed up)
oyster	A kind of bird in the zoo.	(ostrich)

6. *Understanding simple analogies.* Some simple analogies readily understood by Anglo fourth graders may give much difficulty for all those for whom English is a second language.

Water is to drink as bread is to *eat.*
Cowboy is to horse as pilot is to *plane.*
Tree is to trunk as flower is to *stem.*

LANGUAGE AND CULTURE

Language is an integral part of a people's culture. It is the means by which the attitudes and feelings of the group are made known. Anthropologists and linguists have clearly stated this interdependence of culture and language.

". . . the world, as it comes to be perceived by each individual, is in large part filtered through the medium of his mother tongue." [16]

Languages are socially determined. Their uses, form, and content mirror physical setting, historical events, contacts, cultural level, mental climate, and cultural history. The language of a group is an index of most of its char-

acteristics. Conversely, cultural and social structures are affected by the language system. Inadequate command of language retards cultural development and acquisition. The language system and sociocultural context of a society cannot be separated—each is both the cause and effect of the other.[17]

An individual builds his repertoire of thought and action based on the cultural behavior of which he is a part. New ideas must be interpreted in the minds that are to assimilate them. The means by which this is accomplished in language, but language is strictly relative to the culture of its users, intermeshing to the point that one can be understood fully only in the light of the other.[18]

The problem of language in New Mexico has not been the same problem which is faced in other parts of the United States where many different foreign groups have migrated, diffused into the American "melting pot," and in two generations or so, become users of the common language. The Indian and the Spanish-American settled in the Southwest centuries before the Anglo came. Both Oraibi and Acoma are cited by sociologists as being the oldest continuously inhabited villages in the United States and are believed to be 900 to 1000 years old. Civilization that persists for so long a time develops a cultural heritage in which there is pride and allegiance. It is no wonder that these people have resisted absorption into the Anglo culture. It becomes apparent, in this context, why the old Pueblo Indian will insist that his children or grandchildren must know the mother tongue well since this is the very instrument by which his culture will be continued.

FACTORS INFLUENCING THE LEARNING OF ENGLISH AS A SECOND LANGUAGE

The cultural difference, the relationship of language to culture, and the serious degree of educational retardation have been discussed as they relate to the education of the Indian and Spanish-American children in New Mexico. If these children are to succeed academically in the public schools, they must develop a greater mastery of English for communication than they have done in the past. Probably the greatest need in New Mexico's schools is that all these minority groups become more articulate in English. Many different factors influence the child's learning of English as a second language. Some of these are: desire, amount of exposure, socioeconomic status, influence of leaders, schools, educational adjuncts, and elements common to the two languages under consideration.[19]

SUMMARY

This research has indicated that the good teacher will become as sophisticated as possible about the cultural background of the children he teaches. This demands an appreciation on the teacher's part of the contribution which the child's culture has made in the past and its significance to his people in the present—the language, the music, the folk lore, the customs, the religious and spiritual life, the foods, the architecure, the crafts—the whole cultural heritage. Behaviors of children in the classroom will be interpreted both in terms of the life values of the child and the ability he has to communicate in the language of the school. Since lack of intellectual ability has been eliminated as a causal factor in educational retardation, improved techniques in teaching are indicated to overcome the extreme retardation of boys and girls in school. These techniques strongly suggest, first of all, a major effort in the teaching of English as a second language. Beyond this effort, well-defined efforts in remedial teaching in all curriculum areas will be needed to help Indian children achieve successfully in school.

References

1. Shailer Peterson, *How Well Are Indian Children Educated?* (Washington: Bureau of Indian Affairs, 1948).
2. Kenneth E. Anderson, et al., *The Educational Achievement of Indian Children* (Washington: Bureau of Indian Affairs, 1953).
3. L. Madison Coombs, et al., *The Indian Child Goes to School* (Washington: United States Department of the Interior, 1958).
4. Robert J. Havighurst, "Education Among American Indians: Individual and Cultural Aspects," *The Annals of the American Academy of Political and Social Science* (May, 1958), 311: 113.

5. Robert Bunker, and John Adair, *The First Look at Strangers* (New Brunswick: Rutgers University Press, 1959), pp. 138–139.
6. Lyle Saunders, "The Social History of Spanish-Speaking People in Southwestern United States Since 1846," *Proceedings of the First Congress of Historians from Mexico and the United States Assembled In Monterrey, Nuevo Leon, Mexico, September 4–9, 1949* (Mexico City: Editorial Culture, T.G., S.A., 1950), p. 165.
7. Jules Henry, "A Cross-Cultural Outline of Education," *Current Anthropology*, 1, 267–305.
8. Loyd S. Tireman, *Teaching Spanish-Speaking Children* (Albuquerque: University of New Mexico Press, 1948), pp. 45–50.
9. Harlan Sininger, "An Age-Grade Study of the San Jose Training School and Its Two Control Schools," *San Jose Training School,* University of New Mexico Bulletin, School Series, Vol. 1, No. 2 (Albuquerque: University of New Mexico, 1931), pp. 3–10.
10. George I. Sanchez, *The Age-Grade Status of the Rural Child in New Mexico Public Elementary Schools, 1931–1932*, Educational Research Bulletin, Vol. I (Santa Fe: Department of Education, November, 1932).
11. Coombs, *loc. cit.*
12. George Boyce, "Why Do Indians Quit School?" *Indian Education* (May 1, 1960), p. 344.
13. Robert Young, *The Navajo Yearbook, 1958*, Report No. VII (Window Rock, Arizona: Navajo Agency, 1958), p. 8.
14. Maurine D. Yandell, "Some Difficulties Which Indian Children Encounter with Idioms in Reading" (unpublished Master's thesis, The University of New Mexico, Albuquerque, 1959); Veta W. Mercer, "The Efficiency of Bilingual Children in Understanding Analogies in the English Language" (unpublished Master's thesis, The University of New Mexico, Albuquerque, 1960); Christine Dudding, "An Investigation into the Bilingual Child's Comprehension of Antonyms" (unpublished Master's thesis, The University of New Mexico, Albuquerque, 1961; Stephen G. Hess, "A Comparative Study of the Understanding Which Bilingual Students Have of the Multiple Meanings of English Words" (research in progress, The University of New Mexico, Albuquerque, 1960–61).
15. Loyd S. Tireman, "The Bilingual Child and His Reading Vocabulary," *Elementary English* (January, 1955), 32:33–35.
16. Walter Goldschmidt, "Language and Culture: A Reply," *Quarterly Journal of Speech* (October, 1955), 41:279–83.
17. J. O. Hertzler, "Toward A Sociology of Language," *Social Forces* (December, 1953), 32:109–119.
18. Douglas G. Haring, "Cultural Contexts of Thought and Communication," *Quarterly Journal of Speech* (April, 1951), 37:161–172.
19. Loyd S. Tireman and Miles V. Zintz, "Factors Influencing Learning a Second Language," *Education* (January, 1961), 81:310–313.

26. Oglala Sioux Dropouts and Their Problems with Educators

ROSALIE H. WAX

Neither the dropout nor the process of dropping out are well understood. Persons otherwise well informed, including educators themselves, assume on the basis of spurious evidence that dropouts dislike and voluntarily reject school, that they leave it for much the same reasons, and that they are as persons much alike. But, as Miller and Harrison [1] have discovered in the case of urban lower-class youth, dropouts leave high school under strikingly different situations and for quite different reasons. Many state explicitly that they do not wish to leave school and see themselves as "pushouts" or "kickouts" rather than "dropouts." As a Sioux youth in our sample put it, "I quit, but I never did *want* to quit!"

This article has been redrafted and retitled as "The Warrior Dropout," and is to appear in *Trans-Action*. Reprinted by permission of the author.

The research on which this article is based was sponsored by Emory University and supported by contracts (CRP1361 and S-099) under the Cooperative Research Program of the U.S. Office of Education. The bulk of the data was obtained in 1962–1963 by Mr. Robert V. Dumont, Jr., during the course of his highly perceptive, semiparticipant observation among high school students and dropouts. Other helpful materials were obtained by Mrs. Roselyn HolyRock, Mr. Gerald One-Feather, and Mrs. Vivian Arviso One-Feather.

Perhaps the fact that educators perceive dropouts as similar tells us more about the educators and their schools than it does about the process of dropping out. Or to put it another way, an understanding of dropouts provides us with a mirror in which certain important but otherwise concealed aspects of our schools are reflected. In consequence, I shall more easily communicate this mirror image to the reader by beginning with a descriptive analysis of how Sioux boys [2] come to drop out of high school, and by then turning to a comparison between their experiences and those of urban lower-class youth.

PRE-ADOLESCENT EXPERIENCES

The process that alienates many Country Indian [3] boys from the particular kind of high school they are obliged to attend begins early in childhood and is related to the basic structure of the Sioux social system. Sioux boys are reared to be physically reckless and impetuous. If they are not capable of an occasional act of derring-do, their folks may accept them as "quiet" or "bashful," but they are not the ideal type of son, brother, or sweetheart. Sioux boys are also reared to be proud and feisty and they are expected to resent public reproof.

247

While they have certain obligations to relatives, the major instrument of socialization after infancy is the local peer group. From about the age of seven or eight, boys may spend almost the whole day without adult supervision, running or riding about with age mates and returning home only for food and sleep. Even we, who had lived with Indian families from other tribal groups, were startled when we heard a responsible and respected Sioux matron dismiss a lad of six or seven for the entire day with the statement, "Go play with Larry and John." Similarly, at a ceremonial gathering involving a trip to a strange community and hundreds of people, boys of nine or ten might, as a matter of course, take off and stay away until late at night. These unsupervised activities do not cause elders much concern. There is a wide terrain of prairie and creek land for roaming and playing in ways that bother nobody. The only delinquencies about which we have heard Sioux elders complain are chasing stock, teasing bulls, or, occasionally, some petty theft.

Mark Twain, Jean Piaget, and other perceptive observers have noted that the kind of situation here described leads to socialization by the peer group. Among Sioux males it leads to a highly efficient yet unverbalized system of intragroup discipline and to powerful intragroup loyalties and dependencies. During our seventh month stay in a particular reservation community, we were impressed by how rarely the children of the community quarreled with each other. This pacific behavior was not imposed by elders but by the children themselves. As we remarked in our major report:

"Our office contained some things of great attractiveness to them, especially a typewriter, which (the Indian children) were allowed to use. . . . We were astonished to see how quietly they handled this prize that only one could enjoy at a time. A well-defined system of status existed such that when a superordinate child appeared at the side of the one typing, the latter at once gave way and left the machine to the other. A half-dozen of these shifts might take place within an hour, as children came or went, or were interested in typing or attracted to some other activity; yet, all this occurred without a blow or often even a word." [4]

Since we will have more to say later about the Sioux peer group's intense loyalties and dependencies, we add here only that Sioux boys almost never tattle on each other. Again, when boys are forced to take up residence with total strangers, they tend to become inarticulate, psychologically disorganized, or, as so many investigators have put it, "withdrawn."

In ordinary environments the school is where the peer group reaches the zenith of its power. In middle class areas, the power is usually mitigated by the ability of independent children to seek and secure support from parents, teachers, or through them, from adult society as a whole. But when, as in an urban slum area or Indian reservation, the teachers keep aloof from the parents and the parents feel that it is not their place to approach the teachers, the power of the peer group may rise to the extent that the children literally take over the school. The classroom becomes the place where numerous group activities are carried on— jokes, notes, intrigues, teasing, mock-combat, comic book reading, courtship —without the teacher's knowledge and often without grossly interfering with the process of learning. Competent and experienced teachers who have come to terms with the peer group, still manage to teach their charges a fair amount of reading, writing, and arithmetic. But teachers who are imcompetent, overwhelmed by large classes, or sometimes, merely inexperienced, may be faced by groups of children who refuse even to listen. Indeed, as observers, we could not but marvel at the variety and efficiency of the devices developed by the Indian children to frustrate the standard process of formal learning: unanimous inattention, refusal to go to the board or writing on the board in letters less than an inch in height, mumbled and inarticulate responses, whispered or pantomimic teasing of victims called on to recite, and, in some seventh and eight grade classes, a withdrawal so uncompromising that no voice might be heard in the classroom for hours but that of the teacher, plaintively asking questions or giving instructions to which nobody responded.

Most Sioux children attending the day schools insist that they like school and most Sioux parents corroborate this. Once the power and depth of their social life within the school is appreciated, it is not difficult to see why they like it. Indeed, from the children's point of view, the only unpleasant aspects of school are the disciplinary regulations (which, as highly organized juveniles, they soon learn to tolerate or evade), an occasional "mean" teacher, bullies of either sex, or feuds with members of other peer groups. Significantly, we found that notorious truants had usually been rejected by their classmates and also had no older relatives in school to protect them from bullies. But the child who does have a few friends, or an older brother or sister to stand by him, or who "really likes to play basketball," almost always finds life in school more agreeable than truancy.

DAY SCHOOL GRADUATES

By the time he has finished the eighth grade, the Country Indian boy has many fine qualities: zest for life, curiosity, pride, physical courage, sensibility to human relationships, experiences with the elemental facts of life, and the loyalty and integrity that comes with intense internalized group identification. His experiences in day school have done nothing to diminish or tarnish his ideal: the physically reckless and impetuous youth, whose deeds of derring-do and athletic prowess are admired by all. On the other hand, the Country Indian boy is almost completely lacking in the traits most highly valued by the school authorities: a narrow and absolute respect for "regulations," routine, discipline, diligence, and "government property." [5] He is also deficient in other skills which seem to be essential to a rapid and easy passage through high school and boarding school: the ability to make short-term superficial social adjustments with strangers [6] and come to terms with a system which demands, on the one hand, that he study competitively and as an individual and, on the other, that he live in barrack type dormitories where this kind of intellectual endeavor is impossible. Finally, his comprehension of English is inadequate for high school work. Despite eight or more years of exposure to formal training in reading and writing English, many day school graduates cannot converse fluently in this language even among themselves. [7] In contrast, most of the students with whom the Country Indian will be competing in high school have been brought up in town or have attended the boarding school and, in consequence, have spoken English with each other since childhood.

Leaving the familiar and relatively pleasant day school situation for life as a boarding school student in the distant and formidable high school is a prospect both fascinating and frightening. To many young Country Indians the Agency Town of Pine Ridge is the center of sophistication: there are blocks of "Bureau" homes with lawns and fences, a barber shop, big grocery stores, churches, gas-stations, a drive-in confectionary, and even a restaurant with a juke box. While older siblings or cousins may have reported that at high school "they make you study harder," that "they just make you move every minute," or that the "Mixedbloods" or "children of Bureau employees" are "mean" or "snotty," there are the conpensatory attractions of high school movies, basketball games, and the social (white man's) dances that high-light the school year. For the young men there is the chance to play high school basketball, baseball, or football; for the young women there is the increased distance from over-watchful conservative parents; for both, there will be the opportunity to hitchhike or refuse to hitchhike to White Clay, with its beer joints, bowling hall, and archaic aura of Western wickedness. If, then, a young man's close friends or relatives decide to go to high school, he will usually prefer to share in the adventure rather than remain at home and live the circumscribed life of a fellow who must "live off his folks." A young man is also likely to be impelled into enrolling in high school by his elders, for most older Sioux are convinced that "nowadays only high school graduates get the good jobs." Every year, more elders coax, tease, bribe, or otherwise pressure the young men into "making a try at" high school.

THE STUDENT BODY

The student body of the Oglala Community High School is remarkably heterogeneous. First, there are the children of the town dwellers, ranging from well-paid white and Indian government employees who live in neat, government housing developments to desperately poor people who live in tar paper shacks. Second, there is a large aggregate of institutionalized children who have been attending the Oglala Community School as boarders for the greater part of their lives. Some of these boarders are orphans, others come from isolated parts of the reservation where there are no day schools, others come from different tribal areas. But whatever their differences, these town dwellers and the boarders share the advantage that entry into high school is little more than a shift from eighth to ninth grade, so that they possess an intimate knowledge of their classmates and a great deal of local knowhow. High school for them involves no more significant change than going to a new set of classes with new teachers. In marked contrast, the Country Indian Freshman enters an environment that is alien in almost all respects. Not only is he ignorant of the system for bucking the rules, he doesn't even know the rules. Nor does he know anybody who cares to put him wise.

In studying the adolescents on Pine Ridge we concentrated on two areas, the high school and a particular day school community with a Country or conservative Indian population of about 1,000. We interviewed somewhat less than half the young people then enrolled in the high school and, in addition, a random sample of forty-eight young people from the Country Indian community. Subsequently, we obtained basic socioeconomic and educational data from all the young people who had graduated from a particular day school in 1961, 1962, and 1963. All in all, we obtained some 153 interviews from young people between the ages of 13 and 21; some fifty of these were high school dropouts. We used many approaches and several types of questionnaires, but our most illuminating and reliable data were obtained by semistructured and unstructured interviews administered by Indian college students who were able to associate with the Sioux adolescents and participate in some of their activities.

NINTH GRADE DROPOUTS

Many of the Country Indians drop out of high school before they have any clear idea of what high school is all about. In our universal sample, thirty-five per cent dropped out before the end of the ninth grade and many of these left during the first semester.[8] Our first interviews were tantalizingly contradictory. About half of the young men seemed to have found their high school experience so painful they could scarcely talk about it. The other half were also laconic, but insisted that they had liked school. In time, the young men who had found school unbearable confided that they had left school because they were lonely or because they were abused by the experienced boarders. Only rarely did they mention that they had trouble with their studies.

The following statement, made by a mild and pleasant-natured respondent from a traditional family, conveys some idea of the agony of loneliness, embarrassment, and inadequacy that a Country Indian newcomer may suffer when he enters high school:

"At day school it was kind of easy for me. But high school was really hard, and I can't figure out even simple questions that they ask me. . . . Besides I'm so quiet [modest and unagressive] that the boys really took advantage of me. They borrow money from me every Sunday night and they don't even care to pay it back. . . . I can't talk English very good, and I'm really bashful and shy, and I get scared when I talk to white people. I usually just stay quiet in the [day school] classroom, and the teachers will leave me alone. But at boarding school they wanted me to get up and talk or say something. . . . I quit and I never went back. . . .

I can't seem to get along with different people, and I'm so shy I can't even make friends. . . ." (Translated from Lakota by interviewer.)

Most of the newcomers seem to have a difficult time getting along with the experienced boarders and claim that the latter not only strip them of essentials like soap, paper, and underwear, but also take the treasured gifts of proud and encouraging relatives, wrist watches and transistor radios.[9]

"Some of the kids—especially the boarders—are really mean. All they want to do is steal—and they don't want to study. They'll steal your school work off you and they'll copy it. . . . Sometimes they'll break into our suitcase. Or if we have money in our pockets they'll take off our overalls and search our pockets and get our money. . . . So finally I just came home. If I could be a day scholar I think I'll stay in. But if they want me to board I don't want to go back. I think I'll just quit."

Interviews with the dropouts who asserted that school was "all right" and that they had not wished to quit, suggest that many of these had been almost as wretched during their first weeks at high school as the bashful young men who quit because "they couldn't make friends." But unlike the latter, they managed to find some friends and, with the support and protection of this new peer group, they were able to cope with and (probably) strike back at the other boarder peer groups. In any case, the painful and degrading aspects of school became endurable. As one lad put it: "Once you *learn* to be a boarder, it's not so bad."

But for these young men, an essential part of having friends was "raising Cain," that is, engaging in daring and defiant deeds forbidden by the school authorities. The spirit of these escapades is difficult to portray to members of a society where most people no longer seem capable of thinking about boys like Tom Sawyer, Huckleberry Finn, or Kim, except as juvenile delinquents. We ourselves, burdened by sober professional interest in dropouts, at first found it hard to recognize that these able and engaging young men were taking pride and joy in doing exactly what the school authorities thought most reprehensible and that they were not confessing but boasting to our interviewers as they related the exciting and humorous adventures that had propelled them out of school.

Some of the fun and the reckless adventure involved in "raising Cain" is reflected in the verbal account of a bright youth of 15 who had ran away from the high school. Shortly after entering the ninth grade, he and his friends had appropriated a government car. (The usual pattern in such adventures is to drive off the reservation until the gas gives out.) For this offense (according to a respondent) he and his friends were restricted for the rest of the term; that is, they were forbidden to leave the high school campus or attend any of the school recreational events, games, dances, or movies. (In effect, this meant doing nothing but going to class, performing work chores, and sitting in the dormitory.) Even then our respondent seems to have kept up with his class work and did not play hookey except in reading class:

"It was after we stole that car. Mrs. Bluger (pseudonym for reading teacher) would keep asking who stole the car in class. So I just quit going there."

Then:

"One night we were the only ones up in the older boys' dorm. We said

"Hell with this noise. We're not going to be the only ones here."

"So we snuck out and went over to the dining hall. I pried this one window open about this far and then it started to crack, so I let it go. . . . We heard someone so we took off. It was show that night I think. [Motion picture was being shown in school auditorium.]

"All the rest of the guys was sneaking in and getting something. So I said I was going to get my share too. We had a case of apples and a case of oranges. Then I think it was the night watchman was coming, so we ran around and hid behind those steps. He shined that light on us. So I thought right then I was going to keep on going.

"That was around Christmas time. We walked back to Oglala [about 15 miles] and we were eating this stuff all the way back."

[Interviewer:] You took those two cases?

[Respondent:] Naw. We just took what we could carry in our coats.

This young man implied that after this escapade he simply did not have the nerve to try to return to the high school. He insisted, however, that he would like to try another high school:

"I'd like to finish (high school) and get a good job some place. If I don't I'll probably just be a bum around here or something."

Another young man told a similar story:

Int: What year did you go to high school?

Res: I quit three years ago after they kick me out of school.

Int: What happened?

Res: I and two other boys stole a government car and went to White Clay, Rushville, Gordon, and back.

Int: What kind of car?

Res: It was a 1948 model.

Int: How come you are involved with these two other boys?

Res: I don't know. We just decided to steal the car and the other guy said (suggested) it.

Int: Then they kicked you out of school?

Res: No. They weren't going to kick me out, but the week before that, we broke into the bowling alley and took five boxes of candy.

Int: Why did you do that?

Res: I don't know.

Int: Are you willing to go back to school?

Res: I don't know. Since they kicked me out, they probably won't want me back.

(Translated from Lakota by interviewer.)

YOUNG MEN WHO STAY IN SCHOOL

If roughly half the young Sioux who leave high school very early in their career claim that they left because they were unable to conform to the school regulations, what happens to the Country Indian boys who remain in school until the eleventh and twelfth grades? Do they "shape-up," obey the regulations, or, perhaps, even internalize them? We found that most of these older and more experienced young men were, if anything, even more inclined to boast of their triumphs over the rules than were the younger fellows who had left school. Indeed, all but one older male respondent assured our interviewers that they were adept at hookey playing, food and car stealing, and that they were frequent participants at the surreptitious beer parties and the other enjoyments outlawed by the school authorities. Relying on these verbal accounts, we do not know whether, for example, star athletes actually disobey the school regulations as frequently and flagrantly as they claim. But that most Sioux young men between the ages of 12 and 20 (and older) wish to be regarded as hellions who seize every chance to play pranks on the school authorities there can be no doubt at all. To hold any other attitude would be unmanly.

An eleventh grader in good standing explained his private device for playing hookey and added proudly: "They never caught me yet." A twelfth grader and first string basketball player told me how he and some other students "stole" a jeep from the high school machine shop and drove it all over town. When asked why he did this, he patiently explained: "To see if we can get away with it. It's for the enjoyment . . . to see if we can take the car without getting caught." Another senior assured our male staff worker: "You can always get out and booze it up." Still another senior and outstanding athlete remarked:

"Once a bunch of us were restricted —all the guys who work in the bathroom. I didn't care so I took off, went to Holy Rosary homecoming, to White Clay, and then to a dance over to Kyle. But I didn't get slicked. Other times when I try to sneak around, then I get slicked."

The impulse to boast of the virile achievements of youth seem to maintain itself into middle and even into old age. Country Indians with college training zestfully told (male) members of the study how they and a group of proctors had stolen large amounts of food from the high school kitchen and were never apprehended, or how they and their friends drank three fifths of whiskey in one night and did not pass out.

Clearly, the activities regarded as immature or delinquent by administrators and teachers are regarded as part of the world of youthful daring, excitement, agonistic play, and manly honor by the Sioux young men and by many of their elders. They are also, we suspect, an integral part of the world of competitive sports. "I like to play basketball" was one of the most frequent responses of young men to the question: "What do you like most about school"? Indeed, several ninth and tenth graders stated that the opportunity to play basketball was the main reason they kept going to school and one eighth grader who had run away from school several times as a juvenile stated:

"When I was in the seventh grade I made the B team on the basketball squad. And I made the A team when I was in the eighth grade. So I stayed and finished school without running away anymore."

The unselfconscious devotion and ardor with which many of these young men participate in sports must be witnessed to be even mildly appreciated. They cannot communicate their joy and pride in words, although one seventeen year old member of the team that won the state championship tried, by telling how a team member wearing a war bonnet "led us onto the playing floor and this really gave them a cheer."

ELEVENTH AND TWELFTH GRADE DROPOUTS

Our knowledge of dropouts at this level is limited, for many had left the reservation or entered the armed services. Those whom we reached gave various reasons for dropping out. One

said that he was bored: "I was just sitting there doing anything to pass the time." Another said he didn't know what made him quit, "I just didn't fit in anymore. . . . I just wasn't like the other guys anymore." Another refused to attend a class in which he felt that the teacher had insulted Indians. When the principal told him that he must attend this class or be "restricted", he left school. Significantly, his best friend dropped out with him, even though he was on the way to becoming a first class basketball player. Different as they first appear, these statements have a common undertone: they are the expressions of relatively mature young men who find the atmosphere of the high school stultifying and childish.

THE DILEMMA OF SIOUX YOUTH

The intense study of any cross-cultural area is likely to reveal as many tragi-comic situations as social scientific insights. Thus, on the Pine Ridge Reservation, a majority of the young men arrive at adolescence valuing élan, bravery, generosity, passion, and luck, and admiring outstanding talent in athletics, singing, and dancing. While capable of wider relations and reciprocities, they function at their social best as members of small groups of peers or relatives. Yet to obtain even modest employment in the greater society, they must graduate from high school. And in order to graduate from high school, they are told they must develop exactly opposite qualities to those they possess: a respect for humdrum diligence and routine, for "discipline," (in the sense of not smoking in toilets, not cutting classes, and not getting drunk), and for government property. In addition, they are expected to compete scholastically on a highly privatized and individualistic level, while living in large dormitories, surrounded by strangers who make privacy of any type impossible.[10]

The young men who remain in the high school until the eleventh or twelfth grades do not seem to have developed any of the qualities considered essential by the formulators of the school regulations. What they have learned is another and perhaps more efficient way of maintaining their identity and their values on the periphery of an alien social system.[11] They have also grown older, and as more mature youths, are less inclined to commit the extremely compulsive and explosive deeds characteristic of healthy boys in their early and midteens.[12]

If the educational scene were as it was a generation or two ago, then the situation might be bettered by democratizing the schools, involving the Sioux parents in their control. While this system of locally controlled schools was not perfect, it worked pretty well. Today, however, the problem is more complicated and tricky because educators have become professionalized and educational systems have become complex bureaucracies inextricably involved with universities, education associations, foundations, and federal crash programs. Even suburban middle-class parents, some of whom are highly educated and sophisticated, find it difficult to cope with the bureaucratic barriers and mazes of the schools which their children attend, and it is difficult to see how Sioux parents could accomplish much unless, in some way, their own school system were kept artifically small and isolated and accessible to their understanding and control.

THE DILEMMA OF
WORKING CLASS YOUTH

A specific comparison of the Sioux dropouts with dropouts from the urban working class—Negroes, Puerto Ri-

cans, or whites—would, no doubt, reveal many salient differences in cultural background and world view. Nevertheless, investigations so far undertaken suggest that the attitudes held by these peoples toward *education and the schools* are startingly similar. Both Sioux and working class parents wish their children to continue in school because they believe that graduating from high school is a guarantee of employment. Again, many working class dropouts, like the Sioux dropouts, express a generally favorable attitude toward school, stating that teachers are generally fair and that the worst thing about dropping out of school is missing one's friends. Even more important, many working class dropouts assert that they were pushed out of school, and frequently add that the push was fairly direct.[13] The Sioux boys put the matter more delicately, implying that the school authorities would not really welcome them back.

Valuable as the recognition of these similarities may be, they should not be seized on as evidence that the offspring of all disprivileged peoples are alike and that, in consequence, they can all be counted on to respond as a unit to the one ideal educational policy for high school dropouts. Rather, many of the similarities in attitude and experience of working class youth spring from the fact that they are in much the same situation vis-a-vis the monolithic greater society and its one-track educational escalator. It is the schools and their administrators that are so monotonously alike that the boy who is brought up in an ethnic or a little community can but regard and react to them in similar fashion.

A more important and relatively unrecognized point is that while the school poses a dilemma for the working class or ethnic boy, the boy poses a dilemma for the school. In many traditional or urban ethnic cultures, boys are expected and permitted to have a virile adolescence and so become genuine men. Our schools try to deprive youth of adolescence and demand that high school students behave like "mature people" which, in our culture, means in a pretty dull and spiritless fashion. Those who submit to these demands and succeed in school are often able to meet the bureaucratic requirements of future employers, but they are also likely to be lacking in independence of thought and in creativity. The dropout of boys like the Sioux is a failure on their part to become what the school demands. On the other hand, the school has failed to offer them what the boys from the most "deprived" and "under-developed" peoples take as a matter of course—the opportunity to become whole men.

Miller and Harrison, studying working class youth, assert that individuals who do poorly in school are handicapped or disfavored for the remainder of their lives, because "the schools have become the occupational gatekeepers" and "the level of education affects the kind and level of job that can be attained." On the other hand, the investigations of Friedenberg [14] and Henry [15] suggest that the youth who perform creditably in high school according to the views of the authorities and of their peers, are disfavored in that they emerge from this experience as permanently crippled persons or human beings. In a curious way our researches among the Sioux may be viewed as supporting both of these contentions, for they suggest that some people leave high school because they are too vital and independent to submit to a dehumanizing situation. In this respect, we note that the dean of a major school of engineering has recently asserted that the young men who drop out of his institution "include a major share of those with high potential creativity; and that our educational processes tend to destroy the creative potential of a large share of those who survive.[15]

Notes and References

1. S. M. Miller and Ira E. Harrison, "Types of Dropouts: 'The Unemployables,'" *Blue-Collar World: Studies of the American Worker*, edited by Arthur B. Shostak and William Gomberg (Englewood Cliffs, N.J.: Prentice-Hall, 1964), pp. 469–484.

2. For a more detailed report on the educational situation and attitudes of Oglala Sioux adolescents, see "Dropout of American Indians at the Secondary Level," by Rosalie H. Wax and Murray L. Wax (final report, Cooperative Research Project No. S-099, U.S. Office of Education, 1964), mimeoed. In addition to further materials on the boys who are the main subject of the present article, the report also discusses the Sioux girls and the large body of young people who do not even attempt to enroll in high school.

3. Although "Country Sioux" or "Country Indian" might loosely be considered as synonyms for "Fullblood," I have avoided the latter term as connoting a traditional Indian culture which vanished long ago and whose unchanging qualities were a mythology of white observers rather than a social reality of Indian participants. In any case, I use "Country Indian" to refer to the people raised and living "out on the reservation (prairie)" who participate in the social and ceremonial activities of their local rural communities, as opposed to those persons, also known as Indians, who live in Pine Ridge town and make a point of avoiding these backwoods activities. The questions of Indianness and the nature of Indian identity are com-

plex. Those interested should consult Chapter 3 of *Formal Education in an American Indian Community* by Murray L. Wax, Rosalie H. Wax, and Robert V. Dumont, Jr., Monograph #1, The Society for the Study of Social Problems, 1964, as well as Robert E. Daniels, "Cultural Identities among the Oglala Sioux," M.A. thesis, Department of Anthropology, University of Chicago, 1964.

4. Wax, Wax, and Dumont, *op. cit.*, p. 96.

5. These virtues were preached for many decades in the boarding schools operated by the Indian Service. Today those Indians who have graduated from those schools and who, having attained an official post within the Bureau of Indian Affairs, are considered successful by the standards of those ("white") virtues, in turn, preach them to their pupils. One of the administrators of the Oglala High School, an Indian by birth, stated that he had dedicated his life to uplifting his people toward these virtues; strangely, few of his people seemed to appreciate his sacrifices. Compare "Cultural Deprivation as an Educational Ideology," Murray Wax and Rosalie Wax, *Journal of American Indian Education*, III, 2 (Jan., 1964), pp. 15–18.

The social dynamics of contemporary Indian communities are more complex than might appear and have not been discussed, even in anthropological literature. The richest discussions we know of are in as yet unpublished manuscripts of Robert K. Thomas and Albert H. Wahrhaftig of the Carnegic Cross-cultural Educational Project of the University of Chicago.

6. Ralph Turner, *The Social Context of Ambition* (San Francisco: Chandler, 1965).

7. For a discussion of this phenomenon and its causes, see Wax, Wax, and Dumont, *op. cit.*, pp. 80–82; and Wax and Wax, *op. cit.*, "Eighth Grade Dropouts."

8. Also, it should be noted that some twenty per cent of the youth in our sample who had finished the eighth grade did not attempt to enroll in high school.

9. Although the boarding students are given lockers, they are not permitted to lock them.

10. The conflict between congregate living and individuated achievement afflicts college students as well: see E. Jackson Baur, "Achievement and Role Definition of the College Student" (final report, Cooperative Research Project No. 2605, U.S. Office of Education, 1965), Chapter VII.

11. See the manuscript of Thomas and Wahrhaftig.

12. S. M. Miller makes the same point with regard to lower class youth: their acts of delinquency decrease with age, rather than as a result of special programs or therapies. See his "The Outlook of Working-Class Youth," in *Blue-Collar World: Studies of the American Worker.*

13. Miller and Harrison, *op. cit.*, pp. 471f. Other investigators in Detroit and Kansas City, whose work is not yet published, report that working class boys in these cities also feel that they are pushed out of school.

14. Edgar Z. Friedenberg, *The Vanishing Adolescent* (Boston: Beacon Press, 1958); *Coming of Age in America* (New York: Random House, 1965).

15. Jules Henry, *Culture Against Man* (New York: Random House, 1963).

16. Quoted by Lawrence S. Kubie, *The National Observer*, September 27, 1965.

Part III: PROGRAMS AND PROGRESS IN MEETING THE EDUCATIONAL NEEDS OF DISADVANTAGED YOUTH

Americans have always placed great value on equality of educational opportunity. From this belief have sprung many of our educational practices—the ideas of tax support, the comprehensive high school, and even the drive toward social promotion. But past interpretations of what constituted equal educational opportunity emphasized the existence of schools *per se* and the equality of *access* to learning based upon ability. In other words, the nation had assumed that all children had common backgrounds and needs which could be met by providing a uniform set of institutions called schools. If children for one reason or another failed in their attempt to become educated, the problem was theirs, for after all they had received an equal chance.

That this concept has been altered and new assumptions made can be most clearly illustrated by the words of the famous Supreme Court decision in Brown v. Board of Education of Topeka:

"To separate [children] from others of similar age and qualifications solely because of their race generates a feeling of inferiority as to their status in the community that may affect their hearts and minds in a way unlikely ever to be undone. The effect of this separation on their educational opportunities was well stated . . . in the Kansas cases . . . .

"Segregation of white and colored children in public schools has a detrimental effect upon the colored children. The impact is greater when it has the sanction of the law . . . . Segregation with the sanction of law . . . has a tendency to retard the educational and mental development of Negro children and to deprive them of some of the benefits they would receive in a racially integrated school system."

This statement illustrates that public policy has been altered, that new considerations (namely the subculture in which a child lives and the damaging psychological effects of attending segregated schools) must be taken into account. The basic assumption of current school programs for the disadvantaged is but an extension of the Brown decision—children from limited educational backgrounds need to be compensated for their limitations. What does it means to have equal access to education? Most frequently today it means that the school must inject *inequalities* into its programs, that disadvantaged children must receive advantages in schools which enable them to overcome the paucity of their past experiences.

The implications of this new definition for schools are many and profound. Fundamentally, the schools must realize that as institutions they must change. Merely building new schools or hiring more highly trained teachers will not provide equal educational opportunities because the emphasis would remain on making the child fit the school rather than altering the institution to meet the needs of the child. Nor will the schools find a comfortable answer in the creation of more vocational schools. In some respects, this has been the solution proposed by representatives of the power structure, a solution which has been found wanting proponents of a different type of adjustment.[1] The demand, it seems, is for a change in attitude on the part of teachers and administrators from an assumption that children from depressed areas cannot learn to an assumption that they can if those involved in teaching them are willing to make adjustments.

These, then, are the demands on schools: (1) to provide preschool programs which prepare disadvantaged children to enter school; (2) to make adjustments in curriculum and methods at all levels so that disadvantaged children will be enabled to learn; (3) to rule out any inequities in programs and faculty attitudes which might convince disadvantaged youngsters that school is not for them.

What are schools doing to meet these demands? Part III presents a sampling of the new strategies and programs addressed to this problem. The part is subdivided into three sections that deal with the problem, the programs, and the prospects for success.

The first section (The Problem) deals essentially with the relationship between culturally disadvantaged children and schools. The articles by Baldwin and Klineberg emphasize that the school climate as represented by teacher attitudes and materials plays an important part in the adjustment of children to schools. Della-Dora generalizes about the effects of cultural disadvantages on schools and notes some promising directions. Wolman raises the important question of whether minority group children really belong in "slow" classes with the

---

[1] James B. Conant, for example, in *Slums and Suburbs* appears to advance the point that slum children need to develop marketable skills. His viewpoint is severely criticized by Kenneth C. Clark. See the reprint from Clark's work in this book and his book *Dark Ghetto* (New York: Harper and Row, 1965) in which he argues persuasively that the school is responsible for the antischool attitude of slum children.

frequency that they appear there, and Ausubel makes several concrete suggestions to reverse the trend of "cumulative educational deficit" among culturally disadvantaged youth. In two provocative articles, Clark and Rodson suggest several factors that are exceptionally significant in providing equal educational opportunities to all children.

The sheer bulk of descriptive commentary available in the journals on the topic of school programs means that the second section cannot do complete justice to the area. Rather, an attempt is made first to describe the categories of school efforts. For example, Niemeyer discusses general guidelines for school changes, Baynham describes the Great Cities Project, and Friggins deals with the interesting program developed by Dr. Samuel Sheppard. A second group of articles deals with practices and points of view in several subject-matter areas. Although efforts to adjust the curriculum and teaching methodology to the needs of disadvantaged youth are difficult to describe, the articles by Daugherty, Smiley, Ross, Duggans, Edgar, and Lisenbee are excellent illustrations.

The final section contains several evaluations of programs and practices. The early experiences of those in the Head Start programs are discussed in the articles by Robinson. Washington's "Growth and Cultural Conflict" examines the role of the teacher in cultural enrichment. Mackler and Giddings take issue with the terminology used in the discussions of cultural differentiations, making the point that we have perhaps "manufactured" a mental construct of deprivation which does not in fact exist. The last group of articles, a delightful verbal interaction between Guthrie and Kelley, and Austin, provides an excellent insight into two points of view about the schools' role in dealing with the culturally disadvantaged.

27. A Talk to Teachers

JAMES BALDWIN

Let's begin by saying that we are living through a very dangerous time. Everyone in this room is in one way or another aware of that. We are in a revolutionary situation, no matter how unpopular that word has become in this country. The society in which we live is desperately menaced, not by Khrushchev, but from within. So any citizen of this country who figures himself as responsible—and particularly those of you who deal with the minds and hearts of young people—must be prepared to "go for broke." Or to put it another way, you must understand that in the attempt to correct so many generations of bad faith and cruelty, when it is operating not only in the classroom but in society, you will meet the most fantastic, the most brutal, and the most determined resistance. There is no point in pretending that this won't happen.

Now, since I am talking to schoolteachers and I am not a teacher myself, and in some ways am fairly easily intimidated, I beg you to let me leave that and go back to what I think to be the entire purpose of education in the first place. It would seem to me that when a child is born, if I'm the child's

Reprinted from *Saturday Review*, Vol. 46 (December 21, 1963), pp. 42–44. Copyright, James Baldwin. Reproduced by permission of the author.

parent, it is my obligation and my high duty to civilize that child. Man is a social animal. He cannot exist without a society. A society, in turn, depends on certain things which everyone within the society takes for granted. Now, the crucial paradox which confronts us here is that the whole process of education occurs within a social framework and is designed to perpetuate the aims of society. Thus, for example, the boys and girls who were born during the era of the Third Reich, when educated to the purposes of the Third Reich, became barbarians. The paradox of education is precisely this—that as one begins to become conscious one begins to examine the society in which he is being educated. The purpose of education, finally, is to create in a person the ability to look at the world for himself, to make his own decisions, to say to himself this is black or this is white, to decide for himself whether there is a God in heaven or not. To ask questions of the universe, and then learn to live with those questions, is the way he achieves his own identity. But no society is really anxious to have that kind of person around. What societies really, ideally, want is a citizenry which will simply obey the rules of society. If a society succeeds in this, that society is about to perish. The obligation of anyone who thinks of himself as responsible is to examine society and try to change it and to fight it—at no matter what risk. This is the only hope society has. This is the only way societies change.

Now, if what I have tried to sketch has any validity, it becomes thoroughly clear, at least to me, that any Negro who is born in this country and undergoes the American educational system runs the risk of becoming schizophrenic. On the one hand he is born in the shadow of the stars and stripes and he is assured it represents a nation which has never lost a war. He pledges allegiance to that flag which guarantees "liberty and justice for all." He is part of a country in which anyone can become President, and so forth. But on the other hand he is also assured by his country and his countrymen that he has never contributed anything to civilization—that his past is nothing more than a record of humiliations gladly endured. He is assured by the republic that he, his father, his mother, and his ancestors were happy, shiftless, watermelon-eating darkies who loved Mr. Charlie and Miss Ann, that the value he has as a black man is proven by one th·ng only—his devotion to white people. If you think I am exaggerating, examine the myths which proliferate in this country about Negroes.

Now all this enters the child's consciousness much sooner than we as adults would like to think it does. As adults, we are easily fooled because we are so anxious to be fooled. But children are very different. Children, not yet aware that it is dangerous to look too deeply at anything, look at everything, look at each other, and draw their own conclusions. They don't have the vocabulary to express what they see, and we, their elders, know how to intimidate them very easily and very soon. But a black child, looking at the world around him, though he cannot know quite what to make of it, is aware that there is a reason why his mother works so hard, why his father is always on edge. He is aware that there is some reason why, if he sits down in the front of the bus, his father or mother slaps him and drags him to the back of the bus. He is aware that there is some terrible weight on his parents' shoulders which menaces him. And it isn't long—in fact it begins when he is in school—before he discovers the shape of his oppression.

Let us say that the child is seven years old and I am his father, and I decide to take him to the zoo, or to Madison Square Garden, or to the U.N. Building, or to any of the tremendous monuments we find all over New York. We get into a bus and we go from where I live on 131st Street and Seventh Avenue downtown through the park and we get into New York City, which is not Harlem. Now, where the boy lives —even if it is a housing project—it is an undesirable neighborhood. If he lives in one of those housing projects of which everyone in New York is so proud, he has at the front door, if not closer, the pimps, the whores, the junkies—in a word, the danger of life in the ghetto. And the child knows this, though he doesn't know why.

I still remember my first sight of New York. It was really another city when I was born—where I was born. We looked down over the Park Avenue streetcar tracks. It was Park Avenue, but I didn't know that Park Avenue meant *downtown*. The Park Avenue I grew up on, which is still standing, is dark and dirty. No one would dream of opening a Tiffany's on that Park Avenue, and when you go downtown you discover that you are literally in the white world. It is rich—or at least it looks rich. It is clean—because they collect garbage downtown. There are doormen. People walk about as though they owned where they were —and indeed they do. And it's a great shock. It's very hard to relate yourself to this. You don't know what it means. You know—you know instinctively—that none of this is for you. You know this before you are told. And who is it for and who is paying for it? And why isn't it for you?

Later on when you become a grocery boy or messenger and you try to enter one of these buildings a man says, "Go to the back door." Still later, if you happen by some odd chance to have a friend in one of those buildings, the man says, "Where's your package?" Now this by no means is the core of the matter. What I'm trying to get at is that by this time the Negro child has had, effectively, almost all the doors of opportunity slammed in his face, and there are very few things he can do about it. He can more or less accept it with an absolutely inarticulate and dangerous rage inside—all the more dangerous because it is never expressed. It is precisely those silent people whom white people see every day of their lives—I mean your porter and your maid, who never say anything more than "Yes Sir" and "No Ma'am." They will tell you it's raining if that is what you want to hear, and they will tell you the sun is shining if *that* is what you want to hear. They really hate you—really hate you because in their eyes (and they're right) you stand between them and life. I want to come back to that in a moment. It is the most sinister of the facts, I think, which we now face.

There is something else the Negro child can do, too. Every street boy—and I was a street boy, so I know—looking at the society which has produced him, looking at the standards of that society which are not honored by anybody, looking at your churches and the government and the politicians, understands that this structure is operated for someone else's benefit—not for his. And there's no room in it for him. If he is really cunning, really ruthless, really strong—and many of us are—he becomes a kind of criminal. He becomes a kind of criminal because that's the only way he can live. Harlem and every ghetto in this city—every ghetto in this country—is full of people who live outside the law. They wouldn't dream of calling a policeman. They wouldn't, for a moment, listen to any of those professions of which we are so proud on the Fourth of July. They have turned away from this country forever and totally. They live by their wits and really long to see the day when the entire structure comes down.

The point of all this is that black men were brought here as a source of cheap labor. They were indispensable to the economy. In order to justify the fact that men were treated as though they were animals, the white republic had to brainwash itself into believing that they were, indeed, animals and *deserved* to be treated like animals. Therefore it is almost impossible for any Negro child to discover anything about his actual history. The reason is that this "animal," once he suspects his own worth, once he starts believing that he is a man, has begun to attack the entire power structure. This is why America has spent such a long time keeping the Negro in his place. What I am trying to suggest to you is that it was not an accident, it was not an act of God, it was done by well-meaning people muddling into something which they didn't understand. It was a deliberate policy hammered into place in order to make money from black flesh. And now, in 1963, because we have never faced this fact, we are in intolerable trouble.

The Reconstruction, as I read the

evidence, was a bargain between the North and South to this effect: "We've liberated them from the land—and delivered them to the bosses." When we left Mississippi to come North we did not come to freedom. We came to the bottom of the labor market, and we are still there. Even the Depression of the 1930's failed to make a dent in Negroes' relationship to white workers in the labor unions. Even today, so brainwashed is this republic that people seriously ask in what they suppose to be good faith, "What does the Negro want?" I've heard a great many asinine questions in my life, but that is perhaps the most asinine and perhaps the most insulting. But the point here is that people who ask that question, thinking that they ask it in good faith, are really the victims of this conspiracy to make Negroes believe they are less than human.

In order for me to live, I decided very early that some mistake had been made somewhere. I was not a "nigger" even though you called me one. But if I was a "nigger" in your eyes, there was something about *you*—there was something *you* needed. I had to realize when I was very young that I was none of those things I was told I was. I was not, for example, happy. I never touched a watermelon for all kinds of reasons. I had been invented by white people, and I knew enough about life by this time to understand that whatever you invent, whatever you project, is you! So where we are now is that a whole country of people believe I'm a "nigger," and I *don't*, and the battle's on! Because if I am not what I've been told I am, then it means that *you're* not what you thought *you* were *either*! And that is the crisis.

It is not really a "Negro revolution" that is upsetting this country. What is upsetting the country is a sense of its own identity. If, for example,

one managed to change the curriculum in all the schools so that Negroes learned more about themselves and their real contributions to this culture, you would be liberating not only Negroes, you'd be liberating white people who know nothing about their own history. And the reason is that if you are compelled to lie about one aspect of anybody's history, you must lie about it all. If you have to lie about my real role here, if you have to pretend that I hoed all that cotton just because I loved you, then you have done something to yourself. You are mad.

Now, let's go back a minute. I talked earlier about those silent people—the porter and the maid—who, as I said, don't look up at the sky if you ask them if it is raining, but look into your face. My ancestors and I were very well trained. We understood very early that this was not a Christian nation. It didn't matter what you said or how often you went to church. My father and my mother and my grandfather and my grandmother knew that Christians didn't act this way. It was as simple as that. And if that was so there was no point in dealing with white people in terms of their own moral professions, for they were not going to honor them. What one did was to turn away, smiling all the time, and tell white people what they wanted to hear. But people always accuse you of reckless talk when you say this.

All this means that there are in this country tremendous reservoirs of bitterness which have never been able to find an outlet, but may find an outlet soon. It means that well-meaning white liberals place themselves in great danger when they try to deal with Negroes as though they were missionaries. It means, in brief, that a great price is demanded to liberate all those silent people so that they can breathe for the first time and *tell* you what they think of you. And a price is demanded to liberate all those white children—some of them near forty—who have never grown up, and who never will grow up, because they have no sense of their identity.

What passes for identity in America is a series of myths about one's heroic ancestors. It's astounding to me, for example, that so many people really appear to believe that the country was founded by a band of heroes who wanted to be free. That happens not to be true. What happened was that some people left Europe because they couldn't stay there any longer and had to go someplace else to make it. That's all. They were hungry, they were poor, they were convicts. Those who were making it in England, for example, did not get on the *Mayflower*. That's how the country was settled. Not by Gary Cooper. Yet we have a whole race of people, a whole republic, who believe the myths to the point where even today they select political representatives, as far as I can tell, by how closely they resemble Gary Cooper. Now this is dangerously infantile, and it shows in every level of national life. When I was living in Europe, for example, one of the worst revelations to me was the way Americans walked around Europe buying this and buying that and insulting everybody—not even out of malice, just because they didn't know any better. Well, that is the way they have always treated me. They weren't cruel, they just didn't know you were alive. They didn't know you had any feelings.

What I am trying to suggest here is that in the doing of all this for 100 years or more, it is the American white man who has long since lost his grip on reality. In some peculiar way, having created this myth about Negroes, and the myth about his own history, he created myths about the world so

that, for example, he was astounded that some people could prefer Castro, astounded that there are people in the world who don't go into hiding when they hear the word "Communism," astounded that Communism is one of the realities of the twentieth century which we will not overcome by pretending that it does not exist. The political level in this country now, on the part of people who should know better, is abysmal.

The Bible says somewhere that where there is no vision the people perish. I don't think anyone can doubt that in this country today we are menaced—intolerably menaced—by a lack of vision.

It is inconceivable that a sovereign people should continue, as we do so abjectly, to say, "I can't do anything about it. It's the government." The government is the creation of the people. It is responsible to the people. And the people are responsible for it. No American has the right to allow the present government to say, when Negro children are being bombed and hosed and shot and beaten all over the deep South, that there is nothing we can do about it. There must have been a day in this country's life when the bombing of four children in Sunday School would have created a public uproar and endangered the life of a Governor Wallace. It happened here and there was no public uproar.

I began by saying that one of the paradoxes of education was that precisely at the point when you begin to develop a conscience, you must find yourself at war with your society. It is your responsibility to change society if you think of yourself as an educated person. And on the basis of the evidence—the moral and political evidence—one is compelled to say that this is a backward society. Now if I were a teacher in this school, and I was dealing with Negro children, who were in my care only a few hours of every day and would then return to their homes and to the streets, children who have an apprehension of their future which with every hour grows grimmer and darker, I would try to teach them—I would try to make them know—that those streets, those houses, those dangers, those agonies by which they are surrounded, are criminal. I would try to make each child know that these things are the results of a criminal conspiracy to destroy him. I would teach him that if he intends to get to be a man, he must at once decide that he is stronger than this conspiracy and that he must never make his peace with it. And that one of his weapons for refusing to make his peace with it and for destroying it depends on what he decides he is worth. I would teach him that there are currently very few standards in this country which are worth a man's respect. That it is up to him to begin to change these standards for the sake of the life and health of the country. I would suggest to him that the proper culture—as represented, for example, on television and in comic books and in movies—is based on fantasies created by very ill people, and he must be aware that these are fantasies that have nothing

to do with reality. I would teach him that the press he reads is not as free as it says it is—and that he can do something about that, too. I would try to make him know that just as American history is longer, larger, more various, more beautiful, and more terrible than anything anyone has ever said about it, so is the world larger, more daring, more beautiful and more terrible, but principally larger—and that it belongs to him. I would teach him that he doesn't have to be bound by the expediencies of any given Administration, any given policy, any given time—that he has the right and the necessity to examine everything. I would try to show him that one has not learned anything about Castro when one says, "He is a Communist." This is a way of *not* learning something about Castro, something about Cuba, something, in fact, about the world. I would suggest to him that he is living, at the moment, in an enormous province. America is not the world and if America is going to become a nation, she must find a way—and this child must help her to find a way—to use the tremendous potential and tremendous energy which this child represents. If this country does not find a way to use that energy, it will be destroyed by that energy.

28. *Life Is Fun in a Smiling, Fair-Skinned World*

OTTO KLINEBERG

"Readers" are presumably prepared for the purpose of teaching children to read, adding to their vocabulary, developing the capacity to see the interrelationship of ideas; children are helped to understand the structure of sentences and of grammatical forms, to follow the sequence of events, and to become aware of the manner in which they are united and integrated. One reader speaks of the "steady growth of interpretative powers" which is insured through the content of the stories, and describes the situations and plots as containing a "meaningful interplay of the personality, mood, emotion, and purpose of the characters." [5] (This and the following numbers refer to the books listed at the end of the article.) The present writer expresses no opinion as to the contribution of these readers to the ability to *read,* but this analysis of their content raises in his mind, however, some very real questions regarding their contribution to the children's *picture of American society*, the *attitudes* and modes of thinking which are presumably developed, and the desire to *read further.*

First, and perhaps most important, is the picture of American society

Reprinted from *Saturday Review*, Vol. 46 (February 16, 1963), pp. 75–77, 87, by permission of the publisher and author.

which is presented. Margaret Mead and Rhoda Metraux have written about "The Study of Culture at a Distance" (University of Chicago Press, 1953), describing the attempts to understand another culture on the basis of its plays or motion pictures, its books, its manuals of child care, etc. Suppose the visitor from Mars or even from Thailand tried to reconstruct American life from the content of these readers, without any other data to guide him. The resultant picture would be approximately as follows:

The American people are almost exclusively white or Caucasian. The only exception discovered in the fifteen readers refers to a visit to a Western ranch, near which lived an American Indian family, who spent most of their time "making beautiful things . . . to sell to the white people who come to the Indian country." [12] The story told is in general friendly and sympathetic to the Indians, except that they are treated as exotic and "different" not really part of the American scene. Their names—"Big Horn," "Shining Star," etc. —strike Jack, the white American boy, as "funny." [12] This incipient ethnocentrism might have been countered by reminding Jack that many proper names may be considered "funny," depending on one's experiences. What about Longfellow or Bacon? Even "old American" names may refer to occupations (Baker, Tinker), or colors (Brown, Green), or places (Hill, Field); some of the most distinguished names in American history, like Roosevelt, Eisenhower, or more recently Shepherd (or its variant Shephard) also refer, as do most American Indians' names, to places or occupations. There are other stories of Indians, but mostly of Indian children of a bygone day.[14]

The Americans in these readers are almost exclusively North European in origin and appearance. When any mention of ethnic origin appears, which is rarely, it is English, French (Brittany), or Norwegian.[13] Other people and places are visited, including Lapland, Spain, and North Africa, but this is part of travel or foreign lands, and not part of the picture of America. In this particular case, one traveler, on the apparent basis of experience with the North African desert, delivers himself of the following judgment: "A mighty interesting country, Africa,"[13] as if nothing existed south of the Sahara, and as if Africa were one (Arab) country instead of a great many different ones.

To return to the ethnic picture in the United States, the exceptions to the usual North European appearance and origin are themselves significant. An organ grinder is given an appearance which is stereotypically Italian or Greek, with a red scarf instead of a necktie; he appears in the illustration on the cover, as well as several times in the text.[1] A slightly different version of the same, or similar, organ grinder appears in another Reader.[9] There is also an Italian- or Greek-looking peddler who carries a big bag on his back.[14] Finally, there is a story of a discontented horse that works for Mr. Polaski, who "sold fruits and vegetables," and who also "looks" very South-

or Central-European in the accompanying illustrations.[14] The treatment of these characters is by no means unsympathetic, and the last example occurs in a story which is charmingly written, but one cannot help wondering about the extent to which the stereotype—South Europeans are organ grinders, peddlers, and fruit and vegetable vendors—may be strengthened by such a presentation.

Americans in these readers are predominantly, almost exclusively, blondes. A check on the illustrations used in three of the readers found in two of them [3,4] almost 100 per cent blondes, and another [2] with 75 or 80 per cent. There are occasional references to dark skin, but these usually relate to people far away. Pandas, for example, are found in a distant land (India?) with dark-skinned people;[7] in Lapland there are "small dark men";[13] and of course the illustrations for the stories about China, India, North Africa, etc., do show dark people. Not in the United States, however, apart from the exceptions noted above. Negroes are non-existent. One reader has a story called "A Summer in the South," in which a boy and his father go "away down South to see Grandmother." But there are apparently no Negroes even in the South. It is true that Grandmother had a cook whom Paddy liked "almost as well as he liked Grandmother,"[12] but even in the case of the cook, there is no indication of what Charlie May looked like. Either there are no Negroes, or they must not be mentioned. Some years ago, H. E. Wilson ("Intergroup Relations in Teaching Materials," Washington, American Council on Education, 1949) pointed out that in American textbooks foreign nationalities, as well as American minority groups, are either placed in an unfavorable light or treated inadequately. In the readers under review, to speak of "inadequate treatment" of the Negro is an extreme understatement.

Religion, as was to be expected, is rarely mentioned. Only in one reader is there a reference to religious observance, when on Sunday "everyone was going to church" because "this is Sunday, you know." [9] Paddy says, "I always go to church on Sunday, I always do." On a Sunday morning Mr. Carl rolled over in bed until the church bell called, "Come to church! Come to church!" These are the words with which this particular reader closes. No one could argue that in these readers religious (Christian) observance is overemphasized, but again the opportunity might have been taken to give some idea of the range and variety of observance found among the different religious groups that constitute the American people. There is no hint of this in any of the readers examined.

Americans in these readers are all quite well-to-do; not exactly wealthy, perhaps, but certainly quite comfortable, to say the least. The illustrations show, for example, (1) a pleasant home with good furniture, all the children dressed in clean, attractive clothes, with talk about buying new dresses; there are all kinds of toys in the house; the children go out (presumably with their own pocket money) to buy balloons. Again, they live in pretty suburban houses,[2] and the children have money in their pockets with which to buy toys themselves. The farmer has his own tractor, and father brings home a new car, "long and blue and beautiful." [2] In another Reader [3] the family has an attractive home with a car, a television set, toys, and bicycles. In still another, the mother buys her girls new coats; [5] or they already have beautiful clothes and the house a modern built-in kitchen; [6] or the family takes a trip on a big and very luxurious ship; [7] or the boy goes riding on his own pony; [8] or the family lives in "a pretty white house"; [9] or father takes the children to the circus and his boys to the ball game; [11] or they take a train out West.[12] Poverty exists, but usually everything turns out right before the end. Occasionally a boy will do some work in order to earn money, but he then puts away his twenty pennies in his own "bird bank." [9] Not only is there no poverty, but work seems to be readily available to everybody, and is on the whole not only easy but "fun."

In fact, life in general is fun, filled almost exclusively with friendly, smiling people, including gentle and understanding parents, doting grandparents, generous and cooperative neighbors, even warm-hearted strangers. There is an occasional display of anger, but it is usually very transitory. In general, all is peaceful and happy.

In summary, then, life in the United States as it is portrayed in these children's readers is in a general way easy and comfortable, frustrations are rare and usually overcome quite easily, people (all white, mostly blonde, and "North European" in origin) are almost invariably kind and generous. There are other kinds of people in the world, but they live in far-off countries or in days gone by; they evidently have no place on the American scene.

When we turn to the *attitudes* which the content of the readers will develop in the children, we are on less certain ground, since we must depend on inference rather than on direct observation. Certain conclusions can be drawn, however, with a fair degree of probability. There is a great deal of published work which demonstrates that ethnocentric attitudes develop very early in children, and that they are already present at the ages for which these readers are destined. (See for example, "Prejudice and Ethnic Relations," by John Harding et al., Chapter

27 in G. Lindzey, Editor, *Handbook of Social Psychology*, 2 volumes, Addison Wesley, Cambridge, 1954, and K. B. Clark, *Prejudice and Your Child*, Beacon Press, Boston, 1955.) Obviously, the responsibility for this cannot all be laid at the door of school experience, since so many other influences make their contribution. Nevertheless, some of that responsibility must be borne by readers which, by what they omit as well as by what they contain, give the impression that the "true" American is of the fair-skinned "North European" variety. Although this was certainly not the aim of the writers concerned, the net effect would almost certainly be to strengthen the ethnocentric attitudes of those children who share these characteristics, and make all others—of Negro, Puerto Rican, South European, possibly also of Jewish origin—feel that they do not quite belong. Since these and other ethnic groups constitute a substantial proportion of the American school population, it would not be surprising if the readers had an alien quality for a great many of the children who come into contact with them. (The writer is reminded of a Brazilian first reader which starts out telling the children that Brazil has three "mothers," one European, white, one Indian, red, and one African, black, and goes on from there to describe how the present Brazilian population has developed.)

In addition to ethnocentrism, the readers also display what might rather clumsily be called a socioeconomic-centrism, a concentration on those who are relatively well-to-do. Here the problem is rather more complicated, because Americans are in general well-to-do and the amenities described are within the reach of a substantial proportion of the population. For the remaining "one-fourth of a nation" it is part of the American dream that a more comfortable life is attainable. Until it is attained, however, the life portrayed in these readers must represent a very frustrating experience for them. Are *no* other families as poor as ours? Does everybody else live in a pretty white house? Are there no crowded tenements except where we live? Are we the only ones who can't go out and buy the toys we want? On the other side, is it desirable for the well-to-do children to be unaware that there may be poor people living on the other side of the tracks? Surely a more balanced presentation of American life, both from the ethnic and socioeconomic standpoints, would better prepare the children for what they will later encounter and help to correct what would otherwise be a one-sided picture. It may be argued that this will come in time, and that these children are still too young to face that kind of reality. The fact remains that the earliest impressions frequently develop attitudes that persist; it follows that it is never too early to tell children the truth.

There is another striking feature of these readers related to the question of "truth." In addition to the (conceivably factual) accounts of the activities and experiences of children and their families, most of the readers contain a number of stories, which, though fictional in character, deal with animals or with objects such as trains or airplanes which the children have in all probability encountered. These stories are predominantly characterized by *anthropomorphism* (ascribing human qualities to animals) and animism (ascribing life and thought to inanimate objects). Thus a snowman laughs,[1] animals talk to one another,[1,2,8–11,14–15] and cooperate in joint enterprises;[1] trains converse,[10] and so do airplanes and helicopters,[10,11] cars and taxis,[15] and there is even a little red lighthouse, round and fat and "very proud," which carries on a conversation with a new bridge.[15]

There can be no doubt that animistic thinking is widespread among young children, at least in Western society (J. Piaget, *The Child's Conception of the World*, New York, 1929). It has been suggested, however, that this tendency would not be nearly so marked nor so common if it were not for the influence of language (as when we refer to a ship as "she"), the actions of parents and other adults (like spanking the chair that "hurt" the little child), and the stories told as in these particular readers, for example. In any case, animism is a stage *through which* children pass, through which children *must* pass if they are to reach a realistic appraisal of the outside world. The present writer feels that the proliferation of anthropomorphism and animism creates an unnecessary barrier to the intellectual development of children, who should rather be encouraged to make, as early as possible, a distinction which is in harmony with the truth. He finds it hard to believe that animistic distortion is necessary in order to attract the attention of even young children. In fact, he has met children of six who would show a pitying smile at such an insult to their intelligence.

As far as *moral* attitudes are concerned, the readers appear to be on relatively safe ground. They illustrate, without any overt preaching, the virtues of honesty, fair play, cooperation, family solidarity, work and thrift, friendship, independence, cleanliness, courage, and forgiveness. There is even, as has already been indicated, an awareness and acceptance of differences in culture and background, but usually for people far removed in space and time. One could certainly wish for more of this in the case of those nearer home; for these, there are no negative or unfriendly references; they simply do not exist.

In regard to the desire to read further, the editors of these readers, some of whom are personally and favorably known to the present writer, presumably have based their choice of materials on a knowledge of the tastes and interests of children. It is hard to believe, however, that enough is being done to stimulate the *curiosity* of the children, to make them feel that they would like to know more. The readers do contain a number of well-written stories and some delightful poems, but almost no information. Surely, together with the reading of good prose or verse, a reader could do more to instruct the child.

This report concludes with two specific proposals. The first is that the analysis made of American readers be supplemented by a comparison with readers of other countries (France, the Soviet Union, Brazil, and Sweden, for example) to determine what can be discovered from their experience, and also to see what other children, no brighter than our own, can absorb at an early age. The second is the preparation of sample readers designed to give children a more complete and more adequate picture of American life, and capable at the same time of making *important* things *interesting*.

WIDELY USED ELEMENTARY READERS

Dr. Klineberg says of the following books, "These are without exception presented in an attractive format, with hard covers, excellent print, and colorful, attractive illustrations. Although the exact publication figures are not available to the writer, they have been described as representing popular and successful books adopted for general use by many school boards throughout the country."

1. *On Cherry Street*, The Ginn Basic Readers, First Reader (Primer), 1961. O. Oursley and D. H. Russell

2. *We Are Neighbors*, The Ginn Basic Readers, Second Reader, Level I. 1961. O. Oursley and D. H. Russell

3. *Fun With Our Family*, New Basic Reading Program, Scott, Foresman and Co., Second Pre-Primer, 1962. H. Robinson, M. Monroe, and A. S. Artley

4. *Fun Wherever We Are*, Third Pre-Primer, Scott, Foresman and Co., 1962. H. Robinson, M. Monroe, and A. S. Artley

5. *Fun With Our Friends*, Primer, Scott, Foresman and Co., 1962. H. Robinson, M. Monroe, and A. S. Artley

6. *The New Guess Who*, Special Junior Primer, Scott, Foresman and Co., 1962. H. Robinson, M. Monroe, and A. S. Artley

7. *On Four Feet*, The Macmillan Readers, Basal First Reader, 1960. A. I. Gates, M. B. Huber, and F. S. Salisbury

8. *The Little White House*, Ginn, Primer, 1961. O. Oursley and D. S. Russell

9. *Round About*, Alice and Jerry Basic Reading Program; Row, Peterson and Co. First Reader, 1957. M. O'Donnell

10. *Friends and Fun*, Macmillan, Basal Second Reader, 1960. A. I. Gates, M. B. Huber, and F. S. Salisbury

11. *Around the Corner*, Ginn, Second Reader, Level II, 1961. O. Oursley and D. H. Russell

12. *Friendly Village*, Row, Peterson and Co. Basic Second Reader, 1957. M. O'Donnell

13. *If I Were Going*, Row, Peterson and Co. Basic Third Reader, 1957. M. O'Donnell

14. *Finding New Neighbors*, Ginn, Third Reader, Level I, 1961. D. Russell, G. Wulfing, and O. Oursley

15. *Friends Far and Near*, Ginn, Third Reader, Level II, 1961. D. Russell and G. Wulfing

29. The Culturally Disadvantaged: Educational Implications of Certain Social-Cultural Phenomena

DELMO DELLA-DORA

The following material represents the viewpoint of one person looking at the educational consequences of some social-cultural differences found in our present society. Three aspects of the problem which will be discussed are:

(a) Current social-cultural forces which interact with the functions assigned to public schools

(b) Effects of these forces upon the teaching-learning process

(c) Some directions which schools might take to solve the education problems which arise from social-cultural differences.

CURRENT SOCIAL-CULTURAL FORCES OF IMPORTANCE TO SCHOOLS

Newspapers, television, and magazines have been giving a great deal of attention recently to the plight of the large cities. Among the problems cited are (a) exodus of white middle-class families to the suburbs, (b) large numbers of lower-income families in which there is no father or an unstable

Reprinted from *Exceptional Children*, Vol. 28 (May 1962), pp. 467–472, by permission of the publisher and author.

family tie, (c) a rapid influx of lower-class socioeconomic groups into the central city, particularly into blighted or marginal residential neighborhoods, (d) a high rate of unemployment among adults and consequent need for massive social welfare assistance, (e) serious lack of employment opportunities for both high school graduates and nongraduates ("dropouts"), (f) an apparent increase in the incidence of delinquency and crime, and (g) influx of a large mass of low-income families raised in rural areas with relatively little opportunity for formal education.

The largest urban centers are developing a pattern in which the lower socioeconomic group is composed of younger minority-group adults with school-age children who live in the oldest and middle-aged neighborhoods. The middle-class white citizens are older, live in newer homes and either have older children or no children at home. The city is surrounded by segregated white, middle-class suburbs. The combination of increased social welfare costs and reduced property valuation creates a severe financial problem which the cities alone have not been able to solve and which, properly, is not theirs alone to solve. The problems of the cities are really the problems of the state and the nation in terms of their creation. However, relatively little attention is given to city problems by state governments and, until recently, no major consideration was given by the federal government. The relative indifference of state government is better understood when we examine the composition of state legislatures. Here we find that rural representation in both houses of the state legislature is disproportionately great in approximately 35 of the 50 states. In Michigan, for example, 50 percent of the total state population is located in the three metropolitan counties of Wayne (including Detroit), Oakland, and Macomb. Their actual representation in the state legislature consists of nine senators in a senate of 34 members and 47 representatives in a house of 110 members.

Another characteristic of the city, particularly the inner city, is rapidly changing neighborhoods. In Detroit and Chicago, for example, the rural southern white families seem to migrate and emigrate with fluctuations in the employment market, while Negroes apparently remain in the city but change locations frequently. The remaining middle-class and upper-middle-class white families keep moving away from the approaching tide of lower-class movement.

In sum the picture is one of rapid change in population characteristics, involving groups which differ radically in social-cultural makeup and which do not interact very effectively. As indicated, this goes on within a framework in which increasing need for social welfare assistance is accompanied by a decreasing supply of tax revenue from presently available sources.

EFFECTS OF SOCIAL-CULTURAL DIFFERENCES ON THE SCHOOL

Individual Pupils

There is a high rate of illness and nutritional deficiency among the lower economic group families. They are ignorant of good health practices and/or financially unable to carry them out. Children who are hungry, improperly fed, or ill will obviously have reduced efficiency as learners.

Many children lack interest in school and show evidence of low motivation. Apathy as well as emotional and social maladjustment among parents, lack of books or other learning media, and little opportunity for travel all contribute to an educationally sterile home environment.

Student self-concept and level of aspiration are generally low in relation to typical school-centered activities. Evidence of this is found in the study of a large city by Patricia Sexton (1961), in which she reports failure rates as being six times as high among elementary school children whose families earn $3,000 or less annually compared to families earning $9,000 or more. She also indicates that 37 children per 10,000 were identified as very serious behavior problems in the case of lowest income families while none were recorded from the highest income group. Another vital statistic is the dropout rate, which is five times higher among students from lowest income families, compared to those from highest income families.

Pupil-Pupil Relationships

Social class differences are not as great among the elementary school children of a large city as they are among high school students. This is true because the attendance areas of elementary schools are smaller and, therefore, more homogeneous in character. However, even high schools in the large city are much less representative of the total community than the high school for a given smaller community. Sexton reports that, among the seventeen high schools in one large city, median income of families was $5,000–6,000 for five schools, $6,000–7,000 for three schools, $7,000–8,000 for four schools, $8,000–9,000 for four schools, and over $9,000 for the remaining school. Social class differences exist within schools and among schools, compounded by racial differences which are pervasive enough to be considered caste differences.

The testimony brought into evidence before the U.S. Supreme Court favoring school desegregation showed clearly that "separate" cannot be "equal" for education in a democratic society. The segregation which occurs in large cities is in many ways as segregated in terms of social class and caste characteristics as many of the deliberately segregated schools in this country. Students do not have an opportunity to learn and value other students of dissimilar background in this kind of situation.

It would be naive to assume that mere physical integration will automatically bring about social integration or otherwise result in an environment which fosters democratic living more effectively. The data from *Elmtown's Youth* (Hollingshead, 1949) and other studies show that interaction among students takes place primarily along social class lines. As Hollingshead concludes (pp. 444–45),

". . . children's behavior patterns are established primarily by their early experiences in the family and secondarily in the neighborhood . . . similar experiences mold children into similar social types strongly associated with class. . . . As he participates in suc-

cessive social situations, he learns to act in certain ways, to regard himself as a valued member of the group or as an unwanted person. . . . By the time he reaches adolescence his personality is formed. Also, he has developed conceptions of (1) himself; (2) the social structure; (3) his place in it along with appropriate roles and statuses; (4) forms of behavior approved and disapproved; and (5) means of doing what he desires even though it involves the violation of laws and mores."

Thus in both the small-town high school and in the large-city high school the social life in the school is affected materially by social life outside of schools. It determines school friendship groups and also affects learning goals and learning outcomes. Van Egmond (1960), for example, has found in a study of second and fifth grade students that difficulties in peer relations, being disliked by one's peers or being of low status, disrupt pupil motivation and the ability to learn from adults.

Teacher-Pupil Relationships

Teachers generally come from upper-lower or lower-middle class families. They are generally characterized by sociologists as being upward-mobile. A significant number identify strongly with middle-class or upper-class values. The distribution of marks, praise or blame, selection for special-ability classes, determination of promotion or failure, of punishment meted out for infraction of rules, and other kinds of teacher-pupil interaction in school are, at times, affected by social class background of the students. These conclusions are supported by the work of Sexton and Hollingshead and by a number of less comprehensive studies.

For the big-city teacher who favors the behavior and values of children from middle-class and upper-class families, assignment to a low-income neighborhood school may adversely affect treatment of students. There has been a time in the history of each big city's schools when teachers placed in such neighborhoods were either the least competent or the least experienced teachers in the school system. The impact of this process of teacher assignment is readily apparent.

School-Community Relationships

Parents of students in low-income neighborhoods do not feel as close to schools as do parents in higher income groups. Their own educational status, the different social class represented by teachers, less self-respect, a low incidence of familiar stability, and a high incidence of change in home location all contribute to the development of this feeling.

The support ordinarily given to school people through the P.T.A., visits to schools, supportive comments, presence of books at home, and interest in school activities is generally low. School people do not have much opportunity to feel the sense of community through parents or their children, and since they rarely actually live in the community there is very little available to facilitate communication. The barriers to understanding and cooperative action are extremely high. Learning on the part of students, parents, or teachers is inhibited in comparison to the situation in neighborhoods or communities of higher economic levels.

IMPLICATIONS FOR THE SCHOOL

The problems described above and their impact on schools are perplexing for a variety of reasons. A basic question relates to the proper role of the school in our democratic society. What criteria should guide us in determining what the school should *try* to do, much less what it *can* do? The traditional role of schools is conceived to be that of transmitting the culture, the status quo. As such it is a conservator of the existing social system and all the consequences which ensue. On the other hand, the learning problems with which the school must deal do not exist in isolation. American educator and philosopher Joseph K. Hart (Michigan Dept. of Public Instruction, 1960, pp. 2–3), put forth this viewpoint:

"The democratic problem in education is not primarily a problem of training children; it is a problem of making a community in which children cannot help growing up to be democratic, intelligent, disciplined to freedom, reverent to the goods of life— eager to share in the tasks of the age. A school cannot produce this result; nothing but a community can do so."

Schools generally, and big city schools in particular, must increasingly accept this community school concept if they are to provide adequate and equal educational opportunities for all. The conclusion seems inevitable. The problems of living in an urban society cannot be solved exclusively within the confines of an individual home, nor can the schools carry out their responsibility without the active cooperation of other persons and agencies which affect learning attributes. To say that we should "teach the whole child" is a tautology. We have no choice; there is no other way to teach. The so-called "intellect" refuses to be set aside from affective dimensions. Categories of "emotional," "social," and "intellectual" are man-made constructs which are useful for some purposes of analysis but stand in the way if we are examining the total educational goals of public schools in a free society.

TOWARD A SOLUTION

If we can accept the philosophy implied in the foregoing, the nature of our solutions might be in these directions.

Increasing coordinated efforts among schools, local government, and other social and civic agencies. Problems of health, housing, economic well-being, community interaction, and others of importance to learning are problems held in common by many agencies. Schools should initiate action to see that the problems are attacked in a coordinated fashion if no other agency has already done so. In practice this means calling into being some kind of school-community planning group. Each high school could serve as the locus of activity. If not, whatever can be identified as natural communities within the city should form the basis for action groups. The questions to which a community planning group should address itself are:

(a) What is each of us doing to help raise the level of living in this community?

(b) Where do we see an inappropriate or unnecessary duplication of effort?

(c) In what areas can we, and should we, work together?

(d) What do we know about total community needs and problems? Which of these are not being met adequately? What needs to be done? Who *should* do it now? Who *can* do it, in terms of financial and personal resources? What needs to be done to obtain the necessary resources? What are the short term solutions and the long term solutions to these unmet needs and unresolved problems?

A coordinated effort to solve total community problems spearheaded by school people does not imply that the schools should undertake to perform additional societal tasks, nor is it our intention to suggest that social agencies should take over functions of the individual or the family.

The schools may well ultimately perform a lesser number of social functions than many are attempting now as they try to deal adequately with the impact of social-class differences on the teaching-learning process. Local government should probably take on more of whatever additional functions are seen as necessary, including the coordinating function just described. A major criterion for examining solutions to societal problems should involve asking "How can we stimulate and assist individuals and families to help themselves?" The ultimate goal should be to foster self-understanding and self-direction—both for individuals and the basic small unit of society, the family. This should remain as a long-term goal even if the situation warrants something quite different on a short-term basis. People who need help cannot always wait for ultimate or ideal conceptions. Hunger, malnutrition, preparation for a job need to be dealt with when the problems appear. However, because of lack of vision or because we beome enmeshed in the creation of new, inflexible bureaucracy, it is often too easy to retain short-term solutions which infringe on the rights and responsibilities of individuals.

Schools need to carry out a self-study of the impact of social-class differences on students and teachers, school-by-school. The kinds of analyses carried on by Hollingshead and Sexton are examples of a type vital to school operation. How these influences operate in the lives of particular youngsters and teachers needs to be examined by the teachers and administrators who are to evolve solutions. This analysis is necessary both for the school itself and as a prelude to effective cooperative efforts with other social agencies.

Direct teaching aimed at changing attitudes and self concepts should be made available to students and parents. What people think of themselves and others determines how they act. Low level of aspiration and low self-esteem lead to lower than necessary achievement in all areas of living. There is some evidence to suggest that individuals and groups can be assisted in developing more favorable attitudes by means of direct teaching, which it is within the ability of most teachers to do or learn to do. The work of Ellis and Harper (1961) with adults, and exploration of attitudinal change among elementary school children by staff members of the Wayne County Board of Education, offer some evidence to support this contention.

There are other avenues which might be profitably explored by schools in dealing with the issues identified in this presentation. In the interest of brevity they will simply be mentioned without elaboration at this point.

(a) Help expand and diffuse leadership throughout the community.

(b) Give leadership, when appropriate, to constructive community projects.

(c) Practice and promote democratic procedures throughout all phases of school operation.

(d) Use community resources in the instructional program.

(e) Involve all persons affected by the school operation with planning and appraising.

(f) Develop a school program which is genuinely life-centered as a social institution.

SUMMARY

The problems associated with cultural deprivation are problems of class and caste differences. The situation is not unique to big cities but is more apparent and its effects more dramatic in this setting. Schools are involved and affected because these differences radically limit equality of educational opportunity. The problems must be solved not because we are in military competition with Russia and other totalitarian states—nor because we are engaged in scientific and economic competition with all other countries—but because we are citizens of a society in which all persons should be given equal right to develop their individual talents to the fullest.

The most recent publication of the Educational Policies Commission, "Education and the Disadvantaged American" (*NEA Journal,* April 1962), summarizes proposed solutions to the problem in the following manner:

"*Special Characteristics of the School Program.* The successful school program attacks the problem of the culturally handicapped on three fronts, simultaneously. It demonstrates to pupils a close relationship between school and life; it includes remedial services necessary for academic progress; and it arouses aspirations which can alter constructively the courses of young lives.

"*Special Characteristics of the School Staff.* The specialized and administrative personnel, like the teachers, must have preparation designed to promote understanding of the children and parents with whom they will deal. In addition they can learn from each other.

. . . The principal should encourage this sharing and should foster the willingness of teachers to consult with specialists on the staff.

"*Special Characteristics of the Administrator.* In disadvantaged communities, especially, the school should make of itself a neighborhood institution, for its success depends to a considerable degree on the parents' attitudes and the staff's knowledge of family circumstances. . . . Special administrative efforts are therefore required to sustain morale—rewarding good performance and encouraging experimentation."

It is evident that the problems of providing equal and adequate educational opportunity for the culturally deprived will require additional school personnel and additional school services. If we measuse this cost against the actual cost of delinquency, crime, and underproductivity it will be a bargain in terms of dollars. If we measure the cost in terms of unfulfilled human desires, underdeveloped capabilities, and unexplored potential for improving the quality of democratic living—any amount of money needed to do the job will be well worth the expenditure.

References

Della-Dora, D. (Ed.) The community school program: self evaluative check list. Lansing: Michigan Department of Public Instruction, 1958.

Education and the Disadvantaged American, *NEA Journal,* April, 1962 (Vol. 51, No. 4).

Ellis, A. and R. Harper. *A guide to rational living in an irrational world,* Englewood Cliffs, N. J.: Prentice-Hall, 1961.

Hollingshead, A. B. *Elmtown's youth,* New York: John Wiley, 1949.

Sexton, Patricia. *Education and income,* New York: Viking Press, 1961.

A statement of basic philosophy concerning public education in Michigan. Lansing: Michigan Department of Public Instruction, 1958.

Van Egmond, Elmer. Social interrelationship skills and effective utilization of intelligence in the classroom. Unpublished doctoral thesis, Ann Arbor: University of Michigan, 1960.

Working toward more effective education—a report on the Detroit greater cities project after one year. Detroit Public Schools, September 30, 1961 (mimeo).

30. Cultural Factors and Creativity

MARIANNE WOLMAN

Considering the percentage of Mexican Americans in the general school population, one finds them in greater number than one would expect in classes for slow learners. According to their achievement, performance, and test scores they appear to be placed correctly in the special classes, but because of the unexpectedly large proportion, the question arises whether they are all actually of low mental ability. If they are retarded, what is their rate of retardation, their true reading ability, their performance in other school activities? On what other factors are these student evaluations based? Do our teachers actually have opportunities to study how to teach Mexican American pupils more effectively?

THE MEXICAN AMERICAN PUPIL

According to Fargo most attempts to view Mexican Americans in our culture have been made by disciplines other than education.[1] Only little research has been undertaken to consider their educational problems in our public schools. However, some information in this area is available.

McAnulty reported in 1932 that the I.Q. level for various groups of Mexi-

Reprinted from *Journal of Secondary Education*, Vol. 37 (December 1962), pp. 454–460, by permission of the publisher and the author.

can American children ranged from about 78–91.[2] These rather poor test results seem to be typical of the findings of other researchers as well. Intelligence test scores for these children are lower than those given to Anglo-American children of the same age.

McAnulty proposes five causes for these poor test results: (1) unfavorable home background, (2) bilingualism, (3) poor educational facilities, (4) uncontrolled factors, and finally (5) inadequate testing instruments. Nathan emphasizes the inadequacy of the tests themselves and states that to evaluate Mexican American pupils with the same instruments as Anglo-Americans is to operate on an invalid premise.[3]

Fargo states further that it is to be expected that children whose socio-cultural background is completely different from people who designed the tests, and different from children upon whom the tests were standardized, would have considerable difficulty in answering test items correctly. Many of the test items include vocabulary or situations unknown to them. This would be particularly true of children who come from homes of very low socioeconomic status, where no English or only little English is spoken, and where the cultural heritage is entirely different from that of the majority group. Many Mexican Americans who came to the country had previously lived in underprivileged rural or semirural areas and then settled in large cities in the United States.

If Mexican American children do not do well on standardized tests, do they really have no capacity to perform intelligently? Can one legitimately say that their capacity has been adequately measured? Binet himself warned that tests could be used safely only if various individuals had the same or approximately the same environmental opportunities.

Recognizing these shortcomings, efforts have been made to construct culture-free intelligence tests. Allison Davis and his associates at the University of Chicago developed the Davis-Eells tests to estimate the level of intellectual functioning without cultural bias.[4] The tests purport to measure problem-solving ability rather than memory or past learning, and would therefore not discriminate against individuals of lower-class, different cultural background. Unfortunately, the tests have serious limitations. They are difficult to administer, show low reliability, and do not predict academic performance.

To better understand the problems of Mexican American students in the public schools, other factors must also be taken into consideration. The conflict which second generation children face is the conflict of the "old country" traditions and values of their families vis à vis American customs and values. In the public schools the children learn about America, its history, its great men, its cities and government. But the Mexican Americans are never quite included in these achievements of a world in which they have no real part. Their school records are affected by the same factors that influence under-

privileged children of most minority groups—poverty, bad housing, ill health, bilingualism, and segregation.

Mexican American children tend to be classified according to clichés or stereotypes. How do many teachers describe them? Statements are made such as: "They are not competitive, they lack ambition, they are impudent, they are not interested in their school subjects, they are lazy, the dropout rate is very high, those who stay in school just sit through their classes, they have no educational aspirations whatsoever." What does the average teacher actually know about these students, their background, their culture, the structure of their families? Apparently very little.

A CASE STUDY

During the 1961–1962 school year intensive observations were made of a number of Mexican American pupils in public secondary schools in the San Gabriel Valley area. Several of the schools had a Mexican American pupil population of 10–16 percent. A disproportionately high number of the Mexican American pupils was found in low ability classes. The school where the following observation was made includes lower, upper-lower, and lower middle-class students in its over-all population.

An 11th grade Remedial English class was observed, consisting of 20 students, 17 boys and 3 girls, 8 of whom were Mexican, the rest Anglo-Americans. Most of the students' fathers were unskilled or semiskilled laborers; 4 pupils grew up in fatherless homes. Their ages ranged from 16–18; their I.Q. scores on a group intelligence test from 69–98. The Cooperative English Test, evaluating language usage, vocabulary, spelling, and grammar, provided ratings for all except two of a *0 percentile score*, one scored on the first, the other on the second percentile, indicating an almost nonexisting verbal facility. Not all scores which tested school achievement and past learning were available; those recorded were very low. Several of the students were classified "nonreaders"; many of them were 3–5 years below their grade level in reading. School attendance was irregular, some students had spent some time in Juvenile Hall, a few others were on probation. Many of them looked more like grown men and women than like 16–18 year olds. Only 3 of them belonged to clubs sponsored by the school, indicating that they did not participate in extracurricular activities of the school. However, the class climate was warm, friendly, and relaxed.

The teacher, a young woman of Mexican American descent in her first teaching assignment, was able to establish an unusually good relationship with her pupils. All pupils in the class had secured only D's and F's in English during recent years. At the beginning of the 1961–1962 school year, however, the teacher told them that she would disregard the previous grades and assign them grades they actually earned in her class. One pupil did exceptionally well and received "B" in English. He then asked the teacher to *lower* his grade so that he could remain in her class; he had no wish to be identified with better students.

The 11th grade curriculum included a unit of poetry. It seemed very doubtful such an attempt would arouse any interest among her students. The teacher, however, not only expected her pupils to enjoy poetry, but also to *stimulate them to write* poems themselves. She read several poems of American, Spanish, and Mexican poets to them. To give her pupils confidence, she stressed the fact that simple people with deep feelings could write beautiful poetry as well as highly educated men. After several days of class study, the teacher asked the pupils to try to write poems. There were at first some voices of protest, but before long most of them began to work. Not even the teacher, in spite of her trust in her pupils, expected what she received.

Bob

Bob is 18 years old. He has three brothers and one sister. His father died several years ago. His mother works as a dishwasher to support the family. Bob is interested in sports, particularly in track. He has always been a disciplinary problem, difficult to handle in the classroom, as well as on the playground. All except his English teacher consider him an introvert, a worrier who developed ulcers some time ago. He was nicknamed "Ulcer" by his classmates. Plans for his future are uncertain. His I.Q. score is 75, his composite Iowa score 8, and he ranks 0 percentile on the Cooperative English Test.

To Die

The Bars were cold, the man looked
  dry
He saw the sun, and then he knew
The time was near for him to die.

He heard the clock strike six,
And then he saw, the hangman's knot,

He heard the men throw sticks.
And see him die and be a man no more

To Hell, then forever more!

> I have no riches
> I died a debtor,
> I died free-hearted,
> And that was better.

Don

Don is an attractive 17-year-old. He comes from a family of ten. His father works as a laborer at a machine plant.

Don has always been a discipline problem at school; his records show that he is uncooperative in class, disturbs incessantly, is dirty, and pays no attention to his appearance. His *English* teacher describes him as *cooperative*, turning in assignments on time, volunteering for oral reports. He is very artistic and likes to write poetry and short stories. He is fearful and shows severe guilt feelings. There is evidence of extensive masturbation and possible homosexual tendencies. He ran away from home twice and has threatened to do it again. His I.Q. is 92, composite Iowa score 15, he ranks at the first percentile on the English Cooperative Test.

Home

High on a hill stood a young lad,
He was naughty and would not listen
    to his dad,

He stood so high and watched the trees
    sway
For lo' and behold he'd run away.

He soon grew cold, tired and weary,
He wanted to go home but was kind
    of leary.

Soon he saw his dad run up the hill,
He didn't know whether to go or stand
    still.

He soon ran to his father's arms,
And found he had some lover's charms,

This poor lad who had no mother.
Found he and his dad were meant
    for each other.

So, if you ever plan to roam,
You'd soon find out, there's no place
    like home.

Bill

Bill is a self-confident, friendly boy who is anxious to leave school and go to work. He has had a part-time job for several months, selling clothes in a men's store. His mother works as a housekeeper, his father is a carpenter. His school grades are low throughout. He has an I.Q. of 76, a composite score of 11 on the Iowa test, and a 0 percentile score on the English Cooperative. He is quiet and well-behaved in school, and has never given his teachers any trouble. He just sits and waits until school is out.

The Ocean Sound

It's very hard to identify
Those whispering sounds of the ocean
    cry,
It makes you think that we shall die,
And be beyond those clouds up high.

Juan

Juan is 17. His father is a cement worker; his mother, a nurses' aide. He is a very shy, sensitive boy who has many fears. His mother is greatly concerned about him, and gets in touch with Juan's teacher and counselor often. He has an expressive face and looks and acts much more alert than his 82 I.Q. would indicate. Because of his great fears individual testing was suggested. He scored 105 on the Wechsler, with a considerably higher score on the performance than on the verbal test. The English Cooperative Test placed him on the 0 percentile. His achievement in all his school subjects is very low.

Wind

There is a wind, I hate to hear,
A wind of mystery and fear.
They say when it is near,
Its voice will call,
"Come here," "come here."

There is a wind I hate to hear,
A wind of death, a wind of fear.
It's coming! Its voice is near.
Listen, listen, can't you hear?

CONCLUSION

It is clear that the teacher played an essential part, evoking in her pupils intense feelings and a deep sense of poetry resulting in lyrical impression of totally unexpected beauty, unexpected to teacher and pupils. Most striking, the astounding creativity was in an unlooked-for area: the English language. The teacher's belief and trust in her pupils determined the appearance of these poems.

Since the schools have set out to educate all children and to offer them equal opportunities to develop their potentials, it appears urgent to design and to use *reliable, culture-free intelligence tests* in our public schools. Such tests should assess more accurately the true capacity of culturally deprived children and circumvent the false basis on which educational programs for them are sometimes developed. Most teaching in the schools observed is devised by and aimed at middle-class Anglo-Americans. It does not achieve adequate results with pupils of different economic, social, and ethnic backgrounds. It produces negative or contrary results, stifles the development of pupils, their wish to learn; it provokes hostility, opposition, and revolt. It seems that the school should consider ways and means to help the Mexican, Filipino, Negro, poor-white, or other, to achieve security within his own society as a prelude to gaining a feeling of self-worth in the general community.

It appears essential to provide teachers extensive help in attaining thorough knowledge of themselves as teachers, and a clear understanding and appreciation for students who come from various socio-cultural backgrounds. When a teacher is able to overcome classification by stereotype, when the well established clichés are denied and eliminated, he will be able to guide his students to creative experiences.

References

1. Fargo, George, "Criteria for Evaluating Content of Reading Material for Mexican American Pupils in Classes for the Mentally Retarded" (unpublished Master's thesis, UCLA, 1959), p. 13.
2. McAnulty, Edward, "Achievement and Intelligence Test Results for Mexican Children in Los Angeles City Schools," *L.A. Educ. Research Bull.*, Vol. XI, 1932, p. 90.
3. Nathan, Jerome, "The Relationship of English Language Deficiency to Test Scores of Mentally Retarded Mexican American Children" (unpublished Master's thesis, Univ. of Calif., 1955), p. 5.
4. Eells, Kenneth, et al., *Intelligence and Cultural Differences: Study of Cultural Learning and Problem Solving.* Chicago: Univ. of Chicago Press, 1951, p. 6.

31. A Teaching Strategy for Culturally Deprived Pupils: Cognitive and Motivational Considerations

The possibility of arresting and reversing the course of intellectual retardation in the culturally deprived pupil depends largely on providing him with an optimal learning environment as early as possible in the course of his educational career. If the limiting effects of prolonged cultural deprivation on the development of verbal intelligence and on the acquisition of verbal knowledge are to be at least partially overcome, better-than-average strategies of teaching are obviously necessary in terms of both general effectiveness and specific appropriateness for his particular learning situation. Yet precisely the opposite state of affairs typically prevails: the learning environment of the culturally deprived child is both generally inferior and specifically inappropriate. His cumulative intellectual deficit, therefore, almost invariably reflects, in part, the cumulative impact of a continuing and consistently deficient learning environment, as well as his emotional and motiva-

Reprinted from *The School Review*, Vol. 71 (Winter 1963), pp. 454–463, by permission of The University of Chicago Press. Copyright 1963 by the University of Chicago.

tional reaction to this environment. Thus, much of the lower-class child's alienation from the school is not so much a reflection of discriminatory or rejecting attitudes on the part of teachers and other school personnel—although the importance of this factor should not be underestimated; it is in greater measure a reflection of the cumulative effects of a curriculum that is too demanding of him, and of the resulting load of frustration, confusion, demoralization, resentment, and impaired self-confidence that he must bear.

COGNITIVE CONSIDERATIONS

An effective and appropriate teaching strategy for the culturally deprived child must therefore emphasize these three considerations: (1) the selection of initial learning material geared to the learner's existing state of readiness; (2) mastery and consolidation of all ongoing learning tasks before new tasks are introduced, so as to provide the necessary foundation for successful sequential learning and to prevent unreadiness for future learning tasks; and (3) the use of structured learning materials optimally organized to facilitate efficient sequential learning. Attention to these three factors can go a long way toward insuring effective learning for the first time, and toward restoring the child's educational morale and confidence in his ability to learn. Later possible consequences are partial restoration of both intrinsic and extrinsic motivation for academic achievement, diminution of anti-intellectualism, and decreased alienation from the school to the point where his studies make sense and he sees some purpose in learning. In my opinion, of all the available teaching strategies, programmed instruction, minus the teaching-machine format, has the greatest potentialities for meeting the aforementioned three criteria of an effective and appropriate approach to the teaching of culturally deprived pupils.

Readiness

A curriculum that takes the readiness of the culturally deprived child into account always takes as its starting point his existing knowledge and sophistication in the various subject-matter areas and intellectual skills, no matter how far down the scale this happens to be. This policy demands rigid elimination of all subject matter that he cannot economically assimilate on the basis of his current level of cognitive sophistication. It presupposes emphasis on his acquisition of the basic intellectual skills before any attempt is made to teach him algebra, geometry, literature, and foreign languages. However, in many urban high schools and junior high schools today, pupils who cannot read at a third-grade level and who cannot speak or write grammatically or perform simple arithmetical computations are subjected to irregular French verbs, Shakespearean drama, and geometrical theorems. Nothing more educationally futile or better calculated to destroy educational morale could be imagined!

In the terms of readiness for a given level of school work, a child is no less ready because of a history of cultural deprivation, chronic academic failure, and exposure to an unsuitable curriculum than because of deficient intellectual endowment. Hence, realistic recognition of this fact is not undemocratic, reactionary, or evidence of social class bias, of intellectual snobbery, of a "soft," patronizing approach, or a belief in the inherent uneducability of lower-class children. Neither is it indicative of a desire to surrender to the culturally deprived child's current intellectual level, to perpetuate the status quo, or to institute a double, class-oriented standard of education. It is merely a necessary first step in preparing him to cope with more advanced subject matter, and hence in eventually reducing existing social class differentials in academic achievement. To set the same *initial* standards and exceptions for the academically retarded culturally deprived child as for the non-retarded middle- or lower-class child is automatically to insure the former's failure and to widen prevailing discrepancies between social class groups.

Consolidation

By insisting on consolidation or mastery of ongoing lessons before new material is introduced, we make sure of continued readiness and success in sequentially organized learning. Abundant experimental research has confirmed the proposition that prior learnings are not transferable to new learning tasks unless they are first overlearned.[1] Overlearning, in turn, requires an adequate number of adequately spaced repetitions and reviews, sufficient intratask repetitiveness prior to intra- and intertask diversification,[2] and opportunity for differential practice of the more difficult components of a task. Frequent testing and provision of feedback, especially with test items demanding fine discrimination among alternatives varying in degrees of correctness, also enhance consolidation by confirming, clarifying, and correcting previous learnings. Lastly, in view of the fact that the culturally deprived child tends to learn more slowly than his nondeprived peers, self-pacing helps to facilitate consolidation.

Structured, Sequential Materials

The principal advantage of programmed instruction, apart from the fact that it furthers consolidation, is its careful sequential arrangement and gradation of difficulty which insures that each attained increment in learning serves as an appropriate foundation and anchoring post for the learning and retention of subsequent items in the ordered sequence.[3] Adequate programming of materials also presupposes maximum attention to such matters as lucidity, organization, and the explanatory and integrative power of substantive content. It is helpful, for example, if sequential materials are so organized that they become progressively more differentiated in terms of generality and inclusiveness, and if similarities and differences between the current learning task and previous learnings are explicitly delineated.[4] Both of these aims can be accomplished by using an advance organizer or brief introductory passage before each new unit of material, which both makes available relevant explanatory principles at a high level of abstraction and increases discriminability. Programmed instruction can also be especially adapted to meet the greater needs of culturally deprived pupils for concrete-empirical props in learning relational propositions.

Although programmed instruction in general is particularly well suited to the needs of the culturally deprived child, I cannot recommend the small-frame format characteristic of teaching-machine programs and most programmed textbooks. In terms of both the logical requirements of meaningful learning and the actual size of the task that can be conveniently accommodated by the learner, the frame length typically used by teaching machines is artificially and unnecessarily abbreviated. It tends to fragment the ideas presented in the program so that their interrelationships are obscured and their logical structure is destroyed.[5] Hence, it is relatively easy for less able students to master each granulated step of a given program without understanding the logical relationships and development of the concepts presented.[6] In my opinion, therefore, the traditional textbook format or oral didactic exposition that follows the programming principles outlined above, supplemented by frequent self-scoring and feedback-giving tests, is far superior to the teaching-machine approach for the actual presentation of subject-matter content.[7]

MOTIVATIONAL CONSIDERATIONS

Thus far I have considered various environmental factors that induce retardation in the culturally deprived child's intellectual growth, as well as different cognitive techniques of counteracting and reversing such retardation. These factors and techniques, however, do not operate in a motivational vacuum. Although it is possible separately to consider cognitive and motivational aspects of learning for purposes of theoretical analysis, they are nonetheless inseparably intertwined in any real-life learning situation. For example, school failure and loss of confidence resulting from an inappropriate curriculum further depress the culturally deprived pupil's motivation to learn and thereby increase his existing learning and intellectual deficit. Similarly, although a number of practice and task variables are potentially important for effective learning in a programmed instruction context, appropriate manipulation of these variables can, in the final analysis, only insure successful long-term learning of subject matter provided that the individual is adequately motivated.

Doing without being interested in what one is doing results in relatively little permanent learning, since it is reasonable to suppose that only those materials can be meaningfully incorporated on a long-term basis into an individual's structure of knowledge that are relevant to areas of concern in his psychological field. Learners who have little need to know and understand quite naturally expend little learning effort; manifest an insufficiently meaningful learning set; fail to develop precise meanings, to reconcile new ideas with existing concepts, and to formulate new propositions in their own words; and do not devote enough time and energy to practice and review. Material is therefore never sufficiently consolidated to form an adequate foundation for sequential learning.

The problem of reversibility exists in regard to the motivational as well as in regard to the cognitive status of the culturally deprived pupil, inasmuch as his environment typically stunts not only his intellectual development, but also the development of appropriate motivations for academic achievement. Motivations for learning, like cognitive abilities, are only potential rather than inherent or endogenous capacities in human beings; their actual development is invariably dependent upon adequate environmental stimulation. Cognitive drive or intrinsic motivation to learn, for example, is probably derived in a very general sense from curiosity tendencies and from related predispositions to explore, manipulate, and cope

with the environment; but these tendencies and predispositions are only actualized as a result of successful exercise and the anticipation of future satisfying consequences from further exercise and as a result of internalization of the values of those significant persons in the family and subcultural community with whom the child identifies.

Intrinsic Motivation

The development of cognitive drive or of intrinsic motivation for learning, that is, the acquisition of knowledge as an end in itself or for its own sake, is, in my opinion, the most promising motivational strategy which we can adopt in relation to the culturally deprived child. It is true, of course, in view of the anti-intellectualism and pragmatic attitude toward education that is characteristic of lower-class ideology,[8] that a superficially better case can be made for the alternative strategy of appealing to the incentives to job acquisition, retention, and advancement that now apply so saliently to continuing education because of the rapid rate of technological change. Actually, however, intrinsic motivation for learning is more potent, relevant, durable, and easier to arouse than its extrinsic counterpart. Meaningful school learning, in contrast to most kinds of laboratory learning, requires relatively little effort or extrinsic incentive, and, when successful, furnishes its own reward. In most instances of school learning, cognitive drive is also the only immediately relevant motivation, since the greater part of school learning cannot be rationalized as necessary for meeting the demands of daily living. Furthermore, it does not lose its relevance or potency in later adult life when utilitarian and career advancement considerations are no longer applicable. Lastly, as we know from the high dropout rate among culturally deprived high-school youth, appeals to extrinsic motivation are not very effective. Among other reasons, the latter situation reflects a limited time perspective focused primarily on the present; a character structure that is oriented more to immediate than delayed gratification of needs; the lack of strong internalized needs for and anxiety about high academic and vocational achievement, as part of the prevailing family, peer group, and community ideology; [9] and the seeming unreality and impossibility of attaining the rewards of prolonged striving and self-denial in view of current living conditions and family circumstances, previous lack of school success, and the discriminatory attitudes of middle-class society.[10]

If we wish to develop the cognitive drive so that it remains viable during the school years and in adult life, it is necessary to move still further away from the educational doctrine of gearing the curriculum to the spontaneously expressed interests, current concerns, and life-adjustment problems of pupils. Although it is undoubtedly unrealistic and even undesirable in our culture to eschew entirely the utilitarian, ego-enhancement, and anxiety-reduction motivations for learning, we must place increasingly greater emphasis upon the value of knowing and understanding as goals in their own right, quite apart from any practical benefits they may confer. Instead of denigrating subject-matter knowledge, we must discover more efficient methods of fostering the long-term acquisition or meaningful and usable bodies of knowledge, and of developing appropriate intrinsic motivations for such learning.

It must be conceded at the outset that culturally deprived children typically manifest little intrinsic motivation to learn. They come from family and cultural environments in which the veneration of learning for its own sake is not a conspicuous value, and in which there is little or no tradition of scholarship. Moreover, they have not been notably successful in their previous learning efforts in school. Nevertheless we need not necessarily despair of motivating them to learn for intrinsic reasons. Psychologists have been emphasizing the motivation-learning and the interest-activity sequences of cause and effect for so long that they tend to overlook their reciprocal aspects. Since motivation is not an indispensable condition for short-term and limited-quantity learning, it is not necessary to postpone learning activities until appropriate interests and motivations have been developed. Frequently the best way of motivating an unmotivated pupil is to ignore his motivational state for the time being and concentrate on teaching him as effectively as possible. Much to his surprise and to his teacher's, he will learn despite his lack of motivation; and from the satisfaction of learning he will characteristically develop the motivation to learn more.

Paradoxically, therefore, we may discover that the most effective method of developing intrinsic motivation to learn is to focus on the cognitive rather than on the motivational aspects of learning, and to rely on the motivation that is developed retroactively from successful educational achievement. This is particularly true when a teacher is able to generate contagious excitement and enthusiasm about the subject he teaches, and when he is the kind of person with whom culturally deprived children can identify. Recruiting more men teachers and dramatizing the lives and exploits of cultural, intellectual, and scientific heroes can also enhance the process of identification. At the same time, of course, we can attempt to combat the anti-intellectualism and lack of cultural tradition in the home through programs of adult education and cultural enrichment.

Extrinsic Motivation

The emphasis I have placed on intrinsic motivation for learning should not be interpreted to mean that I deny the importance of developing extrinsic motivations. The need for ego enhancement, status, and prestige through achievement, the internalization of long-term vocational aspirations, and the development of such implementing traits as responsibility, initiative, self-denial, frustration tolerance, impulse control, and the ability to postpone immediate hedonistic gratification are, after all, traditional hallmarks of personality maturation in our culture; and educational aspirations and achievement are both necessary prerequisites for, and way-station prototypes of, their vocational counterparts. Hence, in addition to encouraging intrinsic motivation for learning, it is also necessary to foster ego-enhancement and career-advancement motivations for academic achievement.

As previously pointed out, however, the current situation with respect to developing adequate motivations for higher academic and vocational achievement among culturally deprived children is not very encouraging. But just as in the case of cognitive drive, much extrinsic motivation for academic success can be generated retroactively from the experience of current success in schoolwork. Intensive counseling can also compensate greatly for the absence of appropriate home, com-munity, and peer-group support and expectations for the development of long-term vocational ambitions. In a sense counselors must be prepared to act *in loco parentis* in this situation. By identifying with a mature, stable, striving, and successful male adult figure, culturally deprived boys can be encouraged to internalize long-term and realistic aspirations, as well as to develop the mature personality traits necessary for their implementation. Hence, as a result of achieving current ego enhancement in the school setting, obtaining positive encouragement and practical guidance in the counseling relationship, and experiencing less rejection and discrimination at the hands of school personnel, higher vocational aspirations appear to lie more realistically within their grasp. Further encouragement to strive for more ambitious academic and vocational goals can be provided by making available abundant scholarship aid to universities, to community colleges, and to technical institutes; by eliminating the color, ethnic, and class bar in housing, education, and employment; by acquainting culturally deprived youth with examples of successful professional persons originating from their own racial, ethnic, and class backgrounds; and by involving parents sympathetically in the newly fostered ambitions of their children. The success of the Higher Horizons project indicates that an energetic program organized along the lines outlined above can do much to reverse the effects of cultural deprivation on the development of extrinsic motivations for academic and vocational achievement.

References

1. See R. W. Bruce, "Conditions of Transfer of Training," *Journal of Experimental Psychology*, XVI (1933), 343–61; C. P. Duncan, "Transfer in Motor Learning as a Function of Degree of First-task Learning and Inter-task Similarity," *Journal*

of Experimental Psychology, **XLV** (1953), 1–11; and his "Transfer after Training with Single versus Multiple Tasks," *Journal of Experimental Psychology,* **LV** (1958), 63–72; L. Morrisett and C. I. Hovland, "A Comparison of Three Varieties of Training in Human Problem Solving," *Journal of Experimental Psychology,* **LV** (1958), 52–55; and J. M. Sassenrath, "Learning without Awareness and Transfer of Learning Sets," *Journal of Educational Psychology,* **L** (1959), 202–12.

2. See Duncan, "Transfer after Training with Single versus Multiple Tasks," *op. cit.;* Morrisett and Hovland, *op. cit.;* and Sassenrath, *op. cit.*

3. D. P. Ausubel and D. Fitzgerald, "Organizer, General Background, and Antecedent Learning Variables in Sequential Verbal Learning," *Journal of Educational Psychology,* **LIII** (1962), 243–49.

4. D. P. Ausubel, "The Use of Advance Organizers in the Learning and Retention of Meaningful Verbal Learning," *Journal of Educational Psychology,* **LI** (1960), 267–72; D. P. Ausubel and D. Fitzgerald, "The Role of Discriminability in Meaningful Verbal Learning and Retention," *Journal of Educational Psychology,* **LII** (1961), 266–74, and their "Organizer, General Background, and Antecedent Learning Variables in Sequential Verbal Learning," *op. cit.*

5. S. L. Pressey, "Basic Unresolved Teaching-Machine Problems," *Theory into Practice,* **I** (1962), 30–37.

6. D. G. Beane, "A Comparison of Linear and Branching Techniques of Programed Instruction in Plane Geometry" ("Technical Report," No. 1, Urbana: Training Research Laboratory, University of Illinois, July 1962).

7. Pressey, *op. cit.*

8. F. Riessman, *The Culturally Deprived Child* (New York: Harper & Bros., 1962).

9. A. Davis, "Child Training and Social Class," *Child Behavior and Development,* eds. R. G. Barker, J. S. Kounin, and H. F. Wright (New York: McGraw-Hill Book Co., 1963), pp. 607–20.

10. *Ibid.*

32. Educational Stimulation of Racially Disadvantaged Children

KENNETH B. CLARK

Within the past ten years, there has been increasing concern with the problem of providing the maximum educational stimulation for children from socially and racially disadvantaged groups. Probably the most dramatic single stimulus which aroused widespread discussion of this problem, as related to the education of Negroes, was the May 17, 1954, decision of the United States Supreme Court which ruled that state laws requiring or permitting racially segregated schools violated the equal protection clause of the Fourteenth Amendment of the United States Constitution. The decision discussed in rather simple direct language the general social significance of public education in American Democracy. It stated: *

"Today, education is perhaps the most important function of state and local governments. Compulsory school attendance laws and the great expenditures for education both demonstrate

* Brown versus Board of Education, 347 U. S. 483 (1954).

Reprinted with permission from A. Harry Passow, Ed., *Education in Depressed Areas* (New York: Teachers College Press, 1963). © 1963 by Teachers College, Columbia University.
294

our recognition of the importance of education to our democratic society. It is required in the performance of our most basic public responsibilities, even service in the armed forces. It is the very foundation of good citizenship. Today it is a principal instrument in awakening the child to cultural values, in preparing him for later professional training, and in helping him to adjust normally to his environment. In these days, it is doubtful that any child may reasonably be expected to succeed in life if he is denied the opportunity of an education. Such an opportunity, where the state has undertaken to provide it, is a right which must be made available to all on equal terms."

Widespread public discussion of problems of education for any group of children in America necessarily involves discussions of general problems of education affecting all children. Once the emotional reaction to the Supreme Court's desegregation decisions and the various patterns of resistance to the demanded changes have decreased, it will be seen that an effective transition from segregated to nonsegregated schools tends to raise the general level of democratic public education for all children. The interim reports which have been published by the Superintendent of schools of Washington, D. C., indicates that since the desegregation of these schools, there has been a measurable improvement in the average academic achievement level of both Negro and white children.[6,7]

More recently—since the launching of the first Sputnik—some observers have expressed concern about the comparative effectiveness of the American and Soviet systems of public education. These discussions generally resulted in demands for reexamination of standards, methods, curriculum, effectiveness of teaching, and an insistence that the general level of achievement of the students in American schools be raised. It would be expected that discussions of the quality of education in terms of problems of international competition and demands for military superiority would result in the tendency to equate general educational excellence with the specifics of high achievement in mathematics, science, and technology.

An article published in 1956 in the College Board Review [1] presented evidence which pointed to the grave shortage in scientific, technical, and other college trained individuals in America. This evidence indicated that during that year the Soviet Union would graduate 138,000 students in various scientific fields while the United States, at best, would graduate only 78,000 similarly trained students. It was also clear that while the number of individuals receiving Ph.D. degrees in all fields had remained constant during the preceding five years in the United States, it had increased dramatically in the Soviet Union. At that time, that nation awarded nearly twice as many Ph.D. degrees annually as were awarded in the United States. This evidence which suggested at least a quantitative in-

feriority of American education in stimulating and training individuals of superior intellect was being discussed before the Russians launched their first Sputnik. In the six years since the publication of that article, there has been no evidence to suggest that there has been any significant changes in the trends observed at that time. There is still no evidence that America has developed the procedures and facilities necessary to increase the number of trained intellects or that the effectiveness of Russian education has declined.*

In spite of this seeming difference in educational effectiveness, it is questionable whether competition with the Russians and the factor of national prestige are the significant reasons for being concerned with obtaining for each child in America the most effective education without regard to such educationally irrelevant barriers as race, nationality, religion, or low social and economic background. The goals of assuring equality of educational opportunity and providing the most effective education for every child are inherent imperatives of American education in this latter half of the twentieth century.

Any society which is to remain viable and dynamic must raise the educational standards for all of its people and must exploit and use constructively high intellectual potential wherever it is to be found. The argument in support of this is no longer sentimental.

---

* There was a newspaper report to the effect that Premier Khrushchev was publicly dissatisfied with the overwhelming success of the Russian educational system which produced a disproportionate number of "intellectuals." It was reported that he was concerned that an overeducated population would develop a contempt for manual labor. He, therefore, suggested or demanded that henceforth the curriculum in Russian schools must include vocational education and manual training.

The dangers inherent in not developing an effective approach to the discovery, stimulation, and training of superior intellectual potential in all groups of American children seem to be greater than the dangers inherent in an inefficient and wasteful exploitation of our natural material resources. It is now axiomatic that trained human intelligence is the most valuable resource of a civilized nation. Like other natural resources, it must be discovered and transformed creatively into its most effective and usable form. At this period in world history, no nation can afford to waste any of its potential intelligence through indifference, inefficiency, ignorance or the anachronistic luxury of racial and social class prejudices. The economic, social, political, international, and, of course, primary, humanitarian reasons for this are becoming increasingly clear.

Another factor which must be taken into account in understanding these demands for more effective use of the intellectual potentials in previously disadvantaged groups is to be found in the pressure and demands which are coming from these groups themselves. One of the significant changes which characterizes the modern world is the fact that increasing automation in business and industry is relentlessly leading to an increase in leisure for the masses of working people. With this increasing automation and leisure, there will be a smaller proportion of the population required for unskilled or manual work. The educational implications of this social and economic change may be further complicated by the probably irreversible trend toward higher and higher wages and higher and higher living standards for the masses of people who earn their living through wages. If this trend continues, one may expect that there will be a raising of the social-class aspirations of these previously working-class groups and that this will eventually result in an increasing desire for higher education for their children.

Education has been one of the most effective means for social mobility in the American society. This problem in the future may be different from the similar problem in the past only in that it will involve different and larger groups of previously disadvantaged individuals. The rising pressure for higher education which can be expected to come from the presently disadvantaged groups in our society must be met by appropriate and effective adjustments on the part of our educational institutions. If these pressures are not met effectively, then one could anticipate major consequences of frustration among the members of these groups. Some of the social manifestations of these personal frustrations which could be anticipated are: an increase in delinquency and criminality; intensification of bigotry, provincialism, intergroup tensions and hostility; increase in the chances of successful manipulation of the primitive passions of the masses by political cynics, fanatics, or demagogues; an increase in the incidence of emotional instability among those upwardly mobile groups whose aspirations are being blocked; and other symptoms of personal and social disorganization.

Creative educators can help to prevent these personal and social disturbances by making the necessary modifications in curriculum and methods and by providing the educational leadership, guidance, and stimulation which will make it possible for American society to strengthen and improve our system of democratic public education. When this is done, our schools will continue to function as the chief vehicles of upward class mobility and as a major source of social and economic vitality. If it is not done, our schools will contribute to social stagnation and more insidious forms of social-class cleavages and distinctions.

The most compelling argument for providing the maximum educational stimulation for all American children without regard to the social, economic, national, or racial backgrounds of their parents is the fact that the effective functioning of a dynamic democracy demands this. It is one of the cardinal assumptions of our American democracy that significant social changes may be brought about through education—through providing that type of intellectual training and information which will make it possible for the citizen to make the types of decisions which he must make in a democracy —rather than through tyranny or violence. The substance, rather than the verbalization, of democracy depends upon our ability to extend and deepen the insights of the people. Only an educated people can be expected to make the type of choices which assert their freedoms and reinforce their sense of social responsibility.

SOME RESEARCH PROBLEMS AND FINDINGS RELEVANT TO THE EDUCATION OF DEPRIVED CHILDREN

During the past year a number of books dealing directly or indirectly with the problem of the education of children in depressed urban areas have been published. Among the more significant of these books are James B. Conant's *Slums and Suburbs*,[4] Frank Riessman's *The Culturally Deprived Child*,[9] and Patricia Sexton's *Education and Income*.[10]

Dr. Sexton's analysis of the relationship between social and economic status and the quality of education provided for children in the public schools of a northern urban community is a model of objective social science and educational research. The data presented by her demonstrate conclusively that curricula, educational standards, quality of teaching, educational facilities and materials, and academic achievement of the children are directly related to the socioeconomic status of the majority of children attending a particular school. Her findings add another significant dimension to the well-known and often repeated fact that academic achievement varies directly with socioeconomic status. Usually this fact is interpreted as reflecting some type of selective factor wherein individuals of high intelligence attain high socioeconomic status and produce more intelligent children and that higher status families provide their children with more stimulation for academic achievement. The data presented by Dr. Sexton, however, make clear, at least to this observer, the crucial role of the school in determining the level of academic achievement of the children. The traditional interpretation would continue to argue that the standards and quality of the school reflect the limitations of the home and the immediate community from which the child comes and that the school must gear its level to these limitations. This interpretation has so far not been verified through objective research although it is widely accepted as if it were.

Attempts to determine the specific role of a particular school on the average level of academic performance of the children in that school must obtain data on the general attitudes of teachers in that school towards their children—particularly if there is a marked class discrepancy between teachers and students; the expectations of these teachers and the effect of these expectations on the actual performance of their children; and the children's perspective of themselves, their teachers, and their school. It is now imperative that social scientists study with rigorous objectivity and precision the complex and interrelated problems which seem relevant to an understanding of how children from depressed backgrounds can be motivated for maximum academic achievement.

At present, the work of Allison Davis and his colleagues, which demonstrates the educationally depressing effects of the gap between working-class children and middle-class teachers, is an important starting point for future more detailed research. It is important to know, for example, not only the particular attitudinal patterns which the teacher communicates to these children but also the particular ways in which she communicates her attitudes and how these block or facilitate the academic motivation of lower-class children. The empirical data on these specific problems are sparse, and one is required to speculate on the nature of the manner in which these blockages operate. Probably a core factor in the complex inhibiting dynamics involved in the interplay between middle-class and higher-status teachers and working-class and lower-status children is the pervasive and archaic belief that children from culturally deprived backgrounds are by virtue of their deprivation of lower status position inherently uneducable.

Professor Goodwin Watson, in his introduction to Frank Riessman's book,[9] has defined this problem and suggested a general solution as follows:

"In recent decades a spate of anthropological, sociological, and social-psychological studies, many of them mentioned by Professor Riessman, has revealed the appalling gap between our pretensions and our practices. We do not give the same kind of food, clothing, housing, medical care, recreation, or justice to the deprived children that we give to those in comfortably-well-off homes. We don't like to think of class distinctions in American life, so we tend to shy away from these unacceptable facts. Opportunities are far from equal.

"The American public school is a curious hybrid: it is managed by a school board drawn largely from upper-class circles; it is taught by teachers who come largely from middle-class backgrounds; and it is attended mainly by children from working-class homes. These three groups do not talk the same language. They differ in their manners, power, and hierarchies of values. . . .

"Under-cultured children have much to learn from education, but educators could well take some lessons from some of these youngsters. Their language may not be grammatical, but it is often more vivid and expressive than is the turgid prose of textbooks. These children face some of the "facts of life" more realistically than many of their teachers do. Even their pugnacity might be worth attention by some long-suffering, overworked, underpaid teachers. When it comes to making friends and standing by their pals, some children from underprivileged neighborhoods far outshine their priggish teachers.

"The starting point is respect. Nothing else that we have to give will help very much if it is offered with a resentful, contemptuous, or patronizing attitude. We don't understand these neighborhoods, these homes, these children, because we haven't respected them enough to think them worthy of study and attention. Professor Riessman's book is likely to be the pioneer in a series of investigations that will reveal to America that we have neglected a major source of manpower and of creative talent. The stone which the builders rejected may even become the head of the corner."

One may assume that if a child is not treated with the respect which is due him as a human being, and if those who are charged with the responsibility of teaching him believe that he cannot learn, then his motivation and ability to learn may become impaired. If a teacher believes that a child is incapable of being educated, it is likely that this belief will in some way be communicated to the child in one or more of the many forms of contacts inherent in the teacher-pupil relationship.

Because of the importance of the role of teachers in the developing self-image, academic aspirations, and achievements of their students, it was thought desirable to conduct a preliminary study of the attitudes of teachers in ten public schools located in depressed areas of a large northern city. The children in these schools came generally from homes and communities which were so lacking in educational stimulation and other determinants of self-respect that they seemed even more dependent upon their teachers for self-esteem, encouragement, and stimulation. These children, like most deprived human beings, were hypersensitive and desperate in their desire for acceptance.

The findings of this preliminary study revealed that while there were some outstanding exceptions—individual principals and teachers who respected the human dignity and potentialities of their students—the overwhelming majority of these teachers and their supervisors rejected these children and looked upon them as inherently inferior.

For the most, the teachers indicated that they considered these children to be incapable of profiting from a normal curriculum. The children were seen as intellectually inferior and therefore not capable of learning. The qualitative flavor of this complex pattern of negative attitudes can best be communicated by the verbatim reports written by our observers:

"As soon as I entered the classroom, Mrs. X told me in front of the class, that the parents of these children are not professionals and therefore they do not have much background or interest in going ahead to college. . . . She discussed each child openly in front of the entire class and myself. . . . She spoke about the children in a belittling manner. She tried to give each child encouragement, but her over-all attitude was negative in that she did not think much of the abilities of her students. She told me in private that 'heredity is what really counts,' and since they didn't have a high culture in Africa and have not as yet built one in New York, they are intellectually inferior from birth."

Another teacher was described as follows:

"The teacher was a lady of about 50 who had no understanding of these children. She kept pointing to them when talking about them so that even I was slightly embarrassed. She kept repeating "You see what I mean?," which I didn't at all. . . . She took it for granted that these children were stupid and that there was little that she could do with them."

A third description illustrates some of the subtleties of the problem:

"Mr. G. is a rather tense and nervous man. He continually played with his finger or with a pencil or tapped his fingers on the desk. What disturbed him most was the cultural deprivation that most of the students in his school suffered from. He said that often the teacher will refer to everyday facts which the children will be completely ignorant of. He says that it is most difficult if not impossible to teach them."

These and other examples clearly suggest that among many of the teachers who are required to teach children from culturally deprived backgrounds there exists a pervasive negative attitude toward these children. These teachers say repeatedly, and appear to believe, that it is not possible to teach these children. They offer, in support of their conclusion, the belief that these children cannot learn because of "poor heredity," "poor home background," "cultural deprivation," and "low I.Q."

THE PROBLEM OF THE IQ

Probably as disturbing as these examples of rejection of these children on the part of those who are required to teach them, are the many examples of well-intentioned teachers who point to the low intelligence- and achievement-test scores of these children as the basis for their belief that these children cannot be educated. These teachers generally do not base their judgment on conscious racial bias or rejection of these children as human beings or necessarily on their "poor heredity." They point to the realities of a poor environment, cultural deprivation, and lack of educational stimulation in the home as the determinants of low academic achievement of these children. They maintain that these children should not be expected to function up to the academic level of other children because the test

scores clearly indicate that they cannot. Further, they state that to pressure these children for an academic achievement that they are incapable of reaching only creates frustrations and anxieties which will make even more difficult the possibility of adequate functioning on their own level. These individuals, therefore, argue that a special curriculum and a special form of education should be devised for these children from culturally deprived backgrounds who have consistently low IQs and achievement-test scores.

A disturbing aspect of this type of argument is that it does come under the guise of humanitarianism, psychology, and modern educational theory. It becomes necessary, therefore, to look with thorough objectivity at the basis of this argument; namely, the validity of test scores as an index of the intellectual potential of children from culturally deprived backgrounds. Do these test scores indicate some immutable level of intelligence, or do they reflect primarily the obvious cultural and educational deprivations and discriminations suffered by these children?

Modern psychology findings and interpretations would seem to leave no further room for argument that test scores must be interpreted in the light of the general social and cultural milieu of a child and the specific educational opportunities to which he has been exposed. It is generally known that children from deprived educational backgrounds will score lower on available standardized tests. The pioneer work of Otto Klineberg in the 1930's clearly established the fact that intelligence test score will increase on the average as children are moved from a deprived, inferior educational situation to a more positive and stimulating one.[8]

We now know that children who are

not stimulated at home, or in the community, or in school will have low scores. Their scores and, what is even more important, their day-to-day academic performance can be improved if they are provided with adequate stimulation in one or more of these areas. When a child from a deprived background is treated as if he is uneducable because he has a low test score, he becomes uneducable and the low test score is thereby reinforced. If a child scores low on an intelligence test because he cannot read and then is not taught to read because he has a low score, then such a child is being imprisoned in an iron circle and becomes the victim of an educational self-fulfilling prophecy.

Another aspect of the problem of the meaning of the IQ, which is not generally discussed and which seems to have been lost sight of by educators and the general public, is the simple fact that the IQ is merely a score that is offered as an index of a given individual's rate of learning compared with the learning rate of others with whom he can be reasonably compared. This interpretation of the IQ is consistent with the fact that a child with a lower IQ can be expected to take longer to learn that which a child with a higher IQ will learn more rapidly. The IQ itself—at least in the normal ranges and above—does not necessarily determine how much a child will learn or for that matter even the ceiling of what he can learn. Rather it reflects the rate of his learning or the amount of effort which will be required for him to learn. In other words, it is quite conceivable that children with lower IQs, even those low IQs which more nearly reflect inherent intellectual limitations, can and do learn substantively what other children can learn. But it will take a longer time, will require more care and skill on the part of the teachers and probably more encouragement and acceptance of the child.

IQ, SNOBBERY, AND HUMILIATION

Unfortunately, an objective discussion of the problem of the meaning of the IQ is made even more difficult by the fact that this problem has been contaminated by noneducational considerations such as social-class status factors. This point can be illustrated by an examination of the arguments in favor of homogeneous groupings. The most persistent arguments for grouping children in homogeneous classes according to IQs are largely assertions of the convenience of such groupings for overworked teachers. The proponents of the procedure of segregating children according to intelligence for educational purposes seem to base their argument on some assumptions of special privilege, special status, special educational advantages and conspicuous recognition which are to be given to an intellectual elite. It is implied and sometimes stated that these conditions will facilitate the maximum use of the already high intelligence of the gifted children and will reduce the frustrations of those children who are not gifted. It is further suggested that if the gifted child is not given special treatment in special classes, he will somehow not fulfill his intellectual potentials—"he will be brought down to the level of the average or the dull child." So far there seems to be little empirical evidence in support of these assertions in spite of their wide acceptance by the public and by many educators.

Those who argue against this form of educational intellectual segregation must nonetheless eventually demonstrate by empirical research that it is not the most effective educational procedure. Are children who are segregated according to IQ in the classrooms of our schools being educated in a socially realistic and democratic atmosphere? The world consists of individuals of varying levels of intellectual potential and power. Those individuals of high intelligence must be prepared to function effectively with individuals of average or below average intelligence. One important function of the schools is to train children in a socially responsible use of human intelligence. A manifestation of this social responsibility would be the ability of children of high intelligence to use their superior intelligence creatively in working with and helping children of lower intelligence to function more effectively. Children of lower intelligence could be stimulated and encouraged, in a realistic school atmosphere, by the accomplishments of other children. This would be true only if the over-all school atmosphere is one consistent with the self-respect of all children. Children who are stigmatized by being replaced in classes designated as "slow" or "dull" or for "children of retarded mental ability" cannot be expected to be stimulated and motivated to improve their academic performance. Such children understandably will become burdened with resentment and humiliation and will seek to escape the humiliating school situation as quickly as possible.

Probably the chief argument against homogeneous groupings is the fact that children who are so segregated lose their individuality in the educational situation. It would seem that the development of a creative individuality would be among the high-priority goals of education. Homogeneous groupings tend to require that children be seen in terms of group characteristics rather than in terms of their own individual characteristics. This would seem to be true equally for the bright children as it is for average or dull children. Furthermore, it is questionable whether it is possible to establish a homogeneous group of children on any grounds other than the arbitrary selection of some single aspect of the total complexity that is the human being.

It may be argued on the basis of evidence that even the selection of children in terms of similarity in IQ is arbitrary in that the same range of IQs may mask significant differences in intellectral abilities, patterns, interests, and propensities among children who seem similar in level of general intelligence. Any oversimplification of this fact, concretized into an educational procedure, may not be worth the human and social cost.

It is conceivable that the detrimental effects of segregation based upon intellect is similar to the known detrimental effects of schools segregated on the basis of class, nationality, or race.[2] This similarity, if it is found to exist, may reflect the fact that, in general, the average intellectual level of groups of children is related to the social and racial status of their parents. The educational level and achievement of lower-status children are depressed in segregated lower-status schools for those reasons already stated, plus the fact that the morale of their teachers tends to be depressed when they are identified with low-prestige schools. Furthermore, some of these teachers may accept assignments in in these schools because they may be aware of the fact that the staff in these schools is generally not held to the same high professional standards which prevail in schools where it is believed that the children can learn. Teachers in more privileged schools are probably held to more strict standards of professional evaluation and supervision.

Whatever the determining factors responsible for the low educational achievement of children from lower status groups, the fact remains that up to the present, the overwhelming majority of these children attend schools that do not have a systematic educational program designed to provide the extra stimulation and encouragement which they need if they are to develop their intellectual potential. Some school officials may question whether it is the proper function of the schools to attempt to compensate for the cultural deprivations which burden these children in their homes and in the larger community. As long as this is not done by the schools or some other appropriate social institutions, the motivation and academic achievement of these deprived children will remain depressed, inferior, and socially wasteful. What is more, the schools will have failed to provide them with an effective education and thereby failed to meet a pressing contemporary need.

MR. CONANT AND THE EDUCATION OF CULTRALLY DISADVANTAGED CHILDREN

Probably the most widely discussed, if not uncritically accepted, of the recent books dealing with the problem of the education of deprived and privileged children in American cities is James B. Conant's *Slums and Suburbs*.[4] In spite of the fact that Mr. Conant is by training, background, and experience a chemist, college president, and statesman—and not a professional educator or social scientist—he has assumed with the aid of the Carnegie Corporation of New York, the role of educational expert and spokesman to the nation. His book was reviewed extensively—and for the most part praised —by the important education editors of newspapers throughout the nation. In discussing the complexity of educational problems found in the schools in "slum neighborhoods," Mr. Conant coined the phrase "social Dynamite" which has become part of the jargon of these discussions.

Before one engages in a critical analysis of Mr. Conant's assumptions and recommendations for the improvement of the education of deprived and privileged children, it should be stated that this book presents vividly some facts which help to clarify some of the issues related to the basic problem of the inferiority of educational opportunities provided for children of the lower socioeconomic classes in the public schools of the ten largest cities in our nation. For example, the book states that half of the children in deprived neighborhoods drop out of school in grades 9, 10, and 11; that the per pupil expenditure in deprived schools is less than half the per pupil expenditure in a privileged school; and that there are seventy professionals per thousand pupils in privileged schools, and forty or fewer professionals per thousand pupils in deprived schools. Mr. Conant appeals to the conscience of the American public and asserts that this consistent discrepancy "jolts one's notions of the meaning of equality of opportunity."

Critical reading and analysis of this book, however, reveal that Mr. Conant's prescription for this educational disease will not cure the patient, but, on the contrary, will intensify the illness. The implicit assumptions and explicit suggestions, if accepted by American education, would concretize the very discrepancies which Mr. Conant calls "social dynamite" and would lead, if not to an educational explosion to educational dry rot and social stagnation.

The basic assumptions of this book are appalling, anachronistic, and reflect the social science naivete of its author. The unmodified theme that runs throughout the book is that there are two types of human beings—those who can be educated and those who cannot be educated. Those who can be educated live in suburbs and those who cannot be educated live in slums. And for the most part, those who live in slums are Negroes and those who live in suburbs are white. Children who live in the slums should be provided with practical, vocational—job oriented —education and children in the suburbs should be provided with that level of academic education which is appropriate to their level of intelligence.

Mr. Conant's own words are quite explicit: "The lesson is that to a considerable degree what a school should do and can do is determined by the status and ambitions of the families being served." What changes the status and ambitions of the families?

"One needs only to visit such a school (slum school) to be convinced that the nature of the community largely determines what goes on in the school. . . . The community and the school are inseparable."

Why then have schools?

"Foreign languages in Grade 7 or algebra in Grade 8 (recommendations in my Junior High School report) have little place in a school in which half the pupils in that grade read at the fourth grade level or below."

Why are these children reading at the fourth grade level or below?

Mr. Conant is most explicit in his defense of de facto segregated schools and in his support of the outmoded and impossible doctrine of "separate but equal" education for Negroes, and his aversion to the open enrollment program.

"In some cities, political leaders have attempted to put pressure on the school authorities to have Negro children attend essentially white schools. In my judgment the cities in which

the authorities have yielded to this pressure are on the wrong track. Those which have not done so, like Chicago, are more likely to make progress in improving Negro education. It is my belief that satisfactory education can be provided in an all-Negro school through the expenditure of more money for needed staff and facilities."

It would seem as if this opinion is contradicted by the very facts which Mr. Conant presents in his book and describes as "social dynamite." Mr. Conant's lack of social science training and insights probably accounts for his belief that mere money will make a "Negro" school equal—if indeed, he does mean "equal" when he uses the word "satisfactory" in describing education in an all-Negro school. Mr. Conant obviously does not understand the role of such psychological subtleties as the depressed morale, lowered aspirations, inadequate standards of performance which seem inherent in a stigmatized, rejected, segregated situation.

The following gratuitous advice must therefore be rejected:

". . . I think it would be far better for these who are agitating for the deliberate mixing of children to accept de facto segregated schools as a consequence of a present housing situation and to work for the improvement of slum schools whether Negro or white."

It seems incredible that a distinguished American statesman could continue to talk about American schools in terms of the designations "Negro" and "white" as if such racial designations were compatible with the American educational imperatives in this latter part of the twentieth century. This fact merely highlights a general deficiency of this book; namely, that it discusses problems of contemporary education in terms of the static assumptions and procedures of the past rather than in terms of the dynamic imperatives of the future. This book and its recommendations might have been acceptable in the first two decades of the twentieth century. It cannot be taken seriously now when it advocates without adequate supporting evidence:

"An elementary syllabus varied according to socio-economic status of the children: ability groupings and tracks for students in grades 7 through 12; matching neighborhood needs and school services; and generally determining the nature of academic standards and expectations in terms of the 'kinds of schools one is considering.'"

Aside from the archaic educational snobbery which permeates this book —its matter-of-fact assertion of the idea that American education should gear itself to train more efficiently the "hewers of wood and the drawers of water" and provide effective academic education to an "intellectual elite" to be drawn from the socially and economically privileged groups—its author does not seem to understand the crucial role that an imaginative, creative education must play in the contemporary world. He does not understand that it is the function of contemporary American education to discover and implement techniques for uncovering every ounce of the intellectual potential in all our children without regard to their racial, national, or economic background. Creative human intelligence is an all-too-rare resource and must be trained and conserved wherever it is found. It should now be clear that it is not likely to be found in sufficient abundance in the privileged minority. The best of educational stimulation of this group will still produce an inadequate yield. It is now the obligation of our public schools to adopt those procedures, whether open enrollment, Higher Horizon, or other forms of special stimulation and techniques for raising the aspiration of previously deprived children which are necessary to increase the yield of trained intelligence from children whose potential would be lost to a society desperately in need of their future contributions.

Equally important is the fact that Mr. Conant seems unaware of the fact that segregated schools for the privileged suburban white child provide nonadaptive and unrealistic education. He does not seem to grasp that:

"Segregated education is inferior and nonadaptive for whites as well as Negroes. Put simply, no child can receive a democratic education in a nondemocratic school. A white youngster in a homogeneous, isolated, "hot-house" type of school situation is not being prepared for the realities of the contemporary and future world. Such a child may have brilliant college entrance scores, be extraordinary in his mathematical ability, or read and speak a foreign language with skill and precision, but he is likely to be blocked in many circumstances in his ability to use these intellectual abilities with the poise and effectiveness essential to personal and social creativity. A racially segregated school imposes upon white children the inevitable stultifying burdens of petty provincialism, irrational fears and hatreds of people who are different, and a distorted image of themselves. Psychologically, the racially segregated school at this period of American and world history is an anachronism which our nation cannot afford. This point must be made over and over again until it is understood by those who have the power to make the decisions which control our destiny.[3]

CONCLUSION

What recommendations for curriculum and materials for culturally disadvantaged children can now be made on the basis of social psychological research, theory, and the imperatives of the contemporary world?

The available and most relevant research data on the effects of minority status—culturally disadvantaged, rejected, and stigmatized children—on personality development may be summarized as follows:

"As minority-group children learn the inferior status to which they are assigned and observe that they are usually segregated and isolated from the more privileged members of their society, they react with deep feelings of inferiority and with a sense of personal humiliation. Many of them become confused about their own personal worth. Like all other human beings, they require a sense of personal dignity and social support for positive self-esteem. Almost nowhere in the larger society, however, do they find their own dignity as human beings respected or protected. Under these conditions, minority-group children develop conflicts with regard to their feelings about themselves and about the values of the group with which they are identified. . . . These conflicts, confusions, and doubts give rise under certain circumstances to self-hatred and rejection of their own group . . .

"Minority-group children of all social and economic classes often react to their group conflicts by the adoption of a generally defeatist attitude and a lowering of personal ambition." [2]

Upon the basis of these findings it is clear that a fundamental task of the schools in stimulating academic achievement in disadvantaged children is to provide the conditions necessary for building in them positive images of themselves—building in these children a positive self-esteem to supplant the feelings of inferiority and sense of hopelessness which are supported by an all-too-pervasive pattern of social realities. A nonsegregated school situation seems basic (necessary if not a sufficient condition) to all other attempts to raise the self-esteem of these children. A child cannot be expected to respect himself if he perceives himself as rejected and set apart in a compound for those of inferior status or caste.

An important determinant of a reality-based, positive self-esteem for children is the opportunity to have successful experiences in meeting challenges. A minority-group child who is expected to fail will almost always fail. His failure will reinforce his sense of inferiority and the related resentments and hostility. A normal child who is expected to learn, who is taught, and who is required to learn will learn. His experiences of success will generally increase his self-respect, enhance his sense of his own worth. He might not need to engage in compensatory forms of antisocial behavior as attention-getting devices. Nor would he need to escape from the school situation which is a constant reminder of failure and personal inferiority. A single standard of academic expectations, a demanding syllabus, and skillful and understanding teaching are essential to the raising of the self-esteem of disadvantaged children, increasing their motivation for academic achievement and providing our society with the benefits of their intellectual potential.

Some attention should be given to the textbooks and materials which are used in our classrooms in order to be sure that they do not directly or indirectly add to the burdens of already psychologically overburdened disadvantaged minority-group children. Indeed it might be necessary to select or devise materials which would raise the self-esteem of these children at the same time that it broadens the perspectives and deepens the social and ethnical insights of more privileged children. Some students of this problem have been rather specific in their criticisms of available materials.

Frank Riessman [9] quotes Dr. Eleanor Leacock's observation:

"A critical look at basic readers from the viewpoint of their discordance with 'lower-class culture,' reveals at a second look a discordance also with what is real experience for most middle-class children. One might ask how typical are Dick and Jane, or more important, how meaningful are they and their neat white house in the suburbs to children whose world includes all the blood and thunder, as well as the sophisticated reportage, of television. In what sense do Dick and Jane even reflect middle-class ideal patterns in the contemporary world? That such textbook characters help form ideal patterns in the early years is true, but does this not only create a problem for children, when the norms for behavior Dick and Jane express are so far removed from reality? One can even play with the idea of cultural deprivation for middle-class children, since home and school join in building a protective barrier between them and so much of the modern world; and one can wonder what the implications of this protection are for their mental health. Certainly such readers do not arouse interest in reading, which develops in spite of, not because of, their content.

"It would be an exciting idea to have primers which deal more directly with people and events which arouse the emotions of sympathy, curiosity and

wonder in children, texts which recognize whimsy as important in the building of values, which accept the adventurous hero as a valid character for children to respond to, which deal with the 'child's world' as reaching from home and family to the moon. What contrast to the vapid amiability of Dick and Jane! And how important to have basic readers in which some children live in white houses in suburbs, but many more, equally important as human beings, live in tenements, or apartments, or on farms, in the west, the north, the south, so that all children can read about all others, and, as Americans, get to know their world as it is. Nor, it should be added, is the same purpose served by a mechanical translation of Dicks and Janes to other places and periods in upper-grade readers."

The complex problem of increasing the effectiveness of education for culturally disadvantaged children cannot be resolved effectively by fragmentary approaches. Rather the gravity of the problem requires the development of bold, imaginative, and comprehensive approaches. The Junior High School 43 Project, the forerunner of the Higher Horizons Program of the New York City Public Schools, is an example of the possible success of such a comprehensive approach to this problem. This project was designed to test whether it was possible to raise significantly the academic performance of disadvantaged children through the activities of the school itself in spite of the fact that the conditions of home and community deprivations remained constant.

An important aspect of the 43 Project was the fact that in its methodology it did not rely exclusively on test scores as the basis for selecting those students who were believed to have academic potential. Teachers' estimates, the judgment of guidance counselors, and any evidence of the capacity for superior intellectual interests or functioning were some of the criteria, in addition to test results, which were used in selecting those children who were to be involved in the special program of the project. Once these children were selected they were subjected to a special program of educational stimulation. The ingredients of this program were systematic guidance and counseling; clinical services when indicated; a cultural enrichment program which consisted of trips to the theater, museums, opera, college campuses; a parent-education program; and a systematic supplementary remedial program in reading, mathematics, and languages.

The results of this project as reported in the Third Annual Progress Report published by the Board of Education of the City of New York have justified the most optimistic expectations of those who planned and proposed this demonstration of the positive modifiability of human beings. These results may be summarized by the following quotation taken from this report:

"Although it is too early to assess completely the project academically, we have been heartened by some of the progress we have noted. In comparing the achievement of the pupils who entered the George Washington High School from Junior High School 43 in 1953 with that of the project classes that entered in 1957 and 1958, we find a tremendous difference. In the 1953 group, 5 out of 105 pupils (5%) passed all their academic subjects at the end of the first year; and 2 had averages of 80% or better. In the 1957 project group, 38 out of 148 pupils (25%) passed all their subjects at the end of the first year, and 18 had aver-

ages of 80% or better. In the 1958 project group, 43 out of 111 pupils (38%) passed all their subjects at the end of the first year, and 16 had averages of 80% or better.

"The evidence is conclusive that the scholastic accomplishment of the project students is far better than that of previous classes from Junior High School 43."

Those who are still concerned with the ubiquitous IQ, might be interested to note that, of the 105 children who were tested at the beginning of the project and three years later, 78 of them showed an increase in IQ. Forty of these students gained more than 10 points; 13 gained more than 20 points. One child gained as much as 40 points in his tested IQ.

While these measurable demonstrations of the success of this project are impressive, probably of even greater social significance are the positive qualitative and by-product results which were observed. For example, while the drop-out rate from high school for these children prior to the project was around 40 per cent; the drop-out rate for the project children was less than 20 per cent.

The principal of George Washington High School made the following observation:

"In the past, students from 43 were our worst behaved. More teacher and administrative time was spent on them than on any other group. Since we had the project group, this has changed. Not a single student in the project group has been reported to the Dean's office for discipline. Today, they are our best behaved."

The following quotation from the report may serve as summary evaluation of the profound positive effects of this approach to the special education of children from deprived backgrounds:

"Judging by the reactions of the students themselves and our observations of them from day to day, it is our belief that all of them, whether they go to college or end their formal education with graduation from high school, will have higher horizons and a greater sense of commitment and purpose in their lives. In our opinion, it is these expected outcomes that make this project so significant, and so far-reaching in its influence."

Probably the fundamental dynamics for the success of this project is the fact that the project itself raised the self-esteem of these children, increased the aspirations of their parents and bolstered the morale of their teachers. The project and its ingredients of special stimulation, encouragement, and remedial help indicated to these children that someone—the principal, the guidance counsellor, the teacher—believed that they could learn. Someone believed in them—believed in their educability and respected them as human beings. The cumulative effects of these changes in the psychological atmosphere and the changes in the self-image of these children were found in the higher academic achievements and the marked improvement in self-respect and general social behavior.

The special stimulation, the creative approach to the education of these deprived children, can be and should be provided for all children. These positive results can be duplicated in every school of this type. The Superintendent of Schools of the City of New York has extended some aspects of the 43 project to nearly forty other schools. This expanded program is now known as the Higher Horizons Program.

THE CHALLENGE OF THE FUTURE

There are aspects of the problem of raising the level of educational achievement among deprived children which cannot be solved by the public schools and teachers without the help and understanding of the total community and our teacher-training institutions. Certainly the community and its leaders must come to understand the importance of providing adequate education for all children and must through this understanding be prepared to pay the cost of socially effective and democratic education. It can be demonstrated that this would be more economical than the cost of delinquency, crime, bigotry, and other symptoms of personal and social disorganization.

The curricula of our teacher-training institutions must be reexamined to determine whether they make adequate and systematic use of that fund of modern psychological knowledge which deals with such problems as: the meaning of intelligence and problems related to the IQ and its interpretation; the contemporary interpretation of racial and nationality differences in intelligence and academic achievement; the role of motivation, self-confidence, and the self-image in the level of academic achievement; and general problems of the modifiability and resilience of the human being.

The evidence is now overwhelming that high intellectual potential exists in a larger percentage of individuals from lower status groups than was previously discovered, stimulated, and trained for socially beneficial purposes. In order to increase the yield of desperately needed trained intellects from these previously deprived groups, it will be necessary to develop systematic educational programs designed to attain this specific goal. These programs must raise the aspirational levels of these children and their parents. They must change the attitudes of teachers and school officials from one of rejection and fatalistic negation to one of acceptance and a belief in the educability and human dignity of these children. And, of course, the programs must provide appropriate guidance and remedial services designed to compensate for the past educational inferiorities and the deprivations in their homes and communities. It would seem that the chances of success for such an imperative educational program would be minimal in a nondemocratic school atmosphere characterized by intellectual, social, national, or racial segregation.

In providing the necessary conditions for a more effective education of children from lower status groups, the education of the more privileged children at the same time will be made more realistic, more meaningful, and more consistent with the demands of the contemporary and future world. One of the realities of the contemporary world is the fact that the destiny of one group of children is tied to the destiny of all other groups of children. Our schools can no longer afford the luxury of a snobbish status-dominated approach to the hard problems of increasing educational effectiveness for all children. The democratic pressures on our educational institutions are no longer merely verbal or sentimental. They now seem to have the imperative realities of survival.

References

1. Clark, Kenneth B., "The Most Valuable Hidden Resources," *College Board Review,* No. 29, pp. 23–26, Spring, 1956.
2. Clark, Kenneth B., *Prejudice and Your Child,* Boston: Beacon, 1955.
3. Clark, Kenneth B., "Desegregation: The Role of the Social Sciences," *Teachers College Record,* **62** (1), 1–17, October 1960.
4. Conant, James B., *Slums and Suburbs,* New York: McGraw-Hall, 1961.
5. Davis, A., "American Status Systems and the Socialization of the Child," *Amer. Sociol. Rev.,* **6**:345–354, 1941.
6. Hansen, C. F., *Addendum: A Five Year Report on Desegregation in the Washington, D. C. Schools,* New York: Anti-Defamation League of B'nai B'rith, 1960.
7. Hansen, C. F., *Miracle of Social Adjustment,* New York: Anti-Defamation League of B'nai B'rith, 1957.
8. Klineberg, Otto, *Negro Intelligence and Selective Migration,* New York: Columbia University Press, 1955.
9. Riessman, Frank, *The Culturally Deprived Child,* New York: Harper, 1962.
10. Sexton, Patricia C., *Education and Income,* New York: Viking, 1961.

33. Education and the Powerless

DAN W. DODSON

THE CONTEXT

In the large cities of America education is in crisis. The revolution in agriculture has driven the marginal from agriculture. Over one million more of them now live in slums of the large cities than live on all the farms—there are one and one half million more to come. The major portion of these migrants from the rural heritage are Negroes. They bring not only a heritage of poor education, but also a trauma of servitude which is historical. The school systems of these cities are called upon to close the gap between these children of the newcomer and the sophisticated population of well-trained people of the East and West *in one generation.* What is more these children are physically visible so that they speak the same language (approximately) as the remainder of the community, and their residence in America is of the oldest, so the failure cannot be laid on bilingualism as were the rationalizations which explained away the lack of ability to deal with past generations of newcomers.

In addition, the public school has full responsibility for this task of social

Paper delivered at the Third Work Conference on Curriculum and Teaching in Depressed Urban Areas, Teachers College, Columbia University, June 22–July 3, 1964. Reprinted by permission of author.

leadership. Except for the Jewish group, which was composed of people accustomed to living in urban communities, the past experience with mass migrations of peoples with rural heritages relied on parochial schools for the training of a part of their children, so that public education was excused from the total task of closing the gap for these groups. There are still vestiges of Italo-Americans and Polish-American neighborhoods in many cities where the public school was a sort of an annex to the parochial, and in the name of cultural autonomy these children of the marginal were neglected by public education; for to have made education for them commensurate with their need would have made their schools too competitive with the parochial. (One leader from one of these communities was amazed when he found that the achievement levels of his Italo-Americans neighborhood were below those of some of the Negro neighborhood schools. He said, "Thank God! At least one thing we will get out of this (the study of racial imbalance) is good education for all the children." He was amazed to find the gap which still existed between the children from his heritage and the accomplishments of the remainder of the white community.)

As a result of this historical situa-

311

tion, the school systems have little to offer insofar as making the school an intervening agency to take up the slack occasioned by historical neglect of the rural background child in modern-day slums. Vast foundation grants, innumerable conferences, projects utilizing almost every letter of the alphabet have been created to find ways to make these children malleable to the forges of the educational system. To date there is precious little accretion from these experiences to guide program development. Studies, demonstrations, and the "experiments" rarely fail to demonstrate the validity of what the designers set out to prove, but rarely do they give hope that they really have demonstrated that they have found the key to doing what is demanded of public education—closing this academic gap for educationally disprivileged children within a generation. Some despair that it can be done. They would make acculturation a matter of time. Others would even blame the human potential (Shuey, Garrett, et al.), indicating that race itself is a factor. Most try to use the family and the community as scapegoats for their lack of effectiveness as, for example, Conant, who says unless the family and the community are good there is little one can do in the school. Others are now saying that unless there is stimulation in the earlier years it is impossible to do much later. "This deprivation amounts to irreparable loss of ability to deal with abstract symbols," they say. This tends to be a modern version of the stereotype of East Texas fifty years ago when I was a boy. They contended that something closed in a Negro child's head when he was about six. Hence it was impossible to teach him anything beyond that point. Efforts to educate were a waste of money. This current theory amounts to about the same thing. Whatever the ration-

alizations, suffice it to say modern American education has little or no panacea for the children of the Negro slum. Most experience to date indicates that they are not malleable to the forges of the public school system. The experience has largely been one of deterioration of morale and accomplishment for both the students and those who purport to teach them. Clearly business as usual in American Education is not enough if this generation of children are to be salvaged. Neither is business as usual plus a few extra grants from the federal government and the large foundations going to bolster the current approaches to the problem, in this writer's estimation.

THE POWER HYPOTHESIS

During the last few years the power hypothesis has seemed to loom in significance with regard to this problem. It is not contended here that there is a single, simple, unitary pattern of causality. Rather, it is to invite examination of an alternate hypothesis. It is probably impossible for a youth who is a member of a group that is powerless in the community to grow to maturity without some trauma to the perception of himself because of the group's compromised position in the community. This trauma is expressed in various ways. Adler, in his psychology, contended that one who felt inferior tended to overcompensate for his sense of impotence. There are some who do. These we refer to as having a "chip on the shoulder." On the other hand, the vast majority of those who feel extremely powerless resign in apathy. The mass apathy of the slums, it is here contended, results from the pervading sense of powerlessness.

It may be pointed out that this is not restricted to the minority. We all tend to become apathetic about those things we feel powerless about. Witness the apathy in the large city about the bad government, or the apathy over the threat of atomic destruction. To understand the weakness of the school in dealing with such concentrations of impotent populations, it is necessary to review the role of the school as part of the power order. Its major function is to take all the children of the community and teach them their place in the power order. They must teach some that they are "brahmins" and are the academic elite. It teaches 40 per cent that the rewards and recognitions of the schools are not for them; hence they drop out of high school before they finish. The schools must teach all the children the mythologies of the "American Way" in such fashion that all will understand that their failures are their own, rather than those of the system. Otherwise they would rebel and blow the system apart. They must offer hope to the bright ones of the minority that if they meet the demands of the order they will be recognized. On the other hand they cannot offer this escalator to too many, otherwise they will be accused of not having standards.

As with all institutions of the power order, the school tries desperately to work through integrative processes rather than through conflict. This means working through involvement, process, participation, earned leadership roles, and growth through disciplining *to the rules which operate the social order.*

The characteristic approach to the powerless is to get the bright ones involved, get them to take stock in the mythologies of the American Way (which say that all will be recognized according to their ability and initiative), alienate them in their sentiments and sympathies from the group of which they are a part, make them ashamed of their heritage (every minority has wrestled with the phenomena of group self hate among its second generation youths), "sandpaper" them to the dimensions of the order which is, and ultimately transmute them into "ideal Americans." Hence we have never solved the problem of the slum. We have siphoned off the bright youths from the groups, and left the group itself to its own devices. The bright ones, after being transmuted, rarely return to the community to give leadership in solution of problems. With the Negro group this process does not work so well. The reason is that (1) color stands as a barrier to the transmuting process. When the bright one has been alienated and made ashamed of his heritage and is "transmuted" there is no place for him to go. His transmutation is into limbo. (2) The Negro has never been a part of this "American dream." Hence it is hard to sell the mythologies to youths who perceive on every side that they are not for him.

The alternative to this process is that motivation must stem from different sources. There is not time for this alienation, "siphoning off," transmuting process—even if it were desirable. The alternative must be for the group to take power and move under self-direction. It must be possessed by group goals which will require that the youths learn what the schools have to teach in order to prepare themselves to make a worthy group contribution to the autonomous goals of the group itself. The two great issues related to this process are: (1) Will the power order that exists allow such an approach? and (2) Is it possible to help such groups take power?

A significant dimension of the problem is that power has to be taken. It cannot be given. Moe Chusid said it best when he was discussing the

Puerto Ricans in Chelsea. He said they were the majority group. He gave them every opportunity possible to take leadership. But in the last analysis they had to take power. He couldn't give it to them.

SOME METHODOLOGICAL IMPLICATIONS

Concerning Racial Imbalance

One of the first implications of the hypothesis advanced above is related to school assignment policies. The all-Negro school in today's world stands as a symbol of the Negro's powerlessness. It is a reminder of the trauma of a heritage. It represents to the Negro child his rejection by the majority group. It puts him outside the circumference of power and leaves him an alienated soul. Such schools are impossible to maintain as first rate educational enterprises because morale is impossible to achieve, expectations are lowered, standards fall, and most of the time such schools are discriminated against in services. The HARYOU study indicated that children fall back steadily in such situations when their achievement is compared with national norms.

The most basic curriculum decision a board of education makes is the determination of who is going to go to school with whom. This determines whether children are to be brought to the significant encounters to learn the skills of citizenship in a pluralistic world, or on the other hand whether the power order is to leave the minority group segregated in its impotence. The acid test of whether a group has power is its capacity to require the total community to share whatever facilities as exist with all the children.

In this contest it is doubtful that the neighborhood school can maintain its integrity as an educational entity in the years ahead. It is impossible for a community to keep all its schools at the same level of goodness. In most communities one may as well rate the schools as to their popularity or status in the community as to rate them on the collective achievement of the youths to determine their academic standing. Those schools which are less good are harder to staff. The teachers assigned to them are considered less fortunate. The children have less expected of them. They are, as a consequence, traumatized by being required to attend them.

Another aspect of the issue also is pertinent. In such a situation the neighborhood school becomes a turf on which those who have power shield themselves from meaningful encounters with those who are powerless. They are able to attract for the education of their children what cannot be provided for the entirety of the community. They are content to live with such unshared privilege. Hence, it tends to corrupt both the powerful and the powerless. The proposition is hereby submitted that it is impossible to teach *community* in a neighborhood school—the Parents and Taxpayers Groups to the contrary notwithstanding. The neighborhood school teaches the child far more about his worth and the potency of himself and his group than do all the citizenship courses.

In the *New York Times* for Sunday, June 7, 1964, nine out of fourteen houses listed in Mt. Vernon, New York, "For Sale" indicated the name of the school zone in which the property was located. Three others indicated they were also north of the New Haven Railroad. So important did seven of them consider the school to which the property was attached that they put the name of the school next to the name of the town in which the property was located, and before any description of the property itself. Needless to say, none of the advertisements mentioned any of the southside schools. They have the heavy concentration of Negroes. The children really learn the social arrangements of the neighborhood. They study about citizenship in the books. They pass examinations on what the books say and perhaps what the teachers teach. They live what the community teaches. The neighborhood school is the outstanding mentor. Thus racial imbalance becomes a crucial issue in education of the children of the powerless. It cannot be separated from the general sense of apathy and low esteem which the whole culture purveys.

Professional Leadership

Closely related to the problem of racial imbalance is the role of the professionals. In the power order, the bureaucracy, which is the school system, is programmed to teach what the established order thinks is relevant. It scarcely knows any other. In teaching the children their place in the order mentioned earlier, the teaching profession must do two things. It must (1) help the children learn their place in the power order in such a fashion that they and their parents come to believe that the reasons for failure are those of the group and not of the system. Hence there is a variety of myth and ritual involved in achieving this assorting task. Grades are given. It is better if they are objective tests; then they can be better defended. Grouping assigns some to higher status than others. It purports to offer the same opportunity for all to make the first or fastest group. Intelligence scores become the alpha and omega of the educative process. It is understandable that the professional leadership of the schools identifies with and provides the rationalizations for the status position of the power order which is. The major responsibility of the historian is to provide the historical perspective for the power position. When the country was dominantly Protestant, the history was Protestant. When the Catholics came to power also, the history was enlarged to include the Christian heritage. As the Jews come into the power stream, the history is gradually merging into a common Judeo-Christian heritage. When labor was powerless in New York State, it was necessary for them to hire histories which depicted labor's role in building the state. As labor has come into the power order, the histories have become more cognizant of the common contributions. So it is with the Negro, who tends to be powerless. As he takes power, the histories and the literature anthologies will come to recognize his contribution to the common heritage, and will ignore it until he so arrives.

On this point, one must also complain as to the impact of the learned studies of my own colleagues in the behavioral sciences. When one is through reading the proceedings of any of the many conferences held on this problem, he is impressed with their relation to the power order. One wades through such jargon as "low I.Q.," "low social class," "weak ego strength," "lack of a father image with which to relate," "inability to forego immediate pleasures for long range goals," and "cultural deprivation." If a teacher ever had any hope of working creatively with these children of the ghettoes, he would be handicapped if he took us seriously, for the pictures we build in the back of his head would determine what he saw in the human potential rather than what was reality. What does it all mean? Does it not mean that we, too, are the soothsayers for the order which is? Ours is the task of providing the rationalizations for the power order which is, and the explanations as to why it operates as it does.

In the middle of the last century the learned divines afforded the rationalizations for the conditions of the deviants. It was infant damnation. God had damned some before birth; hence the social order could not get creativeness out of them. By the end of the century the psychologists had supplied a "scientific, secular version" of the phenomena. It was the low "I.Q." Today the sociologists are coming up very rapidly with their version. It is "low social class." When one is through reading our "verified hypotheses," he feels like saying "For God's sake, if this is all we see in the human potential with which we work, we had better turn them over to the Black Muslims and resign from the business." Somehow, when youths get a dose of that ideology, and take power, they show considerable imaginativeness, intelligence, and ability. Their "low I.Q.'s," their "low social class," their "weak ego strengths," their "inability to forego immediate pleasures for long range goals," "their lack of the father image with which to relate," and even the demonstrable fact that they perceive differently in the pre-school years does not seem to deter them too much. If the first great hurdle of the depressed area child is the trauma to image occasioned by his sense of impotence, the second hurdle is that of overcoming the mythology built about him by those who purport to serve him.

Another dimension of professional leadership relates to its quality. As school systems have grown larger, they have become increasingly bureaucratic. This means they assign people to increasingly specialized roles so that the teacher of today is the instructor of the common branches of the advanced section of the seventh grade, of a homogeneous neighborhood. She is neither responsible for developing her curriculum (a specialized bureau does that for her), nor her schedule. Someone else specializes in the child's re-creation, his creativity, his psyche, his family, and his guidance. The teacher is an interchangeable part in a vast bureaucratic machine.

As a result of this trend, teaching is rapidly passing from an art in which teacher related to child, to a science in which teacher is increasingly preoccupied with matters of "what and how" in instruction, rather than "who." Very rapidly, the educator as an idea man in the community is being replaced with the operator; the charismatic leader with the bureaucratic leader; the prophet with the priest; the man of vision with the caretaker of the bureaucracy. Unless the educationist can "quicken the spirit" of those he leads, it does not matter much what else he does. This aspect of education has been downgraded in American life in no small measure.

In the past decade there have been millions of dollars spent on the experimentation and demonstration of this nostrum and that, designed to test this or that hypothesis on cultural deprivation. Of all the efforts, the most outstanding job I know about is being done by Sam Shepherd in St. Louis, Missouri. Here a district superintendent took over a traditional slum district several years ago. Within six years he brought the children to slightly above national norms in reading, and almost to comparable advances in mathematics. Although the Ford Foundation made him a grant to assist with testing after he was under way, he had no great resources of outside help to operate a deluxe program. When one tries to examine how he did it, the most that can be seen is the charismatic quality of his leadership.

He had the vision to see the human potential of those he served. He had the wisdom not to believe the clichés the scholars had provided as to why these children were as they were. He had the courage to challenge the stereotypes about their abilities, and he had the quality of leadership to persuade his principals and staff to forget these things they also had been taught and to bear down and hold these youths to the same high standards of expectations as other children were held to.

How do we train people to have charismatic leadership? I frankly do not know. However, I suggest that more attention must be paid to selection of educational staff to make sure bureaucratic requirements, qualifications increasingly written out in job specifications which usually are related to objective tests, do not drive from the schools the last vestiges of uniqueness, which is at the core of creativeness.

Concerning Ideology

Another aspect of the slum situation relates to the role of ideology. Since the Second World War there has been a downgrading of this dimension of the human estate. Man, however, cannot escape the issue of values in human personality.

For this writer there is serious doubt as to whether much can be done for these children who are victims of slum shock and normlessness until and unless some ideology takes hold of life to give it meaning, and structure, and purpose. Granted that the Muslim is considered antisocial, he does stand as testimony to the regenerative power of ideology.

There is enough evidence in the examination of such problems to raise the issue as to whether the major threat

the depressed areas presents to us may be our inability to interpret the ideologies of "our way of life" sufficiently that such youths have an attraction to them. In fact, is not the major threat of our times to all of us the problem that the motivation is increasingly away from inner-direction and self-purpose to outer-direction, which stems from the mass culture? Youths study and make good grades so their parents won't be ashamed of them, rather than because of study to achieve inner purposes. Motivation is not from inner drives and purposes, but outside mass culture pressure.

Mannheim indicated several years ago that the scholar did not have the privilege of standing outside some value system. Neither does the student. Educators would do well to reexamine their own ideological orientation as they work with such youths. Unless they can inspire hope and faith, there is little reason for the slum student to work. In order to do that the educator must be able to impart meanings and values which give orientation and direction to those who sit at his feet.

Methodologies

There are several issues relating to methodology which are puzzling. They will be raised as questions rather than as positions.

CLASSMATES CLIMATES. One of the most pervasive problems of working in culturally deviant schools is the climate of the group or classroom. More teachers fail because they cannot deal effectively with the class as a group, rather than because of their limitations in subject matter. Most educators would contend that classroom climates which are permissive and warm, which unite children in working toward common goals, are more desirable than those which are rigid and formal. How different these can be is illustrated by two schools involved in our evaluation of the Open Enrollment Program of six elementary schools of New York City. In this program Negro children were brought to the host school in the outer part of the city from overcrowded innercity schools by bus. They were distributed proportionately throughout the sections of each grade. They were ethnically identifiable. We studied them in May after a scholastic year of association. In one of these schools whose students were highly motivated, middle-class whites had 44 majority background boys in the fifth grade. Each was asked to make ten sociometric choices—five related to work committees in the classroom and five on the playground. Of the 440 choices these youths made, only one single choice of one Negro youth was made by only one white lad. In other words, there seemed to be only co-racial education in the school. In the other school 84 white boys with comparable sociometric choices, with 840 possible choices, made 118 of their choices from among the Open Enrollment (Negro) youths. This was about the proportion of Negro youth to the total group. Yet the minority children in the situation where the acceptance was almost nonexistent made better progress in their reading than did those where they were well accepted.

Whyte, in his study of an Italo-American group, *Street Corner Society*, indicated that the youth from such a background who wishes to really go ahead and make something of himself, must become an isolate from his group. The question then arises as to whether these permissive classrooms with their methodologies geared to social acceptance, their concern for the isolate—that he be brought into social participation—may be middle-class educational methodologies which we

have adapted to lower social class children without effect. It may be a technique utilized to make "baby sitting" with them palatable without contributing educational merit.

THE ROLE OF TENSION. Closely related to the above factor is that of anxiety and tension. It is doubtful that learning of any consequence is achieved without some tension and anxiety. In some middle-class neighborhoods the school's role is one of shielding the child from such overpowering anxiety that it interferes with learning. In the deviant cultural situations, however, reversal of these roles may be needed. How to induce a certain amount of anxiety without having this considered a rejection of the children is not easy. Again, one wonders if the methodologies validated on middle-class children are useful in these kinds of school rooms?

THE ALTERNATIVES

In conclusion it appears that education in the inner cities is faced with two possibilities in dealing with the powerless. They are not necessarily exclusive, but they are different. The first is the traditional way of dealing with those who are powerless; they can get the bright ones involved; alienate them in their sentiments and sympathies from the group of which they are a part. They can make them ashamed of their heritage and hold out the hope to them that if they will meet the standards of the dominant group they will be recognized. The schools can take them on trips and show them the few of their kind who have made it and hold good jobs. They can persuade some of them to become alienated from their groups and try to aspire to the horizons which the dominant group holds out to them. It will be especially helpful if the teachers will tell them about good jobs they can get.

This is a materialistic culture and it can be figured, in averages, at least, how much it is worth per day to stay in school.

In this context the power order will follow the path of the British as they dealt with colonial possessions—when tension arises, squirt a little more welfare on the powerless. This will keep them sufficiently tranquilized in Egypt that they will not seek out the Promised Land. This will be costly, but it will mean that the power order is not threatened. Those who are transmuted through these processes will not provide leadership in creating dysfunction in the system. Frazier has described them in the *Black Bourgeoisie*. This group will sit on the side lines as long as possible when tension occurs, and come into it only when maneuvered by the mass. Each grant made to provide ever more costly services will give high visibility to those who give it and those who receive it. Each such largesse will further push down the masses of the Negro community, for each grant further reinforces the stereotype that the problem is really the human potential, the children and their parents, and not the society itself. Ultimately, however, under these circumstances the group can be dissolved into the mainstream—if there is time enough.

The alternative to this so-called "integration" approach resides in the Negro group itself taking power and moving under self-direction. In this situation the youth are challenged to learn what the schools have to offer because they need it to prepare themselves to make their maximum contribution to the group's efforts. This approach calls for conflict, i.e., the ability to bring to bear the pressures necessary to make one's interests felt in communal decision making. This does not necessarily mean violence. It means induc-

ing dysfunction into *the system* until the social order comes to recognize the interdependency of the whole to its parts.

This taking of power is the hope of the present revolution. It provides a new faith, a new hope; it gives the powerless a sense of potency which he has not had before. Educators identified with the power structure which is become frustrated and confused when the school boycotts come. They fume about these parents and leaders teaching the children to disobey the law. They do not understand that this "taking power" is the antidote to apathy. They should use the opportunity it affords to assist children to identify with the fight. They should point out the great contribution being made by such leaders as Martin Luther King. His "Letter from the Birmingham Jail" should be among the prize literary compositions of American writers.

In this identification with the revolution should also come the interpretation of the need to study to make oneself capable of carrying responsibility for his share in the undertaking. In the community the school should also identify with this upreaching of the human spirit. There should be encouragement to grapple with the issues so that growth is gained in functioning as a citizen. The infusion of such hope should be a powerful stimulus to learning. Immediately after emancipation the Negroes had great hopes of participating worthily with the white in making the new destiny of the South. They tied their Bibles between the plow handles so they could study as they farmed. Then came the abdication of Federal power and the era of violence in which this light of hope was blown out. Today it is rekindled. This time there will not be abandonment of rights by the Federal government. What was then a mirage must now become a reality. Negroes must learn the art and skill of taking power —as they are rapidly doing. They must learn the responsibilities which go with it—which they are rapidly doing. Out of this process, with a little help, will come a sense that there are no footnotes to this American Creed. It includes Negroes too.

Every classroom should be a laboratory for learning how to take power, how to shield the group from power which is abused, and how to work through shared relationships.

All the great documents of history have been produced by those who were outside the power order as they attempted to interpret the upreach and outreach of the human spirit as it chafed under oppression's yoke. They have not come from those in the power stream who were defending their entrenched positions. Teachers who are handmaidens of the power order should not sell these children of the ghetto short. Out of their protestations is coming the fulfillment of the great-

est faith we have—that all men love freedom and that all men have the capacity to participate worthily in the collective direction of their own destiny. Will we as educators see this upreach as goodness and encourage it, or will we stand in the middle of it and be frustrated by it, and let history pass us by? This is the issue at this time. Those of us who are liberals believe this is a moral issue and not a racial one. We are threatened when the Negro psychologically disengages himself from interracial efforts because he does not trust us. Whether white teachers can lead these students of the depressed areas out of their apathy depends on whether we can sufficiently identify with them in such a way that together we lose the sense of who is Negro and who is white, and therefore see ourselves enlisted together in a common moral encounter. Consequently, it is not for the Negro's sake alone that we are involved in these conferences. It is for the sake of our own souls as well.

34. Some Guidelines to Desirable Elementary School Reorganization

JOHN NIEMEYER

Some of the experimental projects and research which Bank Street College has recently been conducting will be briefly described here because they seem particularly pertinent to the topic before this conference and because they may suggest various lines of new action and thought.

Although Bank Street, from its inception in 1916 as the Bureau of Educational Experiments, has been conducting multiple-discipline research in the area of schools and learning for children up to adolescence, it has in the past five years been working particularly on the question of how the elementary schools in New York City, and presumably in other large urban centers, can raise the learning level of the children of lower social class families, especially those of minority groups.

Since 1943 Bank Street has worked cooperatively with the Board of Education of New York to improve a number of elementary schools, many located in crowded, low socioeconomic

Reprinted from *Programs for the Educationally Disadvantaged,* a report of a conference on teaching children and youth who are educationally disadvantaged, May 21–23, 1962, Washington, D.C., U.S. Department of Health, Education, and Welfare, Office of Education, pp. 80–85.

neighborhoods in the city. In 1957 the superintendent of schools invited Bank Street to try to help a cluster of three integrated elementary schools to strengthen their programs in various ways so as to (1) check the drift away from these schools of white middle-class families; (2) attract to the nearby middle-income housing development then under construction, middle-class families with children who would, hopefully, enroll their children in these public schools.

The field action team for this project consisted of a sociologist, a social psychologist, and an educator working fulltime, as well as four classroom consultants who worked in these three schools parttime. These teacher consultants were public school teachers, selected by Bank Street and then assigned by the superintendent to this particular project. They worked directly with classroom teachers in the three schools to help them strengthen their classroom programs. The other Bank Street team members worked with the principals, the district superintendent, the parents, and certain community agencies. Other aspects of the project included a writing workshop for teachers who wished to prepare materials meaningful to their pu-

321

pils; a preliminary sociological study of a school and the school system; seminars for the 30 principals in that school district; and the beginning of the Parent-Teacher Communication Project.

The most important outcome of this project for Bank Street was the development of our hypothesis as to the cause of low achievement in schools of this kind and a general conclusion about what needs to be done to correct the situation.

Our hypothesis is that the chief cause of the low achievement of the children of alienated groups is the fact that too many teachers and principals honestly believe that these children are educable only to an extremely limited extent. And when teachers have a low expectation level for their children's learning, the children seldom exceed that expectation, which is a self-fulfilling prophecy. A logical concomitant to this hypothesis is the conclusion that the problems of these schools will not be solved simply through "more services" or "changing family backgrounds" but through a functional, and probably structural, reorganization of the schools themselves.

The following areas should be scrutinized for needed reorganization:

THE CHILD, HIS TEACHER, AND THE TEACHING-LEARNING PROGRAM

An effective way to start would be for a school to take a hard look at everything it does and every aspect of the curriculum. It cannot do this productively without looking at the children and asking the question: "What are the interests and needs, the motivational forces for learning, the learning-pattern with which these children come to school?" Is it not possible that these children have resources for the educational program which do not depend upon books, or the arts, or intellectual conversation in the home? May it not be that these children have a deep foundation for educational growth in their day-to-day experience in urban life? And how can the school, without relinquishing its long-range goals, change its approach so as to take advantage of the true educational potential of these children?

A few of the projects which Bank Street is engaged in at this moment seem particularly relevant to this first area of reorganization:

MULTICULTURE "READERS" PROJECT. One specific way in which schools have unconsciously augmented feelings of alienation is by introducing children to the world of reading and books through readers which hold up as an exclusive model the culture pattern of the white middle-class suburban family. The child knows in his heart that the school gives the highest prestige value to books, and yet everything that is familiar to him is excluded from the image of life presented in the books which the school provides. Consequently, Bank Street has a team of writers working to produce readers which will use stories and illustrations to reflect back to children the positive aspects of the variety of community and cultural settings which constitute American society. These will not be books written specifically for minority or low-income groups, but will be books for and about all children. Important, too, is the fact that these books will be published by one of the well-established textbook publishers who have previously been afraid of economic repercussions from the production of books like these. This should help to break down some of the stereotypes which have characterized all instructional materials published for our schools.

SCHOOL ENTRY STUDY. This is a research project studying the relationships among such factors as home background, method of entry into kindergarten, the type of kindergarten program, and apparent success of adjustment to the school world on the part of the child. Both middle and lower social class children are involved, and the public school kindergartens which served as locations are very different in character. From this study should come helpful hints for curriculum changes at the kindergarten level.

CLASSROOM PROCESSES STUDY. In four public schools offering contrasts in racial and socioeconomic settings the classroom life of four second grades and four fifth grades has been examined to clarify mental health implications for children.

THE SCHOOL'S ROLE VIS-À-VIS PARENTS AND COMMUNITY

This is the second area for reorganization. Because Bank Street feels that the school's first job is to cast out the mote from its own educational eye instead of concentrating upon the eye of family background, it does not follow that the school should not do everything possible to help parents help their children learn in school. Neither does it follow that the school can think of itself as a community agency operating in isolation from all other community agencies. Each school operating in a deprived neighborhood needs to work cooperatively with all of the agencies in that neighborhood. Further, certain schools will need to take on some of the responsibilities which usually are thought of as belonging to social agencies and not the school. One elementary school in Philadelphia, for example, has won the cooperation of police and milkmen to the extent that the school learns early in the morning of any child who has been locked out of his home for the night. Such a child is greeted by the principal, given a hot shower and breakfast, and put to bed for several hours. This may seem a far cry from the usual role of the school, but children of this type in this particular school had proved to be drastic disrupting forces and obviously learned nothing during the school day.

All persons speaking at this conference have reported somewhat the same findings that Bank Street has gained: namely, that nearly all parents, even those who are severely alienated or defeated, look upon the school as the one source of hope that their children will have better lives than they have had. Nevertheless, the problem of how the school can help parents help their children in school is not an easy one to solve.

Even though these parents look to the school with hope, many of them are fearful and confused in relation to the school. Furthermore, the school has difficulty in communicating with these parents. Sometimes there is an actual language barrier, but more often the chief barrier is stereotyped thinking on the part of both teachers and parents. There is also the communications barrier which separates different social classes. One mother, speaking of a previous Parents Association meeting, said, "In that there meeting the principal and all the teachers called us dopes—poor slobs that don't know what our kids are getting from school." To which the principal immediately countered, "Why, Mrs. ———, you know very well that no one said anything of the kind in that meeting," and the mother in question replied, "Maybe you didn't say it, but that's what the atmosphere said." However correct or incorrect this parent was in her perception, it is clear that communication between her and the professional staff would be difficult. Two of Bank Street's present projects may be of interest here.

THE TEACHER-PARENT COMMUNICA-TION STUDY. In this project a Bank Street team consisting of a social psychologist and an educator has been working with a school in a depressed area to try to improve the communication between school and parents. In the first phase of the project, most of the kindergarten and first-grade teachers, faced with the necessity for holding periodic conferences with their pupils' parents, worked with the Bank Street team to try to understand the obstacles to effective communication. They evaluated all contacts between the school and parents (a copy of their report is available from Bank Street on request), and the Bank Street team attempted to affect the attitude of the teachers by broadening their cross-cultural understandings. In the second phase of the program, which is now in progress, the attention of the Bank Street team was turned more to the total school situation. Depth interviews have been held with 44 parents. An effort has been made to study the implications of pupil turnover and all the subtle and overt ways in which the school deals with parents.

The plan for the coming year will also include experimentation with a research educator and licensed teacher in the role of assistant to the principal in improving the communications between the school and the parents of the school's children.

STUDY OF A PARENT'S ASSOCIATION IN RELATION TO THE TOTAL SYSTEM OF A SCHOOL. In one of the projects located in a school within a low socioeconomic neighborhood, the attempt is to facilitate change by working with classroom teachers, the principal, and the parents. A research educator with much experience in schools has been assigned to work with the very active Parents Association. The leadership of the association, mostly Negro, is troubled, as is the school principal, about the fact that only a small proportion of the parents participate in the activities of the association. The researcher has assisted the parent committee and, having won its confidence, is now interviewing other parents to ascertain their attitudes toward the school and the Parents Association. In 1962–1963 the researcher's findings were reported in appropriate ways to the parent leadership and the principal as the basis for new practices. One of the purposes of the total project is, of course, to devise better ways for the school to stimulate the kind of participation which gives positive support to the learning of the children in school.

THE INTERNAL ORGANIZATION OF THE SCHOOL AS AN ENTITY AND AS A PART OF A SYSTEM

The third area calls for scrutiny. The school in its effort to educate the "disadvantaged" must begin to study itself as a social system. An individual school is a small culture in and of itself; as such it may operate in certain ways which prevent many of its pupils from realizing their true learning potential. Here is one very practical example: Many schools unconsciously seem to put out an "unwelcome mat" to parents. A parent who comes to one of these schools enters the school office and is faced with a long counter, behind which are three or four secretaries. No one is set up as a receptionist. No names are in evidence. The parent may stand for a long time, shifting from foot to foot, before anyone comes to inquire as to his or her mission, let alone to extend a welcoming hand and smile. Yet the secretaries in question are friendly, warm people, devoted to the school and their work. What has happened is that somehow, subtly, there has been built into the system of the school a deep impersonality in terms of relationships between the school and the parents. Another example, much more serious perhaps, is the condition which exists in most school systems by which each lower rung on the bureaucratic ladder is led to believe that its purpose is to serve the rung immediately above. Somehow, down at the very foot of the ladder is the child in the classroom.

Of help in facing this entire problem should be the sociological studies which have been in process at Bank Street. A number of mental hospitals and one large industry have been studied as social systems, but the American school apparently has not. At the moment Bank Street's chief sociologist, Dr. Donald Horton, and his associates are conducting such a study. The study was begun in some of the schools of New York City but is now being carried out in the town of Brookview in a neighboring state. One particular school in the system is being studied while at the same time the entire school system in a community of 30,000 population is being examined as a whole. The reports on these studies were published in 1965.

Equally important to knowing what changes should take place within our schools is knowing how change can be brought about in the schools, and particularly in the school systems of our large cities. We are all familiar with many of the ways in which educators have traditionally worked to bring about change. Among these methods are inservice courses, the study of children and children's behavior by small groups of teachers, conferences and workshops, assistance to teachers, demonstration schools and classes, bulletins of curriculum bureaus, dicta issued by the superintendent, and so forth. A

recent report done for the Commissioner of Education in New York State takes the position that change can be brought about in a school system only if those in high authority require the change and if they simultaneously provide teachers with demonstration units which offer proof that all of the teachers can do what the demonstration unit is doing. This is not a new approach to the process of change in education, although the author of this particular report would have the goals for change established through research. The prevailing method being used in the programs attempting to upgrade schools in the economically depressed neighborhoods of our big cities is to saturate these schools with all kinds of "special services." It remains to be seen whether the chief change which will result will be upgrading of children's learning or the elimination of the responsibility of the classroom teacher for the learning of each pupil.

The truth is that the process of change in our large school systems is baffling. This process is one which Bank Street is studying intensively. Our hypothesis is that the most productive kind of change process is that which involves intervention at many points in the social system called a school. This calls for actual experimentation. In the school mentioned above in relation to our study of the Parents Association, Bank Street is quite obviously attempting "to intervene," as the researchers say, at all levels of this particular school. Principals in schools like these who wish to bring about change are often baffled by what seems to them to be teacher indifference, if not opposition. The teachers, on the other hand, frequently feel that the principal is interested in his pet projects but does not pay attention to the changes which they, usually as individuals, wish. The parents, or at least the active parents, finally feel obligated to participate in the school but usually do not know why they are participating, and unless they are middle-class parents, for whom having an organization in itself is a satisfying aim, they do not know how to proceed vis-à-vis the principal and the teachers. In a school such as this it is quite apparent that the traditional procedures for attempting to bring about change or to introduce innovations may not be effective. The Bank Street effort to work for change in all phases of the school simultaneously, therefore, may well open up productive new approaches to the problem.

The entire project team meets regularly at Bank Street College with the principal of the school. By the end of the first year the principal has begun to involve more and more teachers. An increasing number of parents are thinking about why they should participate in the school. Also, the principal has seemed increasingly receptive to parent action; rather than regarding it as obstructive, he has come to see it as an opportunity for the school to educate parents about their supportive role. It is not yet certain whether the teachers have begun to lose the suspicion which they seemed to feel at the beginning of the project. (In many of our other efforts to bring about change in schools, work has been done only with teachers who volunteer for the project. It is made very clear to teachers and principal that only those things will be reported about any teacher which the teacher herself decides shall be reported.)

35. The Great Cities Projects

DORSEY BAYNHAM

Travelers to these shores report finding America's great cities disconcertingly alike. Surrounded by layers of suburbs, bound around by concrete expressways, the heart of each great city is characterized either by dilapidation and ruin or by wholesale urban renewal, which in its beginning stages resembles the aftermath of a bombing.

Population trends to the city, mobility patterns *within* the city, and the general air of poverty, deprivation, and hopelessness are comparable in each metropolitan area. And on no other segment of urban life does this overriding pattern, this generally bleak atmosphere, make a greater impact than it does on the public schools.

The challenge to the schools was recognized by big city school superintendents almost a decade ago. Counterattacks, supported by grants from the Ford Foundation and known as the Great Cities School Improvement Program, were launched some six years ago in the largest cities. New York City was not included in the Great Cities School Improvement Program because it had started its own program, Higher Horizons, and has continued to develop on its own. Although final statistical evidence is lack-

ing, reports at this point—midway for many of the projects—are heartening.

Details of approaches to alleviating big-city school problems are as varied as the human beings who direct them. Milwaukee, for instance, has established school orientation centers to prepare culturally deprived children for regular classroom work; St. Louis has set up a combined academic and vocational program aimed at economic independence for students who would otherwise join the army of dropouts; Pittsburgh uses team teaching and flexible programing to tailor education for disadvantaged children.

Though program details differ, certain factors are common to each. Four such factors stand out.

· Awareness that the culturally deprived student is usually poor in communication skills and that this inability causes failure in other subjects.

· Willingness to experiment with a broad range of teaching materials such as filmstrips, records, and television, and with administrative approaches such as team teaching and flexible programing.

· Strenuous efforts to search out and use community help, such as various public health and welfare services or private philanthropic organizations and business and industry.

Reprinted by permission from *NEA Journal*, Vol. 52 (April 1963), pp. 16–20.

• Preparation both in teaching skills and in attitudes of teachers involved in the great city programs and, happily, the concern, devotion, and enthusiasm which ordinarily result from that involvement.

A common denominator in most but not all of the improvement programs is the use of lay personnel—usually with undergraduate degrees—who live in the neighborhood and are knowledgeable about the cities' gray areas. These citizens, some paid, some volunteer, have helped build a bridge of interpretation between school and community.

Although the four factors are irrevocably tied together, individual projects usually highlight one or another factor. The main purpose of the San Francisco program, for example, is "to develop solutions for the reading and language problems of culturally deprived youth." This city makes an across-the-board effort, with project classes in two elementary schools, one junior high school, and three senior high schools.

Small groups of disadvantaged elementary school pupils are taken from regular classrooms and taught by techniques which allow them to look, to listen, and to touch. They are also given a variety of experiences to expand horizons beyond the usual six city blocks area in which most slum children live their daily lives.

Audiovisual devices—filmstrips, tape recorders, records—are used in conjunction with tests to augment understanding and provide motivation. And each part of the San Francisco program makes specific allowances for discussion or reading aloud in order to correct speech patterns, build vocabulary, broaden concepts, and, most important, supply some measure of aspiration.

The same concern for better communication skills has shaped the language arts program set up in Washington, D.C., to aid children "who have the ability to communicate for utilitarian purposes but have not had the background to be able to use English as a form of expression of ideas —which in turn begets ideas." Although the program is used only in the kindergarten and primary grades of fourteen schools, it has affected all grade levels of the schools involved because of the special work of the language arts teachers and strong inservice programs in each school.

Project teachers do not delude themselves that one year of special effort can make up for the slum child's lifetime of impoverishment, but they are encouraged by the results thus far. The results have, in fact, spread beyond the school and show up in the increased number of parents who participate in workshops, language classes, and parent-teacher meetings, accompany children on field trips, and work for the success of book fairs or bookmobiles.

Community-wide influence is also a product of Cleveland's Hough Community Project. Early in the program, the essence of the Hough area's problem was expressed by a boy who asked, "How do I get to want to?"

One of the most effective of this project's community services—aimed at getting area residents "to want to"— has been the project's home visitation program. Project workers visit a pupil's home within three days after he enrolls in a school.

Another effective, and popular, phase of the program provides for parent education through informal group meetings at schools.

The Hough Community Project, like other big city projects, has a strong reading improvement program. Virtually all project teachers teach reading. To prepare themselves, these teachers participated voluntarily in a series of Saturday morning workshops. Reading specialists, however, teach the most severely retarded pupils.

Retardation, whether mental, emotional, or physical, has been attacked in a number of other ways by the Hough project. In the guidance department, an open door policy has led an increasing number of boys and girls to seek counseling services, the major purpose of which is to help build self-confidence and hope for the future. Saturday morning recreation programs have had the indirect effect of curtailing a serious vandalism problem at Addison Junior High. A one-week summer camp gives many pupils their first taste of disciplined living and routine. Finally, a broad range of health services is offered, including physical examinations for newcomers, dental examinations and hearing tests, revaccination, tuberculin tests, and persistent follow-up in cases of referral for correction and treatment of physical defects.

A respected and influential role within the community has also been accorded the Pittsburgh project. In that city, the health department, the recreation department, the housing authority, and the welfare department have joined hands with the school system to improve the life of economically and culturally deprived students. Private and voluntary agencies also have cooperated in such ventures as an experimental study of school construction, a pilot play-school program for preschool children, and a series of public meetings to explain Pittsburgh's major attack method, team teaching.

Three kinds of teaching teams have been organized, primary, intermediate, and junior high; each consists of a team leader, typically four other teachers, a teacher intern, and a team aide. Teams meet at least once a week to determine the purpose, nature, and amount of large-group instruction and to decide upon follow-up activities and which children need specialized instruction. Youngsters are assigned in large groups of from 70 to 120 for subjects which adapt themselves to large-group instruction and in small groups of 5 to 15 for concentrated instruction in subjects for which they need special help.

The Philadelphia School Improvement Project has launched its program on both the community and the school level. The work of Philadelphia's school-community coordinators and language arts specialists was described in a *Journal* article a year ago. Since then, with the addition of two more schools having a sizable population of youngsters of Spanish-speaking parents, the project has added a second bilingual coordinator, under whose leadership Spanish-speaking parents have been encouraged to establish stronger bonds with the schools and to organize community improvement groups.

Extension of the project for three additional years has allowed Philadelphia to intensify its efforts, primarily in the language arts program, to employ additional personnel, and to use a variety of new instructional methods and equipment. Experimentation resulting in positive indications of growth has been carried on in reading, spelling, handwriting, and functional and creative writing. However, the feature unique to the Philadelphia system which has been most helpful in raising achievement levels is the on-school-time in-service training programs for teachers. While the teachers receive this training, their classes participate in a carefully structured literature program. This is a program rich in storytelling, literature films, filmstrips, and recordings. Several thousand dollars per school have gone into classroom library units, books to support the structured literature program, and other books for enrichment.

In Milwaukee, the Great Cities School Improvement Program is trying a unique approach to the problem posed by the constant movement of population within the city's gray area neighborhoods. Orientation centers for children of in-migrant and transient parents have been established to help these children to adjust to the community and to catch up in school work before they are placed in regular classrooms.

The orientation centers provide a variety of psychological, health, welfare, and remedial services. The length of time spent in a center depends upon the needs, the strengths, and the weaknesses of each child. Classes are ungraded and have a maximum of twenty pupils.

Programs for potential dropouts have been established in the school systems of St. Louis and Chicago.

In St. Louis, selected students were divided into experimental and control groups. The experimental group, in addition to regular school services, received special counseling, assistance in getting a job, and further assistance from both school and employer in staying with the job. School personnel worked with an advisory committee representing labor, employers, the Chamber of Commerce, and community agencies; the State Office of Employment Security helped with job placement. At the end of a two-year period, the experimental group had nearly eighteen percent fewer dropouts than the control group.

Chicago's project for potential dropouts involves a number of cooperative employers. The program is divided into three phases: Double C, census and counseling; Double E, education and employment; and Double T, training and transition. The Double T phase is part of a larger Chicago program financed under the Great Cities School Improvement Program. The other two phases, begun under another Ford Foundation grant, are now financed entirely by the Chicago Board of Education.

In the first phase of the Chicago Urban Youth Program, students dropping out of school are referred to a center operated by the Board of Education. Students are then issued invitations to neighborhood-area guidance centers where, during evening sessions, testing and counseling services are provided to determine job skills and further educational needs. Finally, ten evening workshop sessions in this phase usually lead to assignment in either the Double E or Double T program. The latter provides short-term training in specific skills for which there is a job market; the former is a work-study program divided about equally between the two.

Almost all big city projects make provision for in-service education for teachers of children from slum areas. In Detroit, for example, continuous efforts are made to modify the perceptions of those teachers who often bring to their profession a rigid middle-class value system that is quite different from that of residents of depressed communities.

Experiments have been carried on with ungraded primary classes, clock time, core classes, and team teaching. Preprimers and other instructional materials have also been prepared especially for project classes. But whatever changes and improvements in curriculum and methods are launched, the crucial factor appears to be the teacher's attitude. Teacher expectation, in itself, can have a surprising effect on pupils' achievement, and the teacher who expects achievement and who has faith in the educability of his pupils conveys this hope through every nuance of his behavior.

A review of the programs and reports of the Great Cities School Improvement Program leads the observer to a very real and sober appreciation for the program's accomplishments. Big city school administrators and teachers know the problems. Obviously they care. Pupils care and so do parents and segments of the community. But in the face of society's indifference otherwise, will this be enough to do the job?

36. Sam Shepard's Faith

PAUL FRIGGENS

To see Sam Shepard's amazing achievement in education you drive to the sooty Negro slums that spread out from downtown St. Louis, Missouri. Mile after mile the homes are rotting, century-old redbrick tenements, with littered yards and darkened doorways, where idle men sit and talk. In the midst of this blight stands a high-rise housing development, occupied by low-income laborers and domestics and overrun with seven thousand shouting children.

With a young teacher from this school district I knock on the door of a typical apartment in the already run-down-looking development. A young mother, surrounded by her brood and expecting still another child, answers. The rooms are barren, devoid of amenities, but there is one surprising discovery. On the table lies a dictionary. "I makes 'em use it when they studies," the mother says proudly. "I want for my children to get an education and grow up and be *somethin'!*"

Behind that dictionary is the story of Samuel Shepard, Jr., Assistant Superintendent of St. Louis' Banneker School District, a fifteen-square-mile area with twenty-three elementary

Reprinted with permission from the March 1964 *Readers Digest.* Copyright 1964 by the Readers Digest Association, Inc.

schools serving some sixteen thousand "culturally disadvantaged" children—almost all Negro—and staffed by five hundred Negro teachers. Four years ago, when Dr. Shepard discovered that the St. Louis schools were discarding some six thousand used dictionaries for a new edition, he arranged to buy the lot and have them sold for twenty-five cents each to the families in his district.

That secondhand dictionary—for many the first book they have ever owned—is a symbol of Dr. Shepard's accomplishment in the slums. In only six years, the crusading educator has given the lie to the image of Negro inferiority. In his elementary schools he has raised the general achievement level of his Negro pupils to the national norm for whites. Moreover, in attendance some Negro schools outrank the white in St. Louis.

William Kottmeyer, deputy superintendent of St. Louis schools, told me, "Dr. Shepard dares to tell Negro boys and girls, 'Quit crying. Rise above your environment.' In place of unemployment and bitterness Dr. Shepard is giving the Negro training and self-respect."

On a rainy morning I drove out the dismal streets to Dr. Shepard's office at Banneker Elementary School. At the bell, two lines of clean, bright-looking youngsters marched down the corridors, whose walls were dotted with colorful posters: *"Reading is the key that opens all locks,"* one poster promised. Another said, *"There's a place for you in the community—if you're prepared."*

"We keep driving that home," Shepard said. "The Negro is the low man on the totem pole—the last hired, the first fired. He has never prepared himself for a job or had much ambition, because he had little opportunity or place to go. But I tell them that it's a new day; with education and preparation, Negroes can take their places with whites."

Colleagues say that fifty-six-year-old Shepard works fourteen- and sixteen-hour days and stays with a problem like a dog with a bone. A trim, athletic-looking man, highly disciplined and methodical, he weighs himself every payday at the bank, and he keeps fifteen years' weight records in his bankbook alongside his deposit records. Until his rise through coaching and teaching in St. Louis, however, he didn't have much need for a bankbook. Reared in poverty in Kansas City, Missouri, he worked his way through high school, educating two sisters as well. Washing pots and pans, he won his bachelor's and master's degrees at the University of Michigan and twenty-six years later earned his doctor's degree there.

Shepard's crusade was sparked by a decisive event six years ago when the St. Louis secondary schools switched to the "track system" of academic rating—Track 1, superior; Track 2, average; and Track 3, below average. When the St. Louis pupils were given the Iowa Basic Skills tests, the results showed that the majority of Negro children ranked low. Only 7 per cent of Banneker District school children were certified to Track 1; only 10.6

per cent of six thousand youngsters in the primary grades were reading at textbook level. Everybody had expected this. It confirmed studies elsewhere in the United States—that Negro children score on the average anywhere from six months to four years behind white children of the same age and grade.

Shepard refused to accept this rating as permanent. "We know there is nothing inherent in the Negro to explain this showing," he told a meeting of school principals. "Given the same opportunities and motivation, our pupils can measure up to the whites. But first we must show their families the reason for education. We've got to convince them that with schooling their children can get a decent job." With that philosophy the Banneker assistant superintendent launched his program. He attacked the problem on three fronts—parents, teachers, and pupils.

"An impossible task," Shepard was warned. "You can't reach these unschooled parents."

"I don't think we have hard-to-reach parents," Shepard replied. "We merely have parents nobody ever tried to reach before." The educator told me about his district. "In slums there are thousands of Negro homes without a strong father image. Men can't get jobs as easily as women, and so they become mere drones in the family or leave the family without a father altogether. The result is that a pall of insecurity and unworthiness hangs over the home."

"They told me I needed research before I launched my program," Shepard recalls, "but I didn't have time for a study."

And so Sam Shepard set out on the difficult task of getting mothers and fathers to come out to talk about their children's performance in school, with a possible brighter future in mind. At first there was only a trickle of interest, but Shepard persevered. Making the rounds of his twenty-three schools, he spoke night after night, and he concentrated on dollars-and-cents figures. He cited Department of Labor figures to show that a high school graduate can expect to earn maybe $4,500 a year; a college degree is worth $6,300 a year and up; while the unskilled laborer can expect only $2,000 to $3,000—if indeed automation doesn't steal his job.

As this gospel spread, PTA's were organized, and the turnout at these meetings jumped to four hundred and five hundred people. "We can't do much for the kids without your help," parents were told and were given a "Parents' Pledge of Cooperation" listing ways to help their youngsters succeed in school.

"What do you want us to do?" parents inquired at these meetings.

"Manage the homework," Shepard said. "See that your children have a time and a place to study. Give them a good light, and shut off the radio and TV. Above all, make sure they increase their skill in reading. That's the key that will give them a better life than yours." To assist, the schools gave each elementary-school child a homework assignment notebook to be signed each week by the parents. "If your youngster alibis he's lost it," parents were told, "see that he doesn't lose it again."

Shepard also appealed to parents to get their kids to school every day and on time. "People say the Negro is shiftless and can't get to work on schedule. If it's true, then the place to cure this is at school."

While homework and getting to school on time may be routine counseling for white children, it was indeed a remarkable advance in the Negro slums, and it took hold. In response

to these unprecedented appeals, attendance that first year improved, and study habits and scholarship, too.

With the same realistic approach, Shepard set about motivating his principals and teachers. He converted the doubtful and began to weld an extraordinary team.

"The first thing I ask," he said, "is to quit teaching by I.Q." He argued that I.Q. is not a true indicator of ability, that our background and experiences affect our academic performance. He illustrated how teachers are likely to be biased by I.Q. tests. "You know that Mary, for example, tested 119, so you urge her on, draw her out, encourage her performance. But Johnny tested only 74. So when he doesn't respond, you just pat him on the head and say 'You've been a good boy and tomorrow you can clean the blackboard.' However, if you forget the I.Q. and work with and motivate the individual child, he may do infinitely better."

As a second plea Shepard asked that teachers abandon their attitude of condescension. "You've earned a degree or two, live in a better part of town," he pointed out. "You've come up in the world. But don't teach as if you pitied these poor slum kids. They're not stupid."

The assistant superintendent launched his teachers on a regular program of home visits, which, under the appalling conditions, was at first not altogether popular with the staff. But Shepard has continued it, and today home visits are paying great rewards in insight and sympathetic understanding. In the schools I visited, I sensed a heart-warming rapport between teachers and pupils.

Once his program was rolling, the educator looked for new ways to inspire the children. To expand their horizons, Shepard inaugurated field trips to radio and television studios, the St. Louis planetarium, the zoo, museums, parks, the Jefferson Memorial, the famous Shaw Gardens, the city markets. "You wouldn't believe it," a principal explained to me, "but children from many of these poor homes have never ever seen common vegetables —a carrot, for example. They're used to hominy grits and sowbelly. And except for these school trips, they've never been out of their own neighborhood."

These outside experiences paid unexpected dividends. There was the problem youngster from a broken home —with four different last names in the family—who went on one of these trips and reported it for the school paper. "We never had trouble with him since," his principal told me. "He became a reporter from Room 4, and for the first time in his life he was *somebody.*"

As enrichment the Banneker School District inaugurated "Reading Is Fun" programs for advanced students and encouraged the gifted in mathematics, science, music, and art. One group of excited eighth-graders turned up each day for reading class a half hour early. For the less able Banneker children, of course, remedial reading was provided.

By the second year further progress was charted in reading comprehension and vocabulary, where hundreds of students jumped ahead a full year or more. Every child now possessed a library card, and the school libraries stayed open some nights to accommodate avid readers.

Meanwhile Shepard continued to push his program, "Operation Motivation," with the parents. The big thing, the final payoff to all this study and education, he told them, is a decent job with good pay. He organized teams of successful St. Louis Negroes, who made the rounds of the Banneker

schools telling their stories. They're still on the job.

"I call it success in the flesh," says Shepard. "Here is evidence of dreams come true." He then introduces the panel members, who speak about their job experiences.

There are Chester Stovall, director of city welfare in St. Louis and first Negro in the mayor's cabinet; Leon Wheeler, digital computer programer; Charles A. Brown, design engineer with McDonnell Aircraft. Brown recalls that he was the only Negro engineer in his college graduating class, and explains his work on ejection devices for the Gemini two-man spacecraft. "A Negro can make it in science if he's qualified," Brown tells the parents and pupils. "I had four offers of jobs when I graduated from college, all at better than average salaries."

There are other testimonials: from a floor sweeper who won his degree and is now technician in charge of quality control for a soft-drink company; a leading millinery designer, who proudly proclaims, "Now I use my own name on the labels"; a securities salesman; an aerial-map make.

Sam Shepard clinches each session with this telling argument: "You've seen here tonight what a Negro can do. We don't have to live in a jungle all our lives and exist on relief." He closes the meeting with this promise: "You boys and girls can be almost anything you want to be so long as you get an education and you've got the stuff!"

After six years Sam Shepard's faith in his Negro pupils has been amply rewarded. In 1957–58, when St. Louis switched to the track system, the twenty-three Banneker schools had 47 per cent below average (Track 3); 46 per cent average (Track 2); and only seven per cent in the top level, or Track 1. Today the Banneker schools have reversed the picture. Only 11 per cent are in the low division, and 22 per cent are superior. Thus they have gained about a year and a half across the Banneker District and reached the national norm. Hundreds of children even jumped ahead two years in achievement. In one outstanding example, the Dunbar School, eighth-grade reading scores in five years jumped from 7.3 to 9.4—six months over the expectancy of 8.8.

The twenty-three-school attendance figure was remarkable, too. It has jumped from the 80's to 91.1 per cent, and one school has a 95 per cent attendance figure for the year ending last June. As an extra dividend, vandalism in the schools has dropped significantly.

Shepard has received many honors for his achievement, including the "Page One Award" of the St. Louis Newspaper Guild, which saluted him "for service rendered through the public school system to the cause of democracy in the United States." He dis-

claims any miracles. The St. Louis work, he knows, has just begun, and he still has two big concerns. One is that the youngsters' interest and perseverance be kept up through high school. Pulled down by his slum environment, the Negro youngster frequently becomes an early dropout. He goes into the ranks of the unemployed, and all too often turns to delinquency and crime.

Shepard's second major concern is jobs. "There are still barriers of prejudice, and to overcome them we must have superior training," he says.

Shepard's achievement has significance far beyond St. Louis. U.S. cities are gaining rapidly in Negro population, with increasing unemployment, welfare costs, violence, crime. "We are confronted with an inescapable question," says Sam Shepard. "Is the white man going to abandon these cities to culturally deprived Negroes—with resultant chaos—or is he going to help educate them and save the country from disaster?"

37. A Purposeful Language Arts Program

LOUISE G. DAUGHERTY

The Chicago Public Schools endeavor to provide quality education for all the children of all the people who live in the city. The Chicago program in language arts for disadvantaged children is based on the *Curriculum Guide for the Language Arts*. The language arts program of studies, like all other programs of studies, considers the needs of the above-average, the average, and the below-average child in all community areas.

This series of guides, in three volumes (K-3, 4-6, 7-8), is followed by equally appropriate materials that serve the needs of the pupil as he progresses through high school. The *Curriculum Guide for the Language Arts* includes reading, writing, speaking, and listening at all levels as closely interrelated facets of the skills of communication.

The Guide (a) presents the scope and sequence of the required language arts program; (b) provides the structure, framework, and foundation of the local program (there is no ceiling); and (c) stimulates the imagination of the teacher (1, p. xxi).

It encourages the organization of school committees to suggest adapta-

tions suitable to the particular requirements of local environment, thereby helping the classroom teacher to (a) study the guide in relation to individual class and individual pupil needs, (b) use suggestions as a springboard to creative teaching, (c) provide for individual differences, (d) plan, organize, and develop the program within the structure and framework of the guide, and (e) help each child progress as far as his ability and available time permit (1, p. xxx).

To further assist the teacher, each guide points out the characteristics—physical, mental, social, and psychological—of the maturing child. It also illustrates many ways of organizing a room for effective instruction and gives the teacher concrete suggestions in designing a program that will provide for individual differences.

Experiences to bring about the desired objectives in a series of lessons, procedure, and evaluation for the teacher, practices and evaluation for the pupil, and suggested instructional aids are developed for every skill at every level.

Constant evaluation involving every teacher, using a Guide, and a four-year cycle of review, makes the Guide dynamic, modern, and practical.

Increasing attention is being given nationally and locally to the child growing up in below-average communities. Chicago schools seek to overcome factors which militate against the success of the child. Considerations discussed in this article are based on the pupil in the below-average community, and reveal the special interest being shown in helping him realize his potential.

The child who needs special services because he lives in areas of substandard housing, low income, high transiency, and overcrowding may belong to one of several groups. He could be listed as of:

1. Mexican origin—who may be a first or second generation migrant—who must overcome a language handicap.

2. Puerto Rican origin—who has similar adjustment to make.

3. Appalachian origin—who faces deeply rooted suspicion of the new neighbors.

4. Negro origin—who may be the third or fourth generation of a family from the worst sections of the city.

5. Negro origin—who may have southern roots—whose only hope for contributing citizenship lies in the school.

INCREASED STAFF SERVICES

In recent years an increasing number of services in schools in areas of high transiency, overcrowding, and expanding pupil population have made their appearance. Chicago schools' pupil-teacher ratio has fallen from 37.93 in 1954–1955 to 32.5 in 1964–1965 (2, p. 7). This should be kept in mind as additional services are enumerated in the following list:

1. The result of the school building program of 1953–1963 is 1,883 classrooms constructed in the seven districts (out of 21) which are in the low-income, high mobility, overcrowded areas of the city (3, p. 102). This is over half of the total number of rooms constructed in the entire city.

2. Master teachers are freed of classroom responsibilities in order to help beginning teachers and substitutes; such master teachers are assigned to schools having large numbers of newly assigned personnel.

3. Special service teachers are placed in schools having more than 32.5 pupils as a room average. When additional space is not immediately available, special service teachers assist the classroom teacher, work with small groups of children in coaching situations, and help the teachers in routine duties as directed by the principal.

4. Psychological service is offered in the summer to test pupils who could not be treated during the school year.

5. Reading clinics in 12 of 21 districts serve severely crippled readers —elementary and high school—during the regular school day.

6. After-school reading clinics are provided in disadvantaged communities to serve pupils who cannot attend clinics during the regular school day.

7. After-school libraries are used as homework rooms in communities lacking public libraries.

8. After-school reading classes are held in many areas having large numbers of pupils above third grade who are retarded one year or more in reading.

9. Free bus service is provided during school hours for trips of an educational nature.

10. Cultural coordinator services are available to provide free and low-cost cultural opportunities in the performing arts and tours to enrich the child's experiential background.

11. Reading and other subject matter consultant services are available to local schools.

12. Increased attendance officer services, especially in the week before school opens, help the school reach out to the disadvantaged home.

13. Special teachers (nonquota) help foreign-speaking pupils within the local school learn English. These are provided where large numbers of non-English speaking pupils are concentrated. These classes seek to help the child learn English well enough to be enrolled in a regular classroom.

ORGANIZATION AND MATERIALS

Recognizing the special needs of children, local schools can take advantage of additional methods available to them. These additional methods include the following:

1. The continuous development (nongraded primary) plan reduces the number of failures among the slower learners, and allows the academically able to progress as rapidly as they master the required skills (4).

2. Ability grouping in reading reduces certain problems.

3. The regular summer schools provide for the disadvantaged pupils through (a) review of seventh- and eighth-grade work in a regular school program and (b) remedial reading classes of $1\frac{1}{2}$ hours daily for pupils in grades six, seven, and eight.

4. The increased per capita appropriation for textbooks and library books in areas of high transiency allows lost books to be readily replaced and special needs of new, "different" pupils to be more quickly met (3, p. 41).

5. Language laboratories, using the latest electronic equipment for programed learning, are being installed in educational and vocational centers.

At the high school level special English programs for the disabled reader stress the attainment of skill in reading, along with other language arts

skills. Designed for the high school student whose reading abilities range from 6.0 to 7.9, the Essential English program helps the student to establish a sound basis for achievement in all academic areas. The concepts and contents are based upon those presented in the elementary school and in the Basic English course of the high school. They parallel those in the Regular and Honors English guide of the high school.

This kind of sequential development of content promotes movement of students from Basic into Essential and from Essential into Regular or even Honors English at any time along the three-year sequence. If a student remains in Essential English he is placed, during his senior year, in two of the three workshop courses which meet his needs (5, p. iii).

Basic English courses provide for students of low academic potential who enter high school at a level below Essential English.

EXPERIMENTAL APPROACHES

Numerous experiments in improving the quality of education for the disadvantaged child may be found in Chicago's schools. These embrace gifted, average, and overage educationally retarded pupils. They can be found in primary, elementary, and high schools, as well as in the recently created (1962) Educational and Vocational Guidance Centers which serve the elementary pupil who is $14\frac{1}{2}$ to 18 years of age. They may involve increased staff, special groupings of pupils, or cooperation with limited numbers of volunteers. Illustrative programs follow.

Special summer schools assure a laboratory placed in as nearly ideal an educational environment as possible to provide for disadvantaged pupils in their own school district. Features of these special schools include:

1. Grade levels prekindergarten through six.

2. One hundred pupils per grade in 1–6 in classes of 25: (a) Group 1–1½ years below grade level in reading achievement; (b) Group 2—below achievement level for grade; (c) Group 3—at or near standard achievement; and (d) Group 4—above standard achievement for grade (6, p. 59).

3. Staff carefully screened for creativity, ability, interest.

4. Intensive auxiliary services including resource staff and extra materials.

5. Parental involvement.

6. In-service training period daily for all staff.

7. Forty per cent of day devoted to language arts.

Results each summer since 1960 indicate over two times as much learning takes place in all groups as those same groups experience in their home schools in a comparable length of time.

Carver Primary School demonstration center provides an experimental approach to the education of above-average and "gifted" disadvantaged children living in low-income public housing. By grouping children having IQ's from 109 to 130, one experimental class of pupils is organized at each grade level.

Teachers use team teaching techniques to utilize specially developed materials and methods in order to increase motivation in all subjects, but especially in language arts. Supplementary reading materials, special interest groups, field trips to museums, parks, and art galleries are closely related to the unique instructional program. Special efforts to strengthen school-parent relationships are predicated on educating parents to realize the talents of their children and helping them to become more competent

in establishing home conditions in which the gifted child may attain maximum growth (7, p. 45).

Gifted disadvantaged pupils in grades five, six, seven, and eight who attend schools served by the Junior League of Chicago, Inc., may be enrolled in the Junior Great Books Program. Bi-weekly discussion groups, meeting from 3:30 to 5:00 P.M., are led by two trained volunteers assigned by the Junior League (2, p. 73). Started in February, 1964, with initial costs of sets of books defrayed by the Junior League, the program has been expanded in the 1964–1965 school year.

Gifted disadvantaged pupils in their high school years are served by a variety of programs. Each high school provides:

1. "100 Program" for the 100 most academically able pupils in the school, 25 at each grade level.

2. Honors classes in English.

3. Advanced placement classes (at college level and in a limited number of schools).

4. Special interest and club groups.

5. Summer school opportunities, free of charge, including (a) classes for academically talented pupils in English (Fourth Year); (b) special seminars in English-Social Studies; (c) individual and group projects for the gifted; (d) field trips, resource personnel, special counseling (8, p. 55); and (e) opportunities to participate in classes with talented students from many high schools in many differing communities.

Financed by the Ford Foundation and the Chicago Board of Education, the Special Project (District Eleven Project)—one of the Great Cities School Improvement Program studies —provides wider experiences in and out of school for the overage child between eleven and seventeen years of age.

Special nongraded classes with reduced class size, special teaching personnel, and special counselors for pupils and parents are provided. In language arts, teachers develop integrated units based on interest and social maturity rather than on basic texts and workbooks.

Between 4:00 and 6:00 P.M. classes with a variety of activities are conducted in several school buildings. None of the activities is of a recreational nature.

Those activities pertaining directly to the language arts would include (a) a reading clinic, (b) reading classes (ages 14–17), (c) communications arts laboratories (ages 11–13), (d) urban 4-H using library and reading and speaking activities (ages 11–13), and (e) summer library reading groups wherein pupils are escorted in groups to public libraries. (There is no public library in the area which is within walking distance of this group of children.)

Results document that pupils reach high school at higher achievement levels—at an earlier age and in less time—than in previous years under the traditional graded system. Fewer classes in Basic English at the freshman level are needed in the local high school, as all these pupils enter at the Essential English level.

The first elementary graduates of the Special Project classes, designated as potential dropouts, were in the class of June, 1961. It is to be expected that if they persevered in high school they would graduate in June, 1965. Local high school records show a number who graduated in 3½ years, as their names appear on graduation programs in January, 1965.

References

1. Board of Education, City of Chicago. *Curriculum Guide for the Language Arts—Grades 4, 5, 6* (Chicago: Board of Education, 1964).
2. Board of Education, City of Chicago. *Education in the Intermediate and Upper Grades,* Study Report Number Six, 1964 Series (Chicago: Board of Education, 1964).
3. Board of Education, City of Chicago. *Compensatory Education,* Study Report Number Four, 1964 Series (Chicago: Board of Education, 1964).
4. Briggs, Albert A. *What Elementary Schools Are Doing: A Non-graded Primary Program* (Boston: Ginn & Co., 1964).
5. Willis, Benjamin C. "Forward," *Essential English in the Secondary School* (Chicago: Board of Education, 1964).
6. Board of Education, City of Chicago. *Education in the Kindergarten and Primary Grades,* Study Report Number Five (Chicago: Board of Education, 1964).
7. Board of Education, City of Chicago. *Program of Education for the Gifted,* Study Report Number Twelve (Chicago: Board of Education, 1964).
8. Board of Education, City of Chicago. *High School Education,* Study Report Number Seven (Chicago: Board of Education, 1964).

38. Gateway English: Teaching English to Disadvantaged Students

MARJORIE B. SMILEY

Richard, the twelve-year-old protagonist of Warren Miller's *The Cool World,* has this to say about reading:

> Once you know how to read it aint hard to learn almos any thing. Doc say, "Readin. To read Richard. That the beginnin of evry thing. You see if I not right Richard. Man." He say. "When you can read an write why you can do any thing. Do any thing. Be any thing."

This is how Richard sees it. English teachers also see reading as critical in the education of children like Richard, as the *gateway* to work or to further education. Reading is generally central in current programs for educationally disadvantaged students, but there are other important elements too. In such programs, we should consider a number of things.

First, we need to look searchingly at what we hope Richard will find on the other side of the *gateway* we would escort him through. To pose the question more explicitly: what are, what should be the aims of reading instruc-

Reprinted from *English Journal*, Vol. 54, No. 4 (April 1965), pp. 265–274. Reprinted with the permission of the National Council of Teachers of English and Marjorie B. Smiley.

tion for children who are variously described as *underprivileged, deprived,* or *disadvantaged?*

English teachers cannot avoid looking at reading in the larger context of the English language arts. Even though reading may be critical, probably central, in programs designed for educationally disadvantaged children, is it sufficient? What is the place of instruction in spoken English, in listening, in written composition for these children? Is "Doc," whom Richard quotes in the brief passage above, right in his opinion that reading is "the beginning"?

And what of Richard? Who is he? Those who talk about and who design educational programs for underprivileged children often cite Richard or someone like him as a prototype. Is he?

Warren Miller's Richard is a Negro boy who has grown up in Harlem. He has lived in derelict tenements. He has never known a "real" father; his mother is harassed and thus easily angered by her son; his grandmother worries about him but is unable to help him. His well-meaning and conscientious junior high school teacher is just not with it. Alienated from the adults and institutions that might give meaning to his life, Richard searches for manhood and a sense of belonging in the pursuit of a gun and in affiliation with a gang. He tells his story as a part of putting his life in order, with the help of "Doc," from the shelter of a home for delinquent boys.

As a Negro male adolescent, Richard stands for what is the largest group among the millions of children disadvantaged by grinding poverty, by the absence of supportive adults—especially men—to whom he may look as models, and by an educational system that has frustrated and shamed him. As English teachers and as human beings we must remember Richard when we plan English programs for disadvantaged children. But to take Richard as typical of even the most grossly underprivileged adolescents is as mistaken as to forget him. Even among adolescents from the lowest income levels, from broken families, from equally dismal segregated slums, only a very small proportion become delinquent or require intensive psychological help in residential centers. The more we learn about the difficulties which many poor families experience, the more we must be convinced of the extraordinary resilience and inner strength of those often too simply categorized as underprivileged.

As we must learn to differentiate the degrees of psychological damage, of academic and most particularly of reading retardation, while keeping in mind the latent resources of intellect and character among our most deprived students, so we must remember that most of the children even in our nation's Harlems live in intact families, in clean and orderly homes, supported by fathers—and often mothers—who are regularly employed. These children grow up with the same kind of attention, the same parental interest in school achievement that we sometimes seem

to think are to be found only in white upper middle-class homes. The half-truths that have coalesced into a mythology which says that all underprivileged children come from broken—and bookless—homes does incalculable damage: it lowers teachers' expectations, attenuates the curriculum, and alienates children and their parents. Low income parents, white or Negro, differ from middle-class parents in their tendency to buy books and toys and to take their children to the Fair only to the extent that surpluses remaining after rent and necessities are accounted for, and may be limited, of course, to the extent that the parents' own education shapes their choices of books and experiences for their children.

MEANING OF DISADVANTAGED

Nevertheless, these children, like Richard, are disadvantaged educationally. They are disadvantaged, because segregated housing and schools cannot possibly prepare children for a full life in our democracy. They are disadvantaged, because we have not yet succeeded in making the promise of equal opportunity for freedom and for skilled and professional employment a reality, and because every limit on the promise of the future makes the tasks of learning—and of teaching—more difficult. They are disadvantaged further, because most slum schools are themselves underprivileged, though it seems obvious that if we are to look to the schools as the agent which will "allow no man's failure to prevent the success of his son," these schools, their teachers, and their programs must have unusual excellence.

But there are others besides Richard and his somewhat more fortunate Negro classmates who attend slum schools and require our special consideration. Each of our major cities now harbors a Negro ghetto; but in almost every one of these cities there is at least one other ghetto, smaller perhaps, but almost equally deteriorated and only slightly less rigidly segregated. Here most of the other educationally disadvantaged children in our nation live and attend school; today these are chiefly children of Southern rural white families and those from Spanish-speaking Puerto Rican or Mexican families. But even these, who together with Negro children constitute most of the one in three school-age, inner-city children considered educationally disadvantaged, do not complete this roster. There are, in addition, the children of migrant workers, of families marooned in the isolated "pockets of poverty" in the Appalachians, and the often forgotten children on American Indian reservations.

These are the children who are least well served by the watered-down English curriculum too often found in the substandard schools they attend. What can they be helped to achieve in English? What kind of program can contribute most to their special needs? How can English be made truly a gateway to a brighter future for them?

As to the gross effects of educational disadvantage, there are certain symptoms common to all the groups we have mentioned. Each group contributes a disproportionate number to any list of educational and social casualties: to the increasing number of adolescents and young adults who have left school at the earliest legal age, to those whose inadequacies in reading and in oral and written communication and whose poor habits of application bar them from further education, from employment, from the armed services. Since these consequences are overt and socially costly, it is not surprising that educational programs for underprivileged youth have usually been vocationally oriented. With respect to

English these programs have aimed at achieving what is called "functional literacy." Their focus has been primarily remedial or corrective: major attention has been given to reading, infrequent attention has been given to speech, and almost no attention at all to anything that English teachers would consider composition.

SCOPE OF PROGRAM

Despite our almost avid interest in specific materials and methods for teaching reading to disadvantaged students, must we settle for English programs thus limited in aim and in scope? I hope we will not do this: not because I think preparation for work and a view of English as a "tool" for work—or for study in other fields—is demeaning; not because I think that reading can be taught without intensive and systematic practice of its component skills. My reservations are in part methodological. Preparation for work or for academic advancement is a motivating force only for students who already have vocational and academic aspirations. And it is with respect to these aspirations that the children we wish to reach are deprived. As the so far largely unsuccessful efforts to recruit and train young men rejected by the armed services or older men suffering from situational unemployment demonstrate, vocational or vocationally related skills are learned only when the job—or the chance to vote—is realistically and immediately attainable.

This kind of relationship between learning English and its direct practical consequences is not characteristic of most junior and senior high school programs. Within the setting of work study programs, of course, the relation of reading level to vocational advancement may serve to motivate students to improve their reading skills and to master the writing skills essential to secure and perform jobs. Even within the limits of vocationally oriented English programs, moreover, much more attention should be given to the teaching of spoken English than is customary. Sales and office occupations are among the few in which opportunities continue to increase in the face of growing automation. Underprivileged youth must not be passed over for employment or promotion because they speak a substandard dialect. If they are to be prepared for these opportunities in which communication skills are important, they will have to be helped to acquire a level of spoken English that is socially acceptable.

In any event, the aims and scope of programs in English for disadvantaged junior and senior high school students should rest on more than practical and methodological considerations. We are accustomed to justify the teaching of English on quite other grounds. We point to language and literature as uniquely suited to help us give order and meaning to the world we live in. We call upon literature to hold up to each new generation the models which we think will help them shape themselves. In language and literature we believe can be found those persistent strands and those variations that will serve to bind together different generations and different cultural groups. Is this view of the aims and scope of teaching English irrelevant or expendable in the education of underprivileged youth? Is it not rather especially important for those children whose difficulties with life and with learning stem from their deep feelings of alienation? What could be more "useful" than to teach English so that these alienated children may come nearer to possessing a world they now only inhabit?

The abandonment of these tradi-tional aims in so many programs in English for disadvantaged students is almost surely on grounds of expediency rather than conviction. The reasons given, if they are made explicit, are that these students are not interested in the literature of the traditional English curriculum or that their reading level is too low to enable them to read this literature with understanding. But perhaps we should be seeking other explanations. Has the literature selected for elementary and secondary English had the effect of excluding and further alienating many of the children in our classrooms because the characters, problems, and settings are so different from their own experiences and because we have not sufficiently realized what could be done through creative teaching to bridge this gap? Unfortunately, by the time educationally disadvantaged students reach junior or senior high school they have probably developed a strong resistance to reading and their reading skills are not adequate to the demands of much of the literature in the standard English curriculum. Nevertheless, these difficulties can be met by adaptations in materials and methods; they need not and should not limit our larger aims. It is the demands of our increasingly specialized technology that require us to help all youth to achieve the reading level that will qualify them for skilled employment. The essential values of our culture as of any culture can be orally transmitted; certainly they are not bound to a specific reading level or to particular literary works.

PROMISING PRACTICES

To agree that our central aims in teaching English should be the same for all youth does not negate the need for modifications in the methods and materials we employ. Fortunately, mounting social pressure to do something about educating underprivileged children and youth has given rise to a variety of special programs, many of them supported by the federal grants and by private foundation funds. To date the majority of the programs in English has been for elementary and preschool children, but there are enough programs in the secondary school to provide us with a variety of constructive suggestions. Without any attempt at surveying all of these programs, I shall try to cite a number of approaches that seem to me particularly promising, examples chosen from the English programs in Cleveland, Detroit, Houston, Syracuse, New York, and other systems that have given particular attention to secondary school programs for disadvantaged youth. This composite then of many ideas suggests that a good English program for disadvantaged junior and senior high school students would be something like this.

Every English program for disadvantaged junior and senior high school students should begin by introducing specific activities in listening and speaking. A fundamental reorientation of our usual teaching strategy is necessary if listening and speaking are to find their proper place in English classrooms. Instead of our customary practice of telling students, especially these students, what we expect them to learn, we must rather involve them actively in verbal inquiry. We must find ways to have our students ask the questions, make the comparisons, formulate the conclusions. The recent studies of the language of the classroom by B. Othanel Smith, Arno Bellack, and others should be of special interest to teachers of English and to teachers of disadvantaged students particularly. The development of students' skill in questioning, in inquiring which is central to curriculum experimentation

based on early studies of Piaget and the more recent proposals and studies of Bruner and others are usually considered to be appropriate only to intellectually gifted and verbally advanced students. They are equally relevant, equally adaptable to methods of teaching educationally disadvantaged children and youth. We must, of course, take account of the findings of research into social class differences in language patterns that indicate that lower-class children and adults make limited use of complex sentences and subordination and that these limitations restrict the ability to express complex relationships. But these findings should not lead us to the conclusion that students whose language is thus limited cannot learn to perceive and thus to formulate complex relationships. But these intellectual and language skills, which junior and senior high school teachers find already quite well developed among more privileged children, must be explicitly taught to disadvantaged children. They must be taught by making the English classroom—and hopefully every classroom— a forum for students' oral inquiry. They must be taught also by specific exposition and by oral practice.

Some of the difficulties underprivileged children face in learning to read is in the early stages of associating what is heard with the printed symbols for these sounds. One of the most interesting findings of recent research has been the evidence of a high degree of correlation between hearing (auding, as it is called in these studies) and reading. This is a difficulty that many such children have not yet overcome by Grade 7 or 8. These children are unlikely to have had parents with time to read aloud to them in their early years. We do not do nearly enough reading aloud to children in elementary or secondary schools. We do not make nearly enough use of the increasingly rich store of records of poetry, stories, speeches, and plays. And because as English teachers we often find it painful to listen to students who read haltingly, we give least opportunity to read aloud to those students who most need this practice. Most underprivileged children speak a substandard dialect. English teachers, unfortunately, have been taught to set quite rigid standards for spoken English. Children who have not learned these speech habits in their home environments are shamed into holding their tongues—at least in class activities. Classrooms in slum schools are typically either silent or, more usually, frenetically noisy. It is very rare indeed to find a classroom in a slum school in which discussion is taking place. But patient teachers, alert to these children's interests, are able to involve them in discussion, in inquiry. And for children who have not yet learned to deal confidently with the printed word, oral discussion and inquiry are absolutely essential. If discussion is to take place, it is imperative that we learn to accept substandard speech; that we make the extra effort that may be required to understand. This is not to say that we have no obligation to help our students achieve socially acceptable speech patterns. But this aim and the activities necessary to realize it should not be allowed to invade and thus inhibit discussion about ideas or books.

An English program for disadvantaged students should provide systematic experiences in learning to listen with discrimination. There is at least one set of programmed materials using audio tapes already available which is designed to teach listening skills. Every English teacher can use spoken word records to give students experience in listening to increasingly longer and more complex units of oral literature.

SOCIALLY-ACCEPTABLE DIALECT

A comprehensive aural-oral program in English for disadvantaged students should include explicit pattern practice in a socially acceptable dialect. The objective of such an oral language program should, I am convinced, be concerned with the students' mastery of an approved regional colloquial speech. (Printed materials designed to provide practice in realistic spoken English situations are also beginning to be available.) Programs employing practice tapes modeled in part on the pattern practice materials developed to teach English as a second language are in experimental use at elementary, secondary, and college levels. English and speech teachers should seek the aid of linguists and dialectologists to develop programs of this kind appropriate to the requirements of specific school populations. Two cautions should be kept in mind in connection with the introduction of programs of this kind. First, it is extremely important that English and speech teachers who undertake to teach the disadvantaged student a second dialect learn to do so without censuring his native dialect. Teachers of foreign languages do not typically judge their students' native language; teachers of English and speech on the other hand are very likely to start from a correctional point of view. The student too often is taught that his speech is "bad," and that another language, standard English in most cases, is "good." If, on the other hand, an approved dialect is taught as a "second language," teacher and learner together can escape embarrassing and hence inhibiting value judgments of native subcultural dialects.

Finally, the timing of efforts to teach

disadvantaged students a second English dialect should be carefully considered. Ideally, it should be possible to develop a kind of bilingualism in two English dialects in young children. As experience and some experimentation indicate, young children may be able to learn two languages within the context of different language environments, where, for example, one language is spoken at home and another at school. Some underprivileged children do by some means achieve fluency in the English of the school, even though they live in homes and neighborhoods where a socially unacceptable dialect is spoken. Those who have this mastery, however, are unlikely to be among the underprivileged students who are seriously retarded in English in the secondary school. High school students whose spoken English is restricted to a substandard dialect are usually performing below grade level in English, and probably in their other subjects as well. These students must be strongly motivated if they are to attempt a "new" English as teenagers. Successful programs in a second English dialect seem to be tied to and probably depend on students' perception of specific opportunities in employment or on their desire for further education. We would probably be wise, therefore, to place intensive speech pattern practice at these points in students' lives, that is, in the ninth or tenth or twelfth grade.

Perhaps, in the light of the overriding importance of helping underprivileged students master an approved dialect and improve their reading, the allocation of composition to a secondary place in programs for them is justified. Instruction in answering test questions, in letter writing, in precision in filling out forms is customarily included in English programs for these students. These bread and butter skills are important to the future of these students; English teachers need to accept the task of teaching these basic writing skills as worthwhile. But they can and should aim for more. Given opportunity for free oral expression of feelings and ideas in the English classroom, disadvantaged adolescents can be led to put these feelings and ideas on paper. Almost without exception, teachers who have given such students confidence to write about what they know have been agreeably surprised by what they have to say. Given wholehearted acceptance and genuine interest these students, like all students, can begin to accept the always arduous task of learning to write more correctly. As their mastery of spoken English grows and as their exposure to reading increases, the writing of underprivileged students is likely to approximate that of their less disadvantaged classmates.

IMPORTANCE OF READING

But what about reading? It is reading that is popularly and professionally considered the major difficulty of disadvantaged students and thus the major responsibility of English teachers who would help these children qualify for a better future. Reading has been held to be the *gateway* to salvation, to the exercise of the franchise. At one period in our history it was the subject of legislation intended to keep the Negro in his place. Pre–Civil War laws prohibiting anyone to teach a slave to read—or to write—were not uncommon. The most recent extension of the National Defense Education Act includes provisions for preparing teacher specialists in reading as a category of teacher preparation distinctive from—though hopefully not divorced from—English. Thus, while we may disagree with "Doc" in *The Cool World*, in thinking that speaking rather than reading is the best beginning for English programs for disadvantaged students, we cannot escape the conclusion that reading is central in such programs. Eunice Newton, in a recent article in *The Journal of Negro Education,* puts it like this: "If the school cannot teach an educable child to read, there is really nothing else of importance it can teach him."

If we examine the various reading programs for disadvantaged youth that are currently offered in many junior and senior high schools, we find two basically different types, each designed to meet the needs of students with distinctive reading difficulties. One type of program, probably the most common, is that intended to teach beginning or elementary reading skills to students who have arrived at junior or even senior high school reading at first, second, or third grade, or even as "nonreader." These students are still at what Fries describes as the "transfer" stage of reading. Or using Lado's more detailed categories, these students have not yet mastered the four primary reading skills: prereading, or identifying the graphemes; association or "fitting" graphemes and language; the habit of reading what is spoken; and of reading aloud, or speaking what is written. These programs, typically called remedial or corrective, place major emphasis on teaching word attack skills and on vocabulary building. Through these programs, the secondary school undertakes an elementary school task. If they succeed in the initial reading task, learning to read, they have made a critical breakthrough for disadvantaged youth.

But learning to read is only a part of what must be accomplished. Young people who have made this giant and most difficult step are still not qualified either for further education or for employment in highly skilled or semiprofessional levels, where employment opportunities are to be found. Certainly they are far from ready to reap the benefits of reading as a means of enlarging the self and giving order to experience. Once they have learned to read, students are at the point where they can capitalize on this achievement and begin to read to learn and to develop the skills required for those more advanced levels which Fries terms "productive" and "imaginative" stages. In Lado's more detailed breakdown the more advanced reading stages are described as follows: Reading for different kinds of information; reading diversified materials and types; reading for speed and power. Most English teachers would probably agree that these reading skills are appropriate to secondary English programs. Unfortunately, very few English teachers have received explicit instruction in teaching these skills. The teaching of developmental reading is only rarely a systematic phase of junior and senior high school English. Few English courses go beyond vocabulary building and tests of the retention of specific facts. Yet it is only through intensive instruction in the full range of advanced reading skills that underprivileged students can achieve equality with their more privileged classmates. Only by mastering these skills can they qualify for any form of higher education and the kinds of employment open only to those with some education beyond high school. As secondary school English teachers we must not be satisfied to help disadvantaged students over the threshold of basic reading skills; we must turn our attention to the development of methods and materials which will enable these students to read with power.

ADAPTATIONS NOT THE ANSWER

To accept "reading with power" as an aim in teaching English to educationally disadvantaged students is to confront the question: *what* shall be read? The specially prepared reading materials prepared to teach such students elementary reading skills lack the depth, the richness and subtlety of literature. They are thus totally inadequate for teaching critical reading skills. Is *Julius Caesar* the only alternative? Some teachers of slow reading classes report that they can "get through it" in eight weeks. One must question the dramatic impact of such ordeals. Others who think or think they should think that Julius Caesar is part of a heritage which everyone must share compromise by using classic comics. Pressed on whether students who have read a comic book version have really read *Julius Caesar* and thus really shared the heritage, these teachers may shift their defense. Students feel better, they explain, if they think they are reading what other students are reading. Do we really believe fourteen-year-olds are thus deceived?

Adaptations of great books are sometimes defended on the ground that they provide a peg on which to hang discussion of power, loyalty, good and evil which should not be denied adolescents because they are poor readers. But cannot such discussions grow out of contemporary issues presented and discussed on television, even in tabloids? The viewers who watched, without protesting, the street corner murder of a young woman—are they not a more comprehensible and thus more powerful stimulus to a consideration of the evil of apathy than a fourth-grade rendering of Dante's *Inferno?* I think we must ask: whose feelings are wounded if standard works are not read in our classes. The disadvantaged students'? Or ours? Adaptations or cut editions of literary works should be used only when the adaptation retains the essential qualities of the original, or as with the Lambs' *Tales,* has its own literary merit. And since adaptations are usually made of nineteenth-century

novels and reluctant readers are more likely to be attracted to contemporary books, we should probably ask ourselves whether a modern original on the same theme would not be a wiser choice for these students.

Fortunately, there are books mature enough to interest older adolescents which are within their reading range: for example, *The Pearl* and *Lilies of the Field.* Other, more difficult books can be included in the English curriculum for slow readers by teachers who read substantial parts and select the dramatic highlights for students to read in the original. Finally, we need to exploit the rich mine of film, television, and recorded versions of novels and plays as a part of the literature program for disadvantaged students. Students who have seen and discussed the film of *Moby Dick* will be willing and able to read some excerpts from the original novel, for example, the dramatic and ironic incident in which Queequeg rescues his tormentor.

Poetry is the literary form most likely to be omitted from the curriculum of slow and reluctant readers. Teachers who have made careful selections of poetry, however, report that it is enjoyed and understood by a wider range of readers than other literary forms. Traditional ballads and contemporary broadsides in particular can be enjoyed by junior and senior high school students reading at fourth and fifth grade levels. Especially when they are taught through the use of recordings by popular balladists, they enliven the English classroom and make the teaching of simple poetic elements part of the fun. (Incidentally, the use of ballads in contemporary social movements may lead some of these reluctant students to compose their own ballads without realizing that they are engaging in "creative writing.")

To argue that we include adult literature in its original form in English programs for educationally disadvantaged students, however, is not to conclude that other kinds of reading should be excluded. There is a constantly growing list of juvenile books which can serve as a bridge to adult literature for many adolescents. But until recently juvenile books have been singularly inappropriate for underprivileged minority group students in urban centers. Juveniles have been presented a world so white, so orderly, so proper, so committed to happy endings in featureless settings as to provide few possibilities for disadvantaged adolescents to identify with. The exceptions, like *Hot Rod*, which portray a life more "on the wild side" serve to prove this point.

MINORITY GROUP HEROES

Gradually, however, juveniles with minority group protagonists and familiar settings have begun to appear. Some of these, like Louisa Shotwell's *Roosevelt Grady* and Dorothy Hall's *Hurricane*, are good books, because, although each has a young Negro protagonist, they are not formula stories. We know that the children and adults in *Roosevelt Grady* are Negro migrant families only because the illustrations tell us so. The conflict between the young hero and a bully is within the experience of all children; the resolution is credible; the message is implied rather than expounded. Some of the juveniles with interracial casts of character, however, are as contrived as earlier middle-class juveniles are. They are, nevertheless, popular with students who have never seen a book about someone like themselves in appearance.

If we seek books that will give students full rather than stereotyped images of individuals from minority groups, we will be sure to include biographies. They are important in any English curriculum, but especially important to those underprivileged students whose own life space has so few models with whom they can identify. And we can go beyond the biographies of athletes and entertainers, though these are popular and should not be ignored. Biographies of notable Negroes in all fields are available in adult and juvenile books, for example, Charlemae Rollins' sound and readable collection of the stores of forty Negroes in *They Showed the Way*. Unfortunately, there are relatively few biographies at a popular reading level which tell the stories of men and women from other minority groups in the United States.

In the senior high school the literature program for underprivileged students—and for all students—should include books which deal with personal and social issues directly and searchingly. Within this frame it is difficult to see how the curriculum today can fail to include books which confront the reader with the bitter and unresolved problems of racial injustice. We find *The Diary of Anne Frank* and *Hiroshima* on many English reading lists. How many include *The Fire Next Time*, the poignant and little known *A Good Man*, the almost legend-like *A Distant Drummer* by Kelley, Peter Abrahams' *Mine Boy* and *Tell Freedom* and Paton's *Cry, the Beloved Country?* Some of these are fairly difficult, but most can be read by interested adolescents reading at seventh or eighth grade. The magic of a critically important subject and of a well-known name are powerful motivators, even of reluctant readers.

The major contribution of a literature program for educationally disadvantaged students is to help them gain a sense of their own worth and their membership in the American community. It is for this reason that we need to search for books close to the lives of children who have been made to feel excluded from much of the life they see and read about. At the same time, these students also need to read books that tell of lives and times very different from their own. If books about lives like their own can help them order and so control them, books about quite other ways of life may help them give shape to their dreams.

For many of these children, and their teachers, the most important gift of all is the dream of accomplishment. James Aggrey, a modern South African writer, shows us in this parable [1] the dream that must be learned.

Once upon a time, it seems, a man hunting in the forest caught a young eagle. He brought it home and put it among his chickens. The eagle grew in size, but contentedly shared the coop and chicken feed of his domesticated brothers.

One day a naturalist came through the forest and stopped by the forester's hut. "That bird is an eagle!" said the naturalist.

It was, said its owner, but I have trained it to be a chicken. It is no longer an eagle.

No, said the naturalist, it is an eagle still. It has the heart of an eagle. I will show you that it will fly up to the sky as eagles do.

The owner agreed to let the naturalist test his belief. They took the bird up to the roof of the hut and the naturalist said to it. "Fly! You are an eagle, stretch forth your wings and fly."

[1] A paraphrase of a parable by James Aggrey in Peggy Rutherford, editor, *African Voices: An Anthology of Native African Writings* (New York: Vanguard Press, Inc., 1959).

The eagle looked this way and that, and looking down, saw his brothers eating the grain on the ground. Down he jumped and joined the chickens picking at their grain.

"I told you so!" said the owner. "It is a chicken."

But the naturalist begged another chance. And once more he took the eagle to the rooftop and urged it to fly. But again the eagle jumped down to share the chicken feed in the yard.

The owner was glad to be vindicated, but he finally agreed to the naturalist's plea for just one more trial.

The next morning the naturalist rose before dawn and took the bird to the foot of a high mountain. The peaks were beginning to glitter in the rising sun. The naturalist picked up the bird and held it up facing the sun and said: "Eagle, you belong to the sky and not to the earth. Stretch forth your wings and fly!"

The bird looked around; it trembled, it looked up, and suddenly it stretched out its wings and with the scream of an eagle mounted higher and higher until it disappeared in the clouds.

Reading, alas, is not innate to man as flying is to eagles. But unless, like the naturalist, we are able to lift the sights of disadvantaged children to a brighter future than they now see, we are unlikely to teach them English—or anything else. Much, perhaps most, of what must be done for these children must be done outside the English class and outside the school. But, in language, we do have a key to the doorway that must be opened, and in literature a universe of futures to explore.

39. For the Disadvantaged Student— A Program That Swings

FRANK E. ROSS

A friend of mine who works for one of the large automobile companies in Detroit called one Sunday last June and said he was bringing over a car for me to drive. It had no steering wheel. In its place was a flexible shaft topped off by what appeared to be two discs similar to 45-inch record turntables. The driver seats himself, pulls down the shaft so the small turntables rest in his lap. Then he casually rests his hands on the discs and allows his finger tips to steer the auto. Two discs are not really needed, but it is felt that the public could not convert easily to only one. My friend is the head of the department that works on advance designs. His job he says is "To use existing materials to their best advantage in planning ten years ahead."

What a challenge! Yet it is a challenge we, too, in education must accept. In our large industrial cities we now have one in seven youths out of school unemployed. It is predicted that in ten years we will have one in three. That one is the disadvantaged—the culturally different—the newcomer to our cities or the newcomer to our mores.

Reprinted from *English Journal*, Vol. 54 (April 1965), pp. 280–283. Reprinted with the permission of the National Council of Teachers of English and Frank E. Ross.

We can no longer offer to such a student what G. Robert Carlsen calls "the patent medicine approach, in which everyone gets a spoonful from the same bottle." A special program is indicated, and Detroit, among a few other cities, has accepted the challenge.

Who is the child who needs a special program? He has been identified in recent years rather thoroughly. He is bewildered by the world he never made. He is confused, but he realizes he must not show his confusion, for people who have other sets of values consider that a weakness, so he must bluff through with a bravado he did not even know he had. Feign uninterest, real contempt. That's the way to "fake it, Man."

He's a slow learner. That's our word, not his. He has average to low I.Q. That's our measurement, not his. But he knows what we call him; he gets it by osmosis. When we're not very careful, he sees it in our eyes. He picks up nuances in our voices that the linguist hasn't even cataloged yet.

But he gets his revenge. He turns our class attendance books into random checkerboards. He delays the progress of our lessons with his "living it up" in the classroom.

He's insolent, we say. We're from

353

squaresville, he says. We're from nowhere, he says. He's going nowhere, we say.

And so the lines are drawn. The antagonists are identified. The battlefield is the classroom.

Rosemary Wilson, Assistant Director, Curriculum Office, Philadelphia, has asked a heartbreaking and pertinent series of questions, which most of our teachers and most of our curriculum leaders *cannot* answer:

1. What is it like never to hear standard English spoken in your home or community?

2. What is it like never to have had a newspaper, book, or magazine in your home?

3. What is it like never to have seen anyone in your home write anything?

4. What is it like never to have had anyone tell you a story or read to you when you were little?

5. What is it like never to have anyone speak to you except in terms of abuse?

6. What is it like never to have had anyone listen to you tell "what you did in school today"?

7. What is it like never to have traveled more than a few blocks from your home?

8. What is it like to go to a different elementary school every few months as you move from one room or home to another a few blocks away?

9. What is it like to be hungry most of the time, to feel tired and sleepy in school, and not know why?

10. What is it like to have no one to see that you get to school every day?

11. What is it like *never* to have known a kind adult?

Do you wonder really that this child "resents authority," "has undisciplined attitudes"? Do you wonder that his self-image, when he tries to perceive it, is a painful, bleeding sore within his breast?

This is the child we sometimes offer *Silas Marner*. We feed him a diet of noun clauses and a list of 25 spelling words to "have by Friday." He is being programmed every day by parents and by teachers who wring their hands, or wash them, but ultimately do very little to change that program; he is being programmed for a life of frustration, unhappiness, a sense of incompleteness: a human being unfulfilled.

Such children remind us of Vachel Lindsay's "The Leaden-Eyed" [1]

> Let not young souls be smothered out before
> They do quaint deeds and fully flaunt their pride.
> It is the world's one crime its babes grow dull,
> Its poor are ox-like, limp and leaden-eyed.
>
> Not that they starve, but starve so dreamlessly,
> Not that they sow, but that they seldom reap,
> Not that they serve, but have no gods to serve,
> Not that they die, but that they die like sheep.

What program will meet his needs?

Detroit has developed a program that attempts to do the job. It was written in 1961 by gifted teachers, sympathetic, imaginative, aware—the *cognoscenti*. It is a searching call and at once a haven for similar teachers who have rejected the unworkable traditional approach with these children. A single fabric it is, of isolated, successful practices through the years, woven into a course of study and a Gestalt.

[1] Reprinted with permission of The Macmillan Company from *Collected Poems* by Vachel Lindsay. Copyright, 1914, The Macmillan Company. Renewed, 1942, Elizabeth C. Lindsay.

The course has taken into account the considerable research of recent years. We know that these children especially and most children generally have a short attention span. Therefore, now the teacher gives variety to each lesson by doing three and maybe four activities during a forty-minute period. The students may write for five minutes, read for fifteen minutes, have a buzz session on material read for five minutes, and listen to or give a fifteen-minute panel discussion. There is plenty of variety, and it's the spice of *this* life.

We are willing to accept the studies of Ingrid Strom of Indiana University and numerous others who have shown no significant correlation between the study of grammar and its application to writing and speaking. Therefore, language in the course is dealt with relative to history and meaning and not to eighteenth-century foreign word orders.

We acknowledge that children of limited reading ability learn more easily through the ear than the eye. We know, further, that they will make a sometimes lasting impression upon prospective employers with their voices and speech patterns. Therefore, nearly half the course is oral-aural. The students use tape recorders extensively; they give reports, at first from their seats, panel discussions, radio plays, and role-playing skits.

We welcome Paul Diederich's suggestion at Educational Testing Service that students learn to write by writing. Therefore, we require a good bit of writing in English S. Possibly more words get on paper than in some other courses, but it takes the form mostly of "journal jottings." The student maintains a journal in which in the beginning months he writes briefly on any subject that interests him. The student who once faced a piece of paper with tense dread is soon able to relax and pour forth a fountain of words. *De rigueur:* the teacher writes comments on the journal pages regarding the ideas presented but not on the manner in which they appear.

We recognize the appeal to teenagers of the paperback book. This course has no hardbacks. The colorful, cheaper book with the brief insight into its contents blazoned on the cover, with its deceptively small, that is, easy appearance is just what the student will and does read.

The course is different from most classes in other ways. There is no textbook: there is a syllabus in a ringed notebook, college style, for the status-seekers. Circle seating is employed; everyone has a front seat; no one gets lost in the shuffle. Class chairmen often free the teacher to give individual help; class secretaries announce previously determined work; class officers change frequently to give many the opportunity. There is seldom any homework.

Example of a success factor built in: the first test of the course almost guarantees a good score, but the teacher is strongly dependent upon the key. It asks, "Who is the man who introduces the acts on a Sunday evening variety show?" "Don't use that ——— kid stuff!" "Have Gun, Will Travel" is the slogan printed on ———'s calling card."

It was this quiz that Clifton Fadiman sneered about from his tower last year, never knowing for a minute what its object is. No, Clifton, there isn't a Plato in English S, but there are many reclaimed kids.

The most important aspect of English S is the teacher himself, what he is, how he feels, what he does. (No machine will ever teach this course.) English S consists of an over-arching philosophy: this under-achiever, this slow learner, this misfit, is worth saving, capable of saving, and going to be saved. This outcast is going to be incast. It's a rescue operation. A kind of religion, perhaps. The most successful teachers in it certainly have a fervor. The teacher involved has a mission to perform which is at the very roots of his earliest desires to be a teacher. He has always wanted to help those less knowledgeable than himself. Well, he's come to the right place. There are no students *less*.

The teacher through a manual and inservice training workshops is urged to realize that these slow learners are still *learners*. That's where the emphasis must be. However, they are teachable only if they are reachable. The teacher has to be the reacher. (This thought was not composed by Cassius Clay.) Don Schreiber, describing the New York's Higher Horizon Program, said, "Our first job with these kids is the creation of a decent self image. They are encouraged to think they can achieve, and they do achieve. . . ."

Dr. Alvin Loving, now of the University of Michigan, tells about his experience at Miller High School in Detroit. One day when he got home and was looking at his attendance book he discovered he had neglected to take attendance for that day. So he did then, except that he couldn't remember whether a few students were there or not. It was at that moment he realized that if he didn't know whether they were there, they knew he didn't know. There had been no human contact. He made a vow that day to establish a rapport with each student and to practice it each day.

This then is the first concept to practice: pupils are individuals, to be treated on an individual basis, *daily*.

If the teacher has been aware that the students drag behind them a hopeless chain of academic failures, the students know it, too. (That they have the courage to come to class again is amazing.) The teacher's next job is to give them a success experience—every day. The old attitude of "Let's find out what they don't know," or "I've just made a test that will curl their hair" may be fine for college prep students of high ability and stringy hair, but it won't do here. It won't work here; it isn't permitted here. If the teacher wants to beat students, he should try a paddle or a ruler. The welts on their bodies will heal; those on their minds and emotions sometimes do not.

The teacher is then, thirdly, to relax the grip he usually holds on the curriculum, and, through cooperative planning, place some of the decisions in the students' hands. Planning *for* pupils should be distinct from planning *with* them. The teacher needs to plan for specific language skills to be learned by pupils, but he may plan with them what they would like to discover in a certain unit. The manual tells the teacher that English S pupils have successfully shared in planning for the following things:

1. Setting room policies (rules, practices, arrangement)
2. Identifying problems
3. Deciding purposes and objectives for unit study
4. Evaluating learning
5. Devising learning scales
6. Using visual aids
7. Planning field trips
8. Inviting guests to the classroom and planning for such an occasion.

Fourth, the teacher is encouraged to consider the progress of the individual for evaluation, and not to compare each child with other members of the class, or worse still, with some nebulous standard the teacher feels intuitively must exist. If the teacher looks for progress, identifies it for the child and dwells upon it, a chain reaction will develop. The student will bask in this warm sun and grow, and the teacher may develop a resort esprit which will replace his own gloomy conclusion that he is working in a hopeless quagmire.

The attitude of the teacher toward the student and toward the course determines whether all three will succeed. These, then, we have found are the quartet of attitudes that help bring sweet harmony to the education of the disadvantaged child: let students know you like them and respect them; help students achieve some measure of success each day; give students a share in the conduct of the destiny of the class; evaluate the student on the basis of his present performance compared with his past performance.

The student we are working with in ever-increasing numbers in the large cities is a "second son," the disinherited. We have tried to build a program for him that properly fills his void, and we have generally been able to find teachers who are gifted human beings to teach the course we call Communication Skills, English S, with our tenth- and eleventh-graders.

A principal at one of our inner city high schools was curious about the recent attendance of one of the really notorious boys in the school. Hayes, who had never made it to school more than twice a week, was now coming every day. The principal stopped him outside his English S classroom and said, "Hayes, it's good to see you around these days. What is it you find so interesting lately?" Hayes snapped his fingers to some lilting rhythm heard only by himself, and said, "Man, this English S. This program really swings."

40. *Reading and Social Difference*

JAMES H. DUGGINS

I work in San Francisco—in San Francisco's Compensatory Program—a program designed to aid the disadvantaged child—a program the primary emphasis of which in the secondary schools is heightened language skills. I teach English, science, and math to children of the tenth, eleventh, and twelfth grades in an ungraded classroom. The only common characteristic of these children is that none of them can place above the sixth grade on any standardized measure of reading ability.

It is not quite fair to say that there are no similarities among poor readers in the secondary schools. We know almost too much about them. We know them from the vantage point of every behavioral and pedagogical science. For example, we do know how they feel about themselves. Research tells us even how they feel about others. We know what their parents earn, and we can even predict with a fair degree of accuracy the level of their families' reading habits. We know, too, that the poor reader lags behind his peers in the other language arts, speaking, listening, and writing. And we know he

Reprinted from *English Journal*, Vol. 54 (April 1965), pp. 284–288. Reprinted with the permission of the National Council of Teachers of English and James H. Duggins.

is behind in nearly every other school subject.

Despite lavish attention paid to the supposed anomaly of the poor reader in high school, we know, too, he is not in a minority. Some studies estimate that poor readers make up 70 to 80 percent of the public secondary school population of the great cities of this country. And they drop out like paratroopers despite all our efforts.

BASIC PROBLEM:
SOCIAL DIFFERENCE

Essentially, too, we know that this student, this poor reader, is socially different. Despite the frantic screams of some diagnosticians who see monocular vision, handedness, eyedness, large and fine muscle coordination complexities—diagnosticians for whom aphasics peer myopically from behind every flash card —the largest percentage of poor readers is simply socially different. And, let's not be deceived, social difference affects the direction of one's language development.

Our public schools, geared to middle-class values, teach middle-class language patterns. And what else? We teachers are, no matter how it makes us squirm, middle-class people. And verbal ones at that.

Essentially, our problem is not a new one, simply one we feel today is more important to our technical society. We've long talked of the dual standard language of the English classroom. And we do firmly believe, to quote Alan Lerner of "My Fair Lady" that it's "*ow* and *garn* that keep her in her place, not her wretched clothes and dirty face." But despite our own lack of elasticity, we insist these students who are socially different from us stretch to meet the demands of this society at this time.

In our open society these students are simply socially different. Lower class, upper class, and the vast mishmash of shades between are too fuzzy for any of us to *accept*, let alone more than vaguely understand. And what criteria may we use for such ranking of social classes today? Salary? A look at my salary would certainly place some of my plumber's children at a decided advantage. Education? What kind? And for whom? I'd maintain that the greatest single difference evidenced by the children I teach lies in the direction of their language behavior. And we know too much about language to tag it upper, lower, or middle anything.

Language behavior is not normative. We have not yet fallen into the trap of other behavioral scientists who have isolated single criteria and called them "norms." The myth of "General American Speech" and our complete dissatisfaction with the very tests that assume national levels of reading grade placement certainly exemplify the language teachers' refusal to accept the legend of "norms" in language behavior. We know too much about varying patterns of communications to fall prey to mythical standards for language.

But, poor readers in our highly technical society can be seen to be socially different—and more than a little isolated. They are people whose language patterns simply differ from the literacy demands of a highly literate culture. Children who read poorly come from homes where verbal communication is of a very different sort from that of their teachers and more fortunate peers.

And, before we go further, let's forget reading as a separate entity. Reading cannot occur in separation from the other language arts; it is intimately linked to oral communication.

NOISE AND LACK OF PRIVACY

The oral communication of the children I teach develops under conditions quite different from the conditions most of us know. It develops in a world lacking in privacy. Where *is* the privacy in three rooms housing eight people? Children under such circumstances may well sound more aggressive, monosyllabic, and contain more decibels of sound than I feel necessary. But under conditions of their world, more decibels of sound may well be necessary to communicate at all. The noise level—the break through the sound barrier—experienced in these classes is normal in these homes. Only confused outsiders and teachers become angry. The difference is so extreme that being of a clinical bent, I reported 75 cases of suspected hearing loss my first shouting year of public school work. The amount of noise per message unit of communication is but one aspect of sociological difference between communications patterns.

The aura under which this occurs is important, too. Five years ago, as but one example, I was teaching speech to a group of Arabians. As our discussion became more involved, I found them shouting at me. Obviously, when a man screams at you, you scream back. I did. They shouted even more loudly. And, as I became more angry, I shouted even more, too. It was anger that raised my voice. They were having a ball. When communication gets to the pitch of the bazaar, the Arabian's enjoyment is most intense. Certainly my feelings were just the opposite. Now, it may just be—and I firmly believe it is—that a considerable segment of the American public school population of the great cities responds to sound level in a way that is closer to the Arabian than to us teachers. And our school, the world of the great hush, may be a most threatening world to the confused child.

It is no secret either that vocabulary selection and familiarity varies between both geographic and cultural groups. A great deal already has been done to prepare materials which use more nearly the environmental differences of the student. How Negro children of the South ever learned to read when they read stories of an ofay Dick and Jane rolling hoops along the sidewalks of Northern suburbs will always remain a mystery to me. This is not so divorced from reality as it may sound. My children in California have difficulty conceiving a story as real if it contains snow, but, I've yet to find beginning materials that do not somewhere incorporate words such as *mittens, sleds,* and *ear muffs.* One might well ask how different the teaching of such ideas is from the teaching of English to desert peoples. Do teachers really, in New Delhi, in Bali, and in the Philippines—insist their students *cannot* learn when they have difficulty conceptualizing snow scenes and snow gear and the myriad vocabulary surrounding these items. For that matter, is it only the dumb New Yorker who has unclear ideas about the difference between *patio* and *lanai?*

I believe then that the teacher who teaches children who are socially different from himself must exert some real effort to find materials that will have meaning to those students. At least the materials must be close enough to the student's background for him to get

sufficient understanding to want to go on.

Dialect varies from place to place and from group to group, too. How does one teach phonics in the South? For that matter, how do we teach phonics to socially differing groups in the North? As but one illustration of how difficult this can be, the following occurred in my classroom. I had a large class of extremely poor readers, and we'd been working very hard for three weeks on the sounds of vowels. When I felt we could move on to the consonants, I asked, "and who can tell us what a consonant is?" Several answers came—an argument followed and we voted. The tally of the votes revealed that a consonant was "a body of land surrounded on three sides by water." One dissenter who could not accept the finality of this democratic decision raised his hand to insist that "that was not a consonant, but a parenthesis."

VOCABULARY AND LISTENING

I redoubled my efforts to link vocabulary to listening. With this particular group of 17-year-olds who had voted in favor of spelling tests, I had selected fourth-grade lists. I used them for hearing and speech training as well as sight recognition. Each week we'd grunt and groan, sweat and bleed over them. After the disastrous incident with consonants, I changed to the simpler Dolch List of 220 words. With the introduction of these "easier" words, a long, deep sigh burst from a tall, lanky boy nicknamed "Goose" as he said, "That's mo' lak mah stahl." On this certain day one of the words was *want.* Goose asked, "Don't you mean 'won't'?" No, I'd used the sentence, "I want my breakfast." That was indeed *won't,* he claimed. "Ah 'won't' mah breakfast." Phonics work for Goose must indeed be a highly specific learning. To assume that he will learn that method of word attack in the same way as do his socially different peers who speak more nearly like the teachers and the dialect of our books is to waste a good deal of his time.

Goose has other language differences, too. He does not use plurals. His family and peers reinforce this difference in that his "plural-less" patois is completely acceptable to them. *They don't use plurals either!* Not using them, he does not see them; if he sees a plural in print he will either become confused about the word, or disregard it entirely. Currently, his world is circumscribed in a lunch bag containing "two sandwich" and a school attended by "2700 kid."

Significantly, this is but a language difference until he comes to school. Only in school or in the process of social mobility does this become a language difficulty. Because another group, those who write the books, create the tests, and train the employers, perpetuates a myth of correctness, the language of Goose and his peers becomes a problem —and differences become difficulties and handicaps.

On our Coast, Chinese students, for many reasons—docility, studious demeanor, etc.—are nearly universally loved by teachers. And yet the language patterns of Chinese students are nearly identical to the American-born socially different. The Chinese students do not hear American English vowels in the same way, and they do not use plurals either. But, how different is the handling of these students in English. And, perhaps this treatment is part of the reason for their different attitudes toward school.

Just as for aliens, the patterns of verb tenses and subject-predicate agreement vary for the socially different, too. My best students substitute *was* for *were* when reading a printed line. The poorer readers block on *you were,* be-

cause they do not in any other way use this alternate verb form. *I was, you was, he and she was.* My best readers substitute *was* in a line of print, because then it makes sense. Poorer readers block because they do not know what it means, let alone what it says.

The following anecdote perhaps shows this difference in oral usage. My classroom is a "special" room at the top of the building. Because I handle the least able readers in our school, my classes are 90 percent male. My boys and I, of course, suffer the label, the dumb group. One look at me and the crew who march into my room convinces the rest of the school, teachers, and students alike, that Room 501 is for the incorrigibles. One of my favorite and brightest students, Ronald, had just discovered the miracle of the female adolescent when he was referred to me. It was not a joy for Ronald to join the dumb group, and when he saw the lack of girls he knew he'd really been had. He knew a girl, Linda, however, who qualified in every respect for our class. And he begged me: "Get Linda up here." To recommend her, he further offered, "She dumb. She real dumb. But she cute, too." His logic was as refutable as his syntax. But it *did* communicate.

Fortunately, after I'd finally promised to get the eminently deserving Linda into our class, she was taken away to a home for wayward girls and I didn't have to make the promise good. That her deviation of tenses agreed with Ronald's was shown one day when she was caught in the halls without a pass. Spying me she called out to the Hall Patrol, "There Mr. Duggins. He know me, and I knows him." I was so cheered that Linda had learned enough about the language patterns being taught so as to become confused, I signed a pass on the spot. Had poor Linda not begun to *hear* the difference, she'd not have differentiated between the verb forms at all. And, had she learned just a little bit more about passes she'd not have been consigned to a home for wayward girls!

THE FIRST STEP

There is then a correlation between social variation and language behavior. But, what can we classroom teachers do about it? How can we teach socially differing children the language patterns they must understand to become better readers? We can begin by recognizing their language for what it is—different —without moralizing, without judgment, without ascribing it to a *lower* class.

We can conduct and ask for more studies of "noise level and intelligibility." We now know that people can be trained to understand more under varying conditions and amounts of sound. Children who come from communities and homes without quiet may be so trained. I do not mean this to be a bid for uproar in the classroom, but it is possible that we want it too quiet for comfort. Or perhaps we should consider arranging for privacy within the school. Carrels in the classroom and library may lend students a privacy their homes lack. Some of the research with autistic and schizophrenic children would seem to point out some success in the school that gives a student a place all his own.

We can arrange for printed materials centered about the realities our students know. Elementary teachers have capitalized for years upon experience charts and student-dictated stories. Secondary students are not too blasé for the magic of their own names or words in print. Psycho- and sociodrama are effective too. The possibilities in these areas are unlimited.

We can add to a student's understanding of dialect through better presentations of American English pronunciation, heavily emphasizing phonic generalizations in oral-aural work. Better assessments of each classroom could be made, too. Once you know what your class hears, teach—as do the good Americanization teachers—the differences.

Sentence patterns should be taught using oral-aural approaches. Any of a dozen drill books is available. Seat children heterogeneously so they can audit each other and follow a developmental sequence from hearing to speaking to reading and writing. I'd suggest one is better off using a predeveloped course, such as those of Lado or Fries, modifying it only for your individual group. Such already developed sequences have the advantage of slow and careful introduction of vocabulary. Each of the verb forms, for example, is a new item of vocabulary for the socially different child. And one cannot introduce vocabulary too slowly. There may be no limit to how far one goes, but there is a constant limit to how fast.

No classroom teacher of poor readers, socially differing students, should complain of a lack of materials. There are now buckets of reading materials for every class. The contents of the bucket are dependent only upon a greater awareness of the real needs, of the real differences met in each classroom. The cultural plurality which is at once America's diversity and difficulty lends a freshness and vitality to language. If we are to produce constantly more literate peoples, we must understand the differences between language behavior and refine without repression.

41.   History, Reading, and Human Relations: An Integrated Approach

ROBERT W. EDGAR

The work that I am about to describe is an outgrowth of an effort to study the problems of beginning teachers in difficult schools with the ultimate intention of devising an improved program of teacher preparation. Since 1961 a group of us at Queens College have been concerned with bridging the gap which exists between middle-class oriented college students and the youngsters they are likely to teach in the slum ghettos of New York City. The title of our Project, BRIDGE,[1] has been a symbol of our intentions.

The total Project has had three aspects: (1) a small-school-within-a-school organized to facilitate the study of the problems of beginning teachers; (2) a program of participation of undergraduates in after-school centers; and (3) the involvement of college staff members in research and curriculum development related to educationally handicapped children. I shall describe very briefly only one, the first, of these aspects.

In this aspect we set up a center for the study of the problems of the educationally disadvantaged in an all-Negro junior high school in Queens, one

Reprinted from *Social Education*, Vol. 29 (March 1965), pp. 155–158, by permission of publisher and author.

of the five boroughs of New York City. Two hypotheses were used as guidelines in the organization of the center: (1) that the children in this junior high school would learn more if they remained with the same teachers in four academic subjects, including social studies, for the seventh, eighth, and ninth grades, and (2) that inexperienced teachers would have a better chance for success if they had the services of a full-time supervisor. In the three years from 1961 to 1964, this plan was implemented. Eighty-five children were organized in three classes. Fifty-seven of them stayed in the school and in the program for the three years. The withdrawees were replaced by new entrants into the school. In a careful comparison of the intellectual growth of the children in the Project with a control group in the same class in the same school, the Project children gained on the average of five points in IQ scores as measured on the Wechsler Intelligence Scale for Children in two-and-one-half years as contrasted with the control group which gained less than two points. We who participated in the Project are convinced that this form of organization of the junior high schools in depressed areas merits further trial on an expanded scale.

363

However, I am not going to continue with an extended description of that Project. Instead, I propose to discuss a development that emerged from our initial program.

At one point in the BRIDGE Project we made a search for social studies materials to which our pupils would respond. Since they happened to be studying American history at the time, we decided to try out some simple biographical materials with them. The rather remarkable success of that initial tryout has led me to a more formal effort.

Perhaps before I begin my exposition it might be well for me to describe briefly some of the major academic characteristics of culturally deprived children as we got to know them. Our group in 1961 had a mean intelligence of 88 as measured on an individually administered intelligence test. This statistic means that at least half of the children fell below average as compared to a standard group. They ranged from 115 to 65. In reading and social studies information and skills, as they entered the seventh grade, they averaged about the middle of the fifth grade. A substantial number of them read at third and fourth grade levels. It is this lower half of the group that most of us have in mind when we speak of the culturally deprived. They represent an exceedingly difficult problem of adjustment for the teacher prepared to teach academic subjects in secondary schools.

Secondary school social studies is not often successfully taught to these children. Its teachers, untrained in the technicalities of reading instruction for example, are often unskilled in making social studies content comprehensible to such children. They forget that to understand history one must have a highly complex cognitive structure related to the who, when, and where of past events. We have only to recall our own confusions over the names of the leaders in South Viet Nam, Cambodia, or the Soviet Union to remind ourselves that we, too, can be confused over who, when, and where. These children react this way to such names as John C. Calhoun, James Oglethorpe, John Winthrop, Peter Stuyvesant, and to such places as New Orleans, Kansas, West Virginia, and Idaho. A brief but critical examination of the average social studies book reveals the density of its vocabulary especially when proper nouns are seen as vocabulary. The rapid shifts in time, place, and person, typical of social studies, are bewildering to a child who has not yet developed a cognitive system which provides meaningful categories in which new data can be classified.

Too often vocabulary learning in the social studies is treated as a problem in simple repetition. Teachers forget that our functioning vacabulary is a product of meaningful repetition in an endless variety of new situations. How can James Oglethorpe be the name of a full-bodied person when one's complete exposure is a sentence or two stating that he was the proprietor and founder of Georgia and interested in the victims of an oppressive prison system in England? One of my favorite illustrations of a much more meaningful appreciation of what is involved in understanding a word is drawn from Ruth Kraus's *A Hole Is to Dig.*[2] In this brief book for preschool children she uses the word "hole" in eight delightful situations. First there is the title which is repeated in the body of the book and then: "Maybe you could hide things in a *hole*," "A *hole* is to sit in," "A *hole* is to plant a flower," "A floor is so you don't fall in the *hole* your house is in," "A *hole* is for a mouse to live in," "A *hole* is to look through," "A *hole* is when you step on it you go down." All accompanied with delightful illustrations! Even with all this I suppose we would conclude that a child's meaning for the word "hole" is based on substantial first-hand experience. In many misguided efforts to reduce the vocabulary load of social studies material, the need for extensive repetition in a variety of meaningful situations is forgotten. Mere reduction of vocabulary is considered sufficient. However, the reader with a small vocabulary needs not just content with fewer new words, but longer, not shorter, accounts with repeated use of new terms in interesting contexts.

I should like, now, to turn briefly to the academic characteristics of the children. It is a cliche in educational circles to say that the study of a subject is only effective insofar as it produces student interest. Cliche or not, it is true. We as teachers have come to understand that the responses of children are valid clues to whether or not we are meeting their needs. If they respond positively to what we put in front of them, their needs are being met, even if we are not exactly sure just what those needs are and how this specific material meets them. My own contact with culturally deprived children has led me to expect them to respond when the following conditions are met.

1. They will respond when lessons are clearly and simply organized. They want to know what a teacher is trying to teach and how she proposes to teach it. In addition, her purposes must make sense to them. Such objectives as developing democratic attitudes, recognizing the rights of others, and exercising independent critical judgment, though giving larger meaning to the day-to-day efforts of the teacher, are too vague for culturally disadvantaged children to comprehend and act on. They expect to learn information and to develop skills. They recognize and approve efforts directed toward these

ends. In spite of the inadequacy of these goals in the eyes of the teacher, she must at least take account of the pupils' expectations.

2. They understand social, political, and economic ideas or events when human beings are vividly involved in these ideas or events. An extremely interesting characteristic of culturally deprived children is their unusually well-developed insight into the unspoken and often unconscious anxieties, motivations, and feelings of others, especially teachers. Though not academically apt, they are "hep" (or is it "hip"?). They know the score and have many acute perceptions into the significance of the behavior of their elders as well as their peers. This heightened sensitivity can be used to develop their interests in people distant in time and place.

3. They respond to assurance of success. Reacting to a school system which has constantly emphasized their weaknesses, they protect themselves from failure in whatever manner is individually possible and effective. They often refuse to perform, cheat, are insubordinate, or withdraw when faced with exposure of ignorance. Close analysis of these behaviors will reveal that they have a positive, rather than a negative function. A youngster who can sustain any one of these responses avoids failure and preserves his self-respect even though he incurs the teacher's displeasure. During our Project we discovered that the very tests which we used to evaluate the growth of the children such as the Metropolitan Achievement Tests, were viewed by many of the pupils simply as efforts on our part to demonstrate once again how stupid they were. Consequently they resisted taking them.

More of their responses could and should be described, but I think that these three are the most relevant to what I have to say. If you agree with me thus far, our problem of teaching these children has become clearer. We must develop approaches to teaching the basic concepts of social studies which are consonant with the characteristics of culturally deprived children, methods which will reconcile the limitations of their responses with the demands of the subject itself.

In an effort to contribute to the understanding of this problem, Professor Carl Auria of the Queens College Department of Education and I embarked on a cooperative venture with five teachers in three New York City depressed-area schools. These teachers teach American history to eighth graders. In two of the schools all of the children are Negroes; in the other, about two-thirds are Negro and the remainder mostly Puerto Rican.

We have set out to test two hypotheses: (1) that the children in these classes will learn more, retain the learning longer, and be more interested in their studies when material on the Negro is included in their studies than they will using the customary text, and (2) that the children will learn more, retain the learning longer, and be more interested in their studies when their reading on the Negro is in fictional and biographical form rather than in a text. Each teacher is teaching American history to three classes of eighth-grade pupils. In one he is using the customary text; in a second he is using his text plus the text-like supplement that has been prepared by the Detroit Public Schools entitled *The Struggle for Freedom and Rights;* and in the third, eliminating the text entirely, he is using three biographies and two historical novels as the basis for pupil reading.

We are assuming (1) that the emphasis on Negroes will make it more possible for these predominantly Negro children to identify with the people involved in the events of American his-

tory, and (2) that reading materials combining a substantial decrease in the conceptual density with an *increase* in the amount will be more effective in developing historical knowledge, reading skill, and an understanding of human relations in these children than will a text.

This endeavor is only in an exploratory stage. We and the five teachers have had to get to know each other, to develop some security within the group, and to adjust to each others' strengths and weaknesses. In view of our limitations at this stage, we decided to confine our efforts to one historical period, selecting the period 1820 to 1880. It is a period of critical importance to the understanding of the Negro American. It also happens to be a period for which there are rich and varied materials about the Negro.

Our first cooperative task was to make our goals explicit. Since we planned to use different materials to develop an understanding of a given historical period, we had to decide just what aspect of that period we wanted the pupils to learn. We listed all the concepts which seemed relevant to the period, rated them according to their importance, and grouped them into categories: concepts of time, of place, and of people; critical vocabulary; basic social, economic, military, and political concepts; and finally, the Negro as slave and freeman. Though our categories are not of the same order and sometimes overlap, they do provide us with a framework within which we can work.

Having this framework, Professor Auria and I now proceeded to construct an instrument by which we proposed to measure the growth of the pupils. We constructed a test which we hoped would make diagnosis as well as gross measurement possible. We carried over our conceptual categories into the structure of the test. Each conceptual category is approached from several points of view. For example, we want to know how these children view time: (1) Do they think of time from a personal view, that is in relation to themselves, to their own birthdate, or to their age, or to their parents, grandparents, or other personally known figures? (2) Do they think of time in terms of familiar historical figures such as Washington, Lincoln, F.D.R., etc.? (3) Is their concept of time based on the evolutionary development of common objects such as the means of transportation (stagecoach, locomotive, automobile, airplane), of communication, of household appliances, and of dress? (4) Is their concept of time based on the classifications of history—eighteenth, nineteenth, and twentieth centuries, Civil War Reconstruction Period, 1820, 1861, etc.? Our intention is to discover some of the ways they try to build an understanding of chronology as well as to determine their levels of comprehension. The approach to place and people is similar.

This conceptual analysis also became the framework for our lesson planning. Since our five teachers were all experienced in teaching eighth-grade American history, we had little difficulty in relating the concepts of their customary text-based lessons. The teachers quickly absorbed them into the developmental unit which is their customary organization. The Detroit pamphlet was also easily integrated into their customary lesson planning. The transfer to the biography and fiction was not so easily made. Many of the concepts were not directly related to the lives and events of our books. Consequently most of our workshop time was devoted to the elaboration of our methods in using the biography and fiction.

It is now time to describe to you the biographical and fictional material which we used. I have been examining material on the Negro for several years and have occasionally experimented with various books in different junior high schools. Though the idea is not original with me, my approach relies on a classroom library designed to teach a single unit. This somewhat parallels the classroom library based on themes being exploited by Scholastic, among others. The classroom library we are using has *Frederick Douglass* [3] by Arna Vontemps as the basic book. This book is written for the fifth- or sixth-grade reading level, the level of many of the youngsters in eighth grade with whom I have been working. However, its general appearance does not make this fact too apparent to the young reader. The two other biographies are Dorothy Sterling's *Freedom Train; The Story of Harriet Tubman,* [4] and the same author's *Captain of the Planter: The Story of Robert Smalls.* [5] The selections are not capricious for they have been chosen to satisfy certain classroom needs. *Freedom Train* covers the same period at the same reading level. It is, however, about a woman, an illiterate in contrast to Douglass, who risks her life repeatedly to help others escape, another contrast with Douglass. It provides a new view of the same subject. *Captain of the Planter,* on the other hand, is somewhat more difficult and concentrates on the Civil War and the Reconstruction Period. It is suitable for those who are either somewhat advanced or for those who have become ready for more difficult reading as a result of their work in the other books. The fiction, Meadowcroft's *By Secret Railway* [6] and Sterne's *The Long Black Schooner,* [7] add blood and thunder and excitement to the other accounts of the period. They are set in different locales and describe different but related events. The complete library consists of

30 copies of the *Douglass*, 10 of the *Tubman*, 15 of the *Smalls*, 10 of the *Schooner*, and 5 of the *Railway*—a total of 70 books.

At long last we have come to the title of this article, *History, Reading, and Human Relations: An Integrated Approach.* With this library and these books we hope to teach the basic concepts of a given historical period, a few selected reading skills, and some elementary human relations insights. I shall omit further discussion of the basic history goals, assuming that my prior discussion of the conceptual framework of the period gives you some idea of our method of achieving them. I turn briefly to the others.

The three reading skills we chose were: simple recall of factual information, the making of simple inferences, and vocabulary with political, economic, or social significance. To assist us in this endeavor, we developed a homemade workbook. As the pupils read *Frederick Douglass*, they had dittoed workbooks containing five reading exercises, each covering four chapters of the book. An exercise consisted of ten multiple-choice items and a list of ten words drawn from the relevant chapters. The first five multiple-choice questions were simple recall. For example, "What did Mrs. Auld begin to teach Fred?" The correct answer, among a choice of four, was "To read." The next five items demanded simple inferences, that is, the answer was implicit, not explicit, in the book's content. For example, "What effect do you think reading the book *The Columbian Orator* had on Fred?" Answer, "Made him determined to be free some day." The vocabulary for the same exercise included "molasses," "law," "progress," "entitled," and "estimate."

This workbook served both pupil and teacher. For the pupil it met his need for structure and for success. The task was clear. He knew what to do and was able to do it. It was usually easy. Most pupils answered most items correctly. It also individualized instruction. The pupils were able to progress at the speeds adapted to their ways of working. At one point we debated whether or not the exercises would discourage them from reading the book, breaking their rhythm and their interest. Our misgivings were unnecessary. The clear structure and the constant success developed strong motivation.

These exercises also made it possible, in fact demanded, that each teacher follow the progress of each youngster. We in the workshop agreed that teacher correction of the exercises was necessary, desirable, and not onerous. As our study continued we planned to discuss the progress of individual children in our workshops. We tried to keep our attention on the child as well as on our materials and the teacher. In addition, the child's workbook contained a record of his progress with the other books. His homework consisted of extensive reading in three related books, with *The Planter* serving the function of the *Frederick Douglass* in the latter half of the unit.

Our third goal was the development of insight into human relations. We tried to achieve this goal by helping teachers to identify, create, and capitalize on opportunities to use our materials for enlarging understandings of why people think and behave as they do. We were concerned with opportunities to discuss feelings, needs, values, and moral judgments as they affected human behavior. Using a biography, the *Frederick Douglass*, for example, we tried to develop the habit of asking:

How did Fred *feel* when he arrived in Baltimore alone, without a relative or friend, to live as a slave in a strange house?

How would *you feel?* Have you ever slept overnight in a strange place away from your family? How did you *feel?*

Why did Fred work so hard to learn to read? When his lessons were forbidden, *why* didn't he just give up?

Why did Harriet Tubman, with great danger to herself, go back south to help others escape? *Why* didn't she just try to be safe herself?

Why didn't Frederick Douglass do the same as Harriet Tubman? What would you have done? Why?

What was Fred's owner's *view of Fred?* Where did he get such ideas? Was he a *wicked* man? Did all white people agree with him? *Why* did some differ?

What *kind of man* is a slave driver? *Why* do some people beat other people? What does it mean to try to break someone's spirit? When should one *obey?* When should he *disobey?*

In addition we tried to change the image of the Negro American as it is often developed from accounts of his role in history. Instead of presenting him simply as a slave, ignorant, docile, and childlike, we studied those leaders who displayed intelligence, skill, resourcefulness and courage. We portrayed Negroes as participating in the determination of their fate as well as having it determined for them. Negroes were seen as skilled workers, daring rebels, eloquent speakers, brave pilots, and responsible legislators and officeholders.

We also sought to examine the impact of status on the lives of people in the past and the present. We attempted to get at the feelings and reactions of the rejected and lowly person in any society.

What is the effect of being poor, not just on one's food, clothing, housing, but on one's spirit?

What is the effect of being enslaved? Of being excluded? Of being ridiculed?

What price does society pay for these actions?

As we tried to think through the classroom possibilities in this area, we were sometimes blind, insensitive or overly sensitive, fearful, and distrustful of our judgments. As white teachers working with Negro youth we were sometimes afraid that we would enlarge the gap between them and us. But we were committed to an open confrontation of the problem in the faith that rational examination and study lead to better interracial understanding.

Perhaps I can summarize best for you by reiterating a few statements about the culturally deprived that were the basis of our work:

1. Culturally deprived children need a program of studies which satisfies their need for security through clear goals and simple methodology.

2. Culturally deprived children need the reassurance of repeated success experiences. The materials that are read must be well within their grasp and must be more rather than less extensive than customary text materials.

3. Culturally deprived children are person-oriented, not abstraction-oriented. They need materials which place people, not generalizations, in the center of the stage.

4. Culturally deprived children are often acutely aware of the feelings, motivations, and values of people in their environments. This sensitivity can be used in the illumination of the problems of human relations in our past and in the present.

Teachers of the culturally deprived need to develop all the skills that the above four propositions suggest: skill in analyzing their subject to identify its basic concepts, skill in the selection of materials which meet the needs of their pupils at their levels, skill in individualizing instruction in order to diagnose and meet individual pupil needs, and finally, skill in illuminating the problems of human relations. These skills are not beyond the ability of current classroom teachers and they can be learned. Let's hope that social studies teachers will set out to learn them.

References

1. The research was performed pursuant to a contract with the U.S. Office of Education, Department of Health, Education, and Welfare, Project Number 935.
2. New York: Harper and Row, 1952.
3. New York: Alfred A. Knopf, 1957.
4. Garden City, N.Y.: Doubleday and Company, 1954.
5. Garden City, N.Y.: Doubleday and Company, 1958.
6. New York: Thomas Y. Crowell Company, 1958.
7. New York: Scholastic Book Services, 1961.

42.   Teaching Science to the Disadvantaged Pupil

LORENZO LISONBEE

The Biological Sciences Curriculum Study is investigating the feasibility of tailoring a program in biology to fit the needs and abilities of the one-half million slower learners in the biology classes of the nation's high schools. The study finds that it is impossible to separate the socioeconomic factors from the task it is attempting. An estimated 30–50 per cent of these pupils seem to be culturally deprived, disadvantaged Americans. What the BSCS ought to do and can do for these youngsters, whose reading levels range upward from the second grade and whose desires to be taught span from the highly desiring to the stubbornly resistive, remains a question. That they have worth as becoming productive citizens sharing the responsibilities of a democratic society is not doubted. That they need and can learn the minimal science basic to being informed citizens is the consensus of the many who have contributed ideas and suggestions to the BSCS Special Student Project, the first of the major national movements involved with science curriculum revision to become involved with the limited learner and consequently, with the socioeconomic background of its students.

To be disadvantaged is a relative

Reprinted from *The Science Teacher*, Vol. 30 (October 1963), pp. 18–21, by permission of the publisher and author.

matter. If the most disadvantaged student in our American high school were transplanted to many other groups elsewhere in the world, he would be recognized as a very advantaged person, literate and intelligent. He would be able to read and write, add and subtract, and relate a great deal about the so-called civilized world. But in America he is a limited learner, a disaffected youth, a disadvantaged American; he is culturally deprived.

The relativeness in the situation, of course, is due to the present social, economic, and educational status of the large majority of people in America. The median school years completed by adults 25 years old and older in seven states is now beyond the twelfth grade; in three-fourths of the states it is beyond the tenth (6). The large middle class for the past two and one-half decades has placed a premium on education and on becoming skilled. Our technological society has rapidly become more and more technological, consuming in fantastic numbers skilled professional and semiprofessional men and women. There is hardly a place anymore for the unskilled: The machines have taken over the pick and shovel, even the human hand in such skillful "unskilled" labor as cotton harvesting. A distinguishing mark of the disadvantaged is that he does not have

371

the advantage of being skilled in doing something that fits somewhere into the technological pattern of our society.

WHO ARE THE DISADVANTAGED?

A half-dozen books have been written during the past three years on the subject of the disadvantaged American and the culturally deprived. Recent issues of periodicals have been dedicated to this cause (2). The writers, most of whom are specialists in the field of educational sociology, educational psychology, and psychiatry, seem to agree that our disadvantaged citizens are victims of their environment and have a very limited perspective and understanding of the society of which they are a part. They have limited aspirations, not commensurate with their latent abilities. By being deprived, they are further deprived in school with what usually amounts to a second-rate education even in a first-rate school system. They are not understood by their middle-class teachers. They want to learn, but resist the methods of the ordinary educational system to get them to learn. They are not interested in special favors, but do want, like all human beings, to be respected (2, 7–9). They lag in school achievement and do not read at or near their grade level (5, 7, 8). It is estimated that nearly one-half of the slow learners—the low 20–30 percent on the academic scale—in our secondary schools come from the ranks of the culturally deprived, a group which harbors far more potential in ability and aptitude than does the advantaged slow learner group.

The disadvantaged pupils' appearance in our large city schools is increasing at a tremendous rate. The Educational Policies Commission predicts that by 1970, if present trends are not reversed, one-half of our large cities will be inhabited by the disadvantaged Americans (5, p. 10). This would mean that at least one-half of the enrollment in the schools would consist of students from disadvantaged homes. This trend has alarmed a number of spokesmen to the point that the culturally deprived are now in the spotlight. Our large cities have received grants and have budgeted local monies to investigate the problem of the disadvantaged. There are the Great Cities Project, New York's Higher Horizons, Cleveland's Hough Community Project, Philadelphia's School Improvement Project, to name a few (3, pp. 17–20). It is interesting to note that the ranks of the culturally deprived nationwide have not increased; they only seem to be increasing because, heretofore, they have been isolated in remote rural areas, unnoticed. Now that they are migrating to the cities for a better life, they have become conspicuous.

Even though the school dropout rate for this group is high, large numbers of disadvantaged pupils survive their educational experience into and through high school. Compulsory attendance laws encourage many to remain through the ninth and tenth grade. Many pupils stick with it and graduate because they have learned from experience that it is much easier to get a job with a high school diploma than without one. The general tendency to remain in school is reflected in the fact that the enrollments in some of our large city high schools are composed almost entirely of disadvantaged Americans.

SCIENCE OFFERINGS

Of course, these youngsters take science, and they are enrolled in large numbers in the science classes. If you visited the schools in our large cities, you would find most of them in the "general" classes: general science in the ninth grade and general biology in the tenth. You would find that the science program in which these "generals" find themselves is, in the main, entirely lacking in laboratory work and teacher demonstration. High school buildings in the large cities are usually old and were designed back in the days when one biology laboratory for a high school of 2000–3000 students was considered sufficient. Today, in more schools than not, one and only one laboratory remains and is used continuously and exclusively for the honors and college prep classes.

The situation is generally deplored and regretted. One science supervisor in a large city school system remarked that the generals are given a lecture-reading type course, and the higher achievers get an activity program; whereas, perhaps, it should be the other way around. The less able, the less articulate, the less verbal, need the activity in the lab to help them learn. The more able, with a greater power to abstract, are much more at home with textual materials and class discussion than are the less able; but of course, they, too, need the experiences in scientific inquiry provided by the laboratory.

Serious effort is being made in most large city school systems to provide laboratory facilities for all classes in the science program. But the outlook is discouraging. The tax rate in some of our large cities has reached the statute limitation, while property within the school district has devaluated. To add three or four laboratories to each of, say, 50 high schools requires finances which seem under the present circumstances not to be available.

TEACHER AND PUPIL

Associated with the effort and the need to provide laboratory facilities for the less able and the disadvantaged, there seems to be a serious sociological problem involving the pupil and the teacher, a problem which, as yet, has not been recognized or clarified in the literature. In visiting schools during the 1963–64 academic year, a correlation seems to have been observed between the quality of the science program and the socioeconomic background of the school community, other factors being equal. In large city school systems, for example, where the minimum teacher preparation and available monies were the same throughout all the high schools in the system, it was observed that the more deprived the school community, the lesser the quality of the science program.

To illustrate this relationship of economic deprivation and quality of the science program, may I describe my observations in one large city school system. In this district, laboratory facilities are available to all science classes. All the school plants are kept in tiptop shape. To teach in this system, a candidate must pass a qualifying examination and have an accumulation of semester hours of credits in his major field beyond the minimum to meet state certification requirements. Teachers throughout the system are on the same salary schedule. School A is located in an area that is comprised of the so-called culturally deprived, disadvantaged Americans. School officials reported that 10–30 per cent of the students enrolled are absent each day. About one-half of the students who enter in September are not the same one-half who finish in June. Average reading level in the school is seventh grade and the average IQ as measured by verbal tests is 85. In visiting the biology classes, we found the rooms (lab-classroom combinations) to be barren. The class activity consisted mainly of students' taking turns reading from the text, with the teacher interspersing the procedure with comment. As we moved to schools B, C, D, and E, we progressively moved to schools having higher and higher socioeconomic backgrounds. We observed that the quality of the science program improved from school to school. In school D, a biology teacher and his students were working on a research project supported by the National Institutes of Health. The biology lab-classrooms were alive with "biology." In school E, located in a well-to-do upper-middle-class and lower-upper-class community, science was being taught as so many these days say it should be taught. The study of biology was being approached through biology as a science. The students were discovering for themselves important concepts through an investigative approach afforded by the laboratory. The biology lab-classroom was a research lab, with student projects located wherever space permitted.

The most significant part of this narrative now follows: In school E, teacher Mr. Doe was asked how he would react to the proposal that he be transferred to school A, over in the deprived part of town, to set up a science program such as he had in school E, with the understanding that at the end of two years he would then return to his present school. The teacher thought a few seconds and replied, "If the administration insisted that I do this, I would resign." "Why?" "When I teach I must as a teacher and as a human being be stimulated by my students through feedback from them. I put a lot into my teaching; here these youngsters are bright and highly motivated. They find science exciting and are responsive. I have taught students like those in School A. I am fully sympathetic with them. But I cannot get the response from them that I must have to find satisfaction in teaching. These youngsters are unresponsive, to me at least, and unmotivated. Most of them

don't care whether school keeps or not."

The correlation between the socioeconomic background and the quality of the science program seems to exist quite generally over the country. I have often pondered the causes, especially in those cities which provide well-trained teachers and equal financial resources to all. I believe the situation is a fertile field for research. I am inclined to believe that perhaps Mr. Doe provided the answer. It might well be that when a good teacher, full of good intentions, goes the second mile in providing a first-rate science program for these youngsters, he may eventually give up in despair because these youngsters may seem to be unresponsive, unappreciative, unproductive, thus providing no reinforcement for the teacher.

SCIENCE FOR THE DISADVANTAGED

But, the disadvantaged pupil needs to have a first-rate program in science and other basic subjects, and he needs, perhaps more than anyone else, first-rate teachers, and first-rate teaching, for several reasons.

1. He represents a significant segment of our society—a segment that is important and could be more important as a contributor of worthwhile service to society; he is important as a potential voter and important for the fact he is a human being who shares with others the responsibilities of a democratic society.

2. As a human resource this group in our classrooms across the nation is a gold mine of hidden talent. For example, the Cook County Department of Public Aid recently completed a study of 646 dependent youngsters age 16 through 20 who had dropped out of school. The reading levels ranged from grade 2.6 to grade 10, with 40 per cent measuring below grade 6. Yet on the

Beta nonverbal intelligence test, over one-half of these youngsters had IQ's ranging from 90 to 123 (3, p. 30; 7, Chapter 6).

That these youngsters have a great potential in our technological society apparently is not doubted by those who have studied the problems of the disadvantaged. These youngsters deserve good teaching, and they need good teachers, teachers who will tolerate them and respect them, even though they may come from a different class, a different cult than they. Needed are teachers who understand that these youngsters have different values and different aspirations than they, and that these pupils come from a group that often has different family structuring than their own.

A teacher also needs a strong subject-matter background, especially on the secondary level, and herein lies one of the great weaknesses in our attempts to provide a suitable and meaningful education for these pupils. These pupils are often placed into a program wherein the newest, the youngest, the most inexperienced teacher is assigned to teach them. An experienced teacher, an understanding teacher is needed (5, pp. 19, 20). Too often, teachers who have less than a minor in the subject are assigned to teach these classes. If these youngsters are going to be given a valuable and meaningful program in science, they need a teacher who understands science, a teacher who has a good subject-matter background in science and who understands how to teach science to the disadvantaged.

There are a few teachers who do find teaching these pupils rewarding. If somewhere in the professional training of teachers, prospective teachers become aware of this group and the associated educational and sociological problems, more and more teachers would choose to teach these pupils; and many others would do a better job of teaching them. Every methods course should include an hour or two wherein the teacher in training is given opportunity to explore this problem.

In teaching science to the disadvantaged, it is important to help them acquire an understanding of the importance of science in today's world, how it has contributed to our standard of living and to the culture of modern society. These youngsters also need to know how the scientist goes about his work. They also need to gain appreciation for science. To learn these various aspects of science, the disadvantaged as well as other students need to do some actual "sciencing."

In regard to the question of what is the best subject matter for the group, there are two schools of thought: One school is represented by influential voices saying that these youngsters, many of whom will not be going beyond the tenth grade, could best benefit from a program oriented to health and human physiology. They need to know how to take care of their bodies, to know the rudiments of nutrition and sanitary living, and to know how their body works, it is argued. The other school of thought would say that these youngsters have had enough of this type of instruction by the time they reach the tenth grade. They should now be given the opportunity to become familiar with the important basic concepts in science and to be introduced to the processes of science. They are ready and require something new. It is now time to familarize them with the basic scientific principles regarding the world and universe surrounding them and of which they are a part. That these youngsters can grasp these concepts is a proposition supported by a number of current spokesmen. Jerome Bruner's notion that any concept can be taught at any level now seems to be commonly accepted (1, pp. 33, 43, 46, 47). Hubert Evans of Columbia University offers additional hope that our disadvantaged pupils can become sufficiently literate in science when he says,

"Scientific literacy does not require a survey and understanding of the whole of science and technology. A relatively small number of fundamental scientific concepts and conceptual schemes can be identified and, when understood, can form a firm foundation for understanding the nature of the sciences and scientific work and for interpreting the newer developments as they come along" (3, p. 33).

George W. Beadle, Nobel laureate and president of the University of Chicago, recently wrote

"As scientific knowledge grows, it tends to become simpler in one important respect: As the facts increase, the principles often become fewer, clearer, and easier to understand" (3, p. 34).

The advocates of the second school of thought would say that these relatively few basic scientific concepts would and should be the ones given emphasis in a program for these pupils, and in the study of these concepts these pupils can learn best through a discovery approach as offered through laboratory investigations.

PROGRAM EXPECTATIONS

The Biological Sciences Curriculum Study is attempting to prepare a program for the limited learner (low 30 per cent in our academic classes) which consists of a large number of disadvantaged pupils. It is currently working on the premise that these youngsters need and deserve a program which explores important, basic concepts in modern biology. The consensus of biology teachers generally, especially those who have taught the BSCS biology, supports the BSCS premise. The BSCS holds to the conviction that these youngsters will find more interesting adventures in their school experience in science through traveling new roads related to updated concepts in biology than retraveling the byways of health, disease, and nutrition.

During the summer of 1963, three experimental units were prepared, based on this premise. These units explore important ideas in genetics, ecology, and cellular biology. They will be tried by about 1,000 students during the 1963–1964 school year.* The construction of a complete year's program is scheduled for the summer of 1964. It is hoped that through the materials prepared and the program developed and the quality of teaching provided, these youngsters will find the course fascinating and challenging and will want to come back to class day after day. If this can be accomplished, perhaps this program will contribute to the effort to keep these youngsters in school and to provide a program which they appreciate.

In developing the program, the BSCS is cognizant of the associated sociological problems—those that relate to the pupil and his cultural background and to the pupil and his teacher.

* This program has now been put in operation.

References

1. Jerome S. Bruner. *The Process of Education.* Harvard University Press, Cambridge, Massachusetts, 1961.
2. James B. Conant. *Slums and Suburbs.* McGraw-Hill Book Company, Inc., New York, 1961.
3. *NEA Journal,* April 1963 issue.
4. Educational Leadership, 20:3. February 1963.
5. National Education Association, Educational Policies Commission. "Education and the Disadvantaged American." The Association, Washington, D.C., 1962.
6. ———, Research Division. *Research Bulletin,* 40:14. December 1962.
7. Frank Riessman. *The Culturally Deprived Child.* Harper and Row, New York, 1962.
8. Patricia Sexton. *Education and Income.* The Viking Press, New York, 1961.
9. Hilda Taba. *Curriculum Development: Theory and Practice.* Chapters 5, 8, 10. Harcourt, Brace & World, Inc., New York, 1962.

43.   Head Starts in Mississippi

DONALD W. ROBINSON

"These youngsters work mighty hard at their play."

"One of our centers was burned down last night."

"Yes, it's a poverty program, but we're mostly fighting cultural poverty."

"The chief difference between my work here and my work with the Peace Corps in Nigeria is that the Nigerians did not have the problem of a long tradition of humiliation. They are a free and a proud people and they are puzzled by what they hear of segregation in South Africa and America."

"Some of these children have never had contact with a friendly white person."

"They burned crosses at three of our centers last night because today is voter registration day in this county."

"The most important thing is to develop the children's confidence by giving them freedom to do what they want to do."

"We stress the physical well-being of the child, with emphasis on food, exercise, and medical examinations."

"Unfortunately, some of our teachers bring with them the mistakes of their own upbringing and insist on too much regimentation."

"This is an educational job, and they should let the trained educators do it."

Reprinted with permission from *Phi Delta Kappan*, Vol. 46 (October 1964), pp. 91–95.
378

"My only complaint is that there has been no follow-up on the medical problems the examinations revealed. What's the use of examinations if there is no provision for follow-up?"

"Sending Negro children to white-dominated schools is like asking people to send their children to the enemy to be educated."

"The program in this city is fine, but we don't want any of the wild hell-raising activities of that other group."

"Some of these children have never before held a crayon or a fork. They have never seen a toothbrush."

"Some of our teachers don't understand what a preschool should be. They are trying to teach the children the alphabet."

"Our toughest problem has been administration. We have never managed this kind of an operation before. Our people lack experience."

"Our toughest problem has been getting facilities. We don't have school buildings and buses and equipment. We must beg, borrow, or buy every piece of equipment we need."

These random remarks by staff members of Project Head Start centers in Mississippi suggest the variety of viewpoints and the range of problems that prevailed there last summer, and still prevail, since the program will be continued or repeated in many Mississippi communities.

EDUCATION OR INTEGRATION?

Project Head Start in Mississippi was an important part of a three-pronged revolution: to attack poverty, to raise educational levels, and to narrow the chasm that separates whites and Negroes. So long as the project concentrated on the first two goals it enjoyed general support, despite a few reactionary editorials.[1]

When it strayed into the area of promoting an acceptance of the worth of each individual regardless of race, it encountered understandable opposition from the white power structure. When the largest sponsoring organization, the Child Development Group of Mississippi (CDGM), became associated in the public mind with the militant civil rights movement, U.S. Senator John Stennis ordered an investigation, claiming in effect that federal money was being spent to subsidize persons active in the Student Non-violent Coordinating Committee (SNCC) and the Council of Federated Organizations (COFO).

Paradoxically, the leader of CDGM, Dr. Tom Levin, a New York psychologist, is not an advocate of school integration. He claims that the Negro community itself is far less concerned with integrated schools than with securing quality education. Integration today,

he says, means simply "digestion" by the white power structure.

This civil-rights-oriented group [2] has played a vital part in the strengthening of Negro morale and will-to-achieve, by providing an alternative to the traditional school-sponsored programs. The alternative has been a string of eighty-three Negro-planned and largely Negro-staffed community-centered projects throughout the state. Fifty per cent of the central staff was recruited from out of state, to obtain the know-how and experience to make the project go. Only 10 per cent of the 1,500 community center staff members are from out of state, and none of the 2,500 neighborhood volunteers are. The CDGM enrolled 6,000 children and 3,000 adults as of mid-August and had an Office of Economic Opportunity grant of one and a quarter million dollars.

The reason Dr. Levin does not favor school integration is the same reason that explains his opposition to school consolidation. Both situations result in educating students in a strange environment, not in the immediate community where he believes education should take place and can take place most effectively. Integrated schools today remain essentially white-dominated schools, and in these schools in Mississippi the Negro is intimidated and humiliated.

MISSISSIPPI "TURNS A CORNER"

Mississippi has turned a corner. By and large the white public supports current efforts to upgrade the Negro. The business community has learned that an ignorant colored population will remain a costly dependent group, while

[1] For example, "on the face of this undertaking, it appears to be most wholesome and humane, appealing to the most tender senses in assisting infant youngsters who otherwise might be relegated to slum dwelling influence, undesirable home background, and lack of basic necessities. However, as all federal programs are now designed, here is one of the most subtle mediums for instilling the acceptance of racial integration and ultimate mongrelization ever perpetrated in this country."— From the lead editorial in the Jackson *Daily News*, May 21, 1965. And "Wastrels in Congress open the floodgates of needless spending and vote funds for fabulous salaries in a phony war on poverty."— From an editorial in the Jackson *Daily News*, August 6, 1965.

[2] In mid-September, Nathan Cutler, director of audits for the Office of Economic Opportunity, said that officials of the Head Start program at Mt. Beulah, Miss., have used federal funds to bail out civil rights demonstrators, but that most of the money had been recovered by deductions from employees' salaries.

an alert, educated Negro community will contribute to the economy instead of being a drain on it. But most whites want to maintain the separate Negro community, not foster a mixed one.

The *New York Times* recently reported that last year Jackson police pointed with pride to an Army tank they said they were prepared to use if necessary against civil rights demonstrators. This year, after the use of nightsticks brought unfavorable national publicity, police officials instructed their men to "handle them as easy as you can" when arresting demonstrators.

Throughout the state, Head Start centers have had a generally good press. Local newspapers publish sympathetic news accounts, including front page pictures of the integrated staffs. An exception to the rule has been the CDGM, toward whom, as the boldest and most controversial of Head Start types, animus has been intense. The Jackson *Daily News*, for example, headlined the presence of Myles Horton (on the campus of Mt. Beulah Delta Ministry, a Negro theological college at Edwards where CDGM leases facilities), "who has long been identified with leftist causes" and who was accused by the House Committee on Un-American Activities in 1947 of "operating as a stooge for the Communist party within socialist circles."

Dr. Levin is committed to "aggressive compliance with the Civil Rights Act," for he believes that education is a sham if conducted in an atmosphere of deprivation and denial of rights. This spirit is exemplified by the remarks attributed to children attending Freedom Schools in Georgia: "I don't want no white man's freedom. I want my own, Lord. I want my own." And, "I don't like to march. It's more like I have to march. It's my duty. I'm a Negro."

Perhaps the goals of CDGM can best be stated in the words of the director in his letter inviting applications for staff positions: "We will measure the success of the project by two criteria: (1) Have we helped the children to a sense of freedom, responsibility, and self-worth? Have they experienced an expansion of their horizons and skills? (2) Has the community [applied] their own efforts and resources as the central force in the activity of the Child Development Center? Has this been demonstrated by intention to continue the center?"

The application form used in recruiting teachers itself reveals the interest in experience wider than the mere classroom. Such items as these appear in it:

12. Briefly outline the civil rights activities in which you have been involved.

13. List some political, social, and community groups in which you have been active.

14. Have you been in the South? Where? When?

The social consciousness of the organization is also expressed in this statement of its twofold objectives: "We hope to offer an educational program which is unique to children whose incredible poverty is compounded by a racist social structure. Likewise we expect to involve poor rural communities in community action programs in which they define their own problems and bring local resources and ingenuity to bear upon the solutions."

CDGM VERSUS SCHOOL-SPONSORED CENTERS

The white power structure is on the defensive in Mississippi, in education as in every other facet of society. When a local superintendent said of Project Head Start, "We can do this job and we want to do it; it is an educational job, so let the educators do it, not the amateurs," he was really saying, "Let the white-dominated educational establishment control every social and educational project, else we will lose our position of dominance."

The director of a center sponsored by a county school board was at pains to point out that the center was integrated. Negro children were learning to work with white teachers. White teachers had Negro assistants. And the project home economist went into the homes and taught canning.

When the Negro leaders in this community asked for and secured several centers sponsored by CDGM, a brisk and sometimes bitter rivalry developed between the white-dominated and the Negro-dominated programs. The first issue of the *CDGM Newsletter* commented on this rivalry, pointing out that "the people of [this] county want better education for their children. They want a voice in initiating, planning, and carrying out all aspects of this educational program. So they are doing it, and it is working! The Child Development Centers which they have started . . . are beautiful in spirit, in appearance, and in activities for little children who live in this rural area."

SCHOOL OR PRESCHOOL?

The object of Operation Head Start everywhere is to give disadvantaged youngsters the experiences to fill the cultural void in their lives and so make it possible for them to start school more nearly on an even footing with their more fortunate classmates. The child who enters first grade never having held a crayon or a scissors, never having seen a picture book or played with mechanical toys, is likely to feel inferior, perform more slowly, and establish from the beginning an expectation of failure in school. Head Start is designed to prepare underprivileged youngsters for life in school by giving them stimulating play and learning experiences that will develop curiosity, confidence, and physical and intellectual alertness.

Here is how the preschool center is defined in the newsletter issued by the Child Development Group:

Make sure that your program is a nursery school-kindergarten program, not a first grade. . . . If we want to show the federal government and the country that we can run nursery schools for our own children just as well or even better than they, then we need to be sure that we, too, are running preschools. What is a preschool? It is a place where children can find lots to do and lots to play with. It is a play school, not a "lesson" school.

The objective, obviously, is not mere rivalry with the public school centers, but independence. It is the emancipation of the Negro from dependence by creating the intelligent initiative, drive, and independence that should be the goal of every individual in a democracy, both for himself and for others.

The newsletter passage continues to present a lucid description of what a preschool should be, and what most of them actually were in Mississippi:

A nursery school or kindergarten keeps a variety of bought, donated, or homemade toys out all the time on low shelves so the children can constantly see and select the activity of their choice. They are learning to decide, to use their imagination, and to be orderly. Learning how to decide is important because we want adults who can think and arrive at decisions and act firmly. Learning to use imagination is important because we want adults who can figure out problems and get around difficulties (we even want adults with enough imagination to get around impossibilities!). Learning to be orderly, by finding a certain toy always in a certain place and by the child returning it himself to that place, is important because reading . . . spelling, writing, arithmetic, and schedules will also be orderly in public school. . . . Of course our centers are confused in the beginning. But getting the toys out and arranged on shelves made of brightly painted crates or boards and mason blocks is a goal we can work at. It is not just decoration. . . . THE CHILD WILL NOT LEARN HIS NUMBERS AND HIS ALPHABET AND OTHER FIRST-GRADE SUBJECTS AS EASILY NOW AS HE WILL IF WE GET HIM READY FOR THESE LEARNINGS. LET'S GET HIM READY BY LETTING HIM CHOOSE, IMAGINE, AND SEE ORDERLINESS AROUND HIM. THIS IS WHAT WE MEAN BY A READINESS PROGRAM.

A nursery school or kindergarten . . . never baby-sits. Each child at each moment is painting; cutting and pasting; washing the doll dishes; putting on the dressup high heels, and hats; building with blocks; playing with cars, trucks, airplanes, and fire engines; hearing a story; playing a singing game; singing; hearing a record; having a discussion with the teacher; using the outdoor playground; telling a few ideas for the teacher to write down; playing dolls; or doing something else. Children in a nursery school or kindergarten USUALLY CHOOSE FOR THEMSELVES WHAT THEY WILL DO; THEY DO NOT ALL DO THE SAME ACTIVITY WHEN THE TEACHER SAYS IT'S TIME, . . . BUT THEY ARE CONSTANTLY BUSY WITH PLAY ACTIVITIES. THEY DO NOT JUST RACE AROUND IN CONFUSION.

The nursery school or kindergarten teacher sees her job as noticing the unoccupied child and gently interesting him in something. She does not . . . try to pressure him into "doing what the class is doing." . . . She is eager and enthusiastic herself. She is having fun. She is gay and friendly. She tries to give these feelings to the child. . . .

This way each child gets exposed to as many opportunities as possible in one short summer. . . . NOW IS THE TIME TO GIVE HIM WHAT HE WILL NOT GET LATER: MANY EXCITING TOYS, MUSICAL GAMES, ARTS AND CRAFTS, OPPORTUNITIES, AND STORIES TO LISTEN TO.

WHAT WAS ACCOMPLISHED

The first summer of Project Head Start is over, and in Mississippi nearly everyone connected with the program is enthusiastic about its value. They want the centers continued or repeated. Although the informal evaluation appears to be unanimously favorable, official assessments are not yet available. Consultants and evaluators visited every center and reported in depth, but these reports have not been made public. And the attempts at objective measurement of individual pupil progress have not yet been processed by the computer center at Jeffersonville, Mississippi.

The operation of 2600 Head Start centers all over the nation made a radical contribution to the goal of effective education for all of the children of all of the people. The 200 centers in Mississippi contributed to a veritable revolution, for they brought one step closer to reality the proposition that all people deserve equal opportunity and equal respect as individuals. The Child Development Group of Mississippi deserves a great deal of credit for the contribution it made in the face of determined opposition.

44. Growth and Cultural Conflict

An Approach to the School's Role in Cultural Enrichment

BENNETTA B. WASHINGTON

Culture is without question one of the most ill-used, misunderstood words in the English language. In the mind of the so-called average citizen (which includes the insurance executive as well as the street-cleaner) the word "culture" evokes vague impression of stuffy museums, "difficult reading," and music that has no "beat." To the society-conscious matron who must identify herself from the classes beneath her, it may mean supporting a benefit performance of an obscure play by an even more obscure company or having her portrait painted by a fashionable artist.

Even more dissimilar is the way in which the word is understood by well-meaning teachers, educational administrators, and civic groups. They know, of course, that culture is desirable for the youth in their charge, so they glance about the community to find something that smacks of the high-tone, if not the highbrow, gather their students into fairly homogeneous groups, and head them off to a local museum, park, library, or theater, secure in the

Reprinted from *Vocational Guidance Quarterly*, Vol. 1 (Spring 1964), pp. 153–158, by permission of the publisher.

knowledge that they have "culturally enriched" the lives of these students. Or perhaps they are not so secure. Didn't Johnny look more bewildered than awed and Tony more bored than impressed? What did the experience *mean?* What real relationship did it have to their lives? Or was it, as it has often been in the past, a pleasant relief from classroom tedium?

Last spring at Cardozo High School, in Washington, D. C., some students from Silliman College, Yale University, presented a complete performance of *Oedipus Rex,* by Sophocles. For most of these high school youngsters, this was their first chance ever to see a full-length play actually on the stage —and not encased in a television screen. It was produced with costumes, lighting, incense, Greek choral dances, and chants. The voices of the actors were youthful and fervent, and the fervor of the production was transmitted to the watching youngsters.

When Oedipus gouged out his eyes in his unrelenting search for Truth, there was complete, stunned, horrified silence in the auditorium—and after the play there was vigorous applause. Later, interested students gathered

383

on the stage around the actors and fired away questions about why an actor had said a certain line in a particular way, why certain bits of stage business had been included, and what ideas the actors thought Sophocles was trying to present.

This fall, again at Cardozo High School, ten young Americans, all in their twenties, presented a program in which they described to the high school youngsters certain facets of their experiences abroad when they served as Peace Corps volunteers. All of these ten former Peace Corps volunteers are paid teacher-interns in Cardozo for the year 1963–64 under a grant from the President's Committee on Juvenile Delinquency.[1]

In the assembly program, one of the interns described life in Turkey, another described life in the Philippines, another illustrated a Pakistani game of tag, and four others, dressed in native costumes, did an energetic Philippine dance in which the dancers step in and out of long bamboo poles (at Cardozo, they used long window poles) which are rhythmically clapped against each other and against the floor to keep time and to provide a moving

[1] The Cardozo Peace Corps Pilot Project in Urban Teaching utilizes the services of ten returning Peace Corps volunteers who spent two years teaching in foreign countries. These young people have been placed directly in the Cardozo High School classroom to see if they, together with a special staff of master teachers and consultants, can come up with some conclusions about what should be taught in the urban classroom, how it should be taught, and how best to go about training teachers for their gigantic task. The task is to determine whether or not the urban classroom can be a catalyst for the economic, social, and intellectual changes which are required if the public school is to become the way up and out for youngsters caught in the cycle of slum living in which the cultural and economic deprivation of so many families is passed on.

obstacle for dancers. At the end of the dance, the students cheered with the kind of applause usually reserved for a winning touchdown.

CULTURAL ENRICHMENT OR POVERTY

We would all recognize these two assembly programs as programs in "cultural enrichment." I think it is important to understand what we mean by cultural enrichment before any attempt to discuss its possibilities in curbing juvenile delinquency can be undertaken. In the first place, to talk about the need for cultural enrichment is to imply that we are dealing with a condition of cultural poverty. And as each of us here knows, this assumption is only partly correct. To decide whether youngsters from lower socioeconomic groups, many of them Negroes, Mexican-Americans, and Puerto Ricans, are culturally poor, or merely culturally different from the predominant middle-class and upper middle-class American culture, one must of course be clear about the definition of the word "culture."

If by "culture" we mean the "complex of distinctive attainments, beliefs, and traditions constituting the background of a racial, religious, or social group,"—which is one definition of "culture" in Webster—then clearly our students, in some respects at least, are culturally different, but not culturally deprived.

On the other hand, if by culture we mean "conversance with and taste in fine arts, humanities and broad aspects of science, as distinguished from vocational, technical, or professional skill or knowledge, refinement in manners, taste, and thought; delicacy of taste and nicety of breeding"—which is another definition of "culture" in Webster—then, just as clearly, our students, in most respects, are not just culturally different, but are culturally poor.

Obviously, those of us who know and appreciate the existing culture of our youngsters but who also know and appreciate aspects of another culture which most of our youngsters have so far missed, cannot easily choose one definition to the exclusion of the other. For surely our job is not to accept the culture of our students as an anthropologist might accept the culture of some South Pacific Island, as the first definition might imply, for change as well as acceptance is needed. Neither is our job to impose upon our students a haphazard familiarity with theater, opera, modern art, ballet, and concerts—as the second definition might imply, for surely these are only the trappings of culture.

The word "culture" is thus highly ambivalent, and tends, I believe, to obscure our thinking rather than clarify it. When we think about the word "culture," we seem to be faced with a complete dichotomy—yet we continue to use the word without resolving the dichotomy and without facing the question of whether a dichotomy really exists. The words "cultural enrichment" and "culturally deprived" are thus easy labels which may give us a comfortable feeling that we are at least coping with the problem—and it is precisely that comfortable feeling which can keep us from realizing that we have not even *understood* the problem.

CULTURAL AND
PERSONAL INTEGRITY

Our basic problem is not to choose between these unrealistic alternatives, but rather to do what we can to help build in our youngsters fully integrated personalities in which the best of Western culture can play a meaningful part.

We are seeking to develop integrity —integrity in which a youngster neither placidly accepts all of his present values and commitments, nor ostentatiously assumes the forms and trappings of a culture which he might wear like some fancy new coat. In this sense, our task is to try to make the two cultures meet and blend—in the person of the individual.

Actually, we should take care not to glorify a middle-class culture which exists, perhaps, more in our imagination than in reality. I wonder, for instance, how many youngsters in suburban schools are attending concerts or ballet every weekend, or even every month—or even, perhaps, every year. The gap between cultures may not, indeed, be so wide as some would like to believe.

Even the word "gap" may be misleading; it may be much more helpful to think of a spectrum of cultural values, with particular individuals and subgroups. And if we are dealing with individuals on a spectrum, we must realize that each one of these individuals has his own particular cultural conflicts, and each one of these individuals has the potential to become a fully integrated responsible human being in which his own cultural conflict can be an essential part of growth.

Of course I do not want to go so far as to say that there are no meaningful generalizations which can accurately characterize the lower socioeconomic classes as a group, as distinct from observations about individuals in that group. It is fair to say that there seem to be certain general characteristics of cultural poverty which many of our youngsters possess: a lack of basic knowledge and information; difficulty in communicating verbally; and above all, an ignorance of themselves. It is particularly this last characteristic—a brooding, pervasive, and abysmal ignorance about themselves —that is most relevant to our discussion of culture.

LACK OF A UNIQUE SELF-IMAGE

One of the most basic assumptions in all of our Western culture is that self-knowledge is a good in and of itself. It was Socrates who said that the unexamined life is not worth living. This may somewhat overstate the case, but for those of us dealing with youngsters there is another way to state the same essential point: the examined life is far more worth living than the unexamined life. In other words, self-knowledge can be a form of therapy, a force for change, and an inspiration for growth into responsible and creative human beings.

An awareness on the part of students that self-knowledge is a good in and of itself can be partly developed by acquainting our students with some of the great introspective works of Western art and literature. The unrelenting search by Oedipus for the truth about himself was not a lost lesson on many Cardozo students—particularly those ten or twelve English classes that had read and studied the play before the Yale production.

When I speak about a lack of self-knowledge as one of the basic characteristics of cultural deprivation, I mean something much more basic than the lack of self-awareness of various psychological motivations. I really mean that so many of our students have been told for so long by so many voices in our society that they are inferior, that they have no future ahead of them, and that they are just one vast group of juvenile delinquents and culturally deprived youths. Many of them have come to believe not only that these things are true about themselves, but also that there is very little to distinguish one "self" from another in this group.

These youngsters do not know who they are, what they can be, or even what they want to be. They are afraid, but they do not know of what. They are angry, but they do not know at whom. They are rejected, and they do not know why. So they make up answers, and out of their abysmal ignorance of self come strange fancies that they substitute for knowledge. Not knowing who they are, they hide behind an appearance. Not knowing what they want to do, they want and do nothing. They create substitutes to be angry at and to attack violently.

And, perhaps worst of all, they accept without question the world's judgment of them as not simply unlovable, uncultured failures, but as such failures lost in a vast sea of failures. In short, not only do many of our so-called deprived youngsters know little about themselves, but many of them also do not even realize that they are different from the person at the next desk, or the next streetcorner.

THE ROLE OF THE SCHOOLS

We in the schools should be frank to admit that we have played our part in creating and maintaining this feeling of failure and this pathetic concept of self. The schools should be devoted to developing agile minds and strong spirits and unique human beings, each of whom appreciates his own uniqueness. Yet too often we have rewarded the rigid mind and the docile spirit, and too often we have looked upon our youngsters as simply an undistinguishable mass of the culturally deprived. The sharp, intelligent question has been rejected, and the easy answer too often accepted. In the face of this treatment, many of the strong and agile have left our ordered classrooms for the more challenging and seemingly less defeating atmosphere of the streets —where individuality, some of them hope, can be discovered and maintained.

This is an unforgivable failure on the part of the schools, because I submit that the schools are the last and main hope for developing agile, strong, and independent spirits in our youngsters. How can we in the schools meet this challenge?

Questioning Our Curriculum

We can do so partly by a questioning and experimental attitude toward our curriculum. We should face the fact that the traditional curriculum has failed to reach most of our youngsters, and that new kinds of work-study programs, emphasizing individual creativity both on the job and in the classroom, are required. Actually, of course, I suspect that a basic admiration for an agile mind and a strong, creative spirit is why some people think that it is good for our students to hear Mozart played by the National Symphony, or to see Oedipus performed by the Yale players: we have the hope that by appreciating Mozart and Sophocles, our students can themselves realize the potentialities of the creative spirit.

But how many other ways there are of conveying the same values: the school orchestra; the school drama group; the school football team; the history class debating slavery as a cause of the Civil War; the English class discussing the agility of mind and strength of spirit of both Helen Keller and Annie Sullivan in The Miracle Worker; the secretarial class developing a new system for filing to meet a particular office problem—all these, and many others, are ways in which agile minds and strong spirits and vigorous creativity can be nurtured in our schools. In so doing we are enriching the cultures of our students in the most fundamental and most important way possible: we are helping to teach clear thinking, frankness, creativity, and a questioning, probing attitude toward self, life, and society.

But even more important than such an experimental attitude toward curriculum in helping our youngsters develop a positive image of themselves is the relationship that must develop between the teacher (and by teacher I mean anyone whose job it is to guide and instruct) and the student. I am personally convinced that an important part of the student's concept of himself can come from his interaction with teachers. A teacher, by encouraging individuality, can help to create that very individuality that seems, at first glance, to be so lacking among the so-called "culturally deprived."

If we expect our students to question and to reach, we must have teachers who themselves are able and willing to question and to reach. Agile minds in students are not going to be developed either by weakness or domination on the part of teachers. Indeed, as Rousseau said, how do we expect our children to be well-educated unless they are taught by people who themselves are well-educated?

The Teacher Transmits Values

It seems that the real place to focus our attention—if we wish to develop meaningful, long-range programs of cultural enrichment—is upon the problem of training teachers. Teachers must be trained not only in their particular subject fields, but also in the psychology and sociology of the culturally deprived. We must have a constant desire to succeed in the face of tremendous difficulties. We must come to know that nothing is more quickly transmitted to our students than the atmosphere of defeat, and that nothing is more infectious than success, earnestness, and enthusiasm. We must possess a sophisticated sense of dedication and idealism by believing in the importance of the job we are doing. We can show the students the importance of the students themselves in the most dramatic concrete way possible.

In other words, it is the teachers who are primarily responsible for transmitting culture in the schools. If we are going to transmit cultural values to our students, then we must live these values. We cannot talk about America's respect for the individual while behaving disrespectfully toward individuals. We cannot talk to our students about idealism and the satisfaction of a job well done if with every gesture we tell of our own dissatisfaction. No one sees through deception more quickly than adolescents, and perhaps some of our culturally deprived adolescents see more clearly than most the gap between our actions and our words.

Thus when some of our Peace Corps interns get up and perform a Philippine dance, I am less interested in the little piece of Philippine culture which they are demonstrating than I am about the values of naturalness and strength and agility and commitment which they are demonstrating in a much more profound manner just by their presence on the stage clanking window poles together. Now of course there are many kinds of strengths and agilities and commitments—agility in a Philippine dance does not happen to be a quality that many of us have. In fact, I shudder to think of trying it myself. But each of us in the schools has some unique way of showing our students our basic respect for the student as a person, and our dedication to the training of agile minds and strong spirits.

The point is, however, that we in the schools need just the kind of injection of idealism and enthusiasm which American young people have proven they possess by serving in the Peace Corps. Just returned from two years' teaching in the Peace Corps abroad, this large group of concerned young people can perhaps supply some of that commitment to cultural values which I have been discussing here. The challenge is to introduce enough flexibility into our teacher-training institutions and into our certification requirements to make teaching in this country not a threat to idealism and imagination but an outlet for idealism and imagination.

Culture, in this deep sense that I have been discussing, is a set of values—not a series of concerts. Concerts —by Ella Fitzgerald and Louis Armstrong and Peter, Paul and Mary, as well as by Leonard Bernstein and Andre Watts—may help to convey the values, but it is only in the broad setting of a total school program that the values can be fortified and developed. The most important way to build this set of values into the curriculum in a way which the students can absorb is to have teachers who themselves are agile in mind and strong in spirit. The challenge of cultural enrichment is thus really a challenge of teacher enrichment, for it is the teacher who is in the most strategic position to help channel cultural conflict into real growth.

45.   Here the Teachers Treat You with Respect

DONALD W. ROBINSON

The dreary, unshaded rows of 25-year-old barracks at Camp Atterbury, Indiana, do not present an uplifting view for the visitor. What goes on inside these tired wooden shacks *is* inspiring.

Here 554 young men aged 16 to 22 who somehow failed to learn in public school are learning. They are learning self-respect. They are learning the basics of language and arithmetic. And they are learning competence in a useable trade. Their numbers will increase by 100 a week until 2000 or more young men are in this former army training camp learning what the public schools failed to teach them.

A comparison of a Job Corps camp with a public school is nearly impossible because so few facts are available as yet about the camps. Camp administrators are beset with problems of organizing a new program and meeting the difficulties inherent in an enrollment composed largely of fractious youths. They are occupied with the task of developing an appropriate program for youths who until now have always been considered failures; at the same time they try to satisfy the appetite of a public press often hungrier for unsavory stories than for news of

Reprinted with permission from *Phi Delta Kappan*, Vol. 47 (September 1965), pp. 40–42.

constructive programs. In these circumstances it is understandable that camp administrators are protective of their public image and reluctant to advertise statistics or schedules that are likely to be outdated by next week. The three months the camp has been in operation is insufficient time to provide substantial statistical proof of its success.

Yet the evidence of success is everywhere: In the undivided attention of the corpsmen to their classroom work. In the concentration and seriousness of purpose evident in the behavior of every student. In the reading by 18-year-olds who three weeks earlier could not read at all. In the erect postures and confident expressions of men whose bearing had until recently reflected their acceptance of failure. The director announced with justifiable pride that not a single example of classroom disciplinary action has been reported.

This does not mean that 500 near-delinquents have been transformed overnight into 500 model students. There is a troublesome minority in the camp. There are many AWOLs and a high dropout rate. But the majority of the enrollees have found a place where learning is possible because it is geared to their abilities and because they are

389

treated as men, not as overgrown children to be tolerated and "helped" as they were in public school.

The education director is a brisk, businesslike executive with eighteen years of experience as a school administrator. He came to Atterbury from the principalship of a large Eastern technical school.

His faculty is composed of young, alert, experienced teachers, dedicated to the Job Corps as Peace Corpsmen are dedicated to their work. Their average length of teaching experience is six years. They work an eight-hour day and receive salaries ranging from $600 to $800 per month. All meet the standards for state teaching credentials. Faculty meetings are held daily for one hour to work on the immediate problems of improving instruction. Weekly meetings are held to handle administrative routine. On the teaching staff of forty-nine there have been three dropouts, all to accept better positions. Only one staff member has proved unsatisfactory.

Students are grouped by date of arrival and their tested abilities, not by age or grade level attained. Instruction is administered on a nongraded four-track system, with a preponderance of individualized instruction and continuous individual testing.

The educational goals include passing the General Educational Development tests for high school graduation and competence in a vocation. At Atterbury the vocational program, just getting under way, will center on five levels of automotive occupations, ranging from car-washer and service station attendant to skilled mechanic.

Although most of the enrollees have not achieved beyond the sixth-grade level, there are occasional surprises, including the twenty-five who have been identified as having almost the equivalent of a high school education

now. This poses the immediate prospect of expanding the curriculum to include academic work at the eleventh, twelfth, and thirteenth grades.

The discovery that some students are farther advanced than they or anyone else had realized fits the pattern of their identification as school failures. Many of them learned long ago to respond in a way that would not upset the image they and others had of them. The result is cheating in reverse, a common phenomenon in the schools and one deserving of far more attention than it receives.

For those who are sincere in their belief that the academic underachiever poses a major challenge to education, the Job Corps is a momentous undertaking, for in the Job Corps young men who have been underachievers all their lives are beginning to be achievers.

Throughout the country over 10,000 Job Corpsmen in at least forty-eight centers are getting a second chance to acquire the basic education they failed to get in the public schools and many are succeeding. By the end of the year the corps will include at least 40,000 young men and women in more than 100 centers, and by the end of next year at least 100,000.

The Job Corps is a national voluntary program to give poor youngsters an improved chance to succeed. It is aimed specifically at the one million young people who have not completed secondary education, who have been unable to find a satisfactory job, and whose reading and arithmetic skills range from fourth- to seventh-grade levels. It is expected that the average corpsman will spend about a year at the center, but he may stay as long as two years.

In the seven months since the first enrollees arrived at the first Job Corps center in the Cacoctin Mountains near

Camp David, forty-two conservation centers have opened in the national parks, forests, and grasslands, eight men's urban centers have begun operations at former military installations, and five women's centers have been started.

Obviously, it is too early to attempt a thorough evaluation of the Job Corps program. However, if the testimonials to the value of the Civilian Conservation Corps of thirty years ago are any indication, and if the high morale and seriousness of purpose evident at Camp Atterbury are a reliable sign, then the Job Corps should make a significant contribution to American education, offering a specialized program that most public school systems are totally unequipped to offer.

It is impossible to know how deep, how widespread, or how permanent the transformation of the lazy nonachiever in school to the hardworking enrollee at a Job Corps camp may be, but it is real and it is conspicuous.

What qualities of the Job Corps camp make this individual regeneration possible? What advantages enjoyed by the camps produce this vitality in these formerly directionless drifters, who tolerated the school and were tolerated by the school until neither could stand it any longer and they became dropouts? And which of these qualities can be transferred to the public school? Can the school learn to provide the excellent instruction now being offered to these dropouts at Job Corps camps?

Here are a dozen reasons for the apparent initial Job Corps success, based on limited observation at one camp and conversations with staff and students:

1. *All* teachers are superbly competent. All are recently trained, familiar with the latest technical aids, and carefully screened for the job of teaching retarded youth. On this faculty there is no deadwood, no teachers who received their training thirty years ago and have just hung on. The faculty of forty-nine was recruited and employed by Litton Industries, which holds the contract for educational services at the camp. These forty-nine staff members have one and only one responsibility—to teach.

2. These carefully trained and selected instructors operate in a brisk, businesslike manner. They don't wheedle, coax, or bully. They are doing a man's job in an adult atmosphere—and the students respond.

3. This businesslike air is more easily maintained because students are not distracted by the presence of girls. Perhaps public schools might be more effective if boys and girls were separated in some classes while attending the same schools with ample opportunity to socialize at lunch and in student clubs and activities.

4. Classes are small. No class contains more than twenty students, and some of these classes have two or even three instructors.

5. Small classes are possible because of relative freedom from budget limitations. If a hundred additional boys arrive, instructors, equipment, and supplies are made immediately available. There is no need to wait for the voters to approve a bond issue or a tax increase. The funds are available. Consequently equipment is available. Nearly every classroom has a projector and tape recorder.

6. These boys are here of their own choice. Undoubtedly some are pressured by parents and teachers, but technically they are admitted to the Job Corps on their own application, and they may leave (as many do) on their own decision. This helps to create the tone of adulthood, independ-

ence, and responsibility that is reflected in the classroom.

7. And they are away from home. Undoubtedly this cutting of the cord of dependence on parents adds the same kind of zest and motivation to achieve that others derive from going away to college.

8. While students are free from the distracting pressures of parents, teachers, too, are free from the pressures that parents exert on the school. In conspicuous measure the tone of the camp is closer to the adult freedom of a college than the petty regimentation of the typical high school.

9. The boys' morale is high because a camp *esprit* exists. Each boy wears items of Army, Navy or Air Force uniforms, and is entitled to wear the Job Corps emblem on his sleeve.

10. The seriousness of purpose is intensified by the realization by many boys that this is their last chance. They know they have failed in the regular school. They know they have elected to try this special opportunity where everyone is going all out to give them a fair chance. "If you drop out from the Job Corps," they say, "you've really had it."

11. The adult, masculine atmosphere is reinforced by a tone of respect for the individual which in a typical high school seldom reaches the student of inferior academic attainment. The big push has been to recognize the Merit scholar and push the advanced placement program. Even when the school provides remedial classes the connotation of inferiority is inevitably present. These youngsters who are first-class citizens at the Job Corps camp were seldom that in high school.

12. Another advantage enjoyed by the camps cannot be easily transferred to the public schools nor long retained by the camps themselves. This is the Hawthorne effect, the enthusiasm generated by a new program. The camps are riding a crest of energetic action born of novelty, the thrill of innovation, and the challenge to succeed with a new venture. Faculty and students alike are inspired to prove they can succeed where traditional agencies have failed.

46.   Cultural Deprivation: A Study in Mythology

BERNARD MACKLER and MORSLEY G. GIDDINGS

The education of children from disadvantaged areas, although not new to the United States, has recently become a matter of national concern. The differences between the educational attainment of children from white-collar families and children from blue-collar families continues to widen. Ausubel,[7] Hunt,[14] and Deutsch[7] conclude that disadvantaged children are inadequately prepared to perform well in an academic environment and need preschool enrichment programs.[*]

In the past, educators have argued that it is difficult to teach disadvantaged children because their parents are not interested in education and therefore do not present their offspring with favorable educational attitudes. Other arguments have focused on the school's inability to motivate youngsters. At present, the term "cultural deprivation"[†] is used as the frame of reference for explaining academic failure among disadvantaged pupils. Riessman[16] explains the nature of cultural deprivation as "those aspects of middle-class culture—such as education, books, formal language—from which these groups have not benefited."

ERRORS AND DANGERS

Generalizations such as this one are too broad and far too premature in the light of the data from which they are extrapolated. In this instance, they are misleading and inconclusive. The Haryou report[11] and studies by Cloward and Jones,[6] Durkin,[8] Lewis,[15] and Cagle and Deutscher[5] have all indicated that the parents of disadvantaged children are "interested in education" and are interested in their children's receiving a good education. The civil rights movement also attests to this fact. In the past, parents in disadvantaged areas rejected the schools and all they had to offer because of their own poor

[*] Preparation of this paper was facilitated by a grant, 200-4-102, from the Welfare Administration, U.S. Department of Health, Education and Welfare. The authors appreciate the suggestions and criticisms of Thelma Catalano and Herbert J. Gans.
[†] Many educators and social scientists would like to avoid this term or apologize for its usage by indicating its inaccuracy,

Reprinted from *Teachers College Record*, Vol. 66, No. 7 (April 1965), pp. 608–613, by permission of the publisher and authors.

yet "cultural deprivation" continues to be used. See (16, p. 3) for an excellent example of an apology for the use of the concept and its inherent contradictions. Despite this, Riessman uses it "because it is the term in current usage." In all fairness to Riessman, his view is certainly sympathetic to the minority group. Yet he fails to realize that by yielding to the usage of cultural deprivation, the inferiority status of the Negro is maintained, only in a more subtle and confused manner.

experiences and because they had no hope that education was really for them or their children. Today, partly because of the civil rights movement, many parents of disadvantaged children believe and see a hope that the schools can be an instrument for the realization of their own aspirations and the yearnings they have for their children. If Riessman [16] speaks about the anti-intellectualism of the disadvantaged, Hofstadter [13] points out that anti-intellectualism is pervasive in present-day America. Why, then, should the disadvantaged group be be singled out as a prime example of anti-intellectual propensities when the majority of us are anti-egghead?

If these youngsters are to be helped, if they are to be offered equality of educational opportunity, we must discard and avoid the tags, labels, misunderstandings, and myths which have blocked the paths to progress in the past, are doing so at the present time, and will continue to do so in the future. The child from the minority group, particularly the Negro child, is already heir to the characteristics of caste status. As a member of a minority group, he carries the scars of every type of discrimination—legal and forced segregation. He also has limited channels of mobility. Far too often, we have used tags such as "cultural deprivation" as alibis for our failure to provide an adequate educational program for disadvantaged children. Every American Negro child is the victim of the history of his race in the United States.

FOR CLARITY'S SAKE

Again, a closer consideration of the meaning of the words "deprived" and "culture" should help shed some light upon the apparent contradiction of the term "cultural deprivation." Sociologically, the word culture is much broader in meaning than in popular usage. Butts [4] defines culture as:

". . . the whole way of life that is created, learned, held in common, and passed on from one generation to another by the members of a particular society. Culture is the sum total of ways of behaving that a group of people builds up and expects its members to acquire, share and live by. It includes the entire range of social institutions; the organized patterns of behavior, the customs and expectations; the tools and technology; the bodies of knowledge, thought and belief; the cherished ideals, values and sanctions; the forms of creative expression; and the language and modes of communication."

The Thorndike and Barnhart Dictionary [2] defines deprivation as:

"act of depriving; state of being deprived, and deprived as: take away from by force; keep from having or doing. Synonyms are: dispossess; divest; debar.

When these two words are used together, they entail a contradiction in meanings. They suggest, very incorrectly, that a culture can of itself be deprived, or that a culture can somehow deprive its members who depend upon it of the goods, skills, and behaviors which are necessary for survival and adjustment.*

One of the most important aspects of our present scientific-technological society is the rapid changes taking

* At a recent meeting, Mackler presented findings that children in Harlem (this was prior to the riots) were being kept at home and that after-school peer relationships were kept at a minimum for fear of injury in the streets. One of the members of the audience maintained that this was cultural deprivation. If we have not agreed upon the definition of culture, then cultural deprivation becomes simply whatever we choose at different times. At times, education is lacking; in other instances, economic, familial, social, recreational, or peer relationships become focal.

place in it. These changes occur at a faster pace than has ever before been experienced. The changes in our own culture, however, are not all taking place at the same rate. The material changes, by and large, come about more rapidly and are accepted more readily than the changes in institutions. In addition, the changes in ideologies underlying institutional and material change come about relatively slowly. And this resistance to ideological change—the unwillingness, for instance, to accept a minority group member as an equal—which by nature is deeply personal, appears in the persistent but confused utilization of "cultural deprivation" as a central term in educational thought.

The professional person is still *saying* that the minority group member is his equal, but he does not behave this way. The Negro is looked down upon. The white professional is guilty on this score every time he says he has *the* answer, the culture, whereas the black man is "deprived" of *the* "culture." The caretakers, the persons who are publicly responsible for the well-being of others, have reared their heads again, and in the role of always knowing what is best; they dictate on the basis of their subjective values that the white man has the correct culture. Anything else is inferior, inadequate, and deprived. Until the white professional gives up his seat of omnipotence and looks at Negroes as fellow human beings, eye to eye, we shall not see true equality. As in psychotherapy or any comparable interpersonal relationship, when one person continues to define, restrict, or diagnose the other, there is little risk-taking on the therapist's part, little chance of both persons' learning and sharing with each other. And this appears to be the case when one continually uses a term like "cultural deprivation," which dehumanizes both the defined Negro and the white definer. It objectifies both as if there were no possibility for change and growth. It also continues the authoritarian tone of the nineteenth-century white abolitionist, looking down his nose while giving a genuine but arrogant helping hand to the Negro.

PERSONS ABOVE ALL

The literature appears to assume that deprivation leads to one universal reaction. The research by Hebb [12] and his associates at McGill,[3] as by others involved in sensory deprivation studies, reveals that the uniform stimulus of sensory isolation evokes a range of individual differences. Some subjects, although only a few, can adapt in a constructive way. Others show a variety of susceptibilities to deprivation. This variation is important in illuminating the continuum of individual reaction patterns that are available, ranging from adaptive to severely crippling and maladaptive.

A parallel situation seems evident in the concept of cultural deprivation. Given equally severe, incapacitating, external forces, not all children fail. Individuals can and do succeed academically, economically, socially, and personally. Certainly, there is a preponderance of failing response patterns; still, a theory of deprivation—material, cultural, or sensory—must be broad enough to conceptualize more than one type of reaction. To state that deprivation leads to depressed reaction does not allow for individual reactions which, at times, can surmount the most depriving of situations, even concentration camps.[9] The theory must allow for an understanding of the interplay of social forces and individual motivations and how these factors influence success and failure. An adequate theory of deprivation must eventually explain why certain pupils succeed and others do not, given the same social background. And we are still awaiting that theoretical formulation.

Meanwhile, we must recognize that in the United States, the shadow of slavery is still largely with us. Tags or labels like "cultural deprivation" do not help to banish the myth of Negro inferiority. For the enthusiastic worker, especially in the field of civil rights, such labels only complicate the existing problems, social and otherwise. They serve to promote strife and hatred and to perpetuate the myth that disadvantaged children are of inherent inferior ability compared to children from more privileged sectors of our community.

In short, those persons whose behavior and beliefs do not conform to the dominant American culture patterns are by no means without a culture. Realizing this central fact has implications of high importance for education. So long as our perceptions of our race-relations problem are in terms of the absence of culture, rather than of the presence of a different subculture, we will continue to misinterpret our difficulties and their basic dimensions.

PORTRAIT OF ACHIEVEMENT

Visits to homes in disadvantaged areas indicate that the label of "cultural deprivation" is singularly unfortunate. Many such homes are, by many criteria, comparable to those in more privileged areas. Children coming from them do not *all* remain illiterate. They experience success in school as a desired goal, and they sometimes achieve notable success within academic areas. A review of the literature shows that very little is really known about the attainment of academic success among disadvantaged youngsters except that it occurs with far more than chance frequency.

The information herein presented will attempt to describe the "disadvantaged" high achiever in science in a junior high school.[10] The portrait is descriptive rather than explanatory, for no attempt was made to observe the process (or processes) or how the students became this way. The hope here is that until more definitive identification is available, this sketch will help teachers, supervisors, and administrators to identify children from less privileged neighborhoods who show potential in science. And more important, this study may aid teachers in their *expectation* of success and in providing a class milieu that contributes to learning rather than defeats it.

The disadvantaged high achiever in science tends to come from a family background characterized generally as a working-class family in which one or both parents are usually gainfully employed as chambermaids, practical nurses, janitors, porters, or cab drivers. Unemployment is familiar. Usually, one or both parents are immigrants to the city, in many instances coming from the rural South. In more than half of the families, the father is missing from the immediate family. Born and reared in the metropolitan area, the pupil has lived and attended elementary and junior high school in the same metropolitan area and has usually played in the street.

His parents or guardians are interested in the educational enterprise and tell him continually that they are interested. They inquire about his studies and help to budget his study time. They allow him to visit the local library regularly. Generally, he is receiving a free lunch at the school. Assuming that information on lunch applications is a valid evidence of need, one can describe the youngsters as from low socioeconomic circumstances. There are usually many persons living in the home, and there typically is no place which is conducive to study. The overcrowding in many instances is produced not only by the achiever's own large family, but also by persons who rent space in the already jammed apartment.

STANCE TOWARD SCHOOL

Generally well adjusted in school, the achiever enjoys a higher self-estimate and higher aspirational levels than many of his peers. He also expresses himself orally and in written assignments much more efficiently than they characteristically do.

The higher achiever in science, at least in junior high school, shows a general interest in science. He makes contributions to science fairs and science contests. Sometimes he is interested in electronics. He may have flying model aeroplanes as a hobby, or he may show an interest in raising fish in an aquarium. He usually indicates a choice of a scientific or science-related career by the time he is ready to leave junior high school, usually about age 14. In high school, he gravitates toward academic programs, and he is interested and participates in the competitive examinations for the specialized high schools of art and science.

Undoubtedly, disadvantaged pupils across the United States represent a genuine pool of hidden talent. This group has a great potential in our technological society in which we face serious shortages of trained scientific and technical ability at all levels. If high achievers in science, coming from disadvantageous backgrounds, can be adequately described and identified, they can play important social roles while healthily meeting their own strong needs for self-realization.

That some disadvantaged pupils move through the school curricula successfully is an accepted fact. These youngsters can grasp basic scientific principles. They can and must be prepared for a scientifically literate society. In order to help meet future demands and to help solve the present shortage of scientific talent, the recruitment of larger numbers of highly capable youth from disadvantaged groups will be necessary. The identification of the potential high achiever is mandatory if we are to fill the vacancies in the technical manpower pool.

But success in science is only one example of the inherent confusions and contradictions in the notion of "cultural deprivation." Similar examples can be found in the other academic areas. The point is that the successful child coming from disadvantaged areas indicates that some can do well. What is lacking is a means for schools to help these youngsters to alter their views of the situation, to rid themselves of hopelessness, and to dedicate themselves anew to the possibility of altering their circumstances. Teachers need to look freshly at these children and their parents. Parents, although desirous of a better education, are in need of professional guidelines and directions if their attitudes are to be converted into constructive behavior. Here again, the responsibility of the educator is to furnish new modes of teaching that incorporate parents and the community into the curriculum and that guide parents toward self-betterment and improved family life. To start on this road, we must purge ourselves of the concept of "cultural deprivation" and all its derogatory implications. If a concept is needed, then we must seek a more accurate, authentic, and honest term. If we conclude that no term is needed, perhaps that will be all the better.

References

1. Ausubel, D. P. How reversible are the cognitive and motivational effects of cultural deprivation? Implications for teaching the culturally deprived child. *Urban Education,* 1964, 1:16–39.
2. Barnhart, C. *A comprehensive desk dictionary.* New York: Doubleday, 1959.
3. Bexton, W. H., W. Heron, and T. H. Scott. Effects of decreased variation in the sensory environment. *Canad. J. Psychol.,* 1954, 8:70–76.
4. Butts, R. F. *A cultural history of western education.* New York: McGraw-Hill, 1955.
5. Cagle, L. T. and I. Deutscher. Social mobility and low-income fatherless families. Paper read before the Society for the Study of Social Problems, Montreal, September, 1964.
6. Cloward, R. A. and J. A. Jones. Social class: educational attitudes and participation. In A. H. Passow (Ed.), *Education in depressed areas.* New York: Teach. Coll. Bur. Publ., 1963. Pp. 190–264.
7. Deutsch, M. Facilitating development in the pre-school child: social and psychological perspectives. *Merrill-Palmer Quart.,* 1964, 10:249–264.
8. Durkin, Dolores. Children who learn to read prior to first grade: a second year report. Paper read before the American Educational Research Association, Chicago, February, 1961.
9. Frankl, V. E. *Man's search for meaning.* New York: Washington Square Press, 1963.
10. Giddings, M. G. Factors related to achievement in junior high school science among disadvantaged ninth graders in New York City. Unpublished doctoral dissertation, Teachers College, Columbia University, New York, 1965.
11. Harlem Youth Opportunities Unlimited, Inc. *Youth in the ghetto: A study of the consequences of powerlessness and a blueprint for change.* New York: Haryou, 1964.
12. Hebb, D. O. *The organization of behavior.* New York: Wiley, 1949.
13. Hofstadter, R. *Anti-intellectualism in American life.* New York: Alfred A. Knopf, 1963.
14. Hunt, J. McV. The psychological basis for using pre-school enrichment as an antidote for cultural deprivation. *Merrill-Palmer Quart.,* 1964, 10:209–248.
15. Lewis, H. Culture, class, and the behavior of low income families. Paper presented at a Conference on Lower Class Culture, New York: June, 1963.
16. Riessman, F. *The culturally deprived child.* New York: Harper, 1962.

47. Cultural Deprivation—A Few Questions

ERNEST H. AUSTIN, JR.

At a recent meeting of educational leaders, I had this awesome statistic thrown at me several times: By 1970 one out of every two children in our public schools will be culturally deprived or disadvantaged. The current emphasis upon institutes and projects which have been and are being developed at several major universities serves as evidence for this point. Many of these programs follow in the wake of school desegregation. As an aside, I would like to point out the confusion in our thinking which allows us to take advantage of the racial situation in order to do a job which we should have been doing all along.

I have no wish to question or malign the intent of those who support such programs, but I would like to point out some inconsistencies, dangers, and deficiencies which may burden any such project. I contend, specifically, that such undertakings generally are: (1) intellectually unsound; (2) likely to be authoritarian; (3) often directed by incompetents; and (4) philosophically indefensible in themselves.

LACK OF INTELLECTUAL SOUNDNESS

I am inclined to view many of the programs and projects for the cultur-

Reprinted from *Phi Delta Kappan*, Vol. 46 (October 1965), pp. 67–70, by permission of publisher and author.

ally deprived as another hula-hoop phase in which parlor liberals gain publicity for their beneficent undertakings. I am questioning, basically, whether these people have an intellectualized commitment to such programs or whether the programs just happen to be their momentary effort at charity. It is tempting to equate most projects for the culturally deprived with the types of movements that come at Christmastime: primarily visceral as opposed to rational. It is "good" to give food baskets to the needy, and because "good" is intended no one need be overly concerned with the possible consequences of such action. But a child acclimated to a diet of semistarvation can become deathly ill on a rich feast. His pride may also be injured. And, no doubt, he can, as some claim, become habituated to a dependence upon someone or some institution. The point I am trying to make is that, without an intellectual commitment, programs of aid are haphazard and often destructive of the goals to be attained. A grounded and warranted intellectual commitment as well as an emotional attachment is needed in projects for the deprived. This is saying, primarily, that little investigation of evidence is apparent while less than rigorous attention is given to the examination of existing presuppositions held by

399

those involved in programs for the deprived. Also, there seems to be very little time and effort devoted to an examination of possible logical implications following from such projects.

In support of this assertion, I will attempt to show that there is a lack of discrimination in many of these programs of rehabilitation. Early research seems to indicate that there are many positive aspects stemming from cultural deprivation. The question, "Do we want these positive characteristics and can we save them while destroying the negative influences?" is seldom asked. From what is the child to be rehabilitated? And to what? Before these value questions can be answered, we must first define what we mean by "culturally deprived." And it is here that a major problem arises, a problem often overlooked by many programs. Too often we consider "cultural deprivation" and "cultural difference" to be synonymous when in reality there is no deprivation, only difference. This means that "rehabilitation" is not a proper word to use, for it implies that a set of values is wrong when the values are only different. The problem, then, is not to minimize or maximize any particular values but to stress the questioning and reevaluation of *all* values. It is factually possible to do this even if it is psychologically difficult. For example, let me employ two usually accepted generalizations:

Most of our middle-class citizens design their lives on the basis of the future to such an extent that they are bored and dissatisfied with the present. Life is to come. On the other hand, our lower-class citizens concentrate upon the present and neglect the future. Life is in the now.

Here are two "different" values, and we can guarantee that problems will arise from either of them. Should we attempt to stamp out one, or should we question both? If we do the latter, I hypothesize we will find "deprivation" to be a two-way affair. That is, both values are somehow lacking because one class of citizens has been deprived of interaction and communication with another class of citizens. Help for the deprived then becomes a process of reciprocity: each has something to give and something to be taken away. Each class is in a sense both rich and deprived. Each has something to share and something to put aside, something to learn and something to unlearn.

I contend that very few programs take this approach. Help is usually a one-sided process with one class "giving" and the other (primarily minority groups) "getting," which normally means a transfer from one set of problems or deprivations to another set. This happens because most programs are not intellectually grounded. Rather, they are benevolent attempts to impose a particular value system upon a particular group of people. This normal procedure leads into the next point.

DANGERS TO DEMOCRATIC OPERATION

Keeping in mind that the culturally deprived are usually taken to be members of a particular minority group, one wonders how often they themselves are consulted about the matter of their rehabilitation. We in education somehow seem to have decided that it is best to rehabilitate such children. But it seems we have reached this conclusion without much consultation with other interest groups and institutions. Worse, there seems to be little concern whether the culturally deprived enjoy some aspects of deprivation or whether they wish to be rehabilitated. And even if they so choose, how often are they asked to take part in the determination of policies and direction of such rehabilitation? To the extent that their views, arrived at in an informed way, are not elicited and considered, then to that extent programs for the deprived are undemocratic. If the previous description of such programs is reasonably accurate, then most attempts to aid the deprived are good examples of how *not* to be democratic.

INCOMPETENCY IN IMPLEMENTATION

An adequate investigation, I hypothesize, would show that most programs are attempting to educate teachers to work with the culturally deprived through professors, guest lecturers, etc., who themselves have little understanding of the problem because they have never gotten their hands dirty. That is, they have neither been deprived nor have they studied a deprived situation. In such cases, they lack the needed credentials. Perhaps they are theoretically qualified, but without the aid of competent social workers their understanding of the real situation is greatly lessened. A competent social worker knows what an arrest sheet looks like, has personally felt the effects of rampant delinquency, has studied and lived in slum areas where *de facto* segregation is the rule, has firsthand evidence of the ravages of illiteracy, prejudice, venereal disease, and unemployment. He has some understanding of the frustration, loneliness, inadequacy, and violence that such conditions can lead to. To the extent that this knowledge is not employed, then to that extent the possibility of any program's success is also lessened.

PHILOSOPHICALLY INDEFENSIBLE

This is the major accusation. It is implicit in the points already discussed, but it can be explicitly stated. Even if aid to the deprived is taken to be a dual affair in which all involved both gain and lose something, even if the programs are intellectually valid, even if values are shared and reshaped, even if the programs personify democracy in action, and even if all personnel involved are competent—there will still be no successful programs until one other matter is cleared up.

Most projects for the culturally deprived are designed to alleviate results, effects, and consequences. Seldom are plans suggested for the *prevention* of deprivation. That is, most projects are set up to cure the ills or symptoms arising from deprivation, while few have been directed toward identifying and overcoming the causes of deprivation itself. This is a deadly indictment, for it is a judgment of hypocrisy, recognized or not. The statement that opened this paper demonstrates how we cite statistics as unchanging and unchangeable natural law. But the statistical statement that by 1970 one child out of two in our schools will be culturally deprived is a proposition of probability based upon conditions prevailing at this time. That is, the proposition is not logically necessary if steps can be taken to alter the conditions which now breed deprivation. In truth, it is logically if not factually possible that *no* child will be culturally deprived by 1970.

Schools are basically places in which children learn. But there are social conditions which stand as impediments to learning. A poorly clothed and ill-fed child who is cold and hungry is not likely to learn a great deal, except perhaps a lifelong bitterness toward his society. Most programs for the culturally deprived employ escape clauses which allow them to be both modern and conservative at the same time. They bow to intelligently directed social change, then evade the very large philosophic issue by conveniently forgetting it.

The argument employed by these reluctant reformers runs something like this: "While the school does not have the responsibility to see that children are properly fed and clothed, teachers do not recognize that a hungry and cold child is in no condition to learn. And while teachers realize that the school cannot do everything to eliminate cultural deprivation, it must do what it can to *promote* the conditions for learning as well as learning itself."

This is an almost perfect evasion. The schools do not have the responsibility and teachers don't get into trouble by attempting to pin down where the responsibility lies. They can even ignore the question whether anyone has responsibility. One can only guess that the word "promote" signifies lack of intellectual commitment and recognition of the wavering of philosophic position. One also senses the hope that, as at Christmas, small charitable acts will fortify and soothe the conscience to the extent that poverty and deprivation can be neglected for another year. This neglect is the bitter tang of sweet charity, whether it be after Christmas or after school.

From this point of view education is to become both pathological and the protector of entrenched vested interests. Education is pathological when those directing it do not believe that it is necessary for curricular changes to be followed by changes in the surrounding socioenvironmental conditions. To feed a child in school, to adjust his, his teacher's, and his peers' attitudes or self-concepts to reach a harmonious interaction—and then to send him back into the larger social context where these characteristics are not effective—this is to build a pathological personality by withdrawing the child from reality for a part of the day. Social confusion is not simply in us. It

is also "out there" in an existent situation. And to adjust attitudes without a corresponding adjustment and support "out there" is simply to brainwash. Education deals with three elements: the child, the teacher, and the social environment beyond the school. It is this third element which at the present time needs equal consideration, but which is generally neglected in programs for the deprived.

An educational attempt of this sort also serves to protect and foster the power of vested interests in that the school *accepts* surrounding conditions without investigation and criticism, and thus encourages its students to do the same. A school which uncritically designs its program to deal with culturally deprived is, in essence, stamping its approval upon the conditions which breed such deprivation. I would like to put forth a possible counterargument here. It could be said, following the statement just made, that the medical profession, by orienting many of its facilities toward the cure of cancer, also gives approval to the conditions which foster the disease. This would be true *if* no evidence in the form of preventive research could be found. This, fortunately, is not the case. An outbreak of malaria would not only set medical machinery in motion to aid the victims but would also stimulate medical and other authorities to seek out and destroy the source which feeds the disease. Unfortunately, education has yet to become so professionalized, just as it has yet to develop adequate methods of inquiry. Educators cannot honestly evade the question of the source of deprivation by resorting to areas of specialization and divisions of labor any more than a specialist in lung cancer can honestly evade the source of the disease. Millions of dollars are spent in efforts both to cure and prevent cancer and other diseases, yet we live in a nation in which, so the experts say, there should be no poverty. Still, millions are being spent to rectify the *results* of poverty while very little is allocated to determine ways by which poverty can be prevented. This does not speak well of us as an intelligent people.

Many educational proposals directed toward cultural deprivation demonstrate that we are victims of our concepts of what education ought to be and what schools ought to do. Unfortunately, the concepts were formulated from our experience in the schools of yesterdays long since past, and their hold is tenacious. For a long while in our history various groups thrived upon the need for social reform. Most of the plans were visionary and utopian, completely unrelated to existing realities. What these reformers thought (or, rather, felt) "ought to be" was formulated without regard to what "could be." Because of this and other factors, educators are timid about postulating "oughts" which would entail social reform. That they are most willing to engage in educational experimentation and reform only serves to point out their weakness of position. They seem to feel that the only institution that has to be modified is the educational system, never an institution that is political or economic, never the family or our religious structure. These are taboo, untouchable even to reformers. If there are social problems, then all that needs to be done is to have our accommodating educational system make a few magical changes in curriculum and methods, for this will solve the problem of, say, cultural deprivation. One can, of course, make a strong case for this position: The schools are relatively safe places in which to hide.

The negative tone of this article should not be taken to mean that I am opposed to programs which aid the culturally deprived. I am only opposed to indefensible programs. The reader has a right to demand that I cease being solely critical and postulate some "better" solutions. Such solutions can be inferred from what has been said previously, but there is no "the" solution, for these are things which have to be worked out. This "working out" is the essential meaning of democracy. It implies that we can accept the risk involved and develop methods for solving such problems. But—and this is crucial—no attempt to develop such methods will be undertaken until there is a recognition that these problems exist and that they are important. Such an awareness would demonstrate that education can no longer isolate itself from its social context. Teachers would have to acknowledge that it is unfair to educate a Negro boy for a profession generally open only to white men or to educate a Negro girl for a career in cosmetology without *at least* explaining that one occupation is nearly useless and that the other is an extension of an invidious system.

If this article can draw from educators an intellectual and philosophical acknowledgment that changes must be made not only in our educational system but also in the wider social context, then it will have served admirably well, for it is from here that we must start.

I have been advised that this article, because of its attack, is likely to alienate the very persons who are most likely to agree with what has been said and aid those who are opposed to programs for the culturally deprived by furnishing them with ammunition. A professional approach will prevent alienation, and adequate programs will remove any targets for the ammunition which has been provided.

48. Compensatory Education—Some Answers for a Skeptic

JAMES W. GUTHRIE and JAMES A. KELLY

Professor Austin's critical attack upon programs aimed at the rehabilitation of culturally deprived children—compensatory education—is nowhere so logically organized or empirically supported as his four-pronged introductory accusation would lead one to expect. Consequently, it is not possible to refute a number of his unsupported, indeed unsupportable, charges. What follows therefore is an attempt to restore Professor Austin's major derailments to a more accurate track, to analyze the need and justification for compensatory education, and further, to suggest some promising program directions.

The first criticism, "lack of intellectual soundness," is itself somewhat lacking in focus, but it appears to impugn both the intellectual ability and the motives of those advocating compensatory education. This criticism is difficult to meet because it is difficult to understand. If, however, the implication is that no form of empirical or logical rationale exists for compensatory education, Professor Austin errs. The evidence pointing to personal and societal loss resulting from the inability of individuals to gain an education is too weighty and well known to bother repeating here. The fact that culturally deprived children typically are unable to obtain an adequate education is equally well documented.[1] Thus since cultural deprivation leads to less than maximization of human potential, it also leads to individual and societal loss.

Educational programs for the culturally deprived also are charged with being run by "parlor liberals" in search of publicity and lacking in intellectual commitment. No evidence is offered in support of these charges. Nevertheless, the motives of those engaged in compensatory education projects occupy a broad spectrum, perhaps as broad as the array of motives found among professors of education. Thus it is possible that some of the people affiliated with and responsible for culturally deprived rehabilitation programs are so engaged for somewhat less than altruistic purposes. Such a condition, however, does not constitute a valid reason for condemning all persons employed in compensatory education or the programs themselves. Regardless, compensatory education programs should not be evaluated by the motives of the participants and operators;

Reprinted from *Phi Delta Kappan*, Vol. 46 (October 1965), pp. 70–74, by permission of publisher and authors.

rather, judgments should be concerned with the equity and the practicality of the programs.

The second major criticism is that programs for the culturally deprived are likely to be authoritarian and inimical to the democratic process in that the desires of lower socioeconomic groups are ignored and their values transgressed upon. In this connection, it should be remembered that the impetus for a large number of compensatory education programs has emanated from demands presented by civil rights organizations representative of ethnic and lower socioeconomic groups. One needs only to attend school board meetings or public budget hearings in large city school districts to gain proof of this point. Consequently, though no special elections have been held to tap directly their specific demands for compensatory education, it is not accurate to say that the culturally deprived remain unrepresented or their council unheeded.[2]

There is, however, a grain of validity in the charge that rehabilitation projects for the culturally deprived call for replacing lower-class values with middle-class values. In fact, this value transplantation is one of the primary outcomes planned for many compensatory education projects. If the culturally deprived children of poverty-stricken and broken homes can be encouraged to value education, and if they can be equipped with the language skills necessary to profit from it, a large measure of cultural deprivation will have been alleviated.

A degree of authoritarianism is involved in compensatory education programs because a culturally deprived child has no legal choice as to whether or not he will attend school. However, in our society such an option is not open to any child regardless of social status or cultural fulfillment. States charge local school districts with providing educational programs and enforcing compulsory attendance statutes. One justification for compulsory education is that a democracy depends upon educated citizenry for its maintenance. If, as is too often the case with culturally deprived children, the values and actions of some individuals are inimical to the orderly maintenance of society, remedial measures must be taken. It is to our credit that we recognize the cultural cause of much behavioral deviance and consequently attempt to rehabilitate through education rather than ignore or imprison the deviant individual.

Professor Austin's third major criticism—the incompetence of program personnel—is so sweeping that it hardly justifies reply. Literally thousands of compensatory education projects are being tried in large cities alone. Many of these projects are handled by highly trained individuals long experienced in dealing with the day-to-day world of poverty, crime, disease, and squalor. What is needed yet, however, is to continue to focus public attention upon compensatory education in order further to elevate the status and increase the number of competent persons willing to work in the rehabilitation programs. The federal government's actions in the establishment of such projects as VISTA may be an aid in this respect.

Professor Austin claims that compensatory education is philosophically untenable because it is "designed to alleviate results, effects, and consequences," and not "for the prevention of deprivation." Although unsupported, the initial three criticisms were at least relevant. This fourth criticism, which Professor Austin considers to be his major charge, is irrelevant and displays a misunderstanding of the social and psychological concepts underlying compensatory education. The point Professor Austin has so obviously missed is that compensatory education is not only aimed at treating the "symptoms" of cultural deprivation, e.g., lack of linguistic readiness, etc., but is also designed to eradicate the "disease" itself. Cultural deprivation is its own breeding ground. If left untreated it perpetuates itself from generation to generation like mirrors locked face to face. Many children of poverty-stricken parents are seldom taught and seldom see the advantages of delaying immediate personal gratification in favor of present education and future rewards. Thus they drop out of school, doomed to the same despair as their parents and ready to pass the "disease" of misdirected motivation on to their own children. Compensatory education projects are designed to break this cycle and instill in the children of one or two generations both the desire for education and the skills necessary to take advantage of education. To use Professor Austin's analogy, in the same manner that medical experts attempt not only to treat the symptoms of the malaria victim, but also to eradicate the carrier of the disease (the anopheles mosquito), compensatory education strives simultaneously to alleviate the symptoms and rehabilitate the carrier (the culturally deprived individual).

WHAT IS THE PROBLEM?

Professor Austin implies that the compensatory education movement is essentially a vehicle for "do-gooders" to work off their social guilt feelings. Indeed, he questions the equity of differential educational programs in a democratic educational system. To place these issues in perspective, let us examine more carefully the character of the social problems which compensatory education programs are designed to correct and the philosophical grounds on which the corrective actions rest.

Although most members of American society are remarkably affluent, large segments of the population live in conditions accurately described by the word "poverty." In 1959, almost six million families received less than $2000 income. One-fourth of all families earned less than $3400 in 1959. While the median family income for white families was $5643, the median for nonwhite was but $3169.[3] Families with low incomes have been found to have low levels of education, a small proportion voting in elections, a high rate of illiteracy and unemployment, and a high rate of divorce and illegitimacy.

A recent study of large school districts found a correlation of $-.52$ between "percentage nonwhite" and "median family income." Similarly, in the same study, "percentage nonwhite" and "median years of schooling" were found to be correlated at $-.50$.[4] Thus although there are many poor whites, there is a large overlap between racial minorities and the persons at the bottom of the economic ladder. The problem is simply that about one-fifth of the American population lives in self-perpetuating conditions of poverty.

It is probable that the incidence of poverty and of racial discrimination is no greater today than at other times in American history. As a matter of fact, the proportion of our population which is below "minimal" income standards is probably lower today than at any previous time. Similarly, not even civil rights leaders would argue that there is more racial discrimination today than twenty-five or fifty years ago.

Why, then, is so much attention being given today to correcting conditions of poverty and of racial discrimination, and why are the schools being enlisted in a drive to provide special services to children of families with low income? Professor Austin would have us believe that these efforts have been initiated within the public schools and that, by providing such service, the schools are out of step with other agencies of government.

Certainly, public schools have developed and implemented a wide variety of compensatory education programs during the past ten years. Member cities of the Research Council of the Great Cities Program for School Improvement have been particularly active in this regard. Compensatory services have been provided to tens of thousands of children whose home and neighborhood influences have been judged to be "deprived." A simple list of such programs would require many pages. School districts are to be congratulated for what they have already accomplished.

But school programs and services cannot be evaluated in a vacuum; the needs and welfare of society are the criteria against which public schools should be evaluated. And it must be clear that, despite all that has been done, compensatory education programs have not been able to prevent one-fourth of high school entrants from dropping out before graduation; have not been able to provide sufficient vocational training, even to those who do graduate, to insure steady employment; and, evidently, have not been able to interrupt the cycle of economic deprivation, lack of motivation in children to learn, low level of skill acquired in school, low probability of employment, low salaries, etc. Conditions of poverty, unemployment, illegitimacy, and disease—all substantially undesirable social forces influencing young children during their school years—simply have been too powerful for traditional subject matter curricula to overcome.

The facts are plain: Local public schools, working alone, have not been able to correct these social conditions. While local schools have not been inactive, their compensatory education programs have not successfully broken the cycle of poverty which has been at the heart of the civil rights movement and the President's War on Poverty. Thus demands, unsatisfied by local schools, have been focused at the national level, particularly in the last two years. The Elementary and Secondary Education Act of 1965 is a direct outcome of the perception by the President and the Congress that massive action in the form of compensatory education is needed in the immediate future to improve the quality of education provided to low-income families.

WHY COMPENSATORY EDUCATION?

Compensatory education is a major issue, not because of an increased incidence of poverty or racial discrimination, and not because schools have been inactive in recognizing a responsibility to low-achieving pupils from poor neighborhoods. Rather, it is a problem because the predominant values in American society are changing. Conditions of relative poverty and discrimination which were tolerated in an era of social Darwinism during the nineteenth century and the first quarter of the twentieth century are regarded by a growing proportion of Americans as unacceptable and a legitimate object for corrective action by government. The values which determine attitudes toward poverty have changed. If that be "do-goodism," make the most of it.

If there are those among us who fail to see justification for educational programs combatting extensive conditions of poverty—flavored with racial discrimination—a rereading of Myrdal's classic, *An American Dilemma,* is recommended. Myrdal traces to the Enlightenment the direct philosophical roots for an intolerance of poverty and discrimination, and notes that both the French egalitarians, led by Rousseau, and the English libertarians, led by Locke, believed that environment was the primary determinant of character. Although politically the Enlightenment was aimed at limiting the power of government, Myrdal shows that both the egalitarians and the libertarians stood "*for intervention in this one field of education*" (Myrdal's emphasis).[5]

The entire American belief in and commitment to tax-supported, compulsory public schools is at least in part an "intervention" by the state designed to ameliorate social and economic differences by insuring that the poor will become self-supporting and contributing members of society. Compensatory education is merely an extension of the noble concept of "intervention" to one of the major social problems of our time.

AN OLD AND A NEW ANSWER

Whatever one decides is the appropriate role for schools in correcting apparent inequities in society, and the range of alternative educational strategies is large, educators and others will probably agree that education is usefully viewed as a process in which those aspects of our culture judged to be desirable are transmitted to and developed within the person being educated. Schools are not unique as social agencies in working for the maximum total development of each individual's intellectual, moral, emotional, and physical potential as a human being. Certainly the family shares the same goals; churches and voluntary associations work in selected aspects of human development, but the schools remain the major socializing influence outside the family.

It is true, of course, that up to the present time existing school programs have not been able to develop the maximum potential of most students in economically deprived or racially segregated communities. School programs have not been sufficiently potent to counteract the behavior and attitudes acquired at an early age in the home and neighborhood. The general hypothesis upon which compensatory education programs are built is that undesirable behavior patterns and attitudes acquired in the home and neighborhood can be corrected and changed in desirable directions through certain actions of the school. These actions usually involve more intensive participation by the community in school-related activities and programs, or the extension of additional educational services in the school itself.

The community-school concept, which has served rural America so well, is a strategy urban schools should examine carefully while developing their compensatory education programs. Writing in 1940, Cubberley said "The aim has been to make the public school building a center for the life of the community; to extend the work of the school into the homes, and thus influence the civic and social welfare of the people; and to broaden the popular conception of education by making it a life-long process." [6] He continued, "It is only by making the school a center for the community life that the rural and village school can hope to exert the influence which it should. The development of a new and better rural and small-town life is largely a matter of education and guidance, and of the institutions capable of providing this leadership the school easily stands first." [7]

Of course, there are enormous difficulties in getting a school system, particularly a large urban system, to relate directly to the many neighborhoods it contains.[8] To involve the people of these neighborhoods in the total educational effort, the first step must be to persuade professional educators that it is the task of the schools to exercise such leadership. Apparently, teachers in many communities do not feel that this is a legitimate function. Their contact with parents is sometimes limited to occasional "guidance conferences" at which the student's success in the school's subject matter is discussed.

Substantial numbers of today's economically deprived children live in urban ghettos where the school-community relationship is entirely different from that of areas where rural community schools are found. The traditional chasm between middle-class teachers and lower-class parents continues to persist in many cities despite the efforts of a minority of school administrators and dedicated teachers to bring about greater understanding between the two groups. In urban schools today, the school is all too frequently an 8:30 to 3:30, 180-day-a-year proposition both for students and teachers. Indeed, in some cities teachers' unions are demanding that teachers no longer be expected to do *anything* after the close of the school day.

One of the principal elements in the school's attack on conditions of poverty should be the extension of school services to three- and four-year-old children. This has been suggested frequently elsewhere and has been adopted by the federal government as an integral part of the total federally financed compensatory education program. It is precisely by extending educational services down to the ages of three and four that the schools are most likely to be able to "compensate" for the deprivations of home and neighborhood experienced by children of low-income families.

Thus historic changes have been made in the values which underlie the programs of public schools in America. The first of these is that the goal of "equal educational opportunity" must be defined in terms of the achievement by individuals of their maximum potential. For children from low-income families, this can only be accomplished if schools provide unequal services designed to compensate students for the earlier and concurrent acquisition of undesirable values in the home and neighborhood. Second, the federal government has again intervened in public education with programs that will have major economic and social consequences. The government's earlier actions in the land grant college program, the vocational education program following World War I, and the "G.I. Bill" following World War II had profound effects upon the American economy for decades following their enactment. It is unrealistic to expect the Elementary and Secondary Education Act and the War on Poverty educational programs to have less than a historic impact on the American economy and society of the next two decades.

Our society is plainly telling its public educators to reduce the opportunity gap between social ideals and social reality for the one-fifth of Americans who live in conditions of poverty. As our values evolve and we become more affluent, we are recommitting ourselves to the idea of "intervention" through education. The schools have been judged, once again, to be the primary vehicle for the improvement of undesirable social and economic conditions. America can no longer show its poor a different face from the one it shows the majority of its citizens. The challenge to public education in areas of low income is enormous. Unprecedented levels of resources will be made available in the next few years.

The schools have been given broadened responsibilities for leadership. The questions are, can educators recognize social revolution as it is occurring, adapt old concepts about the task of the schools to changing demands from society, and develop the programs required by the challenge?

References

1. See, for example, the research papers and bibliography presented in *Compensatory Education for Cultural Deprivation* by Bloom, Davis, and Hess. New York: Holt, Rinehart and Winston, 1965.
2. Though they are not directly related to compensatory education, it is nevertheless relevant to mention that the "community action" titles of the Economic Opportunity Act require that the poverty-stricken be represented on local committees administering "War on Poverty" funds. Furthermore, analysis of recent tax election results in several big cities reveals that it is precisely the lower socio-economic precincts which are most strongly supporting school expenditures.
3. 1960 U. S. Census data.
4. H. T. James et al. Unpublished findings from "The Determinants of Educational Expenditures in the Great Cities of the United States," U. S. Office of Education Cooperative Research Project No. 2389. Contract No. OE4-10-076, in progress.
5. Gunnar Myrdal, *An American Dilemma.* New York: Harper and Brothers, 1944, p. 1182.
6. Ellwood P. Cubberley, *Public Education in the United States.* Boston, Mass.: Houghton Mifflin Company, 1934, p. 597.
7. *Ibid.,* p. 723.
8. Roald Campbell discussed these difficulties fully in his paper, "Community Extension," prepared for the White House Conference on Education, 1965.

49.   A Parting Shot from a Still Skeptical Skeptic

ERNEST H. AUSTIN, JR.

Once again the issue has been avoided. I find in the Guthrie-Kelly paper no refutation of my contention that prevention of cultural deprivation involves a wideness and wiseness of social planning and reform which will reach into the very guts of our institutional structures. I see no response to the claim that, by their obvious failure to battle the blatant inequalities of these institutions, educators are in effect fostering deprivation. Guthrie and Kelly (hereinafter G. and K.) feel that compensatory education is "noble," and there is no doubt that it is well-intended. But does not the fact that there must be something as pernicious and malignant as "compensatory education" reveal that something is dreadfully and basically wrong, and that something criminal has been and is being done?

Due to faulty scholarship and weak reasoning, G. and K. distort much of my position and confuse much of their own with tautology ("Cultural deprivation is its own breeding ground"), empirical blindness (equation of the environment with the school), and faulty logic (failure to discriminate between "some" and "all"). Since the precariousness of their stand is so ob-

Reprinted from *Phi Delta Kappan*, Vol. 46 (October 1965), pp. 75–76, by permission of publisher and author.

vious, and since my reply must be brief, I will not comment on their many other specific errors. Instead, I will deal with two major points: their stand on authoritarianism (value indoctrination) and their narrow social perspective.

In countering my claim that most compensatory education (hereafter C.E.) is authoritarian—which they do not counter since they inconsistently go on to make a case for authoritarianism—G. and K. cite the fact that many civil rights organizations have demanded C.E. I agree, but these organizations are not necessarily free from authoritarianism themselves; indeed, this may prove to be a very plaguing problem.

There is something frightening about G. and K.'s discussion of authority: "value transplantation" is "primary." One can only wonder how G. and K. came to despise children enough to support forcing a middle-class value system upon them. The authors then advocate "a degree of authoritarianism" and attempt to defend this by reference to compulsory education. The fallacy here is that compulsory education does not dictate a particular school (public or private), a particular program, or a particular "value transplantation." The authors go on to justify compulsory education from a shallow Jeffersonian point of view, that is, de-

411

mocracy rests upon having educated citizens. This is in some degree true, but, as with the Greeks, it all depends upon who the citizens are. We might also ask how it was possible to achieve democracy before the advent of compulsory education. But all of this deals with democracy in a political sense when in reality it has come to mean a way of living together by providing associated experiences which break down artificial barriers between people. This is the real relation between democracy and compulsory education. G. and K. apparently do not believe this; they seem to envision education as indoctrination rather than as inquiry; for example, they make this statement: "If, as is too often the case . . . , the values and actions of some individuals are inimical to the orderly maintenance of society, remedial measures must be taken." It is not difficult to make the point here; the reader need only substitute the word "Jews" for "individuals," and whatever he will for "remedial measures." My concern is not over authority, for there must be that; rather, I want to know how such authority is constituted. And if it is the external *noblesse oblige* authority of G. and K., then I will fight it because it is destructive of democracy.

G. and K. would attack the breeding ground of cultural deprivation via an education which would rehabilitate children by providing them with basic skills and attitudes which, supposedly, would break the cycle of poverty. But some of the most culturally deprived people I know are among the "educated," and it is confusing to equate education with the eradication of a disease-bearing mosquito. For example, what if we find our mosquito to be a part of our corporate economic structure, or an agricultural system which exploits migrant workers, or a power-

ful and avaricious tenant landlord, or an archaic section of our bureaucratic political structure? It is a fanciful and costly dream to believe that the school is a place of miracles and that a larger dose of education emphasizing only skills and attitudes will alleviate cultural deprivation and do away with extensive poverty. Where in their analysis do G. and K. take on the vested interests, the entrenched powers, or the system which is depriving us? Where are the causes of deprivation identified? Where are methods suggested for overcoming such causes rather than "compensating" for them?

In closing, let it be said that my article appears, due to cloudy expression and a surfeit of ignorance on my part, to be a failure. It was not intended as the answer, but as a heuristic device which would prod thinking. This gambit obviously failed with G. and K., perhaps because they are not sufficiently and methodically skeptical. In places, the article is intentionally imprecise, unfair, and unsound. But, and here is the damnable thing, G. and K. did not really expose this. They have one major point of validity: My evidence seems scanty or nonexistent. This, of course, can be escaped by reverting to the purpose of stimulating consideration of C.E. in order that others gather the evidence which will either support or refute my contentions. And I do submit this as partial explanation. But I did not venture forth on complete lack of data; it is available, and the amount increases. For instance, here is a note just received from a professor of elementary education, Dr. Paul C. Burns, who has been associated with the Knoxville, Tennessee, Head Start program:

There are a number of features of government-subsidized programs for the culturally deprived that disturb me. For example, one Knoxville school (which during the regular year has about 10 per cent Negroes as students and is located in a heavy Negro population center) has not a single Negro in its Head Start project. Furthermore, serious questions can be raised as to the competency of a number of persons involved in this program for culturally disadvantaged preschool children. "Beginning first grade instruction eight weeks early" appears too frequently to be the objective, and even this narrow purpose is not well done. Good will and fuzzy thinking are simply not a reasonable substitute for adequate training and experience. On the surface, a number of these projects would appear worthy, but a critical examination reveals a sheer veneer over some pretty shabby programs. The alibi generally given is that adequate time was not permitted to develop worthwhile programs. But any program which is less than desirable should not have been approved for these huge outlays of federal support. The mad escape from thinking about the real problems has deteriorated often into the lowest form of mental activity—simply because we do not know what we are doing has in no way prevented us from madly doing it. The education of children in a democratic society is too important to be as poorly planned (and expensive?), as many of these programs seem to be.

Much more evidence is not included here because of a close association with individuals and organizations whose relations with C.E. programs they are trying to improve would not be enhanced by their public criticism. I can only claim that I am professionally honest and that the evidence is available to those who would care to pursue the topic further.*

* I am in possession of critical letters and statements from which are excerpted the following: "bureaucratic harassment, domination, and rigidity which destroys a balanced program." "Greed for money." "Typical schooling rather than cultural aid." "De facto segregation." "General incompetency in dealing with culturally deprived children—teachers not even trained to communicate with them." "Unwilling to become concerned with value problems." And here is an astute and insightful statement from a very concerned friend employed by a very concerned organization to work with the deprived: "There is, I suspect, much in the culture of poverty that can be admired and yet we go on with the sole goal of totally destroying it and changing these lower-class culturally oriented kids into middle-class-oriented children (notice that I say kids when they're lower class, children when they're middle class). Just a little value judging there. . . ."
One wonders how the above fits Guthrie and Kelly's "literally thousands" of programs. I've heard good things about a few efforts, that is, the Houston, Texas, project, but only nonskeptics would not sickened by many of the others.